Personality Psychology

Personality Psychology:
The Science of Individuality

NATHAN BRODY
Wesleyan University

HOWARD EHRLICHMAN
Queens College and the Graduate School
of the City University of New York

Prentice Hall, Upper Saddle River, New Jersey 07458

Library of Congress Cataloging-in-Publication Data

Brody, Nathan
  Personality psychology : the science of individuality / Nathan
Brody, Howard Ehrlichman.
     p.   cm.
  Includes bibliographical references and index.
  ISBN (invalid) 0-13-046903-7
  1. Personality.   2. Individuality.   I. Ehrlichman, Howard.
II. Title.
  BF698.B69345   1997
  155.2—dc21   97-20128
                                                          CIP

Senior Acquisitions Editor: Bill Webber
Project Manager: Shelly Kupperman
Buyer: Lynn Pearlman
Cover Director: Jayne Conte
Cover Art: Carolyn Mazzucca

This book was set in 10/12 Palatino by BookMasters, Inc. and printed and bound by R. R. Donnelley
& Sons. The cover was printed by Phoenix Color Corp.

Printed in the United States of America

10   9   8   7   6   5   4   3

ISBN 0-13-146903-7

Prentice-Hall International (UK) Limited,London
Prentice-Hall of Australia Pty. Limited, Sydney
Prentice-Hall Canada Inc., Toronto
Prentice-Hall Hispanoamericana, S.A., Mexico
Prentice-Hall of India Private Limited, New Delhi
Prentice-Hall of Japan, Inc., Tokyo
Pearson Education Asia Pte. Ltd., Singapore
Editora Prentice-Hall do Brasil, Ltda., Rio de Janeiro

*For
Erness and Liz,
Sam and Kari,
Jennifer, and
Alan, Melinda, and Aidan*

Contents

Preface

This is a book about research in personality. The operative word in the previous sentence is *research*. Some books that are designed to introduce students to the study of personality are organized according to the theories that have been of historical importance in shaping and defining the field. Any discussion of research in such books is often incidental, intended merely to illustrate the central concepts of various theories of personality. Other books do have a research focus but they still extensively discuss major theories of personality. We have tried to do something different. We do not include a discussion of the major theories of personality. Why? We believe that most of the theories discussed in personality textbooks are primarily of historical significance. Personality research is a vital and exciting scientific discipline that is not closely tied to many of the older theories.

We believe that it is important to understand the details of research and to know something about the controversies in the field and the ways in which these controversies may (sometimes) be resolved. Where we think that the available research permits us to reach a conclusion about some important issue, we state that conclusion. Some instructors and some students will disagree with us—and that is fine. We want our readers to disagree; we also want them to understand why we believe a particular conclusion is warranted. We hope that we are not bland and inconclusive. We would rather be clearly wrong than safe, cautious, and uninteresting.

It is our goal to engage each of our readers in a dialogue. People who read books about personality are usually intensely interested in their own personality. If after reading this book you understand yourself in new and different ways, we will have succeeded. One device that we use frequently is to ask you any of three types of questions. First are questions that we think we know how to answer. We ask them anyway to make sure that you are thinking about the material you are reading. Such questions are used to foster the development of your critical understanding. Second are questions that ask you to think about the implications research findings may have for your understanding your own personality. These are truly personal questions that only you can answer. Third, are questions that we do not know how to answer. These are not personal questions but rather questions that address unresolved issues in the field. Often the most important questions are the ones most difficult to answer. Your answers to these questions are likely to be at least as valid as those that we could provide. We try to explain why some of these questions are difficult, but we do not tell you how to answer them.

Our goal is to convince you that personality research is exciting and maybe even occasionally beautiful and elegant. If, after reading this book, you share these sentiments, we will have succeeded. If, on the other hand, you come away believing that personality research is boring and trivial, we will be content if you at least know why you have reached this conclusion. We respect your right to differ with us, and we respect your ability to understand the outcomes of the research we discuss. We hope you will allow us to enthuse, infuriate, and inform you about a field that we find endlessly fascinating.

Acknowledgments

We wish to thank the following Prentice-Hall reviewers: Jonathan Cheek, Wellesley College; Elizabeth L. Paul, College of New Jersey; and Janet A. Simons, University of Iowa. We also want to express our appreciation to Shelly Kupperman of Prentice-Hall for her diligent work on the production of this book. Special thanks are due to the Queens College students who used an earlier draft of this book in their graduate course in personality and provided many helpful comments and suggestions.

Nathan Brody
Howard Ehrlichman

Personality Psychology

1

Personality and Personality Psychology

What are you like? What are your friends like? Your family? Your teachers? When you think of these people, what comes to mind? Their physical appearance? Their interests, hobbies, style of speaking? Whether they are easy-going or hot-tempered? Whether they are happy or unhappy? One thing is certain: when you think about these people, you won't mix them up. You will undoubtedly think of things that give each of them his or her unique individual qualities. It is also likely that each of these people, and perhaps yourself as well, has at some time seemed something of a mystery to you. Why does one friend act in such a self-destructive manner? Why does another have such a hard time with school? Why is one so cheerful all the time? Questions like these have probably fascinated and perplexed human beings since the beginning of thought. From ancient times to the present, philosophers, playwrights, novelists, and poets have tried to fathom the mysteries of individuality.

Psychologists have also tried. This book is about how they have done so and what they have found: it's a "progress report" on personality psychology. As you will see, many important things have been discovered, many intriguing ideas proposed, and many difficult questions raised (if not always answered). Some of these findings, ideas, and questions may lead you to think about yourself and others in new ways. Others may strike you as common sense. At times you may feel frustrated with the current state of knowledge or the way personality psychologists try to answer questions. At these times, we would encourage you to be open minded. Human individuality is extraordinarily complex, and to study it scientifically is an enormous challenge.

WHAT IS PERSONALITY?

Most people think they know what personality is. But here are some questions that might make you think. Is everything about you part of your personality? Which aspects are and which are not? Do some people have more personality than others? Do animals have personality? Do cars?

Let's deal with the last question first. Of course cars have personality! Alissa's Porsche S/EX definitely has a different personality than Marco's 1970 VW Beetle. But wait, you might say. A car can't have personality—it's just a machine. So what do we mean when we talk about a car's "personality"? Obviously, we are using the term as a metaphor. What we mean is that there is something about these cars that is like personality. We may simply be referring to the fact that they have different characteristics (fast vs. slow; handles well vs. poorly). Or we may be referring to the thoughts and feelings the cars bring out in us. When we say the Porsche is "sexy," we mean it excites us, gives us pleasure, is desirable. A car's personality, then, boils down to (1) a description of its characteristics or (2) our reactions to it. Some psychologists would say that when we talk about people's personalities, we are also just describing or summarizing their characteristics. Some would even say that personality exists more in the eye of the beholder than in the beheld. For these psychologists, the term *personality* is not all that different whether applied to people or to cars.

Other psychologists would disagree. They would say that the term *personality* implies the existence of a living being with an inner mental life consisting of thoughts, feelings, desires, and goals as well as behaviors. Personality is not merely a description of behavior, but involves processes in the person that are responsible for this behavior. People behave as they do, at least in part, *because* of their personalities. To say a person is sociable or aggressive or honest is to say there are inner characteristics that cause him or her to be sociable or aggressive or honest.

From this perspective, cars most decidedly do not have personalities. What about animals? When we asked our students this question, the great majority insisted that animals have personalities. They described their pet dog as friendly, or intelligent, or aggressive. And they argued that this is very different from calling a car sexy. What do you think?

Here is another question. Do some people have more personality than others? We sometimes describe someone as having "lots of personality," often as a way of saying the person makes a strong impact on others or is charismatic. Do charismatic people have more personality than boring people, or are their personalities just different? Virtually all personality psychologists would answer "different, not more or less." But in another way, the idea of some people having more personality than others may make sense. To see this, we need to move on to the question of whether all of a person's behavior is a reflection of his or her personality.

Consider career choice. Some people seem to have a strong sense of what they want to do. They are strongly driven to become an athlete, or a computer scientist, or an artist, or a journalist. Others make their career choices in more haphazard ways. They get a job through a friend or relative, they work 9 to 5, and if they do well maybe they get a promotion. Although both kinds of people are influenced by aspects of their personalities, there is a sense in which inner characteristics in the first kind of person are playing a more influential role. We would argue that not everything we do is equally influenced by personality. Some things we do just because everybody does them. People who sit quietly in church during a sermon are not displaying behavior strongly influenced by their personalities (although the fact that they are in church at all may reflect their personalities). But a person who stands up and starts whistling "Dixie" during a sermon clearly is. So it is possible that some things we do are more strongly influenced by our personalities than other things.

This brings us to the first question we asked: Is everything about you related to your personality? Is "personality" just another word for "person"? If so, personality psychology has a formidable task, because it must be concerned with everything that makes you who you are. From this perspective, personality psychology would not be a subspecialty of psychology, but rather a central discipline drawing not only from general psychology, but from anthropology, biology, sociology, literature, history, cultural studies, and all the other disciplines devoted to understanding people (Maddi, 1980). Obviously, there is no "true" or "correct" answer to the question we have raised. We could *define* personality so that it includes almost everything about people: "The sum total of a person's thoughts, feelings, desires, intentions, and action tendencies, including their unique organization within the person." (In fact, this definition captures much of what is common to definitions of personality given by various psychologists. See Allport, 1961; Chaplin, 1968; Levy, 1970). Perhaps this is what most people mean by the word *personality*. Scientists, however, need not define their subject matter in everyday terms. A definition has a purpose in science: it serves to specify the domain that one intends to study and understand. We believe that this definition takes in too much and sets an impossible goal. Our preference is for a more limited definition that can set a more realistic agenda. As a way of specifying the subject matter of personality psychology, we shall define personality as *those thoughts, feelings, desires, intentions, and action tendencies that contribute to important aspects of individuality*.

Let us compare this definition with the one given earlier. Both definitions focus on psychological processes within the person. Both include cognitive, affective, motivational, and behavioral processes. What are the differences? One difference is that we are placing limitations on the subject matter, specifying that personality psychology focuses on those processes that contribute to individuality. Much of psychology is concerned with processes that do not contribute to individuality at all, let alone to important aspects of individuality.

To illustrate, let us consider Stanley Milgram's classic research on obedience to authority. Milgram (1974) found that many people would administer electric shocks to an innocent victim in a psychological experiment just because they were told to do so by an experimenter. Like many other social psychologists (e.g., Ross & Nisbett, 1991), Milgram was interested in creating situations that influence people's behavior. He had little to say about individuality, even though not every person acted the same way in this situation. Why did some people obey and others not obey? To answer this question, the personality psychologist would examine processes within the individuals that might have led to their different behaviors in this situation.

We also specify in our definition that the processes must contribute to *important* aspects of individuality. Not everything about people is of equal interest to personality psychologists. We want to keep our attention on those aspects that make a difference in a person's life. If you look closely enough, almost every aspect of people's lives has its own unique character, but these differences often play a minor role. It is less important, for example, whether people prefer Burger King or McDonalds than whether they differ in their ability to get along with others. We want to keep the focus on important social and personal outcomes.

Does our definition specifying personality psychology as the study of those processes that contribute to important aspects of *individuality* imply that it is necessary to study individuals one at a time in order to understand what makes each person unique? An influential personality psychologist named Gordon Allport believed that personality psychologists should be especially interested in human individuality. He distinguished between **idiographic** and **nomothetic** psychology, two terms he introduced in his 1937 pioneering text on personality (revised in 1961). *Nomothetic psychology* seeks general laws that can be applied to many different people. Although Allport believed that such laws would be helpful in understanding personality, he claimed that ultimately we can understand the individual only by studying the individual on his or her own terms. For Allport, the goal of personality psychology must be *idiographic*, that is, must be to understand the unique individual; and because each individual is unique, it is also necessary to use idiographic methods to meet this goal. General laws and research geared to discovering them, according to Allport, do not suffice because they do not capture the unique, patterned quality of personality as it exists in individuals. To illustrate how one might study personality idiographically, Allport (1965) used a series of letters written by a woman to her son over the course of twelve years in an attempt to understand the woman's personality. He was able to trace certain major themes and concerns in her life using this **archival material.**

Allport's insistence that the proper study of people is the study of the individual has been echoed by many personality psychologists (Carlson, 1971; Lamiell, 1981; Runyan, 1990). In order to see why, let us consider how nomothetic psychology tries to understand personality. If idiographic psychology is **person-centered,** nomothetic psychology is **variable-centered.** The goal of variable-centered research is to understand a particular characteristic, rather than the whole person. For example, we might want to know how anxiety influences performance on tests. "Anxiety" is considered a **variable** because people vary, or differ, in how anxious they are. The primary tool for studying variables is to compare people who differ with respect to the variable. In other words, we want to compare the behavior of anxious people with the behavior of calm people. Notice that the focus is on the variable, not on the people. We may know nothing else about the individuals in such research other than their level of the variables we are studying. As Eysenck stated, "the unique individual is simply the point of intersection of a number of quantitative variables" (1952, p. 2).

Why might a psychologist (or a student) object to this approach? One reason is that it seems to have nothing to do with our experience of people as complex, living organisms. As Rae Carlson (1971) asked, "Where is the person in personality psychology?" Another reason is that it ignores differences that might remain. For example, suppose two individuals have exactly the same scores on anxiety. Does that mean they are exactly the same? Isn't it possible that the things that get one person anxious (public speaking) are different from the things that make another person anxious (examinations)? Might not one person show anxiety by getting stomachaches while the other shows anxiety by worrying?

For the idiographic psychologist, then, personality must be understood within each individual; for the nomothetic psychologist personality must be understood by comparing people with each other with regard to specific variables. The idiographic psychologist sees the goal of personality psychology as fully understanding each individual's uniqueness; the nomothetic psychologist sees the goal of personality psychology as fully understanding how different variables develop and influence people's lives.

Which approach seems more appealing to you? We guess that most students would say the person-centered approach. They would agree with Allport that a variable-centered approach loses any sense of the real individual, never gets "inside" of him or her, never gives us the flavor of the person's unique individuality. We agree that much personality psychology does seem to present a lifeless picture of the individual. Perhaps that is why we are avid novel-readers and playgoers. We too are fascinated by individuals in all of their richness and complexity. We believe that the great novelists and playwrights have important things to tell us about individuality. But novels and plays are not science. We have no way of verifying the correctness of the novelist's vision. The question isn't whether the person-centered or the variable-centered approach gives more of a feeling for the individual life, but which is more likely to lead to greater scientific understanding.

Let us pursue this line of thinking by returning to the questions we asked earlier about your friends. Why is your friend Marlene always cheerful? Here are some possible answers you might have come up with: (1) She has a "sunny disposition"—it's just in her nature to be cheerful. (2) Her life is going so well—she has a steady boyfriend, she has plenty of money, she is in perfect health, she has an interesting career—who wouldn't be cheerful with all that? (3) She isn't really cheerful at all, she just puts it on so that people will think she is cheerful. (4) It's a phony question—nobody is cheerful, or anything else, all the time.

How can we find out which of these answers is correct? Psychologists using a person-centered approach would study Marlene more closely. If Marlene remains cheerful even when things aren't going well, then answer 2 is not right. If we discover a diary in which she says she is fooling everyone into thinking she is cheerful when actually she is depressed, then answer 3 would probably be right. If we ask a lot of people who know her and find out that she is cheerful only when she is at school (which is mainly where you see her), then maybe answer 4 is closer to the truth.

Now suppose we were actually able to follow her around to observe her behavior and also to interview her friends and family, and were able to come to a conclusion about Marlene that she really is genuinely cheerful much more often than most people. Then we need to ask, why is she like this? Was she born with a cheerful nature? Did she learn to be cheerful in early childhood? Is it the way she was reared? Is she cheerful because of other personality characteristics (interest in other people, high intelligence)? To answer these deeper questions, we would have to find out all kinds of things about Marlene's history. This is what biographers do. By studying letters, diaries, and statements by other people, they attempt to describe and understand the person they are studying. Yet how do we know that the biographer is correct? Different biographers often come up with very different ideas about the same individual.

But suppose we could convince ourselves that we understand why Marlene is always cheerful. What about José? He also seems to be cheerful all the time. Is what we found out about Marlene also true for José? Maybe, maybe not. So now we have to follow José around to find out about him! Nomothetic psychologists would say that this hardly seems like a strategy for scientific progress. Science advances by the discovery of general principles. Although there are undoubtedly circumstances in which it is valuable to study individuals intensively (for example, in biographical studies or in clinical practice), the idea that a primary goal of personality psychology is to understand "what is true of individual human beings" (Runyan, 1983, p. 417) seems to contradict the usual goals of scientific inquiry. Studying individual cases is helpful only if doing so leads to more general understanding.

The nomothetic psychologist would say that what we need to do is study many individuals at once, taking a variable-centered approach. Let us find a lot of people who are cheerful and see if they are also similar in other respects. Rather than focusing on each individual, let's try to come up with some broad principles that apply to many cheerful people. Although we may lose the richness and fascination of the individual by using this strategy, it is more likely to pay off in the long run. For example, by studying groups of people we can discover whether or not genetics can influence people's cheerfulness, or whether there is any evidence that people who grow up in warm, supportive families are more cheerful than those who do not. We can then use these general findings to help us better understand the individual.

Think again of the task of the biographer. Many biographers draw conclusions about the causes of their subject's personality, and these often seem plausible. It would not surprise you if a biographer claimed that John Doe lacked self-confidence because his father treated him with contempt. But it also might not surprise you if a biographer claimed John Doe lacked self-confidence because his mother was overprotective and never let him do anything for himself. By studying many people, we might be able to discover whether people with low self-confidence were more often reared by punitive fathers or overprotective mothers compared with people with high self-confidence. Suppose it turned out that there was no difference between people with high versus low self-confidence in these types of experiences. That finding would certainly suggest that the biographers are on the wrong track. Similarly, you might believe that your friend Marlene was born with her cheerful disposition. But if we study many people and find that genetics plays no role in how cheerful they are, then it cannot be the reason Marlene is cheerful. In short, our understanding of individuals needs to be guided by scientifically valid general principles. Once we have such principles, we can then provide a framework for identifying the sources of each person's individuality. For the nomothetic psychologist, variable-centered research is the key to developing a scientifically meaningful understanding of personality. Furthermore, many skeptics of the idiographic approach would simply point out that despite years of rhetoric, person-centered research has not contributed much to our understanding of personality. This may be true because of resistance to using person-centered methods (Lamiell, 1981). Or it may be true because person-centered methods cannot by their nature lead to scientific understanding.

Our view is somewhat different. We accept the argument of the nomothetic psychologist with regard to goals, but not necessarily with regard to how we meet those goals. We do not think it is a reasonable goal for personality psychology to understand individuals fully in all of their enormous complexity. As with other sciences, the goal of personality psychology must be to develop general principles (Levy, 1970; Maddi, 1980). Nevertheless, we do see a number of roles for the study of individuals. First, many ideas about personality have originated in the intensive study of single individuals. The best-known example is Sigmund Freud's analysis of himself and his patients in developing his theories. The idea that **case studies** are a fruitful source of ideas about personality is commonplace.

Second, because much of personality psychology concerns how different people interpret the situations that face them and how their unique experiences have affected them, it is often necessary to investigate these interpretations and experiences from the individual's point of view.

Third, the distinction between nomothetic and idiographic research may not be as clear as it first appears. Although Allport argued vigorously for idiographic research, he also suggested that the variable-centered/nomothetic and person-centered/idiographic views were more like two sides of the same coin than different currencies. For example, Allport suggested that one way to study the personalities of individuals would be by "particularizing common traits" (Allport, 1961, p. 367). By this he meant that not all personality variables are equally important for all individuals. For some people, aggressiveness might play a major role in their lives; for other people, friendliness or anxiety might play such a role. Allport suggested that those characteristics that people show at unusually high levels are likely to play more profound roles than those on which people are average (see also Paunonen, 1988). Other psychologists have made a similar point. Bem and Allen (1974) and Baumeister and Tice (1988) suggested that consistency of behavior is a major indicator of whether a characteristic is relevant or important for a person. Cheek (1982) suggested that people themselves know which traits are most important for them and can tell us if we ask.

This way of thinking leads to a rapprochement between the variable- and person-centered approaches. We can study variables such as aggressiveness, friendliness, and anxiety, trying to understand as much as we can about their causes and consequences. We can then use this knowledge in understanding individuals for whom these characteristics are of central importance. In essence, this is what all sciences do. Scientists try to establish general laws which can then be applied to the individual cases to which the laws are relevant. Indeed, one could argue that the ultimate test of scientific understanding is whether one can use general laws to understand individual cases (Runyan, 1990). If personality psychology is truly concerned with individuality, the principles we discover must at some point illuminate individuals. As you read this book, we hope you will think about your own personality. The theories and research of personality psychology must be understood and evaluated just as in any other scientific field, in terms of their logical consistency, their ability to explain phenomena, and their methodological soundness—but they also should give us the keys to understanding ourselves.

WHAT'S AHEAD IN THIS BOOK

The primary scientific journal for the publication of research on personality in the United States, the *Journal of Personality and Social Psychology* (JPSP), divides the field of personality into two areas, "Individual Differences" and "Personality Processes."[1] Individual differences refer to the "what" of individuality. What are the ways in which people differ from one another? What is the origin of those differences? What are the consequences of those differences? Personality processes refer to the events inside of us that contribute to individuality, the "how" of personality. Examples include cognitive processes (how we think), emotional processes (how we feel), learning processes (how we learn), and motivational processes (how our needs and goals influence our actions).

It is important to note that ultimately our understanding of individuality must involve processes (Zuroff, 1986). For example, we may find that the tendency to be anxious or calm is an important way people differ from one another. We may find that genetics or early traumatic experiences (or both) may contribute to people's tendencies to be anxious or calm. And we may find that anxious people and calm people tend to engage in different behaviors, such as in their willingness to take risks. But none of this explains what is going on inside the person to produce anxiety. To truly understand individual differences in anxiety, we need to understand the processes that cause people to be anxious or calm. Do such differences reflect different ways of thinking (for example, do anxious people interpret many situations as potentially dangerous)? Do they reflect different degrees of emotional responsiveness (for example, do anxious people have a nervous system that generates anxiety relatively easily)? Do they reflect different goals (for example, do anxious people have unrealistically high goals that lead them continually to experience failure and inadequacy)? Do they reflect different self-images (for example, do anxious people have low self-confidence)? In short, the study of individual differences is not so much an end in itself as a means to identifying and understanding the processes that contribute to individuality.

In this book, we shall discuss both individual differences and personality processes. We begin by focusing on a number of critical issues in the study of individual differences. How do personality psychologists measure individual differences (chapter 2)? What do these measurements actually tell us about people (chapter 3)? How should we decide which individual difference characteristics are most important (chapter 4)?

Next we explore the role of biology in personality. To what extent are individual differences influenced by heredity and environment (chapter 5)? Can we identify brain mechanisms that might influence individual differences (chapter 6)? Does the evolutionary history of our species shed any light on personality processes or individual differences (chapter 7)?

We then move to a consideration of how motivational factors (desires, needs, and goals) contribute to personality (chapter 8). How do conflicting goals within people affect their behavior? Do people have strong needs that channel their lives in particular directions? Are one's life plans and strivings important components of individuality?

The next four chapters concentrate on how cognitive and affective processes influence individuality. Chapter 9 explores the role of unconscious mental activity in personality processes. Chapter 10 focuses on the way in which people think. In this chapter we consider research on intelligence and cognitive style. Chapter 11 focuses on our conscious thoughts and feelings. We examine how the content of our thoughts, especially our thoughts about ourselves, influences our behavior. These thoughts include our beliefs about our ability to function adequately and our interpretation of the reasons for our behavior. We also explore the important issue of how our sense of identity (including our ethnicity and gender) contributes to our views of ourselves.

In chapter 12 we consider the role of personality in three areas of practical concern: psychotherapy, health, and work. Chapter 13 presents a brief conclusion for this book. We try to identify future directions for personality research and give you our guesses about personality psychology in the twenty-first century.

ENDNOTES

[1]Other journals that focus on personality psychology include *The Journal of Personality, The Journal of Research in Personality, Personality and Social Psychology Bulletin, Personality and Social Psychology Review,* and *Personality and Individual Differences.* Personality psychologists also publish in general-purpose journals such as *Psychological Bulletin, Psychological Review, Psychological Science,* and many others.

2

Personality Measurement

CORRELATION AND EXPERIMENTATION

Personality psychology relies heavily on **measurement.** In order to understand how measurement is used in personality psychology, it is important to draw a distinction between two approaches to research often described as "experimental" and "correlational." It is also important to understand what a **correlation** is and what it tells us.

   We usually think of science as a method for understanding the causes of things. Think about these two statements: (1) Children who are good readers usually have parents who read stories to them. (2) Reading stories to children will make them better readers. Are these statements basically the same idea, just phrased differently, or are they really different ideas? Are they both making a claim about cause and effect? Statement 2 certainly appears to be about cause and effect. It says that if we do X (reading to children) then Y will happen (they will become better readers): X causes Y. What about statement 1? Statement 1 says that there is a connection between reading to children and how well the children read, but it does not actually state cause and effect. In fact, there are at least three possible ways statement 1 could be true: (A) reading to children makes them better readers; (B) parents read stories to children who enjoy being read to; these are also the children who become better readers; (C) reading ability runs in families; parents whose genes lead them to be good readers tend to have children whose genes also lead them to be good readers. Possibilities A and B both involve cause and effect, but in opposite directions: in the former, reading to children is the cause, but in the latter it is the effect. In possibility C both the child's reading ability and the parent's tendency to read to the child are caused by something else, the genes that they have in common. So even though statement 1 says there is a relationship between reading to children and their reading ability, it does not make a specific claim about cause and effect.

Now, suppose you wanted actually to find out whether statement 2 is true. After all, if it is true, then we would want to encourage parents to read to their children in order to make them better readers. What could we do to test this hypothesis? Many students would probably say we should carry out a study in which we (1) find a large number of parents with young children whom we could study, (2) determine how often they read to their children, and (3) measure the children's reading skills. If we did this we could see whether or not the children whose parents read to them a lot were better readers than the children whose parents read to them less or not at all. Suppose that is what we find. Would this mean statement 2 is true? The answer is no. In fact, all we would know after doing this study is that there is a relationship between reading to children and how well they read, but we still wouldn't know anything about cause and effect. We wanted to test statement (hypothesis) 2, but in fact all we tested was statement (hypothesis) 1.

So let's try again. Is there a way of testing hypothesis 2? In principle, there is. It involves setting up what is called a **true experiment.** What is a true experiment? We often use the word *experiment* to refer to scientific research of any type, but actually it has a narrower technical meaning. A true experiment is one that allows us to identify cause and effect. It involves **random assignment** of subjects **to conditions.** To see what this means, let us envision a true experiment to test hypothesis 2. As before, let us find a large number of parents who are willing to participate. But this time, rather than simply finding out how often the parents read to their children, we are going to *control* how often they read. Half the parents are going to read one hour a day to their children, the other half will not read at all to their children. This will continue for six months, after which we will find out if the children who were read to are better readers than those who were not read to.

Will this **design** allow us to test hypothesis 2? Actually, that depends on one crucial aspect. Notice that we didn't specify how we would decide which parents will read to their children and which ones will not. One possibility is to ask the parents to volunteer for one condition or the other. But if we did this, wouldn't those parents who normally read a lot to their children volunteer for the read-a-lot condition, and those who did not normally read a lot to their children volunteer for the don't-read condition? If that happened, our experiment would be ruined. Can you see why? In fact, the only way we can be confident that we are testing hypothesis 2 is if there is nothing about the parents or the children that leads them to be in one condition or the other. Each parent-child pair must have an equal chance of being in either. This is what is meant by random assignment. Essentially, we "decide" who ends up in which condition by flipping a coin. Since there is nothing about the children or parents responsible for putting them in one condition or the other, if we find after six months that there is a difference in the children's reading skill, it must be due to the one thing that is different between the two groups: the fact that one group of children was read to and the other was not.[1]

Random assignment to conditions is the *sine qua non* of experimentation. It is also extraordinarily difficult to carry out in real-life situations. Would you be willing to stop reading to your child for six months? Even more important, when it comes to personality variables, random assignment is usually impossible. In our experiment on reading, we were able to **manipulate** the **independent variable.** But suppose we wanted to find out if the reason some children read more than others is that they have superior verbal ability? How could we establish cause and effect? We are claiming that verbal ability is a cause of how much a child reads. But we cannot manipulate verbal ability, randomly assigning children to high versus low verbal ability! All we can do is find out if there is a relationship between verbal ability and how much the child reads. We hope at this point that you see why demonstrating that such a relationship exists is not enough evidence for us to tell what is causing what. Does high verbal ability cause children to read more, or does reading a lot increase the child's verbal ability?

UNDERSTANDING CORRELATION

The kind of research that focuses on relationships is called **correlational research.** Its aim is to discover if different characteristics of people are associated with each other. It often relies on a statistic known as the **correlation coefficient.** You will be reading about correlations throughout this book. The correlation is the workhorse statistic of personality psychology. It tells us about the relationship between pairs of scores. Usually (but not always, as we shall see later), these pairs of scores are obtained from each person in a group (or **sample**) of individuals.

Consider the SAT, an examination you may very well have taken as part of your college application process. If so, you know that you received a score for the verbal section and a score for the quantitative section. What is the relationship between people's verbal and quantitative scores on the SAT? This relationship can be represented by creating a graph in which the horizontal dimension is labeled "SAT-V" and the vertical dimension "SAT-Q." A person's scores on *both* tests are represented by a single point on the graph. When the points of all the participants have been entered, the visual appearance of the dots may be used to infer the relationship between the scores. Look at Figure 2.1a. All of the points in the space fall on a straight line. As scores increase on one dimension, they increase in a comparable way on the second dimension. Thus a person's score on one dimension can be used to predict the score on the second dimension without error. In this case, the statistical index of the degree of relationship between these scores, the coefficient of correlation, would have a value of +1.00. The positive sign indicates the direction of the relationship, and the number 1.00, which is the highest number possible, indicates that it is possible to predict scores on one dimension from knowledge of scores on the other dimension without error.

Now consider the array of scores in Figure 2.1b. Here the scores also fall on a straight line but now the line has a negative rather than a positive slope, since high scores on one dimension are perfectly predictive of low scores on the second dimension. In this case, the correlation coefficient would have a value of −1.00. Here the direction of the relationship is negative, but one can still predict scores from one dimension to the other, without error.

Figure 2.1c presents a different array of scores. Here the points are scattered throughout the graph and there is no obvious relationship between scores on the two dimensions. In this case the value of the correlation coefficient would be .00.

It should be obvious that there are many intermediate degrees of possible relationships between pairs of scores. Figures 2.1d and 2.1e represent intermediate relationships where the correlations are +.60 and −.30, respectively. In these cases, knowledge of a person's score on one dimension helps to predict the second score, but the predictions will be less than perfectly accurate.

Let us summarize. The relationship between pairs of scores may be measured by a statistic called a *coefficient of correlation,* which ranges from −1.00 to +1.00. The plus or minus sign indicates the direction of the relationship, and the absolute value of the correlation indicates the magnitude or strength of the relationship. The statistic may be interpreted as an index of the degree to which scores on one measure may be used to predict scores on the second measure. For reasons that we shall not discuss here, it is conventional to square the value of the correlation and multiply it by 100 to obtain an index of the degree of predictability of one measure by another. This index may be described as a measure of the **percent of variance** in one variable predicted by knowledge of another variable. Applying this formula, a correlation of .5 would mean that knowledge of scores on one dimension accounts for 25% of the variance on a second dimension, and a correlation of .7 means that 49% of the variance may be accounted for in this way.

What size correlations is it reasonable to expect in personality research? That depends. For example, when we are concerned with reliability, discussed below, we want our correlations to be quite high, often .80 or higher. When we are correlating scores on two different personality tests, or correlating scores on a personality test with some real-life behavior, we are usually satisfied to obtain much lower correlations, perhaps even as low as .20. Why is this so? There are two basic reasons: **error of measurement** and **multiple determination.**

Error of measurement refers to the fact that our measures in personality psychology are not perfect. As we will discuss in a moment, no measure is 100% reliable or 100% valid. The score the person gets on a measure is partly a true reflection of what we are trying to measure, and partly just error of

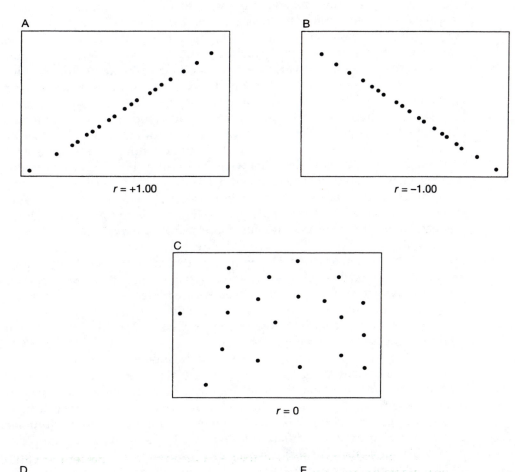

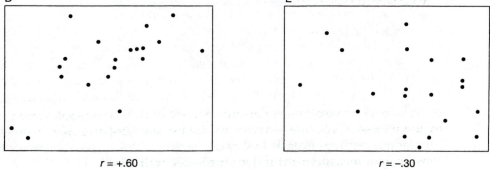

FIGURE 2.1

measurement. Imagine that we are trying to find out if studying more hours for an exam is associated with one's grade on the exam. Let us assume, not unreasonably, that the more one studies, the higher one's grade. But to find this out for sure, we need to measure both variables and then compute a correlation. The course grade is straightforward: we can look it up in the instructor's grade book. Measuring how much one studied might also seem straightforward: we can ask students how much they studied. But suppose they don't remember accurately, so one student who says she studied 6 hours really studied 10 hours, and another student who says he studied 15 hours also really studied 10 hours. All we have to go on is how much the students said they studied, not how much they actually studied, and we have just seen that what they told us is full of error. Suppose the *real* correlation between studying and grades is a whopping +.90; in this case, two students who really did study 10 hours should have very similar grades. But what we are actually correlating is not the true studying time, but what the students told us. If many of the students in our sample are inaccurate in their reports about studying, what correlation would we expect to get? Certainly it would have to be much lower than +.90. Depending on the amount of error, the correlation could even approach zero! In short, error of measurement decreases correlations below what they would be if our measures were perfect.

The second reason correlations in personality psychology are often in the .20 to .50 range has to do with the way things really are. Consider the following hypothesis: highly anxious people do worse in school than people low in anxiety. Suppose this hypothesis is true. What size correlation would we expect to find? If anxiety were the *only* thing responsible for school performance, we would expect a high correlation, limited only by error of measurement. But obviously anxiety is not the only factor. Aptitude, interest, motivation, work habits, other demands on one's time, and many other factors also have an impact. School performance, in short, is caused by many different things, not just anxiety; it is multiply determined. Therefore it is unrealistic to expect a high correlation between any one variable and school performance. If we could identify all of the variables that influence school performance, we might be able to use them together to predict school performance with a high degree of accuracy.

In all of the examples so far, we have computed correlations on pairs of scores obtained from individuals. It is also possible to compute correlations when one score comes from one person and the other score comes from another person. We do this when we have some basis for pairing the individuals. For example, suppose we wanted to know if husbands and wives tend to resemble each other in political attitudes. We would obtain information about political attitudes for each wife and husband. Each couple now has a pair of scores, the wife's score and the husband's score. Using the husband-wife pair as the unit of analysis, we could compute a correlation that would tell us whether liberal wives have liberal husbands, and conservative wives have conservative husbands. In short, correlations can be computed any time that we have a basis for pairing two scores together.

CAUSE AND CORRELATION

We began this chapter by pointing out that relationships between variables do not necessarily tell us about cause and effect. Why, then, would we want to find out about relationships? Knowing that two variables, *X* and *Y*, are correlated does not tell us whether *X* causes *Y*, *Y* causes *X*, or something else causes both. Nevertheless, *if X* causes *Y*, or *if Y* causes *X*, they will be correlated. So the *absence* of a relationship between *X* and *Y* does imply that there is no causal connection between them. Thus finding a relationship between two variables leaves open the possibility that they are causally connected, whereas finding no relationship strongly suggests that they are not causally connected. This fact is important because often some connections between the variables are more plausible than others. For example, there is evidence for a positive correlation between an anatomical abnormality of the heart known as mitral valve prolapse and panic attacks. It is certainly unlikely that panic attacks cause the mitral valve prolapse. It is more plausible that mitral valve prolapse, in some way, increases the likelihood of getting panic attacks. (It is also possible that a third variable, such as a genetic predisposition, may be responsible for both mitral valve prolapse and panic attacks.)

We have seen that in some cases correlation can aid us in choosing among alternative models of cause and effect. In recent years, a mathematical procedure known as **causal modeling** (also called **path analysis**) has been developed to help clarify cause and effect when variables are measured rather than manipulated in experiments. The key to causal modeling is to have data on more than two variables. This **multivariate** approach permits a mathematical analysis (called *structural equation modeling*) to help us choose among different possibilities of what is causing what. One can then carry out statistical tests to see which model the observed correlations best fits.

Consider again the question of the relationship between parents reading to children, children's verbal ability, and parents' verbal ability. Suppose we find that three variables are all positively correlated with each other. We can specify alternative models of cause and effect and then see which model the obtained correlations fit the best. Here are some possible models:

MODEL 1: Parents' verbal ability (PVA) influences how much the parents read to their children (RTC). How much parents read to their children influences children's verbal ability (CVA). However, there is no *direct* effect of parents' verbal ability. This is what the path for Model 1 might look like:

$$\text{PVA} \longrightarrow \text{RTC} \longrightarrow \text{CVA}$$

This model says that the only reason PVA and CVA are correlated is that PVA influences RTC, and RTC has a direct effect on CVA. In this case, we would say that RTC *mediates* the influence of PVA on CVA.

MODEL 2: PVA influences both RTC and CVA. However, PVA has a direct effect on CVA, but RTC has no effect on CVA:

$$PVA \longrightarrow RTC \qquad CVA$$

Note that in this model, the correlation of RTC with CVA is entirely due to a "third variable"—PVA—with which they both correlate.

MODEL 3: PVA influences CVA, and CVA influences RTC—children with higher verbal ability encourage their parents to read to them. The correlation between PVA and RTC is due entirely to the mediating effect of CVA.

$$PVA \longrightarrow CVA \longrightarrow RTC$$

MODEL 4: Here is a fourth model. Can you interpret it?

$$PVA \longrightarrow RTC \longrightarrow CVA$$

To summarize, although it is often difficult to carry out true experiments in personality psychology, correlational research does sometimes permit us to evaluate different ideas about cause and effect.

THE NEED FOR MEASUREMENT

Like other sciences, personality psychology uses numbers to describe the phenomena it studies. Some students find this fact hard to swallow. They say, "How can you reduce personality to a set of numbers?" This attitude represents a misunderstanding of the function of numbers in science. Numbers gain us both precision of communication and ease of comparison. To say that two restaurants both score 10 on a ten-point scale is to communicate quickly that (1) they are as good as restaurants get, (2) they are about equally good, (3) they are only a little better than restaurants that get a score of 8, but a lot better than restaurants that get a score of 2. But the main advantage of numbers is all the things you can do with them. Statisticians and psychometricians have developed sophisticated techniques for analyzing the numbers obtained in personality research. We already saw one example in the correlation coefficient, a simple and clear way of describing the relationship between two variables.

But numbers are not magic. Their value depends on whether they are meaningful. When we say a person is 64 inches tall, we know exactly what that means. Expressing height as a number is straightforward. But what about expressing aggressiveness, or anxiety, or friendliness, or honesty as numbers? Obviously, this is a less straightforward and far more difficult matter. Therefore we must have some way of verifying that the numbers we assign to personality variables are meaningful.

> At this point, we would like you to turn to pages 28–30 at the end of this chapter and take the personality test there. When you are done, return to this page.

To help us explore the topic of measurement, let's look at the test you just took. Was there anything about the test that surprised you? Perhaps you were a bit surprised that you ended up with five scores, not one and not 25 (the number of items). You obtained your score on the five scales by adding up your responses to five sets of items. What justification is there for totaling these particular items? The fundamental justification is that the items are correlated with each other. There is some degree of predictability among the items that form each scale. Because they are correlated, we assume they have something in common. By adding them together we are trying to get a measure of what they have in common. (In chapters 3 and 4 we will discuss the rationale for this procedure.)

Now that we have scores for the five scales, we can ask the key question: Are these scores meaningful? It might be more helpful to turn the question around: In what ways could the scores *not* be meaningful? There are two broad ways: the first has to do with **reliability,** the second with **validity.**

RELIABILITY

One reason the scores might not be meaningful is that they are essentially random. Imagine that you completed the test not by trying to indicate what you actually are like, but by picking a number out of a hat! What would your scores mean then? Absolutely nothing. Although we hope that you didn't pick numbers out of hat, it is possible that your responses are somewhat random. Maybe you have no idea whether or not you are "talkative," so you just put down any number that popped into your mind. The first thing we need to do in evaluating your score's meaningfulness is to make sure your responses are really telling us something about you. How could we find this out? One way is to see whether the scores on the measure are generalizable, that is, to see whether we can predict a person's response on one item from the person's response on another item. If people were responding randomly, there would be no predictability between items. If we find that the items on a scale do correlate with one another (that is, are predictable), then the responses cannot be random: there is something that is causing individuals to respond similarly across different items.

One method often used to test for generalizability of test items (also known as **internal consistency**) is to divide each scale in half (perhaps by using odd-numbered and even-numbered items) and then correlating the scores on the two halves with each other. If the correlation is high and positive, we would have demonstrated **split-half reliability.** (In practice, many psychologists compute a statistic called **coefficient alpha,** which is the average of all possible split-half reliabilities for the scale.)

For personality measurement, generalizability among items on a scale is only a first step for assessing reliability. An important aspect of personality characteristics is that they continue to exist from one time to another. If the BFT is really telling us something about your personality, you should get more or less the same scores if you take the test again. The fact that the test has internal consistency (is generalizable over items) is no guarantee it has **stability** (is generalizable over time). Students sometimes say after they see their personality test scores that they responded the way they did only because of the mood they were in that day. The implication is that if they had taken the test on another day, they would have responded differently. That is certainly possible. In fact, some measures are specifically designed to test moods that change from day to day. But a test score that changes a great deal over time cannot be a reliable measure of a stable personality trait. That is why checking for stability is so important. We do that by giving the test twice to the same group of people and correlating the scores from time 1 with the scores from time 2. This correlation is known as the coefficient of stability, or **test–retest reliability coefficient.** Personality psychologists usually like to see test-retest correlations of +.80 or more, at least over relatively short time periods, anywhere from a week to a few months. It is likely that if your class took the BFT again next week the test-retest correlation would be at least +.80. (The question of the stability of personality over longer time periods will be discussed in chapter 3).

A number of factors influence a test's reliability.

1. *Clarity of items.* Test-takers who understand items are going to respond less randomly than those who do not or who are unsure what the items mean. For example, suppose one of the items on the BFT had been *thoughtful.* This could mean "tendency to think about things deeply," or it could mean "considerate of other people." If your interpretation were to shift over time, you might respond differently at time 2 than at time 1, thereby reducing stability. An extreme case occurs when a test is given in a language in which the test-taker is not proficient. One of the real challenges of creating personality tests is coming up with items that are clear and unambiguous. (That's one reason *thoughtful* is not on the BFT!)

2. *Motivation of test-taker:* If test-takers don't care about the test or if they lose interest in it, their responses may not be reliable. On some tests, items are repeated as a way of identifying unreliable responders. Another approach is to include items like "I have never seen a car" or "I have never brushed my teeth." The assumption is that everybody has seen a car and brushed his or her teeth, so anyone saying "true" to these items is not likely to be providing reliable responses to other items either.

3. *Number of items.* Perhaps the most important way of increasing reliability is to make the test longer. Why? When there are only a few items, each item has a rel-

atively large impact on the total score. Thus if one item is poorly worded or ambiguous, it will add more error if there are a small number of total items than if there are a large number. In addition, **psychometric** analysis indicates that the more items there are on a test, the more likely it is that people will have a large range of scores (known as the test's **variance**), and all else being equal, higher variances produce higher correlations.

Reliability is also important for measures other than pencil and paper tests. For example, when observers are coding behavior, the researcher must be able to show that the method for coding is reliable, one that any judge can follow and get the same results. **Inter-rater** or **inter-judge reliability** can be assessed through correlation of ratings among different judges.

The reason we are concerned with reliability is that we want to be sure our measure is not overly affected by random error. Once we have determined that we have a reliable measure, that we are measuring *something*, we get to the question of *what* we are measuring. How can we find out whether a test measures what we hope it measures? This is the question of validity.

VALIDITY

Suppose you wanted to do research on body types and needed to get a measure of people's weight. Doing this would not present a major difficulty, because there are instruments specifically designed to provide reliable and valid measures of weight. But suppose you don't have the time to weigh each person individually; suppose you need to get a measure of weight from 120 students in a large lecture class, and you can spare only about ten minutes. You might simply ask the students to tell you how much they weigh.

Do you think this measure would be valid, that is, would it be telling you the students' actual weight? Maybe or maybe not. Why might it *not* be valid? Perhaps some students don't know their own weight because they never weigh themselves. Perhaps they do weigh themselves but their cheap scale at home is inaccurate. Perhaps they are self-deceived about their own weight because they have a distorted body image. Perhaps they don't want *you* to know their weight, so they lie. All of these things would make their **self-report** of weight incorrect, and thus invalid.

How could we find out if their self-reports are accurate? One way would be to ask a subset of the students to stay after class, weigh them on an accurate scale, and then correlate their scale weight with their self-reported weight. If the correlation is high, we can be pretty confident that the self-reported weight is giving us valid information. If the correlation is low, we would conclude the self-report measure is not valid and therefore is worthless as a measure of weight.

In this example, we had a **criterion** which we could use to find out if the self-report measure was valid. In general, whenever you have a criterion that is clear and observable (like a scale for measuring weight), validity is easy to determine.

In personality psychology, however, most of what we want to measure does not have such criteria. Personality **constructs** do not exist concretely the way weight does. The BFT is supposed to measure five **dimensions** of personality, as you have read. How would we establish the validity of this test? To put it another way, why should you believe that your scores on the test are telling you something real about your personality? Look at the dimension called "agreeableness," for example. How on earth can we convince you (and ourselves) that the number you obtained is really an indication of how agreeable you are?

Perhaps the first thing we could do is look at the items that make up the agreeableness scale. Do they *look* like they are measuring agreeableness? If they do, we would say the scale has **face validity:** on "the face of it," the content of the scale items appears to relate to agreeableness. Looking more closely, we could ask whether the items include everything we mean by agreeableness. Are there any aspects missing? Now we have a question of **content validity.** If a professor gives you a final exam that includes only a small part of the course material, you could complain with some justification that the exam does not have content validity—it does not adequately cover the domain it is supposed to cover.

Both face validity and content validity are ultimately just a matter of opinion. Neither is convincing evidence that the score is valid. The mere fact that a test looks like it's measuring agreeableness doesn't prove that it is. More convincing would be some empirical evidence of validity. Again, what we want is some evidence of generalizability. We want to see if scores on the test of agreeableness can be generalized to other things. (Recall that for reliability we were concerned with generalization of the measure to itself). What other things would we want to look at? When we were trying to measure weight using self-reports we had a criterion, so it was simple to tell if the self-report generalized to that criterion. Since we have no criterion for agreeableness, our strategy is to identify things that ought to be related to agreeableness.

One common approach to validating personality measures is to obtain ratings of people by their family or friends. Would your friends describe you in the same way as you describe yourself? We can answer this question by obtaining correlations between self-report scores and rating scores for each of the five personality dimensions. McCrae and Costa (1990) obtained correlations between self-reports and peer ratings for a large group of adult subjects. The correlations for personality dimensions similar to those measured by the BFT varied from .37 to .63. If the scores of several raters are averaged, the correlations between self-reports and ratings are somewhat higher. McCrae and Costa (1990) averaged ratings from several peer raters and correlated these scores with self-reports on the same five personality dimensions, and they obtained an average correlation of .59. Consensus ratings remove any idiosyncratic judgments of a single rater and are therefore more reliable. The result is an increase in the correlation between self-reports and ratings.

Does the fact that there is agreement between you and other people provide strong evidence for the validity of a test? Are ratings by others strong criteria in the same way a scale is a strong criterion for weight? This is a difficult question to answer. On one hand, if there is such agreement, then there must be something about you that is causing this agreement. The question is, What is it? It could be that what you think about yourself influences what others think about you. If you think of yourself as agreeable, you may project an image of yourself as agreeable (Ross & Nisbett, 1991). Does that mean you really are agreeable? Perhaps on a deeper level you are a selfish person who uses a "nice guy" image to manipulate others. Perhaps when people rate you they are falling for your image rather than accurately describing your real behavior. If so, it would be desirable to have some evidence that you actually behave the way you and your friends say you do.

In some cases it is possible to obtain such evidence. In structured situations, such as school, it is often possible to obtain behavioral ratings. Studies of children's aggression, for example, have employed observation of actual schoolyard behavior (hitting, pushing, yelling, and so on). If a personality measure of "aggression" was found to be correlated with these behaviors, that would be fairly convincing evidence that the measure was valid. Unfortunately, it is usually difficult to obtain such behavioral measures, especially over a wide range of situations. This is a significant problem, because, as we shall discuss shortly, when we describe personality we most often want to generalize across a number of different situations. Finding that a child acts aggressively at school may not be enough to conclude that the child is generally aggressive: perhaps the aggression at school is in response to a specific problem the child is having there. Perhaps school is the only place the child is aggressive. Also, sometimes a person's observable behavior gives a very different impression than what we would have if we could get "inside" the person. Can you always tell when someone else is upset, nervous, and distressed? One of our students insists that she is a wreck every time she speaks in front of a class, but we have never seen any evidence of it: she appears quite calm and collected. So how can we validate a measure of anxiety or neuroticism if we cannot tell when another person is nervous or not?

This is a problem often faced by personality psychologists as they attempt to measure constructs that often have no clear behavioral manifestation. The process of validating such measures is known as **construct validation.** Construct validation begins with the following question: if this test is a measure of variable *X*, how should people who score high on the test behave in comparison to people who score low on the test? To answer this question, one needs to have a thorough understanding of the construct, that is, a theory about its implications for behavior. From this theory, we can come up with specific hypotheses about differences between high and low scorers on the measure. For example, part of the construct "neuroticism" might be the prediction that people who score high are more likely to show increased autonomic nervous system activity when they are under stress. We could then set up a study to see if this hypothesis is correct. We could select people scoring at the high and low ends of the neuroticism dimension, bring them into the laboratory, assign them a difficult task at which they fail, and see if they differ in their heart rates. If they differ as predicted, we have provided some evidence for the construct validity of our neuroticism measure.

Do you see any problems with this approach? One is that increased autonomic nervous system activity following failure at a task is only one of many predictions that can be made about neuroticism. Is it, by itself, enough to validate a measure of a broad characteristic like neuroticism? In most cases, the answer would be no. To really demonstrate construct validity, one must examine all aspects of the construct and demonstrate that in each case the hypothesized results are obtained. In fact, the search for construct validity is not a one-way street. As we do more research on a variable such as neuroticism, we almost always discover that some of the hypotheses turn out well and some don't. But rather than discarding the construct, we use the empirical evidence to rethink the construct. So, in effect, construct validation is a method not only for finding out what our tests measure, but for refining our ideas about personality variables.

All the types of validity we have discussed involve generalization—positive relationships between our measures and some other indicator of the underlying personality variable. We are looking for convergence among measures (hence the general term, **convergent validity**). We also need evidence that a test is not measuring something else than what we intend: we need to demonstrate **discriminant validity.** We do this by showing that our test does not correlate too strongly with tests that measure other constructs. For example, we do not want a test that is supposed to measure creativity to correlate highly with an IQ measure; if it does, then our test may really be measuring intelligence rather than (or in addition to) creativity.

Early in this section we asked how we can convince you that your test scores measure what they are supposed to measure. We discussed various aspects of validity, most of them involving relationships (usually correlations) between the measure we are trying to validate and other measures. But how do we know when a measure is valid and when it isn't? Unfortunately, there is no magic cutoff for when something is or isn't valid. One rule of thumb is that reliability sets the limit on validity. If you have a test that is only moderately reliable, it can only be moderately valid at best. Because there is no one point at which a measure can be called valid, researchers often provide information on reliability and validity so that others can take this information into account as they evaluate research studies. When such information is not provided, the prudent reader should remain skeptical about the validity of the measures used in the study.

Finally, it is important to remember that all of these attempts to validate test scores involve relationships in groups of people. Even if we can conclude that a test score is fairly valid, that general validity is no guarantee that the score of any one particular person is valid. Keep this caution in mind in regard to your scores on the BFT. You may well disagree with them. Ultimately, you have to decide if the picture of you suggested by the BFT is accurate *for you.* Personality tests are not magic and are not crystal balls. Don't fall victim to the **Barnum effect,** so called after the circus impresario P. T. Barnum ("there's a sucker born every minute"). People often agree with personality descriptions of themselves that are generated completely randomly. We have had students who were amazed that the personality tests they took were so uncannily accurate in describing them, only to find out that they had picked up a different student's results! So don't accept blindly the validity of your personality scores. But if you do decide to reject your scores, you should still try to explain why you received that score. You may find the next discussion helpful in considering why a test result might not be valid.

THREATS TO VALIDITY

You might disagree with one or more of your scores because you feel they are not reliable. But for the sake of the discussion, let's assume the BFT is reliable and your score does not reflect lack of attention, temporary mood, ambiguity of items, and so on. You still might think the score is not valid. Why might a test like the BFT not be valid? What are the **threats to validity** for self-report measures of personality? One possibility is that you have a **response tendency,** assigning numbers to items (at least in part) for reasons that have little to do with the construct the item is designed to measure. Perhaps you tend to use the ends of the rating scale rather than the middle (**extremity tendency**). Or perhaps you do just the reverse, using only middle values and avoiding extreme values. Perhaps you tend to agree with questions, especially when you are not sure how to answer (**acquiescence tendency**). Or perhaps you are consciously or unconsciously concerned with whether your answer makes you look good, in other people's eyes or your own (**social desirability tendency**). All of these response tendencies could produce scores that are invalid because they are not providing accurate information about the characteristic being measured.

SOCIAL DESIRABILITY

Fortunately, research suggests that many of these response tendencies have little major impact on personality scores (Rorer, 1965). The major exception is social desirability. There is no doubt that sometimes responses are influenced by an item's social desirability. Some psychologists believe that one can **control for** social desirability. There are two strategies for doing so. First, one can try to use items that do not have a socially desirable answer. For example, what is the socially desirable answer to "I enjoy collecting stamps"? Douglas Jackson (1984) developed a test, called the Personality Research Form, in which items were carefully chosen to minimize social desirability. Unfortunately, many of the characteristics of interest to personality psychologists have inherently socially desirable answers. Indeed, if you look over the items on the BFT, you will probably have little trouble telling what the socially desirable answer to most of those items would be.

The second approach is to attempt to *measure* people's tendency to respond in a way designed to make themselves look good. The assumption here is that some people are more likely to do this than others. There are a number of tests to measure this tendency. Items from one of these tests, the Marlowe-Crowne Social Desirability Scale, are shown in Table 2.1. Do you notice a pattern to these items? Each is designed to have a socially desirable response. Each is also designed to be very improbable. A person's score on the test is simply the number of items answered in the socially desirable direction. The assumption is that anyone who keeps answering these items in such a direction is revealing a response tendency, because nobody could actually be that good! On the other hand, people who answer in the socially undesirable direction are assumed to be telling the truth (because the items are so improbable).

Suppose we now correlated scores on the MCSDS with scores on a test we are trying to validate. What if the correlation was high? This correlation might mean that scores on the second test are being influenced by social desirability: the reason a person who scores high on one also scores high on the other is that both tests are reflecting social desirability tendency. But suppose the correlation between the two tests was zero? This would mean that scores on the second test are not influenced by social desirability, since people with a strong social desirability tendency are not scoring any differently than people with no social desirability tendency. Which correlation do you think the developer of the second test hopes will be found?

The importance of social desirability as a threat to validity has been hotly debated by psychologists for decades. Certainly, at times people can and will attempt to manipulate their answers on personality tests in order to produce a specific impression (Paulhus, 1984). However, in most personality research there is no payoff for test-takers deliberately to produce an impression on the researcher, if for no other reason than most research studies are carried out anonymously. For such anonymous studies, the more important threat is self-deception, a tendency to bias responses to maintain a positive self-image. Since that tendency may itself be considered a personality characteristic, the issue really boils down to the question of discriminant validity: Is the test I am using really measuring the tendency to self-deception or is it measuring what I intend to measure? When you consider your own test scores on the BFT, ask yourself to what extent you think your responses were influenced by a tendency to maintain or protect your self-image.

TABLE 2.1   Sample Items from the Marlowe-Crowne Social Desirability Scale

1. I never hesitate to go out of my way to help someone in trouble. (T)
2. I have never intensely disliked anyone. (T)
3. No matter who I'm talking to, I'm always a good listener. (T)
4. When I don't know something, I don't at all mind admitting it. (T)
5. I have almost never felt the urge to tell someone off. (T)
6. I never resent being asked to return a favor. (T)
7. My table manners at home are as good as when I eat out in a restaurant. (T)
8. On occasion I have had doubts about my ability to succeed in life. (F)
9. If I could get into a movie without paying and be sure I was not seen I would probably do it. (F)
10. I like to gossip at times. (F)
11. There have been occasions when I have taken advantage of someone. (F)
12. There have been times when I was quite jealous of the good fortune of others. (F)
13. I sometimes feel resentful when I don't get my way. (F)
14. There have been occasions when I felt like smashing things. (F)

VARIETIES OF PERSONALITY MEASURES

Although self-report tests have played a central role in personality research, they are by no means the only kinds of measures available. Intelligence tests, for example, are designed to assess intellectual functioning; they don't ask people to rate themselves but rather try to sample behaviors that require intelligence for correct answers. Ratings by peers, direct behavioral observation, interviews, physiological measurements, projective tests, and responses to specially constructed laboratory situations have all been used in the attempt to measure personality. We will discuss these various types of measures as they come up throughout the book. But regardless of the type of measurement, the goal is the same: to accurately measure aspects of personality that contribute to individuality.

What are these "aspects of personality"? What are we really measuring when we obtain scores on personality tests? How seriously should you take your scores on the BFT? Why should you believe that your rating of 25 adjectives reveals anything profound about your personality? How do we get from words to traits?

BFT

Indicate how true each of the following terms is in describing you:

1 = Not at all true of me; I am almost never this way

2 = Mostly not true of me; I am rarely this way

3 = Neither true nor untrue of me, or I can't decide

4 = Somewhat true of me; I am sometimes this way

5 = Very true of me; I am very often this way

1. __4__ imaginative
2. __4__ organized
3. __3__ talkative
4. __4__ sympathetic
5. __5__ tense
6. __4__ intelligent
7. __4__ thorough
8. __3__ assertive
9. __5__ kind
10. __2__ anxious
11. __2__ original
12. __4__ efficient
13. __4__ active
14. __5__ soft-hearted
15. __4__ nervous
16. __5__ insightful
17. __4__ responsible
18. __3__ energetic
19. __4__ warm
20. __5__ worrying
21. __3__ clever
22. __3__ practical
23. __4__ outgoing
24. __4__ generous
25. __1__ self-pitying

When you have finished, go to the next page.

THE BIG FIVE TEST

You have just taken a personality measure we call the Big Five Test (BFT). It is designed to measure five different aspects of personality. As you will see in chapter 4, looking at these five aspects is considered by many psychologists to be a good way of getting a broad picture of people's personalities. To compute your score on each of the five **scales,** simply copy your answers for each item indicated and add.

Item 1____ + Item 6____ + Item 11____ + Item 16____ + Item 21____ = Scale O ____
Item 2____ + Item 7____ + Item 12____ + Item 17____ + Item 22____ = Scale C ____
Item 3____ + Item 8____ + Item 13____ + Item 18____ + Item 23____ = Scale E ____
Item 4____ + Item 9____ + Item 14____ + Item 19____ + Item 24____ = Scale A ____
Item 5____ + Item 10____ + Item 15____ + Item 20____ + Item 25____ = Scale N ____

What are these scales supposed to measure? You might get some idea by looking at the items themselves. Not all psychologists agree on what to label these five aspects, but to help you remember them, we will use the designations given by John (1990) and McCrae and Costa (1990), which conveniently spell out the word OCEAN.

SCALE O   Openness to Experience. People who score high are described as imaginative, curious, liking variety, and interested in intellectual and/or artistic pursuits. People who score low are described as down-to-earth, conventional, preferring routine, and not intellectually oriented.

SCALE C   Conscientiousness. People who score high are described as well-organized, planful, careful, and thorough. People who score low are described as disorganized, careless, inefficient, and undependable.

SCALE E   Extraversion. People who score high are described as talkative, sociable, having high energy, and assertive. People who score low are described as quiet, solitary, having low energy, and reserved.

SCALE A   Agreeableness. People who score high are described as warmhearted, kind, trusting, and compassionate. People who score low are described as antagonistic, unkind, suspicious, and unsympathetic.

SCALE N   Neuroticism. People who score high are described as emotional, anxious, highstrung, self-pitying, and self-conscious. People who score low are described as unemotional, calm, even-tempered, self-satisfied, and comfortable with themselves.

We have described what very high and very low scorers on these scales are supposed to be like. Most people's scores are closer to the middle. The closer you are to the middle, the less likely you are to show the behavior strongly or consistently. How can you tell whether your score is high, medium, or low? You could compare the five scores. For example, your agreeableness score might be higher than your neuroticism score. The type of measurement in which one person's scores are compared with each other is called **ipsative** scoring. What would this really tell you? If you think about it for a moment, you might realize that it would not tell you much, because the meaning of your score depends on how it compares with scores of other people who have taken the test. To say that a score is high on, for example, the agreeableness scale is to say that it is higher than most other people's scores on the agreeableness scale. The type of measurement in which scores are compared with other people's scores is called **normative** scoring. In order to know what your score indicates, it is necessary to compare it to group **norms.**

Below are norms that we obtained from giving the BFT to a sample of 495 students taking an undergraduate course in personality psychology. The following information is provided for each scale: **mean, standard deviation,** and selected **percentiles.** (The information was calculated separately for women and men. Can you tell why?) This information allows you to tell where your score fell relative to the sample of other students taking personality psychology. You can tell whether you scored higher than most, lower than most, or near the middle of the **distribution** of scores.

Students often ask, "How high does my score have to be to make me a high scorer? Or how low to make me a low scorer?" In fact, there is no real answer to this question, since the scores are **continuous.** Psychologists often describe high scores as about one standard deviation above the mean, and low scores as about one standard deviation below the mean. Or they might use the 25th and 75th percentiles and beyond to define extreme scores. If your score is lower than the 25th percentile, 75 percent of the normative sample got a higher score than you did; if it is higher than the 75th percentile, only 25 percent got a higher score. Obviously, the closer you are to the mean or to the 50th percentile, the nearer your score is to "medium," that is, in the middle.

Openness to Experience

Women:	Mean = 19.4	S.D. = 2.9	25%ile = 18	50%ile = 20	75%ile = 21
Men:	Mean = 20.3	S.D. = 2.8	25%ile = 18	50%ile = 21	75%ile = 22

Conscientiousness

Women:	Mean = 20.2	S.D. = 3.2	25%ile = 19	50%ile = 21	75%ile = 23
Men:	Mean = 18.8	S.D. = 3.3	25%ile = 17	50%ile = 19	75%ile = 21

Extraversion

Women:	Mean = 19.0	S.D. = 3.5	25%ile = 17	50%ile = 20	75%ile = 22
Men:	Mean = 18.8	S.D. = 3.5	25%ile = 16	50%ile = 19	75%ile = 22

Agreeableness

Women:	Mean = 22.2	S.D. = 2.6	25%ile = 21	50%ile = 23	75%ile = 24
Men:	Mean = 18.8	S.D. = 3.3	25%ile = 17	50%ile = 19	75%ile = 21

Neuroticism

Women: .	Mean = 18.5	S.D. = 4.4	25%ile = 16	50%ile = 19	75%ile = 22
Men:	Mean = 16.3	S.D. = 4.9	25%ile = 13	50%ile = 17	75%ile = 20

Return to page 19.

ENDNOTES

[1]It is also possible that something else inadvertently differed between the two groups. We are assuming here that the study has **internal validity** (see Judd, Smith & Kidder, 1991, for a discussion of problems in experimental research).

3

From Words to Traits: The Nature of Dispositions

In chapter 2 you acquired a new description of your personality: a score on each of five dimensions. What does this tell you about yourself? Obviously, this description omits many things. It does not, for example, tell you very much about your interests or your values. Are you a dancer, an athlete, someone who volunteers many hours working in a hospice? Do you like to travel? Are you concerned with the environment or with issues of poverty in the world? Are you religious, black or white, male or female, homosexual, heterosexual, bisexual, or simply unsure about your sexual identity? In chapter 4 we will consider whether or not the five scores you obtained are the best way to describe yourself. In this chapter we want to get a clearer idea of what these scores mean.

TRAITS AND DISPOSITIONS

How are we to interpret the scores you received on the Big Five Test? It is possible to assume that each score is a measure of a trait. A trait may be defined as the tendency of an individual to behave in a consistent manner in many different situations. Each trait is assumed to relate to behavior in a set of situations. For example, a "conscientious" person might turn in assignments on time; she might be inclined to write thank-you notes and she would rarely be late to appointments. The set of situations and characteristic behaviors that define traits are rarely specified. You cannot go to a book that will indicate all of the situations and behaviors that are related to any trait. Nevertheless, there is an intuitive understanding of the kinds of behaviors that ought to be related to many trait dimensions. Although a trait is defined as a tendency to exhibit consistencies in behavior in many situations, it should be obvious that no trait influences behavior in all situations. For example, it is hard to imagine a person sleeping in a conscientious manner or a person being agreeable while sitting in a large lecture hall or driving an automobile on a deserted road.

Thus traits are characteristics that influence some, but not all, behaviors. A given trait may influence behavior in some situations but not in others. Traits may be thought of as **dispositions,** that is, latent tendencies to behave in characteristic ways that are manifest only in appropriate situations. Traits are analogous to physical concepts such as solubility. To say that a substance is soluble is not to imply that the substance is always dissolved, but only that it will dissolve if the right circumstances occur. Some characteristics of persons are not dispositions. Height is a good example. It remains relatively constant; it does not require appropriate eliciting circumstances for its expression.

Traits and *dispositions*, for our purposes in this book, will be considered as interchangeable terms. Both refer to hypothetical characteristics of persons that are manifested in appropriate situations.

ARE TRAITS MYTHICAL?

Are the five scores you have obtained measures of your traits? As was discussed in the last chapter, to ask this question is to inquire about the validity of a trait score, that is, whether it measures what it is supposed to measure. If traits are tendencies to behave in a consistent manner in many different situations, then your trait scores are valid if they accurately describe your tendency to behave consistently. Nothing we have considered up to this point provides evidence for the validity of your trait scores. The fact that your scores are likely to be similar to the scores assigned to you by your friends does not conclusively establish that the scores are valid—you may both be wrong. Your friends' descriptions might even be based on knowledge of how you are likely to describe yourself. Trait scores might be inaccurate for two reasons: (1) Neither you nor your friends might be accurate observers of your behavioral tendencies. (2) The notion that people behave in a consistent manner in different situations may be wrong.

SITUATIONAL SPECIFICITY

Individuals may not be consistent in their behavior in different situations. A person might be conscientious with respect to completing work assignments but not conscientious in fulfilling social obligations. A young woman might be sociable and friendly in interactions with her female friends, but shy, retiring, and withdrawn with someone who is older, or with males. In such a case, a description of her as friendly would not accurately describe the details of her behavioral tendencies.

In 1968, Walter Mischel wrote an influential book in which he argued that the dispositional approach to the description of personality was fundamentally flawed. His conclusions were based on a theoretical analysis of the meaning of traits and a survey of research that related personality descriptions to measures of actual behavior in different situations. Mischel argued that individuals did not behave in the same way in different situations. In his survey of the research, he found that attempts to predict behavior in a particular situation from knowledge of a person's trait rating were rarely successful. The typical correlation between a score on some measure of personality and a measure of behavior in a particular situation rarely exceeded .3, indicating that less than 10 percent of the variance in behavioral measures was predictable. Mischel assumed that the relative lack of predictability was attributable to individuals' tendency to behave in different ways in different situations. If Mischel's analysis is correct, descriptions of personality based on generalized dispositions to behave in a consistent manner are flawed.

Mischel's critique of trait concepts deals with a fundamental issue in personality research. Personality may be thought of as a characteristic that influences behavior in many different situations. If people are not cross-situationally consistent in behavior, conceptions of personality that assume there is some underlying disposition that influences the way in which we respond to the world become suspect. Such an argument, if carried to its extreme, implies that personality is without coherence and structure, that it exists only as a collection of independent tendencies that are expressed differently in different situations. Think about your own personality. Do you carry it around with you in different settings like an aura? If you do, in what sense is it possible to say that your personality influences your behavior in different situations? Is Mischel correct?

THE PRINCIPLE OF AGGREGATION

Epstein (1983) argued that Mischel's analysis was flawed. He noted that measures of behavior were not necessarily accurate indices of a person's behavior in a particular situation. Any single measure of behavior may be subject to errors that do not permit us to obtain an accurate measure of an individual's behavioral tendencies. Consider the following example. Assume that conscientious individuals arrive for their classes on time. In order to test this assumption, we could obtain a measure of the time of arrival of students for a class and relate this score to scores on "conscientiousness" obtained from ratings provided by each student's friends on the same personality measure you took in chapter 2. If a low correlation is obtained, say below .30 as would be expected on Mischel's analysis, the results might be attributable either to problems in the measurement of personality or to problems in the measurement of behavior.

Actually, we have persuasive reasons to believe that it is the behavioral measure that may be at fault in this study. A single measure of behavior may not provide an accurate index of a person's characteristic behavioral tendencies. Perhaps a person who is habitually punctual for class fell down going to class and had to be treated briefly in the infirmary. The student's score for punctuality would not provide an accurate reflection of her behavioral tendencies.

This difficulty can be readily overcome. It is possible to obtain a more accurate index of characteristic behaviors by observing the person on several occasions and averaging or **aggregating** scores. Consider another example. It would not be reasonable to assess the size of a person's vocabulary by asking the person to define one word. It is obvious that a single test item does not provide an accurate index of a person's vocabulary. If the person is asked to define many words, however, an aggregated index of performance might provide an accurate index of vocabulary.

Epstein (1979) designed a study to demonstrate the effects of aggregating observations. He asked a group of college students to keep a record of their positive and negative emotional experiences each day for several weeks and to assign each day a positive or negative score. The correlations between scores assigned on different days were quite low—generally below .20. This implies that it is not possible to predict accurately a student's mood on a single day from knowledge of his or her mood score on another day. Epstein found that aggregated ratings were quite predictive. An aggregated rating of positive scores on all odd days of the study correlated .81 with an aggregated rating of positive emotional scores on all even days. Although it is not possible to predict a student's mood on a particular day, it is quite possible to predict his or her average or aggregated mood score from ratings averaged over several days.

DOES AGGREGATION SOLVE THE SITUATION-VERSUS-TRAIT DEBATE?

Does the principle of aggregation indicate that Mischel's analysis is flawed? Mischel (1979; Mischel & Peake, 1983) accepted part of Epstein's critique. He agreed that single measures of behavior are not reliable indices of a person's behavioral tendencies. But he went on to argue that individuals tend to behave consistently in a particular situation, and so it is meaningful to assert that a particular person tends to arrive on time at classes. A measure of class punctuality based on the aggregation of observations of arrival time would be predictive of a measure of arrival time derived from aggregating several times of arrival. But, Mischel would argue, this analysis does not address the fundamental issue. Although individuals might behave in a consistent manner in the same situation, their behavior in one situation might not predict their behavior in a different situation. An individual who is punctual for class might not arrive at parties on time and might not be conscientious in writing to his grandmother.

Let us consider Mischel's argument in greater detail. He assumes that measures of behavior obtained in one situation are not predictive of measures of behavior for a second situation, even though both situations are assumed to be relevant to a trait. It is possible to argue that Mischel is correct and still develop an argument supporting the trait concept. We will describe procedures that could be followed in a hypothetical study to illustrate our argument:

1. Obtain measures of behavior for a group of individuals in each of twenty situations that are assumed to be relevant to the trait of conscientiousness.
2. Assume further that each individual has been observed several times in each situation and that the measure or index of behavior in a situation for each individual is based on an aggregate index of behavior.
3. Divide the set of situations into two arbitrary groups of ten each.
4. Obtain two aggregated indices of conscientiousness for each individual by averaging the person's score for each of the two groups of ten situations. Note that each of these aggregated indices of conscientiousness is cross-situational, based on aggregating measures of behavior in different situations.
5. Obtain a correlation between the two indices. Can you guess the value of this correlation? It would probably be relatively high—perhaps close to .7. This correlation would imply that individuals who behave in a conscientious manner in one set of situations are likely to behave in a conscientious manner in a different set of situations.
6. Obtain an overall index of conscientiousness for each individual by averaging the aggregated behavioral measures for each of the twenty situations studied. Correlate this measure with a trait rating derived from self-reports or a person's friends. Can you guess the value of this correlation? It too might well be close to .7. What does this tell us? Perhaps individuals assign trait scores to themselves or their friends by observing characteristic behaviors in many different situations, averaging these observations, and then using this average to reach a judgment about the person.

Mischel might, and in fact does, agree that the procedure outlined above would lead to the results we have described (Mischel & Peake, 1982). He would argue, however, that the procedure is fundamentally misguided. By obtaining cross-situational aggregates of behavior, we obliterate the nuanced details of behavior that may be necessary to understand an individual. The argument has now developed in a new direction. Mischel and his critics might well agree that there are cross-situational consistencies in behavior if this consistency is defined as a cross-situational aggregate. At the same time, it should be noted that the cross-situational aggregate score omits a good deal of information about the idiosyncratic pattern of an individual's trait-related behaviors. Two individuals might obtain the same aggregate score on a trait even though they behave in different ways in different situations. The argument between trait theorists and Mischel may be understood as an argument about the appropriate level of abstraction and detail that is necessary to provide an adequate description of an individual's personality.

PERSON–SITUATION PATTERNING

Shoda, Mischel, and Wright (1994; see also Mischel & Shoda, 1994) demonstrated that there are meaningful patterns of individual differences in responses to situations that share psychologically meaningful characteristics. Using as a sample 6- to 10-year-old children attending a six-week summer camp, they obtained many observations of behaviors, consisting of verbal aggression, physical aggression, whining or babyish behavior, complying or giving in, and talking prosocially. These behaviors were noted in response to five interpersonal situations: a peer initiating positive contact; a peer being teased, provoked, or threatened; an adult praising the child; an adult warning the child; and an adult punishing the child. These data could be used to form a profile of each child's characteristic behavior patterns. For example, a particular child might be more likely than other children to respond with verbal aggression when teased, provoked, or threatened by a peer but less likely to respond with verbal aggression when punished by an adult. Each child could be assigned a distinctive profile of behaviors in each of these five psychologically different situations.

In order to determine whether children behaved in a consistent manner across situations, Shoda and his colleagues obtained measures of each child's behavior in each situation. Figure 3.1 presents analyses for four children's tendency to respond with verbal aggression in each of the five psychological situations. Each of the children's profiles are based on observations from two different, randomly selected sets of observations. Child #17 is unlikely to respond with verbal aggression when teased by a peer but is likely to respond with verbal aggression when punished by an adult. This child also is very consistent in these response tendencies. Note that the profiles obtained from two randomly selected sets of observations are virtually identical; the correlation for profile similarity is .96. Child #9 is also relatively consistent in responding with different amounts of verbal aggression in different situations, with the highest levels occurring in response to adult warnings. Child #48 is not very consistent in different situations; note that the correlation for profile similarity for this child is .11. These data indicate that some individuals are relatively consistent in their patterns of response to different situations and others are not.

Table 3.1 presents the average stability correlations for the profiles of four different behavioral responses to the five interpersonal situations. It indicates that the profiles for prosocial talk and whining across different situations are relatively low. Children who are likely to whine more than other children in one psychological

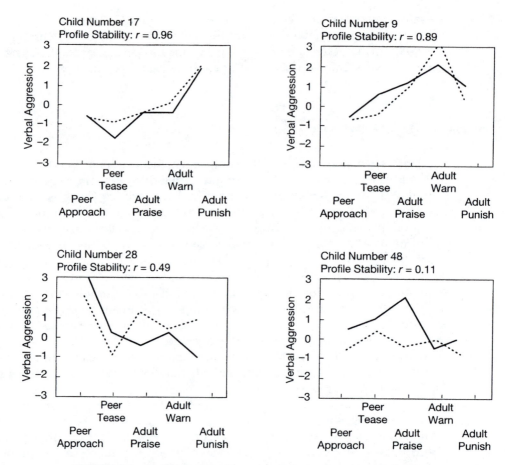

FIGURE 3.1   Individual profiles of verbal aggression across five types of psychological situations. The two lines indicate the profiles based on two different, nonoverlapping samples of occasions in which the child encountered each type of psychological situation, shown as Time 1 (solid line) and Time 2 (broken line). (Based on Shoda, Mischel, and Wright, 1994; reproduced with permission of the American Psychological Association.)

situation in one set of observations may not be as likely to whine more than other children in the same situation as measured in a different set of observations. Compliance and verbal aggression by contrast exhibit greater average profile stability. A child's pattern of verbal aggression in response to different situations is likely to be somewhat consistent across two sets of observations.

The research performed by Shoda, Mischel, and Wright demonstrates that there are some consistent patterns of behavior in different situations that characterize different individuals. It is meaningful to characterize a particular child's be-

TABLE 3.1 Stability of Intraindividual Situation-Behavior Profiles (Based on Shoda, Mischel, and Wright, 1994)

	PROSOCIAL TALK	WHINING	COMPLIANCE	VERBAL AGGRESSION
Correlations	.19	.28	.41	.47

Reproduced with the permission of the American Psychological Association.

havior by noting that he or she is likely to be verbally aggressive when teased by a peer and less likely to be verbally aggressive when punished by an adult. Although this research demonstrates that idiosyncratic patterns of responses to different psychological situations constitute a meaningful level of analysis, the research does not indicate when this level of analysis is optimal.

Consider an analogy. Some of you may have taken the Scholastic Aptitude Test for college admission. The SAT has different subtests including a verbal and a quantitative test. Two individuals may receive the same overall SAT test score but their verbal and quantitative scores may be quite different. Perhaps both students have a total score of 1000, but one student may have a quantitative score of 600 and a verbal score of 400, while the other has 400 quantitative and 600 verbal. It is equally valid to describe a student's performance either as a single aggregate score (1000) or as a pattern indicating relative strengths in quantitative or verbal ability. The former description is analogous to that provided by trait theorists: an aggregated measure that ignores the idiosyncratic pattern of subscores; the latter is analogous to the level of detail preferred by Mischel. Neither description is more fundamental or correct than the other; they complement each other and focus on different levels of analysis. Different levels of analysis might well be appropriate to answer different kinds of questions. For example, knowledge of the pattern of scores might be useful for predicting something about a choice of courses in college. Perhaps students whose Verbal SAT is higher than their Quantitative would be more likely to take courses in the humanities than in the sciences, whereas those with the opposite pattern might likely show an opposite pattern of course selection. Knowledge of a person's total score, on the other hand, might be predictive of a student's overall grade point average.

Consider another hypothetical example. Suppose a person visits a psychotherapist complaining about a tendency to behave in an inappropriately violent and aggressive manner. A trait theorist might want to try to change the person's trait or disposition to behave in a violent way. Someone interested in the situational specificity of behavior, however, might try to discover the specific characteristics of the situations that are likely to elicit aggressive behavior. For example, a male patient might become aggressive when encountering women who reject his sexual advances. Which of these strategies do you think might be more effective? Are there compelling theoretical reasons to assume that one of the two is superior to the other? Do the strategies lead to different methods of therapy?

WHEN TRAITS PREDICT BEHAVIOR

We have sketched a hypothetical analysis of the trait-versus-situation debate. Let's now turn to actual studies that provide evidence for the cross-situational consistency of traits.

Although it is difficult to predict an individual's behavior in a particular situation from knowledge of his or her score on a trait measure, there is evidence indicating that trait measures are sometimes predictive of behavior. Ambady and Rosenthal (1993) demonstrated that judgments of personality traits based on brief observations of a person's behavior could be used to predict ratings of teacher effectiveness. In their study, three ten-second video clips were made of the teaching behavior of thirteen graduate students who were teaching a mock class in a teaching laboratory. They were rated on a number of personality variables by nine female undergraduates on the basis of observations of these video clips. Each teacher was assigned an average rating on each of fifteen desirable rated traits. The trait scores were positively correlated with each other (average correlation between the trait score = .67). Since the trait scores were positively correlated, a global measure was formed that was the average positive trait score assigned to each teacher on the basis of the video clip. Each of the graduate student teachers in this study was also teaching an actual course. The correlations between the ratings assigned to each teacher by his or her actual students and the global trait ratings based on the video clips was .76. Teachers who were rated as active, empathic, confident, dominant, enthusiastic, likable, and optimistic were likely to receive high ratings from their real students.

Ambady and Rosenthal also found that judgments of teacher behavior based on three two-second observations (six seconds total) could also be used to predict teacher effectiveness ratings with comparable accuracy. These data indicate that trait-relevant behaviors can sometimes be assessed very rapidly and that these judgments can be related to an individual's behavior in a particular setting—in this instance in a classroom.

Funder and Sneed (1993) obtained observations of behavior where a male and a female student who did not know each other were asked to say whatever they liked to one another for five minutes. Their interactions were videotaped and recorded. Each videotape was rated on a 62-item behavioral response list by observers who were not acquainted with the students. A second group of students was asked to supply ratings indicating whether each of these 62 behaviors was indicative of each of the Big Five personality traits. The right-hand column of Table 3.2 provides ratings for various behaviors indicative of extraversion. Note that the raters believed that extraverts are likely to have high levels of enthusiasm and energy and to speak in a loud voice. Introverts, by contrast, were assumed to be reserved and to behave in a fearful and timid manner.

Each subject was also assigned an extraversion rating by two acquaintances. The correlations column in Table 3.2 presents correlations between these ratings and the ratings of each of the behaviors that are related to extraversion. The correlations for the behaviors that are indicative of extraversion tend to be positive and the correlations for behaviors indicative of introversion or low scores on extraversion are negative.

What do these data tell us about the meaning of trait ratings of extraversion? The data indicate that laypeople have a reasonably clear idea of the kinds of behaviors that define high and low scores on extraversion. Furthermore, these behaviors can be judged from relatively brief observations of social interactions with a stranger. The ratings of behavior could be combined to form an index of the extent to which an individual behaved in an extraverted manner in this situation. This index would be remarkably predictive of the trait ratings on extraversion

TABLE 3.2 Correlations Between Acquaintance Ratings and Behavior Ratings for Behaviors Judged Relevant to Extraversion (Based on Funder and Sneed, 1993)

BEHAVIORS	CORRELATIONS	MEAN RELEVANCE RATINGS
Fifteen highest positively rated BQ items		
Has high enthusiasm and energy level	.29	4.79
Speaks in a loud voice	.28	4.69
Is expressive in face, voice, or gestures	.30	4.66
Dominates the interaction	.14	4.62
Initiates humor	.20	4.52
Is talkative	.25	4.45
Brags	.01	4.10
Discusses large number of topics	.01	3.76
Exhibits social skills	.30	3.72
Is physically animated	.17	3.69
Seems to enjoy interaction	.16	3.62
"Interviews" partner	.02	3.45
Says or does interesting things	.14	3.38
Engages in constant eye contact	.03	3.38
Makes physical contact with partner	.17	3.34
Nine lowest negatively rated BQ items		
Is reserved and unexpressive	−.32	−4.83
Behaves in a fearful or timid manner	−.33	−4.24
Volunteers little information re self	−.22	−3.79
Shows lack of interest in interaction	−.27	−3.52
Expresses insecurity or sensitivity	−.35	−3.48
Shows signs of tension or anxiety	−.21	−3.24
Keeps partner at a distance	−.31	−3.21
Has awkward interpersonal style	−.33	−2.82
Expresses self-pity	−.13	−2.55

TABLE 3.3 Correlations Between Acquaintance Ratings and Behavior Ratings for Behaviors Judged Relevant to Neuroticism (Based on Funder and Sneed, 1993)

BEHAVIORS	CORRELATIONS	MEAN RELEVANCE RATINGS
Thirteen highest positively rated BQ items		
Shows signs of tension or anxiety	.08	4.25
Has awkward interpersonal style	.07	3.81
Expresses insecurity or sensitivity	.11	3.69
Expresses hostility	.05	3.56
Expresses guilt	.01	3.56
Seeks reassurance	.11	3.50
Expresses awareness of camera/experimentor	−.04	3.31
Expresses self-pity	.10	3.19
Discusses large number of topics	−.03	2.94
Is physically animated	.03	2.88
Tries to sabotage or obstruct	.07	2.81
Acts irritable	.12	2.69
Behaves in a fearful or timid manner	.08	2.56
Three lowest negatively rated BQ items		
Appears relaxed and comfortable	−.12	−3.44
Expresses warmth	.01	−2.56
Speaks fluently	−.14	−2.50

Reproduced with permission of the American Psychological Association.

assigned to a person by his or her acquaintances. Or, to reverse the direction of prediction, trait ratings of extraversion could be used to predict the expression of extraverted behavior in a particular social situation. Although the overall correlations are not provided in the Funder and Sneed article, it is apparent that they would be quite high, perhaps approaching .90.

Table 3.3 presents data for a comparable analysis for ratings of neuroticism. An examination of the data in this table indicates that it would be much more difficult to predict neuroticism ratings on the basis of observations of behavior in a five-minute social encounter with a stranger. The correlations between the behaviors that are assumed to be indicative of neuroticism and ratings of neuroticism by acquaintances are lower than those reported in Table 3.2. Apparently, neuroticism is difficult to judge on the basis of casual encounters.

CROSS-SITUATIONAL AGGREGATES

There are also studies that provide evidence for the cross-situational consistency of traits. In order to determine the cross-situational generality of a trait, it is necessary to observe repeatedly the behavior of a group of individuals in several different situations. This is not easy to do: personality psychologists are usually not given permission, or funds, to observe individuals in their daily activities over extended periods of time. There are, however, situations in which individuals may be repeatedly observed and measures of their behavior obtained. Moskowitz (1982), interested in the trait of dominance, observed 56 children in a nursery school setting for eight weeks, each child being observed for a half hour per week. The observers noted whether or not, in each ten-second interval, the child exhibited any of five behaviors that were assumed to be relevant to dominance: displacement, or the act of taking another child's toy or play space; verbal commands; verbal suggestions; verbal threats; and verbal directions (e.g., telling another child what to do). Each of these indices of dominance was assessed in various situations. The situations could differ with respect to the target of the behavior—a male or female child or a male or female adult. Or they could vary with respect to the extent to which they were constrained by the activity of the teacher; that is, the activity in which the child was engaged might be one defined by the teacher or one that occurred during a free-play period.

These data may be used to illustrate the meaning of the trait concept. Are the different ways of expressing the trait of dominance related to each other? For example, are children who take another child's toy also likely to threaten the child? Moskowitz attempted to predict a child's score on each index of dominance by combining scores on the four remaining indices. The average correlation of an optimal combination of four used to predict the excluded fifth score was .66. This correlation implies that children are relatively consistent in the ways in which they express a tendency to be dominant (or, the converse, submissive). Children who engage in any four of these activities frequently are likely to engage in the fifth activity frequently. For example, if a child behaves in a dominant manner by displacing other children, making suggestions, commanding, and threatening other children, then it is likely that the child will frequently direct other children. There is an underlying coherence to the varying ways in which children express dominant and submissive behaviors.

Are dominance behaviors cross-situationally consistent? Moskowitz attempted to answer this question by obtaining an aggregate index of dominance behaviors in the situations she studied. She found that a combined index of behavior with three of the four types of target persons could be used to predict the frequency of dominance behaviors toward the fourth category of persons. Children who behaved in a dominant manner toward adults and toward their same-sex peers were likely to behave in a dominant manner toward an opposite-sex peer. Similarly, indices of dominance behavior in constrained situations could be used to predict dominance behavior in unconstrained situations. The average correlation was .62, which implies that children who were relatively submissive when engaging in teacher-defined activities were likely to be relatively submissive during free-play activities.

Moskowitz and Schwarz (1982) obtained ratings from teachers of the children studied by Moskowitz. The four teachers rated these children on each of the behavioral indices related to dominance, and their ratings for each behavior were summed to obtain an aggregate index of dominance for each child. These ratings were correlated with an aggregate index of the frequency of the child's dominance behaviors. The correlation was .59. This result indicates that teacher ratings of dominance behavior are related to the frequency of occurrence of these behaviors. Children who are rated as exhibiting dominance behaviors do in fact behave in a dominant way.⌋

Small, Zeldin, and Savin-Williams (1983) studied dominance behaviors in four groups of adolescents attending a summer wilderness or travel camp. They measured eight behaviors which they assumed were related to dominance, and which were similar to the behavioral indices used by Moskowitz in her study of nursery school children. The adolescents were observed for half an hour a day for eight weeks and each instance of a dominant behavior was recorded as well as the setting in which the behavior occurred. Three settings were distinguished: camping, meals, and free time. With three different settings, it is possible to study the cross-situational consistency of behavior. Are individuals who are dominant during meals dominant during free-time periods? One may answer this question by correlating frequency counts of behavior in one setting with those obtained in a different setting. The average correlation across settings was .78, indicating that there was a considerable amount of cross-situational consistency in dominance behavior. Adolescents who behaved in a dominant manner at meals also were likely to behave in a dominant manner during their free time.

In addition, each participant rated all the other participants in his or her group for dominance. Small, Zeldin, and Savin-Williams obtained a correlation between the aggregated measure of dominance based on observed frequency of dominant behavior and an aggregated trait rating of dominance based on ratings by fellow campers. The correlations for the four groups of campers had an average value of .85. These results indicate that frequency counts of behaviors indicative of dominance were highly correlated with peer ratings of dominance.

The results obtained in the Moskowitz and Small, Zeldin, and Savin-Williams studies are impressive. Both studies obtained evidence for cross-situational consistencies of behavior. Can we assume that these studies settle the issue of cross-situational consistency? Are there reasons to be cautious in our assessment of the outcomes of these studies? Note that both studies observe behavior in highly structured settings—nursery schools and summer camps. The cast of characters with whom individuals interact—peers, teachers, counselors—remains constant. If the subjects in these studies were observed in different settings—perhaps at home in interactions with their siblings or parents—their behavior would have appeared to be less cross-situationally consistent. Parents are often surprised when they are informed of their children's behavior in different contexts. Reports of "good" behavior are often met with incredulity and protestations that the child never behaves that way at home and, conversely, reports of bad behavior are often attributed to the influence of other children who lead one's own child astray. We don't want to settle the complex question of the degree of cross-situational consistency by appeal to anecdotes and common observations. Rather, we want to indicate that the issue is complicated. We need more studies similar to those of Moskowitz and Small, Zeldin, and Savin-Williams that obtain measures of behavior in many different situations in order to obtain a clearer understanding of the degree of cross-situational consistency. It is almost impossible to do these studies as the range of possible situations in which individuals are observed becomes extensive. And, for obvious reasons, we do not have many studies of this type.

LONGITUDINAL CONTINUITY

Does personality change? Do you think that your personality will be different in twenty years? Are there relationships between the personality traits you have assigned to yourself and your behavior as a child? The best way to get answers to these questions is to study a group of people for a long period of time.

From Childhood to Adult Personality

Are the personality trait scores that characterize young adults related to childhood behaviors? People behave in different ways in different settings at different ages. Independence in a 3-year-old does not mean the same thing as independence in a college student. A 3-year-old who is aggressive is not likely to be accused of spouse abuse, but a married adult who is aggressive might very well be accused of being abusive to a spouse. If we want to study the relationship between childhood traits and the traits of young adults, we do not expect to search for continuities using exactly the same measures. If there are continuities, we would expect to find them through what are assumed to be age-appropriate indicators of the trait. In the next section we will describe the results of three studies that indicate that the behavior of young children is predictive of personality trait scores obtained several years later.

Predictions from Childhood Personality

Huesmann, Eron, Lefkowitz, and Walder (1984) used a peer rating method to study aggression in a group of 870 8-year-old children. They asked the children to nominate children in their class who behaved in any one of ten aggressive ways, such as: Who pushes or shoves children? Each child's aggression score was based on the number of nominations received from classmates. They also obtained measures of aggression 22 years later for the same children. There were relationships between the earlier peer nominations and evidence of aggressive behavior 22 years later. More continuity was found for aggressive behavior among males than among females. The correlation between aggression scores for males at age 8 and self-reports of aggression derived from a personality test at age 30 was .32. The comparable correlation for females was .20. A better indication of the degree of continuity of aggression can be obtained by aggregating different indices and obtaining a hypothetical correlation between aggregates corrected for errors of measurement. These correlations were .50 for males and .34 for females. These data indicate that children who are described by their classmates as aggressive are more likely to be judged as aggressive as adults.

Aggressive behavior in childhood was also related to criminality. Huesmann et al. divided their sample into thirds on the basis of aggression scores at age 8. Table 3.4 presents the proportion of criminal convictions for male and female subjects whose scores fell in each third of the age 8 aggression scores. Note that the proportion of criminal convictions increases as age 8 aggression scores increase. Males in the top third of the distribution are 2.3 times more likely to have a criminal conviction than males in the bottom third.

Caspi, Elder, and Bem (1987) studied the relationship between ratings of the severity and frequency of temper tantrums for 8- to 10-year-old male children, obtained from their mother's reports, and ratings of these individuals based on interviews twenty years later. Childhood temper tantrum rating scores correlated .45 with a rating indicative of impulsivity twenty years later. In addition, frequency of temper tantrums correlated −.34 with the number of years of education attained. Childhood temper tantrum scores were also related to occupational status; those from middle-class backgrounds who were rated as having many and severe temper tantrums in childhood tended to have low occupational status. Children with high temper tantrum scores obtained less education than children with low scores and had more erratic job histories. The characteristics judged to be present at age 8 tended to endure and influence the way in which these individuals related to the world of school and work.

Harrington, Block, and Block (1983) studied creativity in 4- and 5-year-old children. They assumed that creative children would excel at tasks in which they were to name a number of different things that had a common property. For example, they were asked to name as many round objects as they could think of. A score on this measure was the number of correct responses the child could think of in a limited period of time. Harrington et al. related this measure to personality ratings made by teachers when the children were 11 years old. The teachers were

TABLE 3.4   Proportion of Subjects Convicted for a Crime in New York State before Age 30 According to Gender and Peer-nominated Aggression at Age 8 (Based on Huesmann, Eron, Lefkowitz, and Walder, 1984)

Sex	AGE 8 PEER-NOMINATED AGGRESSION		
	Low	Medium	High
Males	9/90 (10%)	25/163 (15%)	19/82 (23%)
Females	0/49 (0.0%)	2/110 (1.8%)	3/48 (6.3%)

Reproduced with permission of the American Psychological Association.

asked to rank their pupils on 100 personality characteristics. Correlations were obtained between the children's score on the creativity test at age 4 or 5 and each of the 100 personality characteristics. The correlation between creativity test scores and the teacher's creativity rating was .45. This correlation, the highest of the 100 comparable correlations obtained, provides support for the validity of the creativity test. The measures that are related in this study are quite different: the teacher's ratings were based on the child's performance in school and probably in part on the child's writing and artistic productions. Despite the difference in the measures and the kinds of behaviors that are observed at different ages, some characteristic of these children must persist that influences both the way in which the child responds to the test at age 4 or 5 and at school several years later.

From First Year of Life to Childhood Personality

The studies reviewed provide evidence for continuities in personality tendencies present as early as age 4. What is the earliest age at which individual differences in personality are related to later characteristics? Do newborns differ in personality? It is difficult to answer these questions. In order to do so, we would have to study individual differences in behavior in newborns or very young children and relate these to measures of personality obtained several years later in a longitudinal study. There are some studies of this type indicating that characteristics of children observed in their first year do relate to characteristics measured several years later. (We will say more about this issue in chapter 6.)

Continuities in Personality

Three generalizations about continuities in personality are suggested by the research reviewed above. First, the results underestimate the extent to which there are continuities in personality. There are errors of measurement in these studies that tend to decrease the relationships obtained. Consider the Harrington, Block, and Block study. The child's ability to name different objects of a particular category was measured on one occasion. A better index of this ability might be obtained by observing children on several occasions and aggregating the scores. In addition, there might be other ways of measuring a child's creativity at age 4. For example, children could have been asked to draw something and to tell stories. Then the ratings based on their performance could have been aggregated with scores on the test used by Harrington et al. These more comprehensive indices based on aggregates of different kinds of measures obtained on more than one occasion might well have provided a better indication of creativity at this age. So too, teacher ratings might be imperfect indices. Perhaps different teachers assign different meanings to the term "creativity." Also teachers may differ in the accuracy of their judgments. Teacher ratings of the 11-year-olds could have been supplemented with ratings of creative productions (e.g., drawings and writing samples) and children could have been rated by two teachers in successive years. As the accuracy of measurement increases, the correlation between measures increases. Therefore, the correlations obtained from these studies should be thought of as lower-bound estimates of a hypothetical true relationship. These possibilities suggest that personality characteristics manifested in childhood are more predictive of later characteristics than is indicated by the obtained correlations.

Second, there are both continuities and discontinuities in personality. Consider the results of the Huesmann et al. study on aggression. The estimated correlation for continuity between male aggression ratings at age 8 and a combined index of aggression 22 years later was .5. This implies that 25% of the variance in aggression in young adulthood is predictable from childhood aggression ratings. Even though this is probably a lower-bound estimate since more comprehensive measures of aggression would probably yield higher correlations, there are undoubtedly discontinuities in aggressive behavior. Some aggressive children are not aggressive as adults, and some children who are not aggressive become aggressive adults. We need to explain both continuities and discontinuities in personality.

Third, studies relating personality characteristics manifested in early childhood to later personality characteristics use different kinds of measures. Third graders do not have criminal records or engage in the abuse of their spouses. Nevertheless, aggression manifested in childhood is related to aggression in adulthood. The continuities obtained in these studies are examples of what has been called **heterotypic continuity**—continuities between behaviors that have different surface characteristics. The concept is that continuities may be attributable to the continuation of a latent disposition that influences measures obtained in different contexts at different ages.

What accounts for continuities and discontinuities in personality? The studies reviewed here do not really help us answer this question. It would be interesting to compare individuals who exhibited dramatic change in personality and those who did not. Such studies might identify the characteristics of persons or the life events that promote either stability or change in personality. Our understanding of the reasons for change and stability might be different for different personality characteristics. Think about your own personality. Do you think that your characteristics are related to your behavior in childhood? If so, why?

There are many possible explanations for the continuities observed in the studies reviewed here. Here are three possibilities:

1. Children who are rated as being aggressive may come to think of themselves as aggressive. Their aggressive behavior in adulthood may derive from a tendency to live up to their reputation. That is, the perception of others may influence self-perception, and self-perception may act as a kind of self-fulfilling prophecy.

2. There may be environmental influences on personality that are continuous over time. For example, creative behavior in childhood might be influenced by child-rearing practices—perhaps a tendency to encourage imaginative

play—and these same practices might be used when children are older. Parents who encourage imaginative and creative play in 4-year-olds might also encourage similar behaviors in 11-year-olds. Thus continuities in personality might be determined by the presence of related influences at different ages.

3. Personality might be a constitutional characteristic of a person that is present at birth and influences the way in which a person responds to the social environment at different ages.

These three reasons for continuities are not mutually exclusive; all these processes might operate to create stability and change in personality. We shall return to the issue of continuity and change. For now, we leave you with the general conclusion that there are relationships between personality characteristics present in early childhood and personality characteristics present several years later.

STABILITY AND CHANGE IN ADULT PERSONALITY

Does personality change in adulthood? To what extent will your personality trait scores from the test you took in chapter 2 be descriptive of your personality when you are middle-aged or when you are a senior citizen? If you describe yourself as introverted and neurotic as a young adult, will you describe yourself as introverted and neurotic when you are middle-aged? These are questions that we can answer. McCrae and Costa (1990) administered the NEO-PI, a measure of the Big Five traits, to 983 adults at two six-year intervals. Table 3.5 presents coefficients of stability for six-year test intervals for men and women in two different age groups for each of the five personality scores. These correlations are high. With the exception of agreeableness, which was measured with a short form of the scale, the personality dimensions have stability coefficients close to .8. The correlations do not differ appreciably for males and females and they are not different for older and younger adults.

TABLE 3.5   Stability Coefficients for Five Personality Traits (Based on Costa and McCrae, 1988)

	MEN	WOMEN	MEN	WOMEN	
	Age 25–26		Age 57–84		TOTAL
Neuroticism	.78	.85	.82	.81	.83
Extraversion	.84	.75	.86	.73	.82
Openness	.87	.84	.81	.73	.83
Agreeableness	.64	.60	.59	.55	.63
Conscientiousness	.82	.84	.76	.71	.79

Note: Correlations are based on six-year intervals for neuroticism, extraversion, and openness and on three-year intervals for short forms of agreeableness and conscientiousness scales.
Reproduced with permission of the American Psychological Association.

These correlations actually underestimate the stability of self-report measures of personality. There are short-term fluctuations in scores on these tests, for many reasons. An individual may interpret an item differently on two occasions. People may experience temporary mood changes that might influence how they respond to a questionnaire. Shifts of attention or other distractions might also influence a response. Yet short-term stability coefficients provide a baseline to consider long-term stability. If scores fluctuate from day to day, they will surely fluctuate over years. The short-term stability of scores might be considered a baseline to evaluate test-retest correlations over years. The former values set upper boundaries for the latter. When the long-term correlations are corrected by a consideration of the upper bounds set by the short-term values, the corrected correlations are higher. Costa and McCrae (1988a) report correlations of .95, .90, and .97 for the neuroticism, extraversion, and openness scales, respectively. These correlations suggest that the five personality trait scores you obtained will not change much over the adult span. You are quite likely to assign similar scores to yourself 30 or 40 years from now.

Does the fact that your personality descriptions will probably remain relatively invariant mean that your personality, or more precisely, your personality traits, will remain invariant? Note that this question assumes that there is a difference between your scores on self-report measures of personality and your actual personality traits. The scores are an index of the trait—but they may be inaccurate. Perhaps people form a crystallized self-image that is not responsive to any actual changes that occur. For example, you may think of yourself as a neurotic person and this belief may remain relatively constant for the next 50 years even though you may be far less neurotic 50 years from now.

Costa and McCrae (1988a) considered this problem. In order to discover whether or not stability in self-report measures was determined by inaccurate ratings, they obtained spouse ratings for a subsample of 167 adults in their study. The test-retest correlations for spouse ratings for a six-year-period were comparable to those for six-year self-reports. The average correlations for the neuroticism, extraversion, and openness scales were .83, .77, .80, respectively. These correlations inform us that husbands and wives tend to see relatively little change in the personality of their spouses. Do these correlations indicate that personality traits remain constant over much of the adult life span? Not necessarily. Perhaps married couples develop crystallized views of each other's personality as well. Is it possible to design a study to circumvent this objection? It would be desirable to have the results of a longitudinal study in which test-retest correlations were obtained from independent raters during the adult years.

Haan (1981) obtained test-retest correlations for two samples at ages 37 and 47 for a trait related to conscientiousness. The correlations for males and females in the two samples varied between .44 and .56, considerably lower than those obtained by Costa and McCrae for the stability of self-report measures. There are two possible reasons for this difference:

1. Self-report measures of personality may have much higher levels of stability than ratings. Perhaps the former measure is influenced by a crystallized self-image that does not reflect actual changes in personality traits.
2. The ratings used in the Haan study were derived from one rater and may not have been as reliable as descriptions based on aggregate ratings from several raters.

Another way to study the longitudinal continuities in adult personality traits is to relate trait scores obtained on one occasion to outcome measures that are assumed to be influenced by personality traits. Kelly and Conley (1987) obtained personality ratings for a large sample of engaged couples. They had five acquaintances rate each of their subjects on neuroticism, extraversion, and impulsivity (an aspect of the trait of conscientiousness) prior to their marriage. The couples participated in a longitudinal investigation for the next 50 years. Kelly and Conley attempted to predict marital satisfaction and divorce. In addition to trait ratings obtained prior to marriage, they collected information about attitudes toward marriage and family history data, as well as information from the couples about economic status, illness, and tragedies occurring over the adult life span. The best predictors of marital satisfaction and divorce were the trait ratings. Male and female partners in marriages that ended in divorce scored higher in neuroticism than did partners in stable marriages. In addition, males who were rated high in Impulsivity were likely to enter into marriages that ended in divorce.

These results appear to be easily interpretable. Individuals who are neurotic—worried, tense, depressed, and so on—are difficult to live with. Do you think these data have practical implications? Should individuals who are contemplating marriage attempt to obtain personality ratings from their partner's acquaintances? Those contemplating this strategy should not rely on their own impressions of their potential partner's personality traits—love may be blind!

Neuroticism scores predict psychopathology. Levenson, Aldwin, Bosse, and Spiro, et al. (1988) administered a brief version of a self-report personality inventory called the Eysenck Personality Inventory to a large sample of adult male subjects (Eysenck & Eysenck, 1968). Ten years later they asked the same subjects to fill out a standard psychiatric inventory, an inventory used to diagnose psychological disorders as defined by the current Diagnostic and Statistical Manual of the American Psychiatric Association. They found that neuroticism scores on the inventory correlated .46 with a global index of severity of symptoms. Individuals who had high neuroticism scores tended to meet the diagnostic criteria for various forms of psychopathology ten years after filling out the personality inventory.

MODELS OF STABILITY AND CHANGE

Longitudinal studies of personality, then, indicate that personality characteristics initially expressed in childhood are related to later personality characteristics. In addition, they provide evidence that personality traits tend to remain relatively constant for long periods of time. This section will describe three ways of thinking about stability and change in personality.

1. *Personality Traits Do Not Change.* McCrae and Costa (1990) argued that trait scores do not change over the adult life span. In support of their view, they note that test-retest correlations for six- and twelve-year periods for the Big Five personality traits are similar to test-retest correlations for brief periods of time. At the conclusion of their book, *Personality in Adulthood,* they state:

> . . . there is neither growth nor decline in adult personality. A psychology whose purpose was to explain how personality changes with age would have nothing to say. Indeed it becomes more pertinent to explain how personality remains stable.

> . . . Ask not how life's experiences change personality; ask instead how personality gives order, continuity, and predictability to the life course, as well as creating or accommodating change. For the psychologist as well as the aging individual, enduring dispositions form a basis for understanding and guiding emerging lives. (1990, p. 127)

McCrae and Costa's view of personality as constant applies only to the five personality trait scores that you have assigned to yourselves. Other aspects of personality might change. The challenges and events that individuals encounter over the life span do not change personality traits; rather personality traits determine the way in which individuals respond to the events. Consider an example. Psychologists have argued that there is a midlife crisis that creates emotional distress and neurotic reactions. In men, the crisis is attributable to common midlife attitudes and beliefs such as an awareness of mortality, the loss of romantic excitement in marriage, and the realization of limited career options. In women, menopause and a change in child-rearing responsibilities when children leave home are assumed to contribute to the crisis (Levinson, Darrow, Klein, Levinson, & McKee, 1978). McCrae and Costa argued that careful surveys do not find evidence of a peak in emotional distress in middle age. In their longitudinal surveys of adult personality they do in fact find a small subset of male adults who experience a midlife crisis, but these individuals also had high neuroticism scores ten years earlier. They argue that personality, in this instance neuroticism, determined the response to the critical events associated with middle age. McCrae and Costa interpret these results as follows: " . . . [the men] had more than their share of complaints many years earlier, and it begins to seem that they carried their troubles with them. It may be that the *form* of the trouble varies with the period of life in which they happen to be" (1990, p. 166).

2. *Personality as a Blueprint for Change.* Each of us will encounter many crises, challenges, and stressful events in our life. Some of you have recently entered college and may, for the first time, be living apart from your parents. You may form attachments to significant others and these attachments may end. You may experience graduation from school, the birth of a child, a career change, severe illness,

and death of a person you love. Will these events change you? McCrae and Costa would argue that your personality will determine your response to these events. Perhaps they are wrong. Individuals might change. New experiences, especially those that are infused with emotional significance, might lead to changes in personality. Change may be random or it may be systematic. It is possible that the response to dramatic and novel events is unpredictable. Since, by definition, we have not encountered them before, we do not know how we will react to them. And if they do change us, the direction of that change may be difficult or even impossible to predict. If individuals change as a result of encountering novel events, there will be a gradual drift in personality characteristics and each individual will follow an idiosyncratic pattern of change over his or her lifetime.

There is a second and different way of thinking about change in response to novel and dramatic events. If personality characteristics influence the responses to novel events, then the changes that occur in personality might be predictable from a knowledge of an individual's personal characteristics prior to the event. Caspi and Moffitt (1991) argued that encounters with novel events accentuate individual differences in personality. They studied a sample of 348 girls who were born during a one-year period in 1972 and 1973 in New Zealand. They were interested in the effects of menarche on the development of behavior problems. They divided their sample into three groups: those who had early menarche, those with menarche at the usual time, and those who were late in the development of menarche. They found that girls who were in the first group exhibited an increase in behavior problems. Early menarche may be stressful for a variety of reasons. It occurs when girls have few role models to help them respond in appropriate ways. The associated physical changes may cause others to treat them as if they were older and to expect them to behave in mature ways. Caspi and Moffitt obtained ratings of behavior problems at age 9, 13, and 15 from each girl's mother. They also obtained a measure of change in behavior problems for the same girls from age 13 to 15 by subtracting the scale score for girls at age 15 from their scores at age 13. In order to study the impact of personality and the timing of menarche on changes in behavior problems, they divided their sample into two groups: those rated by their mothers as being relatively high in behavior problems at age 9 and those who were relatively low in behavior problems at age 9. Figure 3.2 presents the results of their analysis. Note that the girls who had early menarche exhibited the largest increase in behavior problems. The effect of early menarche was, however, influenced by ratings of behavior problems at age 9. Note that girls who were rated as being high in behavior problems at age 9 showed the largest increase in behavior problems between ages 13 and ages 15. These data indicate that effects of a novel and stressful event served to accentuate preexistent differences in personality.

The Caspi and Moffitt study may be interpreted as indicating that individuals change by becoming more like themselves. Think of a rubbing made by placing a thin piece of paper over an object with a raised design such as a coin. As the paper is rubbed, the underlying design emerges with increased clarity. Personality

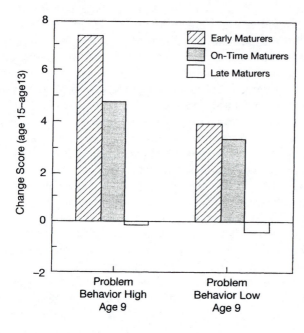

FIGURE 3.2 Changes in behavioral problems from age 13 to age 15 among early-, on-time-, and late-maturing girls stratified by their premenarcheal behavioral problems (high and low at age 9). (Based on Caspi and Moffitt, 1992; reproduced with permission of the American Psychological Association.)

traits may be thought of as the design hidden beneath the paper. As one encounters novel and stressful events, personality traits determine the individual's response and gradually define and clarify the underlying personality structures that are latent within the person.

Caspi and Moffitt note that this model of personality change as an accentuation of preexistent differences needs to be tested in other contexts and with other age groups. Block and Robins (1993) obtained evidence for an analogous change process in a study of changes in self-esteem between ages 14 and 23. In addition to self-report measures of self-esteem, Block and Robins had psychologists rate their subjects' personality characteristics at age 14. They later obtained change scores by subtracting self-esteem scores at age 23 from the earlier scores. They found that changes in self-esteem over this nine-year period were related to the personality ratings of the psychologists who interviewed the subjects when they were 14. Male subjects who were assigned ratings indicative of neuroticism declined in self-esteem. Changes in self-esteem for the female subjects were also related to neurotic characteristics: those who had earlier been rated as exhibiting neurotic tendencies declined in self-esteem. In addition, females who were rated low in extraversion and agreeableness also declined in self-esteem. Can you think of an explanation for the gender difference in this study? Why are changes in self-esteem among females related to a broader set of personality characteristics than among males?

The Block and Robins study indicates that change in personality may be related to personality characteristics present prior to the change. The psychologists who rated the personality characteristics of the subjects at age 14 may have been aware of characteristics that influence one's probable response to events not yet encountered. A person's ability to respond successfully to new challenges and social encounters may be related to that individual's personality traits. Those who exhibit neurotic tendencies at age 14 may be less likely to meet new challenges successfully, and this inability to respond successfully leads to a decline in self-esteem. Changes in self-esteem were not random. They were predictable from a knowledge of personality.

Are the kinds of changes observed in the Caspi and Moffitt and Block and Robins studies rare or common? We don't know. Many of you have recently entered college. College is a novel setting presenting many challenges and opportunities. New friends are made. New attitudes and ideas develop. Many opportunities are provided to join new organizations. Think about your personality traits prior to college entry. Do you think that your extraversion score changed? If you were extraverted, do you think that your extraversion was increased given an opportunity to make new friends, join new organizations, and develop a new persona? If you were introverted, did this fact influence your response to college entry and did your introversion increase?

3. *Change in Personality in Response to New Experiences.* New events that we encounter may actually change us. Perhaps people who enter psychotherapy or who lose a job or who move to a new community may experience changes in their personality. Caspi and Herbener (1990) studied the stability of personality characteristics in married couples. They classified their couples into three groups based on ratings assigned to them on 100 personality characteristics. Ratings were obtained for spouses in 1970 and eleven years later in 1981. Figure 3.3 presents their results. Note that they found that the tendency of individuals to change in personality depends on the degree to which they were similar to their spouses in the initial assessment. Those who were not similar tended to change more than those who were similar. These results suggest that one way to change your personality is to marry someone whose personality is not like yours. Can you explain these results? We think it is likely that individuals who are constantly in the presence of someone who is very different will find it difficult to maintain constancy in their personalities. Imagine the experience of an introverted person being married to an extraverted person. In what ways might an introvert change as a result in this experience. Being married to someone who is quite different is only one of the many possible encounters with new environments that might result in change in a person's personality.

We have identified three possible kinds of changes in personality traits. The traits may remain constant. Change in personality may accentuate previous personality differences. Individuals may change in unpredictable ways over the adult life span. Which of these views is correct? Taken at face value, they appear contradictory. They may, however, all coexist. Personality traits may remain

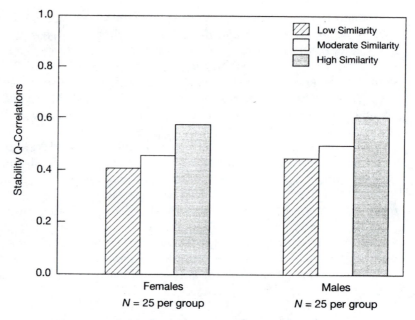

FIGURE 3.3   Intraindividual stability (1970–1981) as a function of dyadic similarity in 1970 Berkeley Guidance Study. (Based on Caspi and Herbener, 1990; reproduced with permission of the American Psychological Association.)

relatively stable. Some changes may be random and unpredictable. And some of the changes that occur may be related to the accentuation of previously expressed traits. We do not have a sufficient body of longitudinal research that focuses on changes in personality to know whether the change in traits is predictable from a knowledge of personality characteristics.

SUMMARY

This chapter presented an analysis of the meaning of the personality test scores you obtained from the self-report test in chapter 2. The trait scores you received based on your self-reports are similar to scores you would receive if you were described by one or more of your friends. And scores are likely to remain stable for brief periods of time.

Trait scores are related to the behavior of individuals in different situations. While it may be difficult to predict accurately from the scores the way in which an individual will behave in a particular situation, the scores are likely to be predictive of an aggregate measure of social behavior.

Trait scores tend to be stable for long periods of time. And they influence the way in which individuals respond to various crises and new experiences they encounter over their life span.

The evidence on the meaning of trait scores is compatible with the assumption that personality is a disposition that is not identical to the score that is a measure of that disposition. It is not the same as a score based on a self-report, or a rating of a trait, or an aggregate measure of how frequently a behavior occurs in situations that are assumed to be related to a trait. We can assume that personality traits are those characteristics of persons that account for the diverse relationships sketched in this chapter. Individuals reveal their personality traits in the course of their social behaviors, and it is these observations made by oneself or others that influence the ratings assigned to a person. Personality traits may be thought of as latent dispositions that influence the behavior of individuals in many different situations and for extended periods of time.

4

The Big Five:
Are We Finished?

Imagine that you are a psychologist who is studying a species of intelligent organisms on a distant planet. You notice that they are not all alike. You consult the local experts and ask how they differ from one another. You are told that they differ in many ways, physically as well as psychologically. Members of this species have a large number of terms in their language that may be used to describe one another. You find this confusing. You ask about a taxonomy, which is defined in Webster's Dictionary as "The study of the general principles of scientific classification . . . the systematic distinguishing, ordering, and naming of type groups within a subject field" (Gove, 1993, p. 2345). Your experts inform you that there are many different taxonomies, but no single agreed-upon taxonomy to describe the ways in which the members of the species differ. They tell you that the taxonomies were developed by experts on the basis of various theoretical notions. Many of the taxonomies had given rise to various measures of individual differences, so there were actually several means available to classify the ways in which individuals differed from one another.

All of this appears to be quite similar to your experience on Earth. John used the analogy of the Tower of Babel to describe the attempts of personality psychologists to develop a taxonomy. He wrote:

> . . . the number of personality concepts, and of scales designed to measure them, has escalated without an end in sight . . . researchers as well as practitioners . . . are faced with a bewildering array of personality scales from which to choose. . . . Even worse,

scales with the same name measure concepts that are not the same, and scales with different names overlap considerably . . . the systematic accumulation of findings . . . continues to be difficult in the present-day Babel of concepts and scales. (1990, p. 66)

There are obvious advantages to an agreed-upon taxonomy, especially if you are a stranger who is not attuned to the nuances of the ways in which members of this new species you are studying differ. You would be able to communicate your findings back to the psychologists on Earth in a simple and comprehensible form if you could indicate to them that members of the species you are studying may be classified with respect to their differences on a small number of dimensions. But the experts assure you that they have not solved this problem.

THE LEXICAL HYPOTHESIS

You decide to try to solve your problem using the techniques that were used to develop the Big Five taxonomy on Earth. If experts cannot solve the problem, perhaps the insights of laypersons may be used to construct a viable taxonomy. Human beings are intensely interested in one another, and there are many English words that may be used to describe a person. Allport and Odbert (1936) found that the dictionary contained 18,000 such words. Perhaps these words, collectively, codify all the essential respects in which individuals differ from one another. The belief that natural language contains descriptive terms that codify the ways in which individuals differ is called the **lexical hypothesis.**

No one should doubt that the lexical hypothesis contains a grain of truth. People are tall or short, thin or fat, old or young, and, at least some of the time, calm or anxious and talkative or quiet. Surely not all of the descriptive words that we use to describe each other are fictitious. But the lexical hypothesis implies far more than this. It assumes that *all* of the relevant dimensions of personality exist in the natural language and that an analysis of natural language provides the basis for an adequate taxonomy of personality. Neither of these assumptions is self-evidently correct. There may be many important dimensions of personality that have not been encoded in natural language. After all, scientists use many terms that are not found in the natural language. Physicists refer to *quarks,* a term of recent origin, to describe a particular class of elementary particles. Perhaps personality psychologists need terms such as *quarks.*

Even if all of the important ways in which people differ are already captured in natural language, it is by no means clear that the best way to understand personality is to study natural language. If there are over 18,000 terms available in English, an adequate taxonomy must provide some procedure to reduce the number to a manageable subset. There might also be better starting points for the development of a taxonomy. We could start with the insights of psychiatrists and clinicians who have studied individuals intensively in psychotherapy. Perhaps we could derive a taxonomy from biological principles. Or, we could develop a taxonomy by a consideration of individual differences in goals and motives. The starting point for the development of a descriptive system for personality is limited only by our imagination and creativity. In this chapter we focus on the lexical system simply because it is the historical foundation of the Big Five taxonomy, which some personality psychologists consider our best current effort to bring order to the confusion surrounding personality constructs.

ORGANIZING THE LEXICON

It is possible to develop taxonomies theoretically. Many examples of such theoretical taxonomies exist including some deriving from the ancient Greek civilization. Murray's taxonomy (1938), one of many that continue to influence contemporary research, is based on a classification of twenty motives. Individuals may differ in their motivations, and an analysis of these differences may be used to describe a fundamental, or perhaps the fundamental, way in which individuals differ from one another (see chapter 8). Psychologists interested in the lexical approach have been less tied to specific theoretical constructs, instead trying to use relatively atheoretical empirical procedures to investigate the lexicon—the collection of terms used in English to describe the ways in which people differ.

The initial problem for any analysis of the lexicon is the reduction of the 18,000 terms to a manageable subset. We can trace an influential approach to this problem initiated by Norman (1967). Norman began with 18,125 words used to describe people. He eliminated evaluative words (e.g., *nice*); words whose meanings were ambiguous (e.g., *mannered*, a word that has two somewhat distinct meanings: having good manners, and having a distinctive style); words whose meanings were usually not known to literate speakers of English (e.g., *scait*); and words referring to anatomical or physical characteristics (e.g., *short*).

This reduction left him with 8,081 words. Norman then noted that these words could be further classified into different types of descriptions of persons. Some described traits construed as broad descriptions of behavioral tendencies: for example, a person could be described as *irascible*. Personality could also be described in terms of temporary moods or states: a person who is irascible might be often be described as *furious*. Personality might be described in terms of the behavior of an individual: an irascible person might yell a lot. Individuals might be described in terms of the effects of their behavior on others: irascible people might be described as *intimidating*. And finally, evaluative terms could be used: an irascible person might be described as *unlikable*. Norman assumed that trait terms could constitute the basis for the development of a taxonomy. After eliminating all non-trait words with which many undergraduates were unfamiliar, Norman was left with 1,600 terms for the description of personality.

Norman's initial explorations of the lexicon should help you to understand why we called this approach *relatively* atheoretical. The method could be distinguished from "armchair" approaches such as Murray's classification scheme for motives. Murray did not systematically survey all of the terms used to describe motivational differences among individuals. His analysis was based on his insights into the nature of individual differences in motivation. But Norman's explorations also carried with them a good deal of "theoretical baggage." For example, it is not self-evident that a description of personality should begin with an analysis of trait terms. It is possible to start with an analysis of actions. One could begin by listing all of the things that humans do (e.g., they yell at each other) and use this classification of behaviors to develop a taxonomy. (Can you think of reasons to prefer a taxonomy based on actions rather than traits? How would these differ?)

Let us go back to the imaginary experiment with which we started this chapter. It should be obvious that a psychologist visiting a strange planet charged with studying the personality of its inhabitants could proceed in a manner similar to that used by Norman. All of the terms referring to stable behavioral dispositions (traits) could be collected to form the basis for the development of a taxonomy. You would not have to know much about the planet's inhabitants to explore systematically the words used by laypeople to describe one another.

Norman's efforts up to this point still left him with an excess number of terms. Norman then went beyond a relatively atheoretical description. Relying on earlier studies and insights, he classified these terms into 75 clusters and tentatively assigned each to one of five dimensions of personality. A psychologist visiting another planet would probably not have been able to do this. The psychologist could, however, have relied on expert informants to cluster the words into those that form similar meanings, thereby arriving at a subset of clusters.

Norman's explorations of the lexicon left psychologists with over 1,400 terms grouped into 75 clusters. These terms may each be analyzed by being converted to a dimension. A term such as *irascible* may be dimensionalized in one of two ways: its negation may be created, leading to a dimension defined by *irascible* at one extreme and *not irascible* at the other; or, a term may be found that is opposite in meaning. An example of terms usually construed as opposite trait descriptions are *extraverted* and *introverted*. Once the set of personality descriptors has been dimensionalized, it is possible to obtain ratings for any individual (either self-reports or acquaintance ratings) on each of the dimensions. Such ratings may be converted into scores on each of the dimensions. For example, the dimensions may be converted into seven-point scales. A statistical technique called **factor analysis** may be used to explore the relationships among the ratings.

FACTOR ANALYSIS

Goldberg (1990) performed a factor analysis of rating scores based on Norman's classifications. He had college students rate their personality on 1,400 dimensions. He used Norman's classification to form 75 clusters and, by summing scores for dimensions that belonged to the same cluster, he obtained a rating score on each of the clusters for each student. He then used factor analysis to analyze the relationships among the cluster scores.

We can illustrate the steps in this factor analysis. Each person has a score on each of 75 dimensions. We first assess relationships between dimensions by obtaining correlations between all possible pairs of dimensions. If there are 75 dimensions, 2,775 correlations are formed, each correlation representing an index of the relationship between two dimensional scores for a group of individuals. If the correlation between extraverted versus introverted scores and talkative versus quiet scores is .50, this would imply that individuals who tend to describe themselves as extraverted also tend to describe themselves as talkative.

Factor analysis, then, is a procedure that attempts to discover *sets* of dimensions that are related to each other by examining their correlations. Consider some hypothetical examples. Suppose all the correlations were equal to 1.00. The 75 dimensions would reduce to a single dimension or factor. If a person's score on any one dimension was known, then it would be possible to predict without error the person's score on every other dimension. What if the scores formed two clusters? Let's imagine in this idealized representation that (1) all of the dimensions numbered between 1 and 37 correlated with each other with a value of 1.00; (2) all of the dimensions numbered between 38 and 75 had a correlation of 1.00; (3) dimensions numbered between 1 and 37 correlated .00 with dimensions numbered between 38 and 75. It is obvious that there are two separate dimensions in this set, or two factors.

Actual sets of correlations are never this clearly structured, of course, and the methods of factor analysis are complicated. We do not propose to explicate them here. But you should understand that the basic approach used is not difficult to understand. Factor analysis is a statistical technique that is designed to discover the number of separate factors that are present in a set of all of the correlations that may be obtained for a set of measures. The end result of the factor analysis is the discovery of a set of factors—groupings of interrelated measures.

A *factor* is a rather abstract concept. It can be thought of as whatever the interrelated measures have in common, that is, whatever is responsible for causing them to correlate with each other. Each measure in our example has a **loading** on each factor. The loading represents the correlation between the measure and the factor. In our idealized example of a two-factor solution for a set of correlations among 75 dimensions, each dimension would have a loading of 1.00 on one of the two factors, because all of the dimensions that collectively define the factor are perfectly correlated with each other. Correlations among variables that define a factor are almost never 1.00, however, and loadings between a dimension and the factor that represents a shared relationship among a group of measures are usually not 1.00 either. By examining the loadings of different dimensions on a factor, it is possible to determine the meaning of the factor. One looks for dimensions that load highly on the factor; these **marker variables,** as they are called, are closely related to the core meaning of the factor. By looking at the marker variables for the factor, one can sometimes develop an understanding of what the several variables that load on the factor share in common.

The end result of a factor analysis is a table representing a group of dimensions and a set of factors. The loadings of each dimension on each factor are displayed. Some of the dimensions may load moderately highly on more than one factor, indicating that the dimension is not a pure measure of the factor but actually is related to two different clusters or factors. Such a measure is sometimes called a **blend.**

When Goldberg factor-analyzed the correlations he obtained, he ended with a set of five factors. These represent the Big Five factors of personality. When you obtained scores for the five dimensions of personality in the test in chapter 2, the ratings you added to form scores were those found to load on the same factor in factor-analytic studies of personality ratings. You were, in effect, obtaining your score on each of five factors.

It should be obvious that the procedures followed to obtain the Big Five taxonomy could be followed by a personality psychologist visiting an alien civilization. All that is really necessary is the presence of a rich descriptive language that indicates the ways in which individuals differ from one another. Self-report or acquaintance ratings may be obtained on each dimension, correlations for all possible pairs of dimensions may be calculated, and the resulting correlations can be factor-analyzed to discover if there are clusters of relationships that may be used to define subsets of measures. The resulting factors may be used as a taxonomy for the description of personality. *Personality* may be defined as a set of scores on each of the factors that are discovered. If the set of factors is relatively small (say five), then individuals may be described in a relatively economical manner.

While we have indicated that there are a number of hidden theoretical assumptions that intrude in this effort, you could probably develop this kind of taxonomy of personality. You would need to know enough statistics to perform a factor analysis (much of the computational work could be done by computers) but you would not need to have the profound theoretical insights of Sigmund Freud (if they are profound).

There are a number of reasons, however, why this method might *not* work:

1. Ratings and self-reports might not be valid.
2. There are few relationships among different dimensions. If all of the correlations obtained tended toward zero, it would be impossible to form clusters of relationships and to discover factors. In such a case the exploration of the lexicon would not lead to a small set of factors. There would be no way of reducing the set of descriptive dimensions to a small and manageable subset.
3. Different individuals might assign ratings in different ways. One might assign high scores on both extraversion and talkativeness to the same person, while another might rarely assign high scores on these two dimensions to the same person. If the structure of relationships among dimensions is not the

same for different people, correlations between dimensions will tend toward zero and it will be impossible to discover a small set of factors that may be used to describe personality.

The method we have outlined presupposes that there are relationships among these several dimensions that are common for different individuals. If personality is structured differently in every person and/or rated differently by each rater, the search outlined above for commonalities will not be successful.

WHAT DO WE KNOW ABOUT THE BIG FIVE?

Generality of the Big Five

Goldberg's study of the Big Five was based on self-reports. We know from several studies that similar factors may be discovered by factor-analyzing ratings. Goldberg's study was based on the analysis of words in English. It is now reasonably clear that something analogous to the Big Five can similarly be found in other languages. German and Dutch descriptions are quite similar (John, 1990). Ratings made by translating dimensions of the Big Five into Japanese and Chinese yield comparable structures. Analysis of ratings in different languages may produce somewhat different structures, but there does appear to be some cross-linguistic similarity of personality ratings.

It is also possible to find dimensions in a variety of other personality measures that relate to the Big Five. For example, Block (1961) developed the California Q sort, consisting of 100 descriptive dimensions, as a basis for describing the judgments of experts in personality assessment. A rater is asked to sort the 100 descriptors into ten piles ranging from characteristics of a person that are most descriptive to least descriptive. The Q sort dimensions were derived not from an analysis of the lexicon, but from the theoretical ideas of psychologists who were experts in the description of personality. When scores on the Q sort are factor-analyzed with dimensions of the Big Five, the Q sort dimensions turn out to have loadings on the five factors (John, 1990).

A number of other personality measures not based on the Big Five turn out to be highly related to the Big Five dimensions. A good example of the attempt to relate the Big Five to other measures of personality is a study by Costa and McCrae (1988a) in which they analyzed a measure of motivation developed by Jackson (1984) called the Personality Research Form (PRF). The PRF consists of 358 true–false items designed to obtain measures of the twenty motives that were initially described by Murray (1938) in his attempts to develop a taxonomy of individual differences in motivation. Costa and McCrae administered the PRF and a measure of the Big Five to a group of adult subjects, then factor-analyzed motive scores and scores on the Big Five. The results of their factor analysis are presented in Table 4.1. It is apparent that each of the twenty scores is related to the Big Five measures. For

TABLE 4.1   Joint Factor Loadings for NEO-PI Factors and PRF Scales (Based on Costa and McCrae, 1988a)

Variable	N	E	O	A	C
	FACTOR				
NEO-PI factors					
Neuroticism (N)	**81**	−17	02	09	−14
Extraversion (E)	13	**83**	13	−03	13
Openness (O)	−09	−07	**78**	04	−11
Agreeableness (A)	−01	15	−18	**72**	−23
Conscientiousness (C)	08	−15	00	23	**77**
PRF scales					
Social Recognition (SR)	**60**	**34**	−10	−19	10
Defendence (DE)	**53**	−07	−13	**−48**	−05
Succorance (SU)	**53**	**40**	**−34**	18	−14
Affiliation (AF)	04	**83**	−13	19	11
Exhibition (EX)	05	**65**	23	**−31**	−03
Play (PL)	−13	**65**	07	−06	**−37**
Understanding (UN)	−02	00	**64**	10	16
Change (CH)	−06	21	**60**	−12	−11
Sentience (SE)	11	29	**53**	13	−09
Autonomy (AU)	**−42**	**−33**	**47**	−26	−10
Harm Avoidance (HA)	21	05	**−52**	**32**	09
Abasement (AB)	06	−14	12	**58**	08
Nurturance (NU)	25	**49**	10	**55**	06
Dominance (DO)	00	**38**	**45**	**−46**	**32**
Aggression (AG)	**43**	07	14	**−68**	−21
Achievement (AC)	05	03	**46**	02	**64**
Order (OR)	−05	12	−25	−17	**64**
Endurance (EN)	−16	07	**33**	15	**52**
Cognitive Structure (CS)	19	07	−23	**−30**	**52**
Impulsivity (IM)	29	11	24	03	**−61**
Desirability (DY)	**−35**	**45**	07	10	**54**

Note: Decimal points are omitted: loadings .30 and higher are given in boldface. NEO-PI = NEO Personality Inventory; PRF = Personality Research Form.
Reproduced with permission of the American Psychological Association.

example, achievement, usually defined as the need to excel in competition with a standard of excellence, is correlated with conscientiousness and openness to experience. Affiliation, the desire to be with other people, is a marker variable for extraversion. We call it a marker variable because of its high correlation with the factor.

The Costa and McCrae study indicates that measures that are based on quite different theoretical assumptions may be related to the Big Five taxonomy. Yet in chapter 8 we shall consider other ways of measuring motives, and some of these may not be related to the Big Five. Undoubtedly many measures of personality are substantially related to the Big Five and many are not. In subsequent chapters we shall consider many kinds of personality dimensions, some of which may be unrelated to the Big Five and others which may be related to one or more of the Big Five dimensions. But these relationships may not help us to understand everything we want to know about the measures. Nevertheless, if the Big Five constitutes an adequate taxonomy of personality, it is useful to try to relate other measures to the factors that have emerged from an analysis of the lexicon.

Blends and Markers

While something comparable to the Big Five can be found in many analyses of personality descriptors, researchers disagree about the measures that define (load) on each factor and about the interpretation of the factors. One reason for this disagreement is that many of the dimensions that define each factor load on other factors as well. As a result, different researchers use different sets of items to define each factor, and consequently, they interpret the factors in somewhat different ways.

Johnson and Ostendorf (1993) attempted to resolve conflicts about the interpretation of the factors. They analyzed fifteen different studies of the Big Five that were based on moderately large samples. Some used self-reports, others used acquaintance ratings; some were in English, others were in German. They calculated average factor loadings for personality dimensions in these fifteen studies. Some of their results are reported in Table 4.2 (see pages 67–71). The table lists marker variables for each of the Big Five factors and also indicates the dimensions that have blended loadings on more than one factor. The "unblended" dimensions that load on each factor may be considered as the most defining and purest measures of the factor. Blended variables provide additional nuances of meaning and indicate the ways in which some dimensions have blended meanings related to two factors. Consider Factor I, extraversion. The purest dimension with the highest average loading on this factor is frank versus secretive. Affectionate versus reserved loads on both extraversion and on Factor II, agreeableness. This dual loading implies that individuals who are likely to be described as affectionate are also likely to be described as extraverted and as frank and in the extraverted direction for all of the marker variables for extraversion (Johnson and Ostendorf identify over 30 marker variables for extraversion). Individuals who are described as affectionate are also likely to be described as mild and gentle rather than as headstrong, the best marker variable for Factor II, agreeableness. Affectionate versus reserved belongs to two clusters of relationships and to two factors.

An examination of the variables listed in Table 4.2 should help you to define the core meanings of each of the five factors. Pairs of factors with their blended and unblended markers may be thought of as forming a geometric space. The unblended marker variables for the space are those that are located on the axes defined by the factor. Blended variables are located in areas that do not coincide with the axes of the space. The axes or coordinates of the two-dimensional space formed

TABLE 4.2 **Factor Loadings for Personality Dimensions in Fifteen Studies of the Big Five (Based on Johnson and Ostendorf, 1993)**

Facet	Facet			FACTOR LOADINGS ACROSS DATA SETS				
				Factor I Extraversion	Factor II Agreeableness	Factor III Conscientiousness	Factor IV Adjustment (vs. Neuroticism)	Factor V Openness to Experience
I+I+	I–I–	Extraverted	Introverted	.71	.03	-.02	.08	-.03
		Frank, open	Secretive	.77	.07	-.06	.04	.10
		Fun loving	Sober	.57	.21	-.19	.06	.23
		Sociable	Retiring, reclusive, unsociable, or solitary	.76	.13	-.05	.11	.02
		Straightforward	Manipulative	.32	.16	.12	.02	-.01
		Talkative	Silent or quiet	.76	-.03	-.01	.01	.02
I+II+	I–II–	Affectionate	Reserved	.61	.44	-.01	.07	.12
		Cheerful	Serious or depressed	.44	.26	.03	.38	.02
I+II–	I–II+	Dominant	Submissive	.47	-.37	.25	.14	.22
I+III–	I–III–	Active	Passive or inactive	.61	.04	.32	.13	.11
		Energetic	Unenergetic or leisurely	.52	.13	.40	.13	.05
I+III+	I–III+	Task oriented	Person oriented	.36	.26	-.34	-.12	.08
I+IV+	I–IV–	Adventurous	Unadventurous or cautious	.53	-.06	-.30	.22	.08
I+V+	I–V–	Assertive	Unassertive	.59	-.03	.21	.26	.22
		Daring	Unadventurous	.43	-.11	-.12	.24	.29
		Forceful	Submissive	.55	-.13	-.03	-.02	.25

(continued on p. 68)

TABLE 4.2 *(cont.)*

				FACTOR LOADINGS ACROSS DATA SETS				
Facet		Facet		Factor I Extraversion	Factor II Agreeableness	Factor III Conscientiousness	Factor IV Adjustment (vs. Neuroticism)	Factor V Openness to Experience
II+II+	Acquiescent	II-II-	Antagonistic	.04	.60	.06	.10	-.10
	Mild, gentle		Headstrong	-.07	.80	.07	.07	.14
	Softhearted		Ruthless	.11	.72	.12	-.12	.12
II+I+	Generous	II-I-	Stingy	.26	.52	.02	.02	.09
	Warm		Cold	.35	.60	.10	.05	.07
II+I-	Diplomatic	II-I+	Outspoken	-.33	.36	.17	-.11	.10
	Humble		Proud	-.16	.25	.00	.00	-.09
II+III+	Courteous	II-III-	Rude	.03	.59	.33	.05	.20
II+IV-	Empathic		Self-centered	.05	.54	.18	.01	-.05
	Agreeable	II-IV-	Critical or disagreeable	.06	.48	.08	.10	.09
	Cooperative		Negativistic, subborn, or uncooperative	.20	.54	.09	.21	.15
II+V+	Open-minded	II-V-	Narrow-minded	.23	.46	.18	.20	.46
	Sympathetic		Callous	.24	.59	.22	-.07	.32
II+V-	Gullible	II-V+	Cynical	.07	.51	-.07	-.11	-.23
	Lenient		Critical	-.06	.56	-.14	.15	-.18

(continued on p. 69)

TABLE 4.2   *(cont.)*

Facet	Adjective (+)	Facet	Adjective (−)	Factor I Extraversion	Factor II Agreeableness	Factor III Conscientiousness	Factor IV Adjustment (vs. Neuroticism)	Factor V Openness to Experience
III+III+	Careful	III−III−	Careless	−.01	.16	.70	−.01	.04
	Fussy, tidy		Careless	−.24	−.06	.67	−.18	.12
	Hardworking		Lazy	.16	.16	.64	.00	.04
	Neat		Sloppy	−.04	.16	.67	.00	−.04
	Punctual		Late	−.01	.16	.59	−.01	−.08
	Scrupulous		Lax or unscrupulous	−.16	.13	.66	−.02	.10
III+I+	Thrifty	III−I−	Extravagant	−.18	−.06	.34	.08	−.07
	Well organized		Disorganized	−.05	.02	.71	.06	.28
	Ambitious		Aimless or apathetic	.23	.01	.62	.10	.12
III+I−	Serious	III−I+	Frivolous	.04	−.11	.54	−.15	.04
	Businesslike		Playful	−.10	−.10	.55	.10	−.05
	Cautious		Rash	−.29	.13	.49	.10	.11
III+II+	Conscientious	III−II−	Negligent	.03	.19	.70	−.02	.10
	Reliable		Undependable	.07	.27	.64	.07	.13
III+II−	Industrious	III−II+	Easy-going	.10	−.06	.42	−.12	.09
III+IV+	Persevering	III−IV−	Quit or quitting, fickle	.06	.05	.56	.21	.18
	Practical		Impractical	.19	.14	.45	.16	.12
	Self-disciplined		Weak willed	.03	.02	.65	.28	.20
	Stable		Unstable	−.10	.16	.37	.15	.19
	Well-read		Unlettered	.19	.12	.43	.40	−.05
III+V+	Clever	III−V−	Naive	.18	−.09	.34	.19	.28
	Learned		Unlearned	.00	.00	.49	.17	.22
III+V−	Rule abiding	III−V+	Rule avoiding	.01	.15	.44	−.26	−.14

FACTOR LOADINGS ACROSS DATA SETS

(continued on p. 70)

TABLE 4.2 *(cont.)*

				FACTOR LOADINGS ACROSS DATA SETS				
Facet		Facet		Factor I Extraversion	Factor II Agreeableness	Factor III Conscientiousness	Factor IV Adjustment (vs. Neuroticism)	Factor V Openness to Experience
IV+IV+	Calm	IV−IV−	Angry, anxious, or worrying	−.02	.11	.01	.60	.05
IV+I+	Confident	IV−I−	Worried	.16	.02	.09	.58	.00
	Guilt free		Guilt ridden	.20	−.01	.10	.68	.03
IV+I−	Unemotional	IV−I+	Emotional	−.33	−.10	.05	.42	−.19
IV+II+	At ease	IV−II−	Nervous	.15	.16	−.01	.69	.06
	Composed		Excitable or moody	.09	.28	.13	.56	.11
IV+III+	Contented	IV−III−	Discontented	.11	.31	.27	.42	.10
	Emotionally stable		Unstable	.11	.12	.36	.63	.07

(continued on p. 71)

TABLE 4.2 (cont.)

Facet		Facet		FACTOR LOADINGS ACROSS DATA SETS				
				Factor I Extraversion	Factor II Agreeableness	Factor III Conscientiousness	Factor IV Adjustment (vs. Neuroticism)	Factor V Openness to Experience
V+V	Artistic	V-V-	Unartistic	-.01	.09	.08	-.06	.62
	Creative		Ordinary or uncreative	.17	.15	.09	.47	.14
	Imaginative		Down-to-earth or simple, direct, or unimaginative	.11	.14	-.11	.01	.49
V+I+	Experimenting	V-I-	Routine	.46	-.07	.08	.14	.47
	Independent		Conforming	.20	-.23	-.01	.17	.48
V+II+	Reflective	V-II-	Unreflective	-.08	.20	-.02	-.04	.42
V+II-	Complex	V-II+	Simple	-.03	-.18	.08	-.06	.32
V+III+	Analytical	V-III-	Unanalytical	-.11	-.07	.31	.05	.46
	Broad interests		Narrow interests	.17	.16	.29	.18	.57
	Cultured		Uncultured	.01	.16	.27	.07	.52
	Curious		Uninquisitive or uncurious	.13	.14	.23	.05	.50
	Intellectual		Unreflective or unreflective, narrow	-.02	.07	.39	.16	.52
	Intelligent		Stupid or unintelligent	.06	.06	.27	.10	.58
	Knowledgeable		Ignorant	.00	.05	.31	.11	.64
	Perceptive		Imperceptive	.09	.07	.29	.13	.53
	Polished, refined		Crude, boorish	.08	.33	.38	.08	.50
	Refined		Unrefined	.03	.04	.16	.15	.41
V+III-	Changeable	V-III+	Predictable	.01	-.05	-.04	-.09	.56
	Unorthodox		Traditional	.03	-.04	-.18	-.04	.55
V+IV+	Aesthetic	V-IV-	Inartistic	.00	.34	.16	.23	.21

by any pair of the Big Five factors may be thought of as being analogous to a space formed by the contiguous 48 U.S. states. This space may be bisected at the longitudinal and latitudinal midpoint of the country by a north–south and by an east–west axis. Some cities and towns lie directly on the axes, others are located off the axes. Any city or town may be located with reference to north–south and east–west axes. In a similar manner, blended and unblended markers may be located in the two-dimensional space formed by pairs of factors.

The Meaning of the Big Five

Caesar wrote that Gaul had three parts. Exponents of the Big Five believe that personality has five parts. Why? What sort of dimensions are these and why are they found in analyses of personality descriptors? We can try to provide an answer to this question by examining the marker variables for each of the Big Five.

The first two factors relate to interpersonal behavior. Factor I, extraversion, has as one core meaning the extent to which individuals prefer to be alone or with others. The factor also seems to be defined by measures of the ability to experience positive emotions (to be fun loving) and to be vigorous and energetic. Some personality psychologists call this factor **surgency,** a term that captures the energetic component of meaning present in its marker variables. Note that this way of defining the factor contains an implicit hypothesis: individuals who like to be with other people are also likely to be fun loving, energetic, and talkative. Why might this linkage occur? One possibility may be that the interpersonal behavior of extraverts is related to their emotional life (discussed in chapter 6.)

Factor II, agreeableness, appears to be related to the characteristic responses of other people to an individual. Agreeable people are those who, for a variety of reasons, are liked by others—they are nice people. The terms that load on both agreeableness and other factors (blends) seem to capture those aspects that are evaluatively positive: warm loads on A and E; courteous loads on A and C; not jealous loads on A and N; open-minded loads on A and O.

Factor III, conscientiousness, is less tied to interpersonal behavior. It relates to the ways in which individuals perform tasks. There is an interpersonal component to this dimension as well; we are interested in whether or not individuals we meet are likely to be careful, hardworking, neat, and organized.

Factor IV, adjustment or neuroticism, is less tied to interpersonal behaviors or activities that are easily observed through casual acquaintance. The markers for this factor relate to a person's emotional life. Those who score high on this factor are prone to experience negative emotions. This dimension does not appear to have as many markers in most descriptions of personality, but it may become a more important descriptive dimension for those who have psychological problems (John, 1990). One reason neuroticism may not be related to a large number of dimensions in ordinary language is that it may be difficult to judge on first encounter. Recall that Funder and Sneed (1993; see chapter 3) found that people were not very successful at judging the neuroticism of individuals they observed for a brief period. This dimension may become more important in long-term relationships. Recall that Kelly and Conley (1987; see chapter 3) found that neuroticism ratings were related to divorce and marital problems.

Factor V, openness to experience, has been the most problematic of the Big Five. This dimension is not invariably found in cross-linguistic analyses and there have been disagreements about its interpretation. In the Johnson and Ostendorf analysis, the marker variables for this factor tend to have somewhat lower loadings than do the marker variables for the other factors—indicating that the hypothetical factor is not as clearly identified with the meanings of its constituent dimensions. There are in fact only three variables with loadings in excess of .60 on this factor: original versus conventional, knowledgeable versus ignorant, and artistic versus unartistic. The factor has been identified as a creativity factor (Johnson & Ostendorf) or as a measure of the extent to which individuals are open to experience (McCrae & Costa, 1990). Many of the marker variables for the factor are difficult to define in behavioral terms; it is relatively easy to determine if someone is talkative but somewhat harder to determine if a person is artistic.

The Big Five factors encompass several levels of analysis and refer to different aspects of behavior: the first two dimensions are primarily interpersonal, the third is primarily task oriented, and the last two refer to a person's emotional or cognitive experiences. These factors describe some of the fundamental ways in which people differ. They are in part the ways in which we describe ourselves and others.

Try to think of people you know who would receive an extreme score on each of the factors. You can also try to do something that is more difficult. Individuals may be described by their score on each of the five factors. Try to assign scores to someone you know well on each of the factors. In what ways, if any, does the combination of scores add something to your understanding of personality? Is the combination the mere sum of its parts or is something added when you consider the five scores together? Does extraversion mean something special when it is combined with conscientiousness, or is extraversion just extraversion irrespective of a person's score on conscientiousness?

BEYOND THE BIG FIVE

Do the Big Five form an adequate taxonomy? We can think of five kinds of limitations.

1. There are disagreements about the structure of the Big Five. Some psychologists prefer a system based on seven factors, others propose three.
2. There is no agreed-upon theory of the origins of the Big Five.
3. Different traits may have different degrees of relevance for understanding different individuals.

4. The Big Five descriptive system is nomothetic. Some psychologists prefer idiographic approaches.
5. There may be serious omissions in a description of personality based on traits.

Disagreements About Structure

The Big Five descriptive system is relatively new. Although it is based in part on research conducted in the 1960s, its acceptance as a descriptive system is of more recent origin. It is likely to undergo revision and has already been challenged in a number of respects.

One source of disagreement derives from the indeterminacies of factor analysis. There may be more than one acceptable factor solution for the same data. Eysenck (1990) proposed a three-dimensional trait theory defined by extraversion, neuroticism, and a trait called psychoticism, which combines aspects of conscientiousness and agreeableness with aggression and antisocial behavior. Zuckerman (1992) reported the results of a factor analysis of self-report dimensions in which he was able to derive both a three-factor solution compatible with Eysenck's theory and a five-factor solution related to the Big Five taxonomy.

Different data may lead to different factor solutions. Obviously, the end result of a factor analysis is dependent on the data that are collected. If actions rather than traits are used as a basis for constructing the dimensions, the results of the factor analyses may be somewhat different. The preference for describing personality in terms of traits may itself be culturally influenced. Shweder and Bourne (1984) asked subjects in the United States and in India to describe an acquaintance's personality. They found that Americans tended to use trait descriptions, whereas Indians tended to describe their acquaintances by their actions. Yet in Norman's study of the lexicon, he discarded personality descriptions that were based on actions. Botwin and Buss (1989) explored the relationship between a description of personality based on actions and the Big Five system. They specified a series of acts that were related to each of the Big Five factors and asked their subjects to indicate the frequency with which they engaged in various acts. They also obtained self-report measures of ratings for the Big Five. When act ratings were analyzed in conjunction with the usual markers for the Big Five, the resulting factor structure was somewhat different from that usually obtained. For example, a conscientiousness factor was obtained that was related to both extraversion and neuroticism. Their data suggest that reports about what people actually do may yield different factor structures from those obtained from trait ratings. Thus the description of personality is at least partially dependent on the kinds of data that are analyzed.

This brief review of alternative taxonomic approaches suggests that the Big Five may be modified as a result of new research, particularly if different kinds of data are analyzed. We have chosen not to describe alternative taxonomies in this chapter—none is as widely accepted as the Big Five—but we do think it is important to remember that the Big Five is a "work in progress" that will undoubtedly be modified.

Origins

Is there a theory that explains the origins of the Big Five dimensions? There is no agreed-upon answer to this question. Buss (1991; see also MacDonald, 1995) suggested that the principles of evolutionary psychology may be used to explain the origins of these five dimensions. Evolutionary psychologists emphasize the importance of judging the behavior of others in order to promote survival. When we assign a trait to a person, we may be evaluating the person. Trait descriptions are not evaluatively neutral, they have good and bad meanings. Most people believe that it is better to be extraverted, agreeable, conscientious, adjusted, and open to experience than introverted, disagreeable, not conscientious, neurotic, and closed to experience. These evaluations may be ways in which we inform ourselves about whether an individual would be a good partner in a cooperative venture. If someone we meet is likely to be sociable, talkative, and frank (i.e., extraverted), such a person might be socially engaging and interested in interpersonal relationships. Similarly, we might want to know if someone is likely to be conscientious and agreeable. Even such traits as neuroticism and openness to experience, which seem to focus on one's inner mental life, may provide important information. Perhaps individuals who are tense, worried, depressed, and anxious would be difficult to live with. And openness to experience might be related to a person's response to new ideas. In addition, judgments of a person's creativity, which is one aspect of the trait of openness to experience, might provide useful information about the value of a person's contributions to a common enterprise.

While we could argue that judgments of a person's position on the Big Five dimensions might be useful to us, and perhaps were useful to our ancestors in selecting individuals with whom to be associated in cooperative tasks that helped them to survive, this evolutionary model is better at explaining why we might want to judge others on these dimensions than why people differ on these dimensions. We could say that these dimensions exist not in persons but only in the eye of the beholder. That is, the Big Five describes the dimensions *we use* to describe people, not the dimensions on which we really differ from one another. But this is precisely the position that we rejected in chapter 3.

If there is an evaluative dimension to these traits and individuals were in fact chosen for their positive attributes, then those with positive attributes would have had a better chance to survive. And if evolutionary pressures operated in this way, genetic characteristics associated with negatively evaluated traits would not have persisted. Why are some people introverted, disagreeable, not conscientious, neurotic, and closed to experience? You can probably develop a scenario in your mind in which these characteristics might help someone survive, but doing so requires an act of imagination that is not soundly grounded in anything we know about our ancestral past. Since people appear to differ on each of these traits, they could not have been subject to consistent natural selection; if they were, natural selection would have arranged for us to be similar in these characteristics just as virtually all human beings have the capacity to learn language (but see MacDonald, 1995, for a different view).

While there are interesting speculations about the ways in which the Big Five may relate to evolutionary ideas, we really cannot derive this taxonomy from the principles of evolution. About all we can say is that these are some of the ways in which people differ. And our judgments about these differences may provide us with useful information, information that may have been useful to our ancestors (although this theory is surely speculative).

Trait Relevance

Are all people well described by their scores on the Big Five? Might some best be described by their position on a subset of the Big Five? As we indicated in chapter 1, some psychologists argued that traits were not equally relevant for all persons, and some psychologists preferred an idiographic to a nomothetic descriptive system. The Big Five is clearly a nomothetic taxonomy that studies the ways in which individuals differ on common dimensions that are assumed to apply to all. In this section we discuss this issue again.

How could we determine which traits are most descriptive and relevant for a person? There is a simple answer to this question. Ask the person. Just as we determine a person's trait scores by the use of ratings, we could determine the relevance of a trait for a person by the use of ratings. Different methods have been used for this purpose. Amelang and Borkenau (1984) asked subjects to indicate whether each of a set of trait terms applied to them. Cheek (1982) asked individuals to indicate whether or not a trait term was appropriate for them. While subjects in psychological studies are often surprisingly compliant in doing what is asked of them, it is not always clear just what they are being asked to do. What does it mean to say of a trait that it is not appropriate for a person or does not apply to a person? Are we asking individuals if they think of themselves in these terms? Is this inquiry analogous to the discovery by a character in one of Moliere's plays that he is in fact a speaker of prose? People in psychoanalysis learn to interpret their behavior in psychoanalytic terms. Few who have not studied psychoanalysis or been in psychoanalytic therapy are likely to describe themselves as having an anal sadistic personality. A low rating of appropriateness for a trait may indicate nothing more than that the individual rarely uses that word to describe behaviors. It is hard to imagine how a dimension such as talkative does not apply to someone. People are generally talkative or silent or they have intermediate positions on the dimension. Or, they may sometimes be silent and sometimes be talkative. In any case, aggregated over situations, a person may be described as having a score on this dimension whether or not the person thinks of himself as talkative or describes this dimension as being a relevant or appropriate description. If trait dimensions refer ultimately to the behavior of individuals, then they must be appropriate descriptors of behavior whether or not individuals think the dimension is appropriate for them.

Appropriateness may be given a different meaning from the one commonly used. Traits are disposition terms, that is, they are relevant to behavior in some situations and not in others. We know that individuals may have choice in selecting situations. Perhaps when they assert that a trait is not appropriate for them, they mean that they avoid or rarely find themselves in situations that are likely to elicit behavior relevant to that trait. (Think of the situations that are likely to elicit trait-relevant behaviors for the Big Five. What degree of choice exists for avoiding some of these situations?)

Are traits that are rated as appropriate more predictive for an individual than traits that are rated as not appropriate? There is some evidence that they are. Amelang and Borkenau (1984) presented subjects with a list of 45 trait dimensions and asked them to rate themselves on each dimension and indicate whether or not that dimension was appropriate for them. They also obtained peer ratings from three friends on each of these trait dimensions. They divided their sample into two groups for each trait: those who rated the trait as relatively appropriate for them and those who rated it as relatively inappropriate. They found that the average correlation between self-reports and peer ratings on traits that subjects rated as appropriate was .35; the comparable correlation for subjects who rated traits as relatively inappropriate was .23. Cheek (1982) reported results for a comparable study using ratings and self-reports for the first four of the Big Five dimensions. He divided his sample on each trait by considering appropriateness ratings. He obtained an average correlation of .47 between self-reports and peer ratings for subjects who rated traits as appropriate for them, and a comparable correlation of .38 for subjects who rated traits as relatively inappropriate. These studies indicate that there is somewhat greater agreement between self-reports and peer ratings for traits that individuals believe are relatively appropriate for them than for traits assumed to be relatively inappropriate—although the differences in the magnitude of the correlations may not be large.

Amelang and Borkenau also obtained test-retest correlations for trait appropriateness for their 45 traits. They obtained a correlation of .71 for trait ratings, but a correlation of .36 for appropriateness ratings. These data indicate that appropriateness ratings are not very stable over time and are not very reliable, one reason why a consideration of these ratings does not dramatically increase the predictive validity of trait ratings.

Trait ratings may be qualified in a number of additional ways. Bem and Allen (1974; see also Chapin & Goldberg, 1985; Kenrick & Stringfield, 1980) obtained consistency ratings for several traits. They found greater agreement between self-reports and peer ratings for traits on which individuals rated themselves as consistent than for traits on which they rated themselves inconsistent. Chapin and Goldberg failed to replicate these findings. Kenrick and Stringfield used a variant of this procedure. They asked subjects to choose from a list of sixteen traits the single trait on which they were most consistent. They found that the correlation between self-reports and peer ratings for the single most consistent trait was .47, while the comparable correlation for other traits was .24.

Baumeister and Tice (1988) argued that individuals differ in the extent to which they do or do not have a trait. They suggested that personality traits are more similar to attitudes than to physical characteristics. Everyone has a height. Not everyone has an attitude toward abortion; a woman might say that she has not thought deeply about the matter and really doesn't know what she thinks about it. If traits are like attitudes, then it makes sense to say that some people really do not have a position on a trait. Baumeister and Tice argued that predictions from trait scores for individuals who are "traited" are more likely to be accurate than predictions from individuals who are untraited on a trait. Strictly speaking, a trait score for someone who is untraited on that trait is meaningless.

How are we to determine if a person has a particular trait? Baumeister and Tice used measures of the variability of responses to questionnaire items as a basis for determining the extent to which a person is traited. Trait scores are typically aggregates of responses to several different items. Individuals differ in the consistency of their responses. Some might respond consistently to all the items relevant to a trait, others might respond inconsistently, sometimes in a way that suggests they have a high score on a trait and sometimes in a way suggesting a low score. For example, two individuals might have the same extraversion score. However, the first person might respond in a moderately extraverted manner to all of the extraversion-relevant items, while the second person might respond to most of these particular items in an extremely extraverted way and to a small subset in an extremely introverted way. Baumeister and Tice assumed that the first person is more likely to be traited for extraversion than the second person. Individuals who respond consistently are more likely to have the trait than individuals who respond inconsistently.

Measures of the consistency of responding to trait questionnaires are called **metatrait** measures. The term refers to a property of a trait measure: the consistency of responses to its components. Do metatrait measures help us to predict things about a person? There is some evidence that they do. Britt (1993) obtained metatrait measures for the gregarious component of extraversion and for a measure of interpersonal locus of control, which is assumed to indicate whether an individual is in control of his or her personal relationships. Britt assumed that these measures would be positively correlated, and that this relationship would be most clearly manifested for those whose metatrait scores indicated that they were traited on both of these measures. Figure 4.1 presents the results of his study. The correlation between these two measures was higher for individuals who were traited on both of the measures than for those untraited on one or both.

Metatrait scores are another way of assessing the degree to which a particular trait score is a valid measure for different individuals. These data provide evidence that consistency of response is another way of modifying the meaning of a trait for individuals. These results, combined with the other studies of trait relevance and appropriateness, indicate that while trait scores are usually valid and predictive for most individuals, predictability may sometimes be improved by considering the extent to which a trait applies to a particular individual. These modi-

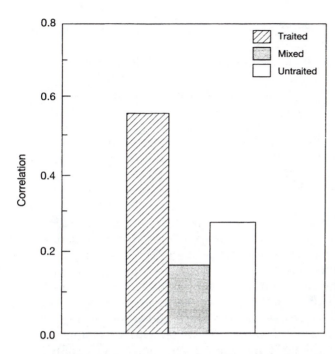

FIGURE 4.1   Correlations between extraversion and interpersonal locus of control as a function of traitedness. (Based on Britt, 1993; reproduced with permission of the American Psychological Association.)

fications of scores serve to make nomothetic traits somewhat more idiographic, but they still leave the nomothetic structure of traits largely intact.

Idiography Reconsidered

Is it possible to develop a description of personality that is more genuinely idiographic? Can we start with truly idiographic descriptors? This issue is basic. Acceptance of the Big Five taxonomy, even with some modifications, commits one to a nomothetic system in which individuals are understood in terms of how they differ from other individuals on dimensions that apply to all. Perhaps personality psychology should place greater emphasis on understanding individual lives. Perhaps it should be more like biography.

There is a simple argument in favor of an idiographic approach. Psychologists try to develop general laws that apply to all individuals. Personality psychology, by definition, is concerned not with what is common to all people but with individual differences and human individuality. It is the study of the unique individual that distinguishes personality psychology from all other branches of psychology. Personality psychology is idiographic by definition.

Is this argument convincing? We can try to answer this question by distinguishing between two different assertions. (1) Personality psychology should be the study of the unique individual. It should focus on human individuality and the characteristics that lead each person to be different from every other person.

(2) The best (or perhaps the only) way to understand human individuality is to describe an individual in idiographic terms.

It is possible to accept the first assertion and reject the second. The study of fingerprints will help us understand the distinction. It is possible to describe a person's unique fingerprints by noting the person's score on each of several nomothetic dimensions. From this example we can conclude that the study of what makes each of us unique may, in principle, be accomplished by the study of laws and principles that apply to all of us. No one doubts that each person is in some way different from every other person in the world, but this truism does not require us to comprehend human uniqueness in idiographic terms.

There is an argument against idiographic descriptions that we find compelling. If carried to an extreme, we reach an absurd conclusion, a *reductio ad absurdum*. If every person must be understood idiographically, then the dimensions used to describe a person must by definition apply only to that person. Such dimensions cannot be expressed in a common language. Therefore, it would be necessary to develop a unique descriptive language in order to understand each person. This task appears to be an impossible one—or one more suited to the skills of a poet than to the skills of a scientist. (We are assuming that personality psychologists are scientists. We hope that we have convinced you by example that this is a justified assumption. You might want to take issue with this claim.)

Let us agree that a completely idiographic description of personality is probably not feasible. Are there ways in which we will need to modify general laws in order to understand the individual case (see Lamiell, 1981, 1982, for a thoughtful discussion of this issue)? Many people believe that they are exceptions to a general rule that applies to most people. We can clarify this belief. We know that it is possible to generalize from self-reports to acquaintance ratings. The usual correlation obtained in such studies is close to .5. This correlation represents a summary of the relationship that is obtained for a group of individuals. If we examine the individuals who collectively form the group, the correlation does not necessarily hold for all or even most of them. Some might have identical self-report scores and acquaintance ratings for a particular trait, others' self-report scores might be higher than the acquaintance ratings, and still others' might be lower. The correlation indicates that there is a moderate relationship between these two measures, but the relationship for individuals in the sample may vary dramatically. Unless the correlation between the measures is 1.00—a value that is never obtained in actual research—it is always the case that a general relationship true of a group may not apply equally or even at all to all members of the group.

Consider another example. Suppose we found that the test-retest correlation for a measure of personality was .00. We would correctly conclude that an individual's score on the first occasion could not be used to predict his or her score on the second occasion. This generalization is a correct summary of an analysis of scores for a group of individuals. If we examine individuals, however, we are likely to find that some have identical scores on both occasions, some have increased scores on the second occasion, and some have decreased scores on the second occasion. What is true of the group is not true of individual members of the group. In this instance, virtually every member of the group is an exception to the general rule.

This analysis leads us to a surprising conclusion. The study of what is true of groups may not lead us to understand what is true of individuals within the group. How are we to discover if any such generalization is valid for a particular individual? Or are we to assume that generalizations based on groups are always likely to be flawed when applied to the individual case?

Some exceptions to a general rule make good sense. One of us once illustrated the meaning of extraversion in a personality class by deriving the following hypothesis: individuals who are extraverted are more likely to study with other people than are introverts. One student, who claimed to be extremely extraverted, said that the generalization did not apply to him, that he invariably studied in complete isolation in a room in the library that did not permit him to see other people. He explained his behavior by stating that he was intensely interested in other people and if he encountered anyone he would be easily distracted from his studying. In this case, his behavior represented a genuine departure from a generalization that is valid for a group, yet his behavior is understandable from our general understanding of what it means to be extraverted.

Some exceptions to a generalization may be dismissed, others may be understood from a fuller explication of the circumstances. Surely these qualifications cannot be used to explain all exceptions to a rule. Some must be genuine instances in which an individual who shares the personality test scores of others still exhibits different behavior. One way to get additional information about this issue is to test hypotheses using data obtained from a single individual. If this process is followed for many individuals, then we can conclude that the general law is valid for each of the individuals tested. Zevon and Tellegen (1982) reported results for a study of this type, in which they analyzed mood states in 23 subjects separately. Each subject described his or her mood on a 60-item adjective list once a day for 90 days. Scores obtained from a single subject could thus be analyzed. It is possible to obtain a correlation representing the relationship between pairs of mood scores for each subject on different occasions, in this case 90 occasions. For example, a correlation of .00 between the dimensions joyful and frightened for a particular person would indicate that a person's score on the joyful dimension could not be used to predict his or her score on the frightened dimension where both scores are obtained on the same occasion. Since there are 60 mood dimensions, there are 1,770 correlations for all possible pairs of dimensions for each subject. After factor-analyzing the correlations obtained for each subject, Zevon and Tellegen found for 20 of their 23 subjects that a two-factor solution was an adequate representation of the structure of moods. One of the factors was a positive mood factor ranging from delighted states at one extreme to sleepy and sluggish states at the other. The second factor was a negative mood factor ranging from distressed to contented moods. These analyses suggest that it is possible to locate mood descriptions in a two-dimensional space formed by the presence or absence of positive and negative mood states. This factor structure was also very similar to the results obtained when mood ratings from a group of individuals on one occasion are factor-analyzed. Whether one studies a group of individuals on one occasion or individuals separately on several occasions, the resultant structure of mood relationships tends to be the same. In this case what is true of the group is true of the overwhelming majority of individuals in that group. This analysis suggests that some of the nomothetic rules of personality structure related to the Big Five are present in the analysis of data derived from single individuals.

Are nomothetic rules always recoverable from an analysis of the single case? The Zevon and Tellegen study may be a special case. The discussion of their study illustrates one approach to the study of individuals. There may be many other ways of understanding the individual case, some of them not leading to the same results.

Omissions

What is omitted from a description of personality based on scores on the Big Five? Consider the following example. Two women of the same age (say 35) with comparable educations (college graduates) live in the same community (Washington, D.C.) and both have comparable jobs: they direct public interest organizations that lobby Congress to pass legislation supporting the goals of their respective organizations. Assume that they have the same scores on the Big Five. All of this information might incline us to assert that their personalities are very similar. Suppose you were told that one woman is head of an organization that lobbies Congress to support abortion rights and the other heads an organization that lobbies to eliminate the right to an abortion. Would you still be willing to assert that they have the same personality? Perhaps the answer to this question might depend on your definition of personality. Whether these women are viewed as having the same personality or not, we are able to infer something about the ways in which they are likely to be different. They would probably experience different emotions if they were told that the Supreme Court had decided to overthrow *Roe* v. *Wade,* the decision legalizing abortion. They might have different religious beliefs and different beliefs about the role of women in society. And they would be likely to have friends with different values, ideas, and lifestyles. If we asked these women what was important to them and what they were trying to accomplish in life, they might very well answer this question in different ways. If this example is persuasive, and we believe that it is, it helps us to understand that individuals may differ on important dimensions related to beliefs, goals, and values, and these characteristics may be relatively independent of their position on the Big Five.

In our example we provided you with information about the social position, age, occupation, and gender of the two individuals we described. Suppose we wished to describe individuals solely on the Big Five. In that case, information about the demographic and social background variables would be omitted. We might then be deprived of relevant information about their lifestyles, friendships, values, living arrangements, and beliefs.

Even if individuals share gender, race, social position, and age, they may differ with respect to the significance they assign to these characteristics. Consider race. Members of a racial or ethnic minority are faced with the problem of defining their identities in terms of their relationships with members of their own minority group and with members of the majority. An example of some of these complexities may be seen in the historical debate among African Americans about their role in American society. Frederick Douglass, a famous African American abolitionist who had been a slave, believed that the ultimate goal of African Americans was to assimilate and be part of the larger American community. He once said in reference to the ideas of Martin Delaney, a prominent African American who disagreed with his assimilationist philosophy, that he Douglass thanked God for making him a man and Delaney thanked God for making him a black man. W. E. B. Du Bois, in his book *The Souls of Black Folks* (1903), argued that African Americans needed to maintain a dual identity both as Negroes and as Americans. He wrote, "In this merging . . . He would not Africanize America. . . . He would not bleach his Negro soul in a flood of white Americanism." African Americans may develop an identity that defines for themselves what it means to be a member of their group in America. Some, like Douglass, may hope for assimilation in American society; others, like Delaney, may wish to foster a distinctive black racial identity. Still others, like Du Bois, have identities rooted in their sense of belonging to two groups, a condition described by Du Bois as having a double consciousness. These examples point to the central role of an identity in defining a sense of oneself. Some psychologists would argue that these kinds of beliefs are the very core of personality. A personality psychology that does not afford a role for what people think of themselves and their position in the world may be incomplete.

McAdams (1992), writing as a critic of the Big Five taxonomy, also argues that the model is incomplete. He refers to it as a "Psychology of the Stranger." He writes:

> . . . we are trait theorists when we have nothing more to fall back on—when the object of our inquiry is new and as yet unpredictable. As the object becomes better known, however, we move beyond traits to more personally meaningful constructs such as goals, strivings, schemata, strategies, and the integrative narratives that provide coherence to the private personality, and we come to consider in detail the history, context, and intricate conditionalities of the individual person's behavior. This kind of broad and deep analysis . . . need not sacrifice all that is nomothetic for the uniqueness of the individual case. What it must forswear instead are a superficiality that comes with general ratings . . . and that comes with knowing little more than what, after an initial meeting, one stranger might know about another. (pp. 353, 354)

We shall have more to say about identity and narrative later in this book.

Let us summarize. People may be understood in terms of their positions on one of several nomothetic dimensions. People may also be understood in terms of their goals, values, sense of themselves, and in a variety of other more personally meaningful ways. Our discussion has proceeded as if these two approaches are antithetical and mutually exclusive. Are there ways of combining these two approaches? It is not easy to answer this question. Many psychologists interested in developing an understanding of personality based on what McAdams calls the integrative narratives that people develop to describe lives do not usually place much reliance on the Big Five. And psychologists who like the Big Five do not usually study the integrative narratives that give meaning and coherence to an individual life. One critic of the Big Five, Pervin (1994), argued that it is irrelevant to an understanding of case history material and individual lives.

Can we integrate these broadly different approaches? We shall try to provide an answer in the last chapter of this book. At this point we want merely to indicate that we do not believe it is possible to understand a person without knowing the person's position on the Big Five or some related taxonomy of traits. At the same time we do not believe that knowledge of a person's scores on the Big Five constitutes an adequate and complete description of personality. We need to know more about a person and we need to understand how to solve the difficult problem of integrating our knowledge of nomothetic traits with our understanding of the "integrative narratives" associated with individual lives.

To return to the problem of our psychologist visiting an alien planet, the methods used to establish the Big Five taxonomy could be applied to the strangers encountered on that planet. But a successful effort of this sort might well leave the psychologist with an impoverished understanding of the personalities of this planet's members.

5

Genetic and Environmental Influences

Why do people have different personalities? The answer is obvious. They have different genes and different environments. In this chapter we shall try to answer the following questions: Would you have a different personality if you were reared by different parents? Would your attitudes be different? Would your scores on the Big Five Test be different? If your family had adopted a child of the same age and gender as you, in what ways would he or she be similar to you? If you had an identical twin who was adopted from birth and reared in a different family, would the two of you be similar? We will review twin and adoption studies of personality traits, attitudes, and intelligence, studies that suggest that each of these personal characteristics is influenced by genes.

THE CONCEPT OF HERITABILITY

There are two fundamentally different ways in which genes could influence our personal characteristics. First, genes can determine characteristics we share with all members of our species. Virtually all human beings have the capacity to learn a language, and this capacity derives from the genetic characteristics that we all share. Second, there are many characteristics that are not shared by all human beings. For example, humans differ in height. Variations in our genes might influence such characteristics. In this chapter we shall be concerned with characteristics that are not shared by almost all human beings.

To what extent do genes influence personality characteristics; or, to use more technical language: Are personality characteristics **heritable**? **Heritability** is a statistical concept, an estimate of the influence of **genotypes** on **phenotypes** in a particular population. A *genotype* is the collection of genes determined for each human being at the moment of conception; *phenotypes* are measurable characteristics of persons. Height and trait ratings are both phenotypes. Heritability estimates, like correlations, vary from .00 to 1.00. If a phenotype has a heritability of 1.00, this statistic implies that variations in phenotypic scores in a particular population are determined wholly by variations in genotypes. If the heritability of a trait is .00, variations in genotypes do not influence variations in phenotypes.

Heritability is a frequently misunderstood concept. It is often assumed to be a *fixed* property of a phenotype. Consider the question, what is the heritability of intelligence? In a very real sense the question is meaningless and has no answer. The question may be reformulated in this way: What is the heritability of intelligence in a particular population at a particular time and place? We insist on this reformulation because the degree to which intelligence, or any other personal characteristic, is heritable may depend on the environments that different groups of individuals encounter. Under certain environmental conditions a phenotype may be very heritable, in a different environment it might not be influenced by a genotype.

Consider the hypothetical impact of two different environments on the development of intelligence. Society A attempts to provide a standard intellectual environment for all children. From birth, several hours a day, children are reared in communal nurseries that use similar methods of child care and expose children to a relatively standardized environment. Elementary schools in this society follow a rigidly standardized curriculum, each day's lesson being specified by a central authority. This description of Society A is not totally fictional. Children reared on communal farms in Israel spend several hours a day from birth in a common nursery. And children in Japan attend elementary schools that follow a rigidly prescribed curriculum that is standardized for all elementary schools (Stevenson, 1991). In Society B, in contrast, there are large differences in the quality of schools and in the intellectual stimulation provided to children. Some children attend superb schools with small classes and excellent facilities; others attend schools that are ill equipped, have large classes, and are staffed by bored teachers.

Is American society more like Society A or Society B? Would the heritability of intelligence be different in these two societies? Heritability would probably be higher in Society A. Why? If individuals with different genotypes are exposed to relatively homogeneous environments, then the influence of genotypes on phenotypes will increase. In the extreme case where there are no variations in the environment, any variations in individuals' phenotypes *must* be caused by genotypes. As environmental variation increases, the possible influence of these variations on phenotypes is likely to increase. Furthermore, even if variations in the usual range of environments have little influence on phenotypes, it is always possible that some variant or modification of the environment may alter the influence of genotypes on phenotypes. Genotypic influences always operate in a particular context and are influenced by the environments encountered. A person who spends most of the first thirteen years of her life locked in a closet is not likely to develop a high IQ, no matter what her genotype might be.

If the heritability of a phenotype depends upon the environment that individuals encounter, then changes in the environment can change phenotypes as well as the influence of genotypes on them. Evidence that a phenotype is highly heritable does not support a notion of biological determinism. Biology is not destiny! Such evidence does not imply that phenotypes are immutable and cannot be changed by manipulations of the environment.

The heritability of height in our society is .92 (Zuckerman, 1991). Variations in this phenotype are substantially influenced by genotypes. Yet individuals born in Japan after World War II were taller than their parents. Genetic characteristics did not change in one generation. Environmental changes, probably better nutrition, led to large changes in a phenotype that is highly heritable. Thus phenotypes that are highly heritable can, in principle, always be altered by the introduction of new and different environments.

Consider phenylketonuria, a genetically determined illness, an enzyme-deficiency disease that leads to the development of mental retardation if the individual is not treated. In order to develop this disease, a child must receive the appropriate recessive gene from both parents. One in four children whose parents do not have the disease but who carry the recessive gene will develop phenylketonuria. Children in America are now routinely tested for this disease shortly after birth. If it is detected and children are placed on a phenylalanine-restricted diet, they develop normal intelligence. Their genotypes do not change—the influence of the genotype on the phenotype (intelligence as assessed by tests in this example) changes.

The influence of a genotype on a phenotype, then, always depends on the nature of the environment. It may not be possible to understand how genotypes influence phenotypes without analyzing the environment of an individual. And, to get a bit ahead of our argument, the way in which the environment influences individuals may be influenced by their genotypes. Genetic and environmental influences are interdependent.

We shall argue that personality traits are influenced by genotypes. This has two implications. First, it leads to the search for biological influences on personality. No one believes that genes directly influence behavior. There are no genes that provide a correct answer to a question on a vocabulary test. Genes can influence our biological characteristics directly but our behavior only indirectly. If genes are related to our behavior, then it is likely that the different bodies, different brains, and different nervous systems with which we begin life influence the way in which we respond to the environment. If we want to understand why individuals appear to respond to the environments they encounter in different ways, it may be useful to understand biological influences on personality, a topic that we will discuss in the next two chapters. Second, and perhaps more surprising, evidence for the importance of genetic influences will lead us to understand **environmental influences** on personality in new and different ways.

METHODOLOGICAL ISSUES IN THE STUDY OF GENETIC AND ENVIRONMENTAL INFLUENCES

Twin studies and adoption studies may be used to study genetic and environmental influences on phenotypes. The twin method makes use of a fortuitous natural event: the existence of two different types of twins—identical or monozygotic twins (MZ) and fraternal or dizygotic twins (DZ). MZ twins derive from a single fertilized egg that is split; they have identical genotypes. DZ twins derive from two separate fertilized eggs; they do not have identical genotypes. Since MZ twins are genetically identical, any differences between them must be attributable to environmental influences. Since DZ twins differ genetically, differences between them may be attributable either to genetic or to environmental differences. Similarity among twin pairs is usually measured by obtaining *separate* correlations for MZ and DZ pairs. Comparisons between these correlations provide information about genetic and environmental influences.

MZ twin pairs can differ only for environmental reasons. DZ twin pairs can differ for both environmental and genetic reasons. If genotypes influence a phenotype, DZ twins should differ more than MZ twins since they have an additional influence that could cause them to differ from one another. This analysis is based on the assumption that the environmental events have equal effects on MZ and DZ twin pairs. The **equal-environments assumption** may be wrong. MZ twins resemble each other more than do DZ twins. Perhaps their physical similarity leads them to be treated more alike and to experience environments that are more similar. Thus MZ twins could be more alike than DZ twins because they experience more similar environments. One way to test the equal-environments assumption is to compare twins who are reared in the same family with twins who are reared in different families. The environment of twins reared in different families is probably more varied than that of twins reared in the same family. If MZ twins reared apart are more alike than DZ twins reared together, we can assume that violations of the equal-environments assumption do not explain differences between MZ and DZ twin pairs. Similarities among MZ twins reared apart provides evidence for genetic influences on a trait.

It is also possible to study relationships between siblings and between children and parents. Such studies are of only limited value in determining the importance of genetic and environmental influences. Siblings reared together share both a common environment and genetic similarity (they share approximately 50 percent of their genes). If they are similar to each other, those similarities may be attributable to their shared environment or to their genetic similarity. Adoption studies provide a way of separating the influence of **shared family environments** from genetic similarity. Many adoptive families have more than one adopted child and some have both natural and adopted children. Comparisons between biologically unrelated siblings reared together (two adopted children, or an adopted and a natural child) provide information about the effects of shared family environments: if those reared together are similar to each other, we can infer that similarities in their environment led to the development of similar phenotypes. So too, if adopted children are similar to their adoptive parents, we can assume that the family environment has influenced the child. If adopted children resemble their biological parents, we can assume that the genes they share with their biological parents have influenced them.

TYPES OF GENETIC AND ENVIRONMENTAL INFLUENCES

There are four kinds of genetic and environmental influences on phenotypes. **Additive genetic influences** cause individuals who are genetically similar to develop similar phenotypes. These influences lead genetically similar individuals to resemble each other—children to resemble their biological parents and siblings to resemble each other. If a phenotype was influenced solely by additive genetic influences, MZ twins, whether reared together or apart, would correlate 1.00; siblings, including DZ twins, would correlate .50; and children would correlate with their biological parents .50 whether or not they were reared by them.[1] Fingerprint ridge counts are determined almost perfectly by additive genetic influences. Lykken (1982) obtained correlations of .96 for MZ twins reared together and .98 for MZ twins reared apart for fingerprint ridge counts. The DZ correlation was .46.

    Nonadditive genetic influences lead individuals who are genetically similar (but not identical) to differ. These influences cause children to differ from their parents, and siblings to differ from each other. If a phenotype was influenced solely by nonadditive genetic influences, MZ twins, whether reared together or apart, would correlate 1.00 on the trait; other types of siblings would correlate no higher than .25 and perhaps as low as .00. Lykken (1982) obtained evidence for nonadditive genetic influences on a trait called "husbandry," defined as an interest in building, fixing, and making things. On a measure of this trait, he obtained a correlation of .55 for MZ twins reared together, .65 for MZ twins reared apart, and .07 for DZ twins reared together. Although MZ twins were similar in their husbandry scores whether they were reared together or apart, DZ twins were not similar at all.[2]

    Nonadditive genetic influences are caused by two genetic phenomena, **dominance** and **epistasis.** In the case of the former, if a gene is recessive, it will not influence a phenotype in the presence of a dominant gene. Consider the case of phenylketonuria. A child will not develop this disease unless it receives the recessive gene from both of its parents. A child may have phenylketonuria even though its parents and siblings do not. In this case, the child would share one member of a gene pair with each of its parents but is phenotypically different from both parents with respect to the disease.

Epistasis occurs when genes at different locations interact with each other. Suppose a phenotype is influenced by three genes at different locations—genes A, B, and C. Assume that person 1 has all three of these genes and that their combined presence causes a high score on a phenotype. Suppose person 2 has genes A and B, but not gene C. Person 2 is genetically similar to person 1, but because they differ with respect to gene C, they are not genetically identical. Person 3, who has none of these genes, is genetically different from person 1 with respect to these genes. It is possible that the influence of any one of these genes is dependent on the presence of the other two. Individuals would receive a high score on the phenotype if all three are present, and a low score if any are not present. If this were true, person 2 would receive the same score as person 3, and both would differ from person 1 for genetic reasons even though person 2 is genetically similar to person 1 and person 3 is genetically different.

Epistasis and dominance cause genetically similar individuals to differ from one another for genetic reasons. Genetic influences can cause family members both to resemble each other and to differ from one another. A phenotype may be totally determined by genotypes in a particular environment, and siblings (other than MZ twins) may not resemble each other at all on the phenotype and children may not resemble their parents. Similarity between parents and children is not a *sine qua non* for the presence of genetic influences.

A third type of influence is **shared environmental influences.** These cause individuals reared in the same family to resemble each other. The environments experienced by children reared together are more similar than the environments of children reared apart. Think of all the ways growing up in the same family produces similar environments. Children reared in the same family live in similar social circumstances. Family social status influences the quality of the schools they are likely to attend, the quality of medical care they are likely to receive, and the interests and values of individuals they encounter in their neighborhood. Those reared in the same family share the influence of the same parents as role models as well as the emotional climate of the same home. If a phenotype was influenced solely by shared family environmental influences, MZ and DZ twins reared together would both correlate 1.00 on the phenotype. Siblings reared together, whether biologically related or not, would correlate 1.00 on the trait.

Finally, there are **nonshared environmental influences.** We tend to think of environmental influences as being determined by the family that rears us, yet a moment's thought will show that children reared in the same family may experience different environments. Environmental influences begin from the moment of conception. Children in the same family may have had different prenatal environments. Lynn (1990), studying differences in the intelligence of MZ twin pairs, found that the twin who was heavier at birth tended to have a higher IQ than the lighter twin. He assumed that this difference was attributable to differences in prenatal nutrition. There are many potential influences of the biological environment that are not shared by children in the same family. For example, one child in a family could experience a serious illness that might have a profound effect on personality.

Children reared in the same family might also be treated differently, or *believe* that they are being treated differently. Parents may favor children who temperamentally or physically resemble them. Children may adopt different roles within the family—mediator, troublemaker, or responsible member of the family. Family circumstances change too. Divorce can alter the composition of the family as well as its economic fortunes. Children who differ in age, although reared in the same family, may be reared in quite different family circumstances at different ages. Furthermore, children reared together may encounter many different influences outside the home and may be exposed to different adults who influence them. Teachers, preachers, coaches, movie stars, and athletes are all potential role models for children. Any and all of these differences might lead children reared together to differ from one another.

We have identified four kinds of influences on a phenotype. Two of them, additive genetic influences and shared family environmental influences, lead biological siblings reared together to *resemble* each other. Two of them, nonadditive genetic influences and nonshared family environmental influences, lead biological siblings to *differ* from one another. Biological siblings reared together may resemble each other and may differ from one another for both genetic and environmetal reasons. However, identical twins can differ from each other only for environmental reasons.

RESULTS OF TWIN AND FAMILY STUDIES: PERSONALITY TRAITS

There are many twin studies of personality traits. In the typical study, MZ and same-sex DZ twins are asked to fill out self-report personality questionnaires. Loehlin (1992) summarized the results of such investigations for the Big Five personality traits. MZ twin correlations are usually close to .5 and DZ twin correlations usually .25 or less. The two traits that have been most extensively studied are extraversion and neuroticism. Table 5.1 presents MZ and DZ correlations for these traits obtained in four large-scale studies, all using large samples and similar measures. The results tend to be consistent. MZ twins are more alike than same-sex DZ twins. These findings suggest that there are genetic influences on extraversion and neuroticism.

There is another important aspect of these data. The two members of MZ pairs do not necessarily respond in exactly the same manner to personality questionnaires. The MZ twin correlation is not 1.00. Why do MZ twins differ? Their differences cannot be attributable to genetic influences: they are genetically identical. Nor can these differences be attributable to differences in the shared environment: they are reared together. The only explanation (other than errors of measurement, which could not account for differences among twin pairs as large as these) is that there must be nonshared environmental influences.

TABLE 5.1   Four Twin Studies of Neuroticism and Extraversion

	NEUROTICISM				EXTRAVERSION			
Samples	MZ–F	MZ–M	DZ–F	DZ–M	MZ–F	MZ–M	DZ–F	DZ–M
U.S. adolescents	.48	.58	.23	.26	.62	.57	.28	.20
Swedish adults	.54	.46	.25	.21	.54	.47	.21	.20
Australian adults	.52	.46	.26	.18	.53	.50	.19	.13
Finnish adults	.43	.33	.18	.12	.49	.46	.14	.15
Numbers of pairs								
United States	284	197	190	122	284	197	190	122
Sweden	2,720	2,279	4,143	3,670	2,713	2,274	4,130	3,660
Australia	1,233	566	751	351	1,233	566	751	351
Finland	1,293	1,027	2,520	2,304	1,293	1,027	2,520	2,304

Note: MZ, monozygotic; DZ, dizygotic; F, female; M, male. Studies: United States, Loehlin & Nichols (1976); Sweden, Flodeurs-Myrhed, Pedersen, & Rasmuson (1980); Australia, Martin & Jardine (1986); Finland, Rose, Koskenvuo, Kaprio, Sama, & Langinvainio (1988).
(Based on Loehlin, 1989) Reproduced with permission of the American Psychological Association.

DZ twin correlations for extraversion and neuroticism tend to be low. Being reared in the same family does not lead DZ twins to resemble each other on these traits. While DZ twins are somewhat similar, their similarity is not dramatically greater than that of strangers who have no relationship to each other.

DZ twin correlations are less than half the value of MZ twin correlations for extraversion. On a simple, additive genetic model we should expect DZ twins to have correlations that are half the value of MZ correlations since they are genetically half as similar as MZ twins. There are two explanations for this result. There may be nonadditive genetic influences that lead DZ twins to differ from one another. Alternatively, the equal-environments assumption may be wrong: MZ twins may be subject to environmental influences that lead them to be similar to each other, influences that may not operate in the same way for DZ twins.

This brief review of twin studies of two of the Big Five personality traits leads to some tentative conclusions. extraversion and neuroticism are both influenced by genetic characteristics and by nonshared environmental influences. When these influences are combined, almost all of the variance in extraversion and neuroticism is explained. There is no need to assume that shared family environments are important influences on extraversion and neuroticism.

Let us examine these conclusions more critically. We begin with what may be the most surprising conclusion: that extraversion and neuroticism are not influenced by shared environmental influences. One possible criticism is that the results for twins are anomalous. Twins may go to great lengths to define themselves as being different from one another. What is true for twins may not be true for other siblings. This objection does not appear to be valid, since non-twin siblings reared together are, if anything, *less* similar than DZ twins. If being reared in the same family led individuals to be similar to one another in personality phenotypes, we would expect that siblings would be similar to one another. They are not. Ahern, Johnson, Wilson, McClearn, and Vandenburg (1982) obtained scores for 54 personality scales from a large sample of siblings and their parents. They obtained an average correlation for siblings of .12; the average correlation between children and their parents was also .12. These results, which are typical, indicate that siblings do not respond in the same way to self-report measures of personality, and children do not resemble their parents on these measures.

The low level of similarity for siblings on self-report measures of personality may be partially or totally attributable to genetic influences. Loehlin, Horn, and Willerman (1981; Loehlin, Willerman, & Horn, 1982) studied biologically unrelated children who were reared together in adoptive families and obtained an average correlation of .04 on measures of personality. These data provide a partial answer to one of the questions we posed at the beginning of the chapter. If you had an adoptive sibling of the same gender with whom you were reared, would he or she be similar to you? The answer for self-report measures of personality: no more similar than any person selected at random. Why are children reared together so different in their responses to personality questionnaires? We shall try to answer this question at the end of this chapter.

Do the twin studies reported in Table 5.1 provide convincing evidence for the influence of genotypes on phenotypes? One could always argue that MZ twins are more alike than DZ twins because they are treated more alike. MZ twins tend to resemble each other physically and tend to share friends in common more than do same-sex DZ twins. An appeal to the violation of the equal-environments assumption of twin studies to explain findings that MZ twins are more similar than DZ twins is plausible. One way to test this assumption is to study twins who were reared in different families. If MZ twins are reared apart and have minimal contact with each other, it is difficult to argue that their similarity is attributable to environmental experiences that are independent of the influence of their genotypes. It is not easy to find twins who are reared apart. When they are found, they may not have been separated at birth and they may have had varying degrees of contact with one another. Often they are reared under similar circumstances (e.g., social class).

There are two contemporary studies of twins reared apart. The Minnesota Study of Twins Reared Apart and the Swedish Adoption/Twin Study of Aging both find that degree of separation and similarity of rearing conditions for twins have a negligible influence on their degree of resemblance. Table 5.2 presents correlations for self-report measures of extraversion and neuroticism obtained in three studies of twins reared apart. The correlations reported in this table are not completely consistent; the studies are based on different samples obtained from different countries. The twins sampled in the Swedish study, with an average age of 59, were older than the twins in the other studies. The Swedish study is based on a systematic sample of all twins who were born in Sweden during a particular period

TABLE 5.2   Correlations for Twins Reared Apart and Together on Extraversion and Neuroticism

Study		MZ Apart	MZ Together	DZ Apart	DZ Together
Shields	Extraversion	.61 (42)[a]	.43 (43)		−.17 (23)
	Neuroticism	.53	.38		.11
Minnesota Study	Extraversion[b]	.34 (44)	.63 (217)	−.07 (27)	.18 (114)
	Neuroticism	.61	.54	.29	.41
Swedish Study	Extraversion	.30 (99)	.54 (160)	.04 (229)	.06 (212)
	Neuroticism	.25	.41	.28	.24

[a]Numbers in parentheses are sample sizes for pairs of twins.
[b]Extraversion and neuroticism scales are derived from measures of affectivity that are correlated with E and N.

and were reared apart. And this study used a brief version of the test for extraversion and neuroticism that is not as reliable as the longer version. Any of these differences could account for the variability in the results (as well as the possibility that correlations based on small samples can vary for purely statistical reasons). Nevertheless, all these data do indicate that MZ twins reared apart tend to be similar on self-report measures of extraversion and neuroticism. On five of the six possible comparisons for these data, they are more alike than DZ twins reared together. For three of the six comparisons, MZ twins reared apart are more similar to each other than MZ twins reared together, although in the Swedish study, with the largest and most systematic sample, MZ twins reared apart are less similar than those reared together. These data indicate that MZ twins continue to be similar on extraversion and neuroticism whether they are reared together or apart. DZ twins, whether reared together or apart, seem to be quite different in extraversion and only marginally similar in neuroticism.

Loehlin (1992) used the results of twin and adoption studies to estimate the relative importance of different kinds of genetic and environmental influences on self-report measures of personality. These analyses should be dealt with cautiously. The results depend on complex statistical assumptions that are somewhat arbitrary, and a full discussion of the procedures and methods followed is beyond the scope of this book. Estimates of heritability based on the results of different studies are not always consistent. And, as we indicated earlier, heritability is to be understood as a property of a population, not of a trait. Heritability estimates may vary over time and for groups of individuals exposed to different environments. Nevertheless, Loehlin's estimates do represent the best current quantitative estimates for the relative importance of the four kinds of genetic and environmental influences on the Big Five personality traits. Table 5.3 presents the results of Loehlin's analyses. The analyses based on the first model allow for the possibility of nonadditive genetic influences. The analyses indicate that the combined genetic influence, including both additive and nonadditive, is close to .50 on self-report measures of personality. Shared environmental influences are low; the highest

TABLE 5.3 **Summary of Loehlin's Analyses of Genetic and Environmental Influences on Big Five Traits (Based on Loehlin, 1992)**

	MODEL 1 ADDITIVE AND NONADDITIVE GENETIC INFLUENCES INCLUDED			
Trait	Additive Genetic	Nonadditive Genetic	Shared Environment	Nonshared Environment
E	.32	.17	.02	.51
A	.24	.11	.11	.54
C	.22	.16	.07	.55
N	.27	.14	.07	.52
O	.43	.02	.06	.49

	MODEL 2 EXCLUDES NONADDITIVE GENETIC INFLUENCES			
Trait	Additive Genetic	Special MZ Twin Environment	Shared Environment	Nonshared Environment
E	.36	.15	.00	.49
A	.28	.19	.09	.44
C	.28	.17	.04	.51
N	.31	.17	.05	.47
O	.46	.05	.05	.44

Reproduced with permission of Sage Publications.

value is obtained on agreeableness ($r = .11$). Nonshared environmental influences are substantial.

The results for the second analysis are different. For the purposes of this analysis, Loehlin assumed that DZ correlations less than half the value of MZ correlations were attributable to special environmental influences that were shared only by MZ twin pairs. Nonadditive genetic influences are not included in the model. As a result, genetic influences are slightly less important. On either analysis, genetic influences and nonshared environmental influences are far larger than the influence of the shared environment.

These studies show that scores on self-report measures of personality traits are heritable. But are personality traits *themselves* equally heritable? Self-report measures are only one way of measuring a trait. Traits were defined in chapter 3 as latent dispositions that are assumed to account for obtained relationships between self-reports, ratings, and behavioral measures. Ideally, a trait should be measured by an aggregate index of all of these kinds of measures. The data reviewed here deal solely with self-reports. If aggregated measures were used, would the influence of genetic and environmental influences on traits be different? It is hard to answer this question since there has not been a great deal of research using aggregated indices for adult measures of personality. Errors of measurement contained in self-report indices are impossible to distinguish from nonshared environmental influences. Furthermore, differences among individuals that are not attributable to the influence of the shared environment or to genetic influences get thrown into the category of nonshared environmental influences. This category is comprised of everything that is left over, both systematic influences and errors of measurement. If errors of measurement of traits were reduced, genetic influences would likely be estimated to be more significant than they are now. Why? The elimination of such errors would reduce the value of nonshared environmental influences, thereby increasing the contribution of the other three influences. Most of the remaining variance is genetic. Therefore, an elimination of errors of measurement would probably lead to an increase in heritability.

This speculative analysis is supported by the results of a study by Heath, Neale, Kessler, Eaves, and Kendler (1992). They performed a study on a large sample of female twins using self-report measures of neuroticism and extraversion and also obtained ratings from their subjects' co-twins. The availability of both self-reports and ratings permitted them to obtain measures that eliminated possible sources of error in each method. They performed an analysis of the heritability of these corrected measures, and the estimates for extraversion and neuroticism were .73 and .63, respectively. These estimates of heritability are approximately 50 percent higher than the estimates derived by Loehlin based solely on self-report measures.

There is an unpublished study available that provides additional information about the heritability of measures of adult personality that are based on more than a single measure. Angleitner and his colleagues (1995) obtained peer ratings from two individuals to generate scores on the Big Five traits for a relatively large sample of MZ and DZ twins. Table 5.4 presents the results. The first two columns provide data on self-report measures of personality. Their results are similar to those obtained in the survey of comparable data by Loehlin. The mean MZ correlation for all five traits is .51 and the comparable DZ correlation is .26. The next two columns, presenting rating data, are based on the average rating for two raters on each personality dimension. The correlations here are slightly lower for both MZ and DZ twins, but the difference between the MZ and DZ correlations are comparable, suggesting that trait scores based on ratings are about as heritable as those based on self-reports. The lower correlations for ratings data imply that nonshared environmental influences may be higher for ratings scores than for self-report scores. (Can you determine why this is true?)

TABLE 5.4   Mean Correlations for MZ and DZ Twins for Big Five Traits Based on Different Measures (Based on Angleitner et al., 1995)

SELF-REPORTS		PEER RATINGS		CORRECTED PEER RATINGS	
MZ	DZ	MZ	DZ	MZ	DZ
.51	.21	.40	.15	.67	.26

The last two columns in the table present an analysis of ratings data that has been corrected for **attenuation.** This is a correction for errors of measurement. For example, the two raters did not always agree about the rating of the same individual. We can assume that each rater provided a rating that contains errors, but it is possible to correct the score. The correction may be thought of as the score that would be obtained if there were no errors of measurement. This notion may strike you as bizarre. What is the point of considering what would be true if there were not errors of measurement when all that is available for analysis are measures that contain errors? One way of obtaining a measure that is relatively free of error is to use many raters. The aggregate score obtained from ten raters whose ratings were positively correlated with each other but had a correlation that was less than 1.0 would be quite close to the hypothetical value of the correlation that is corrected for error *mathematically*—a correlation that is said to be **disattenuated.**

We believe that the correction applied in Table 5.4 is legitimate. The corrected data provide us with a somewhat different picture of the heritability of the Big Five traits of personality. These data—a mean MZ correlation of .67 and a DZ correlation of .26—suggest heritabilities that are above those obtained from uncorrected ratings or from self-report data. The heritabilities that would be obtained from this analysis are closer to those obtained by Heath et al. in their analysis of a phenotype that was based on a combined self-report and co-twin ratings, heritabilities between .6 and .7.

The results of the study by Angleitner and his colleagues are very important: it is the first attempt to study adult personality traits on the basis of results from different peer raters. The study also has the virtue of using a large sample. Angleitner and his colleagues have yet to analyze data for their sample based on an index in which self-report and ratings data are combined. The data they have analyzed, combined with the results obtained by Heath et al., suggest that the conclusions reached by Loehlin based on self-report measures underestimate, perhaps substantially, the heritability of personality.

More studies of this type are needed, including adoption studies and studies aggregating self-reports and ratings by several acquaintances, to provide more information about the heritability of adult personality traits as opposed to the heritability of self-reports of personality. Probably, the heritability of trait measures based on aggregate indices will be found to be higher than that of self-report measures.

If personality traits are heritable, events that are influenced by personality traits may also be influenced by genes. Consider divorce. Kelly and Conley (1987) found that neuroticism was positively related to divorce. If neuroticism is heritable, is divorce heritable? McGue and Lykken (1992) studied divorce in a sample of 1,516 same-sex twin pairs in Minnesota. The correlation for MZ twins was .55 and for DZ twins .16. They estimated that the probability of divorce was .053 for an MZ twin whose co-twin and parents had not divorced. By contrast, the probability of divorce where both partners were MZ twins whose co-twin and parents had divorced was .775. The heritability of divorce was estimated to be .52. The influence of shared family environments on the probability of divorce was estimated by McGue and Lykken to be .00. These data suggest that divorce is more likely to be influenced by the genes received from parents than by the shared family environments, including whether the parents divorced.

Are other individual characteristics subject to the same kinds of genetic and environmental influences as personality traits? For purposes of comparison we shall consider studies of attitudes and intelligence.

RESULTS OF TWIN AND ADOPTION STUDIES: ATTITUDES

Are attitudes heritable? Eaves, Eysenck, and Martin (1989) analyzed twin data on attitudes from studies conducted in Australia and England. They found that MZ twins had higher correlations on attitude scales than DZ twins, suggesting that the attitudes that individuals develop are influenced by their genes. MZ male twins tended to have similar attitudes about the importance of religious beliefs. The MZ correlation for a measure of religiosity was .66, whereas the comparable correlation for DZ twins was .51. Female twins tended to agree in negative attitudes toward minorities: the correlation for a measure of prejudice for MZ twins was .61 and the comparable correlation for DZ twins was .48.

Although these data provide evidence for the heritability of attitudes, the correlations are not like those typically obtained in twin studies of self-report measures of personality. On the latter, DZ twins' correlations usually range between .00 and one-half the value of MZ twins' correlations. For attitude scales, correlations of DZ twins are more than half the value of MZ twin correlations. This pattern is compatible with the assumption that shared family environments influence a phenotype. If they do, correlations among DZ twins will be larger than expected on a model of pure genetic influence. On a simple genetic model, DZ twins are expected to be half as similar to each other as MZ twins. If DZ correlations are larger than that, it is usually assumed that shared environmental influences are present. An analysis of the data for male religiosity suggests heritability values of .30 and values for the influence of shared family environments of .35. This analysis suggests that attitudes are influenced both by genes and by the effects of common family rearing. This certainly seems plausible. Children's exposure to their parents' political and religious attitudes should have a common influence on the attitudes of the children.

Research on genetic and environmental influences on attitudes may be interpreted in a different way. Spouses tend to be similar in attitudes. For example, Eaves and his colleagues reported spouse correlations for religiosity of .52. This similarity in attitudes does not vary with the length of the marriage, a fact suggesting that individuals choose to marry people whose values are similar. In this instance, opposites do not attract.

What is the significance of these results for the interpretation of twin correlations on attitude measures? **Assortative mating** refers to the tendency of individuals to choose mates who are similar to them. If assortative mating is present on a trait that is influenced by genes, a child will receive similar genes from both parents. Thus siblings should share more than 50 percent of their genes and DZ twins should have correlations larger than half the value of the correlations for MZ twin.

This analysis leads to two different interpretations of the data on twin attitudes. The relatively high DZ twin correlations may be attributable either to shared environmental influences or to genetic influences resulting from assortative mating. Which of these interpretations is correct? This question could be answered by means of data obtained from adoption studies. If shared environmental influences are present, adopted children should have attitudes that are similar to those of their adopted parents, biologically unrelated children reared together should have similar attitudes, and MZ twins reared apart should be less similar than MZ twins reared together. Waller et al. (1990) found that MZ twins reared apart were as simlar in religiosity as MZ twins reared together. These data suggest that shared family influences do *not* contribute substantially to an interest in religion.

We don't know if comparable results would be obtained for other measures of attitudes. There has been no appropriate research done that would enable us to determine which of the two interpretations of the importance of shared environmental influences is correct. But, on either analysis, it does appear that the attitudes people develop are influenced by their genes.

RESULTS OF TWIN AND ADOPTION STUDIES: INTELLIGENCE

Are scores on intelligence tests influenced by genes? How important is the shared family environment? In one respect, data for intelligence are different from data for personality traits. Siblings are not very similar in scores on personality tests. By contrast, Bouchard and McGue (1981) summarized many studies of sibling resemblance in IQ and obtained an average correlation of .47. Perhaps siblings are similar in intelligence because of the shared family environment. Relationships between siblings and between parents and children in intelligence might be attributable to the parents' intellectual socialization practices. Parents who are more intelligent might provide an intellectually stimulating environment. While this is a reasonable interpretation of the correlation between siblings, it is not a compelling one. Siblings also share genes, and additive genetic influences might also explain a positive correlation. We shall have to look at adoption studies to understand why siblings are similar in their intelligence scores.

Loehlin, Horn, and Willerman (1989) conducted one of the largest and best controlled studies of adoption—the Texas Adoption Study. They obtained IQ scores for a sample of mothers in a home for unwed mothers whose biological children were adopted shortly after birth. They twice administered IQ tests to the adopted children and to siblings reared in the same home: first when the children were between 3 and 14 years old, and then ten years later. They also administered IQ tests to the adoptive parents. Table 5.5 presents correlations for family members in the study. When the children were between ages 3 and 14, their IQs were related to the IQs of both their adoptive parents and their biological mother. The IQ of the adopted child was also related to that of biologically unrelated siblings. Ten years later the results were different. Older adopted children no longer resembled their adoptive parents and their biologically unrelated siblings. Their IQ continued to resemble the IQ of their biological mother.

The results obtained in the Texas Adoption Study are similar to those obtained in other studies. There are now several studies of older adopted siblings that report near zero correlations between biologically unrelated siblings reared in the same family. For example, Teasdale and Owen (1984) obtained a sibling correlation of .02 for biologically unrelated siblings in a sample of Danish military recruits (see Brody, 1992 for a review of other relevant studies).

Studies of twins reared apart also provide information on the effects of adoption on intelligence. Table 5.6 presents the results obtained in different studies of such twins. Note the close correlations for MZ twins reared apart and those reared together. In both the Minnesota and Swedish studies, the similarity of rearing environments of the separated twins and their degree of contact were not related to the similarity of IQ test scores. Whether MZ twins are separated from birth and have little or no contact, or are separated later in life with extensive contact, does not appear to influence their similarity in intelligence. All MZ twins seem to wind up with similar IQs. DZ twins, whether reared separately or together, are not as similar in IQ.

Parents may influence the early intellectual development of their preschool children. With universal education, the schools become the principal

TABLE 5.5   Correlations for Family Members in the Texas Adoption Study on Intelligence (Based on Loehlin, Horn, and Willerman, 1989)

	TIME 1		TIME 2	
	R	N	R	N
Biological mother and adopted child	.23	200	.26	200
Adopted mother and adopted child	.13	246	.05	246
Adopted father and adopted child	.19	253	.10	253
Adopted children reared together	.11	75	−.09	75
Adopted and natural child reared together	.20	106	.05	106
Natural children of adoptive parents	.27	25	.24	25

TABLE 5.6   Correlations on Intelligence for Twins Reared Apart and Together

Study	TWINS			
	MZ Apart	MZ Together	DZ Apart	DZ Together
Shields	.77 (37)[a]	.76 (34)		
Minnesota Study				
WAIS	69 (48)	.88 (40)		
Raven Test and Mill Hill	.78 (42)	.76 (37)		
Swedish Study	.78 (45)	.80 (63)	.32 (88)	.22 (79)

[a]Numbers in parentheses are sample sizes for numbers of twin pairs.

intellectual socialization influence on the child and parental influences may fade as individuals age. Genetic influences, by contrast, remain important. MZ twins tend to have similar IQ scores as they grow older, whereas DZ twins tend to drift apart (McCartney, Harris, & Bernieri, 1990). Note that in the Swedish study of twins with an average age of 59, correlations for DZ twins whether reared together or apart are quite low. The changing pattern of MZ and DZ correlations for intelligence as individuals age is compatible with the assumption that the heritability of intelligence increases as individuals grow older. Genes are more important determinants of intelligence in old age than they are of intelligence in childhood.

INTELLIGENCE AND PERSONALITY COMPARED

The results of the Swedish study permit us to compare findings for self-report measures of personality and intelligence on the same sample of aged adults. Correlations for MZ twins, whether reared together or apart, are much higher on intelligence than on self-report measures of personality. This finding implies that the heritability of intelligence is higher than that of self-report measures of personality. The heritability of personality for the Swedish data was estimated to be .30, and the estimate for intelligence was .80, a larger value than most estimates of the heritability of intelligence based on younger samples (see Loehlin, 1989). The Swedish study implies that nonshared environmental events are more important influences on self-report measures of personality than on performance on intelligence tests. The study is also compatible with the assumption that the shared family environment is not an important influence on either personality or intelligence. Note that in the Swedish study, DZ twins who are reared apart are slightly more alike in intelligence than DZ twins reared together. The vanishingly small influence of experiences shared by individuals reared together may be the most important thing that psychologists have learned from twin and adoption studies of personality and intelligence.

DO PARENTS INFLUENCE PERSONALITY AND INTELLIGENCE?

The research reviewed permits us to answer some of the questions we posed at the beginning of the chapter. Would you resemble an adopted sibling who was reared with you from birth? Probably not in personality or intelligence, but probably somewhat in attitudes and values. Would you resemble an MZ twin reared apart from you? You would probably be similar in intelligence, be only partially similar in self-report measures of personality, and likely would share some attitudes.

The research that we have reviewed indicates that shared family influences do not lead individuals to be similar in personality and intelligence. Does this result imply that interactions with our parents *do not* have a critical influence on the development of our personality? It is hard to answer this question. Probably there are many environmental influences on personality that have little or nothing to do with the interactions between a child and his or her parents—the books we read, the friends we make, the people we fall in love with, the people we admire, the illnesses we get, and our countless individual experiences may contribute to the development of our personalities. Personality is also probably influenced by experiences with parents, but the impact of these encounters may be different for different siblings reared together. Parents may treat siblings in different ways, and also siblings with different characteristics may respond to similar treatments in different ways. The extended interaction of parent and child, each with his or her distinctive characteristics, may combine idiosyncratically to influence the development of personality.

It is also likely that certain kinds of child-rearing experiences may contribute in a relatively uniform manner to the development of certain kinds of personality characteristics. In his book on *The Antisocial Personality*, Lykken (1995) noted that individuals who are reared by single parents in poverty are far more likely to become juvenile delinquents than are those reared in two-parent, stable families; he estimated that children who are reared by single mothers are seven times more likely to do so. Lykken also argued that some forms of antisocial and criminal behavior may be heritable. He noted, though, that "the modest increase in genetic risk cannot account for the sevenfold increase in the observed risk for delinquency among father-absent children" (Lykken, 1995, p. 204). Lykken argues that in certain circumstances there is an influence of shared family environments.

We need to learn a great deal more about the ways in which encounters with parents influence personality. Our best guess is that interactions between parent and child do influence personality, but it is hard to judge what importance should be assigned to this type of influence. Parental influence often appears to act in such a way as to make siblings different from one another. If this is true, and most of the research strongly supports this conclusion, it is hard to understand the exact way in which we have been influenced by interactions with our parents. Perhaps these interactions are not important. Do you think that you have been influenced by your parents? If so, in what ways?

What about intelligence? Here we have reason to believe that parental influences may be important. Adoptive families are usually intact families with good reputations in their community. The unemployed, the addicted, and the impoverished are not included in significant numbers, if they are included at all, in these samples. What is the impact of the shared-family rearing for children of migrant workers who attend school sporadically and who have poor health care and inadequate nutrition? Such children are unlikely to develop their full intellectual potential.

Capron and Duyme (1989) studied French children whose biological parents differed widely in social background and who were adopted by families with different social class backgrounds. The influence of the biological parents background on the children's IQ was found to be larger than the influence of the adopted parents' social background. Turkheimer (1991) analyzed the results of this study and concluded that there was a relationship between the educational background of the adoptive parents and the IQ of their adopted children at age 14—for every additional two years of formal education completed by the adoptive parent, there was a one-point increase in the child's IQ. Capron and Duyme's study, encompassing such a wide range in social class background, does support the view that, at the extremes, the educational background of adoptive families influences the adopted children's IQ. In most studies of adoption, the social class background of the adoptive families may vary but rarely reaches extremely low social status. Under these circumstances, genes exert a substantial influence on a person's intelligence, and the family environmental influence is vanishingly small.

IMPLICATIONS OF RESEARCH ON GENETIC AND ENVIRONMENTAL INFLUENCES

Genetic Influences

It has been said that parents are environmentalists before their first child is born and geneticists after their second child is born. In the past, psychologists believed that personality was shaped mainly by socialization practices. Many parents believed what psychologists told them, even though their own experiences should have convinced them that children were born different and responded in different ways to the same child-rearing techniques. Children are not blank slates; they come into the world with different response tendencies. Socialization is an interdependent sequence of unfolding influences of children on parents and parents on children.

Once we grant the possibility of genetic influences on personality and other individual characteristics, our understanding of the way in which the environment influences individual differences begins to look radically different. We become skeptical of advice about appropriate methods of child rearing. Consider the advice that parents should read to their children. Studies have shown that children who are read to are likely to develop higher intelligence (Caldwell & Bradley, 1978; Gottfried, 1984), and we are told that reading to a child may stimulate the child's intellect and foster a love of reading. This sounds reasonable, but is it possible that the alleged benefits of reading to a child are illusory?

Consider some of the ways in which our knowledge of genetic influences may complicate our understanding of the alleged benefits of reading to a child. First, children may differ in the extent to which they enjoy this activity. Some may enjoy it, others may not. The extent to which a parent reads to a child may be partially influenced by the genetic characteristics of the child that determines whether the child likes to be read to. Furthermore, children who enjoy being read to may also enjoy school activities, and as a result they become good students and develop their intellectual capacities. According to this analysis, the superior outcomes for children who are read to are caused not by the experience of being read to, but rather by the children's dispositional characteristics that influence the way in which their parents respond to them.

In addition, parents who read to their children may have different genetic characteristics than parents who do not. If the children become better students than children who are not read to, the reason may be the genes they received from their parents rather than the effects of being read to.

The point of this analysis is not to get parents to stop reading to children. We too think that it is a worthwhile and enjoyable activity. As psychologists, however, we are not sure that this activity had a profound impact on our children. The point of our example is to demonstrate how our understanding of the impact of parents on children becomes complicated when we consider the influence of genetic characteristics.

Here is another example. Watching television programs that depict violent and aggressive actions has harmful effects on children. If we attempt to understand a relationship between exposure to television violence and subsequent violent behavior by taking into account potential genetic influences, the analysis becomes complicated. Perhaps children with a genetically influenced tendency to behave violently are attracted to violent television programs. Perhaps parents who permit their children to watch a lot of television are genetically different from parents who do not permit their children to watch violent programs. Thus, a relationship between exposure to violent television programs and aggressive behavior may be caused by the influence of parental genes rather than by the parents' socialization practices.

There is evidence that a child's tendency to watch television may be partially determined by the child's genes. From participants in an adoption study, Plomin, Corley, DeFries, and Fulker (1990) obtained measures of the amount of time parents and children watch television. They obtained a correlation of .15 between the amount of time an adopted child watched television and the amount of time the child's biological mother watched television. Adopted children's television watching was also influenced by the viewing habits of the adoptive mother; the correlation here was .16. In natural control families, the correlation between parent and child in time spent viewing television was .32.

This example points to the complexity in determining the nature of environmental influences on children. Genes may influence the kinds of environmental events one encounters as well as the influence of these events. But what is an environmental event? Watching television my be assumed to be a quintessential environmental event, yet it appears actually to be a kind of hybrid event, neither purely genetic nor purely environmental.

We hope that we have succeeded in complicating your understanding of the ways in which the environment may influence personality. This analysis still does not provide a very clear understanding of the ways in which genes influence personality. The phenotypes we have considered are all probably influenced by many genes, and there are few if any single genes whose location is known that can be shown to influence any of the characteristics considered in this chapter. At present, it is not possible to examine a person's genotype in the laboratory and determine his or her personality genes, yet efforts are underway to identify specific genes related to personality. Ebstein et al. (1996) reported identifying a gene that is related to sensation seeking, a trait related to extraversion involving adventuresomeness and thrill-seeking (Zuckerman, 1983). Research that attempts to identify specific genes that influence personality is in its infancy, although this area is likely to be of increasing importance. The Human Genome Project is attempting to identify the functions of individual genes, and in the coming decades we will likely see many reports relating specific genes to various psychological characteristics. Nevertheless, it will be difficult to discover the genotypes that influence personality. Personality dimensions are probably influenced by more than one gene, and perhaps by epistatic combinations of genes. Even if progress is made in this endeavor, we shall still have to learn something about how the environment acts to shape the influence of genotypes on phenotypes. Remember, biology is not destiny, and no matter what progress we make in understanding the role of specific genes, we will not be able fully to understand personality characteristics by understanding their genetic basis alone. Since personality genotypes cannot presently be directly measured, we cannot trace the impact of environmental events on individuals with defined personality genotypes. Some of this may become possible in the twenty-first century, but for now it is possible only to speculate.

Scarr and McCartney (1983) distinguished among passive, active, and reactive potential influences of genes. Passive influences are those that lead individuals with different genotypes to respond in different ways to the same event. Reactive influences lead individuals with different genotypes to encounter different environmental events. Active influences are choices of genotypically different individuals to create different environments for themselves. Scarr and McCartney assumed that the relative importance of these three kinds of influences changes over time, passive influences becoming less important and reactive and active influences becoming more important.

Here is an imaginary scenario indicating the way in which such influences might work. Children may differ in a genotypically influenced characteristic to respond in a fearful way to threats and dangers encountered in the environment. Children who are genotypically fearful would probably find the environment threatening. This would be an example of a passive genetic influence. Genotypically fearful individuals might be selected by their peers as victims who are easily bullied. This would be an example of a reactive genotypic influence. Thus the child's genotypes might influence the kinds of environmental events the child is likely to encounter. Finally, such a child might learn to select environments that minimize the possibility of encountering frightening events. Perhaps as an adult, such a person might avoid the occupation of firefighter or soldier. This attempt to select environments that are compatible with one's genotype is an example of an active genotypic influence.

This analysis of the way in which genes influence personality is not compatible with the belief that genetic influences are immutable and unchanging. This unfolding pattern of influences provides ample opportunity for potential interventions that will change the impact of the genotype on the phenotype.

Environmental Influences

If children reared together are influenced by experiences that they do not share, it will be necessary to study siblings reared together in order to learn more about the differences in their experiences. Psychologists are beginning to examine differences in the experiences of children reared together. Dunn and Plomin (1990) summarized this new research in a book aptly entitled *Separate Lives*. They reviewed research based on an inventory designed to measure differences in siblings' experiences in parental interactions, sibling interactions, and peer group interactions. Tables 5.7–5.9 present items from the inventory. Dunn and Plomin found that siblings do report differences in their experiences, and these differences were related to personality characteristics. Siblings sometimes report dramatically different perceptions of their experiences together. Here is an example from Dunn and Plomin's book based on an interview with two siblings in England.

> "Well he's nice to me. And he sneaks into my bed at night time from mummy. I think I'd be very lonely without Carl. I play with him a lot and he thinks up lots of ideas and it's very exciting. He comes and meets me at the gate after school and I think that's very friendly. . . . He's very kind. . . . Don't really know what I'd do without a brother.
> —Nancy; 10 years old, talks about her 6-year-old brother Carl

> "She's pretty disgusting and we don't talk to each other much. I really don't know much about her. (Interviewer: What is it you really like about her?) Nothing. Sometimes when I do something wrong she tells me off quite cruelly."
> —Carl talks about Nancy

TABLE 5.7   Selected Items from Sibling Inventory of Differential Experiences: Interactions with Your Sibling (Based on Dunn and Plomin, 1990)

SIBLING INVENTORY OF DIFFERENTIAL EXPERIENCE (SIDE)

This questionnaire is designed to ask about your interactions with your sibling. Compare yourself to your sibling (or one of your own siblings) when you were growing up and living at home. Scoring instructions and comparison scores are provided at the end of the questionnaire.

    1 = My sibling has been much more this way than I have.
    2 = My sibling has been a bit more this way than I have.
    3 = My sibling and I have been the same in this way.
    4 = I have been a bit more this way than my sibling.
    5 = I have been much more this way than my sibling.

	SIBLING MUCH MORE		SAME		ME MUCH MORE
1. In general, who has started fights more often?	1	2	3	4	5
2. In general, who has shown more trust for the other?	1	2	3	4	5
3. In general, who has shown more concern and interest for the other?	1	2	3	4	5
4. In general, who has been more willing to help the other succeed?	1	2	3	4	5
5. In general, who has liked spending time with the other more?	1	2	3	4	5

Dunn, J. and Plomin, R., *Why Siblings Are So Different.* Copyright © 1990 of Basic Books, Inc. Reprinted by permission of Basic Books, a division HarperCollins Publishers, Inc.

Siblings reared together may have different experiences for several reasons. They may perceive small differences in experiences as large differences. Comparisons in the way children are treated in the same family may be vivid components of a child's life. Parental treatment of children may vary with the child's age. Children may notice these age-dependent differences and these observations may be psychologically significant. And children may be treated differently by parents because they are genetically different. Baker and Daniels (1990), who obtained twin data on the sibling inventory of different experiences, found that MZ twins reported smaller differences on the inventory than DZ twins. In addition, they found that biologically unrelated children reared together reported larger differences than biologically related children. These data suggest that the genetic characteristics of children influence either the way in which they are treated or the way in which they perceive their treatment.

Research on the influence of nonshared environmental experiences on personality is just beginning. Twin and adoption studies are more informative about what

TABLE 5.8   Selected Items from Sibling Inventory of Differential Experiences: Parental Interactions with You and Your Sibling (Based on Dunn and Plomin, 1990)

PARENTAL INTERACTIONS WITH YOU AND YOUR SIBLINGS

This questionnaire is designed to ask how similarly your mother and father treated you and your sibling. Compare yourself to your sibling (or one of your siblings) when you were growing up and living at home. If your parents were divorced or if one died, answer the questions for the mother and father with whom you lived for the longest period of time. Scoring instructions and comparison scores are provided at the end of the questionnaire.

1 = In general, this parent has been much more this way toward my sibling than me.
2 = In general, this parent has been a bit more this way toward my sibling than me.
3 = In general, this parent has been the same toward my sibling and me.
4 = In general, this parent has been a bit more this way toward me than my sibling.
5 = In general, this parent has been much more this way toward me than my sibling.

	TOWARD SIBLING MUCH MORE		SAME		TOWARD ME MUCH MORE
Mother:					
1. Has been strict with us.	1	2	3	4	5
2. Has been proud of the things we have done.	1	2	3	4	5
3. Has enjoyed doing things with us.	1	2	3	4	5
4. Has been sensitive to what we think and feel.	1	2	3	4	5

Dunn, J. and Plomin, R., *Why Siblings Are So Different.* Copyright © 1990 of Basic Books, Inc. Reprinted by permission of Basic Books, a division HarperCollins Publishers, Inc.

may *not* be important than about what is important. It is possible that the events that influence personality are idiographic. Each of us may be influenced by unique events. If we wished to study such events, we could ask individuals to describe the experiences that have been most important in their lives (e.g., Moffitt & Singer, 1994).

Here is an example from an autobiographical memoir written by the actor Sir Laurence Olivier (1982). Laurence Olivier attributed many of his personality characteristics to his relationship with his father, an austere Anglican clergyman who was extremely stingy. In his memoir, he described one experience that he believed influenced his personality. In order to conserve water, his father made Laurence and his brother bathe in the same bath water he had used. Since Laurence was the youngest child, he had to bathe in water previously used by his father and brother. As an adult, Laurence Olivier tried to calculate the amount of money his father saved by reusing his bath water. Olivier believed that this experience was emblematic of his relationship with his father and was one of a series of experiences that shaped his adult personality.

The example poses several issues of interpretation given the research reviewed in this chapter. Note that the experience was shared with his brother.

TABLE 5.9   Selected Items from Sibling Inventory of Differential Experiences: Interactions with Peer Groups (Based on Dunn and Plomin, 1990)

INTERACTIONS WITH PEER GROUPS

Think of each item as if your peer group (your main group of friends) has a personality of its own. Even though friends inside each peer group might be quite different, think about how the group is in general. Think about your experience and that of one of your siblings when you were growing up and living at home. Scoring instructions and comparison scores are provided at the end of the questionnaire.

1 = My sibling has had a peer group much more like this than my peer group.
2 = My sibling has had a peer group a bit more like this than my peer group.
3 = My sibling and I have had the same type of peer group in this way.
4 = I have had a peer group which is a bit more like this than my sibling's peer group.
5 = I have had a peer group which is much more like this than my sibling's peer group.

	SIBLING'S PEERS MUCH MORE		SAME		MY PEERS MUCH MORE
1. popular	1	2	3	4	5
2. ambitious	1	2	3	4	5
3. outgoing	1	2	3	4	5
4. lazy	1	2	3	4	5
5. hard working	1	2	3	4	5
6. intelligent	1	2	3	4	5
7. mature	1	2	3	4	5
8. extraverted	1	2	3	4	5
9. delinquent	1	2	3	4	5
10. responsible	1	2	3	4	5
11. successful	1	2	3	4	5
12. friendly	1	2	3	4	5
13. rebellious	1	2	3	4	5

Dunn, J. and Plomin, R., *Why Siblings Are So Different.* Copyright © 1990 of Basic Books, Inc. Reprinted by permission of Basic Books, a division HarperCollins Publishers, Inc.

Did it have the same impact on both brothers? The experience was not the same for both. Did Laurence feel that his experience was worse than his brother's since he was the last to bathe? Does this experience have the significance that Olivier appears to attach to it? Do we usually know the experiences that are critically important in shaping our personalities? If the experiences that have influenced us are unique, and we are not aware of their significance in our lives, how can a psychologist discover the events that are critical in determining individual differences in personality?

THE FUTURE

In summary, it is clear that genes influence many individual differences. And we have begun to rethink the way in which we are influenced by environmental events. At the fundamental biological level we are unable to specify the genes that may influence personality. Studies of adult personality with few exceptions deal with self-report data. There is a need for additional adoption and twin studies of adult personality using aggregated personality indices rather than self-report measures of traits. In addition, we know little about the way in which genetic and environmental events contribute to change in personality. There are few longitudinal studies of adult personality using twin and adoption designs. MZ twins tend to resemble each other in intelligence over much of the adult life span; DZ twins tend to drift apart in intelligence. This means that changes in phenotypes in intelligence tend to be determined by genotypes, and changes in intelligence increase the relationship between phenotype and genotype. Or, put another way, the heritability of intelligence increases as people grow older. There is little evidence for this type of change for personality traits, however. Both MZ and DZ twin correlations decline for self-report measures of personality (McCartney, Harris, & Bernieri, 1990), suggesting that the influence of genes on personality does not increase as individuals grow older. Personality may change over the life span as a result of many unpredictable events that lead individuals with common genotypes to drift apart. Additional longitudinal studies using twin and adoption designs should enable psychologists to understand the way in which genes and the environment combine to change personality over the adult life span.

For the present we can provide only a very broad outline of the influence of genes and the environment on the development of personality. Our outline compels us to recognize the influence of chance and caprice in our lives. We are marked by a biological individuality—created by the random assortment of genes we receive from our biological parents at the moment of conception—that profoundly influences our responses to the social world we encounter.

Endnotes

[1] These correlations assume a completely reliable and valid way of measuring the phenotype, which of course is never the case in measures of psychological characteristics.

[2] MZ twins do not correlate 1.00 on husbandry. Since the correlation is less than 1.00, there must also be environmental influences on this trait. Note that the correlations between MZ twins reared apart and MZ twins reared together are quite similar for this trait. This implies that the environmental influences on husbandry are not those that lead individuals reared in the same family to be similar to one another.

6

Personality and the Brain

DIRECT AND INDIRECT BIOLOGICAL INFLUENCES

We have seen that genetic factors play a role in individuality. This conclusion was based on the repeated finding that people who have more genes in common (i.e., MZ twins, biological siblings) also resemble each other more in their personalities than do people with fewer genes in common (i.e., DZ twins, adoptive siblings). How do genes influence individuality? Genes influence biological structures and processes. Therefore, any genetically influenced differences or similarities in psychological characteristics must reflect differences and similarities in biological structures and processes. But what are these structures and processes and how do they influence personality? Some biological factors might have a relatively direct influence on psychological processes. We saw an example of this sort of influence when we discussed phenylketonuria in the last chapter. It is also possible that linkages between biological factors and psychological phenomena may be relatively indirect. That is, biological factors may influence behavior because they promote different environmental effects.

To understand the difference between these two paths of genetic influence, consider the recent claim that right-handers and left-handers differ in their life expectancy. Coren and Halpern (1991; Halpern & Coren, 1993) reported that left-handers are less likely to live to old age than are right-handers. Although this claim

111

is controversial, and may even be wrong (Harris, 1993), let us suppose for the moment that it is true. The question is, why? A direct biological explanation might be that left-handers have weaker immune systems than right-handers (Geschwind & Behan, 1984). Geschwind and Behan propose that circulating hormones during the prenatal period influence the development of both left-handedness and immune function. Left-handedness is a **marker,** on this view, for a biological characteristic (lower immunological functioning) that could directly influence life expectancy.

Can you think of a way that left-handedness might have an indirect, environmentally mediated effect on life expectancy? Coren and Halpern argue that the reason left-handers are at risk is that they live in a "right-handed world" and therefore are more likely than right-handers to have accidents from using tools or driving cars, both of which (in most countries) are designed for right-handers. The effect of handedness could be reversed if the environment were different: in a "left-handed world" it would be the right-handers who would be at greater risk. Indeed, Halpern and Coren (1993) argue that this is exactly what happens in Great Britain and Ireland, where people drive on the left rather than the right side of the road. You can see now why we call this effect indirect. It involves a biological characteristic (handedness), but the reason for the different outcomes is solely the nature of the environment. In contrast, the immune system explanation is not dependent on the environment but has to do with a direct biological link between handedness and health, both of which are genetically influenced. Of course, many biological influences are some combination of direct and indirect influences. Can you think of some examples?

STUDYING BIOLOGICAL CONTRIBUTIONS TO PERSONALITY

In this chapter we will focus on the more direct biological contributions to personality. One of the difficulties in trying to understand this link is that our knowledge of how the nervous system works is incomplete, particularly in regard to behaviors and psychological processes that cannot be studied in nonhuman animals, such as those most likely to be involved in individuality. Although many researchers have tried to use animal models to help understand human psychological phenomena, the relevance to humans is often problematic. For example, Gray (1982) developed a theory of anxiety based largely on the study of rats. Is "freezing" or "defecating" in a rat the same as anxiety in a human? It should be noted that drug testing often uses such animal models; however, whether a drug has an intended effect on humans cannot be assumed from similar effects in rats or rabbits, and for that reason drug trials with humans are a prerequisite for approval of drugs for human use. With animals, it is possible to use invasive techniques such as brain surgery or electrodes implanted deep in the brain to study brain–behavior relations. The obvious ethical problems of using such techniques with humans limits their usefulness in studying human personality. In recent years noninvasive techniques such as magnetic resonance imaging have been developed for studying brain activity, and there is little doubt that such techniques will become even more powerful and sophisticated. As is true in many sciences, advances in understanding the brain will require advances in technologies (until Galileo invented the telescope there was simply no way of knowing that any other planet than Earth had moons). It is almost impossible to predict what new discoveries and understanding await the development of such technologies.

In the meanwhile, we can use only the knowledge we have and the technical abilities available to us. Therefore, it is important to acknowledge that any theories of how individuality is influenced by biological factors will almost certainly be incomplete, if not entirely wrong. When the ancient Greeks believed that the body influenced behavior through the **humors,** it was natural for them to assert that personality differences reflected differences in the predominance of these causal agents. The ancient Greeks were wrong. Does that mean we should sit around and wait for new developments? Not at all. These developments will grow out of insights and dissatisfactions in ongoing theory and research.

In fact, research on brain and personality has already pointed in some promising directions. We will examine two aspects of individuality for which research points to a role for biological factors: extraversion and neuroticism/anxiety. We will then discuss research on personality differences in infants and young children. We will conclude by examining possible biological contributions to behavioral differences between women and men. But before we begin, let's consider what is involved in a biological study of personality and whether it is likely to be fruitful.

IS A BIOLOGICAL ROLE IN PERSONALITY PLAUSIBLE?

Until early in this century, the idea that personality (temperament, character) was influenced by biological factors was relatively uncontroversial. Yet, by the 1920s this idea had fallen out of favor. Why did this happen? In part, it occurred as a reaction against unscientific claims about biological influences on personality. For example, the nineteenth-century phrenologists claimed that personality characteristics were determined by specific areas of the brain which could be revealed by studying the bumps in people's skulls. The criminologist Lombroso argued that sloping foreheads revealed criminal tendencies. Equally outrageous were claims about racial superiority and inferiority based on "biological" principles. In short, a good deal of bad science served to discredit biological explanations of personality. At the same time, a number of new approaches to understanding human beings were coming to the forefront. Anthropologists and sociologists ruled out specific biological influences in favor of cultural influences. Psychoanalysis, although supposedly based on biology, in reality saw the important influences on personality as essentially psychological. And behaviorism, as propounded most visibly by John B. Watson, argued that all human behavior was learned and that personality was little more than the set of habits each individual had developed through conditioning.

As the century draws to a close, the idea that biology influences personality has again become more widely accepted. Why has this happened? We believe there are five reasons.

1. *Psychopathology.* There have been major shifts in thinking about abnormal behavior in the last 40 years. It is now generally accepted that forms of psychopathology such as schizophrenia, depression, antisocial personality disorder, attention deficit disorder, and obsessive-compulsive disorders, to name a few, are influenced by biological factors. The fact that drugs are often effective in treating or ameliorating these conditions points to at least some involvement at the level of brain biochemistry. If biological factors can influence abnormal behavior, it is plausible to assume that they can also influence normal behavior.

2. *Genetics.* We have already shown how quantitative genetic methods point to a role for the genes in personality. Although some people have been surprised by these findings, if one considers what has long been known about behavioral characteristics of other animals, perhaps it is only the surprise that should be surprising. For centuries, **selective breeding** has been carried out to produce desired behavioral characteristics in animals. Dogs have been bred for aggression, herding behavior, obedience, and many other behavioral characteristics that we would label aspects of personality in humans. (In fact, there are books available to help prospective dog owners select breeds on the basis of their psychological profiles.) Breeding works only if the traits one wishes to breed for are under genetic influence. Lab studies have shown that behaviors such as running speed and fearfulness can be easily bred in rats in a relatively short period of time (Plomin, DeFries, & McClearn, 1990).

3. *Increased knowledge of nervous system and brain–behavior relationships.* It is a cliché that there has been explosion of knowledge about how the brain controls behavior, feelings, and even thoughts. Research in neuropsychology has demonstrated how damage to specific brain areas produces specific changes in people's behaviors. Psychopharmacology and basic neuroscience research have begun to trace out the exact neural pathways involved in various psychological processes. In short, the brain is no longer a "black box," and the more we learn about it, the more easily we can envision how biological factors could influence personality.

4. *Variability in brain structures.* We have little trouble accepting that individual differences in characteristics such as athletic skill are influenced by biology, because we can easily observe that people differ in their bodies (size, muscles, coordination, etc.). What is not generally recognized is that people also vary in their brains. Returning to psychopathology for a moment, recent evidence indicates that there are structural brain abnormalities in the major psychoses; for example, enlarged lateral and third ventricles are associated with schizophrenia (Raz & Raz, 1990). Variations in physical attributes of brains have also been related to handedness and gender (Breedlove, 1994; Witelson, 1989).

5. *Research on brain and personality.* Finally, the case for a biological involvement in personality is strengthened by research demonstrating relationships between personality variables and various aspects of brain functioning. It is this research to which we now turn.

EXTRAVERSION

Genetic research has repeatedly demonstrated that the extraversion dimension is influenced by genetic factors. What could it be about people's brains that could lead them to be more or less sociable, fun-loving, and enthusiastic? We might be tempted to answer this question by saying, "the part of the brain responsible for sociability, fun-lovingness, and enthusiasm." This answer would assume a high degree of **isomorphism** between underlying nervous system processes and personality traits (Zuckerman, 1991). Such isomorphism would make the task of connecting personality dimensions to brain systems relatively straightforward. One would know what one was looking for. An alternative possibility is that there is very little isomorphism—that personality traits are consequences of a complex array of brain processes. In this case, forging links between traits and brain processes would be far more difficult and require far more ingenuity.

Eysenck's Arousal Theory

For almost half a century, Hans J. Eysenck has been trying to understand how differences among people in brain processes can produce differences in the observed behaviors of extraverts and introverts. In 1967 Eysenck published one of the most important books in the field of personality psychology, *The Biological Basis of Personality,* in which he presented a theory of how the brains of introverts and extraverts differ. The challenge was to come up with a way of linking personality to the relatively **nonspecific** functions of the brain. One of the major discoveries at that time was that the brain had a system for regulating levels of **cortical arousal,** labeled the **ascending reticular activating system** (ARAS). Cortical arousal refers to the state of alertness of the organism. We are all aware that sometimes we are alert and sharp, other times drowsy and dull. To some extent, these **states** are influenced by our ongoing environments. We are more aroused at a basketball game or a wild party than in a library or during a quiet conversation with a friend. We also know that such states are heavily influenced by biology (Thayer, 1989). Arousal changes over the course of the day, with some people feeling more alert in the morning, others in the evening. We know that physical fatigue and exercise can influence arousal. We know that stimulant drugs like caffeine increase arousal and sedative drugs like barbiturates decrease arousal. Eysenck suggested that these variations in people's states might also occur as variations in traits: some people might be *generally* more cortically aroused or less cortically aroused than others. Most important, Eysenck was able to come up with a way of tying differences in cortical arousal to the behavioral differences between introverts and extraverts.

In considering the behaviors that make up the extraversion factor, Eysenck noted that they seem to involve activities that produce increases or decreases in arousal. Consider some of the items on Eysenck's measure of extraversion, the

Eysenck Personality Questionnaire: "Can you usually let yourself go and enjoy yourself at a lively party?" "Do you like plenty of bustle and excitement around you?" "Do you prefer reading to meeting people?" The key to linking the arousal concept to extraversion was theorizing that the reason extraverts like to go to parties and the like is that they are attracted to situations that increase their arousal. Introverts prefer quiet activities that do not increase their arousal. Why would some people prefer situations that are very arousing while others do not? In order to understand this, it is helpful to think of cortical arousal as analogous to the volume control on a radio or TV. Imagine two radios, one with its volume control turned up, the other with it turned down. The same signal comes from the broadcast source to the two radios, but because the volume controls are set differently, one radio produces loud sounds and the other produces soft sounds. Cortical arousal may function this way. Two individuals with different levels of cortical arousal experience the same stimulus differently. People high in cortical arousal (volume control turned up) experience stimuli more intensely than do people low in cortical arousal (volume control turned down). Eysenck further assumed that either too much or too little stimulation is unpleasant (that is, one can be overstimulated or understimulated). Can you put these elements of Eysenck's theory together to deduce who would have higher cortical arousal, introverts or extraverts?

Think of the situation of a person with high cortical arousal. If that person goes to a loud, wild party her already high arousal level might go even higher so that she feels overstimulated and uncomfortable. A person with low cortical arousal would not be overstimulated; in fact, the excitement of the party might raise that person's arousal closer to the **optimal arousal level** at which he feels most comfortable. Now think of relatively quiet and unstimulating situations. Under these conditions, the person with high arousal might feel most comfortable, that is, be closer to her optimal arousal level, but the person with low arousal might feel understimulated, and thus bored and edgy. People who prefer less stimulating environments would often be described as introverts; those who prefer more stimulating environments would often be described as extraverts. Through this relatively simple idea that people differ in arousal levels, Eysenck was able to explain some of the important differences between introverts and extraverts. Introverts, having higher levels of arousal, seek out less stimulating environments, while extraverts, with lower levels of arousal, seek out more stimulating environments.

Testing Eysenck's Theory

Eysenck's theory is ingenious, but is it correct? Since 1967, many studies have been carried out to test the theory. As we will see, the research suggests that Eysenck was on the right track but that the theory requires some modifications. But first let's consider how one could test Eysenck's theory. We might begin by asking whether Eysenck's description of the behavior of introverts and extraverts is correct. We know extraverts and introverts differ in their preference for parties because we ask them so in measuring the dimension. But people could like or dislike parties for many reasons not related to the degree of stimulation they provide. (Can you think of some reasons?) What evidence, then, is there that extraverts and introverts differ in their preferences for high versus low levels of stimulation?

Preferences for Levels of Stimulation

Let us examine two studies, one in a natural setting and one in a laboratory. Campbell and Hawley (1982) asked college students whether they preferred to work in a noisy library reading room or in a quieter room. Extraverts more often preferred the noisy room, introverts the quiet room. This difference might be due to differences in preferred stimulation level, or it might be due to the fact that extraverts like to interact with other people. To see if noise level is the crucial variable, it is necessary to eliminate other **confounding** variables. In the Campbell and Hawley study, noise level is clearly confounded with potential for social interaction, so there is no way of knowing which is responsible for the different preferences of extraverts and introverts.

Laboratory studies are often used to try to isolate specific variables and thus prevent such confounds. Geen (1984) set up a study in which subjects were asked to choose a preferred level of noise as background to a paired-associates learning task. Introverts chose noise levels that were substantially lower than those chosen by extraverts. Geen also reasoned that if these noise levels were indeed "optimal," then the best performance on the task would occur when subjects worked with their preferred level. To test this idea, one group of extraverts was assigned to work with the noise level preferred by other extraverts, while another group of extraverts was assigned to work with the level preferred by introverts. Similarly, one group of introverts was assigned to work at the level preferred by other introverts, while another group of introverts was assigned to work at the level preferred by extraverts. The effects of these different levels of background noise on paired-associate learning are shown in Table 6.1.

Extraverts took longer to learn the paired-associates when they worked at the relatively lower noise intensities preferred by introverts than when they worked at the relatively higher noise intensities preferred by extraverts; introverts took longer to learn the paired-associates when they worked at the relatively higher intensities preferred by extraverts than when they worked at the relatively lower levels of intensity preferred by introverts. These data support Eysenck's contention that introverts and extraverts differ in their preferred level of stimulation and that the preferred level is, in some sense, optimal. They do not, however, provide any

TABLE 6.1 Paired-Associate Learning under Different Levels of Noise Stimulation (Based on Geen, 1984)

Personality	MEAN TRIALS TO CRITERION	
	Assigned Introvert Choice	Assigned Extravert Choice
Extraverts	7.3	5.4
Introverts	5.8	9.1

Reproduced with permission of the American Psychological Association.

evidence that the *cause* of these differences involves arousal or any other "biological" factor. To evaluate Eysenck's theory, we need to go beyond demonstrations of differences in behavior and obtain more direct evidence that extraverts and introverts differ in cortical arousal.

Cortical Arousal

How might one provide such evidence? One approach has been to measure responses that more directly reveal nervous system processes. The discipline of **psychophysiology** focuses on measurements of such responses. You are probably already familiar with a number of psychophysiological measures. When we say that our heart beats faster when we see someone we are attracted to, we are referring to a psychophysiological indicator: one's heart rate increases under certain emotional conditions, so one way of "measuring" emotional state is to measure heart rate. Geen (1984) employed several psychophysiological measures to see whether arousal was different for extraverts and introverts during preferred versus nonpreferred noise levels. One of these was a measure of **electrodermal activity.** When people are aroused they often sweat. It is possible to measure the amount of perspiration by passing a small electric current between two electrodes on a person's palm or fingers—the more perspiration, the greater the electrical conductivity. One measure of electrodermal activity involves **skin conductance responses** (SCRs), considered an index of autonomic and central nervous system arousal. If introverts and extraverts differ in cortical arousal, then they should differ in their SCRs to a given level of noise. Geen found that at both higher and lower levels of noise, introverts had more SCRs than extraverts, but the number of SCRs for introverts and extraverts at their preferred level was just about the same. In other words, introverts and extraverts appear to prefer noise levels that produce about the same amount of arousal. Similar results were obtained with pulse rates, another measure of arousal. To summarize, Geen's results support Eysenck's basic idea that extraverts and introverts attempt to produce optimal arousal levels for themselves by seeking different levels of stimulation from the environment.

Eysenck (1967) believed that extraverts are *chronically* less aroused than introverts. It should be relatively easy to test the theory worded in this way: simply place extraverts and introverts in a lab and obtain measures of arousal. Suppose you decided to do such a study. You would immediately have to make some choices. First you would have to decide what measure of arousal to use. Psychophysiological measures, as useful as they are, do not provide a "royal road" to the nervous system. As is generally true of measures in psychology, each psychophysiological measure has a certain degree of specificity. Skin conductance, heart rate, and EEG measures are not simply alternative indexes of some general brain event we call "arousal."

Second, you would have to decide what the conditions in the lab will be and what the subjects will be doing. Should the subjects be simply resting? Should they be involved in a task? Should there be external stimulation (lights, sounds) or should stimulation be kept to a minimum? You might reply that it really wouldn't matter because the theory states that the difference in arousal is chronic, that is, always present. After all, if you measured a person's height, it wouldn't matter what the conditions in the lab were. In fact, many studies have assumed that the difference between extraverts and introverts should emerge under a wide range of conditions (Gale, 1983). This assumption turns out to be false. The conditions under which arousal is measured matter quite a bit. Specifically, differences between extraverts and introverts appear much more reliably when subjects are exposed to stimuli of moderate intensity than when they are in very low- or very high-stimulation conditions (Stelmack & Geen, 1992). Why does this happen? There is reason to believe that at very high levels of stimulation, a process known as **protective inhibition** serves actually to reduce arousal. Protective inhibition is a fail-safe mechanism that seems to prevent the physiological system from becoming dangerously overstimulated. As a result, higher levels of stimulation increase arousal only up to a point, then arousal levels off or even decreases with higher stimulation.

Caffeine is a stimulant; it increases arousal. What would happen to SCRs if introverts and extraverts were administered caffeine? Figure 6.1 shows the results of a study by Smith (1983). Introverts' SCR amplitude was higher than that of

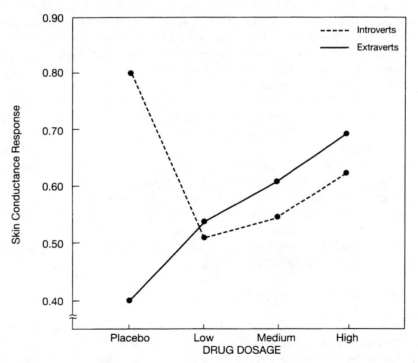

FIGURE 6.1   Effect of caffeine on the amplitude of the skin conductance response for introverts and extraverts. (Based on Smith, 1983; reproduced with permission of Pergamon Press, Inc.)

extraverts in a placebo (no caffeine) condition, but when caffeine was administered, the introverts' SCRs dropped to a level even lower than extraverts' SCRs. Thus the answer to the question of whether introverts and extraverts differ in their SCRs is, "It depends."

What about the low stimulation end? Sometimes psychophysiologists take what they call **baseline** measures. The idea is to see the level of the response under "resting" conditions. The assumption is that "resting" conditions are the same for everyone. But think of the extraverts in a low-stimulation condition. They would be far from their optimal level of arousal. They would be bored. So what would they do? They might very well attempt to increase their arousal through mental activity or even fidgeting. As a result, the so-called resting condition would not be "resting" at all. The extraverts would be producing "paradoxical arousal" to counteract the low level of external stimulation.

Arousal or Arousability?

As you can see, the simple idea that extraverts and introverts differ in chronic arousal is not so simple after all. If you remember the discussion of dispositions in chapter 3, this should not be surprising. One of our main points there was that dispositions should be thought of as potential behaviors. To say someone is aggressive is not to say he is always aggressive, but to say that under certain circumstances he is more likely than most other people to behave aggressively. In the same way, rather than claiming that introverts and extraverts always differ in arousal under all conditions, we could say that they differ in their tendencies to exhibit arousal in response to stimuli. That is, we can subtly shift the emphasis from differences in arousal to differences in **arousability**—from differences in chronic states to differences in responses to stimuli (Stelmack, 1990; Stelmack & Geen, 1992).

Once we draw a distinction between chronic arousal and arousability, we find that there is a good deal of support for aspects of Eysenck's theory. As was mentioned above, introverts do show higher levels of arousal in response to stimuli of moderate intensity than do extraverts. There is also evidence that introverts are more sensitive to stimuli. They often show lower thresholds for detection of very weak stimuli and experience discomfort and pain at lower levels of intense stimuli than do extraverts (Stelmack, 1990).

Is Eysenck's Theory Complete?

There is little doubt that introverts and extraverts differ along some of the lines proposed by Eysenck and that these differences reflect something about the nervous systems of introverts and extraverts. Does Eysenck's theory explain everything about the differences between introverts and extraverts? In particular, can the complex array of differences that make up the E factor of the Big Five be reduced to differences in arousability or sensitivity to stimuli? Earlier we used the analogy of a radio to describe the concept of cortical arousal. But human beings are not radios. The "intensity" of stimuli is not their most important quality. Stimuli have meaning for people and relevance to their ongoing goals. Consider an introvert who lives in an apartment near an airport. Whenever the landing pattern brings jets over his apartment he finds the noise unbearable, the loudness almost painful. And when he tries to sleep at night, even tiny sounds from neighboring apartments annoy him and keep him awake. So far, this is just as Eysenck would predict. However, when he listens to music he turns the volume way up; he enjoys hearing his favorite music loud. Obviously, stimulus "intensity" is not simply a matter of decibels. As Koelga (1992) stated, "Noise is a relative construct. . . . Noise is a function of the person (personality, noise sensitivity, attitudes, interests, momentary mental and physical states) and the situation in which it takes place (a person at home may enjoy loud music but get very annoyed at a neighbor's barking dog)" (p. 251). Eysenck's theory has little to say about the role of these factors in sensitivity, arousal, or preferred levels of stimulation. We would argue that these factors must be taken into account in order for us to understand how extraverts and introverts respond to stimuli. Whether a stimulus is "arousing" may depend on the significance of the stimulus for the individual. Recall that in the Geen (1984) study, the stimuli were irrelevant (and perhaps distracting) with regard to the task at hand.

Beyond the question of responsiveness to stimulation, one must ask whether the crucial difference between extraverts and introverts—the way they interact socially—is adequately explained by Eysenck's theory. Eysenck's notion is that these differences are fundamentally strategies for increasing or decreasing arousal. Obviously, social interaction is a great deal more than that. Remember that Eysenck is not attempting to explain social behavior itself, but rather why some people seek out social interactions more than others do. We must also consider the developmental implications of Eysenck's theory. Children who seek out social interactions are more likely to develop social skills and thus have more rewarding social experiences than children who avoid these interactions. Thus, a biological difference that increases or decreases frequency of social interaction can have effects that radiate out to many aspects of behavior.

Extraversion and Positive Emotions

What about aspects of extraversion other than social interest? Recall that extraverts are described as fun-loving, enthusiastic, and energetic. These components are sometimes given the label **surgency, positive emotionality,** or **positive affectivity.** Extraverts seem to experience life with greater energy and enthusiasm and to describe themselves as more optimistic than do introverts (Marshall, Wortman, Kusulas, Hervig, & Vickers, 1992; McCrae & Costa, 1991). Do you think Eysenck's arousal theory can explain this difference in emotional tone? It has been suggested that the more positive emotional tone of extraverts may be a result of their greater social interest. There is reason to believe that positive affect may be closely tied to social interaction. For example, situations that are described as full of fun and enjoyment often involve other people, so perhaps extraverts are generally in more positive moods simply because they have a greater number of social interactions (Emmons & Diener, 1986). Research suggests this is not the case, however. Extraverts report greater happiness than introverts in both social and nonsocial situations (Diener & Larsen, 1993).

There is another way sociability and positive emotions could be connected. People in good moods may have more desire to interact with others than do people in bad moods. Would you rather go to a party when you are feeling tired or when you are feeling upbeat? Perhaps differences in emotional tone lead to differences in social interest, rather than the other way around. This idea returns us to our original question: Why should extraverts experience more positive emotions than do introverts?

Some theorists have speculated that extraversion may be influenced by brain systems that relate to emotional reactivity (Gray, 1987; Zuckerman, 1991). Gray (1987) proposed that a brain circuit which he labeled the **behavioral activating system (BAS)** determines how sensitive an individual is to signals of reward or nonpunishment. (A different circuit, the **behavioral inhibiting system (BIS)**, determines how sensitive an individual is to signals of punishment or nonreward.)

A number of authors (e.g., Fowles, 1987; Larsen & Ketelaar, 1991; Tellegen, 1985) have used Gray's ideas to explore how extraversion and positive emotions are linked. One idea is that extraverts are more sensitive to reward than introverts are; that is, rewards have a greater emotional impact on extraverts. When exposed to situations with the potential to produce positive affect, extraverts will experience greater positive affect than will introverts.

Larsen and Ketelaar (1991) tested this idea by having subjects imagine being in two positive situations (winning a lottery and having an invigorating, pleasant exercise session). Afterward, subjects rated their mood. Extraverts reported significantly more positive mood than did introverts. In a control condition (imagining driving on a highway and going to a supermarket) there was no difference in reported mood of introverts and extraverts. This result supports the general idea that extraverts are likely to experience positive affective situations more intensely than do introverts, even under conditions that have nothing to do with actual social interaction. Rather, the differences may partly reflect differences in aspects of their brains responsible for positive affect.

What brain systems might be involved in reward sensitivity? Each neuron in the body is innervated by a specific neurotransmitter. One of the major achievements in brain research in the last several decades has been to trace neuronal pathways through the brain that rely on the same neurotransmitter. Figure 6.2 shows a schematic of three major neurotransmitter pathways: for dopamine, for serotonin, and for norepinephrine. The dopamine system has been identified as playing a major role in activity level and the reward-seeking characteristic of the BAS (Cloninger, 1986; Gray, 1987; Panksepp, 1982). According to Zuckerman (1991), the extraversion dimension may largely reflect variation in the dopamine system. This

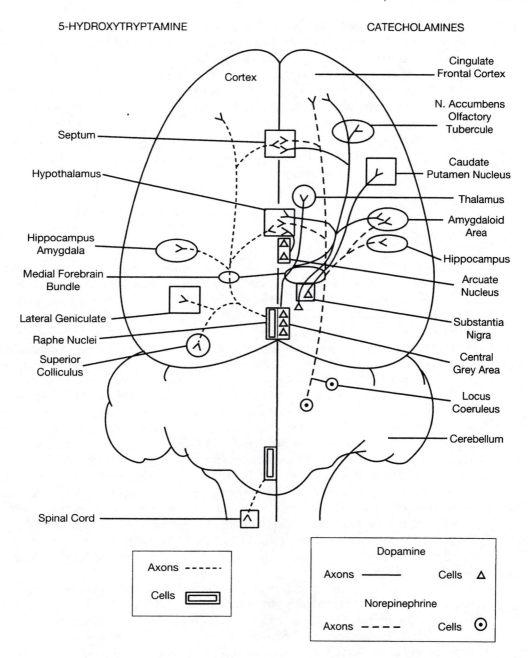

FIGURE 6.2 Schematic representation of serotonin (5-hydroxytrypta-mine), dopamine, and norepinephrine pathways in the rat brain. (From Zuckerman, 1991; reproduced with permission of the Cambridge University Press.)

model suggests a more direct connection between the biological systems and extravert and introvert behaviors than does Eysenck's model. Recent research provides preliminary support for this model. Depue, Luciana, Arbisi, Collins, and Leon (1994) administered a drug that has the effect of activating dopamine receptors, resulting in increased spontaneous blinking and increased secretion of the hormone prolactin. Individuals who exhibit these two reactions are assumed to be more responsive to dopamine. In a sample of eleven volunteers, positive correlations were found between a measure of positive emotionality and spontaneous blink rate ($r = .47$) and prolactin secretion ($r = .75$).

NEUROTICISM   *—defining aspect of the tendency to be anxious vs. calm.*

Anxiety and Stress

The tendency to be anxious versus calm—a defining aspect of the neuroticism factor of the Big Five—is generally agreed to be a core dimension of individuality (Almagor, Tellegen, & Waller, 1995; Eysenck, 1991). Why might some people get upset more easily, more often, and more intensely than other people? Obviously, one possibility is that their lives are more stressful. Undoubtedly, everything else being equal, people are going to feel more anxious under stressful circumstances than under nonstressful circumstances. But everything else is *not* equal: people differ in their tendencies to react with anxiety. It is obvious that different people respond with different levels of anxiety to the same situation (an exam, an airplane ride, a date, public speaking, etc.). A little less obvious is that the concept of stress *per se* is not easy to separate from one's personality. In fact, the term *stress* may be rather ambiguous. Although we can all agree that some situations are more stressful, threatening, and upsetting than others, many everyday situations are experienced as stressful *because* the individual is, in fact, reacting with anxiety and distress. Is taking an exam or going on a date or speaking in public stressful? For some people yes, for others no. Research indicates that the experience of stressful life events is influenced by neuroticism scores. People who are high on neuroticism tend to view more situations as threatening to their well-being, hence stressful, than do people low on neuroticism (Aldwin, Levenson, Spiro, & Bosse, 1989; Ben-Porath & Tellegen, 1990; Watson, 1990).

There is also evidence that people's sense of well-being may be more influenced by their N scores than by stressful life events. Ormel and Wohlfarth (1991) asked people to describe all of their "long-term difficulties" present in the previous four weeks. Long-term difficulties were defined as events of at least two months' duration that most people would consider stressful, such as unemployment, marriage problems, and chronic illness of a family member. The severity of each difficulty was judged in the context of each subject's life situation (for example, unemployed with good chance of getting another job versus a poor chance of getting another job). These subjects had also filled out a questionnaire measuring neuroticism six or seven years earlier, so each subject had scores on long-term difficulties and on neuroticism. Using path analysis (see chapter 2), Ormel and Wohlfarth found that neuroticism had a much stronger direct effect on current psychological distress than did long-term difficulties. Ormel and Wohfarth state:

> "The most salient finding of this study is the strong direct effect of neuroticism on psychological distress. This finding is particularly interesting because neuroticism was measured 6 or 7 years before the assessment of psychological distress. Moreover, the direct effect of neuroticism on distress is strikingly stronger than the direct effects of long-term difficulties. . . . This suggests that temperamental dispositions are more powerful than environmental factors in predicting PD [psychological distress]" (p. 751).

Biological Factors in Neuroticism

Neuroticism is a trait; there is something about people who score high (or low) on measures of neuroticism that causes them to experience more (or less) anxiety and distress than other people do. Many ideas have been proposed over the years to explain the nature of individual differences in neuroticism, not all of them biological in nature. For example, how people interpret situations around them, how they explain their own successes and failures, and how they view themselves may all contribute to the tendency to be anxious or calm. We will discuss these contributions later in this book. In this chapter we will explore the biological factors involved in neuroticism, the factors that must be present to explain the genetic contribution to this dimension. We will focus on theories that look for the source of this individual difference in characteristics of the central nervous system.

How might one investigate biological bases of neuroticism? At first glance, it might appear that of all the Big Five factors, neuroticism would be the easiest and most straightforward to link to biology. Animal models are probably more likely to yield interesting hypotheses for neuroticism than for any other major trait (what is conscientiousness in a rat?). Indeed, one prominent theory of the biological basis of anxiety has been based primarily on studies with rats and other animals, on the assumption that anxiety is basically the same across mammalian species (Gray, 1987). We can also look at the effects of drugs—again, we know drugs can affect anxiety more than other traits. All of this is true because neuroticism, at its core, involves emotional reactions.

The key emotional component of neuroticism is **anxiety.** Like other emotional reactions, anxiety is a complex phenomenon involving cognitive, behavioral, experiential, expressive, and physiological responses. In acute states of anxiety, the physiological component is evident: elevated **sympathetic nervous system** activity (rapid heart rate, shallow respiration, changes in blood pressure, etc.). The biology of this reaction is relatively easy to study. You are probably aware, however, that often anxiety is more like a nagging feeling of unease, a feeling that one's well-being is somehow threatened, that something bad might happen. These kinds of feelings and thoughts are also part of what it means to be an anxious person (or the lack of them, to be a calm person). It is not so easy to see how biology contributes to these more general feelings. Also, neuroticism is not just anxiety. It involves a wide range of negative feelings, including low self-esteem, proneness to depression, irritability, and others (Watson & Clark, 1984).

Suppose you were asked to speculate as to what biological factors might produce differences in the neuroticism dimension? Perhaps the most obvious answer is that people might differ in the ease with which anxiety reactions can be triggered. Imagine two individuals, one whose nervous system has a low threshold for anxiety reactions, the other a high threshold. Figure 6.3 shows how these individuals might react in three driving situations that differ in their objective threat. In situation 1, losing control of a car on an icy road, both individuals experience acute, strong anxiety. In situation 3, driving leisurely on a sunny day, neither individual experiences any anxiety. In situation 2, driving in a heavy rain with low visibility, the person with the low threshold experiences anxiety but the person with the high threshold doesn't. People rarely encounter situations that are obviously life-threatening, like situation 1, and similarly, situations with no threatening possibilities at all are probably also rare. In ambiguous situations, however, a person with a low threshold for anxiety responses would more often experience anxiety than would a person with a high threshold.

Is this a convincing explanation for differences in anxiety-proneness? You might object that we said nothing about the individuals' *beliefs* about how threatening the situation is. Perhaps the difference lies in how they interpret the situation rather than in their threshold for a physiological anxiety response? Perhaps the high-neuroticism person simply believes the world is a more dangerous place than the low-neuroticism person does. We have already noted that people high in neuroticism report more stressful life events. This tendency may reflect cognitive processes rather than physiological responses. (We will discuss cognitive contributions to emotions in chapter 11.) However, one's beliefs about the world may be

	Driver low in N	Driver high in N
	Anxiety experienced?	
Situation 1 Losing control on icy road	Yes	Yes
Situation 2 Heavy rain with poor visibility	No	Yes
Situation 3 Leisure driving on sunny day	No	No

FIGURE 6.3 Anxiety in two drivers differing in neuroticism under different conditions of threat.

a *result* of how one responds physiologically, rather than the other way around. Why would a person be responding with anxiety so often if the world were a safe, unthreatening place? The possibility that people use their own physiological reactions as a way of understanding a situation suggests that the relationship between cognition and physiology could be far more complex than first appears.

Eysenck's Theory of Neuroticism

Eysenck (1967) proposed the plausible theory that the neuroticism dimension reflects differences in the ease with which those areas of the brain that mediate anxiety are activated by stimuli, areas that include structures in the **limbic system** and their connections to other brain areas, including those that interact with the sympathetic nervous system. Activation of the sympathetic nervous system can be observed in psychophysiological responses such as increased heart rate, increased blood pressure, peripheral vasoconstriction (producing the feeling of "cold hands"), increased sweating and electrodermal responses, and increased muscular tension (especially around the forehead). If the neuroticism dimension reflects the ease with which anxiety responses are triggered, it ought to be easy to find differences between people high and low in neuroticism in these psychophysiological indicators of anxiety by simply measuring them during exposure to stressful stimuli. A quarter of a century after Eysenck's proposal, the answer is starting to become clear: studies within normal populations have *not* been successful in linking neuroticism with psychophysiological measures of activation (Eysenck, 1990; Fahrenberg, 1992). When individuals are exposed to a variety of stressors, both in the lab and in the field, there is no consistent evidence that those who score high on neuroticism are more physiologically reactive than those who score low. This is so even when responses are aggregated over different measures and stressors. Does this mean the hypothesis is incorrect? Or does it mean that testing the hypothesis is just more complicated than it first appeared?

Lack of Intercorrelation Among Psychophysiological Measures

One fact about psychophysiological measures of sympathetic nervous system arousal could lead us to say "yes" to both questions: these measures are not highly correlated with one another. Increases in, say, heart rate, are not correlated with increases in, say, electrodermal responses. How can these both be measures of "autonomic arousal" if they are uncorrelated?

These measures do increase in response to stressors when averages of groups of individuals are computed. Yet any given individual in the group might show, say, an increase in heart rate but not in skin conductance, or vice versa. Research on the covariation of physiological responses that are influenced by sympathetic nervous system activity indicates that people differ in which particular responses are influenced by stress. This phenomenon is known as **individual**

response specificity (Stern & Sison, 1990). It means that my sympathetic response might increase my heart rate and respiration, while your sympathetic response might increase your electrodermal activity and muscle tension. It has also been shown that different stressors produce different patterns of physiological activation (**stimulus response specificity**).

The fact that various indicators of autonomic activity are not correlated with one another is one reason why finding consistent relationships between psychophysiological measures and neuroticism is so difficult.

The Problem of Repressors

A second reason concerns the construct validity of measures of neuroticism. A number of studies have suggested that people who score low on neuroticism or anxiety scales may be of two types. One type can be labeled *true low anxious* individuals. They are accurate in describing themselves as calm, rarely distressed, and unworrying. The second type, whom we can label *defensive low anxious* or *repressors,* are not completely accurate in describing themselves in these terms. There is a discrepancy between what they tell us (and perhaps believe about themselves) and how they respond in the face of stress. Weinberger, Schwartz, and Davidson (1979) measured both the behavior and psychophysiological reactions of "true low anxious," "repressors," and "high anxious" subjects under a stressful task. People were classified as true low anxious if they scored low on an anxiety scale and also scored as nondefensive on the Marlowe-Crowne Social Desirability Scale (see chapter 2). Those who scored low on anxiety and as highly defensive on the Marlowe-Crowne were classified as repressors. High anxious subjects were simply those who scored high on the anxiety scale. The task involved quickly making up endings to sentences that contained provocative sexual and aggressive themes. Repressors had more speech disruptions and higher levels of autonomic arousal than true low anxious subjects; in fact, their arousal was as high as or higher than subjects classified as high anxious. Repressors' self-reports of anxiety in a stressful situation were related to their trait anxiety score: they claimed that they were not upset. Similar results were reported by Asendorpf and Scherer (1983), Brown, Tomarken, Orth, Loosen, Kalin, and Davidson (1996), Newton and Contrada (1992), and Weinberger and Davidson (1994).

All of these studies indicate that self-reports of psychological distress can be dissociated from measures of autonomic arousal: what people tell you about their negative emotional experiences may be quite different than what measures of autonomic arousal seem to indicate. If in general those who score low in neuroticism can be either repressors or true low-neuroticism subjects, then studies designed to compare high-neuroticism to low-neuroticism subjects may not be actually doing that: some unknown percentage of the low neuroticism subjects will be repressors. It is not difficult to see why this situation would present a serious problem for research on the psychophysiological correlates of neuroticism.

Acute Anxiety Responses and Neuroticism

Third, and perhaps most important, the premise that *acute* anxiety responses are a key component of neuroticism may be incorrect. Many of the responses that characterize high-neuroticism subjects cannot be described as acute. Chronic worry, dissatisfaction, pessimism, low self-esteem, and low-level feelings of distress, upset, and irritability are far more common in these subjects than are acute anxiety reactions. Yet it is during these acute reactions that the sympathetic fight–flight response is recruited. Although high-neuroticism people may be more likely to experience such acute reactions, to place the entire emphasis on them seems wrong.

Indeed, the description of high-neuroticism individuals seems far too complex to be reduced to thresholds of activation of the visceral brain or sympathetic nervous system. Zuckerman (1991) notes that anxiety involves many different brain systems, many of which are connected to the amygdala. The *amygdala* has been described as a center for assigning emotional meaning to stimuli (Aggelton & Mishkin, 1986). Evidence that the amygdala plays a central role in emotions is strong (Davis, 1992). Electrical stimulation of the amygdala can produce reports of fear in humans (Halgren, 1992). Davis, Hitchcock, and Rosen (1987) have described projections from the amygdala to other structures in the brain that are involved in various components of fear/anxiety reactions (e.g., the hypothalamus). There are also projections that connect the amygdala to areas of the cerebral cortex, especially areas of the frontal and temporal lobes. The picture that emerges is of a set of interconnected brain systems that are involved in a wide range of processes, from perception to thought to expectation to physiological arousal. Perhaps rather than looking at the "lower" components of this system, such as peripheral measures of autonomic arousal, one ought to look at the "higher" components, in particular the neocortex.

Individual differences in anxiety may have as much to do with how the brain interprets stimuli as with strong autonomic arousal reactions. In this regard, it may be that just as the extraversion dimension may reflect sensitivity to reward, or **approach tendencies,** the neuroticism dimension may reflect sensitivity to punishment or **withdrawal/avoidance tendencies** (Tellegen, 1985).

HEMISPHERIC ASYMMETRY AND INDIVIDUAL DIFFERENCES IN EMOTIONS

Davidson (1992) suggests that the left and right sides of the brain may differ in their involvement in approach and withdrawal behaviors and the accompanying positive and negative emotions. One of the most curious aspects of the way the brain is organized is that the two cerebral hemispheres have somewhat different functions. The brain, like some other organs (the lungs, kidneys, gonads) is a double organ, but unlike those organs, the two sides are not duplicates. To some degree they are **specialized** for different functions. You are probably familiar with the idea that the left side of the brain plays a primary role in language functions (speaking, reading, writing, understanding) while the right side plays a major role in certain aspects of spatial thinking. You may be less familiar with the idea that the two sides differ in their role in emotion. Although the exact nature of this difference remains controversial, a good deal of research supports the idea that the right hemisphere plays a major role in the experience of (at least some) negative emotions, including fear.

Studying Hemispheric Specialization

How do we know about this role of the right hemisphere? There are two basic strategies for studying brain function in humans. The first is to study the effects of brain damage, the second is to measure activity in intact brains. The study of brain damage is based on the idea that when a person has a part of her brain damaged, as from a stroke, cancer surgery, or a gunshot wound, it is possible to discover the functions of the damaged areas by looking at **behavioral deficits**. This is how hemispheric specialization for language was discovered: people who had damage in the left hemisphere showed language deficits, but those who had damage in the right hemisphere didn't. Research has indicated also that damage to the left and right sides of the brain may produce different emotional reactions. People with damage to the left hemisphere are more likely to show acute anxiety and depression; those with damage to the right are more likely to express a sense of well-being, and even to deny that there is anything wrong with them (Sackeim, Greenberg, Weiman, Gur, Hungerbuhler, & Geschwind, 1982). Although different interpretations of these patterns are possible (Tucker, 1993), they do suggest that the two sides of the brain are not identical in their involvement in emotions.

The second approach utilizes a variety of techniques to monitor brain activity while individuals engage in emotional tasks. One such technique is **EEG alpha asymmetry.** The EEG alpha rhythm, which can be picked up by electrodes attached to the scalp, is an electrical signal of 8–13 hertz that is believed to reflect the "background" state of the cortical areas that lie beneath the electrodes. High levels of alpha indicate a relatively deactivated state, while low levels indicate a relatively activated state. Imagine you had electrodes attached to your scalp over the areas of the left hemisphere involved in language, and other electrodes over the same location in the right hemisphere. Which would show more alpha activity while you filled out a vocabulary test? Since alpha indicates less activation, we would expect to find more alpha over the right (nonlanguage) hemisphere. In other words, the pattern of asymmetry would be more alpha on right, less on left. We would call this pattern "relative left-hemisphere activation." Many studies have verified this particular pattern during language tasks (e.g., Ehrlichman & Wiener, 1980).

EEG Asymmetry and Emotion

What happens to the alpha rhythm during exposure to emotional situations? Davidson and his colleagues have found that films designed to produce negative emotions like disgust and fear produce a pattern of relative right-hemisphere activation (Davidson & Tomarken, 1989). This pattern was not seen everywhere but was specific to anterior brain areas, in particular the frontal lobes. The finding that EEG asymmetries for emotional experience involve the frontal lobes makes sense and is consistent with results of studies of brain-damaged individuals (e.g., Robinson, Kubos, Starr, Rao & Price, 1984). As was mentioned earlier, the frontal lobes have close interconnections with the amygdala and other subcortical structures involved in emotion. Davidson (1992) suggested that the frontal lobes are likely sites for the convergence of cognitive, perceptual, and emotional processes. Negative emotional feeling, or negative affectivity (NA), is a key component of neuroticism. Thus, if one were to look for a cortical area of the brain that might play a major role in the neuroticism dimension, the right frontal lobe would be a good candidate.

Individual Differences in EEG Asymmetry

Davidson explored the possibility that individual differences in what he calls "affective style" might involve differences in EEG asymmetry. In this research, he reversed the strategy used to test Eysenck's theory of neuroticism. In that research, subjects were selected on the basis of their neuroticism scores: the idea was to see if people high in neuroticism differed from people low in neuroticism in their psychophysiological responses. In contrast, Davidson selected subjects on the basis of their EEG asymmetry, to see whether people who have a pattern of relative left-hemisphere activation differed in their emotional responses from those with relative right-hemisphere activation.

In order to use EEG asymmetry as a basis for categorizing people, it is necessary to show that EEG asymmetry is reliable and valid: the same thing one needs to do for any measure of a consistent characteristic. The validity of EEG asymmetry is indicated by the studies showing shifts in the predicted direction when subjects are exposed to emotional stimuli. Baseline anterior EEG asymmetry tested on two occasions about three weeks apart showed a moderate degree of reliability, $r = +.66$ (Wheeler, Davidson, & Tomarken, 1993), suggesting that it is possible, although with some degree of error, to categorize people in terms of their EEG asymmetry scores.

Tomarken, Davidson, and Henriques (1990) measured frontal EEG asymmetry during a 30-second resting baseline. Subjects were then exposed to a series of film clips designed to produce positive or negative affect. After exposure to each clip, subjects rated their emotional reactions. A small but significant relationship was found between baseline EEG asymmetry and rated emotions: subjects who had a pattern of relative right-hemisphere activation rated their reactions to the negative film clips as more negative than did subjects with relative left-hemisphere activation.

In chapter 3 we discussed the notion that some traits may be more relevant for some people than for others. We described studies in which "traited" subjects (those who are consistent on the trait measure) showed higher correlations than "untraited" subjects (those who are inconsistent on the trait measure). Wheeler, Davidson, and Tomarken (1993) selected subgroups of subjects who showed either a high degree of consistency in their EEG asymmetry over two different sessions or a low degree of consistency. The consistent subjects were assumed to be traited on the EEG asymmetry measure, while the inconsistent subjects were assumed to be untraited. The ratings of negative emotional reactions to film clips were significantly correlated only for the consistent, traited subjects, $r = .49$, indicating a rather strong relationship between baseline EEG asymmetry and how negatively subjects reacted to the films. Again, it was the subjects with greater right-hemisphere activation who showed the stronger negative affect.

The strategy of selecting traited and untraited subjects was also employed by Tomarken, Davidson, Wheeler, and Doss (1992), who found that a questionnaire measure of negative affectivity was correlated with frontal EEG asymmetry for traited but not for untraited subjects. Subjects with stable patterns of greater right frontal EEG arousal had higher negative affectivity scores than those with stable patterns of greater left frontal EEG ($r = .47$).

Davidson's research suggests that people may differ in the extent to which their right or left frontal cortexes are activated and that this difference may influence reactions that may be components of neuroticism. Recall that this discussion of biological aspects of personality started with the recognition that if personality is genetically influenced, there must be biological mechanisms that produce the observed differences in phenotypes. We do not know whether EEG asymmetry is involved, because there have not yet been any genetic studies of EEG asymmetry. There is evidence, however, that EEG asymmetry is present early in life and is correlated with infants' and young children's affective reactions. Davidson and Fox (1989) measured baseline EEG asymmetry in 10-month-old infants, then placed the infants in a situation in which their mothers went away for a period of time. Infants respond differently to maternal separation: some cry a lot, some a little or not at all. Those who cried were more likely to have an EEG asymmetry pattern of greater right-hemisphere activation than those who didn't cry. These results closely parallel those for adults.

TEMPERAMENT IN CHILDHOOD

Davidson and Fox provided evidence that individual differences in EEG asymmetry are related to affective reactions in both infants and adults. Does this mean that biological roots of adult emotional reactions are already present in us when we are infants? To both scientist and nonscientist, the existence of individual differences in infancy seems a convincing argument for biological contributions to personality. There has been relatively little opportunity for **postnatal** experience to influence the newborn or infant, yet newborns and infants display large individual differences in their behavior.

TABLE 6.2   Some Consensual Categories for Describing Infant Temperament

Activity level:	Frequency and intensity of motor behavior; energy output; vigor.
Approach–Withdrawal:	Tendency to approach or avoid novel stimuli.
Attention regulation; distractibility:	Ability to shift attention; tendency to orient to stimuli; soothability.
Negative emotionality:	Fearfulness, distress-proneness, soothability.
Positive emotionality:	Smiling, laughing; sociability.

Biological aspects of personality have traditionally been associated with the concept of **temperament,** which is the characteristic emotional tone or "tempo" of the individual, assumed to be biologically based and to emerge in infancy and early childhood. Many different aspects of infant and childhood temperament have been described over the years (e.g., Buss & Plomin, 1984; Thomas & Chess, 1977). Some consensus on the major temperamental concepts has been achieved recently and these are described in Table 6.2 (Bates, 1989; Rothbart, 1989).

You can probably see that there are similarities between these conceptions of childhood temperament and the adult personality traits discussed earlier. (Extraversion and neuroticism in adults are often described as temperaments.) In fact, factor analyses have found factors in childhood that are similar to those found in adulthood (Rothbart, Derryberry, & Posner, 1994).

Temperament in Infants

How early in life can one detect individual differences in temperament? Obviously, the range of behaviors available to newborns is relatively limited and very dependent on the infant's state. If you went into a nursery, you would see most newborns sleeping and some fussing. Would you be willing to say the fussy babies have more distress-prone temperaments than the ones who are not fussy? Perhaps the fussy babies are just hungrier or gassier. If you observed the infants repeatedly, you might see a pattern: some babies might be fussier than others across many observations. Even so, the behavioral differences might reflect transient characteristics, such as different rates of nervous system maturation.

In order to have any confidence that infant behavior reflects temperament, one would need to demonstrate that measures of infant behavior predict behavior later in life, that individuals retain their position relative to others at two different points in time. It is unlikely that high levels of prediction would be possible, since the measures that are used to define a trait are often vastly different over the course of childhood. We cannot expect the actual behavior to remain the same, so we try to infer what the underlying (latent) characteristic is at each age level. As individuals move through infancy, to toddlerhood, to childhood, to adolescence, and to adulthood, behaviors that might reflect the same underlying dispositions change radically. At the same time, behaviors that seem phenotypically similar, such as activity level, may reflect different underlying processes at different ages (for example, at 7 months activity level may reflect negative emotionality, but at 3 years it might reflect positive emotionality) (Eaton, 1994). Thus one difficulty in determining whether temperament is a stable characteristic is that one cannot look at exactly the same behavior at different ages. Somehow, one must decide which (different) sets of behaviors at different ages reflect the same underlying characteristic (Caspi & Bem, 1990).

Inhibited and Uninhibited Children

Kagan and his colleagues have focused on an aspect of temperament that may reflect individual differences in properties of the child's brain. Certain children seem to avoid many different types of unfamiliar stimuli, including foods, animals, objects, and people. These children may be described as finicky, timid, or shy depending on the type of stimuli they are avoiding, but underlying this behavior may be a general tendency to become behaviorally **inhibited** to the presence of novelty. Other children have a very different reaction to unfamiliar stimuli; they are adventurous, curious, and outgoing, displaying behavior that is **uninhibited.** Kagan and his colleagues hypothesize that these two patterns reflect differences in activity of the limbic system. Inhibited children may have lower thresholds for activation of circuits originating in the amygdala that contribute to distress reactions to novel stimuli, whereas uninhibited children may have higher thresholds for activation of these circuits (Kagan & Snidman, 1991).

Kagan (1989) identified subsets of young children who displayed consistently inhibited or uninhibited behavior patterns when faced with unfamiliar situations. Children's behavior was observed at either 21 or 31 months of age. One group of children, when encountering new people and strange objects in the unfamiliar lab, became shy and fearful; they tended to cling to their mothers, were quiet, and avoided the stimuli. The other group of children were sociable and did not avoid new people or objects. The children who were classified as either inhibited or uninhibited at age 21 or 31 months were tested again in a variety of unfamiliar situations when they were approximately $7\frac{1}{2}$ years of age. The number of spontaneous comments to other children or adults and the proportion of time spent standing or playing apart from any other child were recorded while the subjects were in a play group with seven to ten unfamiliar children. The number of spontaneous comments made during an individual testing session with an unfamiliar female adult was also recorded. Approximately 75 percent of the children were classified the same way at the earlier assessment and at the $7\frac{1}{2}$-year assessment. Thus, over the approximately five years spanned by this study, inhibited children tended to remain inhibited and uninhibited children tended to remain uninhibited.

Notice that while the measures of inhibition were slightly different at each of the two occasions, at those ages both social approach and social withdrawal or

TABLE 6.3   **Proportion of High- and Low-Reactive Infants Displaying Low or High Fear at Both 14 and 21 Months (Based on Kagan et al., 1992)**

Reactivity Category	FEAR SCORE	
	Low Fear (0–1)	High Fear (4 or more)
High Reactive ($n = 77$)	9	43
Low Reactive ($n = 134$)	39	7

Note: Adapted from Table 1 in Kagan et al. (1992) by collapsing over two cohorts.

avoidance could be assessed. How would one assess inhibition earlier in infancy, when social behavior is rudimentary and the infant has limited locomotion? Kagan, Snidman, and Arcus (1992) hypothesized that the limbic circuits they believe underlie inhibition would produce specific patterns of behavior in early infancy. If so, infants who show these patterns should develop into inhibited children. Four-month old infants were stimulated with novel stimuli, including moving mobiles, Q-tips dipped in alcohol, and tape-recorded voices. About 20% of the infants displayed extreme motoric reactions such as movements of limbs and arching of the back, sometimes accompanied by crying and fretting. Kagan et al. labeled this group "high reactive." About 40 percent of the infants responded in the opposite way, showing little evidence of distress through either motor activity or crying and fretting. This group was labeled "low reactive." The remaining infants showed a mixed pattern (either low motor activity with crying, or high motor activity with no crying). The infants were assessed again at 14 and 21 months, in regard to how they responded to a series of events involving unfamiliar people and situations. This time fear was defined as fretting or crying or failure to approach unfamiliar people or objects after being asked to do so. Table 6.3 shows the proportion of infants classified as high reactive or low reactive at age 4 months who displayed low fear (0 or 1 fear reactions) or high fear (4 or more fear reactions) at *both* 14- and 21-month assessments.

Biological Bases of Inhibition

Kagan (1989) suggests that children who show a consistent pattern of responding do so because of underlying biological characteristics. In particular, he suggests that the inhibited children have lower thresholds for activation of limbic circuits that produce sympathetic nervous system arousal. Kagan, Reznick, and Snidman (1988) measured a variety of psychophysiological responses as $5\frac{1}{2}$-year-old children responded to a battery of cognitive tests. Measures included heart rate and heartbeat variability, pupil dilation, muscle tension, and urinary norepinephrine, all of which are influenced by activity of the sympathetic nervous system. By averaging over the set of psychophysiological measures, Kagan et al. computed an aggregate index of sympathetic reactivity of the $5\frac{1}{2}$-year-olds, which was highly correlated with an index of inhibition based on behavioral assessments at 21 months ($r = .70$)

and at $7\frac{1}{2}$ years ($r = .64$). It is interesting to recall that aggregated psychophysiological indices do not appear to be related to self-reported neuroticism in adulthood. It may be that biological factors have more impact in childhood than in adulthood or that behavioral assessment over multiple situations is a better way of measuring personality characteristics than is self-report (as is typically done in research on adults).

CHANGE AND STABILITY IN TEMPERAMENT

Kagan (personal communication, May 19, 1994) and his colleagues have assessed over 600 infants in early infancy and during their second year. About 15% of these infants can be classified as inhibited and about 30% as uninhibited. The remaining 55% either are not extreme in their reactions or are inconsistent across ages. Kagan and Snidman (1991) suggest that those children who show consistency represent separate groups from those who do not. Recall the concept of "traitedness" discussed earlier. Inconsistency may be taken to indicate a lack of an underlying biological trait influencing inhibited versus uninhibited behavior. Yet lack of consistency from one age to another does not necessarily mean that an underlying biological process is not operating. Development involves major shifts in the emotional, cognitive, and social capacities of the individual, much of which undoubtedly involves biological maturational processes. Such shifts could be influenced by underlying biological processes even though there is little stability of behavior from one period to another.

Matheny (1989) obtained measures of inhibition from children at 12, 18, 24, and 30 months of age. The measures included laboratory observations of emotional tone during a variety of play situations, fearfulness during cognitive testing, and mothers' ratings of approach/withdrawal. The age-to-age correlations for these measures are shown in Table 6.4.

Correlations between age periods six months apart (12 to 18, 18 to 24, and 24 to 30) reveal fairly high levels of stability (average correlation .53). Correlations

TABLE 6.4   Age-to-Age Correlations for Temperament Measures Obtained at 12, 18, 24, and 30 Months (Based on Matheny, 1989)

Age-to-Age Interval	TEMPERAMENT MEASURES		
	Emotional Tone	Fearfulness	Approach
12 to 18	.48	.26	.58
12 to 24	.30	.20	.49
12 to 30	.28	.01	.27
18 to 24	.56	.61	.62
18 to 30	.48	.28	.48
24 to 30	.51	.50	.64

Reproduced with permission of the Duke University Press.

between age periods twelve months apart (12 to 24, 18 to 30) were lower (mean = .37), and the correlation between the largest age difference (12 to 30 months) was the lowest of all (.19). This pattern of correlations is typical of longitudinal research: the closer in time the measurements, the higher the correlations. These data suggest that temperament in childhood is a short-lived, age-dependent phenomenon. For unselected subjects, there is little stability over the period from one year to $2\frac{1}{2}$ years of age. If there is so little stability in childhood, how relevant can childhood temperament be to adult personality?

One answer is Kagan's: temperament is consistent for subsets of children. Inhibition is a trait for some but not all children. When the sample of children includes both "traited" and "untraited" subjects, longitudinal consistency should be low. Matheny's study provides a different perspective. The children studied by Matheny were all twins, allowing Matheny to ask whether the lack of consistency over 18 months meant that biological factors were not important. Comparisons between MZ and DZ twins at each of the four ages indicated that heritability for these measures was high. For example, at 12 months of age, the correlation for MZ and DZ twins averaged .70 and .25, respectively, over the three measures. At 30 months, they averaged .63 for MZ and 0 for DZ twins. MZs had significantly higher correlations than DZs in nine of the twelve comparisons (three measures at four ages).

These data might strike you as paradoxical. If there is high heritability for the temperament of inhibition, how can there be such low stability over eighteen months? The solution is evident when one realizes that development is a dynamic process. Development means change. The real question is not whether surface manifestations of temperament remain constant, but whether there are biological factors that systematically influence behavior from age to age. To examine this possibility, Matheny examined patterns of change in MZ and DZ twins. Figure 6.4 shows the age-to-age scores on the emotional tone measures for three pairs of MZ and three pairs of DZ twins. The age changes for the MZ twins are very similar. Both twins in MZ pair A showed negative emotional tone at 12 months but became more positive over the next eighteen months. The twins in MZ pair C did precisely the opposite: they both showed positive emotional tone at 12 months, but by 30 months both were extremely negative. There is much less similarity between DZ co-twins. DZ twins D are each rather consistent over time, and consistently different from each other. DZ pair F move in opposite directions over the eighteen-month period. Matheny computed correlations between profiles for each pair of twins using a composite of the three measures: the correlation for MZ and DZ twins was .79 and .13, respectively. Age to age changes of MZ twin pairs were remarkably consistent, whereas little consistency was found between DZ twins.

In Kagan's research, children selected as extremely inhibited or uninhibited tended to remain that way from infancy through middle childhood. In Matheny's study, unselected children showed moderate to high stability over a six-month interval, but little stability over an eighteen-month interval (although MZ twins

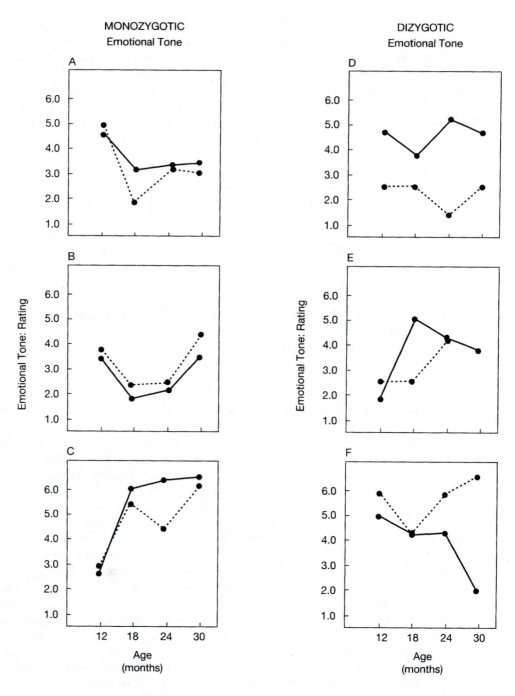

FIGURE 6.4   Illustrative curves for ratings of emotional tone for three MZ and three DZ twin pairs. High scores indicate more negative emotional tone. (From Matheny, 1989; reproduced with permission of Duke University Press.)

were highly consistent in the pattern of change over that period of time). Caspi, Elder, and Bem (1988) found that shyness was stable from age 8 to age 40. As Caspi and Bem (1990) note, "In general, differences between children in aggression, dominance, dependency, sociability, and shyness are preserved from middle and late childhood through adolescence and adulthood" (p. 558). We are still left wondering whether temperament in early childhood is related to personality in adulthood.

Kerr, Lambert, Stattin, and Klackenberg-Larsson (1994) examined the stability of inhibition over a fourteen-year period from infancy to adolescence in a **representative sample** of 212 Swedish children. Psychologists rated the children on a composite measure of inhibition (including, for example, ease of adjustment to the testing situation, emotional dependency on the mother, timidity, and smiling) up to age 6; the children's mothers rated them on scales intended to measure inhibition in social situations each year during the study. From approximately 21 months to 6 years of age, stability of inhibition was significantly higher for those children who were classified as extremely inhibited or uninhibited at age 21 months than for those children who were not classified in these groups. However, when ratings from the full fourteen-year period were examined, there was almost no predictability from 21 months to later childhood and adolescence. The only subjects who showed any stability from infancy to adolescence were extremely inhibited girls, perhaps because inhibition in girls corresponds to sex-role stereotypes and thus may more likely be reinforced by parents and teachers (Kagan & Moss, 1962). Further, subjects rated as extremely inhibited or uninhibited at age 16 years were, on average, indistinguishable in those traits at age 21 months.

One limitation of this study noted by Kerr et al. is that the ratings after age 6 were all done by the subjects' mothers. It is possible that as children move into later childhood and adolescence, mothers' accuracy in judging their children's social behavior diminishes, if for no other reason than that they no longer have as much direct experience of their children's behavior (e.g., in school or with peers).

Caspi and Silva (1995) carried out a longitudinal study of 855 New Zealand children from ages 3 to 18. Behavioral measures obtained at age 3 were used to classify the children into five categories: undercontrolled, inhibited, confident, reserved, and well adjusted. At age 18, the subjects filled out a personality questionnaire. To the extent that continuities were present from 3 to 18, the five groups should differ in predictable ways on the personality measure. The strongest continuities were found for those subjects who had been classified as undercontrolled at age 3 and those who had been classified as inhibited. Undercontrolled children had been observed to be impulsive, irritable, and distractible at age 3; at age 18 they scored higher than other children in negative emotionality and lower in "constraint"—a scale related to Big Five conscientiousness. Inhibited children had been observed to be shy, fearful, uncommunicative, and upset by strangers; at age 18 they scored higher than other children in constraint. Although there were also continuities between ages 3 and 18 for the other three groups, they were generally quite small in size.

CHILDHOOD TEMPERAMENT AND ADULT PERSONALITY

Our discussion of inhibition leaves us with a puzzle. Inhibition, like other aspects of temperament (Pedlow, Sanson, Prior, & Oberklaid, 1993), displays a moderate degree of stability from infancy to middle childhood. Emotional traits such as extraversion and neuroticism display moderate stability from middle or late adolescence to adulthood and high stability thereafter. Yet, stability between early childhood and adulthood, when it has been found, it usually quite small. Many researchers have assumed that the biological roots of adult personality traits should be expressed in infancy and early childhood. The relationships between physiological measures and behavioral indicators of inhibition (Kagan, Reznick, & Snidman, 1988) and strong evidence for a genetic involvement in individual differences in temperament (Matheny, 1989) indicate that biological factors play a central role in emotional behavior during childhood. Yet these biological factors do *not* appear to be the major bases of adult personality. If they were, we should find stronger continuities across the whole life span.

The discontinuities between personality in early childhood and in adulthood could reflect separate bases for individual differences during these two times of life. As Zuckerman (1991) stated: "The idea that all genetic differences are manifest at birth is a misconception. Genes turn on and off according to a timetable during development. Genetically determined traits that are manifest during infancy may have little continuity or relevance for later developing traits" (p. 404). Or perhaps, "the genetic bases of personality can be discerned in infancy and early childhood, but their relationship to later personality traits may not be obvious because their forms and expressions in adult personality may be quite different" (Zuckerman, 1991, p. 405).

Self-regulation

One complication in our trying to understanding how infant temperament relates to adult personality is that infants and children may develop ways of regulating their own behavior. For example, 3-month-old infants may use thumb- or finger-sucking to soothe themselves when they are upset (Rothbart, 1989). Certainly, by later childhood, **self-regulation** is a major aspect of personality functioning. Among the most important self-regulatory processes are those that permit the child to inhibit impulsive responses. Learning norms for social behavior, developing empathy, and recognizing the consequences of one's behavior become crucial aspects of children's ability to regulate their behavior (Rothbart & Ahadi, 1994). It is interesting that the amygdala is fully functioning by the end of the first year of life. In contrast, the prefrontal cortex, which plays a major role in the regulation of emotion and behavior, reaches its peak of synaptic density (interconnections among neurons) at about age 7 and stabilizes to its adult levels at about age 16 (Nelson, 1994). Perhaps up to about age 7, temperament is more or less a direct consequence of limbic system thresholds of activation, but after age 7 it more and more reflects the interaction between limbic system thresholds and prefrontal regulatory processes. Perhaps the highest level of self-regulation occurs when people have insight into their own temperamental tendencies and regulate them to their advantage. Chess and Thomas (1989) state: "Such insight can give the individual the potential for controlling her temperamental reactions when they could be detrimental, as well as using them forcefully when they can be helpful" (p. 384). One notable example of such self-regulation was described by Bill Clinton. In an interview with David Frost, Clinton was asked what was the hardest thing he had ever done. His answer: to force himself to change from a shy, inhibited child to an outgoing adult.

ENVIRONMENT AND BIOLOGY IN TEMPERAMENT

Attachment

A biological predisposition may bias a child to develop a particular emotional tendency, but environmental factors may radically influence the developing personality. Van den Boom (1989) studied the interaction of infant temperament and maternal behavior in the development of **attachment.** According to attachment theory (Bowlby, 1973; Bretherton, 1985; Main, Kaplan, & Cassidy, 1985), the quality of the emotional bond between infants and mothers plays an important role in personality and social development. Infants have a need to be near their mothers. When mothers are not present, infants respond with distress. If the absence is prolonged, infants may become passive and, eventually, emotionally detached, so that when the mother is present, the infant actually disregards or avoids her. Recurrent patterns of mother–infant interactions produce expectations in the infant regarding the availability of the mother.

Attachment researchers typically classify infants on the basis of their reactions in the "Strange Situation" (Ainsworth, Blehar, Waters, & Wall, 1978). One-year-old infants are brought into a room filled with unfamiliar objects. A stranger comes into the room, and shortly thereafter the infant's mother leaves the room. After a brief period of absence, the mother returns. The infant's behavior is observed while the mother is present, when the mother leaves, and after she returns. Research on middle-class American samples found that 62% of infants were classified as *securely attached* (what attachment researchers call category B) (Campos, Barrett, Lamb, Goldsmith, & Stenberg, 1983). These infants explore the room while the mother is present and do not seem overly fearful of the stranger. Although they show distress when the mother leaves, they display signs of pleasure and comfort when she returns. About 23% can be classified as *avoidant* (category A). These infants do not appear upset by the new situation, tend to ignore the mother when she is present, seem indifferent to her absence, and do not seek her comfort when she returns. The remaining 15% can be classified as *anxious/ambivalent* (category C). These infants do not explore the room and remain close to the mother. They get very distressed when she leaves and continue to express distress after she returns. They may seek comfort from her but do not appear to get it. They also may express anger toward the mother when she returns. Infants in categories A and C are generally described as *insecurely attached*.

Are these attachment patterns the result of the mother's behavior toward the infant, of the infant's temperament, or both? Van den Boom (1989) obtained measures of infant temperament at 10 and 15 days of age. Over these two observations, 17% of the sample of 89 infants were classified as "irritable." Interactions between these infants and their mothers, and those of a matched control group of nonirritable infants and their mothers, were observed at home twice each month for the next six months. When the infants were a year old, they were brought into the lab and assessed in the Strange Situation. Infants classified as irritable during the first two weeks after birth were classified in categories A and C significantly more than were infants classified as nonirritable. Longitudinal analysis of mother–infant interactions indicated that mothers of irritable infants more often engaged in behaviors that have been associated with insecure attachment: ignoring the babies, poor soothing skills, and inconsistent responses to the infants' behaviors. Moreover, these behaviors became more pronounced over the six-month period.

The results of this correlational study leave us with the typical "chicken and egg" problem. The infant's early temperament is likely to reflect biological factors. The mother's behavior may be a reaction to the infant's temperament. More irritable babies are more difficult to deal with, so mothers become frustrated when they find their parenting skills inadequate to the task. As a result, they become less responsive to the babies. At 12 months, the babies are insecurely attached. Does the insecure attachment come as a result of the insensitive parenting of the mothers, or is it simply a direct result of the infant's temperament? If the latter, then the behavior of the mother is essentially irrelevant to the attachment pattern observed at 12 months of age: irritable two-week-olds become insecurely attached one-year-olds regardless of parental behavior. Is there any way to choose between these alternatives?

If you recall from chapter 2, correlational studies are limited in answering cause-and-effect questions. Having shown that irritability predicted both attachment and maternal behavior, Van den Boom went on to try to tease out cause and effect by setting up a more experimental study, one that examined the effects of an **intervention** on attachment. One hundred infants were selected who met the criteria for irritability. Mothers of half of these irritable infants were given training in how to interact sensitively with their babies (for example, how to soothe them effectively, how to be aware of their signals, how to play with them when they were not upset). At one year, the infants were tested in the Strange Situation. Of those infants whose mothers had received no training, 28% were classified as securely attached. In contrast, 68% of the infants whose mothers had received training were classified as securely attached. Van den Boom's study does not resolve the question of whether insecure attachment is a direct result of infant temperament or of maternal behavior. To answer that question, one would need a group of nonirritable infants whose mothers are trained to interact insensitively with them! But it does indicate that biology is not destiny. Sensitive mothering can virtually eliminate the relationship between irritable temperament and insecure attachment.

Stress Reactions in Infants

Environmental variables may also influence the stress response itself. Consider two recent studies examining the effects of acute stress on cortisol production. There are two neuroendocrine systems involved in reactions to stress. The sympathetic adrenomedulary system (SAM) is a fast response system that prepares the organism for "fight or flight" and is based on the release of the epinephrine and norepinephrine from the inner parts of the adrenal glands. We have mentioned this system often in our discussion of neuroticism and inhibition. The other system, which is involved in longer-term responses to stress, is the hypothalamic-pituitary-adrenocortical (HPA or PAC) system, based on the release of cortisol from the outer cortex of the adrenal glands. The cortisol response may emerge within fifteen minutes of an acute stressor or may take hours or even days to emerge.

Gunnar, Larson, Hertsgaard, Harris, and Brodersen (1992) measured cortisol found in the saliva of 9-month-old infants after a thirty-minute separation from their mothers. In the "caretaker" condition, the infant's baby-sitter paid no attention to the infant unless he or she fretted or cried. In the "playmate" condition, the baby-sitter played with the infant during the entire thirty minutes. Gunnar et al. found a correlation of .60 between an infant's tendency to become distressed in an earlier situation and salivary cortisol in the caretaker condition. In the playmate condition, there was no correlation between distress-proneness and salivary cortisol. In this study, the behavior of the baby-sitter served as a **moderator variable:** the relationship between distress-proneness and cortisol production was different in the two different baby-sitter conditions. What was the difference between the two conditions? The behavior of the baby-sitter in the playmate condition seems to have eliminated the stressfulness of maternal separation. It should be noted that children low in distress-proneness did not show much of a cortisol response in either condition.

If one were to extrapolate from this study, one could envision two different developmental paths for distress-prone infants. Those infants who have responsive caretakers may infrequently experience high levels of stress; those who have indifferent caretakers may often experience high levels of stress. For the latter child, many life events will be experienced as threatening and upsetting. As more and more stimuli become associated with distress, the growing child becomes more and more fearful and wary. In contrast, for the child who is protected from frequent experiences of distress, even though she or he may have a nervous system that is distress-prone, the world may not be perceived as a fearful and threatening place (Wachs & King, 1994). Thomas and Chess (1977) coined the term *goodness-of-fit* to express the idea that children with different temperaments often

TABLE 6.5   **Number of Infants in the Caucasian American and Japanese Groups Showing Four Patterns of Behavioral and Cortisol Response to Inoculation (Based on Lewis, Ramsay, and Kawakami, 1993)**

	CAUCASIAN AMERICAN	JAPANESE
High behavior/Cortisol increase	10	4
Low behavior/Cortisol decrease	6	9
Low behavior/Cortisol increase	7	15
High behavior/Cortisol decrease	8	2

Reproduced with permission of the University of Chicago Press.

do better under different environmental conditions. This general idea has been incorporated into many contemporary child-rearing handbooks for new parents (e.g., Brazelton, 1983.)

Cultural factors may also play a role in the expression of temperament. Cultures differ in their norms for emotional expression. Lewis (1989) compared Caucasian American to Japanese 3- to 5-month old infants as they underwent medical examinations. All 20 of the Caucasian American infants cried, while only 4 of the 26 Japanese infants cried. Are Japanese infants simply less distress-prone than Caucasian American infants? Lewis, Ramsay, and Kawakami (1993) measured salivary cortisol twenty minutes after infants between 2 and 6 months of age received inoculations. Even though the Caucasian American infants displayed higher levels of distress (crying and facial grimacing) more often than Japanese infants, salivary cortisol was greater in the Japanese infants. Lewis et al. placed each infant in one of four categories based on whether they showed an increase or decrease in cortisol from pre-inoculation to post-inoculation and whether they were crying or quiet by ninety seconds post-inoculation. Table 6.5 shows the number of infants in each category.

In the third and fourth lines of Table 6.5, the observable display of distress and the cortisol response went in opposite directions. For Caucasian American infants, the incongruent patterns were split evenly between low behavior/cortisol increase and high behavior/cortisol decrease. In contrast, Japanese infants who showed incongruent responses were almost all in the low behavior/cortisol increase category. Japanese infants, then, are more likely than Caucasian American infants to show high levels of cortisol combined with low levels of the expression of distress. There is evidence that the emotional expressiveness of infants is subject to learning. It is possible that halfway through the first year of life infants have already picked up cultural norms for emotional display. If you were a temperament researcher, how would you classify those infants who appear low in distress-proneness but show high levels of cortisol following a stressor? Studies such as these underscore the point that observed behavior is not isomorphic with underlying biological dispositions. Experience plays a powerful role in how such dispositions are expressed and how they contribute to individuality.

GENDER DIFFERENCES

In attempting to understand individuality, personality psychologists focus on measured characteristics of people. For example, we may study the extraversion factor by classifying people as extraverts or introverts on the basis of a questionnaire. Personality psychologists have also long been interested in whether classifying people according to existing categories can also help us understand individuality. For example, we might compare older to younger people, or citizens of one country to citizens of another. By far, the category that has been of most interest to personality psychologists is gender. There are many reasons for this interest, the most important probably being the fact that in all human societies, gender is a major category for assigning roles to individuals. Because gender is such an important component of individuality, it will recur at various points in this book. We introduce it here because of the obvious fact that gender is a biological as well as a social category, and also because of research suggesting that some behavioral differences between the genders may be influenced by differences between the brains of females and males (Breedlove, 1994).

Controversies and Misconceptions

The question of whether human males and females differ psychologically has been and continues to be embroiled in controversy. This is an area where science and politics seem to be hopelessly entangled (Eagly, 1995). Part of the reason may be that claims of gender differences were historically used to bolster the superior position of men. The automatic equating of "different" with "better" (or "worse") makes any claim of differences politically charged. It would be comfortable to be able to dismiss this equation; yet, in fact, some aspects of human behavior can be considered better or worse. For example, women have higher life expectancies; boys are much more likely to suffer from learning disabilities; more men commit violent crimes; more women suffer from depression (Nolen-Hoeksema, 1987). Obviously, it would be disingenuous to claim that these characteristics are value neutral. What one *can* say is that one gender doesn't invariably emerge as "better" than the other: some gender differences "favor" females, some "favor" males, and some are just different.

Even more controversial is the idea that gender differences are influenced by biological factors. This possibility suggests to some people that gender differences are "natural" and therefore "good," or that they are unchangeable, thus ensuring gender injustice in perpetuity. We can dismiss the "biology = natural = good" idea easily: good and bad are value judgments, not facts of nature. The second point is more complex and not quite so easy to dismiss. It is a concept called **biological determinism,** the idea that psychological or behavioral characteristics are determined completely by biological factors and thus are resistant to any environmental intervention. We have already seen in our discussions of genetics and temperament that, stated this way, this idea is wrong. One can always envision an environmental event that will change how a biological organism will behave. Biological influences always unfold in the context of environments. It is not nonsensical, however, to assert that under the usual conditions of development some behaviors may be more strongly influenced by biological factors than other behaviors.

Consider the issue of biological versus environmental factors in sexual orientation (Gladue, 1994). At one extreme have been theories in which biology plays virtually no role. From this point of view, learning experiences, cultural norms, or even "free choice" are sufficient to produce different sexual orientations, and individual differences in biological makeup are completely irrelevant. At the other extreme is the view that sexual orientation is entirely determined by genes or by events that change certain areas of the brain during embryonic development, and that the experiences the individual has during childhood play no role whatsoever. Despite the often repeated mantra that development always involves both biology and environment, we believe these theories are not logically absurd; they do make very different claims about the roles of biological and environmental factors. Furthermore, they can be subjected to empirical scrutiny. MZ twins are more often concordant for sexual orientation than are DZ twins. Heritability estimates suggest that from 31 to 74% of the variance in male sexual orientation is genetic (Bailey & Pillard, 1991). Therefore, a completely environmental explanation cannot be correct. Still, it is important to recall our earlier distinction between direct and indirect biological influences. The genetic influence in sexual preference could be very indirect: for example, the genetically based physical appearance of male children might elicit different behaviors from parents and/or peers that could influence sexual orientation. Or it could be very direct, stemming from heritable differences in areas of the brain related to sexual behavior.

Sex Hormones and Gender Differences in Behavior

A small number of behavioral gender differences seem to be influenced by hormones affecting the developing brain. In the last three decades there has been a virtual revolution in the biological understanding of **sexually dimorphic** behavior (that is, behaviors that differ between females and males). Studies of many different species have revealed that certain areas of the brains of males and females differ, often dramatically, and that these differences occur as a result of both biological and environmental influences.

The hormones that most directly influence sexually dimorphic physical characteristics are released by the gonads at certain crucial stages of development. At puberty, sex hormones released by the ovaries, the testes, and the cortex of the adrenal glands produce pubic and axillary hair in both genders, muscles and body hair in males, and breasts in females. As dramatic as these changes are, sex hormones may have even more profound effects during prenatal development. In the first six weeks following conception, there are no physically apparent differences between embryos with XX and those with XY chromosomes. At about six weeks, the Y chromosome causes the development of testes. At about twelve weeks, ovaries develop in XX individuals. The period between six and twelve weeks is crucial for sexual differentiation. The critical variable is the presence or absence of androgens. In XY individuals, the testes produce androgens which cause the male reproductive organs to develop. In the absence of androgens, development "automatically" takes a female path, and XX individuals develop female reproductive organs. Thus, the sex chromosomes influence sexual differentiation primarily by producing either testes or ovaries. The rest of sexual differentiation occurs because of the influence of hormones. As a result, it is possible to manipulate sexual differentiation artificially by altering the "normal" hormonal patterns in XX and XY individuals. This has been done in many species.

Males and females of most species differ not only physically, but also behaviorally, most obviously in behavior that involves reproduction. Research on rats indicates that altering hormone levels at various periods prior to or immediately after birth influences sexual behavior in adulthood. Typical male sexual behavior of rats includes mounting, intromission, and ejaculation; typical female sexual behavior includes lordosis (the raised rump position that indicates sexual interest in many nonprimate female mammals). Introduction of hormones to the brains of female rats right after birth produced an increase in behavior typical of male rats after puberty. This effect occurred only when the hormones had been introduced to a part of the brain (the preoptic area of the hypothalamus) that is known to be involved in sexual behavior. Introduction of hormones to a different part of the hypothalamus reduced typical female sexual behavior. These results suggest that sex hormones have important effects on the developing brain, at least in rats. Hormones produce their effects either by altering the action of genes or influencing nerve cells directly (causing them to connect with other cells or changing their electrical excitability) (Hoyenga & Hoyenga, 1993).

There is little doubt that the brains of women and men differ anatomically. The areas in which these differences are most evident include regions of the hypothalamus (a brain structure involved in motivation, emotion, and sexual behavior) and the anterior commissure and corpus callosum (areas that connect the two sides of the brain). Whether these anatomical differences are caused by sex hormones is not yet known (Collaer & Hines, 1995). Although there is recent evidence linking these anatomical differences to behavioral differences (e.g., Allen & Gorski, 1992), this area of research is clearly in its infancy.

Congenital Adrenal Hyperplasia

Is there evidence that the behavior of humans is influenced by prenatal sex hormones? Obviously, there are indirect influences: prenatal sex hormones determine whether one will be female or male. All societies treat females and males differently and expect females and males to behave differently. What about more direct influences? This is a difficult question to answer because unlike the case of rats, we cannot experiment on humans, changing their prenatal hormones in order to see what will happen. But sometimes unusual prenatal events cause individuals to be exposed to abnormal levels of sex hormones, and these "experiments of nature" can (like the existence of MZ twins) provide insights into the role of biological factors in personality. One of these unusual events is called **congenital adrenal hyperplasia** (CAH) (also known as *adrenogenital syndrome*). In this syndrome, the adrenal glands produce high levels of androgens, beginning during fetal development. Consider the effect of this syndrome on females. The surge of androgen occurs at a point when the external sex organs are differentiating. Since androgen masculinizes the sex organs regardless of chromosomal sex, females with the syndrome develop external genitalia that resemble that of males, even though their internal organs are completely female. Many of these individuals are recognized at birth as having this syndrome. Surgery is performed to create normal female genitalia, and the individuals are put on a lifetime regimen of corticosteroid treatment that counteracts the adrenal glands' overproduction of androgens. These individuals are raised as girls. They look like girls. They identify themselves as girls. They *are* girls. The question that intrigues researchers is whether they *act* like girls. That is, has exposure to prenatal androgens influenced their brains in ways that lead them to behave in any respects more like boys and less like girls?

Let's look at a study by Berenbaum and Hines (1992). It is well-known that girls and boys differ in their preferences for types of toys. The preference of boys for "boy toys" and of girls for "girl toys" is seen very early in life, perhaps as early as 18 months (Caldera, Huston, & O'Brien, 1989). Why these preferences? No doubt you can think of many ways that the environment promotes different toy preferences. Advertising, packaging, parental choice, observation of peers, fears of peer ostracism—all push individuals to choose gender-typed toys (Goldstein, 1994). Given the powerful forces at work, it is hard to imagine that toy preferences reflect anything other than learning and social pressure. Berenbaum and Hines observed the behavior of 3- to 8-year old girls, some of whom had CAH, others of whom were sisters or cousins of CAH individuals but did not have the syndrome themselves. The children were given the opportunity to play with a toy helicopter, dolls, kitchen supplies, a toy telephone, cars, a fire engine, crayons, and construction toys—all of which have been shown in previous research to be favored more by either boys or girls (can you tell which is which?). Neutral toys (books, board games, and a jigsaw puzzle) were also available. Videotapes were made of the children's play, and the amount of time each child spent with each toy was assessed. Raters did not know whether the child was one with CAH or an unaffected (control) child. Figure 6.5 shows the mean time spent with girls', boys', and neutral toys. CAH girls spent more time with boys' toys and less time with girls' toys then did the control girls. Further, while control girls spent more time with girls' toys than with boys' toys, CAH girls showed the opposite pattern. The difference in toy preference between the two groups was more than one-half a standard deviation. When parents were asked whether they encouraged their girls "to act as a girl

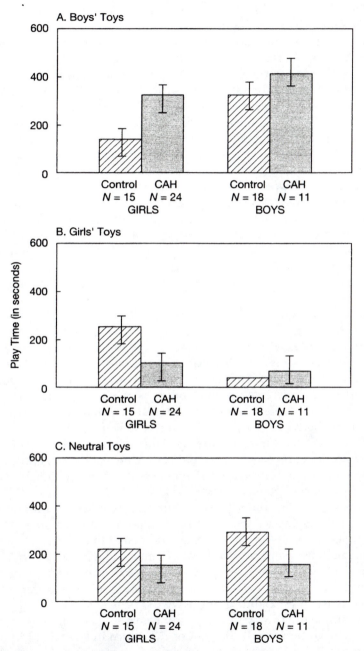

FIGURE 6.5 Time spent in play with sex-typed toys by female and male CAH patients and controls during ten minutes of play. (From Berenbaum and Hines, 1992; reproduced with permission of the Oxford University Press.)

should," there was no difference between parents of CAH girls and parents of control girls—roughly 60% of both sets answered "yes."

The results of this study reinforce those from earlier studies that showed differences between CAH girls and unaffected controls in play patterns, career interest, and interest in marriage (e.g., Ehrhardt, Epstein, & Money, 1968). They are also consistent with results of studies showing that female rhesus monkeys who have been exposed to androgens during perinatal development also tend to show masculine play behavior (Goy, Bercovitch, & McBrair, 1988). Although critics of this type of research have suggested that these CAH girls may be treated differently because their parents know of their hormonal condition, it is not self-evident that this treatment would encourage more masculine behavior (Collaer & Hines, 1995). In fact, it seems equally plausible that parents would work harder to ensure that their child grows up to be a "normal" girl. Of course, studies on CAH girls have not proven that prenatal hormones directly influence activities such as toy preference. As Berenbaum and Hines (1992) note, the effects could be indirect, mediated by temperamental variables such as activity level. This is clearly an area of research where the answers lie in the future, as new technologies allow us to investigate more directly how the brain contributes to sexually dimorphic behaviors.

From Between Genders to Within Genders

You may have noticed that we started by talking about differences between the genders but have shifted to discussing differences within one gender, comparing CAH girls to control girls. In fact, there is almost always greater variation within each gender than between genders. For the personality psychologist, these within-gender variations come closer to our interest in individuality than does the average difference between women and men. Yet sometimes the comparison of women and men can generate insights and hypotheses about individual differences. Understanding the variations in play patterns, career interests, and even sexual orientation within gender may be strengthened when we consider the basis for average differences between the genders.

Consider spatial ability, for example. Many studies have found that the mean score for males is higher than that for females on various spatial tasks (such as imagining how objects look when they are rotated to different positions). Perhaps there is something about how the brains of men and women are organized that partially accounts for this difference. A number of theories about such differences in brain organization have been proposed, although none has received unequivocal support (Halpern, 1992). But suppose we did have evidence to support such a theory, for example the theory that the right cerebral hemisphere is more specialized in males than in females. If the gender difference in spatial ability can be traced back to a gender difference in the specialization of the right hemisphere, then individual differences *within* gender might also reflect differences in the specialization of the right hemisphere. If so, we would have discovered an important cause of individual differences in spatial ability. Note that the range of spatial abilities within gender is much larger than the mean difference between genders (which is about one-half a standard deviation.)

From this perspective, the study of gender differences is not necessarily an end in itself but is, like the other approaches discussed in this chapter, a way of understanding certain aspects of individuality.

7

Personality and Evolution

INDIVIDUALITY AND HUMAN NATURE

Personality psychology has to do with individuality. In seeking to understand the roots of individuality we can focus in on the single, unique individual, we can group people according to their scores on personality measures, or we can look at large naturally occurring groups such as women and men. All of these contribute to individuality: our personalities are partly a result of genetic patterns and experiences that are ours alone, partly a result of characteristics we share with others with similar dispositions, partly a result of being female or male. They are also partly a result of the fact that we are human beings. This may seem a strange idea. After all, if we are all human, how can being human contribute to our individuality?

To understand this perspective, let us once again consider a Martian observing life on earth. The Martian would see enormous variation in the behavior of animals. It (Martians come in only one sex) would notice that some species eat vegetables, others eat meat, and others eat both. Some spend their lives alone while others live in groups. Some fight with other members of their species, others are peaceful. Some mate with just one other individual, others mate with many. For the Martian, the individuality of each animal would be first and foremost a function of the species of which it was a member. The primary fact about a camel would be that it was a camel and not an elephant or a mouse or a spider. Each species has its distinctive patterns of behavior. In observing humans, the Martian would notice that we too have certain ways of behaving that differ from other animals—and from the Martians themselves. To understand the individuality of any particular human, the Martian would need to understand human behavior in general. The Martian would ask: What do humans want? How do they fulfill their needs? How do they solve the basic problems that all life faces: to survive and pass on one's genes to future generations? The answers to these questions would constitute a description of **human nature.**

What are some answers the Martian might come up with? It might look at the huge variety of human societies and be impressed by how different they are. For example, humans speak thousands of different languages, so the Martian might conclude that what is most evident about humans is that they have an enormous capacity to learn and to transmit that learning to one another. The Martian might even conclude that the capacity to learn and transmit that learning (what we might call "culture") is the hallmark of human nature: although other animals seem to have behavioral tendencies built into their genes, distinctively human behavior is entirely a result of learning and culture. Human nature begins and ends with this capacity.

The Martian might not focus on any of these things, however. Although fully aware of the varieties of culture humans have created, it might be more impressed with what is similar among humans. For example, the fact that humans speak different languages might be less significant than the fact that all humans speak some language. The ability to learn a language might be seen as a built-in aspect of human nature. The Martian might see other commonalities as well. For example, it might notice that in virtually all human societies there is some division of labor according to sex, some form of social hierarchy, some set of rules that guide behavior, and many other ways in which humans might appear essentially the same all over the world (Brown, 1991).

Martians are not alone in their bewilderment about human nature. The question of whether and to what extent the human mind and human behavior are a product of learning or of genetic evolution has long been perplexing and controversial to us humans as well. In recent years, a discipline has emerged called "evolutionary psychology" that attempts to grapple with the question of the nature of human nature. This approach asserts that the human mind is comprised of a large number of specific **psychological mechanisms** that have been produced through the process of **natural selection** over the course of millions of years of evolution. In this chapter we shall discuss some of the concepts that form the foundation of this approach and then examine one area to which they have been applied: gender and sexuality.

WHAT IS EVOLUTIONARY PSYCHOLOGY?

Seven million years ago there were no humans. There were also no chimpanzees. There was a creature who was the ancestor of both. Descendants of this creature moved in different evolutionary directions: one line led to the modern chimp, the other led to us. Today we share 98 percent of our DNA with chimpanzees, our closest "relatives" on this planet. It took a long time to get to us: our species, *Homo sapiens,* has been around for only 100,000 years, a tiny fraction of the time life has existed on earth (the great dinosaurs became extinct 65 million years ago). All living things have descended from ancestors who lived before. The line goes back to the beginning of life on earth, a great chain of DNA linking each of us to the earliest molecules that had the capacity to reproduce themselves.

When we look at those organisms closest to us, the similarity of basic structure is obvious: hearts, brains, glands, eyes, and so on. The differences are also obvious. No one would confuse any human with any chimpanzee, and these are the animals closest to us in genetic makeup. Much of what we know about how our body works comes from research on other animals. Because of our shared evolutionary history, many physiological processes are similar among animals. For example, we can learn a great deal about the functioning of the immune system in humans by studying the immune systems of other animals. Yet there are also huge differences. For example, the virus that causes AIDS in humans does not cause AIDS in chimpanzees. Although it is easy to see similarities and differences in physical characteristics, it is much more difficult to judge similarities and differences in behavior.

Psychology has often used animals to aid in understanding people. During much of this century, learning theory was based primarily on the study of rats and pigeons, the assumption being that the basic processes of learning were the same across species. It was also assumed that the processes of learning are the same regardless of what is being learned; that is why so much early research on human learning involved lists of nonsense syllables. Both assumptions are now known to be false.

Consider **observational learning.** One way animals learn is by observing the behavior of others. A monkey that has never seen a toy snake before will not react with fear. However, if the monkey then observes another monkey behaving fearfully in the presence of a toy snake, the observer monkey will also react with fear when shown the snake. Monkeys also do not normally react with fear to flowers. We could train a monkey to react with fear to flowers by shocking it every time it saw a flower. Now suppose we let a second monkey observe the first monkey's fear response. In this case the second monkey will *not* become fearful of the flower. In both cases, the toy snake and the flower, one monkey has observed another monkey acting fearfully, but only in the case of the toy snake does the observer monkey learn to fear the snake (Mineka & Sutton, 1992). Why? During the course of evolution, certain types of stimuli were more dangerous to monkey survival than others. Snakes were more dangerous than flowers. As a result, monkeys are **biologically prepared** to develop fear responses to snakelike objects but not to flowers. Whether or not similar effects occur in humans is controversial (McNally, 1987; Seligman, 1994), although it has been frequently noted that human phobias are generally limited to a small number of stimuli out of the thousands possible, and these are mostly stimuli that would have been threatening during our evolutionary history (such as insects, suffocating closed spaces, and heights).

Whatever "general laws" of learning might exist, it is also true that evolution has programmed different animal species to behave in different ways. If you have ever watched a nature program on animal behavior, you know that even the "simplest" animals have incredibly complex behavior patterns that are determined by their genetic makeup. A baby fawn "knows" to freeze when a predator is stalking. A sea turtle "knows" to seek out a warm beach on which to lay its eggs, and the baby sea turtles "know" to rush immediately into the sea upon hatching. Weaver-bird males "know" how to build a complex nest that will attract females. When "nature calls," your cat "knows" to dig a hole, and your dog "knows" to seek out a fire hydrant! From protozoa to mammals, animals "know" just what they have to do to survive and reproduce.

You might object to our use of the word "know." You might say: These are just instincts; the animals really have no idea what they are doing; they just do whatever their instincts tell them to do. Yet in some sense the animals do "know"—but that knowledge is contained in their genetic makeup and was "learned" over the course of the evolutionary history of their species, rather than over the course of their individual lifetimes.

THE NATURE OF HUMAN NATURE

Are there also things humans "know" that are part of their genetic endowment? Do humans also have preferences, tendencies, and perceptual biases that are built in by evolution? These are the questions that evolutionary psychology tries to address. David Buss (1991) defines the aim of evolutionary psychology as follows: "to identify psychological mechanisms and behavioral strategies as evolved solutions to adaptive problems our species has faced over millions of years" (pp. 459–460).

We left our inquisitive Martian torn between two possibilities: (1) what humans share is their ability to be influenced by the environment (learning and culture); (2) what humans share is a set of specific psychological mechanisms. To put it another way using a computer metaphor, are humans "general-purpose" computers that can be programmed by culture to feel, think, and behave in almost any way imaginable, or do we come into the world with a large number of specific programs designed by evolution to carry out specific tasks?

The idea that human nature is entirely shaped by culture can be dismissed fairly easily. Consider that our sensory capacities limit us to only a small range of sensory input: there are sounds we can't hear and sights we can't see (infrared) and whole senses we lack (like sonar) that other animals possess. So right off the bat (speaking of sonar) we see that we are not totally "general purpose" at all. In fact, there really can be no doubt that our physical structure, including our brain, has been forged by evolution.

The real question is whether there is more to human nature than certain physical limitations combined with an almost infinite capacity to think and learn. That is the view of human nature that has dominated most psychological theorizing in this century. Is it correct? Not according to an alternate view, which argues that humans, like other animals, evolved specific mechanisms for dealing with specific challenges that they faced over evolutionary time. General-purpose mechanisms would not have been adequate to deal with the huge number of challenges our ancestors faced (Cosmides, Tooby, & Barkow, 1992). As Buss (1994) puts it, a mechanism that leads us to choose the most nutritious food would not also lead us to choose the best mate. Each problem requires a specific solution. William James (1890/1950, p. 441) argued a century ago that the complexity of human beings occurs because we have more, not fewer, inborn tendencies than other animals.

"WHY?" QUESTIONS

Evolutionary psychology goes well beyond simply asserting that such tendencies exist. It attempts to understand *why* they exist. In doing this, evolutionary theory provides a way of seeing familiar things in a new light. The key is thinking about the *functions* of behaviors. Evolutionary psychologists, like little children, like to ask "why?" To understand the importance of function in evolutionary "answers," imagine you are with an inquisitive little child, who has just learned from *Sesame Street* that mountains, buildings, and giraffes are "tall." The child starts asking you a series of "why" questions: "Why are mountains tall?" You answer, "Mountains are tall because in the past, tectonic plates collided with each other and pushed up all this earth that had no place to go but up." The child seems satisfied with your answer and goes on to "Why are buildings tall?" "Buildings are tall because people wanted to have space for lots of people on a little bit of ground." The child seems a little less satisfied with this answer. "But why do people want to fit a lot of people in a little ground space?" You answer, "Because land is expensive in cities and it's cheaper to build up than out." The child now seems satisfied and goes on to "Why are giraffes tall?" Getting a bit exasperated, you answer, "Giraffes are tall because they grow that way—it's in their genes." But this is definitely not going to do. "Why do they grow that way?" the child asks. What are you going to say? To explain mountains, all you had to do was describe the physical forces at work. To explain buildings, you had to describe the intentions of humans. What do you have to do to explain giraffes? Why *do* giraffes grow tall? Why *is* it in their genes?

HOW EVOLUTION WORKS

Evolution provides an elegant framework for thinking about function. All characteristics that evolve must somehow serve to reproduce themselves. Why do we eat? One answer is that eating is pleasurable because food tastes good (in a moment we will ask, Why does food taste good?). Another answer is that we can eliminate the unpleasant feeling of hunger by eating. Probably neither of these was your answer though. You probably thought, We eat because we need food to live. Which of these is the correct answer? Well, in some sense all are correct. Clearly, the pleasure of eating and the pain of hunger motivate us to eat. If we felt neither pleasure nor pain, eating would be like trying to remember to take medicine—and probably a lot of people would die from malnutrition! But the function of eating is not to get pleasure or avoid pain; the function is to provide needed nutrients to our bodies so that we can survive.

Imagine that our Martian arrived and saw people eating. Suppose that on Mars people don't have to eat—they get all the nutrients they need by breathing all that red dust. How would Martians understand human eating? They would undoubtedly come up with all sorts of theories about social bonding, religious rituals, and so on, and they might never hit on the idea that eating is done for biological survival. The key to understanding the function of eating is understanding what is needed for humans to survive, or as is often said, what problems need to be solved in order for humans (or any life forms) to survive and reproduce their genes to future generations. Now let's go back to the question of pleasure and pain. Why do you suppose people experience pleasure when they eat? Why do some substances taste good and others taste bad?

The basic ideas of how evolution works were described by Charles Darwin in 1859 in *Origin of Species*. Darwin's essential ideas about evolution have been born out by huge amounts of research, although there have been a number of modifications of his initial formulation as a result of new knowledge about the genetic mechanisms of heredity. (It is amazing to remember that Darwin proposed his theory without any knowledge of genetics.) The basic process that operates to modify species is called **natural selection.** Darwin's fundamental observation was that living things produce many more offspring than the environment can sustain, and as a result, only a small fraction survive and reproduce to send their own genes to subsequent generations.

What determines which offspring contribute their genes to future generations and which do not? If the process was random, there would be no evolution. Darwin realized that the process is decidedly not random. Offspring differ in their hereditary makeup. Recombinations of chromosomes as well as mutations produce genetic differences, some of which will improve an individual's chances of surviving and reproducing, others of which will reduce the individual's chances. Any genetic advantage one offspring has over another will increase the chances it will be the one to send its genes to the next generation.

It is important to understand that this process does not require any intention or desire to pass on one's genes. The combination of overproduction of offspring and genetic variation that affects the chances of survival and reproduction are all that are needed for this process to operate. What is the result of this process? Any genetically influenced characteristic that increases an individual's chances of survival and reproduction will become more numerous in subsequent generations.

WHY IS SUGAR SWEET?

Now we can answer the question about why some substances taste good and others taste bad. Consider the mechanism that produces the sensation of sweetness in the human brain. Human beings experience this sensation when they place sugar in their mouths, because of our brains and because of our taste receptors' combining with the molecular structure of sugar. Sugar is not "sweet" to animals whose brains do not respond this way or who lack these receptors. It is not difficult to understand how the ability to taste sweetness evolved. At some point in our evolutionary history not all individuals had the necessary combination of taste receptors and brain process to experience sweetness. Those who had the ability to experience sweetness gained an advantage in some way, so they were able to survive and to reproduce more than those who didn't. Probably this advantage involved food choice. For example, since sweetness is experienced as pleasant, we prefer sweet, ripe fruit to sour, unripe fruit. Ripe fruit is more digestible and nutritious than unripe fruit. As a result, those of our ancestors who preferred ripe fruit (because they experienced it as sweet) had a slight edge in their nutrition over those who couldn't tell the difference or didn't prefer it (because they couldn't experience sweetness). Over a number of generations, the "sweetness genes" kept getting reproduced at a higher rate than the non-sweetness genes until finally all of the members of the species had the genes to experience sweetness.

What is happening here? Variations in the genetic structure of a species are "tracking" an important environmental variable. Ripeness of fruit makes a difference for survival and reproduction. Evolution has "picked up" on this difference and molded us to take advantage of it. In a sense, we now "know" that ripe fruit is better to eat than unripe fruit—this knowledge was forged by evolution to be part of our nature. This type of characteristic is called an **adaptation,** that is, a characteristic that evolved to solve a problem that made a difference for the chances of reproducing one's genes to subsequent generations. In this case the problem was choosing the most nutritious food.

THE CONCEPT OF FITNESS

From an evolutionary perspective, life forms are simply means by which genes get passed down to subsequent generations. The survival of the individual makes a difference in evolution only if it serves to increase the number of genes passed down. In some species, when individuals finish reproducing, they die. But in most species, the longer one lives the more likely one is to send on one's genes. As a result, organisms have evolved in many ways to increase their chances of survival. These include both physical and behavioral characteristics and are captured by the well-known expression "survival of the fittest." The concept of being "fit" is crucial to evolutionary theory. The term **fitness** refers to how many copies of the individual's genes were passed on to future generations. The individual with the "sweet" genes was more fit than the individuals with the "no sweet" genes because more copies of the former's genes were sent to subsequent generations.

In humans, we are concerned with how various psychological mechanisms promoted fitness in the **ancestral environment**, that is, the environment that existed during the time our species was evolving. Part of the challenge of an evolutionary analysis of human behavior involves imaginatively reconstructing what that environment was like. As we will see later, this is also a pitfall in this approach. For now, it is important to understand that when we talk about fitness in humans, we are talking primarily about fitness in the ancestral environment.

Inclusive Fitness

Fitness does not involve only one's own offspring. Consider the following situation and try to decide who has greater evolutionary fitness. Jack and John are identical twins. Jack never gets married and has no children, but he helps John's family in many ways. In fact, without Jack's financial help, John would have been able to support only one child, but with this aid from Jack, John has had four children. Jill and Joan are also identical twins. They are not close to each other and do not help each other in any way. They each have one child. Compare Jack and Jill. Who is more fit? You might say "Jill" because Jill had one child and Jack had none. Yet if we think in terms of genes, more copies of Jack's genes are going to the next generation than Jill's. Because they are identical twins, all of John's offspring have copies of Jack's genes. So the Jack-John genes have produced four offspring, but the Jill-Joan genes have produced only two.

Suppose the tendency to help one's sibling is itself genetically influenced. Jack has that genetic tendency and Jill doesn't. Because the tendency led Jack to help brother John, more copies of that "helping gene" are in the next generation. The idea that fitness includes not only one's own offspring but also the offspring of those who share one's genes is called **inclusive fitness.** It helps explain why animals often do things to help their relatives. It may also explain certain aspects of human behavior, such as the tendency to be more concerned about the well-being of one's family than that of strangers (Burnstein, Crandall, & Kitayama, 1994), and to favor members of one's own "ingroup" rather than members of the "outgroup" (Tajfel, 1982). In the ancestral environment, individuals were certainly more likely to share genes with their family, tribe, or clan than with "outsiders." Hence, helping members of one's family, tribe, or clan would promote one's inclusive fitness—and if that tendency was itself influenced by genes, the tendency would have evolved to become part of our human nature.

SEXUAL SELECTION

Natural selection occurs when some aspect of the environment favors the survival and reproduction of organisms with certain characteristics more than it does others. However, Darwin recognized that among animals there is another kind of selection that occurs. In sexually reproducing species, it takes two to tango. An individual might survive just fine but unless it can mate (or influence the fitness of its relatives), its genes will not be reproduced; it will not be fit; it will leave no descendants; it will not be part of evolutionary history.

Darwin noticed that mating is not a random process. In fact, many animals expend huge amounts of energy gaining access to mates. There are two reasons why mating is not random. First, all else being equal, the more matings, the more offspring. A male who mates with fifty females will leave more offspring (and more copies of his genes) than a male who mates with one. Males of many species compete with each other for access to females, and the winners pass down more of their genes, including the genes that made them winners. Second, two individuals may have the same number of offspring, but if the offspring of one receive genes that give them a better chance to survive and reproduce, then those genes are more likely to continue to future generations.

The situation isn't so different from that of sweetness. Suppose there are cues that would indicate which of two possible mates had "better" genes. For example, a strong, large individual might have genes that give it better resistance to infections or parasites than a weak, small animal has. Preferring to mate with the strong, large individual would increase the likelihood that one's offspring will be healthy. As a result, any tendency to prefer strong, large individuals as mates would tend to reproduce itself, just as the tendency to prefer ripe fruit would reproduce itself. Over time, this preference would become a powerful part of the species' evolved characteristics.

Animals could also evolve preferences for characteristics in mates that are helpful to them. For example, choosing a mate who has greater access to food or shelter would increase the chances that one's offspring would survive. If so, any genetic tendency to prefer such mates would win out over the tendency not to prefer such mates. Darwin called the evolutionary process that is based on increased mating or preference for certain characteristics in mates **sexual selection.** In coining the term *sexual selection*, Darwin was trying to make the point that the problems organisms have to solve include those that involve survival and those that directly involve mating choices. In fact, in some cases these may work at cross purposes: the huge tails of peacocks hinder their chances of survival, yet they are so preferred by peahens that they continue to be a characteristic of the species.

HUMAN SEXUALITY

An individual who has a long life but fails to reproduce will contribute nothing to future generations (except perhaps through helping kin survive). An individual who has a short life but leaves many offspring will contribute genes to future generations. Our ancestors were those individuals who reproduced the most copies of their genes. Whatever genetically influenced characteristics increased the likelihood that their genes would be passed on were themselves passed on. In order to reproduce, individuals must mate; they must have sex. These facts have led evolutionary psychologists to focus their attention on mating, and particularly on differences between women and men in **mating strategies** (Buss, 1994; Symons, 1979). The focus on sex differences follows from the obvious fact that the roles of women and men in reproduction are very different. As a result, what will increase fitness for one sex is not necessarily what will increase fitness for the other sex.

Parental Investment

There are two major differences between women and men that are important for this discussion. First, women are limited in the number of offspring they can bear. In ancestral times, women probably bore a maximum of eight to twelve children (this estimate is based on studies of contemporary hunter-gatherer peoples). Men, in contrast, can have an almost unlimited number of offspring (the documented world record is 899) (Daly & Wilson, 1983).

The second difference is in what is called **parental investment.** Consider the minimum activity required by a man to mate. If a man copulates with a woman and his sperm fertilizes an egg, he is on his way to producing copies of his genes. Nothing else is required of him. In the jargon of evolutionary biology, sperm represent the **minimal investment** a man must make to produce offspring. The minimal investment of a woman is totally different. If she gets pregnant, she is contributing much more than an egg. First, she will have to carry the fetus for nine months. During this time she will have to feed not only herself, but her offspring. For at least the last trimester her activities will be somewhat limited. Second, she will give birth. In the ancestral environment, this act was undoubtedly risky, sometimes leading to the mother's death. Third, after the baby is born, she will still have to share her food with the child since it will nurse for two to three years, also limiting her activity. Fourth, during most of this time, she will not be fertile. Suppose after three years her baby dies. Her fitness is reduced because none of her genes during that three-year period entered the evolutionary stream, and she has not produced any other offspring. For all of these reasons, women's minimal investments in offspring are much greater than are men's.

Gender Differences in Mating Strategies: Quality and Quantity

There are some rather obvious, and some not so obvious, results from these differences. Remember that evolution works through competition among members of the same species. Those who produce more offspring will have more influence on how the species evolves than will those who produce fewer offspring (the definition of fitness). Characteristics that lead individuals to produce more offspring will eventually become characteristics of the evolving species.

How could a male increase his number of offspring? Since males' minimum investment is low, there is little cost to males of mating with as many females as possible. All else being equal, the more different females a male mates with the greater number of offspring he will have. Consider two males: one has the desire to mate with many different females; the other doesn't. The first male sometimes gets an opportunity to fulfill his desires; let's suppose that over his lifetime he manages to mate with 100 different females. If 25 percent of them have children as a result, he will pass his genes on to 25 individuals. At least some of his male offspring will inherit his tendency to desire many mates, so when they get their chance, they will also try to mate with many females. You can see that in just a few generations, the male with a desire for many mates would leave hundreds of copies of his genes, including the genes that led him to desire multiple sex partners.

Now consider the situation for the male who does not have this desire. He sticks to one mate and becomes father to, at most, twelve offspring. The male children inherit his lack of interest in more than one mate, so they too mate with one female. It is easy to see that over subsequent generations, the proportion of males with the desire for many mates will be much greater than the proportion with the desire for one mate. Thus the desire for many mates would eventually become part of the characteristics of the species.

What about the female who desires many mates? No matter how many mates she has, she will still produce a maximum of eight to twelve offspring. As a result, the female who desires sex with many males will not ordinarily have more offspring than one who desires sex with only one male. Thus there would be little reason to expect the desire for multiple sex partners to evolve in females (although, as we will see, there may be some circumstances that would lead females to seek multiple sex partners).

The first conclusion of this analysis is that the desire for multiple sex partners would have evolved in males far more than in females. Fitness is more closely linked to the *quantity* of mates for males than for females. But quantity is only part of the story. *Quality* of mates is also important. Consider the situation of females. Even though there is not much difference among females in potential number of offspring, it is important to remember that unless these offspring survive and reproduce, the parents' genes will contribute nothing to evolution. Two females may both have eight offspring, but if all of the first female's offspring survive and reproduce, and none of the second female's offspring do, the first female will become an ancestor and the second female will not.

What determines which offspring survive and reproduce? One important factor is the support the female gets from those around her. In particular, think of the advantage a female would have if she mated with a male who stayed with her and contributed **resources** by offering her and her children food and protection, going well beyond the *minimal* parental investment in his offspring. In the ancestral environment, which was probably harsh and challenging, the female who preferred a strong, healthy, committed mate who had resources and was willing to invest them in her and her offspring would have had a huge advantage in fitness over the woman who mated indiscriminantly. So a second conclusion from this analysis is that females would have evolved a strong preference for mates who were willing and able to provide resources to them and their offspring: they would have preferred "dads" over "cads" (Buss, 1994).

Quality of mates can also be an important issue for males. In species in which males invest little in their offspring, the number of mates a male has is likely to be the primary factor in his fitness. However, in species with higher male parental investment, the quality of the female is important to the male. Compared with other mammals, and even other primates, human males tend to invest a great deal in their mates and to maintain long-term relationships with their mates (Kenrick, 1994).

What would constitute a "quality" mate from the male point of view? One very important characteristic would be **fertility.** A male who mates with a female who is infertile will not leave any offspring. A second, related characteristic is health. A healthy female is more likely to bear healthy young and be able to care for them. Age is an important component of both of these. A woman in her twenties has far greater **reproductive value** than a woman in her forties. Imagine two males, one with a strong desire for younger females of reproductive age, the other with no preferences regarding age. The first male mates with a younger female, the second mates with an older female. Which one will produce more offspring? Again, the selection pressure here is enormous. A preference for younger females would give a huge selective advantage over no age preference.

How could a male tell the age of a female in the ancestral environment? Animals do not consciously know the reasons for their preferences and actions. They feel what they feel and do what they do because over the course of evolution these feelings and actions increased the fitness of their ancestors. Our ancestors were no different. They didn't think, "If I choose a younger female I will produce more offspring and thus influence the course of evolution." No conscious intention to produce offspring is necessary. All that is required is a detectable cue that varies reliably with a characteristic that makes a difference to fitness. A male whose genes led him to prefer cues that reliably varied with females' age and health would have had a fitness advantage over a male whose genes did not lead him to prefer these cues. What could these cues be? The cues to age and health are essentially physical. Smooth skin, bright eyes and hair, a lively gait, and full lips are all characteristics that indicate a younger, therefore more fertile, woman. Because a male's preference for these cues would have increased fitness, this preference would then have become part of the evolved mating psychology of men.

Let us summarize. Evolution operates through competition among individuals within a species. Our ancestors were those who were most successful in leaving their genes to future generations. Whatever characteristics led to their success eventually became part of our own evolved human nature. In the area of mating, our female and male ancestors achieved success in different ways. Our female ancestors were those who preferred males with the capacity and willingness to expend resources on their mates and offspring. Our male ancestors were those who desired multiple mates, who preferred young, healthy mates, and who competed successfully with other males to attract or gain access to females.

TESTING EVOLUTIONARY HYPOTHESES: SEX DIFFERENCES IN THE PSYCHOLOGY OF MATING

All of this makes sense, but science demands more than a sensible-sounding theory—it demands empirical evidence. In studies of animal behavior, there is a great deal of evidence supporting many of these ideas (Barash, 1982). We can assume that the environment currently experienced by most animals is fairly similar to the environment in which they evolved. As a result, it is possible to examine how animals' behaviors represent adaptations to their environment. This assumption cannot be made about human beings. In the last 10,000 years, the human invention of culture has had an enormous effect on human behavior, and so it is difficult to use current conditions to test ideas about human adaptations. In fact, most evolutionary psychologists assume that behaviors that were adaptive during our evolutionary past may actually be harmful today. An example is our preference for fatty, salty foods, a preference that made adaptive sense when such foods were scarce but that can be lethal when they are abundant.

Is It Science?

It is at this point that many critics of evolutionary psychology raise their objections (e.g., Kitcher, 1985). We have been talking about an evolutionary process that took place over millions of years, in an environment that no longer exists. Paleoanthropologists try to imagine what that environment was like, and what the social relations of our ancestors consisted of, but these are only educated guesses. We cannot base our views on what other animals do, because there is enormous variation in the mating behaviors of different species. We can look at contemporary hunter-gatherer peoples, but there is no guarantee that their way of life is a model for how our ancestors lived. As a result, these critics say, there is no way to test these ideas, no way to choose one evolutionary scenario over another, no way to prove that any particular pattern of behavior that we observe today was the product of evolutionary processes rather than, say, of culture. In short, evolutionary psychology cannot be tested scientifically.

Evolutionary psychologists respond to this criticism by pointing out that most psychological theories are hard to "prove." At best, one tries to see whether the bulk of evidence supports or contradicts the theory. Certainly, if the patterns predicted by evolutionary theorists cannot be observed in contemporary human beings, then the theory cannot be correct. So we can ask: What evidence is there that males have a greater desire for multiple sex partners than do females, that females prefer males who are willing and able to invest their resources, and that males prefer females who are young and healthy?

Gender Differences in Sexuality

It is curious that despite the importance of sex in human life, and the obvious interest that humans have in doing it, talking about it, seeing it, and obsessing over it, academic psychology has paid very little attention to it. For example, in studies of psychological differences between women and men, sexuality has rarely even been mentioned (Ashmore, 1990; Eagly, 1987; Hyde, 1990; Maccoby & Jacklin, 1974). One would think from reading these books and articles that differences in how men and women can rotate objects in their minds are more important than differences in their sexual behavior! One of the benefits of the recent interest in evolutionary psychology has been to focus attention on sex differences in sexuality, especially with respect to sexual desires and mating preferences (Buss & Schmitt, 1993; Kenrick, 1994). The recent work has shown clearly that sex differences in these areas are among the largest that have been documented. Let us look more closely at the evidence for some the major claims of evolutionary psychologists.

The Desire for Casual Sex

Do men desire casual sex with multiple partners more than women do? In a recent meta-analysis of studies dealing with sexuality, Oliver and Hyde (1993) found that attitudes toward casual sex (along with frequency of masturbation) showed larger sex differences than any other behavioral or psychological characteristics that have been studied. Relatively large sex differences were also found for sexual permissiveness. Unfortunately, there was little attempt to distinguish among *attitudes, feelings,* and *behavior* in this study. Thus, men and women differed very much in actual amount of masturbation (men report engaging in it more often), but not at all in their *attitudes* toward masturbation.

Ehrlichman and Eichenstein (1992) focused directly on desires. They asked samples of students and nonstudents to indicate anonymously which items on a list of "private wishes" they would most want if they could have anything at all with no possibility of any negative consequences. The wishes ranged from "peace on earth" to "health" to "being rich" to "political power" to "time travel." When asked to choose 10 wishes from a list of 48, 25% of men and 5% of women chose "To have sex with anyone I choose." When later asked to rate wishes on a four-point scale ranging from 1 = "This is something I want very much" to 4 = "This is not something I want," 24% of men gave this wish a rating of "1"—compared with 4.5% of women. Fifty-one percent of women gave it a rating of "4"—compared with 22% of men. The sex difference for this wish was over twice as large as the sex difference for any other wish on the list. It was also found for both students and nonstudents, across three different age ranges from 16 to 90, and across three levels of degree of religiousness.

Studies of sex fantasies are also consistent with these results. Women fantasize much more often about sex with someone they are romantically involved with as opposed to someone they just want to have sex with. Men have these two kinds of fantasies equally often (Ellis & Symons, 1990). Perhaps the most dramatic indication of this difference between women and men is an experimental study by Clark and Hatfield (1989). College students were stopped by an attractive stranger of the opposite sex (an accomplice of the experimenter) as they walked on campus. The accomplice said to the subject, "I have been noticing you around campus; I find you very attractive" and then asked one of three questions, randomly chosen: "Would you go out with me tonight?" "Would you come over to my apartment tonight?" or "Would you go to bed with me tonight?" How would you react to such questions? Table 7.1 shows the percentages of women and men who said "yes" to each question.

These results, and many others like them (Buss & Schmitt, 1993) clearly indicate that men are much more attracted to impersonal, casual sex than women are. This doesn't mean women don't enjoy sex as much as or even more than men do; what it points to is a fundamental difference in the *context* for sexual activity. Men are generally ready and willing to have sex with an attractive stranger; women want to know who the person is and what he is like, and want to have some personal feelings about him. These results do not mean that men are never interested in long-term, committed sex. In the study on private wishes, 33% of men gave a rating of 1 to the wish "To have a completely satisfying sexual relationship with one and only one person my whole life." Although women were more positive toward this wish (53% gave it a 1) men actually rated this wish higher than they rated the wish for "sex with anyone." Also recall that men were equally likely to fantasize about romantic and impersonal partners (Ellis & Symons, 1990).

These patterns fit evolutionary thinking closely. For males, both casual sex with many partners *and* committed sex with a long-term partner are strategies that would pay off in fitness. Thus male sexuality seems to involve both of these desires. In contrast, the desire for committed sexual relationships is far stronger in females than is the desire for casual sex. Evolutionary psychologists believe these differences show up in many ways in everyday life, such as in the fact that the vast majority of sexual harassers and abusers are men, in the huge market for pornography aimed at men, and in the ubiquitous institution of prostitution to service male customers (Buss, 1994; Symons, 1979; Thornhill & Thornhill, 1992).

TABLE 7.1   Percentages of Subjects Saying "Yes" to Each of Three Questions (Based on Clark and Hatfield, 1989)

	WOMEN	MEN
"Go out"	50%	50%
"Come to apartment"	6%	69%
"Go to bed"	0%	75%

Cues to Youth and Health

Do men prefer women who show cues to youth and health? Evolutionary psychologists believe that beauty is in the eye, or rather the brain, of the beholder. According to our earlier discussion, males should be attracted to females who are young and healthy. The cues to youth and health are part of what we might call beauty. Our brains process certain patterns of physical features to produce our experience of beauty, just as our brains process certain chemical signals such as sweetness. Both processes are designed to make the objects of our perception more desirable. Beauty is an evolved mechanism, in the beholder, to cause a preference for certain characteristics in the beheld, that would increase the beholder's evolutionary fitness.

Cues to youth and health are major components of physical beauty in women. Many studies have found that youthful complexion, firm muscle tone, lustrous hair, and full lips are desired by men. It should not be surprising that men value youth in potential mates more than women do. This attitude is often considered part of a "double standard" in American society (Kenrick, 1994). However, this pattern is not limited to our society. Buss (1989) found that men prefer younger women in every one of 37 cultures surveyed, and the older the man the greater the difference in age. In fact, men's preference for younger women may even be greater in other cultures than in ours (Kenrick, 1994; Kenrick & Keefe, 1992). Physical appearance of desired mates is also far more important to men than it is to women. In virtually every study that has examined this question, using either self-reports of preferences or content analysis of personals ads, men give greater importance to physical attractiveness as a desired characteristic of mates than do women (Feingold, 1992). In the cultures studied by Buss (1989), this sex difference was found to cut across all continents and racial groups.

Resources

Do women prefer men who are willing and able to provide them with resources? In all 37 cultures studied by Buss (1989), women valued wealth and status in men more than men valued it in women (see Table 7.2). Kenrick, Sadalla, Groth, and Trost (1990) asked college students to indicate the minimum they would accept in a partner with regard to a number of characteristics. The college women indicated that to marry a man, he would have to be in at least the 67th percentile of "earning capacity." In contrast, the college men would require a woman to be only at the 42nd percentile. (Note that the "average" earning capacity would be the 50th percentile.) In personal ads, women mention financial resources as a requirement much more often than men do (Wiederman, 1993). The preference for successful men is not limited to those women who lack their own resources. Wealthier women actually prefer wealthier men more than poorer women do (Wiederman & Allgeier, 1992). In contrast, men's relative lack of interest in a woman's financial situation is the same regardless of the man's own financial situation (Buss, 1989). This is an

TABLE 7.2   Ratings by Women and Men of Importance of "Good Financial Prospect" and "Good Looks" in Choosing a Mate, and Preferred Age Differences between Self and Mate

Sample	Number	GOOD FINANCIAL PROSPECT		GOOD LOOKS		PREFERRED AGE DIFFERENCE	
		Men	Women	Men	Women	Men	Women
African							
Nigeria	172	1.37	2.30	2.24	1.82	− 6.45	+ 4.90
S. Africa (whites)	128	0.94	1.73	1.58	1.22	− 2.30	+ 3.50
S. Africa (Zulu)	100	0.70	1.14	1.17	0.88	− 3.33	+ 3.76
Zambia	119	1.46	2.33	2.23	1.65	− 7.38	+ 4.14
Asian							
China	500	1.10	1.56	2.06	1.59	− 2.05	+ 3.45
India	247	1.60	2.00	2.03	1.97[a]	− 3.06	+ 3.29
Indonesia	143	1.42	2.55	1.81	1.36	− 2.72	+ 4.69
Iran	55	1.25	2.04	2.07	1.69	− 4.02	+ 5.10
Israel (Jewish)	473	1.31	1.82	1.77	1.56	− 2.88	+ 3.95
Israel (Palestinian)	109	1.28	1.67	2.38	1.47	− 3.75	+ 3.71
Japan	259	0.92	2.29	1.50	1.09	− 2.37	+ 3.05
Taiwan	566	1.25	2.21	1.76	1.28	− 3.13	+ 3.78
European–Eastern							
Bulgaria	269	1.16	1.64	2.39	1.95	− 3.13	+ 4.18
Estonia	303	1.31	1.51	2.27	1.63	− 2.19	+ 2.85
Poland	240	1.09	1.74	1.93	1.77[a]	− 2.85	+ 3.38
Yugoslavia	140	1.27	1.66	2.20	1.74	− 2.47	+ 3.61
European–Western							
Belgium	145	0.95	1.36	1.78	1.28	− 2.53	+ 2.46
Finland	204	0.65	1.18	1.56	0.99	− 0.38	+ 2.83
France	191	1.22	1.68	2.08	1.76	− 1.94	+ 4.00
Germany–West	1083	1.14	1.81	1.92	1.32	− 2.52	+ 3.70
Great Britain	130	0.67	1.16	1.96	1.36	− 1.92	+ 2.26
Greece	132	1.16	1.92	2.22	1.94	− 3.36	+ 4.54
Ireland	122	0.82	1.67	1.87	1.22	− 2.07	+ 2.78
Italy	101	0.87	1.33	2.00	1.64	− 2.76	+ 3.24
Netherlands	417	0.69	0.94	1.76	1.21	− 1.01	+ 2.72
Norway	134	1.10	1.42	1.87	1.32	− 1.91	+ 3.12
Spain	124	1.25	1.39[a]	1.91	1.24	− 1.46	+ 2.60
Sweden	172	1.18	1.75	1.65	1.46[a]	− 2.34	+ 2.91
North American							
Canada (English)	101	1.02	1.91	1.96	1.64	− 1.53	+ 2.72
Canada (French)	105	1.47	1.94	1.68	1.41	− 1.22	+1.82
USA (Mainland)	1491	1.08	1.96	2.11	1.67	− 1.65	+ 2.54
USA (Hawaii)	179	1.50	2.10	2.06	1.49	− 1.92	+ 3.30
Oceanian							
Australia	280	0.69	1.54	1.65	1.24	− 1.77	+ 2.86
New Zealand	151	1.35	1.63	1.99	1.29	− 1.59	+ 2.91
South American							
Brazil	630	1.24	1.91	1.89	1.68	− 2.94	+ 3.94
Colombia	139	1.72	2.21	1.56	1.22	− 4.45	+ 4.51
Venezuela	193	1.66	2.26	1.76	1.27	− 2.99	+ 3.62

Ratings were on a four-point scale from 0 = irrelevant or unimportant to 3 = indispensable.

[a] = not significant at $p < .05$

example of how evolved preferences can sometimes override "realistic" considerations in what we find desirable.

Cues to Resources: Dominance and Status

In the ancestral environment, females could not determine the resources a male possessed by looking at his bankbook. A preference for males with resources could have evolved only if there were cues that reliably indicated the presence or absence of resources. One important cue, which is found in many mammalian species, is status in a dominance hierarchy. In the study by Kenrick, Sadalla et al. (1990) on minimum standards for a marriage partner, women required men to be at least at the 44th percentile on "powerful," whereas men required women to be only at the 28th percentile.

Similar sex differences were found for "popular" and "high social status." Sadalla, Kenrick, and Vershure (1987) found that women rated men who were portrayed as socially dominant as being more sexually attractive than were men portrayed as meek and submissive. Kenrick, Neuberg, Zierk, and Krones (1994) presented college students with a series of personality profiles and photographs of other students who were described as "romantically unattached" and interested in meeting others. All of the subjects themselves were currently involved romantically with another person. After viewing the photos and profiles, the subjects were asked to indicate their level of commitment to their current romantic partner. Previous research has demonstrated that men's stated commitment to their current partner is decreased after exposure to *Playboy* centerfolds, and this same effect was found in this study: male subjects who viewed photos of physically attractive women indicated a reduced level of commitment to their current partner. However, for the female subjects, the story was quite different. Physical attractiveness of the males had no effect on women's level of commitment to their current partner. However, after exposure to profiles of socially dominant men (men with leadership qualities and ability to influence others), the level of women's commitment to their current partner decreased. Thus dominance appears to function for women in much the same way that physical attractiveness functions for men.

Effects of Mating Preferences of One Sex on Behavior of the Other Sex

According to sexual selection theory, the preferences of one sex can have a great impact on the characteristics of the other sex. If women prefer men with resources and social status, men will compete with each other to control resources and achieve status. Indeed, the historical record indicates that one of the "perks" of kings, emperors, and warlords has been sexual access to large numbers of women (Betzig, 1986). The evolutionary logic of this is straightforward. Men who achieve power and status have greater access to women (either because of women's preferences or because of the man's ability to control women). As a result they will have many more offspring than men who do not achieve power and status. Whatever genetic characteristics led them to want status and gave them the ability to achieve it will eventually become part of the male psychology in the species. Evolutionary psychologists see the operation of this type of adaptation in the importance men give to status, including the physical aggressiveness that often accompanies altercations between males.

Similarly, if men prefer women who are young and attractive, women will compete with each other on these terms. This perspective is radically different from one that assumes that "our society's" preoccupation with the age and physical appearance of women is a product of the media, with its endless images of impossibly gorgeous young women (Wolf, 1991). In this latter view, standards of beauty, even the concept of beauty itself, is an arbitrary product of society. Evolutionary psychologists disagree. They see both men's and women's preoccupation with female appearance as a result of our evolved psychological strategies: men prefer women who have cues to youth and health, and so women compete with each other to project those cues. These cues may shift somewhat with ecological conditions (for example, what weight is considered attractive may vary according to whether food is scarce or abundant).

Buss (1994) makes the interesting point that the effect of the constant media barrage of models has a negative impact on both women and men. By exploiting these evolutionary tendencies, media images can lead men to become dissatisfied with the appearance of real women, and women to become dissatisfied with their own appearance. But it is because of tendencies deeply embedded in our evolved psychology that these media images have their tremendous force. The endless quest for youth and beauty that seems so crucial to so many women is not an arbitrary creation of the media, but a playing out of an ancient strategy for reproductive success. Media images of tough, dominant men may also lead males to become preoccupied with their physical prowess and social dominance. The evolutionary perspective invites us to look at many of our most common behaviors and wonder what might lie behind them in terms of the ancient patterns that increased or decreased the reproductive fitness of our ancestors.

IS IT CONVINCING?

Do these studies convince you that evolutionary psychology is on the right track? Or, like many critics of evolutionary theory, have you thought of many objections to this approach? Perhaps you don't find the studies convincing because you "already knew" that men try to get sex whenever they can, men like physically attractive women, and women want men with status. We also would see this as a problem. The most convincing evidence for a theory is its ability to make predictions about things that we didn't already know and that could not just as easily be predicted from other theories. In fact, this is what evolutionary biologists do routinely in testing theories of animal behavior. Are any of the studies we have described with humans of this type?

Perhaps the strongest case can be made by studies such as Buss's (1989) that reveal similar patterns among different cultures. It is worth noting that classic anthropological accounts of differences among cultures (e.g., Benedict, 1934; Mead, 1928) were used to support the idea that human behavior is based primarily on culture. Therefore it only seems fair that patterns of similarities among cultures should be used to support the idea that at least some human behavior reflects our common human nature. This is particularly true when the pattern contradicts what a theory based on cultural relativity would predict. For example, do humans in different cultures agree on what features make people good-looking? If you were shown photos of two individuals from a culture with which you have had zero contact, and were told that people in that culture considered one of them good-looking and the other one ugly, would you be able to tell which was which? Cultural relativism would seem to predict that standards of beauty would be arbitrary and differ from culture to culture, whereas evolutionary psychology would predict that cultures will generally agree on who is or isn't attractive, just as they can agree on which facial expressions indicate fear and which indicate happiness (Ekman, 1994). Recent evidence provides some support for the evolutionary view (Cunningham, Roberts, Barbee, Druen, & Wu, 1995).

EVOLUTIONARY ANALYSIS OF JEALOUSY

Buss, Larsen, Westen, and Semmelroth (1992) used evolutionary theory to make predictions about sex differences in jealousy. We know that both men and women get jealous. But is there a basis for predicting what they get jealous about? Buss et al. reasoned that, in addition to the sex differences we have discussed so far, there is another crucial difference between women and men that has profound implications for psychology in general, and jealousy in particular. You may have heard the expression "It's a wise child that knows its own father." Before the advent of DNA testing a man could never be absolutely positive that his mate's offspring was actually his. As a result, **certainty of paternity** becomes a significant issue in evolutionary terms. Suppose a male devotes time and resources to a child who is not his own. On the basis of the discussion so far, you might be able to see why doing this would reduce the male's fitness. The child might live long and prosper with the male's help, but the male's genes would be going nowhere. So imagine once again two males. One is, as John Lennon put it, "born with a jealous mind." He is constantly checking his mate to be sure that she isn't cheating on him. The other male really doesn't care what she does with other males. Which of these two males is more likely to invest resources in his own child with his own genes? Which of these two emotional tendencies—the tendency to be jealous or the tendency not to care—would be more likely to be sent down to future generations?

Evolutionary psychologists contend that the emotion of jealousy is a mechanism that evolved in part to keep men vigilant about the sexual activities of their mates. Does this idea mean females have no evolutionary reason to experience jealousy? Not at all. But it does mean that females should be jealous about different things than men are. According to evolutionary psychology, jealousy is a mechanism that is designed to prevent one's mate from engaging in behaviors that would threaten one's reproductive fitness. For a male, the threat comes primarily from his mate getting pregnant by another male. For a female, the major threat is that her mate will shift his resources from her and her offspring to another female, or even abandon her altogether.

Emotions are designed to keep us focused on the things that matter. We get happy about things that will increase our well-being, we get upset about things that threaten our well-being. For evolutionary psychologists, what "matters" is largely a result of our evolutionary history as a species. One way of determining "what matters" is to find out what situations are most upsetting to people. This strategy was used by Buss et al. to investigate evolutionary ideas about jealousy. Subjects were told to think of a past, current, or wished-for serious romantic relationship and to imagine that the other person became interested in someone else. They were then asked which would upset them more: (1) "Imagining your partner forming a deep emotional attachment to that person," or (2) "Imagining your partner enjoying passionate sexual intercourse with that other person." Sixty percent of the males indicated that they would be more upset imagining sexual infidelity versus 40% who indicated that they would be more upset imagining emotional infidelity. In sharp contrast, only 17% of the females said they would be more upset by sexual infidelity, while 83% said they would be more upset by emotional infidelity. Similar results were found for physiological reactions while subjects imagined finding out either (1) that their partner was having sexual intercourse with another person or (2) that their partner was falling in love with another person. Men showed higher electrodermal activity while imagining sexual infidelity than emotional infidelity; women showed exactly the opposite pattern.

Male Jealousy and Homicide

From an evolutionary perspective, the stakes in ensuring that a male is providing resources for his own progeny are particularly high. As a result, there would have been strong selection pressure for males to avoid investing in other male's offspring. In many species, this is accomplished by the male literally killing infants that are not his own when he gets a new mate. In humans, males have developed many mechanisms to ensure paternity. When these mechanisms fail, men may engage in seemingly irrational acts. Jealousy is the leading cause of homicide by men toward women. Daly and Wilson (1988) reasoned that the evolutionary cost of investing in genetically unrelated offspring would lead children of stepparents to be at particular risk. Using demographic data from the United States and Canada, Daly and Wilson estimated that children living with a stepparent and a natural parent are 40 to 100 times more likely to be fatally abused than are children living with two natural parents. Daly and Wilson's research may be among the best examples of evolutionary psychology leading to research that tells us things we didn't "already know."

CONSIDERATIONS AND CAVEATS

It is important to emphasize a number of crucial points regarding evolutionary psychology. First, the fact that there is variation among cultures or among individuals does not mean evolutionary mechanisms do not exist in humans. A key aspect of evolutionary biology is that behavior often changes with the environment. Many animals, even "simple" ones, change their behavior as situations change. Consider mating patterns: some bird species shift between polygyny and monogamy according to the type of foods available; some fish species actually change their sex according to the distribution of males and females in their environment. An evolutionary mechanism that wasn't sensitive to the changes that the organism is likely to encounter would not be very effective. The astonishing variety of human behaviors does not itself argue for a cultural rather than evolutionary explanation.

An important aspect of Buss and Schmitt's (1993) sexual strategies theory is specifying the conditions under which women and men will prefer long-term versus short-term mating. There is an evolutionary rationale for men to seek both long-term and short-term mates: with long-term mates they can be more confident in the offspring's paternity and can provide resources to the offspring. With short-term mates they can produce higher numbers of offspring. Women seem to gain more in fitness through long-term mating, since multiple short-term mates will not increase her total number of offspring. However, there are conditions under which short-term mating would also enhance fitness. Men are willing to exchange resources for sex, and it is sometimes to women's advantage to engage in such exchanges (Burley & Symanski, 1981). Another reason for short-term mating is to evaluate men before committing to a long-term relationship. But perhaps the most important situation that would lead women to engage in short-term mating is absence of men who are willing to engage in long-term mating. In evolutionary terms, a woman who engages in short-term mating is more fit that one who engages in no mating at all.

Draper and Belsky (1990) have proposed that the environmental conditions in which children grow up may play a large role in their mating strategy. Children who grow up in father-absent households may early in life develop a "model of the world" (Bowlby, 1969) that includes the expectation that men do not invest in their offspring. As a result, both females and males as adults will tend to engage in short-term, low commitment mating.

A second important point to consider in regard to evolutionary psychology is that behavior that once was adaptive may no longer be. One cannot use the criterion of current reproductive fitness as a way of evaluating these ideas.

Mechanisms that led to survival and reproduction in the ancestral environment continue whether or not they still lead to those outcomes. The best example is sexual intercourse itself. In the natural environment, the desire to have sex led to offspring. Yet today it is possible consciously to break the link between sex and offspring by using birth control. That people continue to have sex while using birth control underlines the premise that people do not now actively seek to increase their reproductive fitness, but rather have feelings and engage in behaviors that once increased fitness in the ancestral environment (Symons, 1992).

Third, we would argue that evolutionary mechanisms that are important for personality exist more as preferences and feelings than as behaviors. In fact, we see a close parallel between evolutionary mechanisms and personality dispositions. Both are inputs to, rather than determinants of, behavior. They bias our perceptions, cause us to react positively or negatively to different stimuli, and motivate us to seek out or avoid different situations. The central role of emotions in evolutionary psychology has often been noted (Buss, 1991; Symons, 1979; Tooby & Cosmides, 1992). It is often said humans are the most emotional of animals. Emotions may be necessary for humans because they serve as "guidance systems" (Tooby & Cosmides, 1992). Our ability to imagine almost anything combined with our ability to accomplish almost as much could be quite lethal. If we were really free of evolutionary mechanisms, what would have prevented our ancestors from doing all sorts of things that actually decreased their fitness? To cite a common example, people know rationally that they should take their medication, yet millions fail to do so. But nobody has to remind us to eat; evolved hunger mechanisms that make us feel bad when we don't eat and good when we do eat solve that problem for us.

GENDER DIFFERENCES AND SIMILARITIES

In this chapter we have emphasized evolutionary psychological accounts of sex differences. To the extent that women and men differ in their desires and perceptions, individuality is partly a result of one's gender. However, evolutionary psychology does not assume that women and men are fundamentally different in most regards. Evolution should produce only differences between the sexes that are relevant to differences in what leads to fitness. Even in the area of mating, women and men share certain major similarities. For example, in Buss's study of mate preferences, both women and men rated the characteristics "kind-understanding" and "intelligent" as more important in choosing a mate than either "good looks" or "good financial prospect." Both sexes want mates who are kind and intelligent. This preference makes perfect sense from an evolutionary perspective, since fitness is enhanced in both sexes by mating with individuals who have these characteristics (Buss, 1989). In areas far removed from mating, there is little reason to expect the sexes to differ psychologically.

SCIENCE AND POLITICS

The evolutionary psychology approach to gender differences is controversial. Some of the criticisms of the evolutionary theories are similar to criticisms likely to be addressed to any scientific theory: Are the arguments for the theory compelling? Is the theory logical and coherent? Does the evidence support the theory? Are there better competing theories available? There are, however, additional arguments that are raised about evolutionary theories when they are applied to human beings. These arguments derive from ideological and political concerns. If men and women differ in part for biological reasons, does this fact justify certain social practices that some people might find abhorrent? Does an evolutionary theory of gender differences justify the "status quo"? To put the matter bluntly, are such theories sexist?

The issues raised by such arguments go beyond the usual scientific criticism and enter a realm of political and ideological controversy in which many scientists prefer not to engage. We do not propose to discuss this matter at length, but we would like to address this kind of criticism briefly. First, many scientists would argue that their task is to discover what is true of the world—knowledge is valuable for its own sake, whatever it may or may not tell us about the world. We do not find this position incorrect. In any case whether one approves or not, it is difficult if not impossible to stop scientific research—people will continue to work on topics that interest them.

Second, many evolutionary theorists believe that whatever is known about evolutionary mechanisms does not necessarily indicate that a particular set of social arrangements or personal behaviors is preordained by our biological characteristics. One need only look at the astonishing variety of social arrangements under which humans have lived to know that no particular one is preordained by our evolutionary heritage. Further, although evolutionary analyses may help explain certain behaviors, they do not justify them in a moral, philosophical, or political sense. As we have stated earlier, the equation of "adaptive" with "good" makes no sense in the contemporary world.

Third, knowledge about the way the world works may provide a useful basis for changing the world. Good science may not provide us with good social policies, but bad science is unlikely to provide us with better social policies. Consider, for example, the suggestion that male jealousy with respect to sexual infidelity is an evolved mechanism. If the theory is true, it might provide us with ways to think about changing this tendency—perhaps by teaching men to deal with their jealousy. We do not know how to do this at present, but a correct understanding of the reasons for a particular form of behavior may be useful if one wishes to change that behavior. Knowledge of evolutionary influences may provide a foundation for changing society.

Let us summarize our position. We do not think that anything we have learned about evolutionary influences justifies any particular social arrangement.

Social policy recommendations derived from evolutionary knowledge have little or nothing to do with the knowledge itself. The ideas of evolutionary psychology may be right or wrong. We think they should be judged as scientific ideas on their merits. If we get the science right, we may have a chance to do something useful with the knowledge we have gained. If the science is wrong, we probably will not get the social policy recommendations right either.

8

Motives and Goals

We began the last chapter by asking a lot of "Why" questions. Evolutionary psychologists' answers to "Why" questions about behavior usually refer to the way the behavior influenced fitness in the ancestral environment. But most "Why" questions about behavior are seeking an answer that doesn't go back that far. The questioners are usually asking what the individual was trying to accomplish by the behavior. Why did you date George rather than Jamal? Why did you major in education? Why did you stay home instead of going out? Why did you cut class? Why do you spend so much time working out? Why are you a vegetarian? Your answers to questions like these probably include something about your motives or goals, that is, what you were trying to accomplish through the behavior. Probably also you hoped that attaining these goals would make you feel good rather than bad. In short, we usually expect that people behave in a certain way in order to achieve some goal or to increase their positive emotions (or decrease their negative emotions). In this chapter we define *motivation* as "internal states that impel people to goal-directed action."

EXPECTANCY-VALUE THEORY

Although answers to "Why" questions about behavior often involve motives and goals—what people want to accomplish—obviously what people want is not the only determinant of their actions. Wanting something to happen does not make it happen. People must have the skills and opportunities to make things happen. The choices people make about where to put their energy and time are based not only on what they want, but on what they think their chances are of getting what they want. This line of thinking is widely accepted in one form or another by many psychologists. What people *want* is closely tied to their affective reactions to different possible outcomes; what people *think* is closely tied to their beliefs about themselves and the world. These beliefs include the likelihood that their actions will produce certain outcomes, which in turn will produce certain effects (Bandura, 1989).

The general idea that both desires and cognitions influence behavioral choices can be expressed by a simple equation that lies at the heart of a class of models called **expectancy-value theory**. What one wants is contained in the idea of "value." Outcomes vary from very positive to very negative. That is, every possible outcome has a **valence**—it is something people want to happen or don't want to happen. For most people, winning a million-dollar lottery has high positive value; winning a hundred-dollar lottery has moderate positive value; winning a one-dollar lottery has low positive value. On the negative valence side, losing a lot of money has a higher negative value than losing a little money. We also have expectancies. The simplest type of expectancy has to do with the likelihood that a particular act will produce a particular outcome. Expectancy-value theory states that people's choices are based on (1) the probability that if they engage in a particular activity, a certain outcome will result (expectancy) and (2) how much that outcome is worth to them (value). The result of these two factors is the **behavioral potential**, that is, the strength of the tendency to engage in the specific behavior.

We said that the theory is expressed in an equation. The equation is: $BP = E \times V$. Behavior potential is a result of the product of expectancy and value. Why the product and not the sum? Think about it. Table 8.1 shows some examples of expectancies and values in career choice for a specific individual. Alex is considering

TABLE 8.1   Expectancy × Value Framework Applied to Pursuing a Career

CAREER	EXPECTANCY[a]	VALUE	BEHAVIOR POTENTIAL ($E \times V$)
Medical doctor	.40	9	3.60
School teacher	.75	6	4.50
Astronaut	.01	10	0.10
Volunteer aide	.95	2	1.80
Professional athlete	.10	9	0.90
Factory worker	.75	4	3.00
Nurse	.50	7	3.50
Politician	.15	9	1.35

[a]Expectancy expressed on a scale from 0.0 to 1.0; Value expressed on a scale from 0 to 10.

various career options. The expectancy column represents Alex's beliefs about his chances of being able to enter that occupation. The value column is a rating of how much he would like to enter that occupation, on a 1-to-10 scale. The behavioral potential column indicates that his tendency to choose "school teacher" is the strongest, while his tendency to choose "astronaut" is the weakest. Even though being an astronaut has the highest value for Alex—he would really love to be an astronaut—he simply does not think it is a realistic option, estimating a one percent chance that he could actually become an astronaut. The multiplication is a crucial aspect of the theory. You can see that the BPs for the different occupations would come out in a very different order if the figures were added.

There is little doubt that expectancies and values are crucial determinants of behavior. Yet there is a legitimate question whether both should be considered part of motivation. The term motivation has been used in psychology in many different ways. For some psychologists, it involves all factors that energize or direct behavior. As expressed in expectancy-value theory, these include both cognitive and affective factors. For others, it is primarily the affective aspect that is involved in motivation. In terms of expectancy-value theory, motivation is primarily the issue of why people value the outcomes that they do. Although the equation treats expectancies and values equally, there is some sense in which value would seem to be the more fundamental answer to the question "Why." Consider an outcome that an individual values but has a low expectancy of accomplishing. In many cases, the individual might be able to take action to change the expectancy. For example, a person who wants very much to become a politician but who has a fear of public speaking might enter therapy to overcome that fear, thus changing the expectancy of reaching the desired outcome. Or a person with a strong value might be on the lookout for opportunities that will alter her expectancies.

For the personality psychologist, value seems particularly important, since it seems to reflect core aspects of individuality. Although both value and expectancy, affect and cognition, are always involved in behavioral choice, an argument can be made for focusing on them as separate, albeit interconnected, sources of individuality. This is the approach we take in this book. This chapter focuses primarily on motives, dealing with such questions as: How many motives do people have? Are people aware of their motives? How can we assess people's motives? How do individual differences in motives contribute to individuality? Chapter 11 focuses on the role of beliefs about the self and the world and on the crucial role of people's explanations for their own successes and failures on future behavior.

WHAT ARE PEOPLE'S MOTIVES?

What motivates people? As is so often the case, answers to this question depend on whether one is looking at small, specific, and immediate units of behavior (often called *molecular* or *microlevel* analysis) or at broader, more general, and longer-term units (often called *molar* or *macrolevel* analysis). At the molecular level, there may be an infinite number of "motives." Why did the person cross the street? To get to the other side. Every behavior a person engages in to produce some outcome has an *intention* associated with it. People can almost always tell you the intention. Furthermore, people's stated intentions have been found to be excellent predictors of their immediate behavior (Ajzen & Fishbein, 1977). Ask people what they are going to do in the next minute, and you will find a very high correlation between what they say and what they do.

Does that mean every action has its own motive attached to it? From the point of view of understanding people's behavior, this approach is unsatisfactory. First of all, it merely shifts the "Why" question from "Why did the person act a certain way?" to "Why did the person have the intention to act a certain way?" Second, stated intentions may be highly related to immediate actions but probably not to actions in the more distant future. As McClelland (1985) noted, "a student's statement that he or she intends to study right now will predict behavior fairly well; the same type of statement applied to 'studying hard next year,' however, should be greeted with some skepticism, because it is not known what attractive alternative courses of action the student will face, whether or not the courses taken will be interesting or not, and so on" (pp. 14–15). McClelland is pointing out that a stated intention takes many determinants of action into account in addition to motives. The farther into the future one goes, the less are people able to anticipate all the factors that will contribute to their actions.

A third reason for doubting the explanatory power of intentions is that while we can ask people about their intentions, it is hard to ask, say, chickens. Yet we all know that they also cross the street to get to the other side. In seeking parsimony, behaviorists have argued that if we don't need the concept of intention for chickens, we don't need it for people either. To say the chicken walked across the street because it wanted to get to the other side is to use circular reasoning. How do we know the chicken intended to get to the other side? Because it just walked across the street. Why did it walk across the street? To get to the other side. In the late nineteenth and early twentieth centuries, many scientists proposed lists of "instincts" to explain human behavior. Bernard (1924) counted about 6,000. Virtually any behavior you can think of was "explained" by naming an instinct for it! This was circular reasoning with a vengeance.

We have rejected the simple idea that intentions are the same as motives and have warned against assigning a motive for every action (McClelland, 1985). Where does that leave our initial question, "What motivates people?" There is, in fact, no empirically based answer to this question. Different theorists have proposed different ideas, some emphasizing the importance of one or two motives, and others proposing many more. Some theorists have emphasized the biological roots of motivation; others have focused on motives that are learned. Some have viewed human motivation as a process that releases tension or energy so that people can

TABLE 8.2   Major Issues in Motivation Theory

1. Number:	One, two, or many?
2. Source:	Biology or learning?
3. Process:	Release of tension, homeostasis, equilibrium or increase of tension, challenge-oriented
4. Aim:	To satisfy selfish desires or to fulfill creative potential
5. Consciousness:	Aware of one's own motives or not aware of them

maintain their equilibrium; others have claimed that humans often go out of their way to increase tension or energy and often seek out difficult challenges. Some theorists see humans as motivated basically by selfish desires; others take a more positive view, emphasizing human growth and creativity. Some believe motives are often unconscious; others think motives are usually conscious (see Table 8.2).

Psychological Hedonism

The question "What do people want?" has perplexed thinkers about the human condition for thousands of years. One rather obvious answer is that people want either to obtain pleasure or to avoid pain, or, to use the language of learning theory, to obtain rewards or to avoid punishments. From this perspective, when you ask "Why did so-and-so do such-and-such?" the answer must always involve one of these two motives. Many philosophers and psychologists have proposed this type of answer, and in some sense it is probably quite accurate. Virtually all behavior can be described as approach (moving toward objects or situations that will satisfy needs, desires, wishes, goals—or will be experienced as pleasurable) or avoidance/withdrawal (moving away from objects or situations that interfere with needs, desires, wishes, goals—or will be experienced as painful) (Lang, Bradley, & Cuthbert, 1992). The idea that motivation is centered around the pursuit of pleasure and avoidance of pain is called **psychological hedonism** (Allport, 1961). We have seen that such a formulation may even underlie some personality traits in that people may differ in their sensitivity to signals of reward or punishment (Gray, 1987).

You might object to this idea by pointing out that people often engage in activities that bring pain and difficulty rather than pleasure. Athletes, for example, often work out to the point of pain; volunteer firemen risk injury or death; individuals committed to a social cause may sacrifice their lives for that cause. More commonly, people often claim they don't like what they are doing, but they do it anyway. Murray (1938) argued that even in these cases, the principles of hedonism are at work: " . . . introspection will reveal that the man is determined (consciously or unconsciously) by thoughts of something unpleasant (pain, criticism, blame, self-depreciation) that might occur if he does not do what he is doing. He goes to the dentist to avoid future pain or disfigurement, he answers his mail in order not to lose social status, and so forth. If it is not the thought of expected unpleasantness that prompts him, it is the thought of expected pleasure, possibly in the very distant future. Visions of heaven after death, for example, have often encouraged men to endure great suffering on earth" (p. 92).

One can also object to the principle of hedonism on the same grounds used in the discussion of intentions. What determines why any particular outcome is pleasurable or painful? In the case of physical pain and pleasure this might not be too difficult to answer, but much human behavior does not have direct physical consequences, especially the behavior of interest to personality psychologists. Psychological pleasure and pain is a murkier area. Why does one person find helping others satisfying? Why does another person find creating artworks enjoyable? Why does a third suffer when speaking in public? One could accept the importance of hedonism and still believe that a finer-grained analysis of human motivation is necessary to understand the sources of psychological rewards and punishments. As we will see, Henry Murray proposed that human motivation can be analyzed into at least twenty different motives, each of which operates according to the principle of hedonism.

FREUD'S THEORY OF MOTIVATION

We begin our discussion of motivation theories with Sigmund Freud's psychoanalytic theory. Freudian psychoanalysis is based fundamentally on conceptions of motivation (Mackay, 1989). Although Freud is not a contemporary theorist, his ideas had a profound influence on the psychology of motivation. An awareness of many of his ideas is part of the intellectual heritage of all personality psychologists, a background that many contemporary writers assume the reader possesses. We too assume that you have some exposure to Freud's ideas; we will not cover all aspects of his thinking here, but rather, will highlight his ideas about motivation. Historically, many other theories of motivation have been proposed either as alternatives to Freud or as elaborations of his basic ideas.

Freud believed that virtually all human behavior is motivated. We said earlier that motivation involves internal states that impel the organism to goal-directed action. By this definition, not all action is motivated. For example, if we ask you to stop what you are doing and just say the first number that comes into your mind, it is obvious that the number you think of was not motivated—it was not based on an internal impulse and had no goal. But Freud felt that this perceived "obviousness" indicates a superficial understanding of the roots of behavior and the nature of human mental life. If one were to go into the matter in depth, a person with suitable training and understanding would discover that even the apparently simplest behaviors often have roots deep in the individual's psyche. In *The Psychopathology of Everyday Life*, Freud (1904/1948) described many types of behaviors that seem unimportant or random on the surface but that, on deeper analysis, reveal motivated behavior. You have probably heard of "Freudian slips." You can find many examples of these in "bloopers." Many years ago the slogan for Wonder Bread was "Wonder Bread—for the best in bread." In one famous blooper, the announcer said instead: "Wonder Bread—for the breast in bed." For Freud, such slips often reveal real wishes that people either are trying to keep private or may not be aware of themselves. These wishes are the result of basic impulses that are unacceptable to society, especially those concerning sex and aggression. These impulses push for expression and, despite people's attempts to keep them down, often come out in disguised form, such as slips of the tongue, lapses of memory, accidents, and misperceptions. They also are expressed in neurotic symptoms and in dreams and fantasies.

To get a flavor of how seemingly random behavior can reveal deep motives, consider the following excerpt from *The Psychopathology of Everyday Life:*

> I shall tarry a little longer at the analysis of chance numbers, for I know no other individual observation which would so readily demonstrate the existence of highly organized thinking processes of which consciousness has no knowledge . . . I shall therefore report the analysis of a chance number of one of my patients. . . .
>
> While in a particularly happy mood he let the number 426,718 come to his mind, and put to himself the question, "Well, what does it bring to your mind?" First came a joke he had heard: "If your catarrh of the nose is treated it lasts 42 days, if it is not treated it lasts—6 weeks." This corresponds to the first digit of the number ($42 = 6 \times 7$). During the obstruction that followed this first solution I called his attention to the fact that the number of six digits selected by him contains all the first numbers except 3 and 5. He at once found the continuation of his solution:
>
> "We were altogether 7 children, I was the youngest. Number 3 in the order of the children corresponds to my sister A., and 5 to my brother L.; both of them were my enemies. As a child I used to pray to the Lord every night that He should take out of my life these two tormenting spirits. It seems to me that I have fulfilled for myself this wish '3' and '5,' the *evil* brother and the hated sister, are omitted."
>
> "If the number stands for your sisters and brothers, what significance is there to 18 at the end? You were altogether only 7."
>
> "I often thought if my father had lived longer I should not have been the youngest child. If one more would have come, we should have been 8, and there would have been a younger child, toward whom I could have played the role of the older one."
>
> With this the number was explained, but we still wished to find the connection to the first part of the interpretation and the part following it. This came very readily from the condition required for the last digits—if the father had lived longer. $42 = 6 \times 7$ signifies the ridicule directed against the doctors who could not help the father, and in this way expresses the wish for the continued existence of the father. The whole number really corresponds to the fulfillment of his two wishes in reference to his family circle—namely, that both the evil brother and sister should die and that another little child should follow him. Or, briefly expressed: *If only these two had died in place of my father.* (Freud, 1904/1948, pp. 134–135)

Although Freud changed his ideas over the course of his life, he always believed that human motivation was based on a very small number of drives or instincts. By the end of his life in 1938 he had come to classify the basic motives of human beings as the **life instinct (Eros) and the death instinct (Thanatos)** (Freud, 1940/1949). Freud believed that his ideas were grounded in basic biological and evolutionary principles. The life instinct was in the service of the species. It involved sex, love, and human bonding. The death instinct (which he also called the *destructive instinct*) represented the tendency of all living things to return to complete inactivity and dissolution. The overarching principle of motivation for Freud was the **pleasure principle:** " . . . [people] strive after happiness; they want to become happy and to remain so. This endeavor has two sides, a positive and a negative aim. It aims, on the one hand, at an absence of pain and unpleasure, and, on the other, at the experiencing of strong feelings of pleasure . . . the purpose of life is simply the programme of the pleasure principle" (1930/1961, p. 23).

For Freud, pleasure occurs when tension is released or reduced. The most intense pleasure, according to Freud, is based on bodily sensations—the pleasure of eating when hungry, eliminating when one "has the urge," having an orgasm after a buildup of genital tension. These bodily impulses comprise what Freud labeled the **id.** The id is made up of the basic biological instincts forged by evolution. It is a portion of the mind that is unconscious, primitive, and demanding of immediate gratification of biological urges. Freud labeled the energy of the id **libido;** he believed that the discharge of libido was the key to human psychology.

According to Freud, the complexity of the human mind was built on the idea that immediate gratification of impulses—of id-based wishes—was an impossibility for human beings. What set us apart from other animals, who had similar instincts, was that we live in civilization, and civilization requires that such instincts be suppressed and molded into acceptable forms. The **ego** is the aspect of the mind that takes reality into account. Operating by the **reality principle,** the ego attempts to satisfy the impulses of the id in a way that would not result in increased pain rather than pleasure. In a social world, the person who tries to gratify every wish instantly will not thrive. The id, which is nonrational and knows only what it wants, cannot deal with the demands of reality. In addition, society, via the parents, inculcates in people sets of rules—"thou shalt nots" as well as images of what ideally one ought to be and do—that further limit the ability of the id to gratify instinctual impulses. The portion of the mind devoted to following the rules of society was labeled by Freud the **superego.** When the person transgresses, the superego is able to turn some of the instinctual energy against the individual, who then experiences guilt. The interactions of these tendencies—biological instincts, the demands of reality, and the demands of society—produce a complex drama of conflict and deception, mostly self-deception, as the individual attempts to satisfy id impulses while taking both reality and society into account.

We have said that for Freud the most powerful human instincts involved sex and aggression. Freud's view of humanity was not very positive. He was in a long tradition of thinkers from Plato onward who saw humans as basically brutish creatures who needed to be tamed by civilization. Today we often identify this view with the Enlightenment philosopher Thomas Hobbes, who felt that left to their own devices, humans would murder, rape, steal, do whatever they wished to satisfy their brutish desires. This is not a popular point of view in the late twentieth century. Yet in recent years we have seen the horrors of genocide in Rwanda and ethnic cleansing in Bosnia. Individual acts of murder and atrocity blare across our headlines every day. Human history is full of unspeakable cruelty. Freud believed that human beings were at their core creatures of selfish passions. After witnessing the carnage of World War I, he found it self-evident that

> . . . the inclination to aggression is an original, self-subsisting instinctual disposition in man. (1930/1961, p. 69)

> . . . men are not gentle creatures who want to be loved, and who at the most can defend themselves if they are attacked; they are, on the contrary, creatures among whose instinctual endowments is to be reckoned a powerful share of aggressiveness. As a result, their neighbor is for them not only a potential helper or sexual object, but also someone who tempts them to satisfy their aggressiveness on him, to exploit his capacity for work without compensation, to use him sexually without his consent, to seize his possessions, to humiliate him, to cause him pain, to torture and to kill him. . . . Who, in the face of all his experience of life and of history, will have the courage to dispute this assertion?" (p. 58)

Selfish passions also lie at the heart of the life instinct, according to Freud. Human sexual impulses push for satisfaction. As Westen (1990) has put it: "Psychoanalysis repeatedly leads one to think about what one does not wish to think about. It is an approach to personality that one does not care to discuss with one's mother" (p. 53). In Freud's time and social milieu, respectable, "civilized" people did not indulge their sexual and aggressive impulses; self-control was strongly encouraged (despite the fact that beneath the surface of social respectability there was a vigorous trade in prostitution and pornography). As a result, people's sexual and aggressive feelings were subject to a great deal of pressure not to be directly expressed. Freud believed that most people **repress** these impulses and the wishes that accompany them. But repression does not make them go away; it merely keeps them out of consciousness. The impulses still express themselves in various ways, from works of art to neurotic symptoms, to dreams, slips of the tongue, and, under the proper conditions, to overt actions. But Freud believed that for most people they produced anxiety—feelings of dread that unacceptable impulses in us are pushing for action. So in addition to having these basic instincts, people are also motivated to try to reduce the accompanying anxiety. The **defense mechanisms** represent strategies, almost always unconscious, to prevent anxiety from becoming overwhelming.

Freud's ideas about motivation touch on all of the issues in Table 8.2. He attempted to reduce the number of basic motives to a small number. He viewed motivation as coming from innate, biological processes. He conceived of motivation as the release or reduction of tension and the restoration of homeostasis. The aim of motives was entirely selfish; even "noble" motives could be shown to reflect the selfish desires of the id. Most of our deepest motives come from the unconscious, and we expend a great deal of energy making sure they remain there.

HENRY MURRAY

If Freud was the most influential theorist emphasizing a small number of basic motives, Henry Murray was the most influential theorist emphasizing that human behavior requires a larger number of motives to be comprehended. Much of Murray's thinking on motivation is contained in a landmark book published in 1938, *Explorations in Personality*. Murray believed that people differed in the strength of different motives. By categorizing and assessing each person's motives (along with other cognitive and affective variables), Murray felt it would be possible to provide a comprehensive picture of the personality.

Murray and his colleagues intensively studied 54 college men, using a wide variety of assessments including standardized questionnaires, projective tests, interviews, autobiographies, and observations of behavior. He and his collaborators developed a list of needs that seemed to cover all of the motivational tendencies to be found in this sample of men. Table 8.3 provides a list of the needs along with brief descriptions. Notice that some of the needs, such as Sex and Harmavoidance, are "bodily" or what Murray called *viscerogenic needs* in contrast with *psychogenic needs*. Notice also that viscerogenic needs such as eating or drinking are not included in this list, not because they are unimportant for survival, but because Murray believed they played a minor role in individuality: everybody needs air and water but not everybody has an equally strong need for sex or avoidance of pain. In addition, the needs that are most important for understanding personality are those whose satisfaction cannot be "taken for granted." In contrast to the need for air, the need for sex "ordinarily depends upon the co-operation of another person, is commonly interfered with by rivals, is highly unstable, and is hemmed in by all kinds of social restrictions. This is enough to account for its importance" (Murray, 1938, p. 79).

Murray defined needs as hypothetical constructs that represent forces in the person that influence perception, fantasy, thought, intention, and behavior by seeking to transform "unsatisfying situations" to "satisfying situations." Needs are "provoked" by **press**. Press are actual or imagined features of the environment that may benefit or harm the individual. Different needs are provoked by different press, and the strength of the aroused need is determined by the power of the press to harm or benefit the individual. To understand the relationship between needs and press, let's look at Murray's description of one of the needs: *n* Dominance (Murray used a small *n* to indicate needs, a small *p* to indicate press).

n Dominance (*n* Dom)

Desires and effects of n Dom: To control one's human environment. To influence or direct the behavior of others by suggestion, seduction, persuasion, or command. To dissuade, restrain, or prohibit. To induce others to act in a way that accords with one's sentiments and needs. To get others to cooperate. To convince others of the "rightness" of one's opinion.

Press: Others who are of lower status or inferior in some way; or who are deferential, compliant, or willing to take blame; or who are of higher status or superior in some way; or who exhibit dominance or rivalry.

TABLE 8.3   Illustrative List of Murray's Needs (Based on Murray, 1938)

NEED	BRIEF DESCRIPTION
Abasement	To submit passively to external force. To accept injury, blame, criticism, or punishment. To surrender. To become resigned to fate. To admit inferiority, error, wrongdoing, or defeat. To confess and atone. To blame, belittle, or mutilate the self. To seek and enjoy pain, punishment, illness, and misfortune.
Achievement	To accomplish something difficult. To master, manipulate, or organize physical objects, human beings, or ideas. To do this as rapidly and as independently as possible. To overcome obstacles and attain a high standard. To excel oneself. To rival and surpass others. To increase self-regard by the successful exercise of talent.
Affiliation	To draw near and enjoyably cooperate or reciprocate with an allied other (an other who resembles the subject or who likes the subject). To please and win affection of a cathected object. To adhere and remain loyal to a friend.
Aggression	To overcome opposition forcefully. To fight. To revenge an injury. To attack, injure, or kill another. To oppose forcefully or punish another.
Autonomy	To get free, shake off restraint, break out of confinement. To resist coercion and restriction. To avoid or quit activities prescribed by domineering authorities. To be independent and free to act according to impulse. To be unattached, irresponsible. To defy convention.
Counteraction	To master or make up for a failure by restriving. To obliterate a humiliation by resumed action. To overcome weaknesses, to repress fear. To efface a dishonor by action. To search for obstacles and difficulties to overcome. To maintain self-respect and pride on a high level.
Defendance	To defend the self against assault, criticism, and blame. To conceal or justify a misdeed, failure, or humiliation. To vindicate the ego.
Deference	To admire and support a superior. To praise, honor, or eulogize. To yield eagerly to the influence of an allied other. To emulate an exemplar. To conform to custom.
Dominance	To control one's human environment. To influence or direct the behavior of others by suggestion, seduction, persuasion, or command. To dissuade, restrain, or prohibit.
Exhibition	To make an impression. To be seen and heard. To excite, amaze, fascinate, entertain, shock, intrigue, amuse, or entice others.
Harmavoidance	To avoid pain, physical injury, illness, and death. To escape from a dangerous situation. To take precautionary measures.
Infavoidance	To avoid humiliation. To quit embarrassing situations or to avoid conditions that may lead to belittlement: the scorn, derision, or indifference of others. To refrain from action because of the fear of failure.
Nurturance	To give sympathy and gratify the needs of a helpless object: an infant or any object that is weak, disabled, tired, inexperienced, infirm, defeated, humiliated, lonely, dejected, sick, mentally confused. To assist an object in danger. To feed, help, support, console, protect, comfort, nurse, heal.
Order	To put things in order. To achieve cleanliness, arrangement, organization, balance, neatness, tidiness, and precision.
Play	To act for "fun" without further purpose. To like to laugh and make jokes. To seek enjoyable relaxation of stress. To participate in games, sports, dancing, drinking parties, cards.
Rejection	To separate oneself from a negatively cathected object. To exclude, abandon, expel, or remain indifferent to an inferior object. To snub or jilt an object.
Sentience	To seek and enjoy sensuous impressions.
Sex	To form and further an erotic relationship. To have sexual intercourse.
Succorance	To have one's needs gratified by the sympathetic aid of an allied object. To be nursed, supported, sustained, surrounded, protected, loved, advised, guided, indulged, forgiven, consoled. To remain close to a devoted protector. To always have a supporter.
Understanding	To ask or answer general questions. To be interested in theory. To speculate, formulate, analyze, and generalize.

Notice that the press consist of people either who provide an opportunity for *n* Dom to be satisfied or who are threats to the satisfaction of *n* Dom. When either type is encountered, *n* Dom may be aroused. When none of these press are perceived in the situaiton, *n* Dom will not be aroused. The strength of the press and the strength of the need both contribute to whether or not the need will be aroused. Some situations contain such powerful press that virtually anyone will have the relevant need aroused. For example, *n* Sex may be aroused in most people by the seductive behavior of an attractive individual. Some individuals may have such a strong need that even very weak press may arouse the need. For example, a person with a very strong *n* Sex might have the need aroused by the mere presence of another person.

In Murray's view, needs are essentially unconscious. People may know what they find attractive or unattractive, rewarding or punishing, pleasant or unpleasant, but they may not know that the reason for these reactions is a need within them. In other words, they have no direct knowledge of *why* they react as they do. A person may feel good helping another but not realize that the other is a press that has aroused his *n* Dom, which he is satisfying by helping (thereby placing himself in the dominant position relative to the other person). When an action does satisfy a need, it becomes part of a "complex" or "thema" associating the press, need, and action. Such themas are stored in memory and can be activated by a variety of external stimuli and internal cognitive activities.

Once a need is aroused, it tends to persist until satisfied. However, not all needs are easily satisfied, and those that are not may remain latent. A need that can be satisfied leads to "overt behavior (physical or verbal) that seriously engages itself with real objects. It is latent (unmanifested, subjectified, inhibited, covert or imaginal) when it does not lead to serious overt behavior, but takes the form of desire, resolutions for the future, fantasy, dreaming, play, artistic creation, watching or reading about the exhibition of the need in others" (Murray, 1938, pp. 252–253). Murray believed that many needs are latent and that a thorough understanding of personality requires a way of assessing these needs. The fact that needs are often unconscious and latent led Murray to emphasize the importance of indirect means of assessing them.

The Thematic Apperception Test

In the intensive study of 54 men reported in *Explorations in Personality,* many methods of obtaining information were employed. Murray felt that the most productive methods were those modeled on the psychoanalytic technique of **free association.** Freud believed that the true sources of people's behavior and feelings are unconscious, so the analyst needed ways of getting at material that patients could not directly express. Free association and dream analysis were based on the idea that important information would be expressed when patients were least able to guard against threatening, unconscious material. Another way of getting people to express such material is to focus their attention on an ambiguous, external stimulus and describe what they see. The best known example of such a **projective technique** is the Rorschach inkblot test. Murray used these ideas to develop the *Thematic Apperception Test* (TAT). To quote Murray:

> The test is based upon the well-recognized fact that when a person interprets an ambiguous social situation he is apt to expose his own personality as much as the phenomenon to which he is attending. Absorbed in his attempt to explain the objective occurrence, he becomes naively unconscious of himself and of the scrutiny of others and, therefore, defensively less vigilant. To one with double hearing, however, he is disclosing certain inner tendencies and cathexes: wishes, fears, and traces of past experiences." (p. 531)

Subjects were shown a series of pictures of people in ambiguous situations or relationships and were asked to make up stories about the pictures. The pictures included a person with whom the subjects could identify (i.e., of same gender and similar age). The instructions were as follows:

> This is a test of your creative imagination. I shall show you a picture and I want you to make up a plot or story for which it might be used as an illustration. What is the relation of the individuals in the picture? What has happened to them? What are their present thoughts and feelings? What will be the outcome? Do your very best. Since I am asking you to indulge your literary imagination you may make your story as long and as detailed as you wish." (p. 532)

What was revealed by these stories? Because Murray and his colleagues had information from many other sources about the subjects, it was possible to get an idea where these stories came from. There were "four chief sources from which the items of the plots were drawn: (1) books and moving pictures; (2) actual events in which a friend or member of the family participated; (3) experiences (subjective or objective) in the subject's own life; (4) the subject's conscious and unconscious fantasies" (Murray, 1938, p. 533). Murray noted that all of these could be revealing about the subject's personality. The books, movies, and events that were recalled were not a random sample of those the person had experienced. Rather they were just those experiences that made the deepest impression and persisted in memory, presumably because they reflected in some way the subject's own "preoccupations."

Murray and his colleagues used the TAT stories to help them understand the needs and other personality characteristics of their subjects. The goal of this research was to produce a "biography" of each subject. This biography would differ from usual biographies in that it was based on systematic material gathered from the subjects themselves which would be discussed and interpreted by a panel of experienced, sensitive experts. Murray called this approach **personology.** Although he believed that these biographies fell "short of the portrayal of personality in good literature," he saw their strength as making "matters which novelists only suggestively touch upon, explicitly intelligible" (p. 608).

CONTEMPORARY RESEARCH ON NEEDS

Some psychologists today believe that personology is a viable and important aspect of personality psychology. Yet, as we discussed in chapter 1, the more traditional view of science is that progress is gauged by our ability to make generalizations that can help us understand many cases. Murray and his colleagues certainly intended to do this. By creating coherent and meaningful biographies, they tried to show that their constructs and methods were useful for understanding the subjects. Yet another traditional aspect of scientific inquiry is skepticism. We have a right (perhaps a duty) to ask: "How do you know? What is your evidence?" In the case of *Explorations in Personality,* the evidence is entirely subjective. How do we know that the biographies are accurate, or that constructs such as needs really are useful in understanding people? How do we know that the interpretations of TAT stories tell us about the individual who told the story rather than the psychologist who interpreted it?

In the late 1940s and early 1950s a number of psychologists attempted to subject some of Murray's ideas to more rigorous research. Their first task was to come up with a method for measuring needs. Like Murray, they believed that needs should emerge in fantasies such as stories told to TAT pictures. They first sought to demonstrate that this basic assumption was correct. To do this, they decided to manipulate a need experimentally and then compare the TAT stories of subjects in whom the need had been aroused with stories told by subjects in whom the need had not been aroused. They selected a need that is relatively easy to arouse: the need for food (Atkinson & McClelland, 1948). Subjects were sailors serving at a submarine base. The sailors wrote stories to TAT-type cards under one of three conditions: one hour after they last ate, four hours after they last ate, or sixteen hours after they last ate. Analysis of the stories indicated that the hungrier sailors' stories differed from those of the less hungry sailors primarily in references to hunger and to objects associated with preparing food or eating, such as plates and forks. Interestingly, there was no difference in fantasies that actually involved the act of eating. Atkinson and McClelland concluded that the stories did not represent "wish-fulfillment" in the Freudian sense, but rather the subjects' preoccupation with activity relevant to the goal of eating.

The next step was much more difficult: how to come up with a method for scoring the presence of psychogenic needs that did not depend on subjective interpretations and could be shown to be valid. The food study provided a possible solution. If a way could be found to arouse a specific psychogenic need, it should be possible to arouse the need in some subjects and not others, and then compare their TAT stories. If this was done a number of times with a number of different samples and different ways of arousing the need, then it might be possible to derive a scoring system empirically by noting how the stories of people in whom the need was aroused differed from the stories of people in whom the need was not aroused.

MOTIVE INCENTIVES

Over the past 40 years, David McClelland, John Atkinson, and their students have pursued research on a subset of the needs described by Murray. In a moment we will describe theory and research on four such needs: the need for achievement, the need for power, the need for affiliation, and the need for intimacy. In order to understand this work, we must discuss the crucial concept of **incentives.** Each need or motive is defined by the incentives that satisfy it, or, to put it in terms of psychological hedonism, by the occurrences that increase positive affect or decrease negative affect. The existence of an incentive is inferred from the affect that accompanies it. For example, McClelland (1985) argued that "consistency" is a natural incentive for humans. He inferred this from the fact that people seem to find various inconsistencies unpleasant and often seek to resolve them. Social psychologists have studied consistency in many different guises. For example, the well-known work on **cognitive dissonance** is based on the premise that people find inconsistencies between their beliefs and their behaviors to be unpleasant. Direct evidence that people find such inconsistencies unpleasant has recently been provided by Elliot and Devine (1994).

The relationship between motives and incentives is sometimes clear-cut (for example, what is the incentive for need for food? Food!). However, for complex **social motives** such as achievement, the incentives that satisfy them are not always so obvious. For example, one might think of money as an incentive, yet money can symbolically represent many different incentives (McClelland, 1985). Huge amounts of money might be an incentive for the power motive, increasing amounts of money for performance might be an incentive for the achievement motive, a gift of money might be an incentive for the affiliation motive. As we discuss the social motives of achievement, power, affiliation and intimacy, we will see how these issues are important in understanding the role of motives in individuality.

ACHIEVEMENT MOTIVATION

We said that the incentives for social motives are not always obvious. Unlike hunger and sex, "social motives" are hypothetical constructs, or, as Murray put it "convenient fictions." To state what the incentives are for the need for achievement is to invent a *theory* of what you mean by "need for achievement." The usefulness of the theory is then evaluated as to its ability to help us understand the phenomena on which it focuses. McClelland (1985) states that the primary incentive of the need for achievement is "doing something better" (p. 228). In other words, McClelland is suggesting that an important human incentive is "doing something better," and he is labeling the motive that is served by that incentive "need for achievement." People who have a strong need for achievement are people who get positive feelings from doing something better. Saying that "doing something better" is the incentive for the "need for achievement" is a theoretical statement, not a statement of fact.

What does McClelland mean by "doing something better"? He rightly points out that people often "do better" for a variety of reasons, such as pleasing one's parents or teachers, maintaining a positive self-image, or finishing a job in order to have more leisure time. These cases all involve different incentives and different motives. A person who "does something better" to please a parent is satisfying a different need than is a person who "does something better" to have more leisure time. "Doing something better" becomes an achievement incentive only when *it is done for its own sake:* when the goal is "success in competition with some standard of excellence" (McClelland, Atkinson, Clark, & Lowell, 1953/1992). That competition may be with another person, with oneself, or with an internal notion of what constitutes "doing something better."

As was mentioned above, the strategy used by McClelland, Atkinson, and their colleagues for developing a way of scoring individual differences in motives was to arouse the motive experimentally in some subjects and not in others and then to discover empirically how their TAT stories differed. The key to arousing *n* Achievement was setting up situations in which the hypothesized incentives for the motive were present. In the first studies, Atkinson and McClelland used a variety of situational factors. Subjects were told that a set of tasks involved an important cognitive ability. In some cases false norms were given to produce an illusion that the subjects had done either very well or very poorly on the tasks. A different group of subjects were told their performance on the tasks didn't matter because the experimenters were only trying to find out some things about the tasks themselves, which were in a preliminary stage of development. TAT stories told under achievement-arousing conditions were very different from those told under the relaxed conditions of the second group, particularly with regard to elements involving "doing something better," such as whether a character in the story anticipated positive feelings at success, behaved in a way to promote success, and showed a capacity to overcome obstacles on the way to accomplishment (Atkinson, 1982; Koestner & McClelland, 1990). Over the next few years, a number of investigators replicated these basic findings in a variety of samples in the United States and elsewhere (Atkinson, 1982).

Scoring Need for Achievement

The differences in TAT stories told under arousing versus relaxed conditions became the basis of a coding manual, a set of instructions for scoring the need for achievement (McClelland, Atkinson, Clark, & Lowell, 1953). An individual's *n* Achievement score is based on a **content analysis** of stories told in response to a standard set of TAT-type pictures. In evaluating each story, the coder first decides whether it includes achievement imagery, that is, whether it contains references to success in competition with some standard of excellence, unique accomplishments, or long-term involvement with an achievement goal. Specific examples of each of these is provided in the manual along with discussion of what story characteristics meet scoring criteria and what do not. Examples of elements that meet the scoring criteria for achievement imagery are given in Table 8.4. If a story contains at least

TABLE 8.4   Examples of Achievement Imagery Used in Scoring for the Achievement Motive (Based on McClelland et al., 1992)

The scorer must first decide if the story contains any reference to an achievement goal, that is, success in competition with some standard of excellence. An achievement goal may be inferred by the scorer in the absence of an explicit statement of such a goal.

1. *Competition with an explicit or implicit standard of excellence:* "He wants to prove that he is capable of making minor repairs." "The boy wins the essay contest and feels proud." "She feels bad that she didn't study harder and decides she will do so in the future." "He is studiously and carefully preparing his homework."

Illustrative story: "An operation is taking place. The persons are the doctor, patient, nurse, and a student. The patient must have been sick at one time to be on the table. The student is observing the doctor doing his job along with the nurse. The doctor is concentrating on his work. The student is attending the doctor's movements, the nurse probably thinking about her boyfriend. *A good job is wanted by the doctor* and student. The doctor will complete the operation, give a lecture on it, the student will ask questions on the work, the nurse will take off on her other duties."

2. *Unique accomplishment:* "She is writing a book that will be hailed as a breakthrough in medieval scholarship."

Illustrative story: "The boss is talking to an employee. The boss has some special job that he wants done, and this man is an expert in that particular phase. The boss wants the employee, and engineer, to start working on a *specially designed carburetor for a revolutionary engine.* The employee is thinking out the problem. The job will come off okay, and the engine will *revolutionize* the automobile industry."

3. *Long-term involvement:* "He is studying in order to get into a top medical school."

Illustrative story: "A boy, Jim Neilson, 18 years old, is *taking an examination for entrance in the Army Air Corps.* He has studied very hard in high school *hoping all along that he will some day be a fighter pilot.* Now that he sees how difficult the examination is, he is very worried that he may fail it. He is thinking so much about his failing it, he cannot concentrate on the test itself. He will just barely pass the test and will later become a cadet, then a pilot."

Reproduced with permission of Cambridge University Press.

one such element, additional aspects of the story are evaluated further, such as whether there is an explicit statement of a character in the story wanting to reach an achievement goal ("He wants to be a doctor"), whether characters in the story engage in activities to further achievement goals ("He will study hard to pass the medical boards"), whether a character anticipates success or failure ("He feels the teacher will give him an A"; "He worries that the paper might not be good enough"), whether there are obstacles to success ("His paper was almost done when the computer crashed"), whether the plot of the story centers on achievement (called a "thema"), as well as other elements.

The subject's *n* Achievement score is simply the total number of elements that meet the criteria specified in the twenty-page coding manual. It should be evident that coding a story for achievement (or any other) motivation is not a simple matter. The manual is long and detailed in order to provide the different coders with a common and specific set of criteria, allowing for intercoder reliability. Although it takes some time to learn to score the stories, trained scorers show high levels of agreement (reliability coefficients ranging from .85 to .95) (McClelland, 1985).

The coding manual can be used to assess whether different situations arouse *n* Achievement in randomly assigned subjects, or it can be used (under neutral conditions) to assess individual differences in **motive dispositions,** defined by McClelland (1985) as a "recurrent concern about a goal state that drives, orients, and selects behavior." The coding manual can also be used for verbal materials other than TAT stories. In fact, any verbal material can be coded for achievement (as well as for other motives). As we will see, the flexibility of content analysis methods has permitted psychologists to study historical figures as well as college sophomores.

The theory of achievement motivation states that people with high *n* Achievement should have that need aroused under certain conditions but not under others. French (1955) provided three different incentives for subjects to perform well on a digit-symbol substitution task. One group of subjects was told in a casual, friendly way: "We are just experimenting today and we appreciate your cooperation very much. We want to find out what kind of scores people make on these tests." A second group was told in a formal and serious manner that the test involved "a critical ability—the ability to deal quickly and accurately with unfamiliar material. It is related to general intelligence and will be related to your future career. Each man should try to perform as well as possible." A third group was told that "the five men who make the best scores in five minutes will be allowed to leave right away—the others will have more practice periods and more tests."

What were the incentives in these three situations? Certainly the second condition embodies McClelland et al.'s ideas of what ought to arouse achievement motivation, since the incentive for "doing better" is clearly evident. The other two conditions would not appear to involve this incentive.

How do you think people high in *n* Achievement would perform in each of these three conditions? If "doing something better" really is the key incentive for people high in *n* Achievement, they ought to perform best in that condition, compared with people low in *n* Achievement. To test this prediction, the motives of all

TABLE 8.5   Digit-Symbol Performance of Subjects Hight or Low in *n* Achievement Under Three Different Incentive Conditions (Based on French, 1955)

Performance Incentive	AVERAGE DIGIT-SYMBOL PERFORMANCE	
	Low *n* Achievement	High *n* Achievement
"To please experimenter"	15.4	17.7
"To demonstrate intelligence"	16.7	29.8
"To leave early"	22.5	18.2

Reproduced with permission of the American Psychological Association.

the subjects were scored. Table 8.5 shows how they performed. Those high in *n* Achievement performed much better when they were told that the task tested their ability; in the other conditions they performed about the same as subjects low in *n* Achievement. Only in the second condition did the incentive arouse their achievement motive and lead to increased performance.

The "fit" between incentive and motivation was also evident in another aspect of this study. Imaginative stories were also coded for the *affiliation motive* (see section on this motive later in the chapter). French (1955) argued that pleasing the experimenter would function as an incentive for people high in *n* Affiliation. The results supported this hypothesis: in the "Please experimenter" condition, the correlation between *n* Affiliation and digit-symbol performance was a significant .48; in the other two conditions, it was near zero. Thus, whether a motive will influence performance on a task depends on the way the task is presented, and specifically what incentives are perceived by subjects. People's motives must "contact" relevant incentives before they can have an impact on behavior.

Natural Incentives for *n* Achievement

In the French (1955) study, the same task was linked to different incentives (and hence different motives) through the use of different instructions. However, life is (we hope) not an experiment. The incentives in situations are usually inherent in the situation itself, not arbitrarily imposed by an experimenter. What are some characteristics of situations that provide incentives for people high in *n* Achievement? What characteristics of a task might be particularly important for the incentive "doing something better"? Two aspects that have received a good deal of research attention are how easy or difficult the task is and whether the task provides feedback about how well the person is doing on it.

> Before you continue reading, go over to a wastepaper basket and place it at one end of a hallway. Now find a piece of scrap paper and roll it up into a ball. Go into the hallway and toss the paper ball into the wastepaper basket. After you are done, continue reading.

Although you might not have realized it, you had to make a choice about how far away from the basket you stood when you tossed the paper ball. If you stood right up next to the basket, you probably got the ball in. If you stood all the way at the end of the hall, you probably didn't. Why would a person choose to stand close up, far away, or somewhere in between? Atkinson and Litwin (1960) used a ring toss game (where the task is to toss a ring over a peg) to examine people's "risk-taking" preferences. The subjects could stand anywhere from 1 to 15 feet from the peg. The most preferred distance was about 9 to 11 feet. Why do you think this was the case? One possibility is that in this type of situation, subjects will try to maximize their positive affect and minimize their negative affect (Atkinson, 1964). Who would be more likely to experience positive affect (i.e., pride) when tossing a ringer? Subjects who stood right next to the peg were not likely to jump up and down if they tossed a ringer, but subjects who tossed a ringer from 15 feet might well feel a rush of pride. So why didn't everyone stand 15 feet away? Recall what we said earlier about expectancy-value theory. If the object is to maximize positive affect, there are two basic things one needs to take into account: the affect that the act will produce (value) and the probability that the act will produce the desired outcome (expectancy). So even though tossing a ringer from 15 feet would produce the highest positive affect, the chances that a subject could actually do it is pretty remote. By choosing a moderately difficult level of challenge, subjects increase their chances of actually experiencing positive affect.

Atkinson and Litwin (1960) measured n Achievement from brief essays written by subjects and also obtained scores from a self-report measure of anxiety about test taking. They assumed that the choice of distance from the peg would be influenced by both of these characteristics. People high in n Achievement should be particularly sensitive to the aspects of the situation relevant to their motive and thus be particularly likely to choose a level of challenge that would maximize their positive affect. Atkinson and Litwin called this the "motive to approach success." What would the effects of test anxiety be in this situation? Atkinson and Litwin assumed that people scoring high in test anxiety would be more focused on failure than on success, that their goal would be to avoid the negative affect resulting from failure. Atkinson and Litwin described people high in test anxiety as having a high "motive to avoid failure." In choosing their distance from the peg, these subjects might not find a realistic challenge particularly appealing; they might instead want to choose either a closer distance (thereby increasing the chances that they won't fail) or a farther distance (so they could blame their failure on the task difficulty rather than their own lack of ability).

By measuring both n Achievement and test anxiety, Atkinson and Litwin were able to classify subjects into four groups: high n Ach, low test anxiety; high n Ach, high test anxiety; low n Ach, high test anxiety; low n Ach, low test anxiety. Figure 8.1 shows the percentage of shots that subjects in each group took at each distance from the peg. While subjects in all groups preferred intermediate distances, this preference was particularly strong for subjects high in n Ach and low in test anxiety. Several other studies have also shown that people high in n Ach have a greater

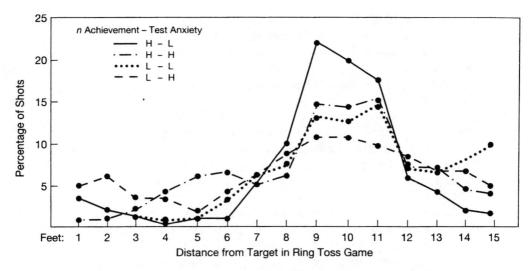

FIGURE 8.1   Percentage of shots taken from each line for subjects classified as High or Low simultaneously in *n* Achievement and Test Anxiety. H – L (*n* = 13); H – H (*n* = 10); L – L (*n* = 9), L – H (*n* = 13). (Based on Atkinson and Litwin, 1960; reproduced with permission of the American Psychological Association.)

preference for tasks of intermediate difficulty or moderate levels of risk than do people low in *n* Ach (McClelland, 1985; Weiner, 1992). There is also evidence that people high in *n* Ach work harder and perform better at such tasks than they do at either very easy or very difficult tasks (Karabenick & Yousseff, 1968; McClelland, 1985).

Affect or Information?

Moderate difficulty or risk appeals to those high in *n* Ach because it maximizes the positive affect they experience from success. In Murray's terms, moderate risk is a press for *n* Achievement because it allows the person to experience positive affect for success.

There is another way of looking at preference for moderate risk. If the incentive for the achievement motive is "doing something better," it is necessary that individuals have some way of assessing whether or not they are doing something better. Weiner (1980) argued that intermediate task difficulty optimizes the opportunities for an evaluation of one's performance. What do you learn about your ring-tossing ability if you stand too close or too far from the peg? Nothing. To find out about your ring-tossing ability, you should choose a distance at which you are not sure whether you can hit the peg. In this view, choice reflects a cognitive rather than an affective process: people high in *n* Ach choose intermediate risks because intermediate levels of difficulty tend to be most informative, or "diagnostic," not because they are looking to maximize their feelings of pride.

A study like Atkinson and Litwin's cannot tease these two explanations apart because the intermediate choice maximizes both information and affect. Studies that have separated task difficulty from diagnosticity (for example, by informing subjects that a very difficult or easy task is a more valid measure of an ability than is a task of moderate difficulty) suggest that people prefer tasks that provide information about their abilities regardless of the difficulty level (Trope, 1986). Since these are usually confounded, the greater preference of people high in *n* Ach for moderate challenge could reflect the desire for feedback about their abilities. Although this finding might appear to indicate that the incentive for *n* Ach is purely cognitive, that would not be a necessary conclusion. Trope points out that feedback about one's abilities can be very affective. Perhaps people want such feedback because they wish to feel pride about their abilities. Or affect may have little to do with it. Perhaps people want feedback because they wish to know the truth about themselves. Trope labels the first incentive "self-enhancement," and the second incentive "self-assessment." Self-enhancement involves attempting to maximize positive feelings about oneself (pride) and to minimize negative feelings about oneself (shame). Self-assessment involves obtaining accurate information about oneself, regardless of whether it produces positive affect, negative affect, or no affect. Thus the issue here is no less than whether people are motivated by hedonics (to feel good about themselves) or by knowledge (to know the truth about themselves).

The Role of Uncertainty Orientation

These different explanations of the preference for intermediate levels of challenge are based on different ideas of what incentives are relevant in risk-taking situations. It could be that both informational and affective incentives are important. Or it could be that informational incentives are important only insofar as they relate to anticipation of future affective consequences. Another possibility is that for some people the affect that comes from "doing something better" is an important goal, while for others the informational goal is primary. Sorrentino and Short (1986) believe that people differ in their **uncertainty orientation.** Some people are oriented toward attaining clarity about themselves or their environment and will embrace opportunities to find out more. They are attracted to situations in which they do not already know what will happen or what their capacities will be. Hence they are labeled *uncertainty oriented.* In contrast, *certainty oriented* individuals prefer situations that confirm what they already believe, and they avoid those that might lead them to change their beliefs. (Rokeach, 1960, had earlier described these characteristics as "open-minded" versus "closed-minded.")

Sorrentino, Hewitt, and Rasko-Knott (1992) carried out research to examine how uncertainty orientation and achievement motivation contributed to risk-taking behavior in the ring-toss task used by Atkinson and Litwin. Uncertainty orientation and *n* Ach were assessed with projective techniques; fear of failure and certainty orientation were assessed with self-report measures. A resultant uncertainty score (uncertainty minus certainty) and a resultant achievement motivation score (*n* Ach minus test anxiety) were computed for each subject. The results supported the idea that both affective and informational incentives influence risk taking. As expected, subjects who were high in resultant achievement motivation took more of their shots from a distance judged to be moderately risky than from easy or difficult distances. Subjects high in uncertainty orientation also preferred to shoot from an intermediate distance. Moreover, the effects were additive: the preference for the intermediate distance was strongest for those who were high in both achievement motivation and uncertainty orientation. In contrast, those who were high in certainty orientation and fear of failure ("fear threatened") avoided intermediate risks, preferring to shoot from very close or very far (see Figure 8.2). As

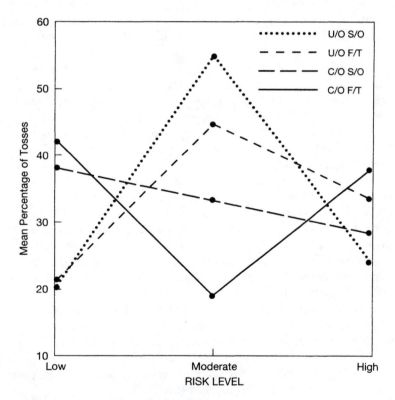

FIGURE 8.2   Mean percentage of tosses at each risk level for Uncertainty Orientation × Achievement-Related Motive combinations: U/O S/O = uncertainty-oriented, success-oriented persons, *n* = 49; U/O F/T = uncertainty-oriented, failure-threatened persons, *n* = 21; C/O S/O = certainty-oriented, success-oriented persons, *n* = 20; C/O F/T = certainty-oriented, failure-threatened persons, *n* = 50. (Based on Sorrentino, Hewitt, and Rasko-Knott, 1992; reproduced with permission of the American Psychological Association.)

Sorrentino et al. state: " . . . differences due to achievement-related motives reflect the affective value in risk-taking situations relating to pride in accomplishment and fear of failure. However, behavior also reflects information value, as assessed by uncertainty orientation, relating to approach or avoidance of knowledge about one's abilities" (1992, p. 527).

Some Consequences of High Need for Achievement

Moderate risk, knowledge of results (feedback), and personal responsibility for outcomes appear to be important factors in arousing the achievement motive. As a result, those high in *n* Ach ought to gravitate toward occupations that provide these features. Mahone (1960) linked career choice to preference for moderate risks. He found that college students who were high in *n* Ach were more likely to aspire to careers that were realistic for their IQ, GPA, and major than were students low in *n* Ach. McClelland has long contended that entrepreneurship is ideally suited to those high in *n* Ach. Business provides opportunities for feedback in the form of profits and losses, allows a good deal of personal responsibility, and often involves taking realistic risks. McClelland (1985) cites a large amount of research supporting this idea. In both the United States and many other countries, including some in Asia and Africa, men who are in business occupations tend to have high *n* Ach scores. In addition, businessmen with high *n* Ach scores tend to do better than businessmen with lower *n* Ach scores. In what McClelland describes as "the most definitive study," Kock (1965 as cited in McClelland, 1985) found that *n* Ach scores of owner-managers predicted increases in the company's gross value of output, number of workers, and investment in expansion. McClelland (1961) also found correlations between economic development and achievement themes in cultural artifacts such as children's storybooks.

Not all aspects of business are related to the incentives relevant for *n* Ach. Consider corporate managers. What is "doing something better" for a manager, and how would he or she know? Corporate management does not appear to provide the incentives for the achievement motive; in fact, people high in *n* Ach might not be at all suited for management. However, incentives for other motives might well be present. In particular, successful managers appear to be higher in the power motive (see below) than unsuccessful managers. Interestingly, managers high in the affiliation motive seem to make worse managers, perhaps because they are too concerned with being liked (McClelland, 1985).

Students often assume that need for achievement is highly related to success in school, but research has often shown that this expectation is incorrect. *n* Ach is not an important predictor of GPA. Why? It is important to remember that people get good or bad grades for a variety of reasons. *N* Ach will be reflected in good grades only if the incentives relevant to *n* Ach are present in the school setting. To the extent that students in a class must follow rules, give back what the teacher wants, or deal with material that is either too easy or too hard, there is no reason to expect *n* Ach to predict grades (Koestner & McClelland, 1990).

Achievement Motivation in Women

The studies that led to the scoring system for *n* Ach were all carried out on male subjects. When a similar set of conditions for arousing *n* Ach was used with female subjects, no differences were found between TAT stories told under arousing versus relaxed conditions (McClelland et al., 1953). As a result, virtually all of the research on *n* Achievement was carried out on male subjects. One wonders why nobody tried to understand *why* the achievement arousal conditions failed to influence females' TAT stories. When researchers began to take another look at achievement motivation in women, they discovered that social roles and opportunities played a major role. Recall that in the early studies, the conditions that increased achievement imagery in men's stories did not have the same effect for women. However, McClelland et al. (1953) did find that while conditions emphasizing cognitive abilities important for career success had no effect on women, there was some evidence that *n* Ach imagery increased when the women believed *social* competence was involved. Perhaps achievement incentives can exist in areas other than the settings emphasized in the early research on achievement motivation.

This idea led Elder and MacInnis (1983) to explore need for Achievement in women who pursued various goals in their lives. They obtained data about women who, as high school students in the 1930s, had participated in a longitudinal project known as the Oakland Growth Study. In early adolescence these women had taken the TAT, and later in high school they provided information about their life goals. Virtually all of the women wanted to marry and raise a family, but some also wanted careers. Elder and MacInnis (1983) classified the girls into two groups—one having wholly domestic interests (wife/mother) and the other having both domestic and career interests. You might think that the career-oriented girls would have higher *n* Ach scores than domestically oriented women. However, that expectation reflects the idea that "achievement" is something one does in the workplace. From the perspective of the *incentives* for *n* Ach, it is possible to envision how both career and domestic interests could provide them. As described by Elder and MacInnis: "Two goal frameworks (family-centered/domestic and career-oriented) specify different lines of action for women's achievement concerns. The first entails achievement through marriage and parenting, whereas the second involves achievement through education and work life" (1983, p. 394). Thus for both career-oriented and domestically oriented girls, those who were high in *n* Ach might differ from those who were low.

This idea was studied by correlating *n* Ach scores with various measures taken during high school and later in adulthood, computing them separately for domestically oriented and career-oriented women. Table 8.6 shows correlations

TABLE 8.6   **Correlations Between TAT Achievement Imagery in Adolescence and Measures of Social Status and Peer Relations in Adolescence and Outcomes in Adulthood for Domestically Oriented and Career-Oriented Women (Based on Elder and MacInnis, 1983)**

	DOMESTIC	CAREER
Junior High (self-report)		
Wishes to be attractive, popular	.50	.02
Unhappy; lacks friends	−.54	.43
Senior High		
Humorous (peer ratings)	.35	−.23
Popular (staff observations)	.39	−.07
Oriented toward going steady	.31	−.31
Conversational topics (self-report)		
Sports	−.12	.32
Teachers	−.13	.31
Clothes	.26	−.29
Being glamorous	.50	.02
Outcomes in adulthood		
Age at first job	−.18	.18
Age at first child	−.01	.39
Marital satisfaction	.37	.08[a]
Number of children	.35	.00[b]

[a]Difference not significant.
[b]Difference significant at $p < .10$.
Reproduced with permission of the American Psychological Association.

for a subset of measures which were significantly different (except where noted) between the two groups. These data indicate that *n* Ach played a role for both career and domestically oriented women. For example, in Junior High girls with higher *n* Ach scores were less unhappy than girls with lower *n* Ach scores (correlation of −.54), but only if they were domestically oriented. For the career-oriented girls, just the opposite was the case (correlation of +.43). In Senior High, domestically oriented girls high in *n* Ach talked about being glamorous more than domestically oriented girls low in *n* Ach, but there was no relationship between *n* Ach and conversation about glamour among career-oriented girls. In adulthood, *n* Ach was related to age at first child for career-oriented women but not for domestically oriented women, whereas *n* Ach was related to marital satisfaction and number of children for domestically oriented women but not for career-oriented women. In general, one can see that high *n* Ach subjects with wholly domestic aspirations emphasized those social behaviors that fostered goals such as popularity and attractiveness and were more successful at achieving their goals (as indicated by higher marital satisfaction and more children). In contrast, high *n* Ach subjects with career and domestic aspirations placed less emphasis on their social lives and tended to put off having children to a later age.

   A person's motives will be aroused in situations that provide appropriate incentives for the motive. However, not all situations are equally available to all people. The fact that there are fewer female than male entrepreneurs in the United States, for example, does not mean women have lower *n* Ach, it may simply mean that entrepreneurship has been less available for women. There is little reason to believe that *n* Ach itself differs between women and men (Stewart & Chester, 1982). As social barriers based on gender continue to erode, we can expect that high *n* Ach people of both sexes will seek out vocations that maximize the incentives for their motives.

IMPLICIT AND SELF-ATTRIBUTED MOTIVES

   McClelland has long argued that people are not necessarily aware of their motives. Methods such as the TAT allow individuals' concerns to emerge naturally. Yet, as we have seen, coding verbal material such as TAT stories is time consuming and requires a good deal of training. Personality psychologists often prefer methods that can be used to gather large amounts of data more easily—hence the popularity of self-report, true–false, or multiple-choice measures. It is not surprising, then, that a number of questionnaire measures of *n* Achievement have been developed. There is nothing wrong with this method in principle, but in practice it has proven to be a problem, since the fantasy measures and self-report measures of *n* Ach do not correlate with each other, that is, they lack convergent validity. Since both methods cannot be measuring the same thing (otherwise they would be correlated), it is unfortunate that they have the same name. Many studies of so-called achievement motivation use self-report measures and discuss their theories and results as if they measured the same thing that McClelland and Atkinson talked about.

   McClelland, Koestner, and Weinberger (1989) argue that motive measures taken from picture-story tasks like TAT and motive measures based on self-reports are measuring fundamentally different things. Fantasy measures can be described as *implicit* because individuals are not attempting to describe themselves; in contrast, self-report measures can be described as *explicit* or *self-attributed*. The crucial difference between the two is that for self-attributed motives people are relying on their cognitive representations and beliefs about themselves, that is, the self-concept (see chapter 11). People's self-concepts may be heavily influenced by their values and may be highly evaluative. Thus, people who believe themselves to be high achievers may be motivated to behave as they believe a high achiever should behave, even if they are unresponsive to the natural incentives for the achievement motive. On the other hand, people who have high implicit *n* Ach may not think of themselves as high achievers but may respond positively to incentives such as moderate challenge and experience satisfaction from "doing better."

   In order to differentiate these two types of achievement motivation, McClelland, Koestner, and Weinberger (1989; Weinberger & McClelland, 1990) use the traditional *n* to designate motives coded from verbal material and *san* (**self-attributed need**) for motives measured by self-report questionnaires. *San* motives

TABLE 8.7   Differences Between Implicit Motives and Self-Attributed Motives (Based on McClelland et al., 1989)

	IMPLICIT MOTIVES	SELF-ATTRIBUTED MOTIVES
Origins:	Biologically based; similar motives in animals	Social values; self-concept
Incentives:	Affect that comes from doing or experiencing things involving natural incentives	Knowledge that one has behaved according to self-concept, values, or social norms
Number:	Limited number that exist in all people but in different strengths	Indefinite; depends on individual's specific self-concept
Effects:	Long-term behavioral trends	Short-term influence tied to intentions, goals
	Activates relatively spontaneous behaviors; operant	Activates limited choice of specified behaviors; respondent
Awareness:	Relatively unconscious	Conscious; verbally encoded
Acquisition:	Learned from experiences with natural incentives in early childhood; prelinguistic	Learned from explicit rules and teaching by parents and others; linguistic
Brain substrate:	Midbrain structures	Necortex; language areas
Assessment:	Best assessed by indirect means such as projective tests	Best assessed by self-report
Affect:	Enthusiasm, energy, interest	Tension, frustration, relief

focus on unmet goals that are part of the self-conception. They tend to be activated when individuals are made aware that a situation is relevant to their self-image. Thus people who think of themselves as high achievers will work hard when encountering a situation explicitly defined as an achievement situation. Implicit motives, in contrast, focus on natural incentives, regardless of how the situation is explicitly defined. People high in *n* Ach will not work hard just because a situation is defined as an achievement situation; what is crucial is whether or not the situation provides relevant incentives. Thus these two types of motives function very differently.

Table 8.7 lists differences between implicit and self-attributed motives cited by McClelland. It can be thought of as a set of hypotheses about how motives measured by thought sampling differ from motives measured by self-report. McClelland, Koestner, and Weinberger (1989) provide some supporting evidence for these hypotheses.

One hypothesis is that *n* motives are acquired in infancy from direct experience whereas *san* motives are acquired after the development of language through explicit teaching. Results of a longitudinal study support this distinction. The sample consisted of 38 males and 40 females, about half of whose parents were classified as white collar and about half as blue collar. Mothers' reports of their child rearing practices were obtained when the subjects were 5 years old. Motive measures were obtained when the subjects were 31 years old. Two aspects of child rearing were consistently related to *n* Ach scores (as measured by the picture-story method at age 31): scheduling of feeding and severity of toilet training. Subjects whose parents imposed feeding schedules on them or who were strict in the demand for toilet training during the first two years of life obtained higher *n* Ach scores at age 31 than did subjects whose parents were less rigid about feeding and less strict about toilet training. The correlations with adult *n* Ach were .33 (for feeding) and .41 (for toilet training). This basic pattern was found for all subsamples (i.e., males and females, white collar and blue collar) as well as for the full sample (McClelland & Pilon, 1983). The correlations between *san* Ach and feeding and toilet training, in contrast, were .06 and −.10, neither of which approached statistical significance. However, another aspect of child rearing did correlate significantly with *san* Ach ($r = .31$) although not with *n* Ach (−.10): the degree to which the mothers set tasks for their children. McClelland, Koestner, and Weinberger (1989) interpret these results as follows:

> Setting high standards early in life for moderately difficult mastery of internal states is associated with adult n Achievement but not with adult san Achievement. Learning when to be hungry and when and where to defecate and urinate should provide some intrinsic pleasure from self-mastery in all children. And parents who emphasize the importance of these learnings apparently succeed in developing an affectively based interest in mastering challenging tasks that lasts into adulthood. On the other hand, setting explicit tasks for the child to learn and perform is significantly associated with adult san Achievement but not with adult n Achievement. Explaining what tasks a child is to carry out certainly involves more linguistically coded information than does teaching a child when to be hungry by scheduling feeding, and probably more than is involved in consistently putting the child on the toilet and demanding performance. Furthermore, in this sample at this period in history, toilet training was reported to be complete for the majority of children by 19 months . . . so that the learning occurred before language comprehension was developed as highly as would be necessary to understand what was involved in carrying out instructions to perform various tasks. The later emphasis on carrying out tasks, however, did develop a self-attributed need to achieve that persisted into adulthood." (p. 699)

According to McClelland, Koestner, and Weinberger (1989) different incentives are relevant for implicit and self-attributed motives. Consequently, individual differences in implicit motives should be related to behavior when "natural" incentives are present, while individual differences in self-attributed motives should be related to behavior when "social" incentives are present. Spangler (1992) carried out meta-analyses to see if this pattern would be found in the area of achievement motivation. Spangler coded studies for whether they involved natural incentives (what he labeled "activity incentives") or "social incentives." Activity incentives included moderate risk taking, task contingency, achievement work content, time pressure, and high objective relationship between performance and some achievement-related outcome in the immediate situation. Social incentives included challenging goals set by an experimenter, achievement-oriented instructions in an experiment, achievement work norms, and pretreatment experimental manipulations. According to McClelland, Koestner, and Weinberger (1989), TAT measures of *n* Ach ought to predict behavior when activity incentives are present while questionnaire measures of *san* Ach ought to predict behavior when social incentives are present. Although the magnitude of the correlations was not high, the meta-analysis provided some support for this prediction. Spangler (1992) notes that since none of the studies was explicitly designed to test the prediction, no study contained the optimal set of characteristics for comparing *n* Ach to *san* Ach. However, on the basis of the correlations in the meta-analysis, he estimated that under conditions that maximized either activity or social incentives, there would be a high level of prediction for *n* Ach and *san* Ach, respectively.

The importance of the distinction between self-attributed and implicit motives is shown in research by Woike (1995). College students filled out the Achievement scale of Jackson's Personality Research Form, a self-report measure of Murray's needs, and wrote stories to TAT pictures. Every night for two months, the students wrote down what their "most memorable experiences" had been for that day. The experiences were later coded by the experimenter as either "routine task experiences" (e.g., "studied psych," "worked a double shift") or "affective task experiences" (e.g., "had a very productive meeting," "Professor M really liked my paper"). Woike predicted that individual differences in explicit (*san*) achievement motivation as measured by the PRF would correlate with the number of routine task experiences reported by subjects, while individual differences in implicit (*n*) achievement motivation as measured by the TAT would correlate with affective task experiences. Table 8.8 shows the results. Although the correlations are not high, the pattern is as predicted.

What is the relationship between implicit and self-attributed motives? The near-zero correlation between them means that the two types of motives are congruent for some people and incongruent for others. When these motives are working at "cross-purposes," individuals may experience conflict and tension. Someone whose self-image is wrapped up in the idea of achieving (high *san* Ach) but who does not get pleasure from doing well (low *n* Ach) might be quite unhappy and frustrated. In fact, Weinberger and McClelland (1990) suggest that it is just such a person who might benefit from the self-exploration of psychoanalytic therapy.

TABLE 8.8   Correlations Between Two Types of Achievement Motives and Two Types of Most Memorable Experiences (Based on Woike, 1995)

Achievement Motive	MOST MEMORABLE EXPERIENCES	
	Routine Task	Affective Task
Explicit	.21[a]	−.07
Implicit	−.06	.27[b]

[a]$p < .01$.
[b]$p < .001$
Reproduced by permission of the American Psychological Association.

INTRINSIC AND EXTRINSIC MOTIVATION

The work of McClelland, Atkinson, and their colleagues has focused on individual differences in motive dispositions. There is also a huge literature on the motivational *processes* that influence behavior. In McClelland's terminology, this literature is concerned with how different incentives influence performance. A number of investigators have drawn a distinction between **intrinsic motivation** and **extrinsic motivation** that is similar to McClelland's distinction between natural and social incentives (Deci, 1975; Lepper & Greene, 1978). Deci and Ryan (1985; 1992) assume, as do many other psychologists (Allport, 1961; Csikszentmihalyi, 1975; White, 1959), that a major human motive is to feel competent and self-determined. This innate need is experienced as interest and curiosity and leads to behaviors that are engaged in for their own sake, that is, for rewards that are intrinsic to the behavior itself. Intrinsic motivation is what leads people to seek out challenging activities that provide feedback regarding their competence and that they experience as being under their own control. When people engage in activities because of external rewards, pressures, or demands or in order to live up their own self-concepts, motivation is described as extrinsic.

Much of the research on intrinsic and extrinsic motivation has focused on the environmental conditions that increase or decrease each type of motivation. An early and often repeated finding concerns the effects of external rewards. Imagine you were playing a video game which you found challenging and interesting—say a game like Tetris, in which you have to fit shapes into each other as fast as you can. You play the game because it is inherently enjoyable. Now imagine that someone tells you he will give you a nickel for each 1,000 points you get. Great, you say. Now you can have fun *and* earn some money. So you play hard, you get your money, and you feel fine. Now imagine that the person says to you, "Okay, that's all the money I have, but you can play some more if you want." Do you think you would continue to play? In fact, studies have shown that under these conditions people seem to lose interest in the game after the external reward is withdrawn. That is, compared with people who have not been externally rewarded, those who have been rewarded will spend less time playing the game after the reward stops. What has happened is that the intrinsic motivation for playing the game has been *undermined* by the extrinsic motivation produced by external reward. Deci and Ryan (1992) argue this happens because people come to feel that their behavior is no longer self-determined when they receive external rewards, and apparently once this happens, it is hard to get back the feeling that one is doing the activity for its own sake. Intrinsic motivation can be undermined by "any external event that is experienced as pressure to perform in a particular way or to attain a particular outcome" (Deci & Ryan, 1992, p. 17), such as when other people impose goals or deadlines.

The consequences of fostering either intrinsic or extrinsic motivation can be profound. Intrinsic motivation leads to greater persistence by athletes (Vallerand, Deci, & Ryan, 1987), greater work satisfaction (Deci, Connell, & Ryan, 1989), better school performance and adjustment (Grolnick & Ryan, 1989), and greater creativity (Amabile, 1985). For example, Amabile (1982) had two groups of girls aged 7 to 11 make collages. One group was set up to be competitive, with prizes given for the best collage. The other group was noncompetitive. Collages produced under noncompetitive conditions were judged by artists to be more creative than those produced under competitive conditions with reward. It is important to emphasize that much, if not most, "achievement" behavior is extrinsically motivated (Ryan, Connell, & Grolnick, 1992). Success in school, for example, may depend more on whether one responds to the extrinsic incentives and controls of highly structured school settings than on whether one finds the material inherently interesting. Not everybody, however, responds to extrinsic incentives. Students may feel alienated and bored if they don't care about the external rewards (e.g., grades) or if doing well in school is not important to their self-image. And even those who do well under the pressure of extrinsic motivation may not experience much joy in their activities—relief perhaps, but not joy.

Koestner and McClelland (1990) draw attention to the parallels between the work on intrinsic/extrinsic motivation and *n* Ach/*san* Ach. These research traditions are largely complementary. The conditions that foster intrinsic motivation are just those that provide incentives for *n* Ach, and the conditions that foster extrinsic motivation are just those that provide incentives for *san* Ach. Although these two traditions have developed mostly independently of each other, it seems clear that they are converging on a perspective that emphasizes the fact that humans have both natural, inherent motivational tendencies and those that are developed in their interactions with society. This distinction provides an important framework for understanding achievement behaviors.

POWER MOTIVATION

What do these have in common: trying to convince someone of your point of view; seeking political office; teaching; wearing a Rolex watch; seducing someone; helping someone; mugging someone; selling used cars. In each of these cases, a person seeks to have *impact* on others, to do something that controls them, influences them, or impresses them. Although any one of these actions could be carried out for other reasons, a person who repeatedly told stories to TAT pictures that included these kinds of actions would be indicating a recurrent concern for having impact on others. Why would a person seek to have impact on others? According to McClelland (1985), the reason is to experience feelings of power. Such feelings provide a natural incentive for the **power motive.** People with a strong power motive experience positive affect when they feel they can have impact on others.

Like *n* Ach, *n* Power is scored from verbal material such as stories told to TAT-type pictures. Table 8.9 describes the coding system for *n* Power used by Winter and his colleagues (Winter, 1992). This system was developed the same way the *n* Ach system was developed: by comparing stories told under conditions intended to arouse the power motive with stories told under relaxed conditions. Conditions used to arouse the power motive included taking the role of the experimenter in

TABLE 8.9   Brief Description of Coding System for the Power Motive (Based on Winter, 1992)

The story is first scored for the presence of any of the following three types of power imagery:

1. Someone shows power concern through actions that in themselves express power by being forceful (e.g., "They plan to attack an enemy supply area"), by giving help that has not been asked for (e.g., "The mother is interested in teaching her son basketball"), by trying to control other people by regulating their lives (e.g., "The welfare worker arranged to transfer the kid to the country, to bring him under a new influence"), by trying to persuade, convince, or bribe someone (e.g., "The junior executive is trying to get her point across"), by trying to impress someone (e.g., "The man is urbane and sophisticated; he knows the right places in town to be seen in").
2. Someone does something that arouses strong positive or negative emotions in others (e.g., "She has taken him to a small café. He is enchanted by the atmosphere, shows his delight").
3. Someone is described as having a concern for reputation or position (e.g., "He has taken her out because he likes her, but also because he wants to find out how his boss rated him on his last rating").

If a story contains any power imagery, the entire story is then scored for the following power subcategories:

1. Prestige of the actor (e.g., "These are top-ranking military people. . . .")
2. Stated need for power (e.g., "She wants to have an affair with him. . . .")
3. Instrumental activity (e.g., "The man is emphatically trying to make a point.")
4. Block in the world (e.g., "The girl resists his advances.")
5. Goal anticipation (e.g., "The man is thinking that he is convincing his boss.")
6. Goal states (e.g., "He will lose his reputation and become bitter.")
7. Effect (e.g., "The girl takes her mother's advice, is successful, and frequently looks to her mother with respect.")

research, watching a film of John Kennedy's inauguration, seeing a multimedia presentation of inspirational speeches, observing a demonstration of hypnosis, and role-playing being in an activist political group (Winter, 1992; Winter & Stewart, 1978).

It is striking how different many of the actions are that involve having an impact. How one's power motive is expressed is influenced by cultural, situational, and personality factors. For example, social class values influence whether men will express the power motive through aggression or other means: working-class men are more likely to do so through aggression than are middle-class men (Winter, 1973). It is important to remember that although we can discuss motives one at a time, in the real world each motive is influenced by other motives and goals, as well as by fears, habits, values, and capacities. For that reason, it is often difficult to find very strong correlations between motive scores and real-life outcomes. Nevertheless, research does support the idea that people high in *n* Power seek opportunities to have an impact by holding office or pursuing careers in teaching, clergy, therapy, journalism, or business management, and that they are concerned with prestige (McClelland, 1975; Winter, 1973). A number of laboratory studies indicate that those high in *n* Power are more likely to form coalitions and to attempt to influence others in small group discussions (McClelland, 1985).

Power Motivation in Women and Men

Who do you think gets higher scores on TAT measures of *n* Power: (1) men, (2) women, (3) neither? In fact, a great deal of research indicates that there is no consistent tendency for either women or men to score higher (Winter, 1988). In addition, power-arousing conditions such as those mentioned above influence TAT stories of women and men in much the same way (Stewart & Winter, 1976) and many of the correlates of *n* Power are found for both (Stewart & Chester, 1982; Winter, 1988). This is not to say that gender has no influence on how *n* Power is expressed. For example, Mason and Blankenship (1987) found more college men above the median in *n* Power reported being abusive to their partners in close relationships than did those below the median, but there was no relationship between partner abuse and *n* Power in women.

One aspect of power motivation that occurs much more in men than in women is what Winter (1988) calls "profligate, expansive impulses": . . . "Thus, among men, *n* Power usually predicts drinking, drug use, physical and verbal aggression, gambling, precocious and exploitative sexuality, and reading 'vicarious' or sexually-oriented magazines" (p. 512). The fact that these activities are not correlated with *n* Power in women suggests that when women engage in such activities, something other than *n* Power is responsible. Why does *n* Power express itself in profligate expansive impulses in men but not in women? It is tempting to explain this difference by citing differences in sex-role stereotypes, our culturally based, shared ideas about what behaviors are appropriate for men and for women. In this view, it is acceptable for men to express power (or their desire to feel power) in these ways.

Winter (1988) suggests that this explanation is wrong. He carried out a series of studies in which brief descriptions of individuals were given to subjects, who rated them as to how powerful (influential, potent) they seemed to be. Half the descriptions were of a profligate individual, half were of an individual who was not profligate. For some subjects, the person being described was named "John," while for others the person was named "Jane." The same basic results were found when the subjects were college students, working-class high school students, and mental health paraprofessionals: there was no tendency for profligate John to be rated as more influential or potent than profligate Jane; in fact, both were rated as less influential than their nonprofligate namesakes.

Winter (1988) acknowledged that these studies are only suggestive and that more research on the impact of sex-role stereotypes on the expression of power should be carried out. He proposed an alternative explanation for why n Power correlates with profligate, expansive impulse in men and not in women. This alternative brings us back to the idea mentioned earlier that the effect of any motive (or any personality characteristic, for that matter) often depends on the other motives (or characteristics) of the individual. Winter's proposal is that individuals who have been given responsibilities as children are more likely to express n Power in "responsible" ways, whereas those who did not have such training are more likely to express n Power in profligate ways. Girls are more often given responsibility training than are boys. If this theory is correct, then one ought to find *within-gender* differences that parallel *between-gender* differences: girls who received responsibility training should become women who channel n Power responsibly, and girls who did not receive such training should grow up to channel n Power in a profligate manner; the same difference should hold for boys. Thus responsibility training is seen as a moderator for the expression of n Power.

In order to test this idea, Winter reasoned that having a younger sibling was a major factor in whether or not a child received responsibility training. Accordingly, subjects were divided into two groups: those who had younger siblings and those who didn't. Correlations were then computed between n Power and behaviors that reflect "responsible power" (e.g., office holding) versus "profligate power" (e.g., sex, aggression, drinking). Table 8.10 shows the correlations for women and men college students. These data were based on reanalyses of data collected for other purposes, hence the behaviors that make up responsible and profligate power vary from sample to sample. Generally, responsible power is reflected in office holding, number of organizational memberships, canvassing for organizations, and owning pets, while profligate power is reflected in number of sexual partners, drug and alcohol use, frequency of swearing, and hostile behavior. The results are partially supportive of Winter's hypothesis: for subjects with younger siblings, there is generally a positive correlation between n Power and responsible

TABLE 8.10   Correlations of *n* Power with Responsible and Profligate Power-Related Behaviors for Subjects with or Without Younger Siblings (Based on Winter, 1988)

	WOMEN	
	With Younger Sibs	Without Younger Sibs
Responsible power	+.23	−.26
Profligate power	−.11	+.55
	MEN	
	With Younger Sibs	Without Younger Sibs
Office holding	+.45	+.05
Been in physical fight	−.24	+.11
Profligate behavior	.00	+.67

Note: Women's data aggregated over three samples; men's data reflect two different samples for "physical fight" and "profligate behavior."
Reproduced with permission of the American Psychological Association.

power behaviors, whereas the same correlations are smaller and sometimes reversed for subjects without younger siblings. In contrast, profligate behavior tends to correlate positively (and quite substantially) with *n* Power only for subjects without younger siblings; for subjects with younger siblings the correlations are small and inconsistent. Perhaps most important, a similar pattern is observed for women and men. Thus, in attempting to explain what appeared to be a gender difference, Winter has developed a broader conception of how *n* Power expresses itself in both men and women. Does this mean gender is irrelevant? Obviously not. There is still the fact that men are much more likely than women to express *n* Power in a profligate manner. Winter's (1988) analysis suggests that this is so because women are given more responsibility training than men; if men received the same amount of responsibility training, the "sex difference" in the expression of *n* Power would disappear.

AFFILIATION AND INTIMACY MOTIVES

Barbra Streisand sang that "People who need people are the luckiest people in the world." Whether or not that is true, such people might very well score as high on *n* Affiliation, a motive defined as the need to be with people and expressed as a concern for establishing, maintaining, and restoring positive relationships with others (McClelland, 1985). *N* Affiliation is scored from verbal material such as stories based on TAT cards. As was true for *n* Achievement and *n* Power, the scoring system for *n* Affiliation is based on differences in stories of those subjects in conditions designed to arouse the motive versus subjects in neutral conditions. Once again, it is instructive to consider carefully the situations that were used to arouse *n* Aff. In one study, fraternity members sat together in a group and publicly stated their opinions of other members, thus providing subjects with a rather clear picture of how liked or disliked each was. In another study, the subjects in the arousal condition were freshmen who had been denied membership in fraternities at a college where virtually all students were fraternity members (Shipley & Veroff, 1952). Stories told by these subjects were compared with stories told by students who had not participated in the group session and by students who were accepted into fraternities. The main differences in the stories involved concerns about rejection and loneliness, along with activities designed to produce or maintain positive relationships with others. Thus *n* Aff appears to be best described as a fear of losing relationships with others—a fear of rejection (McAdams, 1988; McClelland, 1985).

What types of conditions provide incentives for people high in *n* Aff? Recall that French (1955) found a correlation between *n* Aff and digit-symbol performance when the incentive was to "please the experimenter" (see page 194). McKeachie (1961) found that college students who were high in *n* Aff obtained higher grades in a class in which the teacher was warm and friendly than in a class in which the teacher was not. The desire of those high in *n* Aff to create and maintain positive relationships with others is also seen in their tendency to avoid interpersonal conflict (McClelland, 1985). This motive may lead them to be particularly sensitive to the interpersonal ramifications of their actions, a concern that sometimes may interfere with other goals. For example, McClelland and Boyatzis (1982) found that individuals high in *n* Aff tended to be unsuccessful as corporate managers, perhaps because they were overly concerned with whether their subordinates liked them. Research also suggests that people high in *n* Aff are not particularly popular (McClelland, 1985). Their anxiety about rejection and attempts to avoid it may not be perceived by others as very appealing. Maybe Barbra was wrong.

Do you believe that the only reason people want to be with people is fear of loneliness or rejection? McAdams (1980) certainly didn't. He believed that people can be motivated by a desire for *intimacy*—for close, warm relationships characterized by openness, contact, joy, and sharing. He attempted to find out what the effects on TAT stories would be in conditions that ought to arouse an intimacy motive. The conditions consisted of (1) initiation ceremonies for sororities and fraternities, (2) a campus party, (3) couples who were in love, and (4) a psychodrama designed to facilitate closeness and communication. TAT stories told under these conditions were contrasted with those told by subjects in neutral condition. The resultant scoring system is described in Table 8.11 (McAdams, 1992a).

The construct validity of the intimacy motive scoring has been supported by a number of studies (McAdams, 1992b). For example, McAdams, Jackson, and Kirshnit (1984) found that subjects high in intimacy motivation stood closer to other people, used the word *we* more often, and were generally more intimate in their interactions (the correlation between the intimacy motive score and an

**TABLE 8.11   Brief Description of Coding System for the Intimacy Motive
(Based on McAdams, 1992a)**

The story is first scored for the presence of either of the following two types of intimacy:

1. An encounter or relationship between people produces or expresses positive affect (i.e., love, friendship, happiness, peace, or tender behaviors such as kissing, holding hands, and so on): "The man loves his family"; "They greeted each other warmly"; "She is reminiscing about the fun they had together in Italy."
2. Exchange of information that is reciprocal, involves an interpersonal relationship, or is designed to help another person in distress: "He struck up a conversation with her"; "They confide in each other regularly"; "This picture depicts two people who are sitting by a river discussing their relationship"; "They will listen to her and comfort her."

If a story contains either (1) or (2), the entire story is then scored for the following additional categories:

3. Psychological growth and coping (e.g., "She has learned a great deal about life from him.")
4. Commitment or concern (e.g., "He feel responsible for their well-being.")
5. Time-Space (e.g., "The three men in the preceding picture get together every year to hunt deer and shoot the bull.")
6. Union (e.g., "They decided to get married.")
7. Harmony (e.g., "They found they had much in common.")
8. Surrender (e.g., "These two people happen to meet on a bench next to a river.")
9. Escape to intimacy (e.g., "Her father wants her to be chaste and pure. But she will run off with her lover and they will become gypsies.")
10. Connection with the outside world (e.g., "She liked the speed of the horses, the fresh air, and the countryside.")

Reproduced with permission of Cambridge University Press.

aggregated measure of intimacy behaviors was .70). College students high in intimacy motivation also reported more positive interpersonal experiences with others (McAdams & Constantian, 1983), and were described by their friends as more "sincere" and "loving" than were students low in intimacy motivation (McAdams, 1980).

McAdams (1988) has been interested in how people construct their "life stories." In thinking about our lives, each of us has constructed a narrative, with characters, themes, and important incidents. McAdams believes that certain events in people's lives play a central role in these narratives; he calls these *nuclear episodes*. In order to explore the relationship between life stories and motives, McAdams (1988) had two samples of subjects describe high points in their lives (peak experiences) and positive experiences that occurred in their childhood. These experiences were coded for power and intimacy themes and then correlated with the subjects' motive scores based on the TAT measure. Table 8.12 shows these correlations. In the table, the events that are important in people's life stories are shown to be strongly related to their motive scores. Whether this connection means that people selectively remember those events that are consistent with their motive concerns (in which case reports of autobiographical

TABLE 8.12 Correlations of Power and Intimacy Themes in Combined Peak and Positive Childhood Experiences with Power and Intimacy Motive Scores in Two Samples (Based on McAdams, 1988)

	SAMPLE A	
	Power Motivation	Intimacy Motivation
Power Themes	.62	−.02
Intimacy Themes	.01	.40
	SAMPLE B	
	Power Motivation	Intimacy Motivation
Power Themes	.53	−.07
Intimacy Themes	−.10	.49

events are much like TAT stories) or that people's experiences reflect their enduring motives is impossible to tell from correlational data of this kind. In either case, it appears that people's motives are expressed in both imaginative stories and autobiographical recollections.

CONTENT ANALYSIS OF ARCHIVAL DATA

McAdams (1988) was able to look at power and intimacy themes in people's autobiographies using the same coding system used in scoring TAT stories. In fact, any verbal material can be analyzed by means of such coding systems (Smith, 1992). It is not even necessary to obtain the material in formal research. Already existing or archival material can also be coded. McClelland has carried out a great amount of research using material as varied as children's stories, folk tales, and works of literature to assess the **collective motives** of whole societies. McClelland (1985) assumes that when recurring themes of achievement, power, or affiliation/intimacy are found in such materials from a specific social group, they may signify strong levels of that motive in the group. By analyzing such materials, McClelland and others have suggested that such social trends as economic development may be related to fluctuations in levels of achievement motivation in the social group as a whole.

McClelland's research has covered large time frames and a wide range of verbal materials and has focused on collective motives. Perhaps more pertinent to issues of individuality, Winter (1987) analyzed the inaugural speeches of U.S. presidents for affiliation/intimacy and power themes. He found that power imagery in speeches was positively correlated with a number of aspects of presidential "outcomes" such as historians' consensus on "greatness" ($r = .40$), entry into war ($r = .52$), and importance of decisions ($r = .51$). Affiliation/intimacy imagery was correlated with reaching arms limitation agreements ($r = .43$). Winter (1993) also used content analysis to analyze the motives of diplomats involved in international crises and found that increased power motivation was associated with escalation of the crises and increased affiliation/intimacy motivation with peaceful resolution of the crises. Although such correlational data do not prove that social motives of presidents and others are what determine war and peace, they do show how psychological measures can add to our understanding of people and events far removed from our laboratories filled with college sophomores. As Winter (1993) put it: "From the perspective of personality psychology, these studies suggest that personality theory and variables can be translated into objective measures that can be applied at a distance to individuals and groups. As a result, rigorous personality research can now be extended to include history, biography, political science, and related fields, and the personality 'laboratory' can be expanded to include libraries and archives, the past as well as the present" (p. 542).

GOALS

We said earlier that people's immediate actions are closely related to their intentions or goals. We also pointed out that as an answer to "Why" questions, a person's stated intention or goal ("I worked hard so I could get a good grade in the course") often leads to yet another "Why" question ("Why did you want to get a good grade in the course?"). For the personality psychologist, knowing a person's intentions or goals is often just a first step to understanding what aspect of the person's individuality has led to that intention or goal. Motives such as *n* Achievement, *n* Power, and *n* Intimacy provide a basis for understanding why individuals have the goals they have.

Yet motives like *n* Ach are not very good predictors of a specific person's specific behavior. We could know that a person has a high need for Achievement or Power yet have very little idea how that need will influence his or her actions. As we have seen, there are many different ways for such needs to be expressed. Many psychologists find that concepts such as needs are too far removed from the behaviors they wish to understand, too distant from the concrete realities of people's lives, too *decontextualized* to provide a real understanding of how individuals negotiate their way through the thicket of daily living. For these psychologists, it is often less important to know *why* a person has particular goals than to know *what* those goals are and *how* they influence behavior. For example, in the area of work motivation, Locke and Latham (1990) have shown that certain types of goals lead to higher levels of job performance than other types of goals; difficult, specific goals produce higher levels of performance than do easy, vague goals. Assigning a goal of producing 25 widgets per hour will result in more widgets than assigning a goal of producing as many widgets "as you can." Locke and Latham note that in work settings, goals are ordinarily set for people by others, so their focus is less on the reasons individuals have certain goals and more on the effects of goals on behavior. This approach to studying goals emphasizes how situational factors influence people's commitment to goals, how knowledge of results influences goal-directed performance, and how people's beliefs about their ability to achieve goals affect goal choice, goal commitment, and task performance (see chapter 11).

The approach of Locke and Latham is designed to explicate the general principles that guide goal-directed behavior, with the hope that such principles can be used to influence behavior in applied settings. Goal concepts have also been used by psychologists interested in individuality. These psychologists attempt to assess people's goals and to understand how their goals are related to various aspects of their lives. Goals can range from the very general to the very specific. For example, you might have a general goal of "being a good person." This goal does not specify the exact behaviors that one might engage in to meet the goal, nor does it contain a clear criterion for what constitutes meeting the goal. A very specific goal, such as "renting a video to watch tonight," is more closely tied to a specific behavior and has a defined point at which the goal has been accomplished. This very specific type of goal is closely related to the concept of "intention" that we discussed earlier.

PERSONAL STRIVINGS

Emmons (1989) has argued that goal concepts that occupy a "middle level" between general social motives such as *n* Ach and specific goals and intentions are optimal units for personality research. He uses the term **personal strivings** to describe "what people are typically trying to do." To get a flavor for Emmons' approach, you might take a few moments to produce a list of your own personal strivings. Make a list of fifteen things "that you typically or characteristically are trying to do in your everyday behavior." Examples are "'trying to persuade others that one is right,' 'trying to seek new and exciting experiences,' 'trying to be attractive,' and 'trying to avoid being noticed by others'" (Emmons, 1989, p. 96). The strivings may be positive (something you are trying to accomplish) or negative (something you are trying to avoid). It doesn't matter whether you are being successful or not—the focus should be on things you are *trying* to do. Include only those strivings that involve a repeating or recurring goal, not strivings that are temporary and short-lived. Begin each item on your list with the words "I typically try to . . . . "

If you follow these instructions, you will produce a list of strivings that can be used in a variety of ways. You could explore them further by thinking about specific goals, plans, and activities that are associated with each striving. For example, if you listed "trying to spend more time relaxing," you might specify that this involves planning a vacation, having a drink before dinner, and/or going to the movies (Emmons, 1989, p. 98). You might also think about how each striving is related to more general motivational dispositions. For example, "trying to make a good impression on others" might be related to *n* Power or *n* Affiliation. This exercise highlights the *hierarchical* aspect of personality concepts. It may help you connect the very specific level of your most immediate personal concerns with the more abstract concepts such as motive dispositions.

Nomothetic Analyses of Idiographic Strivings

Perhaps you found the exercise worthwhile as a means of thinking clearly about yourself because the striving list was generated by you, not by us—that is, it was idiographic rather than nomothetic (see chapter 1). In fact, one of the distinguishing features of many contemporary goal concepts is this idiographic flavor. As we discussed in chapter 1, the problem with idiographic assessment is that it rarely leads to generalized understanding. In fact, although many contemporary goal concepts have idiographic content, the research strategies that employ these concepts are most often nomothetic.

In the case of personal strivings, the nomothetic aspect enters in a variety of ways. One way is through "striving assessment scales." After subjects generate their lists of strivings, they are asked to rate them on a series of scales: "degree of striving" indicates how valuable and important the striving is and how committed the person is to it; "success" indicates how much the striving has been accomplished or is likely to be accomplished; "ease" indicates whether there are opportunities to fulfill the striving and how difficult it is to do so. As soon as different subjects rate their idiosyncratic strivings on the same set of scales, the resulting data become nomothetic. These nomothetic data can then be used to ask questions such as, "Do people whose strivings are felt to be important experience more positive affect than people whose strivings are felt to be unimportant?"

A second way of treating strivings nomothetically is to ask subjects to indicate how their strivings affect each other. For example, a person might judge "to be honest" and "to present myself in the best light" as incompatible strivings, which produce internal conflict. Other nomothetic measures of strivings might include ambivalence about strivings (both wanting and not wanting a goal) and differentiation of strivings (are strivings independent or interdependent; does a particular striving require few or many plans for its fulfillment) (Emmons & King, 1988, 1989). In short, while the *content* of strivings is idiographic, the research questions entail creating some sort of nomothetic variable on which people can be compared with one another.

Emmons and his colleagues have carried out a number of studies using nomothetic analyses of personal strivings. Emmons (1986) found that the value one places on strivings (how much joy one experiences if the striving is successful and how much unhappiness if it is unsuccessful) correlated .39 with positive affect and .34 with a measure of how satisfied one is with one's life ("subjective well-being"). Ratings of the importance of strivings correlated .52 with subjective well-being. The extent to which one feels one's strivings have been fulfilled in the past was also related to positive affect ($r = .36$). Negative affect was related to pessimism about the future prospects of fulfilling one's strivings ($r = .34$) and to conflict and ambivalence about one's strivings ($r = .33$ and .52, respectively).

The role of conflict and ambivalence was studied further by Emmons and King (1988). They noted that a key characteristic of motivation in psychoanalytic theory is the ubiquity of conflict between motives, in particular between the desires to satisfy id impulses while avoiding superego feelings of guilt. Psychologists of many persuasions often identify mental "health" with an "integrated personality," whereby one's motives, goals, and behaviors work together rather than at cross-purposes (recall our earlier discussion of implicit and self-attributed motives). Further, conflict between motives has also been suggested as a factor in physical health.

Emmons and King (1988) wondered whether conflict between personal strivings might also affect physical and mental well-being. College students generated lists of fifteen strivings, which were then organized into a 15-by-15 matrix so that each striving could be compared with every other striving. For each cell in the matrix, subjects indicated how being successful in one striving would affect the other striving on a scale from -2 = very harmful to $+2$ = very helpful, with 0 indicating no effect. This procedure permitted Emmons and King to compute an average conflict score for each of the fifteen strivings in each subject's list. Subjects were also asked to rate each striving on a scale indicating whether fulfilling it might make them unhappy (0 = not unhappy at all to 5 = extremely unhappy). A high score on this question was taken to indicate ambivalence about a goal. Examples include "to be all things to all people" and "to avoid being aggressive if I feel I've been wronged" (p. 1042). In these cases, although the individual wants to "be all things to all people," she also feels that being this way might actually make her unhappy.

Subjects were also given a set of measures designed to assess physical and psychological well-being, essentially measures of physical symptoms and positive and negative affect. Correlations between average conflict and ambivalence scores and these measures of well-being indicated that both conflict among strivings and ambivalence about individual strivings were associated with increased negative affect, depression, anxiety, and physical symptoms. In addition, conflict and ambivalence were correlated with each other ($r = .26$). A measure of physical symptoms taken a year later was also related to the conflict ($r = .31$) and the ambivalence ($r = .41$) measures. In a second study, the conflict measure correlated .27 with the number of times subjects had visited the college health center.

Why do conflict and ambivalence about strivings have a negative influence on well-being? Emmons and King (1988) speculate that people tend to spend more time thinking about strivings that are conflictual than about those that are free of conflict. At the same time, people are less likely to act on strivings about which they are in conflict or ambivalent. This combination of *rumination* and *inhibition* may produce autonomic stress (Pennebaker, 1985). In a third study, Emmons and King used an **experience-sampling method** to assess people's thoughts and actions about their strivings. Subjects wore watches with alarms set to go off at random times during the day. When subjects heard the alarm, they filled out a form to indicate what they had just been thinking about and what the main thing was that they were doing. This continued every day for three weeks, after which subjects were asked to indicate for each thought and action whether it was related to any of their fifteen strivings. It was then possible to compute how much time each subject thought about and acted upon each striving. Each individual's fifteen strivings now had four scores: a conflict score, an ambivalence score, a time spent thinking about score, and a time acting upon score. As was predicted, people spent more time thinking about strivings about which they were in conflict ($r = .17$) or ambivalent ($r = .14$), but they spent less time actually doing anything about these strivings ($r = -.17$ for conflict, $r = -.27$ for ambivalence). (Although these correlations are not high, it is important to realize that many factors can influence ongoing thought and action, so high correlations are not to be expected.) Emmons and King further reported that negative affect was associated with increased rumination about strivings ($r = .36$) and with decreased striving-related action (inhibition) ($r = .41$). Thus strivings about which people were in conflict or ambivalent tended to be thought about more but acted upon less than were strivings about which they felt little conflict or ambivalence. Further, rumination about such strivings and inhibition of actions related to them were correlated with negative affect, including anxiety and depression.

Although you may be tired of hearing this, we must reiterate that correlational research of this sort does not indicate the direction of causality. People who have high negative affect may be just those who judge their strivings to be unimportant and who are in conflict about them. It is possible that people's feelings about their strivings may cause them to feel anxious and depressed, but these studies by Emmons do not allow us to draw this conclusion. Although there appears to be some relationship between feelings of well-being and strivings, it is premature to conclude that feelings about strivings are responsible for people's sense of well-being (Emmons, 1986).

Personal Strivings and Motive Dispositions

What is the relationship between personal strivings and motive dispositions? We have already indicated that motive dispositions such as *n* Achievement, *n* Power, and *n* Affiliation occupy a higher position in the personality hierarchy and hence are more general and abstract than personal strivings. As was discussed earlier, lower-level motive constructs such as personal strivings may represent specific contextualized expressions of these higher-level motive dispositions. At the same time, McClelland's analysis of motive dispositions suggests that in some respects they are quite different from personal strivings. Most important, motive dispositions are assumed to be unconscious, while personal strivings are assumed to be accessible to self-report. Further, motivational dispositions are relatively independent of the existence of situational opportunities (although the aroused motive state may require such opportunities). In contrast, personal strivings may be very much affected by situational opportunities, beliefs, and values. Indeed, it is because they are tightly connected to these factors that they are considered more contextualized than motive dispositions. Perhaps this discussion has reminded you of McClelland's distinction between implicit motives and self-attributed motives and has raised the question whether personal strivings might be more related to the latter than to the former.

To examine these issues, Emmons and McAdams (1991) had college students generate lists of strivings, fill out scales from a self-report measure of Murray's needs (the Personality Research Form, Jackson, 1984), and write stories to a set of six TAT-type pictures. The strivings were then coded into motive categories based on the coding manuals for achievement, affiliation, intimacy, and power (Smith, 1992). The TAT stories were coded for achievement, intimacy, and power. Table 8.13 shows the correlations between striving categories and TAT motives. People whose strivings reflected mostly achievement also scored relatively high on the TAT measure of *n* Ach, and similar patterns were found for intimacy and power. The results suggest that when people are asked to reflect consciously on their strivings, they come up with material thematically similar to what they write in response to TAT pictures. Although this result might appear to undermine McClelland's claim that motivational dispositions are "unconscious," results for the questionnaire measure of motives suggest otherwise. Generally, these correlations were lower than those for TAT-measured motives, the highest being .33 between the category of achievement strivings and the PRF achievement scale. Thus, using McClelland's language, people's lists of strivings are more related to their implicit motives than to their self-attributed motives.

These results indicate that strivings—what people say they are typically trying to do—may be considered expressions of more general social motives. As McClelland et al. (1989) noted, how social motives are expressed in different people depends on opportunities, values, roles, and cognitive schemas. This having been said, it is legitimate to question how much lists of strivings really increase our

TABLE 8.13   Correlations Between Strivings and TAT Stories Coded for Social Motives (Based on Emmons and McAdam, 1991)

Striving Category	TAT MOTIVE SCORE		
	Achievement	Intimacy	Power
Achievement	.37	−.28	.05
Intimacy	−.02	.42	−.13
Power	.14	.07	.41

understanding of individuality. Consider these strivings listed by a subject high in *n* Power:

Be assertive when I feel violated or taken advantage of

Avoid confrontations

Force friendships into deeper intimacy than other is willing or ready for

Arrange things so I get my own way

Be the peacemaker in a crowd or relationship

It is true that to some extent we get a "richer," more contextualized picture of this person from these strivings than from the statement "high in *n* Power." But recall that the statement "high in *n* Power" is meaningful only in connection with the body of theory and research that is the basis for our understanding of *n* Power. In fact, these strivings are just the types of activities and goals that have already been linked to high *n* Power. As we look at this list, what impresses us is not so much the specific strivings as the overall pattern, the coherence among them, which is embodied in the phrase "high in *n* Power." Although it might seem on the surface that the more detailed one gets in describing people, the better one understands them, we wonder if the opposite might not be closer to the truth: the details take on significance only when placed in the context of a more general conception (Funder, 1991). Thus Emmons and McAdams' demonstration that strivings are systematically related to motives seems most important to us as further evidence for the construct validity of the measures of social motives.

LIFE TASKS

An important aspect of individuality can be seen in the strength of different people's social motives and personal strivings. Not all goals, however, originate in motive dispositions. Many originate in situations that are encountered, particularly those connected to transitions in life. For example, moving to a new city engages goals related to finding a new home, new doctors and dentists, and new friends. Some of these transitions are normative for certain age groups within a culture. For example, in the United States many young adults leave their parental homes to enter college or to set up their own households. These transitions engender goals such as those mentioned above, as well as goals of a more "psychological" nature, such as feeling independent and establishing a sense of identity. Cantor and her colleagues have referred to such goals as **life tasks,** defined as "the problem(s) that individuals see themselves as working on in a particular life period or life transition" (Cantor & Zirkel, 1990, p. 150; see also Little, 1989, for discussion of a similar concept labeled *personal projects*). Life tasks are closely linked to the specific circumstances of people's lives within a particular time frame. Whereas personal strivings are assumed to persist over long periods (because they are expressions of underlying dispositions), an individual's life tasks are expected to change with changing sociocultural patterns and expectations.

Individuality enters into the analysis of life tasks in three basic ways. First, people may construe the same life tasks differently. Second, people may emphasize one life task more than another. Third, people may utilize different strategies for carrying out a life task. Each of these aspects has been the focus of research by Cantor and her colleagues (see Cantor & Langston, 1989, for a review); here we wish to emphasize the third aspect, what Cantor (1990) calls the "doing" rather than the "having" of personality. From this perspective, life tasks can be thought of as problems to be solved. Just as people use different strategies to solve intellectual tasks, life tasks also can be approached in many different ways. How they are approached reflects personal dispositions (e.g., needs), beliefs about the self, and the possibilities offered by the situation (Cantor, 1994).

Life Tasks in the Context of People's Lives

Cantor and her colleagues have studied a number of life tasks faced by college students, including establishing independence, forging an identity, succeeding in academic pursuits, finding and having friends, and establishing intimacy. Their research has demonstrated that students' pursuit of their goals is very much influenced by contextual factors. For example, Cantor, Acker, and Cook-Flannagan (1992) found that the task of establishing intimacy has very different ramifications for women college students who are in ongoing romantic relationships than for those not romantically involved.

The study of life task strategies is particularly useful for understanding the specific ways in which people in specific settings deal with specific challenges in their lives. Consider the important life task faced by college students of doing well in courses. Harlow and Cantor (1994) studied a strategy used by some students who felt that the task of doing well academically was both very important and very difficult. Fifty-four members of a sorority at a midwestern university generated ten current life tasks and then indicated which ones were connected to the tasks of "doing well academically; getting good grades" and "making friends; getting along with others." The importance of these two "consensual" tasks is indicated by the fact that 69% of the self-generated life tasks fit into one of these two categories. The women were then asked to rate their tasks on a set of scales similar to those used by Emmons and King (1988). Subsequently, the women provided information about their friends and acquaintances, participated in an experience-sampling procedure, and filled out a questionnaire about their life satisfaction.

A group of women was identified whose ratings of "doing well academically" indicated a heightened concern with grades combined with a feeling that this task was difficult. This group of "outcome-focused" women was compared to women who either didn't care much about doing well academically or who did care but felt the task was not difficult and were not preoccupied with grades. The main issue Harlow and Cantor were interested in was the strategies students with an outcome focus used in pursuit of this task. They hypothesized that these women would tend to bring this task into situations other than those involving actual academic work. In particular, they expected the academic task to intrude into situations that are usually not a place for working out academic problems, namely when socializing with other students.

Information about how students saw different situations was obtained from the experience-sampling procedure. The students were asked to rate how relevant each situation they encountered was to their various life tasks. As can be seen in Figure 8.3, outcome-focused students much more often indicated that the task of doing well academically was relevant to social settings than did the non-outcome-focused students. For the latter group, the task of "finding intimacy—dating" was the most relevant for social settings; yet, as Figure 8.3 shows, for outcome-focused students it was no more relevant than was the task of academics. The experience samples also showed that the tendency to bring academic concerns into social settings occurred most often when the outcome-focused women were experiencing academic difficulties.

The close connection between academics and socializing for outcome-focused women is further indicated by the finding that their social satisfaction (as indicated on the Life Satisfaction Questionnaire) was highly correlated with their positive experiences in the classroom (.49) but only moderately correlated with their positive experiences while relaxing with other students (.27). In contrast, there was no relationship between social satisfaction and positive experiences in the classroom (−.03) for non-outcome-focused students, but there was a strong relationship with positive experiences relaxing with other students (.48).

How did outcome-focused women make social situations relevant for academics? Analysis of the experience-sampling data indicated that when they felt things were not going well academically, they used social settings to seek

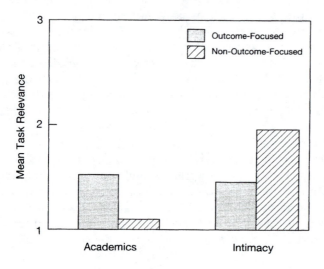

FIGURE 8.3   Mean relevance of the academic and intimacy life tasks while socializing *(1-not relevant, 2-somewhat relevant, 3-very relevant)* (Based on Harlow and Cantor, 1994; reproduced with permission of the American Psychological Association)

reassurance from other students about their academic performance. Although this strategy may have helped them feel better about their academic task, it appears to have interfered with their social satisfaction: the correlation between seeking encouragement from others and social satisfaction was −.58. Furthermore, an end-of-semester survey indicated that outcome-focused students lost contact with more people than non-outcome-focused students.

The detailed analysis of life task strategies is useful for an understanding of how goals are translated into behaviors and outcomes in specific situations. The Harlow and Cantor (1994) study draws attention to the possibility that people's goals may sometimes extend to "atypical" domains and that pursuit of one life task may interfere with pursuit of others. The more contextualized a research focus, the more likely it is to aid in an understanding of the specific situations or individuals studied. Whether it is also contributes to a more general understanding depends on whether the research has a strong theoretical rationale or is explicitly linked to higher-order constructs such as needs.

MOTIVES, GOALS, AND TRAITS

In chapter 3 we discussed the concepts of dispositions and traits. We said that dispositions are latent characteristics that are revealed in behavior under certain conditions. Many psychologists use the term *trait* to refer to a kind of disposition: those that produce consistent behavioral patterns in the person. Where do motives and goals fit into this scheme? According to Murray (1938), needs (motives) are dispositions. They are part of the individual's psychological system whether or not they actually produce overt behavior. Indeed, some needs may never or only rarely express themselves in behavior. A person with a strong need for Power may never have the opportunity to express the need, or the need may be in conflict with other needs, or the person may lack the ability to fulfill the need. But the need is there, nonetheless, and will be revealed in instruments like the TAT. Other needs may be expressed frequently in overt behavior, in which case the consistent behaviors that make up a trait can be observed. More specifically, when consistent behaviors reflect one's motive disposition, we may speak of a "motivational trait" (Murray, 1938, p. 713). As Read and Miller (1989) note, a sociable person and a lonely person may have the same goals, but the lonely person may lack the skills necessary to get and maintain friendships. It is important to note that neither Murray nor anyone else claims that all traits are motivational. Some traits may reflect temperament, others may reflect cognitive abilities, and still others may indicate expressive styles (Allport, 1937; Cattell, 1965; Guilford, 1975).

How do motives fit into a system like the Big Five? On one level, you might be tempted to think that the traits that are part of the Big Five are all motivational. If you look at the list of needs in Table 8.3, you might not find it hard to pick out those that could correspond to extraversion, conscientiousness, agreeableness, neuroticism, and openness. In fact, you may recall that in chapter 4 we discussed a factor analysis of the Personality Research Form that produced a factor structure very similar to the Big Five (see Table 4.1). For example, need for succorance was related to neuroticism, need for affiliation to extraversion, need for sentience to openness, need for nurturance to agreeableness, and need for achievement to conscientiousness (Costa & McCrae, 1988). These relationships led McCrae (1994) to state that "One might conclude from such findings that the structure of motives is equivalent to the structure of traits" (p. 151).

People's goals (strivings, projects, life tasks) may also be connected to traits such as those described in the Big Five model. For example, judgments of the stressfulness and enjoyableness of personal projects were related to neuroticism and extraversion, respectively (Little, Lecci, & Watkinson, 1992). In a study of individuals who volunteered to help people with AIDS, Snyder (1993; Snyder & Omoto, 1992) found that the volunteers' goals were often related to their personality characteristics. For example, people who said they volunteered because they felt a humanitarian need to help others tended to have high scores on measures of nurturance, empathy, and social responsibility; volunteers who said they wanted to feel better about themselves tended to score low on measures of self-esteem.

There is little doubt that motives, traits, and goals are interrelated. Yet it is not obvious that a view such as McCrae's quoted above is correct. Recall that McClelland argues strongly that self-report measures such as the Personality Research Form measure something very different from what fantasy and thought-sampling techniques measure. Virtually all of the research relating traits to motives has incorporated such self-report measures. The relationship between *implicit* motives and traits is much less clear-cut. Further, almost all of the research on goals has dealt with goals that people know they have, that is, conscious goals. Yet, it is quite likely that people also have goals that are not consciously accessible. To the extent that motives and goals are not conscious, self-report measures such as those that dominate contemporary research on traits and goals may be missing a large piece of the action.

9

Unconscious Processes

Imagine the following scenario. John is interviewing an applicant for a job in a small firm. During the interview, John thinks, "This applicant is more capable and experienced than I am." John is jealous. In his report of the interview, he denigrates the abilities of the applicant and recommends rejection of her application for the job. During his weekly psychotherapy session, John mentions this interview, and his therapist thinks it is worthwhile to explore John's response to the applicant. In what ways might different beliefs about conscious and unconscious processes influence the goals of therapy? We will sketch some possibilities.

1. John is aware of his thoughts and the experience of jealousy. He might even know why he thought the applicant was better than he was and why he was jealous. John reports these thoughts to the therapist and the report is **veridical,** that is, it is an accurate portrayal of the reasons for John's actions. The therapist's role in this instance might be devoted to helping John clarify and talk about what he already understands.

2. John is aware of his experience of jealousy and the thought that the applicant is more competent than he is, but he is reluctant to reveal these thoughts to the therapist and therefore disguises the reasons for his action. John chooses to suppress his knowledge of these reasons. In this instance the therapist must either

infer the patient's true reasons for his action or create conditions that will encourage John to be truthful in order to understand John's actions.

3. John knows why he acted as he did but he does not want to admit the truth of what he already knows to himself. He would not like to think of himself as a jealous person and refuses to admit that fact to himself. The therapist might create the conditions that would help John to think about something that he would rather not think about—to accept a truth that could be conscious but is either suppressed or avoided.

4. John does not know why he acted as he did. The true reasons for his actions are unconscious—outside of his awareness. He is not aware of the experience of jealousy and not aware that he had the thought, "She is better than I am." In this case, the therapist would have to help him discover why he acted as he did. Why might a person be unaware of the reasons for an action? A Freudian might argue that John is repressing the impulses or beliefs that underlie his actions. If intense negative emotions accompany the true reasons for an action, a person might use repression as a defense that blocks access to consciousness. In order to help a person understand the reasons for his actions, the Freudian therapist might have to help the person confront painful memories that had been blocked from conscious awareness.

We assume that you decided to take a course on personality because you were curious about your own behavior. Which of the beliefs about the relationship between thought and action do you think is correct? Do you think you usually know why you do what you do? Do you try to deceive yourself or others about the true reasons for your actions? Are you puzzled about *why* you do what you do? Are you inclined to believe that the true reasons for your actions are buried in your unconscious?

Psychologists are inclined to answer these question in various ways. If people generally know why they do what they do, then the psychologist does not have to discover what is unknown. If people do not know why they do what they do, then the psychologist cannot rely solely, or predominantly, or at all, on the reasons people give for their behavior. Different beliefs about the unconscious also structure our deepest insights into personality. If we want to understand a person, do we have to understand the contents of that person's conscious mind or unconscious mind?

We don't know the answers to any of these question. Some personality psychologists think they have the answers, but these answers would undoubtedly differ from each other. We will tell you about some research that may help you to think about these questions in a critical way.

ACTS AND REASONS: CAN WE EXPLAIN WHY WE DO WHAT WE DO?

Intention and Voluntary Movement

What is the simplest possible voluntary action that a person might be asked to perform? Moving a finger could certainly be thought of as an extremely simple voluntary act. Suppose we asked you, as an experiment, to move your finger from time to time. Let's assume that you are a reasonably cooperative person and you decide to comply with this request. If you were asked, "Why did you move your finger?" you might answer, "Because I was asked to." But how did this intention translate into action? What determined the actual moment that you moved your finger? Try to introspect—to think of what is going on in your mind before you move your finger. Most people who are asked to do this say that they were aware of their intention to move their finger before they moved it. Someone might say, "I experienced an urge to move my finger and then I moved it."

Libet (1985) studied the causes of voluntary movement of the wrist or fingers. Libet told his subjects to flex their fingers whenever they wanted to. The responses were voluntary and under the control of the subject. He recorded the time of occurrence of each response. He wanted to know what the subjects were aware of right before they made the motor response. Subjects reported that they experienced an intention to make the response before the response actually began. Libet was interested in the exact timing of the intention to move the finger in order to discover whether or not the intention preceded the movement and whether it occurred before other possible events that predicted the movement. In order to time the experience of the intention to make the movement, the subject was asked to look at a screen with a dot moving in a circular fashion to mimic a second hand on a watch. The subjects reported the position of the dot on the screen when they were aware of the intention to act, and from this location, the experimenter was able to determine exactly when the awareness of the intention occurred. Typically it began approximately 190 milliseconds before the motor response (slightly less than one-fifth of a second).

Why did the subject perform this motor act? We could say that the subject formed a conscious intention to act and this intention caused the act to occur. This answer certainly seems plausible and is compatible with the way we analyze many of our more complex actions. A professor asks a question in class. A student raises her hand. If we were perverse enough to ask the student why she raised her hand, we would generally be content with the answer, "I wanted to answer the question you asked." Note that we assume that there is an intention to act that the person is conscious of and that this intention initiates the action.

In his experiment on the initiation of motor action, Libet also monitored the electrical activity at the scalp. He found that there was a change in this electrical activity that invariably preceded the initiation of the motor response. The change in electrical activity is called a **readiness potential.** The average time of occurrence of the readiness potential was approximately 535 milliseconds prior to the finger movement. Figure 9.1 shows the timing of the three events studied by Libet: the occurrence of the readiness potential, the awareness of the intention to act as measured by the reported location of a dot on a screen, and the actual response of moving a finger. This figure indicates that while the intention to move occurred before the actual finger movement, the readiness potential occurred even earlier—before there was an awareness of an intention to move the finger.

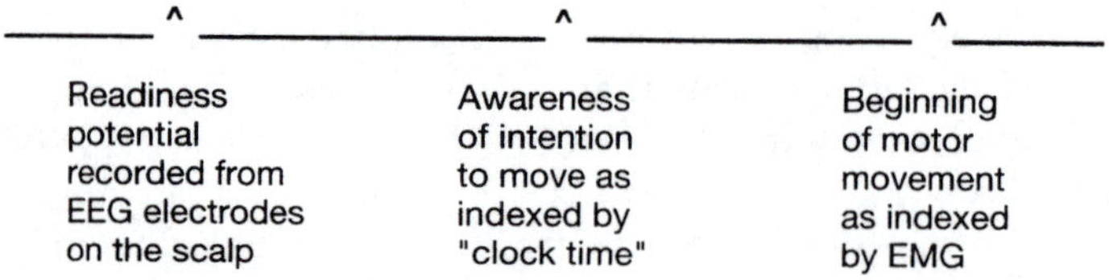

^	^		^

Readiness
potential
recorded from
EEG electrodes
on the scalp

Awareness
of intention
to move as
indexed by
"clock time"

Beginning
of motor
movement
as indexed
by EMG

FIGURE 9.1   Libet's time line. (Based on Libet, 1985)

How do you interpret these results? Are you still sure that the intention to move causes the subject to move the finger? One could argue that the movement occurs not because of the intention to move but because of changes in the brain that precede the awareness of the intention. If this is correct, what is the role of the conscious intention? Here is a radical answer: it has no role. It is, to use a philosophical term, **epiphenomenal.** That is, it accompanies the act or, in this instance, even precedes the act, but it plays no causal role in the initiation of the act.

Are there problems with this interpretation? You may have noticed that there may be a flaw in the experiment. Perhaps subjects are aware of the intention to move their finger before they indicate that they are aware. The timing of the awareness of the intention is determined by the report about the location of a dot on a screen. Perhaps there is a 500 millisecond time lag between the awareness of the intention to move and the observation of the location of the dot.

In order to rule out this interpretation, Libet used the same timing method in a control experiment in which subjects were asked to report the location of the dot when they first experienced a pinprick on their skin. The clock time in this case was coincident with or even slightly before the occurrence of the stimulus. There does not appear to be a time lag between the occurrence of a sensation and the awareness of its occurrence as reported by the clock procedure used by Libet. If we accept the timing of the conscious intention to act as valid, we are forced to conclude that the *conscious* intention could not have caused the act, since events occurred prior to the awareness of that intention that signal the occurrence of the act. The awareness of the intention may be caused by events in the brain that signal the subsequent occurrence of the motor act. Since the brain events *precede* the awareness of the intentions, they can cause the mental event (the awareness). The converse cannot be true—unless you are willing to believe in "backward causality," whereby the cause of an event can occur after the event occurs. If intentions have a causal role in initiating an action, then the intentions must occur prior to an awareness of their occurrence.

Libet's study suggests that our beliefs about the role of conscious intentions in controlling action may be flawed. If you find this experiment convincing, are you prepared to generalize these findings? Would you argue that you don't really know what made you have an argument with your friend? Are most of our actions controlled by events that we are not aware of? Is consciousness epiphenomenal—like a ghost in a machine creating idle chatter in the mind? If we want to understand the true reasons for an individual's behavior, must we disregard the reasons offered by the person? Libet's study, however it is to be interpreted, surely does not provide answers to all of these complex questions. Perhaps we can come closer to answers by describing the results of some other studies.

In summary, Libet argued that events that occur in the brain can initiate voluntary actions before the awareness of the intention to act occurs. If intentions are the initiators of actions, Libet's study suggests that intentions are brain processes, not experiences. This analysis also suggests that our beliefs about the reasons for our actions may be wrong.

Effects of Facial Muscles on Affective Judgment

Are there other examples of bodily changes that we may not be aware of that influence the occurrence of mental events? Zajonc, Murphy, and Inglehart (1989) studied the effects of changes in facial musculature on emotional experiences. In one of their studies they had German-speaking subjects read a story that had many words containing the German vowel *ü*. In order to pronounce this vowel sound, it is necessary to align the musculature of the face in a manner that is similar to a frown. They also had their subjects read stories that did not contain this vowel sound. The stories were matched for length, semantic content, and emotional content. The stories containing the *ü* vowels were rated by their subjects as being less pleasant and were not as well liked as the corresponding stories without this vowel sound. The experiment indicates that arrangements of the musculature of the face in a form that is analogous to what occurs during emotional experiences influences a person's emotional state and judgments. It is highly unlikely that subjects were aware of the subtle influence of changes in the muscles on their emotional state.

These interpretations of the Libet study and the Zajonc, Murphy, and Inglehart study still leave us with relatively little information about the role of the unconscious in our behavior. Both studies deal with unconscious influences on behavior that is of little importance. Our concerns are not centered on moving fingers and judging stories. Not much is at stake for a person in performing either of these actions. When we act in more consequential ways, our conscious intentions and thoughts may be more deeply engaged in determining our actions.

Cognitive Dissonance

Is it possible to demonstrate unconscious influences on behaviors that are important to a person? We can try. **Cognitive dissonance theory** assumes that individuals strive to maintain consistency among their beliefs. For example, if I know that I smoke and I also believe that smoking leads to cancer, these two beliefs are dissonant. I try to eliminate my cognitive dissonance, perhaps by doubting the relevance to me of research on the relationship between smoking and cancer. I might assert that smoking leads to cancer only in genetically vulnerable individuals and I am not genetically vulnerable since no one in my family has had cancer. This new belief reduces the cognitive dissonance.

Zimbardo (1969) used cognitive dissonance theory as a basis for investigating cognitive influences on motivation. He designed a series of experiments in which he induced a motivational state in his subjects. For example, in one study the subjects were asked to skip breakfast. After they participated for a period of time, Zimbardo asked them to continue in the experiment—their doing so causing a delay in their lunch. If a subject was induced to continue in the experiment and was not given very persuasive reasons for doing so, the knowledge that he is hungry and also that he has agreed to a further delay in eating creates a state of dissonance. The dissonance could be eliminated if the belief that he is hungry is modified. If such an effect occurs, he would exhibit a decrease in hunger attributable to a process of reasoning. Cognitive dissonance theory assumes that individuals engage in a soliloquy in which they reason as follows: "I am hungry and I have agreed to delay eating for no good reason. That doesn't make much sense. But I am really not that hungry so it is okay to delay eating."

Zimbardo, Cohen, Weisenberg, Dworkin, and Firestone (1969) reported the results of a cognitive dissonance study of pain. Subjects who received a series of electric shocks were given an opportunity to continue in the experiment. One group, assigned to a low-dissonance condition, was given ample justifications for continuing in the experiment: they were paid well for continuing and they were told that they would be making an important contribution to knowledge. A second group of subjects, assigned to a high-dissonance condition, was not given persuasive reasons to continue. The subjects in both groups were subsequently given electric shocks. Zimbardo and his colleagues assumed that those in the high-dissonance group would not find the shocks as painful as subjects in the low-dissonance group, that the former would reason as follows: "I have agreed to receive additional shocks and I don't really know why I have done so. But this is not really a bad thing because the shocks are really not that painful." This process of reasoning serves to eliminate the cognitive dissonance. The researchers predicted that these subjects would exhibit a cognitive control of pain that would reduce their pain.

Zimbardo et al. measured the response to the electric shock in several different ways. They asked subjects to rate the painfulness, they permitted subjects to decide the level of shock that they were willing to tolerate, and they obtained measures of physiological and behavioral responses. They found that responses of those in the high-dissonance condition indicated that the shock was less painful to them relative to those in the low-dissonance condition.

This experiment does not provide any evidence for unconscious processes. The results suggest that thought processes can control response to pain. In order to explain the results of this experiment, it is necessary to assume that subjects reasoned in a particular way. We are usually aware of our thought processes and therefore it is reasonable to assume that the thought processes that influenced the behavior of the subjects in the Zimbardo et al. experiment were conscious processes.

How could we actually determine if the thought processes that are assumed to influence the response to pain in this study were conscious? Nisbett and Wilson

(1977) proposed three tests of the hypothesis that subjects are conscious of their thought processes:

1. We could ask the subjects about their reasoning processes. If the subject was conscious of the thought processes that influenced the response to pain, we would expect that the subject would be able to tell the experimenter about them.

2. We might assume that it would be relatively easy to control the verbal report about pain, but it would be harder to control the physiological and behavioral indices of pain. If this assumption is correct, conscious processes could influence a person to *say* that the shocks are not painful, but this change in verbal response might not extend to the control of physiological responses or even to the decision to tolerate high levels of shock.

3. There should be a positive correlation between the verbal report about the painfulness of the shocks and the level of the shocks that subjects are willing to tolerate and about the intensity of the physiological responses to the shock.

These tests contain an implicit theory of conscious influences on behavior that assumes that individuals are generally aware of their thought processes. If this is correct, the subjects in the dissonance experiment should have been able to tell the experimenter about their experiences. If behavior is controlled by our conscious processes, we should expect to see clear evidence of changes in the verbal reports of pain as a result of dissonance manipulations. The changes in beliefs about pain might influence a person's physiology indirectly. Any influence that conscious states have on behavioral and physiological indicators should be indirect. (You might find this argument unconvincing. Perhaps conscious processes are only poorly reflected in our verbal reports.)

Nisbett and Wilson (1977) reviewed the Zimbardo cognitive dissonance and related studies and argued that they failed to meet the three tests outlined above. (See also Brody, 1988, chap. 6; Quattrone, 1985). First, when subjects were asked to describe their reasoning processes in the Zimbardo et al. study, they could not report the presence of the reasoning process that was assumed to determine the changes in their behavior. When they were told the dissonance explanation of their behavior, they denied that this described their reasoning processes. It could be argued that subjects were not able to report the presence of this reasoning process because it never occurred—that cognitive dissonance theory is wrong. The problem with this argument is that it leaves us without an explanation of the behavior of the subjects in the experiment. How else would you explain the differences in response to pain for the high- and low-dissonance subjects?

Second, there was very little effect on the verbal behavior of the subjects. Subjects in the high-dissonance condition said that they found the shocks just as painful as did subjects in a control group who were not asked to continue in the experiment. The assertion that the dissonance manipulation reduced the level of pain is based on their physiological and behavioral responses. The high-dissonance group responded physiologically and behaviorally in the same way as a control group who received shocks of much lower intensity. What appears to have happened in this experiment is that subjects in the high-dissonance condition *said* that the shocks were painful but then were willing to accept high levels of shock before asking the experimenter to end the experiment and exhibited physiological and behavioral responses that were typical of individuals exposed to much lower levels of shock. Zimbardo (1969) obtained analogous results in experiments on the dissonance manipulation of hunger. Subjects in a high-dissonance condition who agreed to postpone eating when they were hungry without being provided with strong reasons for this delay would say that they were hungry although if given an opportunity to eat they would not eat much and their blood sugar levels would be similar to those of individuals who were not hungry. Thus the dissonance manipulation of thought processes had its strongest influence on physiology and behavior, not on verbal reports about psychological states.

Third, the correlations between pain ratings and behavioral and physiological responses to the shock stimulus were close to zero. A subject's rating of the painfulness of the shocks could not be used to predict his physiological or behavioral response. We can say that the verbal reports and the behavioral and physiological responses to the shock stimuli were unrelated to each other and were determined by different influences—they were **dissociated.**

The results of the Zimbardo et al. study fail to meet each of the three tests proposed by Nisbett and Wilson for the presence of conscious influences. They concluded that these results, as well as the findings of a number of related studies, are best interpreted as providing evidence for *unconscious* influences on behavior. On their analysis the results obtained in this experiment may be interpreted as follows: Subjects in the high-dissonance condition engage in the process of reasoning suggested by a dissonance theory analysis. This process of reasoning is not accessible to awareness. Because it occurs in the unconscious, subjects are not able to reproduce this reasoning process when they are asked about it in postexperimental interviews. The unconscious reasoning process reduces the physiological and behavioral response to shock—in effect subjects are not in pain, or at least not in intense pain. The reduction in pain caused by the unconscious reasoning processes is not in awareness.

If you accept this analysis of the results of the Zimbardo et al. study, do you think that such processes of reasoning are common or rare? Do we often have unconscious thoughts that change our psychological states? Could a person be angry without knowing that she was angry and could this anger be manifested even though she denies that she is angry? If such processes occur, it would be necessary to investigate the unconscious thought processes in order to understand the reasons for the behavior. We could not accept at face value assertions about the presence or absence of psychological states such as pain. Verbal statements about a person's pain, or level of hunger, or degree of sexual arousal, or jealousy might be incomplete in providing clues about a person's psychological state. They are not the same as the state. A person may be in pain in some sense (perhaps physiologically), or hungry, or sexually aroused, or jealous even if the person states that he or she is not any of these things. When a verbal report about a state seems to disagree with other ways of determining the state, we may say that there is a dissociation between verbal reports and other indices of the state. In the Zimbardo et al. experiment it was possible to reconstruct tentatively the subjects' thought processes. In real life we are usually not able to test these kinds of hypotheses. We might note in many instances that individuals act in ways that belie their assertions about the reasons for their actions or that do not appear to be congruent with their verbal reports. If a person professes lack of anger at another yet acts, perhaps in subtle ways, in a manner that indicates he is angry, we might be inclined to distrust the accuracy of the person's assertion. This analysis suggests that the report might not be intentionally deceptive (although it might rightly be understood as being self-deceptive).

If we can recognize the discrepancy or dissociations between reports and actions, how are we then able to discover if the dissociation is a product of a self-deception or an intentional deception? Can you think of instances in which you now believe that your understanding of your actions was based on self-deception? Can you think of instances in which your reports to others about your psychological states and the reasons for your actions were deliberately deceptive?

RESPONSES AND AWARENESS

Perceptual Defense and Subception

Conscious processes are those things of which we are aware; *unconscious processes* are those things that are not in our awareness. We cannot touch or directly observe awareness: it must be inferred from various responses, typically from verbal reports. We have already seen that reports about experience may not always tell you what is going on in a person's mind. How, then, can we determine what a person is aware of?

Let us begin again with an experiment, one with a serious flaw (see if you can spot it). Imagine that you are a subject in an experiment conducted almost 50 years ago by McGinnies (1949). You are a male college student who is asked by a female experimenter to recognize words that are presented to you in a tachistoscope, a device that allows a visual stimulus to be presented for very brief periods of time. The words are presented for durations below what appears to be your threshold for correct recognition of the words. The duration of presentation is increased until you are able to identify the words. Among the words presented are ordinary English words and a class of words chosen by the experimenter as **taboo,** words such as *Kotex* and *whore* (remember, this was almost 50 years ago!).

McGinnies found that the threshold for recognition of the taboo words was higher than that for the ordinary words. In other words, the presentation times required to accurately recognize the taboo words were higher than the times required to recognize ordinary words. McGinnies also recorded skin conductance responses (called *galvanic skin response* or *GSR*) as the words were presented. He found that the GSRs to the taboo words were larger than the GSRs to neutral words *before* the taboo words were correctly recognized. Although the taboo words were presented below the threshold for correct identification, the GSR provided evidence that subjects had an emotional reaction to them. McGinnies interpreted these results as an instance of **perceptual defense.** Subjects unconsciously recognized the taboo words, which evoked an emotional response, which in turn created a barrier or a defensive process that inhibited conscious recognition of the taboo words.

Do you find McGinnies' interpretation of these results convincing? There may be a simpler interpretation. Subjects in a psychological experiment might be somewhat reluctant to report that they were seeing taboo words unless they were quite sure of what was being presented to them. A subject who reports seeing the word *whore* when actually being presented with the word *where* might well be suspected of being demented or at least hypersexed. Surely ordinary social conventions might dictate considerable caution before uttering a taboo word in the setting of a psychological experiment.

Is it possible to design a study to demonstrate something analogous to perceptual defense without being subject to the kind of criticism directed at the McGinnies experiment? Lazarus and McCleary (1951) developed an emotional response to neutral stimuli (nonsense syllables like *VUZ*) by a conditioning procedure in which the neutral stimuli were paired with shock. These emotionally conditioned nonsense syllables and the control nonsense syllables were presented to subjects via a tachistoscope. Again, the presentation times were below the threshold of correct recognition and were increased until subjects were able to identify the nonsense syllables correctly. They also obtained GSRs to the stimuli. When Lazarus and McCleary looked only at those trials on which the subjects had not correctly identified the nonsense syllables, they found that the GSRs to stimuli that had been associated with shock were higher than the GSRs to the other stimuli. They interpreted these results as providing evidence for a process analogous to perceptual defense that they called **subception.** They assumed that subjects were able unconsciously to perceive the emotionally significant stimuli, as indexed by the GSR, even though they were not consciously aware of the stimuli, as indicated by their inability to identify them correctly.

Do Verbal Reports Tell Us Everything a Person Knows?

Lazarus and McCleary assumed that the GSR was more sensitive than the verbal response since the former indicated the presence of an emotional response while the latter indicated that subjects were not able to identify the stimulus. Although their interpretation is not as easily dismissed as the interpretation by McGinnies of his experiment, it is possible to provide a somewhat different interpretation of this experiment.

We can define subception as a phenomenon that occurs because of a discrepancy between two different responses, in this case a GSR and a verbal report that attempts to identify which of several nonsense syllables is tachistoscopically presented. Lazarus and McLeary believed that there was a dissociation between the verbal report and the physiological response. Before we accept their interpretation, we might want to think a bit more about verbal reports. An individual may know more about a stimulus than is revealed in the initial verbal response. Therefore we cannot exhaustively determine the nature of the subject's knowledge from a single verbal response about the stimulus.

It is easy to demonstrate that a person may know more or be aware of more than she knows that she is aware of. Here is a classic demonstration of this phenomenon. Blackwell (1952) presented subjects with a task in which they had to guess the location of a very dim and briefly presented dot of light in one of four clearly demarcated quadrants on a screen. If the subject's initial response was wrong, the subject was asked to respond again. The probability of correctly identifying the location of the light by chance is now .33, since there are three possible remaining locations. Subjects exhibited greater than chance accuracy in locating a light. Even if they were wrong on their first two responses, their third response exhibited greater than chance accuracy. This experiment demonstrates that subjects may have more information about a stimulus than is exhausted in an initial verbal response.

There is a difference between what may be called an **objective threshold** for the identification of an event—that is, the level of presentation at which the subject has obtained no information about an event— and the **subjective threshold**— that is, the level of presentation at which the subject *believes* that he or she has no information about the event (Dagenbach and Carr, 1985). One of us once did an experiment in which subjects were presented with words that had positive or negative emotional meanings (Brody et al., 1987), shown at the edge of a screen and written vertically rather than horizontally. The subjective threshold for most subjects was close to 50 milliseconds; most subjects indicated that at that presentation time (1/20th of a second) they were not able to see the word clearly, since the letters were blurred. They were aware that letters were on the screen but they said they were not able to tell what was written. When they were asked whether they had been presented with a good or bad word at presentation times that were below their subjective threshold, they reported that they had not seen the word clearly and that their judgments were based on guesses. At presentation times of either two or three milliseconds, the subjects were accurate in close to 75 percent of their judgments. Chance performance would be at 50 percent since half the words were either good or bad half of the time. Presentation times of two or three milliseconds were still above the objective threshold but below the subjective threshold for correct recognition of the words.

The difference between objective and subjective thresholds is widely recognized. Virtually all psychologists interested in **subliminal perception**—the perception of stimuli that are below threshold—agree that it is possible to make accurate judgments and be influenced by stimuli that are below subjective but above objective thresholds (Greenwald, 1992; Holender, 1986); however, they disagree about whether or not it is possible to be influenced by stimuli that are below objective thresholds.

We can use this analysis of the difference between objective and subjective thresholds to explain the results of the subception experiment. *Subception* was defined as a discrepancy between two responses. On those trials in which subjects in the Lazarus and McCleary experiment were not able to identify the words, GSRs were larger to syllables paired with shock than to syllables that were not paired with shock. This result does not really indicate that subjects were not aware of the syllables that were paired with shock. If, after an incorrect first response, they are given a second chance to guess which syllable was presented to them, their second verbal response will have a better than chance probability of being correct. In other words, subjects know more about the stimulus presented to them than they are able to reveal in their first verbal response. The subception experiment, which we have said indicates that subjects know more about a stimulus than is revealed by a single verbal response, provides additional support for the notion that our judgments of the nature of a subject's awareness depend on the ways in which we try to judge that awareness. People always seem to have more information about something than they think they do.

Let's summarize. Individuals may have more information about a stimulus than they know that they have. A single verbal response may not always exhaust a subject's knowledge. We cannot begin to understand what a subject is aware of without considering whether or not we have exhaustively examined his knowledge. You can have information about something without knowing that you have this information. We cannot measure awareness directly, we can only infer it from various response indices. Unless we take great pains to study many possible responses, it is easy to conclude wrongly that individuals are not aware of something when they are.

The phenomenon of discrepancy among different response indices of psychological states occurs in several areas of research on unconscious influences. Kunst-Wilson and Zajonc (1980) studied the effects of exposure to stimuli that individuals were not able to recognize. Subjects were tachistoscopically exposed to a set of polygons several times. The exposures were quite brief and subjects were not able to "see" the polygons. In order to ascertain whether subjects had clear information about the polygons, they were given a test in which they were presented with pairs of polygons, one of which had actually been shown and the other of which was similar but had not been presented to them. The subjects were asked to choose the one of each pair that had been shown. The probability of correct performance on this task by chance is 50 percent. If the appropriate level of stimulus presentation is chosen, subjects will not be able to perform this task with greater than chance accuracy—indicating that they cannot recognize the stimuli that had been shown (Seamon, Marsh, and Brody, 1984). If the pair of polygons is presented at above threshold durations and subjects are asked to choose the one of each pair that they like, they tend to choose the one that was previously presented. It is well-known that subjects prefer stimuli that are familiar to those that are unfamiliar. These preferences develop even for stimuli that subjects are not aware of having previously seen. Such preferences persist for as long as a week (Seamon, Brody, and Kauff 1983).

CONSCIOUS AND UNCONSCIOUS PROCESSES COMPARED

What difference does it make if psychological processes are conscious or unconscious? If you know that you are angry, will you behave differently than if you are angry but are not aware of being angry? Our review of research on unconscious processes has not addressed this question. We have argued that some of our actions may be controlled by events of which we are not aware (e.g., the Libet study). But this fact does not indicate that the influence of such out-of-awareness events is qualitatively different than is the influence of events in awareness. We argued that people may not always know what they know about something. Attempts to assess people's knowledge and awareness directly may not provide an adequate index of what a person knows. But does knowing something without knowing that we know it have a different influence on us than it would have if we did know that we know it?

Consider a simple example. Suppose you are sitting in a movie theater and someone flashes the following message on the screen, "Buy Coca Cola." The message is flashed briefly—above the objective threshold but below the subjective threshold—so that the audience is not aware of seeing it. If some attempt were made to ask individuals to distinguish between messages that were sent and those that were not sent (for example, by asking if the message concerned food or cars), they could in some way indicate that they have information about the message that was sent although they might not know that they have this knowledge. How would this message that you do not know you have received influence you? Would it have a different influence on you than it would have if you were aware of seeing it? Does its unconscious or partially unconscious status lead you to an irresistible impulse to buy Coca Cola? Is the influence of such an unconscious stimulus stronger than it would be if you were aware of seeing it? Does the unconscious stimulus influence you in ways that are qualitatively different from the influence it would have if it were conscious?

These questions embody a fundamental issue about unconscious processes. Probably most psychologists would indicate that there is very little evidence to suggest that the subliminal Coca Cola message would lead to an irresistible influence to purchase a Coca Cola nor would it influence you in some qualitatively different way than would the same message presented above subjective thresholds for awareness. Subliminal messages of this sort are likely to be ineffective in influencing someone. If they have any influence at all, that influence is likely weaker than it would be if the message were clearly in awareness (see Greenwald, 1992).

But this thinking does not settle the general question that we have raised about qualitatively different conscious and unconscious influences.

Why would conscious influences be qualitatively different from unconscious influences? We sometimes think of conscious and unconscious processes in terms of a spatial metaphor, each with a distinct location in the mind. If they occupy different regions, then it is possible that the laws that govern one region may be different from those that govern another. While this metaphor may appear plausible, it is not one that is acceptable to all psychologists. Some psychologists argue that consciousness is unitary, that the alleged independence of unconscious and conscious processes is a mistaken idea (Holender, 1986; Shanks & St. John, 1994). They say that different ways of assessing conscious processes may well give us somewhat different impressions of what individuals know, but this possibility still does not imply that there are qualitatively distinct processes associated with conscious and unconscious experiences. We will not attempt to resolve this controversy here. We will, however, describe several studies that may be interpreted as providing evidence for qualitatively distinct conscious and unconscious influences.

Implicit Memory

Psychologists interested in memory distinguish between **implicit** and **explicit memory** systems. Explicit memories refer to knowledge that can be intentionally retrieved. Implicit memories refer to memories of events that influence us that we cannot intentionally recall. Early evidence supporting this distinction came from an observation made by the French neurologist Claparede. Claparede studied a patient with Korsakoff's syndrome, an alcohol-induced disease that in extreme form appears to destroy memory for any episode after the onset of the disease. One manifestation of Korsakoff's syndrome is that patients do not know if they have previously encountered someone, thus are not aware that the physician who is introduced to them is the same physician they encountered even as recently as a half hour before. Claparede pricked the hand of one patient with a hatpin. When he returned to see the patient, the patient was reluctant to shake his hand. When he was asked why, the patient responded, "Sometimes pins are hidden in people's hands." The patient was not aware that this belief was related to a memory of a previous encounter with Claparede.

More recent studies of implicit memory in Korsakoff's patients provide additional evidence that the deficit in their ability to intentionally recall episodes does not extend to their performance on various measures of implicit memory (Graf and Schacter, 1985; Schacter, 1987). For example, they respond similarly to normals on tests of the effects of previous exposure to words. If a person has previously encountered the word *scalp*, when then asked to complete a word using the stem *sca*, the person is likely to complete it with *lp*, recreating the word *scalp*, even though such alternatives as *scar* and *scan* have much higher probabilities of occurrence without previous exposure to *scalp*. Korsakoff's patients exhibit these effects even though they do not recall having seen the word and may not even recall seeing a list of words.

Normal subjects too exhibit influences of previously encountered stimuli that they do not know they have encountered. For example, Jacoby and Witherspoon (1982) asked normal subjects to spell homophones such as *reed* and *read* that were spoken aloud to them. If the subjects had a single previous visual encounter with the word *reed*, they were more likely to choose this infrequent spelling of the word over the more common spelling. This effect occurred even if the subjects were not aware of having previously encountered the word *reed*.

The extreme independence of explicit and implicit memory systems exhibited by Korsakoff's patients is related to anatomically localized brain damage (Squire, 1992). If different parts of the brain are involved in implicit and explicit memory systems, it is reasonable to think of conscious and unconscious processes as having different locations, and, by extension, if these different kinds of memory are supported by different parts of the brain, they may function in qualitatively distinct ways.

Measures of implicit and explicit memory are influenced in different ways by different experimental manipulations. For example, Jacoby and Dallas (1981) found that word stem completion effects (a measure of implicit memory) persisted with relatively little change for long periods of time. Other studies have indicated that the ability to recognize previously presented stimuli declines rapidly with time. Implicit and explicit memory have also been shown to be differentially influenced by the way in which individuals study test items. If subjects are asked to answer questions about the meaning of words they are studying (elaborative processing) as opposed to indicating whether or not a particular letter is present in a word (nonelaborative processing), the ability to recognize previously presented words is enhanced. By contrast, measures of implicit memory are unaffected by elaborative or nonelaborative processing of words (Graf, Mandler, & Hayden, 1982; Jacoby & Dallas, 1981). These results indicate that different experimental manipulations may have different effects on measures of implicit and explicit memory.

Priming

The influence of previously encountered words on word stem completions is sometimes called **priming.** The effect of priming is to change subsequent responses to stimuli because of previous stimulus exposure. Meyer and Schvǎneveldt (1971) demonstrated priming influences in a task in which subjects were required to determine whether a sequence of letters was a word in English or merely a collection of meaningless letters. This task is called a **lexical decision task.** It was found that if a word is preceded by a word with a related meaning, the time taken to solve the lexical decision task is decreased. For example, subjects are able to ascertain that the letters *s–h–i–p* constitute a word in English somewhat more rapidly if they are preceded by the word *boat* than if they are preceded by a word unrelated in meaning to the word *ship*.

Marcel (1983a; 1983b) demonstrated that it was possible to obtain lexical priming effects for words that subjects were not aware of seeing. In his experiments the priming stimulus, the word *boat* in the example, was presented tachistoscopically, followed by a dense pattern of letters in different orientations that covered the screen. If the second stimulus—the dense pattern of letters called a **pattern mask**—is presented immediately after the onset of the first stimulus *boat*, subjects report that they are not aware of seeing the word *boat*. They may not even be able to discriminate between words that were presented and words that were not presented to them if the words are followed by a pattern mask. The word *boat* in this instance is presented below the subjective threshold of awareness. Even though it is presented subliminally, it will influence the time taken to reach a lexical decision about the second word, in this example *ship*. Thus subliminal stimuli decrease the time taken to reach a lexical decision in the same way that do stimuli presented above the subjective threshold of awareness.

In addition, the influence of the prime stimulus may depend on whether it is presented above or below threshold. Marcel attempted to demonstrate that the influence of a prime stimulus varied according to whether it was presented subliminally or supraliminally. He used polysemous words that had two meanings, such as *palm*, which refers both to a kind of tree and to a part of the hand. Subjects were presented with three-word sequences and instructed to reach a lexical decision about the last word presented. Consider the sequence, *tree–palm–hand*. Although the word *palm* would act as a prime for *hand* if it were presented in a two-word sequence, the three-word sequence leads to a delay in reaching a lexical decision. In this sequence the wrong meaning of the word *palm* is primed by the first word (*tree*) and this results in a delay or interference in the processing of the word *hand*. Marcel also investigated the effects of presenting the second word in a three-word sequence subliminally. If the sequence *tree–palm–hand* includes a pattern mask after the word *palm*, rendering the word subliminal, the priming effects of the word *palm* are different. Rather than interfering with the processing of the word *hand*, and causing a delay in the lexical decision, the word *palm* facilitated the processing of *hand*, leading to a more rapid lexical decision. The effects of the same stimulus—the word *palm* in our example—are opposite depending upon whether the word is subliminal or supraliminal.

Why did Marcel obtain these results? Why does a polysemous word have different influences when it is subliminal than when it is supraliminal? Marcel argued that the different effects obtained may be understood by reference to the way in which conscious and unconscious processes function. He argued that conscious processes act to restrict awareness. Consciousness is inherently selective, focusing on one of many possible meanings and fixing a particular meaning for an experience. Unconscious processes by contrast are not selective. Multiple meanings can coexist. If individuals have unconscious awareness of many things, then these multiple states of awareness can each influence and serve as a prime for the next event.

Groeger (1988) also reported qualitatively different effects of words depending on whether they were presented subliminally or supraliminally. In one of his experiments subjects were visually presented with words followed by a list of different words that were either structurally similar or similar in meaning to the original word. The second list did not contain the first word presented although the subjects were not told this. The subjects were asked to select a word from the second list that was identical to the first word presented.

In one condition the first word was presented below the threshold for subjective awareness, so subjects were not aware of seeing the word. In another condition, the same words were presented at longer durations that permitted the subjects to obtain partial information about the word without being clearly aware of the actual word. When the subjects were asked to select the word that they had seen from the second list, those who were not aware of seeing the original words tended to select words from the second list that were similar in *meaning* to the first words seen. Thus the subliminal words had a priming effect based on shared meaning. If the first words had been presented for a longer duration, however, the subjects selected words that were *structurally* similar from the second list.

Groeger obtained similar results in an experiment on the auditory presentation of words. Subjects were given a choice of selecting words that were similar in meaning to the first word or that sounded similar to the first word. In comparison to a control group of subjects who were not exposed to the first word, subjects tended to select words that *sounded* similar to the first word if the word was presented supraliminally, and they tended to select words that were similar in *meaning* to the first word if the word was presented below the threshold of subjective awareness.

The results of Groeger's experiments are somewhat surprising. They suggest that subjects may be aware of the meaning of a word before they are aware of its structural properties. Perhaps the subliminal or preconscious awareness of the meaning of the word is superseded by an awareness of the structural properties of the word that is then followed by a clear understanding of the word, permitting both its structural and semantic properties to be present in awareness.

Both Groeger's and Marcel's experiments suggest that individuals attain an understanding of the meaning of stimuli in stages. At different stages of processing of a stimulus, different meanings may be present, and the result is qualitatively different priming influences of the stimulus.

WHAT ABOUT FREUD?

Although ideas about unconscious influences on behavior certainly precede Freud (see Ellenberger, 1970), it is Freud more than any other theorist who argued that understanding unconscious influences was critical to an understanding of human action. Most of the research we reviewed was performed by cognitive psychologists or by psychologists who may be interested in personality but are not particularly committed to Freudian ideas. Whether or not contemporary research on the unconscious supports Freudian ideas is debatable. Many psychologists who are interested in unconscious phenomena are inclined to argue that while there is good support for the proposition that individuals are influenced by events of which they are not aware, this research does not provide evidence for the view of unconscious influences developed by Freud (Erdelyi, 1992; Greenwald, 1992; Kihlstrom, Barnhardt, & Tataryn, 1992). While the evidence we reviewed is compatible with a Freudian conception, Freudian analyses of the unconscious contain a number of additional assumptions that are not strongly supported by contemporary research.

The Freudian model assumes that the unconscious is capable of sophisticated reasoning processes and that ideas remain unconscious because of their emotional content. Freud believed that many of the things that are unconscious are emotionally threatening and individuals go to great length to prevent these ideas from being conscious. Various *defensive processes* in one way or another are devoted to disguising unconscious thoughts or preventing their access to consciousness. Unconscious impulses are expressed in disguised form, influencing dreams, slips of the tongue, and various forms of psychopathology. In order to provide some insight into the nature of unconscious processes from a Freudian perspective, we will present a simplified version of a case history.

Wachtel (1977) described a case in which a man had a phobia that prevented him from driving a car. Attempts to remove the fear of driving were not particularly successful. A further exploration of the man's fears and desires suggested to the psychoanalytically oriented clinician that the fear of driving was related to an unconscious aggressive impulse. For this man, a car represented an instrument of violence and destruction, and the inability to drive therefore was a way of defending against the unconscious desire to use the car as a weapon to harm someone. In order for this phobia to be cured, the unconscious impulses and thoughts that were expressed in the phobia had to be dealt with. Once the individual was able to consciously understand the reasons for his phobic response and "work through" the reasons for his unconscious impulses, he was able to resume driving.

This case history assigns a rather complex set of capabilities to unconscious thoughts. The analysis assumes that an unconscious impulse can give rise to an intense negative emotional state and initiate processes that prevent the thought from reaching conscious awareness. In addition, it is assumed that the unconscious impulse may be expressed indirectly, in this case in terms of a fear of driving, leading to a profound alteration in a person's ability to act in certain ways for reasons that are not transparent.

The experimental literature we reviewed does not provide evidence for this kind of motivated unconscious process that is capable of an indirect and disguised influence on action. Does this lack of evidence imply that a Freudian conception of the unconscious is unsupported? Not necessarily. It would be more correct to say that the kinds of experimental literature that many contemporary psychologists interested in research approaches to personality and cognition find convincing does not provide support for a Freudian model of the unconscious.

Is a Freudian model of the unconscious without empirical support? Not necessarily. The empirical support for the existence of these phenomena derives, for the most part, from clinical observations and experience, not from studies conducted in the laboratory. Should we accept the observations of clinicians? This is a complex question (see Grunbaum, 1984, for a discussion of the empirical support of psychoanalytic concepts derived from analytic sessions). We do not intend to present a full discussion of this complex question here. We do have some brief comments to offer.

The clinical setting in which a patient discusses psychological problems in the presence of a psychoanalytically oriented clinician may not provide an ideal setting for the validation of complex theoretical notions. The situation is not one in which great care is taken to obtain objective and unbiased data. Psychoanalytic therapy may be construed as a mutual educational process in which the patient is taught to construe problems in terms of psychoanalytic concepts and the interpretation provided by the patient is then taken as evidence for the existence of the concepts. The evidence provided by the contents of such sessions does not necessarily constitute unbiased and convincing empirical support for the concepts.

Silverman's Psychoanalytic Research

Is it possible to test psychoanalytic concepts directly? There is at least one contemporary research program that attempts to test psychoanalytically derived clinical concepts in laboratory settings. Silverman (1976; 1983) initiated such a research program. In his early research he presented subjects with subliminal messages designed to arouse unconscious conflicts. He assumed that the arousal would be manifested by an increase in symptoms that were thought to be related to these conflicts. In one of these studies, Silverman, Bronstein, and Mendelsohn (1976) used male homosexuals and stutterers as subjects. They assumed that male homosexuality was related to an unresolved Oedipal complex and that male homosexuals would therefore have unconscious conflicts centered on their sexual attraction to their mothers. Stutterers were assumed to have unconscious conflicts related to anal regressive tendencies. Freud assumed that individuals could develop conflicts that had their origins in an anal period in childhood when conflicts surrounding toilet training and the ability to release and hold back anal products became a metaphorical model for the way in which individuals related to the world. Psychoanalytic interpretations of stuttering construe this behavior as a metaphorical expression of the unconscious conflicts deriving from the anal period.

Silverman et al. assumed that subliminal presentations of stimuli designed to arouse anal conflicts would increase stuttering for their subjects who stuttered and would have little or no effect on male homosexuals. Conversely, subliminal presentations of stimuli that were designed to arouse Oedipal conflicts would be expected to arouse homosexual desires in male homosexuals but would have little or no effect on stutterers.

Silverman et al. presented their subjects with different subliminal messages. To arouse anal conflicts, they presented a picture of a dog defecating with the words "Go shit" written on the stimulus. To arouse Oedipal conflicts, they presented a somewhat brooding picture of an older woman embracing a younger man with the words "Fuck Mommy" written on the stimulus. The stimuli were presented subliminally below the objective threshold for awareness. To assess the presence of homosexual arousal, they had their subjects rate the attractiveness of male nudes. To assess the effects of the subliminal stimuli on stuttering, they had observers (who were not aware of which stimulus had been presented) rate the extent of stuttering behavior. They found that individuals who were prone to stutter exhibited an increase in stuttering after the stimulus designed to arouse anal conflicts. They were relatively unaffected by the stimulus designed to arouse Oedipal conflicts. By contrast, the male homosexuals rated the male nudes as more sexually attractive after the stimuli that were designed to arouse Oedipal conflicts and were relatively unaffected by stimuli designed to arouse anal conflicts.

Silverman and his colleagues also investigated the influence of a subliminal stimulus that was designed to ameliorate unconscious conflicts. The stimulus "Mommy and I are one" is assumed to recall childhood feelings of a symbiotic relationship with the mother (feelings of "oneness") and these feelings are assumed to reduce unconscious conflicts (for a review of these studies see Hardaway, 1990; Silverman & Weinberger, 1985; Weinberger & Hardaway, 1990). This stimulus has been used to reduce phobias and used in various efforts to change behaviors in clinical settings. Silverman, Martin, Ungaro, and Mendelsohn (1978) used subliminal presentations of the "Mommy and I are one" stimulus in a study of the effects of a weight loss program. Woman in this program were assigned either to a group that received subliminal presentations of the "Mommy" stimulus or to a control group that received the subliminal stimulus "People are walking." Twenty-four weeks after the end of their treatment, the women who received subliminal presentations of the "Mommy" stimulus were 15 pounds lighter than their pretreatment weight, and the women who received the stimulus "People are walking" were 6 pounds lighter.

Parker (1982) assigned law students to one of three groups: one group received the subliminal stimulus "Mommy and I are one," a second group received the subliminal stimulus "Prof and I are one," and a third group received the subliminal stimulus "People are walking." He studied the effects of these stimuli on the performance on examinations in a law school course and found that both groups that received messages referring to oneness had greater improvement on their exam scores than the group that received the message "People are walking."

The research initiated by Silverman and his colleagues provides laboratory support for unconscious influences on behavior that are compatible with a Freudian model of the unconscious. The research is controversial, however. A recent survey of expert opinion of researchers interested in unconscious influences found that only 16 percent of these researchers were willing to accept the kinds of phenomena that Silverman and his colleagues studied as established empirical results (Greenwald, 1992). This skepticism may derive in part from a disinclination on the part of many research psychologists to accept psychoanalytic hypotheses as valid. Perhaps the researchers surveyed were indulging in an irrational prejudice against psychoanalytic theory. Perhaps not. Certainly, there may be legitimate reasons to be skeptical of the kinds of phenomena generated by this research program (see Brody, 1988, chap. 6). Yet a recent meta-analysis found positive effects of the subliminal stimulus "Mommy and I are one" (Hardaway, 1990). On the other hand, in a number of studies in which the control stimuli also had positive emotional meanings (e.g., Parker's study using the stimulus "Prof and I are one") the effects were similar to those obtained with the stimulus "Mommy and I are one," although the influence of some of these other stimuli was not always as great. These results suggest that the effects of the subliminal stimuli used in this research may not always be due to the particular meaning assigned to the stimuli in psychoanalytic theory. Perhaps the word *Mommy* by itself might lead to the development of a positive emotional state.

In the last analysis, we suspect that the truth value assigned to these studies may depend on a person's prior commitments and belief systems. If you accept the validity of psychoanalytic hypotheses, you might be inclined to believe that it is possible to create and ameliorate unconscious conflicts by presenting subliminal messages, although we should indicate that some psychoanalytically inclined theorists might be skeptical about the ease with which conflicts can be created and ameliorated by such messages. If, on the other hand, you are rather skeptical of psychoanalytic hypotheses and find them far-fetched, you are unlikely to accept an orthodox interpretation of these results. We leave it to our readers to arrive at their own views of the meaning of this body of research.

THE UNCONSCIOUS AND PERSONALITY

Social Behavior

Many contemporary studies of unconscious processes are conducted by cognitive psychologists and do not deal with the kinds of social behavior that are of interest to most personality psychologists. Nevertheless, it is possible to use some of the techniques used by cognitive psychologists to study social behavior. Here are two examples.

Lewicki (1986) designed an experiment to demonstrate that individuals might be influenced by unconscious thoughts in a social situation. In one of his experiments subjects had a preexperimental interview in which they were insulted by a female experimental assistant. The assistant asked the subjects two innocuous questions and then asked them, "What is your birth order?" The subjects in this experiment were not familiar with the term "birth order," and when they asked for clarification, the experimenter responded either in an irritated manner (saying "Don't you really know the meaning of 'birth order'?") or in a neutral manner.

After the interview the subjects were asked to go into another room and se-lect whichever of the two experimenters was free to administer the experiment. When the subjects walked into the room, they found that both experimenters were free, so the subjects had to make a choice. One of the two experimenters re-sembled the interviewer who had previously insulted the subject (e.g., the inter-viewer and the experimenter both wore glasses). Eighty percent of the subjects who had had the unpleasant encounter chose the experimenter who did not re-semble the first experimenter. By contrast, 42.9% of the subjects who did not have an unpleasant encounter chose the experimenter who did not resemble the first experimenter.

Lewicki gave the subjects a questionnaire asking them about the reasons they chose one of the two experimenters. Almost all endorsed an item that read, "My choice was completely random." The subjects did not appear to be aware of the re-semblance between the experimenter they tended to avoid and the person who in-terviewed them, and they were not aware that this resemblance influenced their social behavior.

It should be noted that Lewicki did not conduct an extended postexperimen-tal interview with the subjects. Such an interview might have revealed that the sub-jects were aware of the resemblance or even that this was one of the reasons for their choice. Even if this awareness was present, Lewicki's experiment suggests that subjects were not aware that they had this knowledge and their initial reports about their actions may be understood as the subjects' own interpretation of the reasons for their actions. In other words, it is possible to interpret these results in two different ways; (1) the reasons for the subjects' actions were out of awareness in the unconscious; (2) the subjects were aware of the reasons for their action but they did not know that they had this knowledge, which might have been obtained in an extensive interrogation. In any case, the experiment demonstrates that we may behave in many ordinary situations with relatively limited understanding of the reasons for our actions.

Bargh, Bond, Lombardi, and Tota (1986) used a priming study to demonstrate that subliminal stimuli could influence personality judgments. Subjects were pre-sented with a list of 100 words below their threshold for the accurate discrimina-tion of the words. The words referred either to a set of *kind* personal characteristics or to a set of *shy* characteristics. Then the subjects were asked to rate the personal-ity characteristics of an individual who was described to them. The ratings that the subjects assigned to the person were found to be influenced by the characteristics of the words previously encountered. After this, the subjects were shown sets of three words and asked which of each three had been presented to them sublimi-nally. They were not able to tell with better than chance accuracy. Yet even though the stimuli were subliminal and close to the objective threshold for identification of the stimuli, they influenced judgments of personality characteristics.

The Lewicki study and the Bargh et al. study both suggest that some of our ordinary social judgments and behaviors may be determined by thoughts and cognitive contents that are not in our awareness.

Traits and the Unconscious

Trait psychologists often assess personality using self-reports and ratings. This approach to personality implicitly assumes that individuals are able and willing to judge their personality characteristics and the personality characteristics of others. Is this always true? If it were not true at least some of the time, we would not have been able to find studies providing evidence for the construct validity of trait ratings. Yet reports may not *always* be valid. If people are able to suppress or repress their awareness of their personal characteristics, surely they might provide inaccurate reports about their own personal characteristics or characteristics of their acquaintances. It is not hard to guess where such distortions are likely to occur. Some personality characteristics are negatively evaluated: we generally do not think that it is a good thing to be high on neuroticism and low on agreeableness (the low end of agreeableness is related to hostility). In order to receive a high score on a measure of neuroticism, a person would have to respond in a way that obviously indicates that he or she is not well adjusted. Some people may choose to describe themselves in a positive way even though they believe that they are neurotic, or they may have neurotic tendencies that they are not aware of (recall the discussion of social desirability in chapter 2).

Can we obtain empirical evidence of distortions in personality judgments that may be related to unconscious influences on behavior? Shedler, Mayman, and Manis (1993) studied individuals who rated themselves as low on neuroticism. They also asked these individuals to describe their earliest memories. The data derived from these descriptions of early memories were used by a clinical psychologist to judge the person's psychological adjustment. They reasoned that individuals who described themselves as neurotic were probably neurotic, and that individuals who described themselves as nonneurotic or as well adjusted might constitute two separate groups: one who were actually low on neuroticism, and one who said they were low on neuroticism but who might actually be defensive or poorly adjusted. This last group are those who report a distorted view of their personal characteristics.[1]

Shedler et al. in this way divided their subjects into three groups: individuals who said that they were high on neuroticism, individuals who said that they were low on neuroticism and were judged to be well adjusted by the clinician who independently judged their responses to the early memory test, and individuals who said that they were low on neuroticism but were judged by the clinician to be poorly adjusted. Shedler et al. compared the cardiac reactions of these subjects in stressful situations. Their results are presented in Figure 9.2. Note that the subjects who were judged to be poorly adjusted who said that they were low on neuroticism were likely to exhibit an increase in their heart

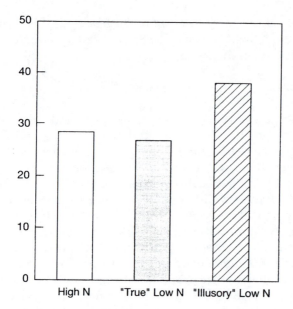

FIGURE 9.2 Maximal cardiac reactivity change from baseline for subjects scoring high on the Eysenck neuroticism scale and judged distressed by clinicians (High N), subjects scoring low on the Eysenck neuroticism scale and judged not distressed by clinicians ("True" low N), and subjects scoring low on the Eysenck neuroticism scale and judged distressed by clinicians ("Illusory" low N). (Based on Shedler, Mayman, and Manis, 1993. Reproduced with permission of the American Psychological Association.)

rate response to stress. These data provide an indirect index suggesting that the judgments of individuals whose self-reports of their adjustment disagreed with the independent judgment of the clinician are less likely to be able to respond to stresses in their life.

Do the results of the Shedler et al. study provide evidence for unconscious influences on behavior? It is difficult to answer this question. The study clearly indicates that individuals who exhibit discrepancies between their self-reports and ratings assigned by others may behave in different ways than individuals who do not exhibit such discrepancies. This study provides us with relatively little information about the *reasons* for the discrepancy. The subjects who describe themselves inaccurately may in fact be aware that their reports are deceptive; perhaps they really believe that they are poorly adjusted and choose to present a false description. Or these subjects may genuinely believe that they are well adjusted.

Davidson (1993) also obtained data indicating that individuals who exhibited discrepancies between their self-reports of their psychological states and the reports of raters of those states were more likely to exhibit psychophysiological responses to stress. In her experiments, subjects rated themselves on measures of hostility. These measures are related to agreeableness: individuals who score low on agreeableness may be viewed as hostile and antagonistic to others. Self-report scores on measures of hostility were compared with ratings of hostility obtained from acquaintances of the subject. Davidson was interested in the effects of suppression of hostility. She assumed that individuals who said they were hostile but who were rated as being low in hostility by their acquaintances were able to suppress their hostile behavior. She measured changes in blood pressure in response to a stressful situation. Figure 9.3 presents her data. Note that the largest increases in blood pressure occurred for subjects who rated themselves as being high in hostility but who were rated by their friends as low.

Davidson's results suggest that the hyperreactive physiological response to stress she obtained for subjects who exhibited discrepancies between their self-reports and the ratings assigned to them were not caused by unconscious influences. After all, these were subjects who said that they were hostile. Their hyper-reactive physiology might be related to their attempt to deceive others.

If we consider the results of both the Shedler et al. study and the Davidson study, we might argue that individuals who exhibit discrepancies between their self-report and the ratings assigned to them by others are more likely to exhibit stressful responses than individuals who do not exhibit such discrepancies. Similar results are obtained in these two studies for individuals who assign negative characteristics to themselves but are viewed positively by others, and for individuals who assign positive characteristics to themselves but are viewed negatively

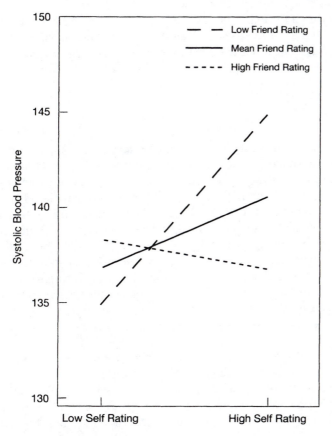

FIGURE 9.3   Reactive systolic blood pressure levels for varying self- and other hostility ratings. (Based on Davidson, 1993; reproduced with permission of the Duke University Press.)

by others. Perhaps we are less able to handle stress when we try to construct an image of ourselves that is not in agreement with the way we really are.

What these studies do not tell us is whether or not individuals are aware of these discrepancies. Do subjects in Davidson's studies know that their self-perceptions are not shared by their acquaintances? Are they consciously attempting to present a false image of themselves? Is the suppression of their hostility unconscious even though they are aware of this trait? Are the subjects in the Shedler et al. studies aware of the discrepancy between their self-reports and how they are judged by others? Is it possible that the subjects who described themselves as well adjusted but were perceived as maladjusted may have thought of themselves as truly maladjusted but were reluctant to admit this to others? Are they suppressing their knowledge of their maladjustment, are they deliberately deceptive, or do they truly believe that they are well adjusted? If we assume that they are genuinely maladjusted, is this maladjustment something of which they are aware (in consciousness) or something that they are not aware of (in the unconscious)?

The Davidson and Shedler et al. studies do not tell us much about conscious and unconscious influences on behavior, but they do indicate that discrepancies between self-reports and ratings for negative traits are informative. Where such discrepancies occur, we have reason to suspect deception. Whether the subjects are aware of these deceptions and whether they are conscious or unconscious remains to be determined.

CONCLUSION

Psychologists who are interested in unconscious influences on personality have not attained a consensus about unconscious influences on behavior. There are, however, some generalizations that do appear to be strongly supported. Perhaps the most fundamental of these is that different approaches to assessing a person's conscious states may yield different results. We simply cannot assume that a person's description of his psychological states is invariably veridical. People can know things that they do not know that they know. There is no doubt that we can be influenced by things that we do not know we know. There is even some tentative evidence that such things may have an influence on us that is different from their influence when they are fully in our conscious mind. We may also be influenced by things that are totally out of awareness—that are truly in our unconscious—although this idea would probably not be accepted by everyone.

If people are not always accurate in their reports about their conscious processes and the reasons for their actions, we cannot understand individuals solely by relying on their own descriptions of the reasons (Westen, 1992). If we want to understand why a person did something or why individuals may not always be able to report accurately on their psychological characteristics, we shall have to use methods other than simple faith in what people tell us. As psychologists, we may be able to know things about a person that he or she does not know. In this sense the psychology of personality is more than the study of a person's conscious mind.

Endnotes

[1]This research should remind you of our discussion of repressors in chapter 6, which you might want to review in the context of this discussion.

10

Cognitive Form

In chapter 9 we discussed unconscious thought processes. In the next two chapters we shall deal with other aspects of thought processes. In this chapter we shall consider personality dimensions that are based on the way in which people think. The next chapter will consider differences in the content of thought.

INTELLIGENCE AS A DIMENSION OF PERSONALITY

Are differences in intelligence a dimension of personality? Many psychologists believe that intelligence is not a dimension of personality. It is not substantially related to the Big Five trait dimensions. There are, however, at least two persuasive reasons to think of intelligence as a personality dimension. First, most people believe that individuals differ in intelligence and that these differences are important. Buss et al. (1990) asked men and women in different countries to describe the attributes of an ideal marriage partner. They found that in all of the countries studied, intelligence was a valued characteristic for both men and women.

If it is true that individuals believe intelligence is an important characteristic, then by implication, people routinely judge the intelligence of others. Are they able to judge accurately the intelligence of people they encounter? To answer this question, Borkenau and Liebler (1993) videotaped subjects who entered a room, sat down, and read the text of a weather report for 90 seconds. The videotapes were shown to groups of college students, who were asked to rate the intelligence of the videotaped subjects. The correlation between scores on tests of intelligence and the judges' ratings was .38. Evidently, people are able to judge the intelligence of people they meet relatively quickly and these judgments are surprisingly accurate even when they are based on minimal information.

A second reason intelligence might be considered a personality dimension is that it is related to success in school situations and to a person's occupational status. Individual differences in intelligence are related to important social outcomes.

If people are able to judge individual differences in intelligence and if these differences influence the ways in which people are treated and the ways in which they lead their lives, it would appear that intelligence is a dimension of personality. Many books on personality do not include intelligence as a dimension of personality. Its inclusion is somewhat arbitrary. We do consider intelligence as a dimension of personality simply because, as we shall see, individual differences in intelligence are related to a person's social position.

HOW IS INTELLIGENCE MEASURED?

We could measure intelligence in the same way that we measure personality traits. We could ask people to rate their intelligence or we could obtain ratings from friends and aggregate these ratings. We generally do not measure intelligence in this way, however. Usually we measure intelligence by observing an individual's behavior. If we want to measure the size of someone's vocabulary, we ask the person to define words. We present the person with several different kinds of intellectual tasks to solve and note the number of correct answers given. The problems presented are diverse. They might include solving analogies, defining words, solving puzzles involving blocks, and repeating digits in a backward order—any and all kinds of tasks that seem to require some kind of reasoning or thought process. A score on this type of test is a cross-situational aggregate index of performance (you might want to refer to the discussion of cross-situational aggregate measures in chapter 3). It is an aggregate because it is a summary of performance on different tasks. It is a cross-situational aggregate because it aggregates performance on tasks that are deliberately selected to measure different kinds of cognitive skills.

The Positive Manifold

It is possible to obtain a score for performance on each of several kinds of tests of cognitive skills. For example, a score on a vocabulary test may be obtained by aggregating performance on several vocabulary questions; a score for memory tests could be obtained by aggregating performance on items requiring a person to repeat without error a series of numbers or letters. Spearman (1904) was one of the first psychologists to study relationships among scores obtained on different kinds of intellectual tasks. When he examined a correlation matrix of different measures of intellectual ability, he noted that all of the measures were positively correlated—they formed what is called a **positive manifold**. His results have been repeatedly supported.

Many different kinds of measures of intellectual ability form a positive manifold. This means that individuals who excel in one kind of intellectual task are likely to excel in other kinds. To the extent that this is true, the choice of tasks that are used to develop a measure of intelligence is not critical. Since all of the tasks are related to each other, an aggregate score based on any subset of measures of intelligence will tend to be highly correlated with an aggregate score based on any other set of measures. This tendency is called the **principle of indifference of the indicator**. The aggregated score is sometimes described as a measure of *g*—Spearman's term for **general intelligence**—defined as that which is shared or common to all of the different measures of intelligence that form a positive manifold.

What Should Be Included in a Definition of Intelligence?

It may occur to some of you that there is something wrong with our discussion of general intelligence. We stated that all measures of intelligence form a positive manifold. But how do we know what constitutes a measure of intelligence? If something is positively correlated with other measures of intelligence, it is a measure of intelligence; if not, it is not a measure of intelligence. This is not a very satisfactory definition; it is a circular definition that "begs the question." Rather than providing an answer, it buries the question. We think that there is a better way of answering this question. We can indicate what kinds of abilities form a positive manifold and what kinds of things may not be part of the manifold. Doing this should help us come to a better understanding of the nature of the claim that measures of intelligence form a positive manifold.

Gardner (1983) developed a theory of multiple intelligences that assumes there are six kinds of intelligence: linguistic, logical-mathematical, spatial, bodily-kinesthetic, musical, and personal intelligence (the ability to understand one's own emotions and the behavior of others, sometimes called *social intelligence*; see Goleman, 1995). Measures of the first three kinds of intelligence form a positive manifold (Carroll, 1993). Measures of the other three kinds are usually not strongly related to the measures that form a positive manifold and are not usually included in the set of traditional measures of intelligence. Musical ability, physical skills, and social and personal intelligence are probably not related to each other. On the other hand, people who excel in either linguistic or spatial or mathematical-logical intelligence are likely to excel in the other two.

Whether we want to think of intelligence as one thing or as many things depends, in part, on the way in which we choose to define intelligence. Many people might believe that an intelligent person would have good social skills. Such a person might be tactful and skilled at understanding the emotions of another person. If your definition of intelligence encompasses social skills, then you would probably be justified in concluding that measures of different kinds of intelligence do not form a positive manifold.

What, then, is included in the set of abilities that *do* form a positive manifold? The most comprehensive answer to this question is contained in Carroll's extensive studies of this issue. Carroll (1993) studied patterns of relationships among different kinds of intellectual tasks obtained in over 450 studies. Using the same factor-analytic techniques, he reanalyzed all of the studies. This comprehensive analysis of the literature provided the basis for what he called the *three-stratum theory of intelligence,* which is summarized in Figure 10.1. Intellectual abilities are depicted as forming a hierarchical order. The third stratum contains a single general ability, *g,* which is related to eight second-stratum abilities. The second-stratum abilities, reading from left to right in the figure, are ordered in terms of their relationship to *g,* with the abilities on the left assumed to be better measures of *g* than those on the right. Each second-stratum ability is related to several more specific and narrow tasks. A complete picture of an individual's intellectual abilities would require scores for each of the three strata abilities.

The measures of intelligence in Carroll's hierarchy form a positive manifold, justifying his decision to postulate *g* as a single general ability that is related to all the other abilities in the hierarchy; *g* is the common thing they all share. Carroll's comprehensive analysis provides another answer to the question, Is intelligence one thing or many things? The simple answer is, it is both. While many measures of intelligence tend to be related to each other, measures of intelligence that rely on similar kinds of reasoning or skills correlate more highly with each other than those that measure different skills. Tests of verbal ability such as those measuring vocabulary and the ability to solve verbal analogies will tend to be highly correlated with each other, more so than these tests are with tests of spatial reasoning such as the ability to draw from memory a map of the path to be followed between two campus landmarks. This pattern of correlation implies that there are specialized intellectual abilities as well as a single general intellectual ability. Two people may have the same aggregate score but different patterns of scores on different kinds of measures. Thus if we describe a person's performance on a diverse set of intellectual tasks in terms of a single measure (*g* score), we lose information about the person's distinctive pattern of strengths and weaknesses in different kinds of intellectual tasks.

g AND REASONING

People who score high on tests of intelligence (i.e., those who have high *g*) excel at solving intellectual puzzles and at giving the right answer to questions asked by psychologists. Is it possible to relate this ability to more fundamental processes of reasoning? Do people who have different scores on tests of intelligence reason differently? Perhaps these questions are too general to answer in a comprehensive

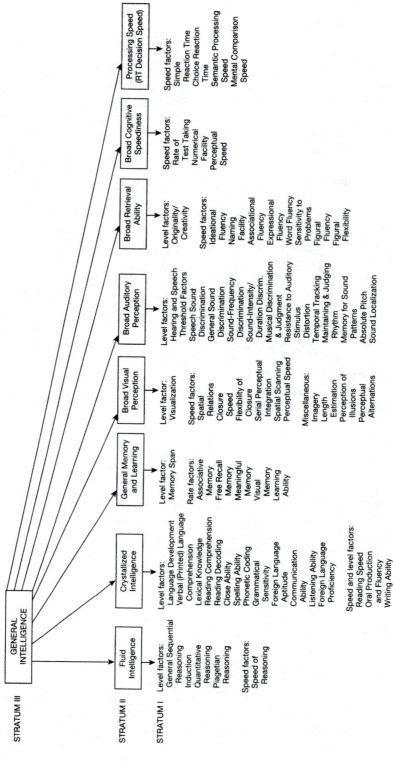

FIGURE 10.1 Carroll's three-stratum theory of intelligence. (Based on Carroll, 1993). Reproduced with permission of the Cambridge University Press.

manner. We do know, however, that people who differ in intelligence differ in performance on a variety of elementary and complex intellectual tasks.

Elementary Information Processing

Individual differences in intellectual skills are first manifested in the first six months of life. There are tasks that can be presented to infants during that time that predict performance on intelligence tests given as late as age 8 (Colombo, 1993). Recently, Rose and Feldman (1995) extended this research to age 11. They found that measures of infant information processing obtained in the first year of life predict scores on tests of intelligence obtained at age 11. These studies are longitudinal, relating scores of the same children at different ages. We shall have to wait to learn whether or not the performance of infants on these measures will predict the performance of older children and young adults. Longitudinal research cannot be hurried!

What kinds of measures of performance in infancy may be used to predict early childhood intelligence? Infants can be presented with a novel stimulus (a pattern of lights) and their attention to the stimulus can be noted (one way of doing this is to note whether or not the infant looks at the stimulus). If the stimulus is repeatedly presented to the infant, there is a decline in attention to it. This reaction is called **habituation.** Habituation may measure the ability of an infant to develop an internal representation of the stimulus (something that represents a model of what the stimulus is like). Once the infant realizes that the stimulus has not changed, attention declines. Infants who habituate rapidly score higher on later tests of intelligence than infants who do not. The correlation between measures of habituation obtained in the first several months of life and scores on tests of intelligence in childhood is close to .4. This result has been obtained in several different studies. These data imply that the complex skills that are measured in tests of intelligence are related to individual differences in information-processing skills that are manifested in the first several months of life. There is evidence that such skills can be measured even earlier than six months. Sigman, Cohen, Beckwith, and Parmalee (1986) found that performance on a test of attention administered to newborn babies predicted scores on tests of intelligence when the children were 8 years old.

Individual differences in intelligence are also related to performance on elementary information-processing tasks in adult samples. Raz, Willerman, and Yama (1987) measured college students' ability to detect differences in pitch between tones lasting 10 or 20 milliseconds. Correlations between pitch discrimination and scores on intelligence tests ranged from $-.42$ to $-.52$. The negative correlations indicate that subjects who had low pitch thresholds (they were able accurately to tell the difference between tones that were relatively similar in pitch) tended to have high scores on tests of intelligence.

There are other relatively simple information-processing tasks that are related to performance on tests of intelligence (see Brody, 1992, chap. 3). For example,

Kranzler and Jensen (1989) summarized research on **inspection time** tasks, tasks requiring subjects to discriminate between two stimuli that are clearly different. A stimulus is presented briefly followed by a second stimulus that prevents the first one from being examined (the second stimulus is called a *backward mask*). In one common inspection-time task, two vertical lines are presented that clearly differ in length, followed by two heavy black lines that cover up each of the first lines and prevent additional inspection. Subjects are to indicate which of the two original lines was longer, and the shortest inspection time permitting subjects to do this is noted. Kranzler and Jensen summarized all of the inspection-time studies using a meta-analysis in which they averaged all the correlations between IQ and inspection time. They obtained an average r of $-.29$, indicating that subjects who do not require long inspection times to discriminate the difference between two lines tend to score higher on tests of intelligence.

Vocabulary Size and Intelligence

Scores on tests of intelligence are also related to differences in more complex intellectual skills. Measures of the size of a person's vocabulary are good measures of g. Thus a person's score on a vocabulary test may be used to predict his score on other tests of intellectual ability. Why? There is an obvious answer: the size of a person's vocabulary depends on exposure to words, and individuals who read a lot and whose parents use unusual words are provided with the opportunity to develop a large vocabulary. While this obvious answer contains a grain of truth, it does not provide a complete explanation for individual differences in vocabulary. Children reared in the same family with common exposures to their parent's words may differ in the size of their vocabulary. Something else may be at work. In order to understand this, it is necessary to think about the process that permits us to learn the meaning of unusual words. Most of the words we can define have probably never been formally defined for us. We rarely learn the meaning of words by memorizing a dictionary definition. How, then, do we learn the meaning of words? We may figure out their meaning by inference, that is, we may encounter a new word in a sentence and infer its meaning from the context in which it is used. In order to do this, we need to solve an intellectual puzzle and we need to store in our memory the possible meanings we have inferred. Repeated encounters with the same word may help us to develop a more refined and exact meaning for the word.

In order to test these ideas, Sternberg and Powell (1983) presented high school students with passages containing nouns that occurred very infrequently in English, words that could not be defined by the subjects prior to their exposure to the passages. In this study the *prior* exposure of subjects to these unusual words did not vary. The subjects' ability to define these words after this controlled exposure correlated $+.62$ with IQ. These data suggest that the size of a person's vocabulary may be determined by skill in decoding the meaning of words from the context in which they are used.

In summary, a score on a test of intelligence is related to one's ability to solve a variety of intellectual tasks. This ability is related to individual differences in reasoning processes. The complex skills and knowledge structures that are measured in tests of intelligence are probably related to differences in how individuals process information, differences first manifested during infancy. Individual differences in intelligence are also related to such elementary skills as the ability to discriminate between two briefly presented lines differing in length and two briefly presented tones differing in pitch as well as to the complex intellectual skills required to decode the meaning of words from the context in which they are used.

THE SOCIAL RELEVANCE OF INTELLIGENCE

We have seen that people differ in their ability to solve intellectual puzzles. How do these differences relate to other aspects of a person's life? Is this ability analogous to the ability to rotate one's thumbs in opposite directions? We might marvel at such an ability but we do not assume that it tells us anything fundamental about a person. Or, are individual differences in ability to solve intellectual puzzles a more consequential index? We shall try to convince you that they are.

INTELLIGENCE AND EDUCATION

Individual differences in intelligence relate to performance in school. Children who score high on tests of intelligence tend to get better grades, do better on examinations, and get better scores on tests of knowledge of the skills and concepts taught in school. The correlation between scores on tests of intelligence and performance on measures of academic accomplishment is usually close to .5 (Lavin, 1965). A good example of the predictive relationships is found in a study by Feshbach, Adelman, and Fuller (1977). They administered IQ tests to two large samples of kindergarten children before most of them had learned to read. Then they obtained reading achievement test scores for these children when they were in the first, second, and third grades. In one sample, the correlations between IQ in kindergarten and later reading achievement increased from .32 in the first-grade to .45 in the third grade. In the second sample, the comparable correlations increased from .42 to .45. These results indicate that IQ tests given at the start of a child's education predict academic performance measures obtained several years later.

The relationship between IQ and what children learn in schools is ubiquitous. It is difficult if not impossible to create an educational setting in which scores on tests of intelligence are not predictively related to what children learn. Cronbach and Snow (1977) surveyed studies of the relationship between individual traits and school performance where some attempt was made to study variations in educational practices. They concluded their comprehensive survey as follows: "We once hoped that instructional methods might be found whose outcomes correlate very little with general ability. This does not appear to be a viable hope" (Cronbach & Snow, 1977, p. 500). Cronbach and Snow noted that although there were educational practices that might benefit individuals who had low or who had high scores on tests of intelligence, their review of the research literature convinced them that pupils who score high on IQ tests always learn more than pupils who score low on IQ tests.

Does performance in school tell us much about what happens to people *outside* of school? It is evident that school performance clearly relates to the amount of education obtained. If you are a good student in high school, you are more likely to go to college than if you are not a good student. And if you are a good student in college, you are more likely to go to graduate or professional school. In our society, the amount of education that a person obtains is related to occupational status. High-status occupations are those that tend to require high levels of education. You can't be a lawyer or a doctor without going to professional school, and it is unlikely that you can be the president of a bank or the chief executive officer of a company without having a college degree. Those jobs that do not require many years of formal education tend to have low status and prestige. If this is true, and scores on intelligence tests predict educational performance, and educational performance is related to the amount of education a person is likely to receive, then scores on intelligence tests should predict the amount of education that a person receives and, ultimately, the prestige level of a person's occupation.

Intelligence, Social Class, and Education

If we are to consider the influence of intelligence on occupational status, we also have to consider one's childhood social class background. The social class status of the parents predicts the child's intelligence, success in school, and amount of education received. Social class background is usually measured by educational background, occupational status, and family income. Perhaps the relationship between intelligence, amount of education, and ultimately occupational status is nothing more than an indication of the extent to which the American educational system is designed to confer educational and social advantages to children with privileged social backgrounds.

There are many ways in which children whose families are socially privileged may receive an advantage in the American educational system. Social class background is related to the quality of the school one attends. Children with socially privileged parents are likely to attend better schools that, among other things, spend more per pupil, than other schools. If such children are having problems in school, their parents may be able to hire a tutor; if their high school academic credentials are not strong enough to ensure admission into a selective college, their parents might be able to send them to a boarding school for a year in order to enhance their academic skills; if their Scholastic Aptitude Test scores are not satisfactory, they may be able to afford courses designed to increase their performance (although it should be noted that such courses may not be especially beneficial; see Messick, 1980); if such children have difficulty writing an effective essay for a college application, their parents may be able to hire an admissions counselor to help them; and if one of their parents is a graduate of a selective college and a substantial contributor to that college, the admissions office might evaluate the student's application favorably. Social privilege may contribute to the amount of education that a student receives in diverse ways.

It is possible to analyze relationships among social class background, education, intelligence, and ultimate occupational status. First, it should be noted that there is a positive correlation between social class background and intelligence. White (1982) performed a meta-analysis of all the studies relating IQ to social class and obtained an average r of .33. The relationship is not strong, however. We also know from the discussion of research in chapter 5 on the heritability of intelligence that biologically unrelated adults who were reared in the same family tend to have zero correlations in intelligence, a result implying that part of the relationship between social class background and intelligence is influenced by genes and is not solely attributable to social advantages. Similarly, a child's score on a test of intelligence is not solely or predominantly determined by social background. Thus children with the same social background as well as children reared in the same family may all differ in intelligence.

It is possible to study the independent influence of children's social class background and intelligence test scores on the amount of education they will eventually receive. Longitudinal studies of these relationships indicate that children's IQ is more predictive of the amount of education they will receive than are indices of their social class background (Duncan, Featherman, & Duncan, 1972; Jencks, 1979.) Benson (1942) reported a correlation of .57 between the IQ scores for sixth grade pupils and the number of years of education they obtained. Jencks found that the correlation between childhood IQ and the number of years of education has remained constant in American society and is usually found to be in the high .50s in different studies.

The correlations between IQ and the amount of education received are higher than the correlations between social class background and education. Duncan et al. developed a path analysis to assess the independent contributions of childhood IQ and social class background to the number of years of education and ultimately to occupational status. Their analysis indicates that the independent contribution of intelligence, controlling for social class background, accounts for approximately 29% of the variance in the number of years of education. The independent contribution of social class background accounts for an additional 15% of the variance. Together these indices account for 44% of the variance. Childhood intelligence scores are almost twice as predictive of the number of years of education that a person will receive than are indices of the person's social class background.

Intelligence and the Choice to Continue One's Education

How does intelligence influence the amount of education that a person receives? Rehberg and Rosenthal (1978) investigated the determinants of the decision to continue education after high school. Their study was a longitudinal investigation of the decision processes of 2,000 students who attended ninth through twelfth grade in the same high school. They obtained information about each student's social class background, intelligence test score, parents' expectations for higher education, the particular curriculum selected, and the intentions of friends to continue their education. They related these measures to the students' *plans* to continue their education after high school, and, at the conclusion of the study, to the actual *decision* to continue education. They found that, for ninth graders, social class background was more predictive of plans to continue their education than was IQ; after graduation, IQ was more predictive of the actual decision to continue.

Rehberg and Rosenthal's analyses indicate that intelligence influences experiences in school, changing the impact of some of the influences that are important at the start of high school. Students whose IQs are high are likely to get better grades than students with low IQs. Academic performance may influence the kinds of courses that students take, the kinds of encouragement they receive from their high school counselors, the characteristics of the other students with whom they associate, and their own sense of the extent to which higher education is appropriate for them. The influence of IQ on extent of education, as found from the Rehberg and Rosenthal study, documents a process that is also likely to occur at elementary and postgraduate levels. Individual differences in intelligence influence performance in elementary school. Academic performance in elementary school may influence parental beliefs about whether or not higher education is appropriate for a child. And a child's performance in elementary school may influence that child's liking for school and her plans for additional education. Something analogous to this process probably occurs at the college level as well; the educational performance of a student influences the decision to seek admission to professional schools or to graduate school.

Thus individual differences in intelligence have diverse influences on individuals' educational experience. They influence school performance, which in turn may influence motivation and the schools' response to students. This process exemplifies the relationship between individual differences and the impact of the environment on individuals. The educational environment is not monolithic—it consists of a range of possible influences that may have different effects on different people. How the educational system impacts on a person may depend on the characteristics of the person and the way in which the individual uses the opportunities that are made available. The amount of education a person receives may be understood as an example of what Scarr & McCartney (1983) call *niche selection*—the selection of environments that are compatible with a person's genetic capabilities. Individuals with high intellectual ability tend to structure their interactions with the educational system to create an environment that fosters the continued development of their intellectual skills and abilities. At the same time, it should be realized that the American educational system does not provide an environment that is sufficiently flexible to encourage all students to develop their abilities. It does provide advantages to socially privileged students that are not related to a student's intelligence.

INTELLIGENCE AND ANTISOCIAL BEHAVIOR

Intelligence is related to criminality. Although there are social class influences on both criminality and general intelligence, general intelligence appears to exert an influence on criminal behavior that is independent of social class influences. McGarvey, Gabrielli, Bentler, and Mednick (1981) obtained criminal records for a group of over 4,000 Danish males. After controlling for social class background, they obtained a correlation of −.17 for the relationship between scores on intelligence tests given as part of a universal military induction program and the frequency of criminal convictions. Individuals who had low IQ were slightly more likely to be convicted of criminal offenses than those who had high IQ, and this relationship was independent of social status. The relationship, however, is quite weak. Intelligence cannot be used to predict criminal behavior with much accuracy. The relationship between criminality and intelligence is much weaker than the relationship between intelligence and educational performance.

Personality characteristics related to antisocial behavior may also influence the development of intelligence. In chapter 3 we discussed a longitudinal study by Huesmann et al. indicating that children who were rated as aggressive by their classmates were more likely to exhibit antisocial and aggressive behavior as adults. Huesmann, Eron, and Yarmel (1987) used the data from this study to investigate the relationship between childhood aggressive behavior and the development of intellectual skills. They obtained measures of intellectual ability and aggressive tendencies for children at age 8 and then 22 years later when they were 30. The correlation between the aggression scores at age 8 and a measure of intellectual competence (the Wide Range Achievement Test) at age 30 was −.21. The correlation between age 8 IQ and intellectual competence at age 30 was .49. It is possible to use childhood IQ and aggression scores together to predict age 30 intellectual skill. The combined correlation (actually a multiple correlation) between these two measures and age 30 intellectual skill was .61. Thus age 8 aggression scores add significantly to the ability to predict intellectual competence at age 30. Children who were rated as aggressive were less likely to develop their intellectual skills than children who were rated as nonaggressive. It is interesting to note that intelligence at age 8 did not add to the ability to predict aggression scores at age 30. These data imply that aggressive tendencies influence the development of intellectual competence, but intellectual competence does not influence the development of aggressive tendencies.

Intelligence, aggressive tendencies, and criminality are related to each other in complex ways. Why? School performance may contribute to these relationships. Children who score low on intelligence tests and who are aggressive may have more difficulty in school than children who score high on intelligence tests and are not aggressive. Children who are not successful in school are less likely to develop their intellectual abilities and may be more likely to engage in criminal behavior as adults than children who are successful in schools. This analysis is very speculative. We are not aware of research that attempts to study these relationships simultaneously.

ADDITIONAL CORRELATES OF INTELLIGENCE

Intelligence has been related to many other variables. Humphreys, Davey, and Kashima (1986) related scores on a health questionnaire to intelligence for a sample of over 10,000 American high school students. They found 43 items that were related to scores on intelligence tests for their sample. They then tested these relationships on a new sample of over 10,000 high school students and found that the correlation between scores on the health questionnaire and on intelligence was .40. The correlation between a measure of social class background and scores on the health questionnaire was .22, indicating that intelligence test scores are more strongly related to self-reports about an individual's health than is social class background.

What accounts for the correlation between intelligence and self-reports about health? Perhaps individuals who score high on tests of intelligence are more likely to report that they are healthy, whether or not they actually are (see chapter 12). Perhaps intelligent individuals are more likely to follow a healthy lifestyle, or possibly the opposite may be true and individuals who follow a healthy lifestyle are likely to develop higher intelligence. Perhaps there are factors that influence both intelligence and health. For example, nutrition may be related to both. We don't really know why intelligence and reports about health are related. The relationship may be an artifact of the way in which health is measured in this study, or all of the possibilities offered above may be partially true.

There are many other variables that have been related to scores on tests of intelligence. Brand (1987) compiled a list of such variables, shown in Table 10.1. It is obviously extensive. Some of the relationships may be attributable to social class influences or to the influence of formal education. Although we have a reasonably good understanding of the influence of intelligence on education, relationships between intelligence and other variables are not as well understood.

TABLE 10.1   Correlates of General Intelligence (*g*) in the Normal Population (Based on Brand, 1987)

POSITIVE CORRELATES

Achievement motivation
Altruism
Analytic style
Anorexia nervosa
Aptitudes: cognitive abilities; "abstractness" of integrative complexity
Artistic preferences and abilities
Craftwork
Creativity, fluency
Dietary preferences (low sugar, low fat)
Educational attainment ($r \approx .60$)
Eminence, genius
Emotional sensitivity
Extracurricular attainments
Field independence
Health, fitness, longevity
Height
Humor, sense of
Income
Interests, breadth and depth of
Involvement in school activities
Leadership
Learning ability
Linguistic abilities (including spelling)
Logical abilities
Marital partner, choice of
Media preferences (newspapers, TV channels)
Memory
Migration (voluntary)
Military rank
Moral reasoning and development
Motor skills
Musical preferences and abilities
Myopia
Occupational status

Occupational success
Perceptual abilities (for briefly presented material)
Piaget-type abilities
Practical knowledge
Psychotherapy, response to
Reading ability
Regional differences
Social skills
Socio-economic status (achieved)
Socio-economic status of origin (parental)
Sports participation at university
Supermarket-shopping ability
Talking speed
Values, attitudes

NEGATIVE CORRELATES

Accident-proneness
Acquiescence
Aging
Alcoholism
Authoritarianism
Conservatism (of social views)
Crime
Delinquency
Dogmatism
Falsification ("Lie" scores)
Hysteria vs. other neuroses
Impulsivity
Infant mortality
"Psychoticism"
Racial prejudice
Reaction times
Smoking
Truancy
Weight/height ratio, obesity

Brand, C.R. (1987). "The Importance of General Intelligence," in Modgil, S. and Modgil C. (eds.), Arthur A. Jensen, *Consensus and Controversy*. Reprinted with permission of Falmer Press, England.

COGNITIVE ABILITIES, SOCIAL BEHAVIOR, AND PERSONALITY

We have taken the position that intelligence is an important individual difference that relates to a variety of important life outcomes. Perhaps the same could be said for other types of abilities as well. For example, high levels of athletic or musical talent can also have a major impact on one's life. So can physical appearance. Probably you could come up with other individual differences that influence important outcomes in people's lives. Are these all part of personality? From our definition on page 3, intelligence and talent probably do merit inclusion as part of personality, but physical appearance does not. Our physical appearance may influence people's reactions to us, and it may influence our self-esteem (Hatfield & Sprecher, 1986; see chapter 11) but physical appearance is not itself a psychological variable. Intelligence and talent are psychological in nature, yet many psychologists do not include these as part of personality either. For these psychologists, abilities are similar to physical characteristics: they may influence our lives, but they do not involve social behavior, emotions, or motivation. As we have noted, whether one considers cognitive abilities to be part of personality depends on one's (fairly arbitrary) definition of personality.

There is another way of thinking about personality and intelligence that does not depend on definitions. We can ask whether cognitive abilities are related to emotion and motivation. Do people who differ in their cognitive abilities also differ in ways everybody agrees are part of personality? In one sense, the answer is obviously "yes." For example, an intellectually brilliant student who is also conscientious is going to differ in many ways from an intellectually brilliant student who is lazy. This is no more than saying that people's characteristics influence each other. It doesn't indicate whether people with different abilities also have different personality characteristics. Consider the Big Five traits. Do you think that people with lower or higher intelligence would differ on any of the Big Five dimensions? Research indicates that, with the possible exception of openness (McCrae, 1987), there is little correlation between the Big Five and IQ.

But perhaps this is still the wrong way of thinking about personality and intelligence. Perhaps there are aspects of how people think that have direct influences on their social behavior. Our social behavior clearly involves attention, memory, and problem solving. Perhaps individual differences in these cognitive processes are connected to how one negotiates the social world.

Field Dependence-Independence

One of the most intriguing attempts to link cognitive abilities and social behavior has been the work on **field dependence-independence** (FDI) begun over 40 years ago by Herman Witkin and his colleagues (Witkin, Lewis, Hertzmann, Machover, Meissner, & Wapner, 1954). Witkin did not set out to discover a new personality dimension, and the history of FDI is a fascinating example of how research findings can lead to new theoretical conceptions. Witkin was originally interested in a question that seems to have little to do with personality: How do people know which way is up? At the time, some perception psychologists believed that people's sense of up and down was based on visual cues, such as walls, trees, flagpoles, windows, and so on. Other perception psychologists believed that our sense of the upright was based on our ability to sense the pull of gravity (from our kinesthetic, tactile, and vestibular senses). To find out which was more important, Witkin (Asch & Witkin, 1948; Witkin, 1949) put the visual and gravitational cues in conflict. Imagine the following situation: you enter a small cubicle that looks like a small room (it even has a picture on the wall) and you sit down in a chair. The only thing you can see is the room itself; you can't see outside the room. The "room" is attached to a mechanical device that allows it to be rotated, that is, tipped to the left or the right; the chair, which you are strapped into, can also be rotated. Suppose the room and the chair are both rotated to a position 28 degrees off true vertical. Since you and the room are still lined up on the same axis, the visual field looks normal to you rather than tipped. The question is, do you feel tipped to one side? If you were using only the visual cues to determined upright, you would feel yourself to be sitting vertically. On the other hand, if you were using only the gravitational cues you would feel tipped. With the room remaining tilted, the subjects were asked to adjust the seat so that they were sitting truly vertical, like the flagpole outside the lab. Some of them used the gravitational cues totally and were able to place themselves in the true vertical position. Others used the visual cues totally and said they were already sitting upright (even though they were actually tilted). Most people were affected by both sets of cues, but some more by the visual field and some more by the body cues.

The finding of these differences among people intrigued Witkin and led him to explore whether these individual differences were limited to this specific situation or were related to behavior in other situations. One such situation is the **Rod and Frame Test** (RFT; Figure 10.2). The subject sits in a completely dark room

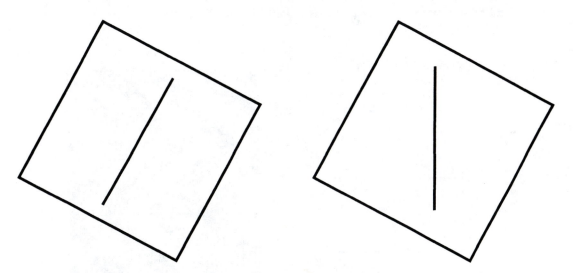

FIGURE 10.2   The Rod and Frame Test. The subject's task is to set the rod to true vertical. The figure to the left shows how a field-dependent person would set the rod; the figure to the right shows how a field-independent person would set the rod.

and views a large luminous square frame, which is tilted. Inside the frame is a luminous rod. The subject's task is to set the rod to true vertical while the frame remains tilted. Witkin found correlations in the .5 to .6 range between these two situations: people who were able to set their body to true vertical in the tilting room were also likely to set the rod to true vertical in the RFT; people who were influenced by the tilt of the room were also influenced by the tilt of the frame (Witkin et al., 1954). For these people, the axes of the frame seemed to define up and down, as if the frame were not tilted at all. Witkin coined the terms *field independent* (FI) and *field dependent* (FD) to denote those people who were less influenced by the visual field versus those who were more influenced by it.

Witkin then asked whether FI and FD individuals differed in ways that had nothing to do with perception of the vertical. He considered the possibility that the inability to locate the true vertical in a tilted visual field might be part of a more general difficulty in overcoming the effects of the visual field. For example, consider Figure 10.3, which shows an item from the **Embedded Figures Test** (EFT). On the EFT, subjects have to locate a simple figure hidden within a more complex figure. To accomplish this, one must be able to break up the complex figure into unrelated lines and shapes so that one can trace the simple figure. Witkin found that people who had trouble with this task also tended to be more influenced by the visual field in perception of the upright. Field dependence-independence was evidently more than the ability to tell which way is up. How much more?

What do the ability to locate the upright when the visual field is tilted and the ability to identify a simple figure within a complex embedding field have in common? In other words, what leads FD and FI individuals to perform differently on

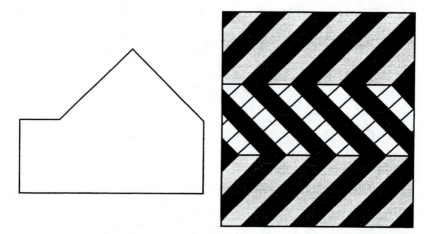

FIGURE 10.3   Example of an item on the Embedded Figures Test. The subject's task is to outline the simple figure that is embedded in the complex figure to its right.

these tests? The answer is not obvious, and Witkin and others came up with somewhat different answers over the years (Witkin et al., 1954; Witkin, Dyk, Faterson, Goodenough, & Karp, 1962; Witkin & Goodenough, 1981). Field-dependent individuals seem to be strongly influenced by the dominant appearance of the visual field; field-independent individuals seem to be able to separate the visual field into components. FD individuals respond to the field "as given," whereas FI individuals "restructure" information to meet their immediate goals. Witkin suggested that these tendencies might be general characteristics, not limited to perceptual tasks like the RFT and EFT. Performance on these tasks was merely a reflection of a more general **cognitive style** that cut across many aspects of people's functioning. To explore this idea, Witkin and colleagues (and many others) studied differences between FD and FI individuals in areas such as psychopathology, career choice, and learning styles.

FDI and Social Behavior

Most intriguing has been the extension of the FDI theory to social behavior. Witkin has drawn analogies between social functioning and perceptual functioning. In the social world, other people are the most important objects in the stimulus field. An individual with a cognitive style of dependence on external frames of reference would be more likely to attend to and be influenced by other people, as compared to an individual whose style is to restructure information internally. As Goodenough has written: "If the field-dependent cognitive style involves a reliance on the external stimulus field, then people ought to play a particularly significant role for the field-dependent person. In contrast, field-independent people should function with a greater degree of separateness from the immediate social context in which they find themselves" (1978, p. 182).

Two studies illustrate how FD and FI individuals differ in social situations. The first one studied the effects of **deindividuation** on a variety of behaviors, including cheating (Nadler, Goldberg, & Jaffe, 1982). Deindividuation is said to occur when people feel anonymous. One of its effects is to loosen internal standards of behavior and increase the influence of external standards (Spivey & Prentice-Dunn, 1990). When people are in a deindividuated state they tend to "go along with the crowd," accepting whatever standards of behavior people around them appear to be using. However, when people are made aware of their own individuality (for example, by being publicly identified by name), they tend to rely more on their own personal standards of behavior.

Nadler et al. set up a situation in which subjects observed other individuals cheating. Subjects were tested in groups of three, only one of whom was a real subject (the other two were accomplices of the experimenter). Half the subjects were in a condition in which their identity was made salient (e.g., they gave their names and where they lived, and the lighting in the room was bright); the other half were in a condition that fostered feelings of anonymity (e.g., they revealed nothing about who they were, and the lighting was dim). All the subjects had been selected on the basis of earlier performance on the Rod and Frame Test as relatively field independent or field dependent. They were given a test of general knowledge and were told that if they answered enough questions correctly they would receive a financial bonus. The questionnaire was rigged so that half of the questions had no correct answer. After the subjects began working on the questionnaire, the experimenter left the room. Each confederate then got up and went over to the desk, where the experimenter had left the answer sheets. Imagine you were in this situation. Would you do the same as the other "subjects," or would you resist cheating?

Previous research has suggested that people are more likely to follow the lead of others when they are anonymous. Nadler et al. predicted that FD people would be more affected by the conditions of anonymity versus identifiability than would FI people. Why did Nadler et al. make this prediction? Remember that FD people are more likely to be affected by prominent external frames of reference, and anonymity tends to make external standards more prominent. Just as the looming frame in an otherwise completely dark room becomes a powerful influence on FD people's sense of the vertical axis, the behavior of others under conditions of anonymity should also powerfully influence FD people. And just as FI people can ignore the frame in determining the true vertical axis, they should also be unaffected by other people's standards of behavior whether they are anonymous or identified. Nadler et al. found clear support for this prediction. Many more of the FD cheated when anonymous than when identifiable. In contrast, there was little effect of anonymity versus identifiability for the FI subjects (see Table 10.2).

There are two things about this study worth emphasizing. First, remember that FDI was measured by means of the RFT. It is quite remarkable that performance on a task that requires finding the true vertical when a frame is tilted is related to complex social behavior such as the effects of anonymity on cheating. Second, this study is an example of a **person–situation interaction**. Notice that neither FDI nor anonymity had a **main effect** on whether subjects followed the confederates' lead. It would be wrong, on the basis of this study, to conclude that anonymity causes all people to shift to external standards; this study suggests that the effect of anonymity depends on whether one is FD or FI. It would also be wrong to conclude that FD people are always more influenced by others than are FI people.[1] In this study, the difference between FD and FI depended on the level of

TABLE 10.2   Number of Field-Dependent and Field-Independent Subjects Who Cheated under Conditions of Anonymity or Identifiability (Based on Nadler, Goldberg, and Jaffe, 1982)

	FIELD DEPENDENT		FIELD INDEPENDENT	
	Anonymous	Identifiable	Anonymous	Identifiable
	8	1	4	5

Note: 10 subjects per cell.
Reproduced with permission of the American Psychological Association.

anonymity. When person–situation interactions exist, both personality character-istics and aspects of the situation must be taken into account to predict behavior.

The second study of FDI and social behavior was on conflict resolution. Olt-man, Goodenough, Witkin, Freedman, and Friedman (1975) had college students meet in pairs to discuss differences of opinion on a variety of "choice dilemmas" such as whether a person should have a risky operation for cancer. The students were told that pretesting had determined that they had different opinions but that their task was to resolve their differences by finding common ground. The students had been previously tested on the RFT and EFT and designated as relatively FI or FD, so that it was possible to set up three types of pairs: two FI subjects, two FD subjects, or one FD and one FI subject. Oltman et al. predicted that the FI–FI pairs and the FD–FD pairs would differ in their ability to resolve their disagreements. Which pair do you think would be most likely to reach agreement? Table 10.3 shows the percentage of dilemmas for which the pairs were *unable* to reach a con-sensus. Clearly, two FI subjects are much more likely to resist compromise than two FD subjects.

Why should performance on tests like the RFT and EFT predict whether peo-ple will be able to reach agreement? The FI style is to separate oneself from exter-nal frames of reference and to use one's own standards for making judgments. In contrast, the FD style is to give greater attention to and to be influenced by exter-nal frames of reference. Just as FI subjects are less influenced by the tilting frame or the complex figure, they are also less influenced by the point of view of others.

Further evidence that FD people pay more attention to others comes from an-other part of this study. The subjects (college students) were asked how many other participants in the research they knew. FI subjects knew (by name) an average of 2.0 subjects out of the 39 others. FD subjects knew an average of 4.1 names, a highly significant difference. Witkin and Goodenough (1977) suggested that the greater attention of FD people to others is part of what they call an "interpersonal orienta-tion," in contrast to the more "impersonal orientation" of FI people.

Many studies have revealed differences in behavior of FD and FI individuals that seem on the surface to be far removed from finding the true vertical in a tilted frame or locating an embedded figure. There is also evidence that FDI is related to personal characteristics that can be observed by others. Kogan and Block (1991) analyzed data from 105 18-year-old women and men who had been tested on the RFT and EFT and who had also been described by examiners using the California Q-Sort.

TABLE 10.3 **Percentage of Problems That Pairs Were Unable to Resolve as a Function of Field Dependence-Independence Makeup (Based on Oltman et al., 1975)**

COMPOSITION OF PAIR	PERCENTAGE OF PROBLEMS NOT RESOLVED
FI with FI	35%
FD with FI	18%
FD with FD	5%

The description of FI individuals included "wide range of interests," "values intellectual matters," "insights into own motives and behaviors," "personally charming," and "perceptive of interpersonal cues." The description of FD individuals included "self-defeating," "concerned with self-adequacy," "self-indulgent," exhibiting "repressive" tendencies, and "judges people in coventional terms."

Field Dependence, Intelligence, and Personality

How does FDI relate to our original question about intelligence and personality? Witkin labeled FDI a cognitive style because he believed that it reflected how people approach the world rather than how well they do. Yet measures of FDI look a lot like ability measures: there is a right answer and a wrong answer, and the dimension is scored in terms of correct performance. Attempts to find tasks on which FD people do better than FI people have not been successful, and these include tasks such as detecting the emotion expressed in the face of another person, supposedly a measure of "social sensitivity" (Hoffman & Kagan, 1977; Sabetelli, Dreyer, & Buck, 1979). In short, tests of FDI are clearly measures of ability and, like other such measures, are part of the positive manifold (which is why it has been so difficult to find tasks on which FD people do better). In particular, it has been suggested that the EFT (and perhaps the RFT as well) is a measure of "spatial ability" or "fluid ability" or even g (McKenna, 1984). If so, the large body of research on FDI may be viewed as evidence that aspects of intelligence have important relationships to social behavior and personality. Performance on these ability tests, which do not themselves involve actual, self-reported, or rated social behavior or personality, predict people's behavior in areas far removed from the measurement procedure. Although Witkin's theory of FDI provides a way of understanding these relationships, which would not have been predicted by usual concepts of intelligence, it remains an empirical question whether measures of FDI predict social behavior beyond what would be predicted by measures of spatial ability. If not, we must rethink what it is about spatial ability that leads people with different levels to behave differently in the social domain.

The work on FDI constitutes the most ambitious attempt to understand how intellectual factors might interact with social behavior. Many other cognitive and intellectual styles have also been proposed over the years. It is likely that what some have called "cognitive style" is actually the interaction of traditional personality traits with cognitive abilities. For example, Kagan (1966) proposed that some children may be more impulsive than others in approaching cognitive tasks. However, impulsivity in carrying out cognitive tasks is likely a reflection of a disposition toward impulsivity that can emerge in many situations, social as well as intellectual. Has one gained additional knowledge or understanding by claiming that impulsive behavior on a cognitive task reflects an "impulsive cognitive style" rather than simply a general trait of impulsivity? Similarly, Sternberg (1994) describes a "thinking style" that involves creating one's own rules and formulating new ways of doing things. There is no doubt that some people do use their abilities in this way, but is this anything more than being high on openness to experience or unconventionality? Just as we questioned whether or not field dependence is empirically discriminable from spatial ability, we must also ask whether various other cognitive styles are empirically discriminable from more well-established personality traits.

Mischel (1990) has noted that "Historically, personality psychologists tried to 'partial out' the role of intelligence, adhering to the traditional dichotomy between 'abilities' and 'personality.' In spite of these efforts, cognitive competencies (e.g., as tested by 'mental age' and IQ tests) proved to be among the best predictors of social development and interpersonal adjustment" (p. 118). Earlier in this chapter we discussed the relationship between intelligence and important social behaviors such as school achievement and criminality. Whether or not intelligence should be considered part of personality, there is no doubt that people's ability to reason, to learn, to solve problems, and to understand the world in which they live plays an important role in their lives. We hope that the historical division of labor between those who study personality and those who study intelligence will continue to break down and that we will learn much more about how intelligence contributes to individuality.

CONCLUSION

We believe intelligence is an important dimension of personality. People judge the intelligence of others they meet and believe that individual differences in intelligence have important social consequences. When we attempt to measure intelligence objectively, we find that scores in childhood have important social consequences. In seeking to understand the ways in which individuals differ from one another and how these differences might influence their social behavior, we cannot ignore individual differences in intelligence.

Endnote

[1]See also Mausner and Graham (1970) for another example of a person–situation interaction involving FDI and social influence.

11

Our Thoughts, Our Feelings, Our Selves

Do you believe that you are a superior person with admirable qualities—one who has high **self-esteem?** How stable are your beliefs about yourself? Do they remain the same or do they fluctuate? Think about your performance on the next exam in your personality class. Do you think you are likely to receive a good grade? If you received an A on the exam, how would you explain your success? Would you be inclined to attribute your success to your brilliance? Or would you attribute it to luck, or to hard work and effort? Are you a person who is given to introspection? Do you focus on your private thoughts and experiences a lot? Are you concerned with the way in which you are perceived by others? What is your conception of gender? How does it influence your actions? Do "real" men cry, and do "real" women change the oil in their cars?

What do all of these questions have in common? They all refer to the ways in which we think about ourselves and our actions. In this chapter we will explore research designed to inform us about individual differences in our thoughts about ourselves and our actions. We shall try to discover if the contents of our thoughts influence the way we behave. In addition, we shall consider how thoughts are related to our feelings.

SELF-ESTEEM

We can describe ourselves and we can evaluate ourselves. I may say that I am tall or short—a descriptive statement. I may say that I am a superior or an inferior person—an evaluative statement. Most people seem to evaluate their personal characteristics. There are many self-esteem measures that require subjects to endorse or reject evaluative statements about the self (Wylie, 1974). Scores on self-esteem scales are negatively correlated with scores on the neuroticism scale of the Big Five (McCrae and Costa, 1990). Individuals who view themselves as being well-adjusted are likely to score high on self-esteem measures. This does not imply, however, that measures of self-esteem are nothing more than measures of one of the Big Five personality traits. Researchers interested in self-perception have developed distinctive theoretical concepts about the self, and these concepts are used to design studies that inform us about the ways in which individuals who differ in self-esteem behave.

People are likely to endorse items on a test of self-esteem that suggest that they have positive characteristics. Perhaps people do things to enhance their self-esteem. People might also tend to see their performance in a more positive way than is warranted.

Are our views of ourselves more positive than is justified by our true characteristics? Is this true of all people or only of individuals who are high in self-esteem? It is possible to contrast two different views of self-esteem. (1) People are generally accurate in their self perceptions. This is sometimes called the *correspondence view*—that is, self-perception corresponds to reality. (2) People distort their views of themselves in order to enhance their self-esteem. John and Robins (1993) designed a study to test these different notions about the accuracy of self-perceptions. They asked several groups of graduate students who were enrolled in Master of Business Administration programs to rate their performance in a group discussion in which they were asked to evaluate employees on the basis of written materials presented to the group. The performance of each group member was ranked by experienced assessors who observed the discussion, by each of the five other participants, and by the person. This procedure permitted John and Robins to obtain two external measures of each participant's performance—by peer participants and by expert observers—and compare them with a self-reported ranking.

The results support five conclusions about self-esteem. First, there is evidence in support of the correspondence theory. Individuals judge the quality of their performance in a relatively accurate manner. The average correlation between individuals' self-rankings and the rankings assigned by peers was .32.

Second, individuals are less accurate in their self-rankings than they are in the rankings of others. The average correlation between rankings assigned by participants to other participants was .45. There must be biases in self-judgment.

Third, biases tend to be self-enhancing. Individuals tended to rank their own performance higher than they were ranked by their peers or by the assessment staff. Fifty-eight percent of the individuals ranked themselves more highly than their peers ranked them.

Fourth, although most individuals distorted their own views of their performance in a self-enhancing manner, this was not true of all subjects. Approximately one-third ranked their performance lower than they were ranked by the others. These data imply that some individuals may underestimate the quality of their performance.

Fifth, self-reports about the quality of performance on this task were related to personality characteristics. Each participant was judged by the staff assessors for narcissism, defined as "self-admiration that is characterized by tendencies toward grandiose ideas, fantasized talents, exhibitionism, and defensiveness in response to criticism; and by interpersonal relations characterized by feelings of entitlement, exploitativeness, and lack of empathy." Narcissism ratings were correlated with self-ratings, and those rated high in this trait tended to rate themselves higher on performance than their peers or the staff rated them (r for peer ratings between narcissism and the degree of positive distortion in ratings $= .55$). These results indicate that individuals differ in their tendency to distort the quality of their performance in a situation.

How do beliefs about the self influence behavior? The John and Robins study provides information about how individuals evaluate their performance, but not about the influence of self-esteem on behavior.

Is self-esteem associated with superior performance on a task? Baumeister, Heatherton, and Tice (1993) were interested in the relationship between self-esteem and goal-setting behavior. They studied the performance of subjects in a video game. After playing the game, the subjects were assigned a goal of exceeding a level of performance that was slightly above their previous average performance. If they did so, they would win a prize. They were also given the option of choosing a still higher level of performance in order to win even more money. In their experiments Baumeister et al. informed some of their subjects that the task might be one in which they could "choke" and therefore they might want to choose a conservative goal. They found that subjects who had high self-esteem performed better than subjects with low self-esteem when they were not informed that they might choke, that is, when there was not a possible threat to their self-esteem. When the subjects were informed that they might choke, individuals with high self-esteem did not perform as well as those with low self-esteem. Individuals with high self-esteem set unrealistically high goals for themselves that they were not able to attain. As a result, they earned less money at the task than individuals with low self-esteem.

The John and Robins and the Baumeister, Heatherton, and Tice studies both focus on what might be called the dark side of self-esteem. Having high self-esteem is generally perceived as a good thing. Most of us probably want to feel good about ourselves, and people who have high self-esteem may generally perform better at many tasks than people with low self-esteem. At the same time, individuals may distort their interpretations of experience in order to enhance and preserve their self-esteem. Such enhancements may lead to unrealistic perceptions of their own performance. And, when their own positive view of themselves appears to be threatened, they may select unrealistic goals and perform in a less competent manner.

Components of Self-Esteem

Is self-esteem one thing or many things? When you evaluate yourself, do you think of yourself as being generally competent (or incompetent) or as competent in different activities? Is your self-esteem dependent on your competence in activities and spheres that are important to you? People's self-esteem appears to depend on their view of their competence in many different activities, and they tend to have a differentiated view of their abilities. One of the authors has a terrible sense of direction and frequently gets lost. He thinks of himself as having poor spatial ability. On the other hand, he thinks of himself as being good in things that involve verbal ability. Some of you may believe that you are poor in athletics and good in math. It seems obvious that each of us has strengths and weaknesses and that we are not equally talented in everything. Self-esteem may be described as the result of a combination of people's various beliefs about their abilities and talents.

　　How do we form a global estimate of our self-esteem? Consider some possibilities. Your self-esteem may be nothing more than the average of your view of your abilities in different domains. You may have a profile of your relative standing in several areas—your social skills, your academic skills, your leadership skills, and so on. Your global self-esteem may simply be the average of your ratings in each of several domains. Or it may be more complicated. It may involve additional complexities in how you combine your beliefs about your competencies in different areas. Some theorists (e.g., Rogers, 1961) argue that what is important is not your view of your ability but your view of your ability relative to an ideal—what you would like to be. Perhaps you think that you are very good in math—maybe in the top 10 percent of college students—but you have the ideal view of wanting to be in the top one percent. In this case you would have a self-ideal discrepancy between your ability and the ability you would like to have. By contrast, if you believe that you are average in physical attractiveness and your ideal physical attractiveness is also average, your self-ideal discrepancy would be small or nonexistent for attractiveness. It may be that your self-esteem is dependent on your self-ideal discrepancies rather than on your average ratings. If so, you could have a very positive view of your various abilities but still have low self-esteem because you have ideals that you have not attained.

　　William James wrote in his famous nineteenth-century textbook of psychology: "I who for the time have staked my all on being a psychologist, am mortified if others know much more psychology than I. But I am contented to wallow in the grossest ignorance of Greek." (1890, p. 310). James believed that self-esteem was determined by beliefs about abilities in those areas that were important for a person. He assumed that individuals differed in the areas that were important to them. If James is correct, self-esteem should be determined from a person's views of his or her talents in those areas that are important to the person. In calculating a self-esteem score, it would be necessary to weight ratings in different domains by the importance assigned to them. James's self-esteem, for example, would depend much more critically on his beliefs about his skills as a psychologist than on his beliefs about his knowledge of Greek.

Marsh (1993) tested various rules for combining ratings to predict a person's global or total self-esteem. He asked college students to rate their abilities relative to other students in each of ten domains. In addition, he obtained data on the importance each student assigned to each domain, and asked them to rate their self-ideal discrepancy in each, that is, whether they were close to or far from their ideal in each domain. He used these ratings to predict their scores on a measure of self-esteem. Marsh found that he was able to predict self-esteem simply by averaging the abilities ratings students assigned to the ten areas. The correlation between the average rating and a measure of self-esteem was .51. Marsh found that more complex ways of combining the data did not substantially improve prediction. For example, a weighting based on the importance of a domain to the individual did not meaningfully increase the ability to predict global self-esteem. Similarly, a consideration of self-ideal discrepancies did not add to the ability to predict self-esteem.

Marsh's study indicates that our global or overall self-esteem is determined principally by the average ratings we assign to our competencies in each of several domains. While we may each feel that some domains are more important for us than others and that we may be closer to our ideal level of competency in some areas than in others, a consideration of these idiographic ways of perceiving our individual competencies does not add appreciably to our ability to predict an overall or global self-esteem score.

We argued that self-esteem is based on an averaging of self-esteem scores across specific domains. This doesn't mean that knowledge of scores in specific domains is not useful. If you want to predict whether a person will choose a math elective, knowing about that person's estimate of math ability is more important than knowing about the person's global self-esteem. Since domain-specific self-esteem scores cannot be predicted from an aggregate score, it is useful to know what a person believes are his or her competencies in various domains in order to predict the person's behavior. Later in this chapter, we will see that even if discrepancies between self and ideal self may not improve the ability to predict global self-esteem, such discrepancies may be related to a person's emotional experiences.

Self-concepts, in addition to containing beliefs about various competencies, may also consist of beliefs about the kind of activities and behaviors that are appropriate and that are consistent with our self-concept. One of the authors heard a woman on a radio call-in show discussing her decision to buy a car. She had narrowed her choice to a Volvo and a Lexus. She liked the Lexus, which she perceived as a glamorous and exciting car, but she was reluctant to buy it because her friends tended to drive Volvos and she saw herself as a "Volvo" person—that is, a person who was sensible and not glamorous. She believed that buying a Lexus would not fit her personality, that people who bought Lexus cars were not like her.

The woman described above was engaging in prototype-matching behavior. Niedenthal, Cantor, and Kihlstrom (1985) argued that people use this strategy to make decisions about the kinds of situations they choose. Situations are broadly defined to include, among other things, friends, the things we purchase, and the organizations we join. We may have beliefs about the kinds of people who choose any of these situations. We have often found that college students have strongly defined beliefs about the kinds of students who attend different colleges. One of us teaches at Wesleyan. His students often say that students at Amherst and Williams, two other comparable liberal arts colleges in New England, are "business types" who would like to get a job working for a large corporation, whereas students at Wesleyan are more "artistic" and individualistic and wouldn't fit into the corporate world. These beliefs may not be accurate, but they are cited as reasons for the choice of Wesleyan over Amherst or Williams. Individuals who choose a particular situation because they believe that the people who are likely to choose that situation are similar to themselves are engaging in prototype-matching behavior.

ATTRIBUTIONS

Attributions are explanations for the causes of events. Consider an example. A man has an argument with his wife and he hits her. How are we to explain his behavior? Consider some of the ways in which explanations might differ. We could attribute this behavior to characteristics that are *internal* to the person or that are *external* to the person. If we assert that the person is aggressive and violent, then we are assuming that there are characteristics internal to the person that caused his behavior. If we assert that his wife provoked him and acted in a way that was likely to cause him to strike her, then we are attributing his behavior to something that is external to him.

Attributions may also differ with respect to their *stability*. We might assert that this behavior occurred because the man is habitually violent and aggressive. This action reflects a stable characteristic of the person. Alternatively, we might attribute this event to labile characteristics that are unlikely to be enduring. A mild-mannered man who is not habitually angered might have been given a drug by a physician that made him unusually irritable and uncharacteristically violent. Or, his wife, who is usually calm and well adjusted, may have been upset about something and uncharacteristically acted in a way to anger her husband.

The husband's behavior may have been *controllable* or *uncontrollable*. We may assume that the husband's behavior was caused by dispositional and traitlike behaviors that cannot be controlled or modified. Alternatively, we might assume that the husband could learn to control his aggression.

The behavior that we seek to explain might be understood as a *global* or as a *local* event. If we believe that the husband is habitually aggressive in many different contexts, then we would understand this event as a manifestation of a general behavioral tendency. Or we might believe that the behavior is uncharacteristic of the person or specific to a particular set of circumstances that are not likely to arise again.

Finally, we might view this behavior as *intentional* or as *unintentional*. Perhaps the husband had been angered by something that occurred earlier in the day and had planned to act aggressively toward his wife. He might even have imagined the exact form of his aggressive actions. Alternatively, his actions might have been unplanned and unintentional—caused by a momentary and passing sense of rage.

Attributional Styles

It is obvious that there are many different explanations that we might offer for actions or events and that these explanations may differ in several rather general ways. We develop explanations for events in which we ourselves are not involved and for events in which we are the actors. Individuals may differ in the habitual explanations that they develop for the things that happen to them. These differences may be an important aspect of personality, providing us with insights into how we think about the world and ourselves. These **attributional styles** or beliefs might influence our behavior.

Consider the attributions that individuals develop for failures. If I fail at a task, I might attribute that failure to stable, global, and internal characteristics. Here is example. I am driven once to a house in a new location. I need to find that house on a second occasion and I get lost. Why did I get lost? I would assume that I have little or no spatial ability. My attribution for this failure is stable (I have always had poor spatial ability and there is nothing that I can do about it; it is habitual and enduring); internal (my failure to find the house is caused by something in me); and global (I always get lost and I do poorly at all tasks that require spatial ability). This kind of attributional style may promote a sense of helplessness and may cause me to give up and to fail to solve tasks that I might actually be able to solve with more effort.

Alternatively, I could have assumed that my failure was attributable to a temporary detour that led me to deviate from the path I intended to follow. In such a case it was attributable to a cause that is local, unstable, and external. If I were given a similar task the next day, I might assume that I was capable of solving it. Nothing in my attributions about the previous failure ought to lead me to believe that I was not capable of doing so.

Is this analysis correct? Do people have different kinds of attributions for failures and do these differences actually influence the way they behave? There is evidence that they do. Peterson, Seligman, and Valliant (1988) assessed the attributional styles of 99 Harvard graduates based on their responses to a 1946 questionnaire about their wartime experiences. The subjects had graduated from Harvard between 1942 and 1944, had good academic records, and were judged to be well adjusted and in good health in 1946. These men were asked to describe difficult wartime experiences they had had. The attributions they offered for each event were independently judged by four judges, on three dimensions: stable vs. labile, internal vs. external, and global vs. specific. Each subject was assigned a composite score that reflected the degree to which he attributed events to internal, stable, and global characteristics. It was assumed that individuals who used this type of attributional style would be less likely to develop constructive strategies to cope with adversity. They are pessimists who believe that there is little or nothing they can do to overcome adversity. Individuals who believed that adverse events were attributable to external characteristics that were unlikely to be recurring and that were not attributable to their own failings (external attributions) were characterized as optimistic.

Peterson, Seligman, and Valliant related attributional style scores to measures of physical health based on physical examinations administered every five years from ages 30 to 60. They found that health measures were not related to attributional style between 30 and 40, a period when most of these individuals were healthy. Health status measures obtained in middle age, however, *were* related to attributional style measures obtained when the subjects were in their mid-twenties. The correlations between an attributional style for difficult wartime experiences that was stable, internal, and global and poor physical health was highest at age 45 ($r = .37$) and ranged from .18 (at age 50) to .25 at age 60. Pessimistic subjects had poorer health than optimistic subjects as judged by the results of their physical examinations. (We shall discuss the relationship between personality and health in chapter 12.)

Can you explain the results obtained by Peterson, Seligman, and Valliant? What causes individuals with pessimistic attributional styles to develop poor health? Do they fail to follow medical advice? Do they experience more stress because they fail to take actions that are likely to solve personal problems? Why do people develop these kinds of attributional styles, and if they result in negative outcomes, can they be changed or are they influenced by enduring dispositions that are difficult to change? To what do we attribute individual differences in attributions? We shall return to these questions after considering additional research relating attributional styles to behavior.

How do you explain academic failures? Suppose you were asked to develop an explanation for your inability to understand the points a lecturer made in class. To what would you attribute this inability? If you believed that your understanding was attributable to your lack of intelligence, you would be endorsing a stable, internal, and global attribution for your failure. If, on the other hand, you believed that your failure was attributable to the inadequacies of the professor—who is vague and fails to explain concepts clearly—then you would be attributing your failure to external, labile, and specific events. Peterson and Barrett (1987) used an attributional style questionnaire to obtain measures of the extent to which college students explained academic failures in a global, stable, and internal way. They related overall scores on this measure obtained during the first two weeks of college to the students' first-year grade point average (GPA). Students who attributed their failures to external, labile, and specific causes tended to get better grades than did those who attributed them to internal, stabile, and global causes. If you believe that you are the kind of person who always fails (perhaps because you think that you are stupid) and that there is nothing you can do about it, you are likely to have a low GPA.

Mastery-Oriented and Helpless Children

Dweck and her colleagues studied children's attributions about success and failure on intellectual tasks (see Diener & Dweck, 1978; 1980; Dweck & Leggett, 1988). Diener and Dweck (1980) asked children in the fourth, fifth, and sixth grades a series of questions about attributions for failure. Those who tended to attribute failures at different tasks to lack of effort were designated as "mastery oriented." Such children believe that if they worked harder they might not fail in the future. Children who did not attribute failures to effort were designated as "helpless." Such children don't believe that their own lack of effort is responsible for their failures and so they feel there is little or nothing that they can do to improve their performance.

Diener and Dweck asked the children to solve a series of problems and noted whether or not the children used appropriate strategies. The children were given hints that enabled them to solve the first eight problems; then they were presented with four more problems that they could not *immediately* solve using the strategies that worked for the first eight problems. However, by pursuing those strategies, they could find the correct answers. Any other strategies were clearly not appropriate for these trials. The researchers noted whether children continued to use the strategies that could lead to correct answers or abandoned them in the face of failure and used strategies that could not lead to successful performance.

Diener and Dweck found that there was little or no difference in the performance of mastery-oriented and helpless children during the first eight trials when they had all received helpful hints. However, the two groups differed on the set of four trials that could not be solved immediately using those strategies. Table 11.1 indicates the number of children in each group who improved, remained the same, or deteriorated in their use of various strategies to solve the second set of problems.

TABLE 11.1   Number of Helpless and Mastery-Oriented Children Whose Hypothesis-Testing Strategy Improved, Remained the Same, or Deteriorated (Based on Diener and Dweck, 1980)

GROUP	IMPROVED	SAME	DETERIORATED
Helpless	4	19	33
Mastery oriented	15	33	8

Reproduced with permission of the American Psychological Association.

Most of the mastery-oriented children improved or remained the same, while most of the helpless children shifted to inappropriate strategies and as a result their performance deteriorated.

Although all of the children experienced success before failing at these problems, the mastery-oriented and helpless children responded differently to the experience of success. Ninety percent of the mastery-oriented children believed that they would succeed if presented with similar problems in the future. Only 50 percent of the helpless children believed that they would succeed. Mastery-oriented children tend to attribute success to ability, whereas helpless children tend to attribute it to luck and to a belief that the problems were easy. Helpless children appear to be convinced that they do not have the ability to do well, and even when they succeed this ability is not likely to be diagnostic of future success. Mastery-oriented children have faith in their abilities and assume that additional effort will overcome adversity. These beliefs influence the way in which these children respond to failure (and success).

Dweck and Leggett (1988) assumed that these children have different beliefs about intelligence and its influence on their performance. Table 11.2 presents a summary of their theoretical analysis. Mastery-oriented children who believe that their intellectual ability is a fixed and unchanging "entity" and who believe that they have high ability may seek challenges designed to confirm their view of their ability. By contrast, individuals who believe that their ability is fixed and who think that they have low ability become helpless in the face of challenges. Children who believe that intelligence is malleable and that it changes in response to learning experiences are likely to be mastery oriented whether or not they believe their intelligence is low or high. If you think that you have low ability but that your ability may increase through learning, you may seek intellectual challenges that are likely to increase your ability. The belief that abilities may be changed may counteract the effects of the belief that one has low ability. If you believe that you have low

TABLE 11.2   Theories, Goals, and Behavior Patterns in Achievement Situations (Based on Dweck and Leggett, 1988)

THEORY OF INTELLIGENCE	GOAL ORIENTATION	PRESENT ABILITY	BEHAVIOR PATTERN
Entity (Intelligence is fixed)	Performance (Goal is to gain positive judgments/avoid negative judgments of competence)	High	Mastery oriented (Seek challenge; high persistence)
		Low	Helpless (Avoid challenge; low persistence)
Incremental (Intelligence is malleable)	Learning (Goal is to to increase competence)	High or Low	Mastery oriented (Seek challenge that fosters learning; high persistence)

ability but that this condition is remediable, you may be willing to work hard to improve your ability.

Origins of Explanatory Styles

Why do people differ in explanatory styles? The studies reviewed here suggest that beliefs about the reasons for our actions influence the way in which we respond to events. Where do these beliefs come from? Perhaps we develop attributions from the feedback we receive from significant others in our lives. If children are told by parents and teachers that they are stupid, they may come to believe that this is true and that there is little or nothing that they can do in response to their failures. If children are told that their failures are attributable to lack of effort or if they are provided with procedures that enable them to develop a sense of their ability to solve problems, they may come to develop a sense of mastery. While this is certainly a plausible view of the origins of attributions, it may be oversimplified.

Schulman, Keith, and Seligman (1991, as cited in Peterson, Maier, & Seligman, 1993) found that scores on an attribution questionnaire were heritable. They obtained heritability estimates for these scores that were comparable to those of other personality dimensions. There was also little evidence of shared family influence, suggesting that child-rearing practices are not a strong influence on attributional styles. It is unlikely that children reared in the same family who probably attend the same schools would systematically encounter different kinds of feedback from teachers for their performance on intellectual tasks.

If these speculations are correct, then why do people develop different attributions? Perhaps their attributions are partially correct. Perhaps their beliefs about their abilities and the reasons for their performance are based on accurate assessments of their experiences. While some of these beliefs may be overgeneralized and may lead people to respond in less than adequate ways to the challenges in their life, others may provide accurate guidelines for performance. We know that people differ in intellectual ability, partly for genetic reasons, and these differences do influence intellectual performance in a wide variety of situations. From this perspective, attributions should not be thought of as semiautonomous concepts that independently influence behavior in ways unrelated to a person's enduring characteristics. Consider two extreme positions. (1) Attributions are nothing more than the accurate generalizations we draw from our life experiences. (2) Attributions are unrelated to our characteristics and behaviors—they are simply a set of autonomous beliefs that we come to develop that determine how we behave. If this were true, all we would need to do to change people's behavior is to get them to develop new ideas about the reasons for their actions.

Probably both of these extreme views are wrong. For most of us, attributions are related to our life experiences and have some basis in a realistic appraisal of our actions. Yet our beliefs are not always accurate and may contain false and counterproductive generalizations. Think of a task that is difficult for you. Perhaps you are not a naturally talented athlete. You might correctly assume that you do not have the coordination required to be a good tennis player. While your belief may be grounded in reality, it might also be overgeneralized. Perhaps you could be a better tennis player if you practiced and tried hard to succeed. Maybe you falsely generalized initial failures and have assumed that improvement is impossible. Perhaps you need to develop attributions that are simultaneously accurate and nondestructive. You may want to think about your attributions for an important event in your life. Try to answer these questions: Is your attribution accurate? Where did it come from? Are you generalizing appropriately or inappropriately from past experiences? If your attributions for failure are helpless and pessimistic, do you think that this approach will contribute to an inability to cope with related negative events? Do you think you could change your attributions? If you were to change them, do you think your ability to respond in a mastery-oriented way would be enhanced?

Attributions about Others

We have considered the attributions that individuals develop for the experiences they encounter. We also have attributions about the behaviors of others.

If we are in an intimate relationship with another person, the attributions that we have about the actions of the other person may influence the relationship. Consider a negative event that might occur in a hypothetical relationship. Perhaps Janet is criticized by Joe for being late for a social engagement. Janet might attribute the criticism to a characteristic of Joe (Joe is hypercritical) or to a personal characteristic of her own (I am always late—Joe's criticism was caused by my behavior). The attribution might be global or local: Janet might believe that Joe always criticizes her, or she might believe that she is invariably guilty of failing to fulfill her social obligations, that being late is only one symptom of a pervasive behavioral tendency. Such attributions are global; the behavior is seen as part of a more general dispositional characteristic. Alternatively, Janet might assume that she is generally conscientious in fulfilling her social obligations and her tendency to be late is not part of a broader pattern; or, if she believes that the criticism was due not to her behavior but to Joe's attitude, she might believe that Joe is not generally critical of her and that this was a local event. Janet might similarly believe that the attribution was stable or labile: If Janet thinks she is always late or that Joe is always critical of her lateness, this would be a stable characteristic. If she thinks that she is rarely late and therefore rarely provides a reason for Joe to criticize her, or if she believes that Joe is unlikely to persist in his criticism, then she is attributing the criticism to causes that are unlikely to recur or to endure in the relationship.

What kinds of attributions are likely to contribute to dissatisfaction in a relationship? If you believe that the negative things that occur are your partner's fault and are part of a general disposition related to other difficulties and that this is a stable pattern of behavior, then you might well be unhappy in your relationship. If Janet thinks that Joe is hypercritical and is always complaining about her behavior and that he is unlikely to change this tendency, she is unlikely to find her relationship with Joe satisfactory.

Fincham and Bradbury (1993) studied the attributions of married couples in a longitudinal study. They measured their attributions for hypothetical negative events that occur frequently in relationships, such as "My spouse does not pay attention to what I am saying." They obtained an attribution score for each husband and wife pair indicating the extent to which negative events were attributed to stable and global characteristics of the partner. In addition, they obtained a measure of marital satisfaction both at the time of filling out the questionnaire and one year later. They found that an attributional style that attributed negative events in a relationship to stable and global characteristics of one's spouse was negatively related to marital satisfaction. Husbands' composite attributional style score correlated with their initial satisfaction −.39 and correlated with their marital satisfaction one year later −.37. The comparable correlations for wives were −.51 and −.38. These data indicate that attributional styles are predictive of current and future marital satisfaction. People are not satisfied with their marriage when they attribute the negative things in it to the enduring and global characteristics of their spouses.

Do these results imply that people could become more satisfied with their marriages if they learned to attribute the negative events to their own actions and to characteristics that were specific and labile? Perhaps, perhaps not. It is possible that some attributions are accurate. Perhaps one's spouse really does cause a lot of negative things to happen because of enduring and broad dispositional tendencies that are difficult to change. Do we become happy in our marriage if we falsely attribute negative things to our own actions or if we falsely believe that each negative event is unlikely to recur or to be understood as part of a more general pattern? It is difficult to know whether our attributions are accurate or false. Some negative attributional styles are in fact grounded in reality.

SELF-EFFICACY

Think about a challenge you have faced in your life. Perhaps you wanted to lose weight or to quit smoking or drinking. Or you may have wanted to achieve some positive goal, such as to get an A in a course. You probably had some beliefs about your ability to attain these goals. People may develop two sorts of beliefs about their ability to attain their goals (Maddux, 1991). **Outcome expectancies** are beliefs about the likelihood that a certain behavior will lead to a certain goal. For example, I may believe that if I reduce my caloric intake to 1,500 calories per day, I will lose weight. **Self-efficacy** expectancies are beliefs about one's ability to perform the actions that will lead to the expected outcomes. For example, I may believe that restricting my food intake to 1,500 calories per day will lead to loss of weight, but I may also believe that I am not capable of restricting myself to this level of caloric intake. In such a case, I would have low self-efficacy.

In chapter 8 we saw that according to expectancy-value theory our actions are determined jointly by beliefs about the likelihood that a behavior will produce a certain outcome and the value we place on that outcome. Self-efficacy theory argues that in order for a person to undertake actions that will lead to the desired goal, it may be necessary to believe both that the actions will produce the desired outcome and that the individual is capable of performing the necessary actions. If self-efficacy is low, people may not attempt to perform the actions. For example, I may not try to restrict my food intake if I believe that it is exceedingly unlikely that I can stick to the 1,500 calorie diet.

The concept of self-efficacy was introduced by Bandura in 1977 to explain the results of studies of the effects on behavior of observing others performing various actions. Bandura attempted to demonstrate that individuals who are exposed to models either on film or in real life are able to perform the acts performed by the models. We can learn by imitation. For example, if a child who is afraid of dogs is shown a model who is able to pet a frightening dog, the child may exhibit less fear in subsequent encounters with dogs.

Bandura noted that the tendency of an observer to emulate the actions of a model seemed to vary with the model's characteristics. Children were more likely to emulate child models than adult models. Why? Bandura (1977) reasoned that the tendency to emulate was influenced by the beliefs developed by the observer. A child observing an adult's behavior might reason that adults are capable of doing many things that children cannot do and thus the child may not develop a belief in her ability to perform the actions. If a child who is mildly dog phobic observes a child acting in a fearless manner, she might come to believe that she too is capable of performing the same actions. Indeed, if the model is observed to be initially fearful and to overcome her fear, that might lead the child to believe that she too might overcome her fears and behave in a similar manner.

This analysis of Bandura emphasizes the role of self-efficacy. At the heart of the theory is the assumption that self-efficacy beliefs control behavior. People are likely to undertake actions toward desired goals that they believe they are capable of performing; they are not likely to undertake such actions if they believe they are not capable of performing them. Change self-efficacy beliefs and you change behavior.

Do self-efficacy beliefs control actions? Let's consider some evidence. Bandura, Adams, and Beyer (1977) designed a study to test the effects of different techniques to reduce snake phobias. They assigned subjects who were snake phobic to one of three groups: a no-treatment control group, a group that was asked to perform various behaviors with snakes (a participant group), and a group that was exposed to models who performed various actions with snakes. When assessing changes in the subjects' self-efficacy beliefs about their ability to perform these actions as a result of treatment, they found that those assigned to the participant group had the largest changes in self-efficacy, followed by the subjects assigned to view the behavior of models; subjects in the no-treatment control group had the lowest self-efficacy scores.

Then, to test the relationship between self-efficacy changes and behavior changes, they asked their subjects to perform a number of actions with a snake. Again, they found that those from the participant group were able to perform more actions with the snake than were those in the modeling group, and those in the control group were least capable of performing these actions. Not only did the groups who differed in self-efficacy beliefs differ in behavior, but also within each group there was a strong relationship between self-efficacy beliefs and behavior. Those subjects who developed the strongest efficacy beliefs also were able to perform many of the behaviors with the snakes. These results demonstrate that efficacy beliefs are predictive of behavior. Subjects are likely to perform actions that they believe that they are capable of performing.

Bandura and his colleagues included another test in which they presented the same subjects with a new snake that had a different appearance than the original snake, and they attempted to predict the subjects' behavior in this situation. They had two sources of data that they could use for predictive purposes: measures of the subjects' actual behavior with the first snake, and measures of efficacy beliefs indicating whether or not a subject believed she was capable of performing actions with a new snake. Which of these two sources of data would provide more accurate predictions of subjects' behavior? They found that they could predict the behavior of the subjects in the new task more accurately from their efficacy *beliefs* than from their *behavior*. Fifty-two percent of the subjects who were able to perform all of the required actions with the original snake were not able to do so with the new snake. Only 24% of those who expressed the highest efficacy beliefs were unable to perform all of the actions. In this instance, the subjects' beliefs about their capabilities were more predictive of their behavior in a new situation than the actual behavior they had exhibited in a similar situation.

Efficacy beliefs have been related to many different kinds of behaviors. Candiotte and Lichtenstein (1981) evaluated the effectiveness of different treatments designed to help people stop smoking and found that efficacy beliefs correlated .57 with a measure of relapse. Those who believed they were likely to stop smoking after treatment were more likely to do so.

Cozzarelli (1993) studied efficacy beliefs about the ability to cope with the stress of an abortion. She asked women who were about to undergo an abortion to fill out a questionnaire indicating their efficacy beliefs about ability to perform such acts as thinking about children or babies comfortably, continuing to have good sexual relations, and watching television shows or reading stories about abortion. She related the efficacy scores to a composite measure based on both mood and depression taken thirty minutes after the abortion and three weeks later. She obtained correlations of $-.77$ and $-.67$, respectively. Women who had strong efficacy beliefs about their ability to perform specific acts that were related to coping with abortion were less likely to experience depression and negative mood states after the abortion.

Cozzarelli also obtained measures of self-esteem, optimism, locus of control (a measure of generalized beliefs in one's ability to control the things that happen in one's life), and depression prior to the abortion. These were correlated with the efficacy and post-abortion adjustment measures. Figure 11.1 presents a summary of a "path" model that summarizes these relationships. Reading the path coefficients from left to right provides a model of the way in which these measures are related

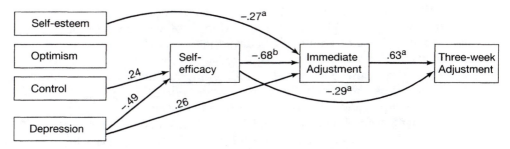

FIGURE 11.1 Personality variables and initial depression as joint predictors of three-week psychological adjustment. (Higher scores indicate high self-esteem, optimism, perceived control, self-efficacy, and *poorer* psychological adjustment; [a]$p < .05$, [b]$p < .01$.) (Based on Cozzarelli, 1993). Reproduced with permission of the American Psychological Association.

to post-abortion adjustment. Self-efficacy is related to the pre-abortion depression measure and is weakly related to the measure of control. The self-efficacy measure has a strong relationship to adjustment following abortion (the path coefficient—a measure analogous to a correlation that represents the independent influence of one variable on another—is $-.68$). Immediate post-abortion adjustment influences adjustment to abortion three weeks later. Self-efficacy, in addition to being the strongest influence on immediate post-abortion adjustment, has an independent influence on the measure of adjustment obtained three weeks later (the path coefficient is $-.29$). The self-efficacy measure is the only pre-abortion measure that has an independent influence on adjustment to abortion three weeks after the abortion. These analyses indicate that post-abortion adjustment is related to a woman's efficacy beliefs about the ability to perform specific acts indicative of adjustment to abortion. Efficacy beliefs appear to be a better predictor than more general personality measures of depression, self-esteem, locus of control, and optimism.

Changing Efficacy Beliefs

Efficacy beliefs appear to be strongly related to behavior. Individuals have a good deal of knowledge about how they will respond to specific challenges in their life, and their beliefs about their abilities to perform various actions seem to influence their behavior. How could we use this research to influence behavior? Could we change a person's behavior merely by changing efficacy beliefs? Assume that you want to stop smoking. You might say that you don't think you would be successful; you have tried to stop before and have been unsuccessful. You might have specific efficacy beliefs: perhaps you believe that you will not be able to resist smoking after a leisurely dinner accompanied by two or more glasses of wine. According to the research that we have reviewed, these beliefs are likely to be accurate. Now suppose we tried to brainwash you. Perhaps we could hypnotize you and tell you that you will be able to stop smoking and that you will not want to have a cigarette after a leisurely dinner that included wine. Would this procedure stop you from smoking? Why might it not? For one thing, you would not be likely to change your behavior if you did not really believe that you could do so. It might not be easy to change efficacy beliefs. It's easy to tell someone that she can do something, but if she doesn't believe what she is told, telling her might have little influence. How could we get someone to truly change her beliefs?

Bandura and Schunk (1981) suggested that one way to change efficacy beliefs is to provide tangible evidence that the individual could accomplish a goal. This may be accomplished by allowing a person to achieve success at tasks that lead to a goal. If you want to lose weight, you can set a goal of thirty pounds, or you can divide the task into more manageable units such as one pound per week. If you are able to attain the subgoal or **proximal goal,** then you may produce a true increase in self-efficacy.

Bandura and Schunk studied elementary school children who had difficulty with subtraction. These children participated in a special instructional program designed to help them learn to do subtraction problems. The children were randomly assigned to groups that differed in the goals assigned to them: one group was assigned a proximal goal (to complete six pages of instructional materials every day), a second

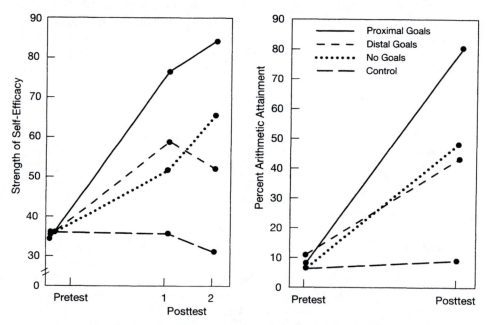

FIGURE 11.2 The left panel shows the strength of children's self-percepts of arithmetic efficacy at the beginning of the study (pretest), and before (Post$_1$) and after (Post$_2$) they took the subtraction posttest. The right panel displays the children's level of achievement on the subtraction tests before and after the self-directed learning. (Based on Bandura and Schunk, 1981) Reproduced with permission of the American Psychological Association.

group was assigned a **distal goal** (to complete all 42 pages of materials), and a third group was not provided with a specific goal. Figure 11.2 presents the changes in efficacy beliefs for children assigned to each of the three experimental groups and for children in a control group who were not participating in the instructional program. Children in the proximal-goal group developed stronger efficacy beliefs about their ability to perform subtraction problems than did children in the other three groups. Did these efficacy beliefs influence behavior? Figure 11.2 presents the relevant data. The children assigned proximal goals exhibited the best performance on math tests.

The Bandura and Schunk study demonstrates that efficacy beliefs that are changed as a result of tangible evidence that a person can accomplish a goal are accurate predictors of behavior. What would happen if efficacy beliefs were changed without such tangible evidence? Suppose a person convinces you that you can accomplish a goal although the change in your efficacy beliefs is not based on your observations of your behavior? Biran and Wilson (1981) used two different methods to reduce phobias—a behavioral method and a "cognitive restructuring" method. The behavioral method required subjects to perform a series of actions that were guided by the psychologist. The cognitive restructuring procedure was designed to eliminate irrational beliefs that were contributing to the phobia. Those assigned to a cognitive restructuring experience changed their efficacy beliefs although they had no opportunity to observe their own behavior in response to the phobic stimuli. Subjects in the guided exposure conditions actually observed their behaviors. Efficacy beliefs were more predictive of the behavior of subjects in the guided exposure conditions than in the cognitive restructuring conditions. In the former, the relationship between efficacy beliefs and actual behaviors was 96% congruent when exposed to the original phobic stimuli and 92% congruent when exposed to a novel stimulus. The comparable congruence numbers for the cognitive restructuring situations were 71% and 64%, respectively. These data indicate that efficacy beliefs are not likely to be completely accurate predictors of a person's behavior where these beliefs are not derived from the actual observation of one's own behavior. Why?

We will try to answer this question. If efficacy beliefs control behavior, then it should not matter whether or not the beliefs are derived from the observations of one's own behavior. The finding that efficacy beliefs deriving from such observation are in fact more predictive of what a person will do suggests that efficacy beliefs are not always predictive. Perhaps they become predictive because past behavior is a guide to future behavior. If we have an opportunity to observe our behavior in a situation, then we have an accurate basis for predicting our future behavior in a similar situation.

Bandura would argue that this cannot be quite right. Why? Recall that the results of the Bandura, Beyers, and Adams study suggested that efficacy beliefs were more accurate predictors of how a snake-phobic person would respond to a new snake than were previous behaviors with a different snake. If this is correct, then efficacy beliefs must reflect something more than the observation of previous behavior. Perhaps not. In the Bandura, Beyers, and Adams study each behavior is classified in one of two ways: the subject performed an act, or the subject did not perform an act. If one of the acts was to pick up a snake and hold it, then according to the psychologist's recording procedure, the subject either is able to do it or is not able to. But the subject may have a good deal more knowledge than that about his behavior. Perhaps he knows that although he was able to accomplish this act, it was very difficult to do. Perhaps he has information that he experienced tremors and felt great fear, information that might lead him to reason that although he was able to do this once he would not want to do it again nor would he be successful if he tried to do it again. Another subject might accomplish the same act but learn that it was relatively easy and that he was not anxious when he did it, and so he thinks he would be able to do it again. Note that these two subjects have different efficacy beliefs that are based in part on differences in their responses to the same situation. The psychologist, however, who is using a relatively crude system of classifying behavior, would classify them as having responded in the same way. If the subject's knowledge of prior behavior influences efficacy beliefs, then efficacy beliefs may be predictive of behavior because they are based on past behavior—not because they exert an independent influence on behavior. We do what we believe we can do (and we don't do what we believe we cannot do) when what we believe we can do is based on our observations of what we have done before.

SELF-CONSCIOUSNESS

Do you think about yourself a lot? Do you pay attention to your inner feelings? Do you try to figure yourself out? People who are asked these kinds of questions answer them in different ways. Those who respond "yes" are said to be high in **private self-consciousness** (Fenigstein, Scheier, & Buss, 1975). They are assumed to focus their attention on their inner feelings and thoughts.

Individuals may also be induced by an experimental procedure to pay more attention to their feelings and thoughts. Carver and Scheier (1981) assumed that people who were placed so that they could observe their behavior in a mirror would be more likely to focus their attention on their personal thoughts and feelings. In a series of experiments they randomly assigned individuals to groups that performed a task either in the absence of a mirror or with a mirror placed in an unobtrusive location in the room. Although the subjects were able to see their reflection, no special instructions were provided in regard to the mirror.

Scheier and Carver (1977) asked subjects to rate their mood in response to positive and negative statements with a mirror either present or not present. Table 11.3

TABLE 11.3   Mean Mood Ratings in the Presence or Absence of a Mirror (Based on Scheier and Carver, 1977)

STIMULUS	NO MIRROR	MIRROR	Row Means
Positive statements	8.1	8.9	8.5
Negative statements	6.0	4.4	5.2
Column Means	7.0	6.6	6.8

Note: The higher the number, the more positive the mood.
Reproduced with permission of the American Psychological Association.

presents the results. When a mirror was present, subjects rated their moods more positively when presented with positive statements and more negatively when presented with negative statements. These results imply that focusing on one's inner states intensifies one's affective experience to external stimuli.

In another experiment they found that the effects of the mirror were paralleled by the effects of individual differences in self-consciousness. They had male subjects view a series of slides designed to elicit positive and negative emotions. They assumed that males would like to look at pictures of female nudes and that such slides would elicit positive emotions (do you agree with this assumption?). They also presented slides that were assumed to elicit negative emotions such as disgust (for example, pictures of dead bodies). The subjects were asked to assign a pleasantness rating to the slides. Table 11.4 presents the results. Subjects who were high in self-consciousness tended to view positive slides as more pleasant and negative slides as less pleasant than subjects who were low in self-consciousness. These results imply that individuals who tend to focus their attention on their inner states are likely to have more intense emotional experiences when presented with emotional stimuli.

Does self-focused attention influence behavior? Scheier (1976) studied the influence of an anger induction on the behavior of individuals who differed in self-consciousness and in whether they were exposed to a mirror. An agent of the experimenter who pretended to be another subject attempted to anger a fellow subject by criticizing the problem-solving skills of the subject, who had been asked to solve difficult problems. After being exposed to this anger-inducing experience, the subjects were asked to act as a "teacher" and to deliver an electric shock to a "learner" every time the learner made an incorrect response. The learner was the confederate of the experimenter who had attempted to anger the subject in the first phase of the experiment. The subject was told that the level of shock delivered to the learner could be controlled by choosing from an array of buttons. No shock was actually delivered. Scheier noted the level of shock chosen by subjects in different experimental groups.

Scheier assumed that subjects who were angered by the learner would express their anger by choosing higher levels of shock than subjects who were not

TABLE 11.4   Mean Pleasantness Ratings for Positive and Negative Slides for Subjects Differing in Private Self-Consciousness (Based on Scheier and Carver, 1977)

Stimulus	PRIVATE SELF-CONSCIOUSNESS		
	Low	High	Row Means
Positive slides	22.6	24.6	23.6
n	18	14	
Negative slides	12.5	10.0	11.3
n	10	15	
Column Means	17.6	17.3	17.5

Note: The higher the number, the higher the pleasantness rating.
Reproduced with permission of the American Psychological Association.

angered by the learner. The experience of anger should be more intense for subjects who are high in self-consciousness and who were performing the task in the presence of a mirror. As Table 11.5 shows, the data support all of his assumptions. Subjects who were angered delivered higher levels of shock than subjects who were not angered. Those who were angered and were high in self-consciousness delivered higher levels of shock than those who were angered and were low in self-consciousness. Subjects who were angered and who were with the mirror delivered higher levels of shock than those who were angered who performed the task in the absence of a mirror. The highest levels of shock were chosen by subjects who were angered, who were high in self-consciousness, and who performed the task in the presence of a mirror.

Carver and Scheier's studies indicate that people differ in their response to their inner states. The influence of inner states on our behavior may depend on the extent to which we attend to those states. Individuals who attend to their inner states are likely to find that those states have an enhanced influence on their behavior.

THE SELF IN THE SOCIAL CONTEXT

The Independent and Interdependent Self

When you think about yourself do you think of the ways in which you are different from others? Do you think that it is important to attend to your inner feelings and beliefs? Do you want others to understand you and to respond to you as a unique person? If you are like many (perhaps most) American college students, you probably answered these questions in the affirmative. Markus and Kitayama (1991) believe that this way of thinking about the self is a characteristic of Western cultures that emphasize what they call an *independent* conception of the self. Asian cultures emphasize what they call an *interdependent* conception of the self,

TABLE 11.5   Mean Shock Intensities Delivered by Subjects in Each Treatment Group (Based on Scheier and Carver, 1976)

	NO ANGER		ANGER	
	No Mirror	Mirror	No Mirror	Mirror
High self-conscious	2.9	2.7	4.1	4.9
	(11)	(10)	(11)	(11)
Low self-conscious	3.0	2.5	3.3	3.9
	(12)	(12)	(12)	(12)

Note: The higher the number, the higher the shock intensity. Parentheses contain the number of subjects per group. Main effect means: High self-conscious (3.6), Low self-conscious (3.2); Anger (4.1), No anger (2.8); Mirror (3.5), No mirror (3.3).
Reproduced with permission of Duke University Press.

TABLE 11.6 Summary of Key Differences Between an Independent and an Interdependent Construal of the Self (Based on Markus and Kitayama, 1991)

FEATURE COMPARED	INDEPENDENT	INTERDEPENDENT
Definition	Separate from social context	Connected with social context
Structure	Bounded, unitary, stable	Flexible, variable
Important features	Internal, private (abilities, thoughts, feelings)	External, public (statuses, roles, relationships
Tasks	Be unique	Belong, fit in
	Express self	Occupy one's proper place
	Realize internal attributes	Engage in appropriate action
	Promote own goals	Promote others' goals
	Be direct: "say what's on your mind"	Be indirect: "read others' mind"
Roles of others	Self-evaluation: others important for social comparison, reflected appraisal	Self-definition: relationships with others in specific contexts define the self
Basis of self-esteem[a]	Ability to express self, validate internal attributes	Ability to adjust, restrain self, maintain harmony with social context

[a]Esteeming the self may be primarily a Western phenomenon, and the concepts of self-esteem should perhaps be replaced by self-satisfaction, or by a term that reflects the realization that one is fulfilling the culturally mandated task.
Reproduced with permission of the American Psychological Association.

whereby the self is thought of as being interconnected with others. Table 11.6 presents their summary of the differences in independent and interdependent construals of the self.

Markus and Kitayama developed the consequences of these two different ways of construing the self. Yoshida, Kojo, and Kaku (1982, as cited in Markus and Kitayama, 1991) asked Japanese children in the second, third, and fifth grades how they would evaluate a child who described his superb athletic talent in a modest, self-restrained way versus a self-enhancing way. The children were asked to decide whether the person was a good person and whether he was a talented athlete. Figure 11.3 shows their results. There was a clear influence of grade level. The older children tended to view the person who described his abilities modestly as a good person. The fifth graders viewed the person who described his abilities in a self-enhancing way negatively. The older children, in contrast to the younger children, came to believe that the person who described his abilities in a self-enhancing way actually had inferior ability to the person who described himself in a modest way. Markus and Kitayama view these differences as an example of a socialization process in Asian countries that emphasizes the importance of modesty and self-restraint. The American child may be taught that "the squeaky wheel gets the grease." Japanese children are taught "the nail that stands out gets pounded down."

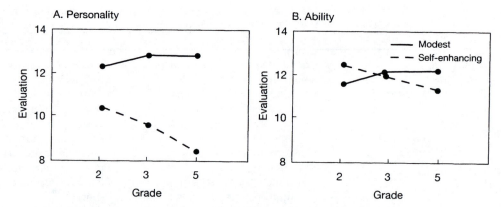

FIGURE 11.3   Mean evaluations by Japanese second, third, and fifth graders. (A: Personality of target person. B: Ability of target person. Drawn from results reported by Yoshida, Kojo, and Kaku, 1982) (Based on Markus and Kitayama, 1991)
Reproduced with permission of the American Psychological Association.

Markus and Kitayama's analysis reminds us that the way we think about ourselves may depend on the culture in which we are reared. Perhaps many of us have been told to "know ourselves." We may believe that we should look inside of ourselves to find the ways in which we are unique and then should act in such a way that we express our uniqueness. According to Markus and Kitayama, to know oneself in the context of an Asian culture may be to understand one's relationship to other individuals and to act in a way that fulfills the goals of an interdependent society.

Group Identity

We all belong to many groups. Which of the groups to which you belong is important in defining your personal identity or self-concept? Do you think of yourself in terms of gender, or race, or sexual orientation? Perhaps you define yourself in terms of some other dimension of human difference—the candidates for definition are legion. You could think of yourself as belonging to the group of exceptionally tall people or short people. Perhaps you think that your membership in a particular religious or ethnic group is important to your identity. What is the relationship between your group identity and other dimensions of your personality? Do people who have strong group identities differ in other dimensions of personality? Can you be well adjusted or have high self-esteem if you do not identity with a group to which you nominally belong? If you have or plan to have children, do you think their psychological well-being depends on the degree to which you can encourage them to be firmly identified with a particular group?

All the preceding questions are addressed to you; they are not questions that we as psychologists are able to answer. We can, however, tell you something about research on the self-concept of African Americans that is at least tangentially relevant to these questions. The research originated in the 1930s. Clark and Clark (1939a; 1939b; 1947) asked a group of African-American 6- and 7-year-old children a series of questions about black and white dolls. Some of the questions were designed to elicit information about the child's racial identification, such as "Give me the doll that looks like you; Give me the doll that looks like a Negro child." Other questions were designed to elicit questions about preferences among the dolls, such as "Give me the doll that is a nice doll; Give me the doll that looks bad." The Clarks reported that some of the children preferred white dolls although they were able to identify their own racial status. Clark and Clark (1950) interpreted their data as providing support for the concept of self-hatred. They assumed that the African-American children who preferred white dolls had a negative self-concept, that they accepted the negative views of their own characteristics held by many white Americans.

The doll-play research is historically important. It was even cited in the Supreme Court's landmark decision, *Brown v. Board of Education of Topeka*, the ruling that segregated public schools were unconstitutional. The Court argued that segregation contributed to a negative self-concept for African-American children and was psychologically harmful to them. Despite its enormous historical importance, however, the doll-play studies have been subject to a number of empirical and conceptual critiques (see Banks, 1976; Cross, 1991). The data from the early studies were somewhat ambiguous: by age 7 the majority of the African-American children preferred black dolls. Banks reviewed many of the doll-play studies done prior to 1976 and found that, although there was some evidence for consistent rejection of black dolls by white children, there was very little evidence of consistent preference for white dolls among African-American children. Banks argued that these data provided more support for prejudice among white children than they did for the presence of self-hatred among black children.

The inferences drawn from the doll-play studies are dependent upon a number of implicit assumptions. Two of these appear to be critical: (1) African-American children who exhibit occasional or even consistent preferences for white dolls (or, more generally, white cultural products) have a negative view about African-American people and culture. (2) African-American children who prefer white dolls (and cultural artifacts) have a negative self-concept. These assumptions, combined with the interpretations provided to the somewhat ambiguous findings of the early doll-play studies, led many social scientists to assume that African Americans had lower self-esteem than white Americans.

Rosenberg and Simmons (1971) were among the first social scientists to challenge this conclusion. They administered a self-esteem test to a large sample of white and African-American children attending public schools in Baltimore. They found that the black children had marginally higher self-esteem than the white children. Their findings were confirmed in a number of other studies using direct measures of self-esteem, including data obtained from a large sample designed to be representative of the population of U.S. tenth graders (Bachman, 1970; see also Cross, 1991; and Porter & Washington, 1979).

The apparent contradiction in the conclusions drawn from direct measurement of self-esteem and from the doll-play studies may be attributable to several factors. The doll-play studies used younger children, many of whom may not have had a stable sense of self; there are methodological differences between a direct measure based on self-report data and the quasi indirect or projective procedure in which doll preferences are used to infer self-esteem; the direct measurement studies were conducted after the development of black consciousness movements and subsequent enhancement in the self-esteem of African Americans—perhaps the notion that black is beautiful leads African Americans to have a positive self-concept. Although all of these methodological concerns may have contributed to the different interpretations derived from the doll-play studies and the direct measurement of self-esteem studies, perhaps the most important consideration may derive from the assumption that there is a positive correlation between group identity and self-esteem. Cross (1991) reviewed studies of the relationship between what he calls "group" and "personal identity" among African Americans. He asserted that "the mental health characteristics of Blacks, including any propensity toward self-hatred are not, and have never been, easily predicted by measures of racial identity" (Cross, 1991, p.117).

If African-American children occasionally express preferences for white cultural objects, does this preference imply that they have rejected their African-American identity? The answer could be yes if one assumes that there is a unidimensional continuum with preferences for white or for African-American culture, artifacts, and persons at each extreme. Such an assumption, however, may not fit the reality of attitudes among African Americans. It may be more correct to assume that members of minority groups have independent attitudes toward their status as a member of a minority group and as a participant in a culture that is not defined by that membership. Writing at the turn of the century, W. E. B. DuBois, in his book *Souls of Black Folk,* wrote as follows about his sense of double consciousness as a black person and as an American:

> . . . the Negro is a sort of seventh son, born with a veil, and gifted in second sight in this American world—a world which yields him no true self-consciousness, but only lets him see himself through the revelations of the other world. It is a peculiar sensation this double consciousness, this sense of always seeing oneself through the eyes of others, of viewing one's soul by the tape of a world that looks on in amused contempt and pity. One ever feels his twoness—an American, a Negro: two souls, two thoughts, two unreconciled strivings; two warring ideals in one dark body, whose dogged strength alone keeps it from being torn asunder. (DuBois, 1903).

Phinney (1990), some 85 years later, reviewed research on the identity concepts of members of minority groups. She argued that minority group identification could not be construed in terms of a unidimensional continuum but required an analysis based on two independent continua—one representing attitudes toward the majority and one representing attitudes toward the minority. A person who is strongly identified with both majority and minority culture might be described as *integrated* or *bicultural*. A person who identified with the majority culture and rejected the culture of the minority group to which he belonged could be described as *assimilated*. Someone who identified with his or her minority group and rejected majority cultural identification could be described as *separated*. Theoretically, someone could reject both minority and majority status; such a person might be described as *unintegrated* or *unformed* with respect to this issue. From this perspective, an attraction for aspects of white culture does not imply a rejection of African-American culture among African Americans. Preference for white dolls may not have implied a tendency to reject African-American cultural identity among children.

Let's summarize this analysis of research on racial identity among African Americans. The early evidence for the widespread presence of self-hatred and negative self-esteem among African Americans did not have a strong empirical foundation. The interpretations of the research were based on several assumptions that are problematic. Preference for white culture does not imply rejection of black culture. Attitudes toward one's status as a member of minority group are probably not related to self-esteem. Apparently people who endorse and people who reject the culture of a group to which they nominally belong may have high (or low) self-esteem.

Sex and Gender

Almost all people are assigned to one of two mutually exclusive groupings at birth: we are designated as males or females (there are some individuals, *hermaphrodites*, born with ambiguous sexual characteristics and so the assignment to one of these two categories is ambiguous). How do men and women differ on psychological characteristics? Are our beliefs about how men and women differ accurate? We may have stereotypes in mind that lead us to attribute characteristics to males and females that they do not actually possess.

We cannot discover if a belief about the world is accurate without knowing what is true of the world. Meta-analyses are used to obtain measures of the magnitude of gender differences in psychological characteristics (see chapter 2). Differences between the means of males and females are expressed in terms of differences in standard deviations, differences called **effect sizes**. Thus if females have scores on a measure that are one standard deviation higher than the scores of males, the effect size for this variable would be 1.00. When effect sizes are small, the distributions of male and female scores are likely to overlap more than when effect sizes are large.

Swim (1994) asked college students to estimate the magnitude of mean gender differences on several psychological characteristics, then she compared these estimates to the actual magnitude of these differences that were obtained in meta-analyses. Her results support two generalizations. First, estimates of the magnitude of gender differences are generally accurate. The perceived magnitude of differences correlated .78 with the obtained magnitude of these differences. Second, perceived differences were more likely to be underestimates of the actual magnitude than overestimates, although for the most part the differences in estimated and obtained differences were relatively small. Table 11.7 presents Swim's results. Swim's results are limited in at least two ways. First, college students may be reluctant to assign gender differences to people, and their beliefs may not be representative of the beliefs held by others in our society. Second, Swim did not examine some characteristics where gender difference is relatively large. These include, not surprisingly, characteristics related to physical strength and abilities; the effect size for the speed at which a person can throw a ball is 2.18, indicating that on this characteristic there is relatively little overlap between males and females (Thomas & French, 1985). There are other characteristics, related to sexual behavior, where there are relatively large gender differences. For example (as was discussed in chapter 7), males are far more likely to assert that they wish to have

TABLE 11.7   Meta-Analysis Results versus Perceived Effect Sizes (Based on Swim, 1994)

CHARACTERISTIC	META-ANALYTIC EFFECT SIZE	PERCEIVED EFFECT SIZE	ACCURACY
Restless	.72	.32	A
Emerge as leader	.49	1.04	O
Math tests	.41	.29	A
Math SAT	.42	.47	A
Help in a group	.42	.03	U
Help when alone	.20	.07	A
Aggression	.29	1.03	O
Verbal SAT	.11	−.16	O
Verbal tests	−.06	−.63	O
Happy	−.07	−.23	A
Influence by persuasive messages	−.16	−.31	A
Influence by group pressure	−.32	−.48	A
Involved in conversations	−.32	−.83	O
Decode nonverbal cues	−.43	−.98	O
Gazing during conversations	−.68	−.70	A

Note: Regardless of the original meta-analysts' presentation of their findings, a positive effect size presented here represents a higher mean for men. A = meta-analytic and perceived *d* are not significantly different. O = meta-analytic and perceived *d* are significantly different and perceived *d* is in the stereotyped direction. U = meta-analytic and perceived *d* are significantly different and perceived *d* is in a nonstereotyped direction.
Reproduced with permission of the American Psychological Association.

many sexual partners than are females (effect size = .80.) Some gender differences are of intermediate size, large enough to assert that males are generally higher (or lower) on some characteristic but not large enough to produce distributions without considerable overlap. For example, males are generally higher on tests of spatial ability. Here the magnitude of the difference depends on the kind of spatial task being examined. On the ability to rotate a visual image rapidly the effect size is as high as .94 (Linn & Peterson, 1986) while on some other spatial tasks the differences tend to be lower. Most estimates of gender differences in general spatial ability are close to .5, indicating that the mean scores for women and men differ by about a half a standard deviation (see Hoyenga & Hoyenga, 1993). Women tend to score higher on tasks requiring them to judge nonverbal behaviors. Eagly (1987) estimates effect sizes for ability to decode the meaning on nonverbal behaviors as .43; on average, women are better at this task than men by slightly less than one half a standard deviation.

Gender differences in many psychological characteristics vary in subtle ways dependent upon how the characteristic is defined and measured. It is possible to assert that men are, on average, more aggressive than women, but this sort of global generalization may not do justice to the details of the gender differences. For example, Eagly and Steffen (1986), in their meta-analyses, found larger differences for measures of physical aggression (effect size = .40) than for measures of psychological aggression (effect size = .13.).

Summaries of mean differences in meta-analyses on quantitatively varying characteristics may not highlight some gender differences that are in fact large and socially significant. In a recent comprehensive survey of gender differences, Hoyenga and Hoyenga (1993) indicate that in the literature the largest difference is in arrest rates for committing violent crimes. Figure 11.4 presents differences in arrest rates for violent crimes as a function of age and gender. Arrest rates for violent crimes by men peak at a rate in excess of one percent of the male population in young adulthood, more than ten times the peak rate of female arrests for violent crime. Similar gender differences in violent crime (and crime in general) are found in all cultures in which these differences have been studied.

This brief discussion of the nature of sex differences indicates that these differences may best be understood if we are precise about how men and women tend to differ in their characteristic behaviors. Global descriptions of general differences—for example, men are more aggressive than women—may fail to capture some of the ways in which these differences are expressed.

Effect sizes may fail to do justice to other aspects of gender differences. Score distributions may differ in several ways. For example, they may differ in means and in variability. If two distributions have the same mean but differ in variability, the more variable distribution will have more low and more high scores. Hedges and Newell (1995), analyzing data from several large-scale surveys on gender differences in the distribution of intelligence, found that mean gender differences were small and inconsistent. When they examined the variability of scores on intelligence test, they found that men tended to be more variable in their scores than

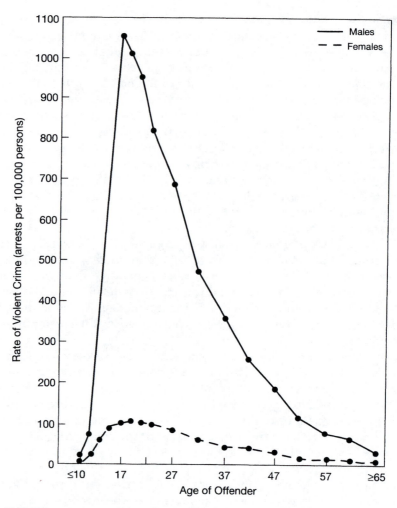

FIGURE 11.4   Arrest rates for violent crime in the United States as a function of age and gender. (Based on Hoyenga and Hoyenga, 1993)

women and therefore were more likely to have scores that were either very high or very low.

These differences can become socially significant. They explain some of the sex differences found in a program developed by psychologists at Johns Hopkins to foster unusual mathematical talent in adolescence. They gave the SAT test of quantitative abilities designed for high school seniors to selected seventh graders. They were able to find seventh graders who scored 700 or above on this test, a score that would be unusually high for a high school senior. The ratio of males to females meeting this criterion was 12 to 1. These results were obtained among students who did not differ in mean performance on tests of mathematical ability and did not differ in their formal study of math in the public schools.

Can you think of an explanation for this phenomenon? Do you think the best explanation is likely to be found by studying biological differences or differences in cultural expectations for men and women? Any explanation must explain both the absence of sex differences in means and the differences in variability. We do not know of any such explanation. Consider the kinds of problems that any attempts to explain this might encounter. Suppose one were to argue that men are encouraged to develop unusual intellectual abilities and women are encouraged to be moderately but not extremely intelligent. Such an explanation might help explain why there are more men with very high scores, but it would also imply that men should have higher mean intelligence scores. And this explanation will not help us to understand why men have more very low scores. Perhaps we need to use different explanations for more men being at the low end than we need to use to explain the excess number of high scores. Our guess (and it is only a guess) is that society may permit and even occasionally encourage a kind of monomaniacal pursuit of intellectual interests in men while encouraging women to develop more well-rounded social skills. But we are not very satisfied with this explanation.

We have considered gender differences in means and in variability. There is a third kind of difference that may also be informative. Men and women may have the same scores or even the same distribution of scores on a particular measure but the correlations between the scores and other measures may be different for men and women. The meaning of a score, or, more technically, the construct validity of a measure, depends upon its relationship to other measures. If the same measure has a different pattern of relationships with other measures for men and women, then the measure may be assumed to be measuring different things for men and women. Differences in the meaning of depressive illness in men and women provide an example of this phenomenon. Hoyenga and Hoyenga (1993) summarized studies comparing differences in the structure of relationships surrounding depression. Table 11.8 presents their summary of some of the differences in depression between men and women. An examination of these data clearly indicates that men and women respond in different ways to depression. The differences are complex and not subject to a single overarching explanatory scheme. They may relate to differences in social roles and possibly to biological differences. In any case, it is clear that depression has a somewhat different meaning in men and women.

Masculinity and Femininity

Virtually everyone thinks of himself or herself as either male or female. And, as we have seen, men and women do differ, often in subtle ways, on several psychological characteristics. Saying this tells us relatively little about the ways in which people think about themselves. A person could say, "I am male and that fact

TABLE 11.8   Sex Differences in the Structure of Depressive Syndrome in Females and Males (Based on Hoyenga and Hoyenga, 1993)

The sexes differ not only in overall frequency but also in symptom patterns displayed within the various depressive syndromes.

1. Clinically depressed females more often report excessive eating and weight gain as a symptom (loss of appetite and weight loss is the most common eating symptom in both sexes).
2. In nonselected populations, females are more likely to report that they eat when they become depressed; women also are more likely to report crying, becoming irritable, and confronting their feelings; males are more likely to report becoming aggressive and engaging in sexual activity.
3. Factor structure of depression scales is different for males and females, both in nonselected populations and among depressed subjects.
4. Working females are more likely to go to health services and males simply to miss work when depressed.
5. The personality factors that differentiate depressed males from depressed females are the same as those that differentiate nondepressed males from nondepressed females.
6. Psychomotor agitation (nervous activity) seems to be more common in female depressives; retardation (inactivity) may be relatively more common in males.
7. Among depressed college students (rating scale measure), males are more socially withdrawn, express more motivational and cognitive problems, use drugs, and have somatic symptoms (e.g., aches and pains); women have greater lack of confidence, lack of concern over what happens to them, more self-blame, more crying spells and irritability, and are more hurt by criticism.
8. Depression is associated with decreased instrumentality (as measured by sex role scales), but this may be an effect rather than a precursor of depression.
9. When under stress, college student females report feeling more depressed and anxious than males do, and females say they are more likely to express their feelings; males become more active in response to stress; stress from school or from intimate relationships depressed personal self-esteem only in females.
10. Age of onset of bipolar and unipolar syndromes is the same for both sexes, although female/male ratio for bipolar onset may be greatest from ages 30 to 75.
11. Incidence of depression before puberty is the same in both sexes; female incidence of depressive episodes increases at puberty.
12. Males are more likely to commit suicide; females are more likely to make nonfatal suicide attempts.

defines who I am—my thoughts, values, and actions." Or a person could say, "I am male—so what?" Terman and Miles (1936) constructed a scale to measure a personality variable they called *masculinity versus femininity*. The scale consisted of a large number of items that were endorsed differently by men and women. Since the distributions of scores on the scale for men and women were quite different, scores could presumably be used to predict a person's gender. Approximately one percent of males had a score below the mean for females and one percent of females had a score below the male mean. Terman and Miles assumed that masculinity and femininity defined opposite ends of a continuum, and individuals could be located at some point on the continuum. They also assumed that males who scored low in masculinity/high in femininity and females who scored low in femininity/high in masculinity were likely to be maladjusted. However, the items on the Terman and Miles scale did not have a consistent theoretical rationale and coherence (see Morawski, 1985): they included items such as "dislike being alone" and "dislike foreigners" (masculine items) as well as "dislike riding bicycles" and "dislike bald-headed men" (feminine items).

In the early 1970s psychologists developed measures of masculinity and femininity that were based on the assumption that each of these characteristics is independent, that is, individuals could be high on both measures, low on both measures, or high on one and low on the other (Bem 1974; Spence & Helmreich, 1978; Spence, Helmreich, & Stapp, 1974). Bem developed a scale called the Bem Sex Role Inventory (BSRI) by asking college students to indicate which of 200 socially desirable personality traits would be more desirable for a man to have and which more desirable for a woman. For example, "independence" was chosen as a trait that was desirable in a man, "nurturance" as a desirable female trait. Bem defined femininity as the set of traits rated as more desirable for females than for males, and masculinity as the set of traits rated as more desirable for males than for females. She selected 20 traits for each of the two dimensions and asked 1,000 college students to indicate the degree to which each trait was a correct description of their personality. The self-report ratings were summed, permitting her to assign a masculinity and a femininity score to each of her subjects. The correlation between these scale scores for men was .11 and the comparable correlation for women was −.14. These data supported Bem's belief that masculinity and femininity were independent constructs and not the end points of a bipolar continuum.

Spence and Helmreich developed a measure called the Personal Attributes Questionnaire (PAQ) by asking judges to select personality traits that are typical of men and of women (note that there was a subtle difference in their procedure and that followed by Bem: Bem asked judges to select personal characteristics that men and women *ought* to have, whereas Spence and Helmreich asked for characteristics that men and women *do* have). They then asked men and women to rate themselves on those characteristics that had been selected as typical. Some of the traits were rated as being positive (such as masculine traits "independent," "active," and "self-confident") and some as negative (such as masculine traits "arrogant" and "cynical"). They too found that scores on masculinity and femininity were uncorrelated.

Bem believed that the old Terman and Miles assumption that adjustment was related to having gender-appropriate personal characteristics was wrong. She believed that individuals who were *androgynous* (defined as being above the median on both masculinity and femininity scores) would be able to deal in a flexible way with many different situations. Moreover, she assumed that being androgynous conferred advantages that exceeded the benefits of having either masculine or feminine traits alone. This aspect of Bem's theory has not been consistently supported. Most of this research has entailed obtaining correlations between scores on the BSRI or the PAQ and measures of self-esteem and adjustment. These studies have indicated that there are relationships between masculinity and femininity scores and measures of self-esteem, but there is relatively little evidence that being balanced on both dimensions (i.e., being androgynous) conveys some special advantage on self-esteem. Individuals who have moderate scores on femininity will tend to obtain higher scores on self-esteem if they are high rather than moderate on masculinity. Most relationships between self-esteem and scores on the BSRI are attributable to scores on masculinity; femininity is only weakly related to self-esteem. Masculinity is estimated to be nine times more predictive of self-esteem than is femininity (Lubinski, Tellegen, & Butcher, 1981; 1983), and this is true for both men and women. Even the relationship between masculinity and self-esteem may derive in part from item overlaps in the scales used to measure these traits (Whitley, 1983; 1985; 1988).

There seems to be relatively little relationship between a person's tendency to assign to himself or herself traits associated with masculinity and femininity and psychological adjustment. Men and women can probably be neurotic whether or not they have stereotypical masculine or feminine personality characteristics. This conclusion is similar to the one we presented in our discussion of self-esteem and identification among African Americans. How you respond to a category that you nominally belong to may have little or nothing to do with your psychological adjustment or self-esteem.

Although it is clear that men and women are willing to endorse traits that are believed to be feminine and masculine, it is not at all clear that scores on the BSRI or the PAQ define masculinity and femininity. Spence (1983) believes that the PAQ is *not* a measure of masculinity and femininity. She prefers to think of the scale as a measure of what she calls "instrumental or self-assertive behavior" and "expressive behavior or interpersonal orientation." Therefore it is more appropriate to assume that the PAQ is a measure of personality traits rather than of masculinity and femininity *per se*.

The distinction between personality traits and concepts of masculinity and femininity is crystalized in a study by Lippa (1995) in which a different method is used to assess gender-related differences. Lippa asked males and females to rate their preferences for different occupations (e.g., being an art teacher), activities (e.g., making a speech), and hobbies (e.g., fishing). He was able to distinguish between occupations, activities, and hobbies that are preferred by males and those that are preferred by females. A score based on the extent of these preferences can be used as a measure of masculinity or femininity. Lippa calls this a *gender diagnosticity* measure. He administered it to samples of male and female college students and also asked them to fill out both the BSRI and the PAQ as well as measures of the Big Five personality traits. The gender diagnosticity scale was far more predictive of actual gender than were scores on the BSRI and the PAQ. The correlation between masculinity scores on gender diagnosticity and being a female rather than a male was $-.89$ (the correlation was negative because Lippa arbitrarily assigned a higher value to being female than to being male). The comparable correlation on the PAQ was −.34 for the masculinity scale and .29 for the femininity score. The correlations for masculinity and femininity as assessed by the BSRI were −.17 and .31, respectively. These data indicate that preferences for occupations, activities, and hobbies are far more predictive of a person's gender than are self-reports about a variety of general personality traits.

Lippa also found that, unlike the BSRI and PAQ, the gender diagnosticity measure was not strongly related to the Big Five personality traits. Lippa developed indices based on optimal weightings of the Big Five scores to predict scores on the gender diagnosticity measures and the masculinity and femininity scores on the BSRI and the PAQ. (The optimal indices were actually multiple correlations.) The correlation between the gender diagnosticity score and an optimal index of Big Five trait scores was .26, while the comparable correlations for the BSRI and the PAQ were all in the low .70s. Lippa noted that these results imply that the Big Five traits account for more than seven times as much variance in masculinity and femininity scores than in gender diagnosticity scores. Lippa's research supports Spence's interpretation of the meaning of masculinity and femininity on the PAQ: they are really not measures of gender-defining characteristics, but rather are measures of general personality traits that are weakly linked to gender.

Lippa's research provides a compelling demonstration of a simple generalization: men and women differ more on their preferences for different occupations, activities, and hobbies than they do on general personality characteristics.

COGNITION AND AFFECT

What is the relationship between our thoughts and our feelings? Think of the last time you were angry or sad, frightened or joyful. What caused you to have those feelings? Did they just "happen" or did they occur because of an event in your life? Why did the event evoke an emotion? And when you were in the emotional state, did you think about things differently? If you were joyful, did you feel warm and caring toward the people around you? If you were sad, did the world appear a dreary, hopeless place? How do our thoughts affect our feelings? How do our feelings affect our thoughts?

What Causes Emotions?

When you last experienced an emotion, you were probably emotional *about something*. It is very likely that this "something" mattered to you; you felt that it could benefit or harm you in some way. Shaver, Schwartz, Kirson, and O'Conner (1987) asked students to describe episodes in which they felt different emotions. They then coded the students' accounts and subjected them to a statistical technique called hierarchical cluster analysis, which allowed them to group elements of the accounts together to produce **prototypic emotion scripts**. The scripts for fear, sadness, anger, joy, and love are shown in Figures 11.5 to 11.9. The elements are grouped into large boxes corresponding to *antecedents* (the situation that provoked the emotion), *responses,* and (for the negative emotions) *self-control procedures*. If you look at the antecedents in these figures, you will see that in almost every case, a harm or threat of harm (for the negative emotions) or a benefit (for the positive emotions) is involved. People respond emotionally when they feel that what is happening has personal significance for their well-being.

This point of view forms the basis for a number of emotion theories (e.g., Frijda, 1986; Lazarus, 1991a; Ortony, Clore, & Collins, 1988). Lazarus (1991a; 1991b; 1991c; Smith & Lazarus, 1990) has presented a compelling account of the role of personal significance in emotion. In Lazarus's view, emotions occur when, and only when, people evaluate an encounter as having personal significance. Lazarus calls such an evaluation an **appraisal.** This process of evaluation has two aspects. First, a **primary appraisal** must be made concerning the possible benefits or harms in the encounter. Primary appraisals have three components, which can be expressed as questions: (1) Is this encounter relevant to me? If the answer is yes, there is a high likelihood that an emotion will occur. What determines whether a "yes" or "no" answer is given? Lazarus believes that the answer depends entirely on one's motives and goals. Encounters are relevant to the extent that they move us toward or away from our goals. This is another way of saying that we must have a *stake* in what is happening in order for the emotion process to be instigated. Lazarus calls this aspect of appraisal, *goal relevance.* (2) Is the encounter likely to be beneficial or harmful? Is it likely to thwart or facilitate our goals? If a goal is thwarted, the emotion will be negative; if a goal is facilitated it will be positive. This appraisal component, which Lazarus calls *goal congruence,* begins to differentiate one emotion from another. (3) What specific goal is involved in the encounter? What personal concern is at stake? The answer to this question further differentiates among emotions. For example, if the answer to question 1 is "it is relevant," and to question 2 is "incongruent with my goals," then we already know that a negative emotion will occur. If the answer to question 3 is "the goal involves a moral transgression," then the specific negative emotion will be *guilt.* Lazarus calls this third component of primary appraisal *type of ego-involvement.*

Secondary appraisal refers to how the individual might react to the encounter, or what Lazarus calls *coping options.* The fundamental question is: "'What, if anything, can I do in this encounter, and how will what I do and what is going to happen affect my well-being?'" (Lazarus, 1991a, p. 134). It is not enough to believe that an encounter threatens or enhances a self-relevant goal; one must also take into account one's resources, the abilities one has to deal with the situation. Consider two individuals walking alone at night on a dark street. The sound of rapid footsteps approaching from behind is heard. One individual reacts with extreme fear; the other does not. Why? The second individual is a black belt in karate

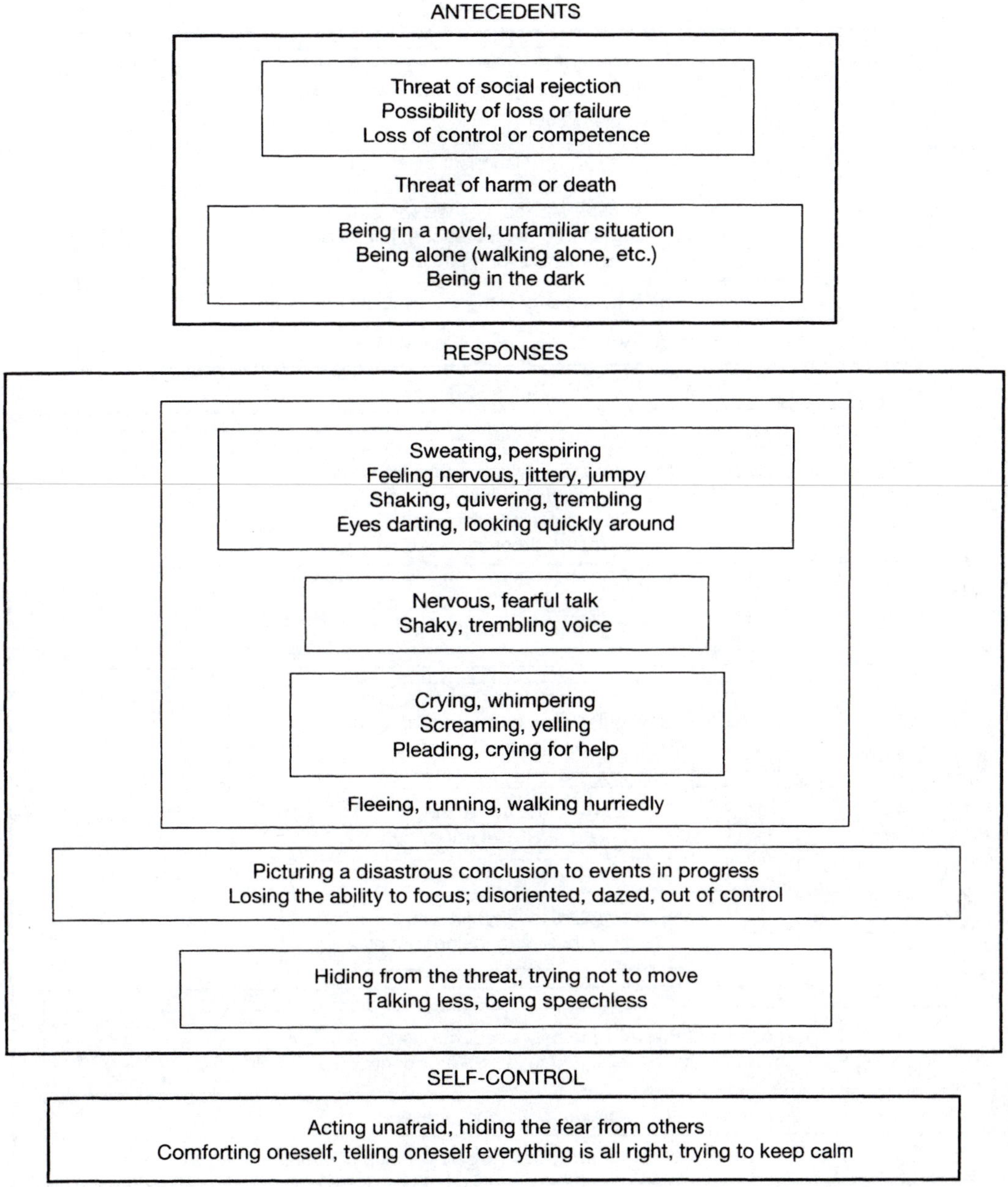

ANTECEDENTS

Threat of social rejection
Possibility of loss or failure
Loss of control or competence

Threat of harm or death

Being in a novel, unfamiliar situation
Being alone (walking alone, etc.)
Being in the dark

RESPONSES

Sweating, perspiring
Feeling nervous, jittery, jumpy
Shaking, quivering, trembling
Eyes darting, looking quickly around

Nervous, fearful talk
Shaky, trembling voice

Crying, whimpering
Screaming, yelling
Pleading, crying for help

Fleeing, running, walking hurriedly

Picturing a disastrous conclusion to events in progress
Losing the ability to focus; disoriented, dazed, out of control

Hiding from the threat, trying not to move
Talking less, being speechless

SELF-CONTROL

Acting unafraid, hiding the fear from others
Comforting oneself, telling oneself everything is all right, trying to keep calm

FIGURE 11.5   The prototype of fear. (Based on Shaver et al., 1987)
Reproduced with permission of the American Psychological Association.

ANTECEDENTS

An undesirable outcome; getting what was not wanted;
a negative surprise
Death of a loved one
Loss of a valued relationship; separation
Rejection, exclusion, disapproval
Not getting what was wanted, wished for, striven for, etc.
Reality falling short of expectations; things being
worse than anticipated

Discovering that one is powerless, helpless, impotent

Empathy with someone who is sad, hurt, etc.

RESPONSES

Sitting or lying around; being inactive, lethargic, listless
Tired, rundown, low in energy
Slow, shuffling movements
Slumped, drooping posture

Withdrawing from social contact
Talking little or not at all

Low, quiet, slow, monotonous voice
Saying sad things

Frowning, not smiling
Crying, tears, whimpering

Irritable, touchy, grouchy
Moping, brooding, being moody

Negative outlook; thinking only about the negative side of things
Giving up; no longer trying to improve or control the situation

Blaming, criticizing oneself

Talking to someone about the sad feelings or events

SELF-CONTROL

Taking action, becoming active (either to improve the situation or to
alter one's feelings)
Suppressing the negative feelings; looking on the positive or bright
side; trying to act happy

FIGURE 11.6   The prototype of sadness. (Based on Shaver et al., 1987)
Reproduced with permission of the American Psychological Association.

ANTECEDENTS

Predisposition to anger, either because of previous similar or related experiences or because of stress, overload, fatigue, etc.

Reversal or sudden loss of power, status, or respect; insult
Violation of an expectation; things not working out as planned
Frustration or interruption of a goal-directed activity
Real or threatened physical or psychological pain

Judgment that the situation is illegitimate, wrong, unfair, contrary to what ought to be

RESPONSES

Obscenities, cursing
Verbally attacking the cause of anger
Loud voice, yelling, screaming, shooting
Complaining, bitching, talking about how lousy things are

Hands or fists clenched
Aggressive, threatening movements or gestures

Attacking something other than the cause of anger
(e.g., pounding on something, throwing things)
Physically attacking the cause of anger
Incoherent, out-of-control, highly emotional behavior
Imagining attacking or hurting the cause of anger

Heavy walk, stomping
Tightness or rigidity in body; tight, rigid movements
Nonverbally communicating disapproval to the cause of anger
(e.g., slamming doors, walking out)

Frowning, not smiling, mean or unpleasant expression
Gritting teeth, showing teeth, breathing through teeth
Red, flushed face

Crying
Feelings of nervous tension, anxiety, discomfort

Brooding; withdrawing from social contact

Narrowing of attention to exclude all but the anger situation;
not being able to think of anything else
Thinking "I'm right, everyone else is wrong"

SELF-CONTROL

Suppressing the anger; trying not to show or express it
Redefining the situation or trying to view it in such a way that anger is no longer appropriate

FIGURE 11.7 The prototype of anger. (Based on Shaver et al., 1987)
Reproduced with permission of the American Psychological Association.

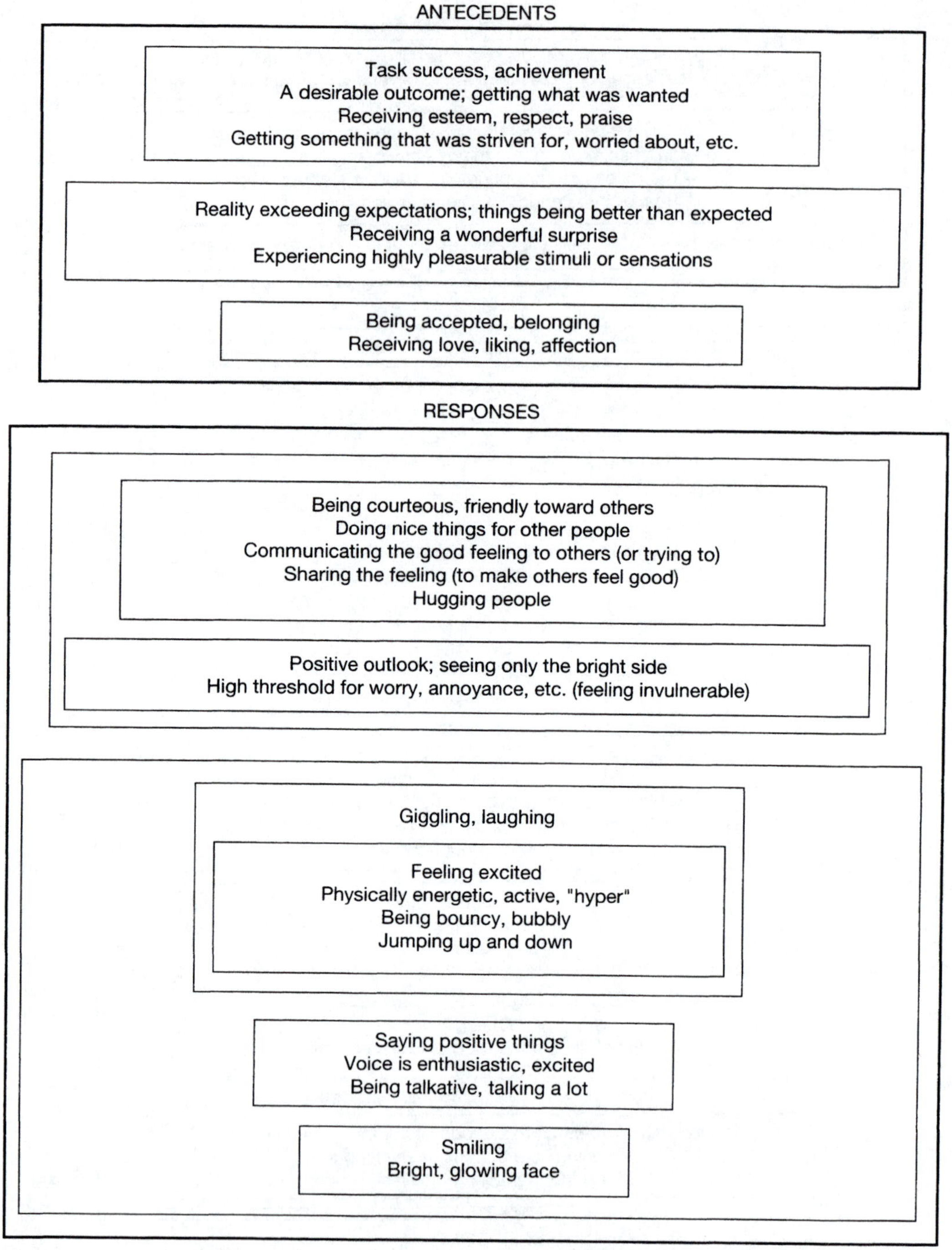

ANTECEDENTS

Task success, achievement
A desirable outcome; getting what was wanted
Receiving esteem, respect, praise
Getting something that was striven for, worried about, etc.

Reality exceeding expectations; things being better than expected
Receiving a wonderful surprise
Experiencing highly pleasurable stimuli or sensations

Being accepted, belonging
Receiving love, liking, affection

RESPONSES

Being courteous, friendly toward others
Doing nice things for other people
Communicating the good feeling to others (or trying to)
Sharing the feeling (to make others feel good)
Hugging people

Positive outlook; seeing only the bright side
High threshold for worry, annoyance, etc. (feeling invulnerable)

Giggling, laughing

Feeling excited
Physically energetic, active, "hyper"
Being bouncy, bubbly
Jumping up and down

Saying positive things
Voice is enthusiastic, excited
Being talkative, talking a lot

Smiling
Bright, glowing face

FIGURE 11.8 The prototype of joy. (Based on Shaver et al., 1987)
Reproduced with permission of the American Psychological Association.

ANTECEDENTS

O offers/provides something that P wants, needs, likes
P knows/realizes that O loves, needs, appreciates him/her
P finds O attractive (physically and/or psychologically)

Exceptionally good communication
O inspires openness, trust, security, etc. in P

Having spent a lot of time together, having shared special experiences

RESPONSES

Being forgetful, distracted, etc.; daydreaming
Being obsessed with O, not being able to take
eyes or thoughts off O

Wanting the best for O, wanting to give to O
Wanting/seeking to see, spend time with, spend life with O

Saying "I love you"
Expressing positive feelings to O

Wanting/seeking physical closeness or sex with O
Kissing
Touching, petting
Hugging, holding, cuddling

Eye contact, mutual gaze

Feeling excited, high in energy, fast heartbeat, etc.

Feeling/acting self-confident, assertive, invulnerable
Seeing only the positive side; everything seems wonderful
Feeling happy, joyful, exuberant, etc.
Feeling warm, trusting, secure, etc.

Feeling relaxed, calm

Smiling

FIGURE 11.9 The prototype of love. (Based on Shaver et al., 1987)
Reproduced with permission of the American Psychological Association.

and has dealt with this kind of situation before. She is not scared because she appraises her ability to deal with the situation positively. In contrast, the first individual has no such skill and feels extremely threatened.

Each emotion is linked to a particular set of appraisals that together make up a **core relational theme.** When a particular core relational theme is experienced, the linked emotion occurs. Lazarus views this process as part of our evolutionary heritage. Emotions evolved because they were adaptive reactions to critical aspects of encounters with the environment, particularly encounters involving other people. Frijda (1988) expresses the tightness of the link between appraisal and emotion succinctly: "in goes loss, out comes grief; in goes frustration or offense, out comes anger" (p. 349). Table 11.9 summarizes the core relational themes that Lazarus believes are the source of a variety of emotions (cf. Plutchik, 1980).

What evidence is there that specific emotions are linked to specific patterns of appraisals? A number of researchers have attempted to study this question by asking subjects either what led up to an emotional experience or what emotional experience they thought a particular encounter would produce. These studies tend to support the idea that emotions are linked to appraisals. For example, positive emotions occurred in situations appraised as goal congruent, and negative emotions occurred in situations appraised as goal incongruent (Frijda, 1987; Roseman, Spindel, & Jose, 1990; Smith & Ellsworth, 1987).

Although appraisals are cognitive, they need not involve long drawn-out thought processes; they can occur virtually instantaneously, especially if the core

TABLE 11.9   Core Relational Themes for Each Emotion (Based on Smith and Lazarus, 1990)

Anger	A demeaning offense against me and mine.
Anxiety	Facing uncertain, existential threat.
Fright	Facing an immediate, concrete, and overwhelming physical danger.
Guilt	Having transgressed a moral imperative.
Shame	Having failed to live up to an ego ideal.
Sadness	Having experienced an irrevocable loss.
Envy	Wanting what someone else has.
Jealousy	Resenting a third party for loss or threat to another's affection.
Disgust	Taking in or being too close to an indigestible object or idea (metaphorically speaking).
Happiness	Making reasonable progress toward the realization of a goal.
Pride	Enhancing one's ego identity by taking credit for a valued object or achievement, either our own or that of someone or group with whom we identify.
Relief	A distressing goal-incongruent condition that has changed for the better or gone away.
Hope	Fearing the worst but yearning for better.
Love	Desiring or participating in affection, usually but not necessarily reciprocated.
Compassion	Being moved by another's suffering and wanting to help.

relational themes have been experienced often (directly or vicariously) in the past. Sometimes we just have a feeling that an encounter is relevant to our goals without clearly articulating the connection. Appraisals can also be unconscious. In some cases, the appraisal may be encoded in language; in other cases, it may occur in a nonverbal form (LeDoux, 1993).

Self-Discrepancy Theory

One of the most important "triggers" for emotional reactions may be the appraisal that one is not meeting standards of behavior necessary to achieve important goals. These standards may be established very early in life and may function automatically later in life. Any event that "reminds" people of the failure to meet such standards may precipitate a negative emotion. These ideas are central to a theory developed by Higgins (1987) and his colleagues called *self-discrepancy theory*. Higgins's theory deals with the relationship between beliefs about the self and emotions. It illustrates the ties between thoughts and feelings.

Self-discrepancy theory starts from the premise that people have beliefs about themselves that may be incompatible with each other. These beliefs can be divided up into three *domains of the self*. First, there are attributes we believe are true about us, such as that we are kind, or fun to be with, or athletic. These beliefs about what we actually possess represent the domain of the **actual self**. We also have beliefs concerning how we wish we could be. If only we were smarter, or better looking, or less nervous, or taller, then we would be able to achieve our most wished-for goals. The characteristics that we believe would make us happier and our lives more rewarding comprise the domain of the **ideal self**. Finally, we have beliefs about characteristics that we think we should have in order to fulfill our sense of duty, obligation, or responsibility. We may feel that to be a worthwhile person we should be more caring, or disciplined, or talented. These attributes make up the **ought self**. The *actual* self corresponds to what is often called the self-concept; the *ideal* and *ought* selves represent standards or *self-guides* that influence our self-appraisals.[1]

When the actual self is discrepant from the ideal or ought self, people may experience negative affect. For example, Table 11.10 shows the attributes of the three

TABLE 11.10   Example of Actual/Ideal and Actual/Ought Self-Discrepancies

ACTUAL	IDEAL	OUGHT
Underachiever[a]	Rich	**Honors student**
Fun-loving	Charismatic	Thorough
Ordinary looking	**Look like a model**	Talented
Athletic	Concerned about others	Courageous
Impulsive	Energetic	**Less impulsive**
Moody	**Cheerful**	Better daughter

[a]**Boldface** characteristics on the same line are mismatches.

domains of the self of Felicia. The bold print shows areas of discrepancy. Felicia has two actual/ideal discrepancies (or mismatches) and two actual/ought discrepancies. According to Higgins's theory, when anything activates these constructs in Felicia's memory, she will experience negative affect. In particular, anything that activates material in her memory related to "ordinary looking/looks like a model" or "moody/cheerful" will produce feelings of dejection (sadness, disappointment, dissatisfaction). Why dejection? Recall that in appraisal theory, emotions result from specific patterns of appraisal. Dejection-related emotions result from an appraisal that one is not able to achieve one's desired goals or from an absence of positive outcomes. Higgins believes that one need only be reminded of those areas where one feels that one lacks what is needed to achieve goals in order to experience dejection.

If the attributes of "underachiever/honors student" or "impulsive/less impulsive" are activated, Felicia will experience a different sort of negative affect: agitation-related emotions (fear and anxiety), the result of a discrepancy between beliefs about oneself and how one believes one ought to be. This feeling may derive from early childhood when violations of parental norms led to punishment, or it may represent the feeling that by not meeting standards of right and wrong one is at risk for social exclusion.

To summarize, Higgins believes that the relation between our sense of who we actually are and our sense of who we would like to be or should be can place us at risk for experiencing dejection-related or agitation-related emotions. The attributes that make up these three domains differ from person to person. Further, some people have many discrepancies between the actual self and the ideal or ought selves, while others have few discrepancies. Individuals who frequently experience emotions like sadness are believed to have many actual/ideal discrepancies; those who experience emotions like anxiety are believed to have many actual/ought discrepancies.

It should be emphasized that the individual may be unaware of these discrepancies. Furthermore, they may be activated without the individual's having any idea what is going on. Automatic activation of self-discrepancies was demonstrated in a study by Strauman and Higgins (1987, study 2). Subjects filled out a "Selves Questionnaire" that asked them to list attributes they actually possess, attributes they wish they had, and attributes they felt they ought to have. Four weeks later some of the subjects were recruited for a supposedly different study on "thinking about other people." Only those subjects who were either high on actual/ideal mismatches and relatively low on actual/ought mismatches or were high on actual/ought mismatches and relatively low on actual/ideal mismatches were included in the second part of the study.

In this session the subjects verbally completed sentences that began with "a ____ person . . . ," the experimenters filling in the blank either with attributes that were unrelated to the subject's actual, ideal, or ought selves or with attributes that were mismatches. For example, a person who included "lazy" as an attribute of the actual self and "industrious" as an attribute of the ideal self would have to complete the sentence: "An industrious person. . . . " In all cases, the more positive attribute was used. The basic hypothesis of the study was that simply completing sentences about people that involved a mismatch would activate dejection or agitation, depending on whether the mismatch was actual/ideal or actual/ought. Furthermore, this would happen automatically, since subjects were not aware that the second session had anything to do with the previous session or that the attributes had been tailored for them.

The dependent variables were self-reported mood, skin conductance responses, and speed of vocalization (previous research has shown that dejection tends to decrease motor speed while agitation tends to increase it). Self-reported mood was assessed before and after the sentence completion trials. Table 11.11 shows the results. Subjects whose mismatches were of the actual/ought type shifted mood toward agitation; subjects whose mismatches were of the actual/ideal type shifted mood slightly toward dejection.

Of the eight sentences each subject had to complete, four were mismatches and four were unrelated to the subject's actual, ideal, or ought selves. Thus trial-by-trial comparisons of sentences with and without mismatches could be made for the skin conductance and verbalization measures. Table 11.12 shows that there was lower skin conductance and slower verbalization on actual/ideal mismatches than on trials that were unrelated to the subjects' self-attributes, but higher skin conductance and faster verbalization on actual/ought mismatches than on trials that were unrelated.

These results demonstrate a number of aspects of self-discrepancy theory. First, mood-sensitive measures such as skin conductance and verbalization rate can be changed from moment to moment as subjects are exposed to attribute labels that correspond to areas of mismatch. Second, the nature of the mood change depends on whether the mismatch is an actual/ideal or an actual/ought discrepancy. Third, these effects can occur even when the context of the mismatch does not directly involve the self. Fourth, exposure to a number of these mismatches can change overall mood.

Higgins's theory can account for both state and trait affect. People can experience shifts in their mood state from moment to moment as discrepant aspects of themselves are brought to their attention. To the extent that we all have at least some such mismatches, we are all vulnerable to such shifts of mood. Some people, however, have more and stronger mismatches than others, which should make them particularly vulnerable to dejection (actual/ideal mismatches) or anxiety

TABLE 11.11   Shift in Mood for Subjects with Actual/Ideal and Actual/Ought Discrepancies (Based on Strauman and Higgins, 1987)

	DEJECTION	AGITATION
Actual/Ideal Discrepant	+.08	−.35
Actual/Ought Discrepant	−.09	+.51

Reproduced with permission of the American Psychological Association.

TABLE 11.12   **Difference Between Subject Unrelated and Mismatch Trials on Skin Conductance and Verbalization Time (words per second) (Based on Stauman and Higgins, 1987)**

	SKIN CONDUCTANCE	VERBALIZATION TIME
Actual/Ideal	−.20	−.28
Actual/Ought	+.50	+.48

Reproduced with permission of the American Psychological Association.

(of actual/ought mismatches). In contrast, people with few mismatches should be generally less vulnerable to negative affect.

Can Emotions Occur Without Cognitions?

Although there can be little doubt that appraisals play a central role in emotional processes, there is nevertheless continuing controversy surrounding Lazarus's claim that appraisals are both **necessary and sufficient** for emotion to be generated. The idea that they are *sufficient*—that appraisals can, on their own, generate emotion in normal human beings—is not in question. But to say they are *necessary* is to claim that any time an emotion occurs there must be an appraisal process operating; that is, there can never be an emotion in the absence of appraisals. This idea is vigorously opposed by a number of emotion researchers in what has sometimes been called the *affect-cognition debate* (e.g., Zajonc, 1984).

As you undoubtedly know, there are many psychoactive drugs that can influence emotional states. Some drugs reduce feelings of anxiety; others reduce feelings of depression. Drugs that activate the norepinephrine system may elicit anxiety. Izard (1993) argues that these drugs have a direct impact on emotional neural systems that underlie emotional experience. These circuits can also be activated by electrical stimulation of the brain. When low levels of electrical stimulation were applied to brains of patients during neurosurgery, the patients sometimes reported experiences of joy, fear, or anger. As soon as the stimulation stopped, the experiences ceased (Heath, 1986).

Another example of emotion in the absence of appraisal concerns the effects of facial expressions and posture on emotional experiences. The idea that one's facial expression can influence how one feels is an old one. If you believe that "putting on a happy face" can make you feel better, or walking around with a frown can make you feel worse, then you agree with Charles Darwin and William James that facial expressions can influence our experience of emotions. Ekman (1992) and Tomkins (1962) asserted that certain **basic emotions** are closely linked to facial expressions, so that if the proper expression is made, that emotion will be experienced. Ekman and Friesen (1978) carefully studied facial expressions of individuals experiencing different emotions and came up with a precise description of exactly how the facial muscles are patterned (called the FACS—Facial Action Coding Scheme). Support for the idea that these expressions are biologically linked to emotion comes from findings that these specific expression–emotion links occur all over the world, in both industrialized and preindustrialized societies (see Russell, 1994, and Ekman, 1994 for a discussion of this research).

Levenson, Ekman, and Friesen (1990) directed college students to move their facial muscles in specific ways to produce these emotions; for example: (1) pull your eyebrows down and together; (2) raise your upper eyelid; (3) push your lower lip up and press your lips together. Students were asked whether they experienced any emotions while holding their face in the given pattern for ten seconds, and if so to rate the emotions' intensity. Videotapes were then used to check whether the muscle pattern accurately corresponded to the FACS criteria (can you tell which emotion was linked to these instructions?). Sixty-six percent of the trials in which the subjects accurately produced the facial expression of the target emotion produced a report of that specific emotion; in contrast, only 27% of the trials that were judged as not meeting the criteria produced a report of the target emotion. In addition, physiological measures of heart rate, skin conductance, and finger temperature also differed as a function of the facial pattern, suggesting that facial expressions influence autonomic activity as well as emotional experience.[2]

Some emotions are associated with specific bodily postures. Darwin (1872) noted that when people feel pride, they tend to hold their head high and stand erect; when they feel shame or humility, they tend to slump. Weisfeld and Beresford (1982) confirmed that pride is associated with an erect posture: students who had received high grades in an exam stood more erect than those who had received low grades. One's posture in turn has also been shown to influence emotions. A number of studies found that instructing people to adopt either an upright or slumped posture influences their self-reported stress, well-being, and depression (Riskind, 1984; Riskind & Gotay, 1982). Stepper and Strack (1993) found that when subjects were asked to assume different manipulated postures under the guise of studying how different work positions influence performance ("ergonomics"), those in an erect posture reported greater pride than those in a slumped posture when told they had done exceptionally well on an achievement test.

These studies suggest that emotions can be influenced by people's facial expressions and body posture. Do they refute Lazarus's claim that appraisals are necessary for emotions to be experienced? Although facial expression and posture can influence the intensity of emotions, and may bias subjects toward more negative or positive feelings, it is less clear that they can produce full-blown emotions such as anger, fear, or joy (Izard, 1990; Matsumoto, 1987; Winton, 1986). The fact that drugs and electrical stimulation can directly elicit (sometimes strong) emotions does, however, suggest that not all emotional experiences require appraisals (Izard, 1993).

Why has this issue been at the center of emotion theory and research for the past couple of decades? If emotions are a crucial aspect of personality, we need to know what aspects of individuality influence them. An appraisal theorist such as Lazarus emphasizes the importance of goals, beliefs, and knowledge. If you want to understand why Jerome is feeling sad, you need to understand Jerome's motives and goals, his understanding of the possibilities that a given situation provides, and his beliefs about his ability to deal with those possibilities. For example, if Jerome is often angry, this fact would suggest that Jerome often feels that important goals are being threatened and that he blames someone else for this. If he feels dejected, then important goals are not being met, and he feels helpless to do anything about the matter. If his appraisals are very general and involve large aspects of his life (for example, the goal of "being a success"), then Jerome might be chronically depressed. An appraisal theory, then, attempts to unravel the mystery of our emotions and moods by analyzing the cognitive components that produce core relational themes. No matter how irrational one's emotions may seem to be, there is an underlying logic to them, based on our appraisals of core relational themes.

The idea that emotions and moods can be generated by processes that bypass appraisals leads to a very different view of the nature of emotions. If Jerome is often angry, it is possible that those brain circuits associated with anger (Panksepp, 1992) are chronically activated, or are set at a lower threshold than most people's. If he is sad, it may be because levels of neurotransmitters have been influenced by his physical state (e.g., an illness). Thus the understanding of individual differences in emotional tendencies, which seem to be such an important aspect of personality, differs crucially between appraisal and nonappraisal theories.

A partial rapprochement between these views is possible. If we accept that emotion refers to a process that includes feelings, thoughts, and action tendencies, then we can agree with Lazarus that all emotions and all moods must involve all three of these components. However, we can also agree with Izard and Zajonc that not all emotions are precipitated by appraisals. All we need to add is that each component can trigger each other component. A shift in neurotransmitter levels might precipitate feelings of tension and increased autonomic activity, but subjects will experience anxiety only if they appraise these physical events in a certain way. Such an appraisal might occur because the physical experience brings to mind other times when such feelings were experienced, which will often be under circumstances of threat. Or perhaps the feelings themselves make the individual feel vulnerable and unable to cope (Lazarus, 1991a). This line of thinking suggests a certain fluidity in the connections between thoughts, feelings, and actions.

How We Feel Affects How (and What) We Think

It is Sunday afternoon. You are at home. The day is dreary—cloudy and rainy. The telephone rings. You answer and a voice asks you to participate in a survey on how satisfied people are with their lives. You agree, and the person asks you, "All things considered, how satisfied or dissatisfied are you with your life as a whole these days?" Now imagine the same thing happening on a bright and sunny day. Do you think your rating of your life satisfaction would be influenced by the weather? Schwarz and Clore (1983) found that people rated their life satisfaction significantly lower on rainy days than on sunny days—but only when the interviewer did not mention the weather. When the interviewer casually asked the subjects, "By the way, how's the weather down there?" the difference between rainy and sunny days disappeared (see Table 11.13).

Why would subjects rate their life satisfaction lower on a rainy day, but only when the weather was not brought to their attention? The subjects were asked to make a snap rating; they didn't have much time to think about it. As a result, they may have used whatever information they had available at the moment to make their rating. One source of information about life satisfaction is how you feel. We know that people's moods are influenced by the weather; people feel less happy on rainy days than on sunny days (Cunningham, 1979). So the rainy day subjects used a kind of "shorthand" (what is known in the cognitive psychology literature as a **heuristic**): if I feel down, I guess my life satisfaction isn't very high. Why didn't this happen when the weather was brought to subjects' attention? Once they became aware of the weather, they could attribute their negative mood to the rainy day; as a result, it was no longer a source of their judgment about their over-all life satisfaction.

This study shows that current mood can influence judgments of life satisfaction. A great deal of research supports the more general idea that mood can influence all sorts of judgments (Bower, 1991; Forgas, 1995). Much of this research has been carried out in laboratory settings in which mood was induced by a wide range of situations including happy and sad music, success and failure experiences, happy and sad films, hypnosis, repetition of positive and negative statements, and even fragrant and foul odors. These studies frequently find **mood-congruence** effects, whereby judgments are shifted in the direction of the mood produced in the laboratory. For example, Salovey and Birnbaum (1989) induced happy and sad moods in college students and then asked them to rate the likelihood of future negative health-related events (such as developing high blood pressure) happening to them in comparison to other students. Subjects who were placed in a happy mood judged that they would be far less likely than other students to experience negative health events, while those who were placed in a sad mood expected to have only slightly fewer negative health events than other college students. (The fact that both groups thought they would "do better" than other students reflects the pervasive phenomenon known as *unrealistic optimism* or *self-enhancing bias*, to which we referred earlier; Taylor & Brown, 1988; Weinstein, 1980.)

TABLE 11.13   **Effects of Weather on Judgments of Life Satisfaction (Based on Schwarz and Clore, 1983)**

	NO MENTION OF WEATHER	CASUAL MENTION OF WEATHER
Rainy Day	4.86	6.71
Sunny Day	6.57	6.79

Note: Ratings were made on a 10-point scale with 10 = most satisfied.
Reproduced with permission of the American Psychological Association.

Mood also can prime material in memory (Blaney, 1986; Bower, 1981, 1991). For example, people in positive moods are more likely to recall happy experiences than are people in negative moods (Ehrlichman & Halpern, 1988; Teasdale, Taylor, & Fogarty, 1980). The priming of memories may be one way in which mood influences judgments. Positive moods may increase the chances that more positive information will come to mind, while negative moods may increase the chances for negative information. Since judgments typically use information stored in memory, a tendency to retrieve either more positive or negative information could influence the judgment process. For example, Forgas and Bower (1987) induced good or bad moods through (false) feedback on a "personality test." Subjects were then asked to read a number of statements describing individuals and to form impressions of the individuals. Subjects who were made happy by very positive feedback made more positive judgments of the individuals described, and also recalled more positive information about those individuals, than did subjects who were made unhappy by very negative feedback (see Figure 11.10a and b).

Judgments of oneself can also be affected by moods. Brown and Mankowski (1993) found that subjects in whom a happy mood had been induced rated themselves more positively on a set of adjectives than did subjects in whom a sad mood had been induced. In a separate study, subjects reported on their naturally occurring moods and rated themselves on a set of adjectives every day over the

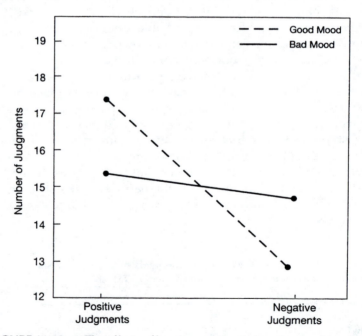

FIGURE 11.10a The effects of happy or sad mood on the number of positive and negative person-perception judgments made by subjects. (Based on Forgas and Bower, 1987) Reproduced with permission of the American Psychological Association.

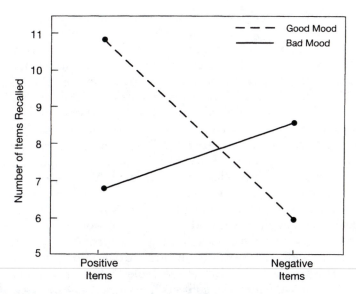

FIGURE 11.10b   The effects of happy or sad learning mood on subjects' ability to recall the positive and negative details of target characters. (Based on Forgas and Bower, 1987) Reproduced with permission of the American Psychological Association.

course of six weeks. On a day-by-day basis, their moods and self-ratings were highly correlated: when in relatively happy moods self-ratings became more positive, when in relatively unhappy moods they became more negative. Brown and Mankowski (1993) also found that individual differences in self-esteem were related to the strength of the association between mood and self-ratings. Subjects with low self-esteem were more influenced by their moods than were subjects with high self-esteem, and this was particularly true for bad moods. Bad moods seemed to have a much greater impact on shifting self-judgments in a negative direction for those low in self-esteem than those with high self-esteem.

To some extent, then, our views of the world and of ourselves are influenced by our moods. This influence is not always as straightforward as the mood-congruence notion suggests. If you think about times that you have been in good or bad moods, you may remember how your moods seemed to affect your thoughts, memories, and outlook. Everything may have seemed full of promise and possibility when you felt good, and possibly you could seem to think only about the worst aspects of life when you felt bad. But you might also recall quite opposite experiences. Perhaps when you were feeling down, you actively shifted your thoughts toward a more positive focus in an attempt to get out of your bad mood. In fact, a number of researchers have noted that bad moods sometimes do not produce mood congruence, and they may even produce **mood-incongruence** effects (Parrott & Sabini, 1990), whereby bad moods make memories or judgments more positive. This effect can occur when individuals try to counter a bad mood by thinking thoughts that will put them in a better mood.

Smith and Petty (1995) considered the role of self-esteem in people's tendency to engage in this type of "negative mood regulation." In one study, subjects high and low in self-esteem were given either a neutral or sad mood induction and were then asked to make judgments about a series of newspaper headlines, some of them positively toned and some negatively toned. They were then asked to recall as many of the headlines as they could. Correlations were computed between self-reports of mood and the emotional tone of the headlines recalled. For subjects low in self-esteem, there were positive correlations between how sad the subjects felt and the tendency to recall more negative headlines in both neutral and sad mood induction groups. Thus, regardless of whether they had been exposed to a sad mood induction or not, those subjects low in self-esteem who reported feeling relatively sadder also recalled more negative headlines; that is, they showed a mood congruence effect. However, quite a different pattern was found for subjects with high self-esteem. These subjects showed a small mood-congruence effect in the neutral induction condition, but a very large mood *in*congruence effect in the sad mood induction condition: the sadder the individuals felt, the more likely they were to recall positively toned headlines (see Table 11.14). Apparently, when exposed to a sadness-inducing situation, subjects high in self-esteem were able to bias their recall toward the headlines that would make them feel better, whereas for subjects low in self-esteem sad mood triggered negative (mood-congruent) memories.

The studies by Brown and Mankowski and by Smith and Petty both point toward the importance of self-esteem as a moderator of mood-cognition effects. Those low in self-esteem seem more susceptible to mood congruence, especially when the mood is negative. This pattern can produce an unfortunate tendency to remain "stuck" in negative thoughts and feelings, because when such individuals feel bad, their thoughts become more negative and may in turn prolong their bad mood, and so on. In contrast, those high in self-esteem seem to be more likely to engage in cognitive activity that will counteract their bad feelings.

Earlier in this chapter we discussed the concept of explanatory style as a cause of affective reactions. People who tend to attribute bad occurrences to internal, stable, global factors seem to be prone to depression. There is also evidence that temporary mood states can influence the kinds of attributions people make. Forgas (1994) interviewed people about conflicts they had in intimate relation-

TABLE 11.14   Correlations Between Mood State and Positivity of Recalled Headlines for Subjects High or Low in Self-Esteem (Based on Smith and Petty, 1995)

Self-Esteem	MOOD INDUCTION CONDITION	
	Neutral	Sad
Low	.38	.44
High	.30	−.71

Note: Positive correlation indicates mood congruence; negative correlation indicates mood incongruence.
Reproduced with permission of the American Psychological Association.

ships. Some of the subjects were interviewed just after watching a sad movie, some were interviewed just after watching a happy movie, and some were interviewed before going into the movie theater (control group). Subjects were asked to rate the causes of a recent serious conflict with their intimate partner on globality, stability, and internality. As is shown in Figure 11.11, those who had just seen a sad movie tended to make "depressive" attributions for the conflict, whereas those who had just seen a happy movie had the opposite pattern of attributions.

Once we accept that affect can influence thoughts and perceptions, and that moods and emotions can be provoked by things like facial expressions, posture, fatigue, drugs—or for that matter, unconscious appraisals—it becomes clear that we have a "chicken and egg" situation. Consider Barbara and Phil. Barbara is the kind of person who is not afraid to take on challenges, to deal with potentially dangerous situations. Phil avoids challenge and stays away from anything that could possibly hurt him. Phil frequently feels worried and anxious, Barbara hardly ever does. The (cognitive) chicken: Phil has low self-efficacy; he doesn't think he can handle things well; he feels vulnerable; his secondary appraisal is that all sorts of situations are beyond his ability to cope. He also believes the world is a dangerous place, with germs, terrorists, and disapproving people. So he often experiences anxiety. Barbara is self-confident and self-assured; she believes in herself; she thinks she can cope with almost anything. She views the world in positive terms, focusing on its promise and potential for growth. The (emotional) egg: Phil is biologically disposed to experience anxiety; his nervous system is sensitive to threat; his emotional reactions are swift and strong. As a result, he has a low threshold for perceiving threat; his anxiety triggers associations that paint the worst picture of the world around him; he stores and recalls threatening information more readily than nonthreatening information. Barbara has high levels of "energetic arousal" (Thayer, 1989); she is biologically disposed to have energy and enthusiasm. She is

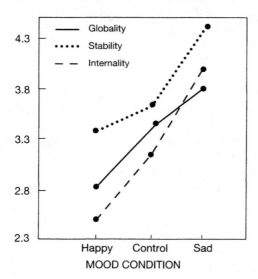

FIGURE 11.11 Patterns of attributions made for a serious conflict with one's partner by subjects in happy, control, or sad mood states. (Based on Forgas, 1994) Reproduced with permission of the American Psychological Association.

sensitive to signals of reward. As a result she sees opportunity around her rather than danger; positive events are recalled more easily than negative events; she is an optimist.

So which came first? Is appraisal the cause of affect or is affect the cause of appraisal? The research suggests that both are true: "People may be expected to differ in thresholds for particular emotional response modes, in the readiness with which they appraise events in a particular way, and in resources for coping with particular events" (Frijda, 1993, p. 330). Both affect and cognition play a crucial role in individuality.

CONCLUDING THOUGHTS

In chapters 9, 10, and 11 we examined the role of thought in personality. In chapter 9 we argued that we may be influenced by unconscious thoughts. In this chapter we discussed relationships between beliefs and actuality—what we think about ourselves and what we are actually like. Our view is that we cannot come to understand personality merely by ascertaining what people believe about themselves. We are more than our beliefs about ourselves. We also think that we cannot understand a person unless we know what a person thinks about herself. Running through much of our discussion has been the question of whether thoughts drive actions and affects or whether the direction of causality is from action and affect to thought. There is at least one kind of evidence that suggests that thoughts are the *result* of affects and actions rather than their cause. Attributional styles and personality dispositions related to the tendency to experience negative and positive affects (e.g., neuroticism and extraversion) are highly heritable; we argued in chapter 5 that the heritability of these personality characteristics when they are measured appropriately may be close to .7. It is exceedingly unlikely that genes directly influence thoughts. They can influence physiological structures that may influence our reactions to events and ultimately our cognitions about these reactions, but since the genetic influences precede the development of thoughts about ourselves, the thoughts cannot be primary.

A second line of evidence also suggests that thoughts are derivative. Davidson's research (see chapter 6) on the lateralization of affect in infants indicates that dispositional tendencies to experience negative affect are related to brain functioning in preverbal infants. If infants who have not developed language differ in their tendencies to experience negative emotions, this fact suggests that there are influences on emotions that precede the development of cognitions.

Thus our beliefs may be influenced by both our bodies and our brains. But this does not mean that our thoughts about ourselves are irrelevant. The things that we believe are important to us and help to define who we think we are. Our thoughts may be influenced by our genes and our physiology, but they are unlikely to be determined solely by these influences. There is ample evidence that individual differences in what we believe change the way we react to events and the ways in which we behave. Change thought and you often change behavior. Thoughts therefore may be quasi-autonomous: once present, they may change the direction of our behavior. Thus we believe that a personality psychology based solely on our beliefs about ourselves will be incomplete. So too will be a personality psychology that neglects the role of thought.

Endnotes

[1]Higgins (1987) distinguishes two "standpoints on the self," one representing our own views and the other representing the views of others such as our parents. Most research, however, has focused on the "own" viewpoint.

[2]However, the claim that each emotion has a specific pattern of autonomic activity associated with it remains controversial (Cacioppo, Klein, Berntson, & Hatfield, 1993).

12

Applications

Can we change personality through therapeutic interventions? How do we use our knowledge of personality to select people for jobs? How does personality relate to physical health? Are there personality characteristics that predispose individuals to become ill? In this chapter we shall try to provide answers to these questions.

PERSONALITY AND THERAPY

Go into any bookstore and look at the section on psychology. You are likely to find it filled with books offering advice on how to change and improve your personality. Many magazines contain columns providing advice on psychological topics. Colleges provide counseling services. People consult clinical psychologists, counselors, psychiatric social workers, and psychiatrists for help in solving psychological problems. It is not always clear whether a particular problem in a person's life can be solved without changing her personality. Suppose a woman is disturbed by insomnia. She might consult her physician, and the physician might treat it as a physiological problem. Perhaps a different sleep position or a change in diet would solve this problem. Or the problem might be construed as a psychological one involving some aspect of her personality; perhaps the woman has unconscious conflicts leading to feelings of anxiety and tension that interfere with her sleep. She might consult a psychoanalytically oriented clinician, who might attempt to explore her unconscious conflicts.

Consider another example. A college student goes to the University Counseling Service to obtain information about career choices. He is confused about what to do after he graduates. His problem might be solved satisfactorily by his counselor's giving him brochures about any additional training required for some professions that interest him. Alternatively, his problem might be solved through an extended exploration into the reasons for his indecision about an appropriate vocation. Perhaps he has problems making decisions. Perhaps he selects occupations that are not challenging. Perhaps he believes that his parents have unrealistic aspirations for him, and his inability to commit to an occupation may be a way of expressing opposition to them. Presumably these psychological aspects to his problem cannot be solved without some attempt to alter his personality.

People may also consult mental health professionals for the treatment of psychological problems that are designated as a form of mental illness described in the American Psychiatric Associations's *Diagnostic and Statistical Manual* (DSM IV). It is estimated that 20 percent of adults will suffer from a diagnosable mental disorder at some time in their life.

Have you ever considered visiting a mental health professional? What kinds of problems can be solved by such professionals? Are various kinds of therapies successful? Obviously these are rather general questions and they do not lend themselves to simple answers.

DOES THERAPY WORK?

How could we discover if some kind of therapy is beneficial? We could ask people who have been treated if the treatment helped them. Why might this not be a satisfactory approach? People might not be accurate in their assessment of the benefits they had obtained from a particular form of treatment. Why? One important reason is that they might falsely attribute changes to the treatment when in fact they would have improved without treatment. Someone takes an aspirin and asserts that his headache improved, but perhaps it would have improved even without taking the aspirin.

There is a good reason to believe that people will generally improve even if they are not treated. People usually seek treatment for a psychological problem when it is troubling them. A person does not usually seek treatment for depression if he is not feeling depressed. If we obtain measures of psychological well-being at two different occasions from a group of people and correlate them, the value of the correlation will usually be positive but it will always be less than 1.00. Thus, for purely statistical reasons, a person who has extreme scores on the first occasion will be expected to have less extreme scores on the second occasion—a statistical phenomenon called **regression toward the mean.** Therefore, if people enter therapy when their psychological problems are intense and their scores are extreme, we would expect their scores to be less extreme when we test them later even if they are not in treatment.

Choosing a Control Group

How can we overcome the "regression toward the mean" problem? Use a control group. We need to compare individuals who have been given treatment with individuals who have not, in order to determine whether treatment is effective. What kind of control group? Sometimes the control group consists of matching individuals in treatment to individuals who have not received treatment. You might compare a group of alcoholics who seek treatment with a group of alcoholics who are matched to the first group in such variables as social class background, length of time they had been alcoholics, and the severity of their alcoholism. Is this procedure satisfactory? It is certainly better than not having a control group at all. But it is also less than ideal. Why? The matched group may differ from the treated group in subtle ways that are not obvious, and they certainly will differ in one critical way: the matched group is not matched on the decision to seek treatment. Perhaps those who seek treatment are ready to change in a way that those who have not sought treatment are not.

How could we choose a more appropriate control group? One way is to use what has been called a **wait-list control.** Individuals who seek treatment through a clinic may be told that it is not available at the present time but that it will be available later. Comparisons between groups of individuals randomly assigned to a wait-list control group or a treatment group should provide information about the effectiveness of the treatment.

Is a wait-list control group ideal? There is at least one major difficulty with it: it does not control for the belief that one is in treatment. Individuals who believe that they are in treatment are likely to improve irrespective of the nature of that treatment. The belief that someone is doing something for your problems often causes you to improve. This phenomenon is called the **placebo effect.** Researchers interested in testing the efficacy of a drug almost always include a **placebo control** in which some individuals are given a chemically inert substance and their response is compared with that of the group given the drug. A **double blind** procedure is sometimes used in which neither the patient nor the physician is aware of which drug is being prescribed.

How is a placebo control used for psychological treatment? Sometimes it is possible to use a pill placebo just as in the standard drug experiment. Patients who seek therapy for their psychological problems may be randomly assigned to a group who are told that they will be helped by a drug (which is actually a placebo). Other forms of placebo could be used as well. A person might be told that she would be helped by receiving subliminal messages, and she is seated in front of a tachistoscope that presents flashes of light but no actual messages.

The Length of the Follow-Up

Suppose a psychologist was able to show at the end of treatment that individuals assigned to some kind of psychological treatment condition were improved relative to individuals in a placebo group. What else would you want to know? You might want to know if the improvement is likely to continue. A test for improvement at the end of therapy does not tell us if an individual is likely to relapse. In evaluating the effectiveness of cancer treatments, it is conventional to report five- and ten-year survival rates. This monitoring is an implicit way of recognizing that some treatments may be effective in the short run but may not confer any long term benefits.

Criteria for Improvement

We have not discussed the most complex issue in the evaluation of therapy. How do we know someone is improved? What do we measure? First of all, we could ask the person. Surely the patient or client is the best judge of whether she is improved. Perhaps, perhaps not. As we indicated earlier, sometimes one's beliefs might be at variance with reality. Suppose a person enters therapy with a specific goal. Assume that person is a compulsive gambler and entered therapy with a goal of learning to control this behavior. At the end of therapy, she might believe that her gambling has been cured or arrested and that she is no longer likely to gamble. If we discovered that she continued to gamble, however, we would have objective reasons to doubt the validity of her self-report.

Things are not always this simple. A person may say that he believes his depression is substantially improved, but other ways of measuring depression such as clinical interviews or physiological indices may indicate that the individual is still depressed. Would you assign credibility to this self-report or would you be inclined to doubt its validity?

There is no easy solution to the choice of an appropriate measure of improvement. The choice is in part dependent upon theoretical issues about the goals of therapy. If someone believes that the goal is to help people understand unconscious conflicts in their lives, then an ideal measure of therapeutic success would be evidence that the person had resolved or learned to deal with the consequences of unconscious conflicts. If someone believes that the goal of therapy is to reduce the discrepancy between the self and the ideal self, then self-report measures of self-ideal discrepancies would be the appropriate index of improvement. If someone believes that self-reports could be distorted, then one would not place much faith on such a measure.

There are compelling reasons to distrust virtually any measure of therapeutic outcome. Self-reports may be inaccurate, and a patient's need to justify the time and expense of therapy might lead to positive distortions. Therapists too have a vested interest in judging the outcomes of their patients in a favorable manner. Independent evaluators who conduct clinical interviews of patients are ultimately dependent upon self-reports, and while they may be trained to evaluate such self-reports and to discriminate between truth and distortion, their interviews are conducted under artificial conditions. They do not have direct knowledge of the everyday behavior of the individuals they are evaluating. Evaluations based on re-ports by significant others and peers may miss subtle changes in patients. Or such evaluations may be colored by previous evaluations, leading significant others and peers to discredit actual improvements. Observations of behavior typically are too limited for a comprehensive picture of behavior characteristics. Physiological mea-sures also are subject to a variety of errors and often fluctuate over time. In addi-tion, such measures are rarely available for more generalized complaints. For example, how do we measure a physiological change indicative of improvement in the attitude that life is without meaning?

In short, people seek psychological assistance for many different conditions. Different theories may specify different measures as indices of improvement, but there is disagreement with respect to which measures are appropriate. Also there are persuasive reasons to believe that any measure is subject to error that may lead to an incorrect inference about changes as a result of psychological intervention.

Using Multiple Indicators

While we cannot solve the question of choice of measure, there are some common-sense notions that may be useful. We always want to have evidence of validity. To establish validity, we need to examine data about the relationship between a measure and other measures. Therefore it is useful to obtain several measures of outcome. Our belief in the validity of a measure would surely be enhanced if it were supported by the results of other measures. For example, if someone asserts that he is no longer depressed, we would be inclined to accept that statement as being true if an independent psychological interview indicated that he is not depressed, if his spouse and friends note a decline in his level of de-pression, and if physiological indices of depression also exhibit an appropriate change. Where the evidence of improvement is confined to a single measure, however, or is contradicted by the results of additional measures, we may be skeptical about the validity of a claim for improvement.

A Model Study

We now have an idea of the kind of study that would provide evidence for im-provement following therapy: individuals should be randomly assigned to a treatment or a placebo condition, improvement should be indexed by changes on several independent measures, the improvement should be observed at the end of therapy, and the improvement observed should be sustained over time.

Paul (1966) performed a study that fulfills these criteria. He asked 96 students with anxiety about public speaking to be subjects in his study of the effectiveness of various forms of therapy. The subjects were randomly assigned to one of five groups:

1. A systematic desensitization group, who were taught to relax while thinking about giving a speech. In this form of therapy the relaxation response is initially paired with thoughts about situations that are only slightly anxiety

arousing. After the subject can accomplish this, the relaxation response is paired with increasingly anxiety-arousing situations.

2. Insight-oriented psychotherapy.

3. A placebo consisting of a chemically inert pill that subjects were told was a tranquilizer, accompanied by occasional meetings in which the subjects were given support and attention.

4 and 5. Two different nontreatment groups—a wait-list control group who were told that they would be given treatment in the future, and a noncontact group who were assessed at the beginning of treatment and at the end of the study but who were not told that they would be given treatment in the future.

Each subject who was provided with an active form of treatment had five treatment sessions extending over a six-week period.

Paul used a variety of methods to assess change. At the end of treatment, the subjects were required to give a speech, during which anxiety ratings were provided by observers. Self-reports about the subjects' anxiety during the speech were also obtained. In addition, physiological measures of anxiety were obtained during the speech. Figure 12.1 presents Paul's results, the percentage of subjects in each group who exhibited decreased anxiety from initial assessment to assessment at the end of treatment on each of the three types of measures. The majority of subjects assigned to the control groups showed relatively little improvement. Depending on the measure, from 48 to 72 percent of those assigned to the placebo

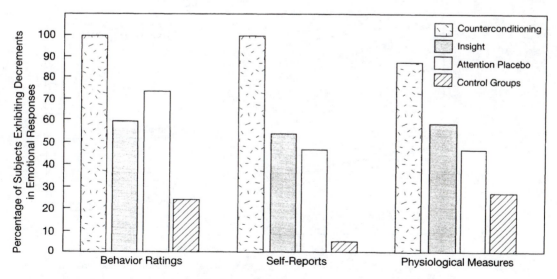

FIGURE 12.1 Percent of subjects in each of the four conditions who displayed decreases in anxiety as measured by behavior ratings, self-reports of emotional disturbance, and measures of physiological arousal. (Based on Paul, 1966)

or psychotherapy groups improved. Almost all of the subjects assigned to the systematic desensitization treatment exhibited improvements.

Paul used a six-week and a two-year follow-up to discover if the improvement was sustained. He obtained ratings of performance during a speech and he administered a number of self-report scales to assess anxiety and the tendency to become anxious in various situations, including an exam and an interview (see Paul, 1967). Figure 12.2 presents some of the follow-up results. Paul found that the

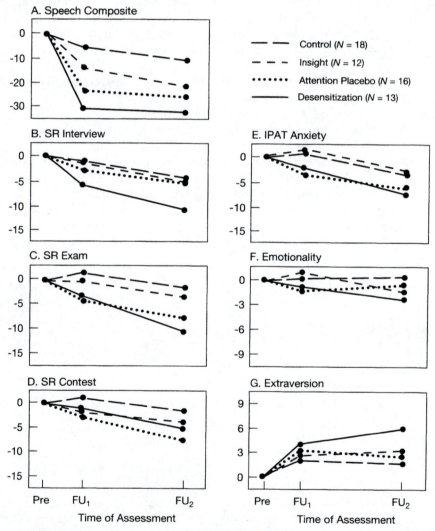

FIGURE 12.2   Mean change from pretreatment to six-week follow-up (FU$_1$) and two-year follow-up (FU$_2$) for subjects retained at FU$_2$. (Based on Paul, 1967)

improvements were sustained for a two-year period. On the speech composite measure, the subjects assigned to the desensitization treatment exhibited a 33 percent improvement over their performance at the beginning of treatment. Subjects in the untreated control groups exhibited a 12 percent improvement. About half of the improvement was attributable to a placebo effect; note that subjects in the placebo group (and in the insight psychotherapy group) both exhibited a 25 percent improvement on this measure.

The improvements obtained as a result of treatment were not confined to the focal issue addressed in treatment, that is, anxiety about public speaking. Note that subjects in the desensitization group showed improvements in their self-reports about anxiety in interviews. Subjects in the other treatment groups did not differ on this measure. The improvements obtained for the desensitization group in speech and in self-reports about anxiety in interviews were not manifested in more general measures of anxiety. These subjects were not improved relative to subjects assigned to a placebo on measures of anxiety and emotionality that are related to the Big Five dimension of neuroticism.

We presented some of the details of the Paul study in order to indicate that it is possible to perform methodologically sophisticated research assessing the benefits of a particular form of therapy. We also want to use the study to address five additional issues:

1. Paul's study fulfills our criterion for an exemplary study of therapy outcome: it includes a placebo control, improvement is demonstrated on several different kinds of measures, and the improvement is sustained for a two-year period (an unusual length of time for studies of therapeutic outcome in psychology, which rarely extend more than six months after the conclusion of therapy). The study benefits from focusing on a relatively narrow and well-defined behavioral problem. This focus allowed Paul to obtain relatively direct measures of change on a relevant variable. For psychological problems that are less behaviorally defined and focused, it is considerably more difficult to obtain direct behavioral measures of change.

2. Paul did not deal with an actual patient population. His study used solicited subjects, that is, subjects who were asked to volunteer who may have been experiencing a personal problem. Subjects who seek treatment may have more severe problems that are less responsive to psychological interventions. Or, they may be more motivated to improve.

3. Improvement that is clearly present is likely to be manifested in several different ways. If people have really changed, then different methods of assessing change will usually exhibit somewhat comparable results. That was certainly true in the Paul study.

4. When a person solves a problem, the results may generalize, leading to improvements in other situations. Paul's subjects who were assigned to the

desensitization condition reported that they were also less likely to feel anxious in an interview.

5. While changes may occur in specific areas in a person's life and some of these changes may generalize to other related behaviors, it is hard to change broader personality dispositions. Note that Paul's subjects did not exhibit changes in measures of anxiety or emotionality related to neuroticism.

META-ANALYTIC STUDIES OF THE EFFECTIVENESS OF THERAPY

We surely don't want to reach conclusions about outcomes of psychotherapy based on one study. Are there conclusions that are supported by a broader range of studies? There are now thousands of studies of therapy outcome in the literature. Research on this problem was substantially influenced by an analysis of these studies in 1980 by Smith, Glass, and Miller, who were the first to use meta-analytic techniques to investigate therapy outcome. They studied outcomes in several hundred studies in which some form of therapy could be compared with a control group. One difficulty in using meta-analysis to assess therapy outcomes is that the studies investigated are quite diverse. Therapies may differ on several dimensions including the theoretical orientation and training of the therapist, the duration of the therapy, differences in patient populations ranging from psychotics to delinquents to people with marital problems, and differences in how outcomes are assessed. Therefore, a single composite effect size may mask considerable diversity in the effectiveness of different forms of therapy.

On the other hand, some of these differences in therapy can be systematically investigated. The question of whether duration of therapy matters can be answered by examining effect sizes for studies that differ in the duration of therapy. What about therapist credentials—do psychiatrists get better results than psychologists? What about experience—do experienced therapists get better results than inexperienced therapists? What about patient variables—do schizophrenics change more in therapy than manic-depressive patients, and do young patients change more than old patients? What about measures of therapy—are changes larger for self-report than peer ratings? And it is possible to study whether outcomes vary according to some complex combination of variables—does psychoanalytically oriented therapy administered by therapeutically experienced older women for obsessive compulsive male adolescents produce unusually large benefits when the benefits are assessed by self-report indices of improvements? The questions that can be addressed are limited solely by the variations in the existing data base. And while a question as specific as that about the psychoanalytically oriented middle aged female therapist probably cannot be answered with the available data base, with the thousands of studies of therapy outcomes that are available it is possible to answer many detailed questions. It is beyond the scope of this book to attempt a detailed analysis of the large number of meta-analytic investigations of therapy outcomes, but we will venture some broad generalizations.

The Basic Findings

Smith, Glass, and Miller reported an effect size of .81 for all measures of therapy aggregated across all of the studies. This result has been repeatedly supported by additional studies of therapy outcome. Patients assigned to therapy groups are usually found to be improved relative to those assigned to control groups. Differences of this magnitude correspond to a result in which the average patient who had been assigned to a therapy group would be placed at the 75th percentile of patients assigned to the control group on the typical measure of psychological health. So people do get better following treatment.

Smith, Glass, and Miller reported a number of additional findings that have generally been supported in the subsequent literature. Duration of therapy did not affect outcome. Patients who were treated for short periods of time seemed to change as much as patients whose treatments were longer. Notice that this conclusion is based on comparisons across studies. Can you think of a problem here? Perhaps studies of long-term treatment had different kinds of patients than studies of short-term treatment.

Credentials and experience of therapists didn't seem to influence therapy outcome. It didn't matter whether a therapist had a Ph.D or an M.D. or was still in training. Type of therapy also didn't seem to be very important. There was some evidence that behaviorally oriented therapies were slightly more effective than traditional psychotherapies, but for the most part people in therapy tended to get better irrespective of the theoretical orientation of the therapist.

Some Complications and Qualifications

The Smith, Glass, and Miller findings have generally been supported in subsequent meta-analyses. The number .81 is relatively large, exceeding many comparable numbers for the benefits of other kinds of interventions designed to improve physical conditions or educational performance. While it is an impressively large number, it may nevertheless be necessary to develop a more nuanced understanding of its meaning. We believe five qualifications are needed in order for us to understand the relevance of these findings for more general issues in personality research.

Placebo Effects

First, about half of the effect size of therapy is attributable to the placebo effect. Smith, Glass, and Miller found the effect size for psychotherapy versus placebo treatments to be about .40.

Inadequacies of Design in Many Studies

Second, many of the studies of therapy outcome include solicited subjects rather than patients who sought psychotherapeutic services. Many of the studies do not include follow-up data, although those that do often reported that the effects obtained were sustained over time. Follow-ups that were included rarely extended beyond six months. Few of the studies used a variety of measures of outcome, and when several measures were used, the changes were not invariably present on all of them. Some of these shortcomings can be overcome by aggregation of results over many studies—indeed, that is one of the strengths of meta-analysis. On the other hand, there is some truth to the adage, garbage in garbage out. Meta-analyses can only partially overcome the inadequacies of the summarized studies. While there are thousands of studies of therapy outcome, only a small number of them include a variety of outcome measures, placebo controls, and follow-up data for individuals who seek treatment.

Failure of Some Well-Designed Studies to Show Effects

Third, there are some carefully done studies of outcome where the results indicate that therapy is only marginally effective. Elkin et al. (1989) designed a large-scale clinical trial of therapy outcome based on the model used to investigate the effectiveness of medical treatments. In these treatment studies individuals at different clinical locations are randomly assigned to different specified treatments (i.e., a protocol exists that describes the treatment to be used). The results from the several locations are then aggregated in order to discover whether a treatment is effective. This study, sponsored by the National Institutes of Mental Health, was one of the largest studies ever done of therapy outcomes for a psychological treatment.

Patients who were moderately to severely depressed were randomly assigned to one of four treatment groups: a cognitive behavior therapy treatment for depression, interpersonal psychotherapy, a drug treatment (imipramine), or what was called a managed care treatment. The managed care included a pill placebo but it was not a pure placebo condition. Patients were asked to periodically visit their psychiatrists, who refrained from active forms of treatment but who did ask the patients about their progress and reaction to drug therapy. The researchers thought it would be unethical to assign seriously depressed patients to a pure placebo condition that did not allow for monitoring their progress and for intervention in a crisis situation.

The patients were assessed at the end of treatment and then after six months. Two measures were used to assess outcome: a self-report measure of depression, and a rating scale based on a standard psychiatric interview. The results of the study are somewhat complex, depending on the sample analyzed (are patients who drop out to be included?) and the measure used to assess improvement. At the end of treatment, patients assigned to the psychotherapy and the drug treatment were marginally more improved than those in the managed care group. These differences were not always significant, however. The benefits of these two forms of treatment were confined to the subset of patients with the most severe form of depression. At the six-month follow-up, there were no significant differences among the patients assigned to different treatment conditions (Shea, 1994). Active forms of treatment were not superior to managed care.

Lack of Outcome Differences among Therapeutic Treatments

Fourth, there is the dodo bird problem. Everyone has won and all must have prizes! Meta-analyses of therapy usually indicate that all forms of therapy are about equally effective. Sometimes there are subtle differences in outcomes for different kinds of patients or therapies, but the effects are usually small and it is generally accepted that most therapies improve patients and that differences among therapies are small.

There is an additional aspect of the dodo bird problem. Recall that Smith, Glass, and Miller found that it extends to therapist training and experience: it doesn't appear to matter much if the therapist is a psychologist or a psychiatrist, or is relatively experienced or inexperienced. The irrelevance of therapist training extends to whether the therapist is professionally trained or not. Strupp and Hadley (1979) randomly assigned 30 patients who sought therapy to a group treated by professional therapists or to a group treated by college professors who had no formal training in psychology. The patients were typical of those who seek therapy, including people who were highly anxious or depressed. At the end of therapy, there were no significant differences on several measures of change. Meta-analyses of studies contrasting treatment by professionals and treatment by individuals without formal training have concluded that professional training is not related to treatment outcome (Berman & Norton, 1985; Christensen & Jacobson, 1994; Durlak, 1979). People who seek help for psychological problems seem to get better, whether the person who assists them is formally trained or not.

A study by Seligman (1995), however, may challenge this assumption about the irrelevance of the therapist's training. He obtained data from a survey of readers of *Consumer Reports* about the results of therapeutic interventions for a variety of psychological problems. His study has the virtue of including a large sample probably representative of many of the predominantly middle-class patients who seek therapeutic interventions from various professionals. (Did you notice the word *middle-class* in the previous sentence? Does that raise any questions in your mind?) Seligman found that duration of therapy influenced patients' reports about their improvement. Those who had been in therapy for more than six months were more likely to report being improved than those in therapy for less than six months. Those who sought help from psychiatrists, psychologists, and social workers were more likely to report improvement than were those who sought help from marriage counselors and physicians. Figure 12.3 presents a summary of the data he obtained.

Does the *Consumer Reports* survey provide convincing evidence that duration of therapy and training of therapists influence therapeutic outcomes? It is difficult to answer this question. In some respects the survey does provide valuable

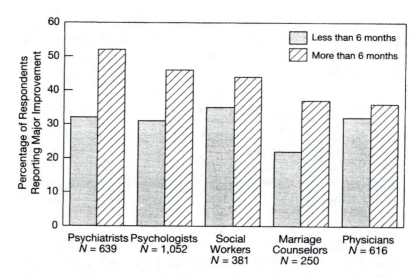

FIGURE 12.3   Percentage of respondents ($n = 2.738$) who reported that treatment "made things a lot better" with respect to the specific problem that led to treatment by psychiatrists, psychologists, social workers, marriage counselors, or family doctors, segregated by those treated for more than and less than six months. (Based on Seligman, 1995) Reproduced with permission of the American Psychological Association.

information about the reactions to therapeutic interventions among a large sample of individuals who are likely to be representative of individuals who seek therapy. On the other hand, the study is not a true experiment in which subjects are assigned at random to different conditions, so it is possible that the kinds of individuals who stay in therapy for long periods or who seek treatment from different kinds of therapists may be systematically different. Quite apart from the issue of experimental control, there are a number of reasons why these findings should be judged cautiously.

Depending on the training of the therapist, from 48% to 64% of patients in long-term therapy (more than six months) reported that therapy did not make things a lot better (see Figure 12.3). If the data for improvements in more general characteristics are examined, such as in work and social domains or other personal domains, the percentage of patients who believed that long-term treatment did not make things a lot better ranged from 63% to 79%. The *Consumer Reports* survey thus indicates that approximately two-thirds of patients in long-term therapy do not believe they have made major improvements in general psychological functioning, and approximately one-half believe that they have not made major improvements in the symptoms that led them to seek therapy in the first place.

Some of the benefits of long-term as opposed to short-term therapy may be attributable to regression toward the mean. It is possible that the test–retest correlation for measures of psychological well-being decreases as the period of time between testing increases. Why? People who are distressed at one time are likely to be still distressed a short time later, but if we measure their distress several months later, the earlier measure is less likely to be as predictive. If this is true, individuals who are in therapy for long periods of time may simply be exhibiting a larger regression toward the mean effect than those in therapy for brief periods. We need a control group of individuals not in therapy to determine the degree to which benefits of long-term improvement are attributable to regression effects that increase with the passage of time.

The *Consumer Reports* survey does not really inform us directly about the benefits of "treatment" with nonprofessionals. It did find that treatment by psychiatrists, social workers, and psychologists was superior to treatment by marriage counselors and physicians, but the latter two groups may not constitute ideal comparison groups. People who seek treatment by marriage counselors are probably seeking help with their relationship with a significant other. Their ability to resolve their difficulties may depend in part on their partner, and poorer outcomes for this group may be the result of the actions of someone not being treated. Patients who seek help from physicians may not have received as much attention and concern as those who were treated by mental health professionals. The *Consumer Reports* survey does not tell us much about the benefits of treatment with individuals who devote time but are not trained as professionals.

There is one finding in the survey that may be relevant. Patients who received help from Alcoholics Anonymous had an average improvement score of 251 on a scale ranging from 0 to 300, a value that was significantly better than that attained by the three groups of patients treated by mental health professionals, whose scores on this scale varied from 220 to 226. Of course, patients in Alcoholics Anonymous are not comparable to those treated by mental health professionals. Why? They are more likely to be alcoholic, for one thing. It is interesting to note that individuals who seek help from Alcoholics Anonymous do not usually receive treatment from trained mental health professionals. Although the *Consumer Reports* survey indicates that mental health professionals are more effective than family physicians, it also shows them to be less effective than nonprofessionally trained counselors who are members of Alcoholics Anonymous. Therefore, the *Consumer Reports* survey does not provide convincing evidence about the benefits of long-term treatment with mental health professionals as opposed to equally intense treatment by individuals without professional training.

How Enduring Are Effects of Therapy?

Fifth, we know relatively little about the enduring effects of psychological treatments. Psychological problems frequently endure for long periods of time and individuals may be at risk for recurrent problems. Lewinsohn, Zeiss, & Duncan (1989) found that the ten-year relapse rate for depression was 89 percent. If a person has experienced one depressive episode, the probability is .89 that he or she will experience one or more other episodes sometime during the next ten years. Mannuzza et al. (1991) compared a group of 18-year-old males from the community with a group of 18-year old males who had been treated in childhood for

hyperactivity or attention deficit disorder. All subjects were interviewed by psychiatrists. Forty percent of the discharged patients were assigned ratings indicative
of the presence of adult forms of attention deficit disorder, versus 3 percent of those
in the control group. Fifty percent of the discharged patients were assigned one or
more labels described in the *Diagnostic and Statistical Manual* of the American Psychiatric Association, versus 16 percent of the control group. These data indicate that
a decade after treatment, subjects with attention deficit disorder are three times
more likely to be diagnosed as exhibiting a psychological disorder than individuals selected at random, and they are sixteen times more likely to be judged as exhibiting signs of an attention deficit disorder.

Vaillant (1983) reported the results of a 50-year longitudinal study of alcoholics. He summarized the results of his study using a one-third rule. After 50
years, one-third of young adult alcoholics are either dead or severely debilitated
from the prolonged effects of abusing alcohol. One-third are nonalcoholic—they
are either abstinent or social drinkers. One-third continue to have problems controlling a tendency to drink. Valliant's summary of the available literature on the
effects of treatment for alcoholism suggests that this one-third rule is as valid for
those who receive treatment as for those who do not. Some alcoholics recover
whether in treatment or not. Many, whether in treatment or not, continue in their
tendency to abuse alcohol.

These data support the notion that people who exhibit psychological problems are likely to find that these problems recur in their lives. From this perspective, there is a mismatch between what we know about the enduring
character of psychological problems and the results of therapy outcome. The
outcome studies inform us about improvements likely to occur six months or,
rarely, two years after treatment. They do not tell us about the effects of treatment ten years or even thirty years later. Yet that is the ultimate test of the effectiveness of therapy. Do those who have received treatment for their problems
have an enduring decrease in the probability of suffering psychological distress
over their life span?

CHANGING PERSONALITY

Genetic Influences

What are the implications of these findings for understanding more general issues
of change in personality attributed to therapeutic interventions? We believe it is
difficult to change personality. Individuals who are prone to experience psychological distress may have an enduring problem that is likely to influence their behavior over the life span. One reason this is so is that genetic influences may
contribute to recurrent problems over long periods of time.

Kendler et al. (1993) studied the heritability of depression in a large sample
of female twins. They measured depression in their sample on two occasions in two

different ways—once by a self-report index, and a year later by a standardized rating scale based on a psychiatric interview. They obtained heritabilities for their self-report index, for their rating scale measures, and for a more comprehensive index based on the combined measures. They found, in agreement with other studies, that depression measured on a single occasion was moderately heritable, with heritabilities close to .40. The heritability of their combined index was .70. MZ twins were more likely to be concordant for depression than DZ twins when concordance measures were based on a comprehensive index of depression than when it was based on a single measure of depression. Kendler et al. noted that depression had generally been thought of as a moderately heritable condition that could be reliably assessed on a single occasion. They argued that their data indicate that depression might better be thought of as a highly heritable condition that is assessed with moderate reliability by data obtained on a single occasion.

This analysis leads us to think about psychological problems in terms of the presence of a disposition that may be expressed at different times over the life span. The influence of genotypes on the underlying disposition may be greater than their influence on any particular measure or manifestation of the disposition. Genes may influence the probability that a person will become depressed in response to various stresses. Whether a person is depressed at any given time may depend on the relationship between genes and environmental stresses. This way of thinking is compatible with the findings reported by Lewinsohn et al. on ten-year relapse rates for depression.

One may influence behavior by influencing the environment that a person encounters. The environmental events that influence depression may be of two types—exogenous and endogenous. **Exogenous events** are events that are not attributable to a person's actions. If a person loses his job because a factory closes, this is an exogenous event. **Endogenous events** are those that occur because of the influence of the person who experiences the event. If a person is fired from a job because he is chronically late, or drunk on the job, or argumentative, then his job loss is, in part, the result of his own actions. The events that create stresses may be complex combinations of endogenous and exogenous events.

Genetically influenced dispositions can contribute to psychopathologies in two ways. First, people may respond to the distresses in their lives differently. Some may experience distressing events without profound disturbance, others may be distressed for long periods of time. For example, some widows and widowers may be able to pick up the threads of their lives without grieving extensively, while others may grieve for years with little evidence of psychological healing. Second, individuals who are prone to experience distress may be more likely, as a result of their own actions, to experience endogenous events that are distressing (Ormel & Wohlfarth, 1991). The tendency to experience stressful endogenous and exogenous events can accumulate over long periods of time. Individuals who respond adversely to stress and who are prone to experience endogenously created stresses in their lives will, over time, be prone to depression.

Co-Morbidity

The propensity to experience psychological difficulties is often a general disposition. Psychological problems are usually co-morbid, that is, the probability that you have one condition increases the probability that you have a second condition. Co-morbidity is more often the rule than the exception among psychopathological conditions. For example, individuals who are bulimic are frequently depressed. Drug addicts often abuse alcohol. People who are depressed are often anxious. Levenson et al. (1988) found that a brief measure of neuroticism correlated .5 with a combined index of all forms of psychological problems obtained ten years later. If people have a generalized disposition toward psychological difficulties, it may be expressed in alternative co-morbid ways at different times over the course of a person's life.

Some of the co-morbidities may be attributable to genetic influences. That is, there may be genotypes that predispose individuals to more than one form of psychological distress and those genotypes may be expressed in different ways at different times. Martin and Jardine (1986) asked a large group of twins to fill out anxiety questionnaires and depression questionnaires. They found that the anxiety score of one member of a twin pair was more predictive of the depression score of the other member for MZ than for DZ twins. How do we interpret this difference? If anxiety and depression are influenced by the same genes, we would expect that genetically identical individuals will be more alike on these two dimensions than genetically different individuals. And that is precisely what Martin and Jardine found.

The existence of co-morbidity among psychopathologies raises questions about the breadth of change in personality attributed to therapeutic interventions. Does therapy profoundly alter the underlying disposition, or does it influence only one of several possible forms of expressing the underlying disposition?

What You Can Change and What You Can't

We have provided some speculations about change and stability in personality and psychopathology and about the results of outcome studies. Let's try to tie these together. People who reach a decision to talk to someone about their problems and who make a commitment to change are likely to become less distressed. It doesn't matter very much who you talk to, or for how long you talk, or what you talk about as long as your talk, or other activities, is focused in one way or another on your psychological problems. At the same time, there is evidence that psychological problems endure in one form or another over the life span. Do the changes that result from talking about your problems substantially alter your lifetime risk for experiencing various forms of psychological distress? We don't really know the answer to this question. One reason therapy may not profoundly alter the disposition to experience distress is that the changes that occur as a result of therapy may be superficial—therapy may alter the *symptoms* of the heritable disposition that may be expressed in different ways in different circumstances and at different times over the course of a person's life without altering the underlying disposition.

In his book, aptly entitled *What You Can Change and What You Can't*, Seligman (1994) introduces the concept of "depth" as a clue to understanding change in personal characteristics. He uses gender identity to illustrate this concept. The core of gender identity, Level I, refers to the sense that one is a man or woman. This belief may occasionally not be congruent with one's external appearance. You can believe that there is a mismatch between your body and your gender identity, and this belief may be so profound and unalterable that your sense of disjunction can be resolved only by surgery to make your body compatible with your identity. Level II refers to your choice of sexual partner, whether homosexual, heterosexual, or bisexual. Level III refers to the particular forms of sexual activity that are eroticized, especially for males. Many males exhibit preferences for particular sexual acts or parts of the female anatomy. Preferences that are unusual or socially prohibited are called fetishes. Level IV refers to gender roles—attitudes and preferences.

Seligman believes that these levels are differentially influenced by events that occur at different times in a person's life. For example, transsexuality and homosexuality may be influenced by genes and by prenatal events; fetishes may derive from experiences in adolescence; cultural norms may influence attitudes, interests, and preferences. Seligman also believes that these characteristics are arrayed in terms of the possibility of change. It is difficult to change one's core sexual identity even when doing so leads to cross-sexual identity. Homosexuality has not been responsive to psychological interventions (we do not endorse the effort to change this form of behavior, we simply note that when people have tried to change this it has not been easy to do so). At least some features of gender role are very responsive to cultural changes. We have lived through changing expectations for educated women. When the authors were undergraduates, women were expected to marry shortly after finishing college, work briefly if at all, and then stay home and care for children. Many women students now believe that they should finish college, work for a lifetime, marry late if they choose to marry, and maintain their careers after their children are born, if they choose to have children. Having experienced the changes, we can attest to their profound nature.

Without endorsing all aspects of Seligman's analysis, we do find the general notion of a hierarchy and the notion of depth attractive. Our therapeutic interventions may be more successful with levels of personality that are peripheral rather than core. We may be able to help individuals deal with crises, help them to overcome some problems such as difficulty with public speaking, and provide them with useful tools to deal with recurrent problems, such as ways of dealing with anger. However, it is somewhat unlikely that we can alter core dispositional tendencies that precipitate crises in a person's life.

Do you find this analysis persuasive? What aspects of your personality do you think you can change and what aspects do you think will endure? Are they arrayed along a continuum of depth? If they are, why do they array themselves this way? Are there alternative ways of thinking about depth?

If psychological treatments do not change core dimensions of personality, does that fact mean that those of us who are predisposed to experience psychological distress (those high on neuroticism) are doomed to continued psychological distress during our lives whether we enter therapy or not? Perhaps this view about the benefits of therapy is too negative. Certainly, it is not a popular view or one encountered in many treatments of this topic in textbooks of personality. Indeed, a frequent criticism of trait theory presented in personality textbooks is that it does not really explain change, especially change in response to therapeutic interventions. In our view, this criticism fails to address a critical question: Do people really change their core personality dimensions? If not, a theory that emphasizes continuity of personality should be praised rather than condemned.

PERSONALITY AND WORK

What do you want to be when you grow up? Surely you tried to answer this question one or more times during your lifetime. What determined your answer? Did your personality influence your occupational choice? Once you enter an occupation, in what ways will your personality characteristics influence your satisfaction and success on the job? Freud noted the importance of two human activities in defining success in life: our ability to work and our ability to love. In this section we relate personality research to the world of work.

THE ORIGINS OF INTERESTS

What kinds of activities do you enjoy? Do you like outdoor activities? Do you like to attend parties where loud music is played and people are likely to drink and take drugs? Do you like to work with your hands and make things? We all enjoy different activities and we have different views of our skills. Perhaps you think you are better at working with people than working with your hands. How do we develop interests and beliefs about our abilities? Are they related to our personality? Are they influenced by genes? Do we develop our interests by being exposed to the activities and interests of our parents?

We can use the techniques of behavioral genetics discussed in chapter 5 to look for answers to these question. Lykken, Bouchard, McGue, and Tellegen (1993) administered a battery of tests designed to measure occupational and leisure-time interests to a large sample of adult MZ and DZ twins who were reared together and to a smaller sample of MZ adult twins who were reared apart. They factor-analyzed their battery of 191 test items and obtained 39 separate factors, which were further factor-analyzed, leading to the development of 11 superfactors that define occupational and leisure activities. Table 12.1 presents a brief description of these superfactors.

**TABLE 12.1   Superfactors Based on the 39 Interest-Talent Factors
(Based on Lykken et al., 1993)**

SUPERFACTOR

1. Intellectual and Educated
    Writer, Reading, Self-Educating, Public Official, Mental Vigor, Musician or
    Performing Artist, **Industrial Arts, Blue-Collar Interests, Socializing**
2. Breadth of Interests
    Travel, Wilderness Activities, Leisure Mean, Vocational Mean, **Home Activities,
    Passive Entertainment**
3. Self-Esteem
    Talent Mean, Well Adjusted, Hardworking and Productive, Mental Vigor, Persuasive
    and Assertive
4. Adventurous versus Harm-Avoidant Occupations
    Risky Activities, the Law, the Military and Police, **Working with Food, Personal
    Service Work**
5. Solidarity
    Blood Sports, Attractive Personality, Interpersonal Warmth, Public Official, **Physical
    Fitness**
6. Artificer versus Athlete
    Arts and Crafts, Industrial Arts, Sewing and Weaving, **Athletics and Coaching,
    Physical Fitness**
7. Religious Orientation versus Sensual Indulgence
    Religious Activities, **Gambling, Swinger**
8. Personal Attractiveness and Charm
    Physical Appearance, Attractive Personality
9. Agrarian Activities
    Working with Animals, Farmer or Rancher, Wilderness Activities
10. Male Physician
    Medical and Dental, Scientist and Explorer
11. Female Physician
    Medical and Dental, Interpersonal Warmth

Note: Negatively loaded factors are shown in boldface. Superfactor scores were computed as the sum of the scaled item responses of the positively loaded factors minus the corresponding sum for the negatively loaded factors, if any. Vocational Mean is the mean score on the 100 vocational interest items: Leisure Mean is the mean interest in the 120 leisure-time activities; Talent Mean is the average self-rating on the 40 talent items.
Reproduced with permission of the American Psychological Association.

The superfactors define broad patterns of occupational and leisure activities. Lykken et al. obtained correlations for their twin samples on individual items as well as on factor scores. These are presented in Table 12.2. The correlations reported in the table have a number of interesting properties. There is relatively little difference between correlations for MZ twins reared apart or together. The correlations for DZ twins are about half the magnitude of those for MZ twins and are lower than the correlations for MZ twins reared apart. The correlations for the factors are slightly higher than those for individual items.

TABLE 12.2   **Mean Twin Correlations for Items, Factors, and Factors Corrected for Instability (Based on Lykken et al., 1993)**

	ITEMS	FACTORS	CORRECTED FACTORS
MZT	.32	.49	.66
MZA	.34	.42	.58
DZT	.14	.23	.30

Note: MZT = MZ reared together; MZA = MZ reared apart; DZT = DZ reared together. Reproduced with permission of the American Psychological Association.

Lykken et al. administered their test battery to a subset of the same subjects three years later, thereby obtaining test–retest correlations for all of their measures. It is possible to obtain a correction for unreliability for these correlations. Fluctuations in interests are excluded from this measure and only those interests that remain relatively constant are included. The correlations reported in Table 12.2 suggest that the heritability of single items in the battery is slightly greater than .3, the heritability of factor scores exceeds .4, and the heritability of stable superfactor scores exceeds .6. How do you interpret these results? We think they indicate that genes influence broad dispositions and that environmental influences are stronger on the specific manner in which these dispositions are expressed.

Note in Table 12.2 that MZ twins reared apart are not substantially different from those reared together and that DZ correlations are not more than half the value of MZ correlations. Both of these results indicate that shared family influences are not a determinant of adult interest patterns.

How might genes influence individual difference in interests? Surely we don't inherent genes for an interest in scientific work (superfactor 10) or for such items as listening to public radio, an experience that wasn't available in our ancestral history. Heritable interest patterns develop from the interaction of genetic dispositions and experiences and the ways in which we select from the cafeteria of experiences that are available to us. Consider an interest in sports. Genes might influence factors relevant to athletic skill such as strength and coordination. Genes might have something to do with whether a boy who is interested in football becomes a tackle or a wide receiver—the physical demands of the positions vary. Personality traits such as conscientiousness and extraversion might relate to the extent to which a person develops athletic skills and the choice of team or individual athletic activities. Cultural opportunities have a great deal to do with the choice of specific activities; for example, soccer is more popular in Europe than in America, and basketball is more popular in urban, predominantly African-American communities than tennis.

The research on the heritability of interests suggests that the influences that shape the way people relate to the world of work begin at the moment of conception. Other research provides evidence that temperamental characteristics first manifested in childhood may influence work-related interests. In chapter 3 we presented two studies that make this point. Harrington and Block demonstrated that it was possible to measure the early manifestations of creativity in 4-year-olds. Caspi found that children who had many intense temper tantrums exhibited frequent job changes as adults. These results indicate that the ways in which individuals relate to the world of work are predictable from behavior patterns that are first manifested in childhood.

Furthermore, interests that are developed in early adolescence may be predictive of the interest patterns exhibited by young adults. Lubinski, Benbow, and Ryan (1995) administered an occupational interest inventory to a sample of intellectually gifted individuals at age 13 and at age 25. These tests were designed to obtain measures of the vocational interests identified by Holland (1985), the psychologist whose work has had the broadest impact on research on vocational interests. Holland identified six vocational interest themes: *Realistic*—an interest in working with gadgets; *Investigative*—scientific interests, especially in mathematics; *Artistic*—an interest in creative expression in the arts; *Social interests*—expressed as an interest in helping professions involving working with people; *Enterprising*—an interest in leadership roles involving economics; *Conventional*—an interest in structured work environments, a setting where the rules of work are defined by others such as an office setting.

Table 12.3 reports the correlations that were obtained in this fifteen-year longitudinal study. Note that the correlations between each of these broad vocational interest patterns tend to be higher with the same interest pattern score than with different interest pattern scores (these results provide evidence for the existence of convergent and discriminant validity—see chapter 2). Realistic, artistic, social, and conventional interests remained relatively stable over a fifteen-year period.

While it is undoubtedly true that vocational interests change, over the life span, sometimes in unpredictable ways, there is at least some continuity, starting from conception to early childhood to adolescence in the development of work-related interests and personal characteristics.

PERSONALITY AND PERSONNEL SELECTION

When education ends, it is time to get a job. How does personality relate to your ability to succeed at the job? Are there any personal characteristics that are predictive of occupational performance? This is the traditional question that is asked by the personnel psychologist. What do I have to know about a person in order to predict his or her success on the job? If there are several applicants for a position, which person should be selected? Are the characteristics that predict success in one job likely to be the same that predict success at another job? How do we determine which people will be successful in a particular job?

Answers are available to some of these questions. Recent research in personnel psychology has relied on meta-analysis to develop generalizations about personality characteristics that are predictive of success in job-related contexts. There

TABLE 12.3   Convergent and Discriminant Test–Retest Correlations of Holland's RIASEC Themes over Fifteen Years (Based on Lubinski et al., 1995)

Time 1[a]	TIME 2[a]					
	R	I	A	S	E	C
Realistic	**.51**	.28	.06	.17	.09	.11
Investigative	.12	**.21**	−.03	.07	.13	.15
Artistic	.04	.05	**.48**	.18	.05	−.02
Social	.14	.11	.19	**.52**	.24	.18
Enterprising	.17	.11	.06	.32	**.27**	.24
Conventional	.24	.16	−.10	.26	.31	**.44**

[a]Time 1 = Age 13; Time 2 = Age 28.

Note: For $rs > .14$, $p < .05$. Convergent test–retest correlations are the diagonal entries presented in bold. ($N = 162$; 48 female, 114 male). RIASEC = Realistic, Investigative, Artistic, Social, Enterprising, and Conventional.

Reproduced with permission of the American Psychological Association.

are at least two general characteristics that are related to success in many different jobs: general intelligence and conscientiousness.

Intelligence

Meta-analyses of the relationship between intelligence test scores and various criteria of occupational success—such as supervisor ratings or measures of job performance both in military and civilian occupations—have consistently reported positive correlations. Perhaps the most interesting studies of this type have used actual measures of work-related performance on tasks that are part of subjects' everyday job responsibilities—for example, an auto mechanic might be asked to repair cars, and the ability to diagnose and repair the defect, as well as the quality of the repair, might be measured. Hunter and Hunter (1984) obtained correlations between a measure of general intelligence and job samples for fourteen occupations. The uncorrected correlations ranged between .3 and .4. When these were corrected for unreliability of measurement, the average correlation was .54. These results indicate that general intelligence predicts about 25 percent of the variance in actual job performance.

In addition to general intelligence, there are many specialized intellectual abilities, such as spatial ability. To what extent are these more specialized abilities predictive of job-related performance? For the most part, it is general intelligence that relates more to success in a job. When attempts are made to predict job-related performance via a battery of intellectual ability tests, the g score (in a sense the aggregate score) is usually more predictive than are narrow ability measures, and after the general score is used for prediction purposes the specialized ability scores usually do not add substantially to the ability to predict job performance.

Olea and Ree (1994) used a variety of ability tests to predict the performance of a large sample of pilots and navigators who were in training. They had six measures of performance for each of the subjects, including four measures of job-related performance. General intelligence was the best predictor. When they added to the equation ability scores and tests of knowledge specifically related to skill as a navigator or pilot, the increments in accuracy of prediction were relatively small. For navigators, the correlation between general intelligence and a composite index of performance was .31; the addition of specific ability scores increased the correlation (actually a multiple correlation) to .34. The addition of specific ability measures to the prediction equation for pilots added to the ability to predict job-related performance; the uncorrected correlation increased from .18 to .32.

These prediction correlations are usually corrected in various ways. It is usual to correct them for unreliability of measurement and sometimes for **restrictions in range of talent** (see chapter 2). This is a correction for the usual practice of excluding those with low scores prior to their selection for training. If you throw out all of the people with low scores, then you reduce the correlation between a measure used to predict a criterion and the criterion.

The exact corrections to be used and the ways in which these corrections are made is a subject of considerable complexity and occasional disagreement among personnel psychologists. We will not consider these issues here. We simply want to indicate that when various corrections were applied to these correlations, the increments in the predictability of criteria related to success as a pilot or a navigator were small. For example, the corrected correlation between general intelligence and an overall competence index for performance as a pilot was .31 and the corrected value of the correlation that included g plus specific abilities and job knowledge measures was .40. This study is representative of the typical finding in research on predicting job performance. General intelligence is a relatively consistent predictor of performance in many occupations, and most of the predictive relationship between a battery of measures of intellectual ability and job performance is attributable to g.

Not only is general intelligence related to performance in a job, it is also related to change in employment. Wilk, Desmarais, and Sackett (1995) studied changes in jobs for a large sample of young adults over a five-year period. The individuals were engaged in full-time work in 1982, when they were between 17 and 23, and later in 1987. Wilk et al. used a classification of job complexity which ranked jobs on a 10-point scale. Level 1 jobs include tending machines, buildings, plants, and animals. Level 10 jobs include chemists, engineers, and physicians. They found that ability measures obtained at the first assessment were predictive of job change for this five-year period. Table 12.4 compares the mean general intelligence score of those who changed to a job of equal, lower, or higher complexity. The data are quite consistent. Individuals whose job in 1987 was classified as being lower in complexity than the job they held in 1982 had lower scores on ability measures than individuals who held a job of equal or higher complexity in 1987. Similarly, those whose job classification in 1987 was higher in complexity than the job they held in

TABLE 12.4 Movement Across Occupational Aptitude Levels from 1982 to 1987 and General Intelligence (Based on Wilk et al., 1995)

1982 Job Complexity Level	1987 JOB-COMPLEXITY LEVEL		
	Lower	Same	Higher
10			
Mean	1.07	1.42	
n	43	28	
9			
Mean	0.63	0.78	1.26
n	84	48	3
8			
Mean	0.79	1.23	1.01
n	40	19	12
7			
Mean	0.06	0.19	0.42
n	305	211	114
6			
Mean	0.31	0.69	0.75
n	77	128	77
5			
Mean	− 0.12	0.08	0.43
n	234	338	130
4			
Mean	− 0.05	0.26	0.27
n	34	30	123
3			
Mean	− 0.47	− 0.19	0.10
n	42	71	119
2			
Mean	− 0.28	− 0.29	0.06
n	72	60	169
1			
Mean		− 0.43	− 0.04
n		524	752

Note: Scores are means for general intelligence scored on a scale in which the mean score = 0, and scores 1 standard deviation above and below the mean = + 1 and − 1, respectively.
Reproduced with permission of the American Psychological Association.

1982 had higher scores on ability measures than those who had a job of equal or lower complexity in 1982.

These results support what is called the **gravitation hypothesis:** over time, individuals tend to find jobs that are commensurate with their initial characteristics. Why do you think this happens? Do employers use tests of ability to select employees, so that individuals with high ability are more likely to obtain jobs that are higher in complexity? Do people who have high ability become bored with jobs that do not require high ability and therefore seek employment commensurate with their ability? Do people with low ability who find themselves in high-complexity jobs get fired? Probably all of these things occur. Of course intellectual ability is only one of several influences on job performance. Many people with high ability are not very successful at jobs, at school, or in their personal lives. Do you have a friend who seems to have high intellectual ability who cannot function even in an academic setting?

Conscientiousness

How is performance on the job related to personality traits? Meta-analyses of studies relating measures of the Big Five to job performance measures—usually supervisor ratings—suggest that conscientiousness is the personality trait that is most consistently related to measures of work-related performance (Barrick and Mount, 1991; Hough et al., 1990). People who obtain high scores on conscientiousness describe themselves as responsible, dependable, persistent, and achievement oriented. Such individuals tend to be rated highly by supervisors and to be viewed as being more competent employees than those who score low on conscientiousness.

The correlations between self-report measures of conscientiousness and job performance ratings are not high, usually close to .2. Why are the correlations low? Here are some possibilities. conscientiousness is just not that important. Job performance is determined by many skills, and the traits measured by self-report measures of personality are just one of many influences. Also the fact that a person is conscientious in general tells us relatively little about his or her tendency to be conscientious in a job-related context; the issue of the cross-situational predictability of trait measures may be important. In addition, perhaps conscientiousness is important but it is not adequately measured by self-reports. Or perhaps conscientiousness is predictive in certain jobs and not in others.

Mount, Barrick, and Strauss (1994) used observer ratings and self-reports to obtain indices of the predictive validity of measures of conscientiousness for a sample of 105 sales representatives. They found that self-report measures of conscientiousness were weakly related to supervisor ratings of performance: $r = .19$, a value typical of those reported in the literature. They had three other ratings of conscientiousness available to them: ratings by the supervisor (both on overall job performance and on conscientiousness), ratings of the employee's conscientiousness by customers, and ratings of conscientiousness by co-workers. In each case, the correlations between ratings of conscientiousness and supervisor ratings of job performance were higher than those for self-report measures of conscientiousness. While self-report measures of conscientiousness accounted for only $3\frac{1}{2}$ percent of the variance in supervisor ratings, a predication equation that included all of the ratings of conscientiousness as well as self-report measures accounted for 20 percent of the variance in supervisor ratings, a value corresponding to a correlation of .45.

These data certainly indicate that ratings of conscientiousness when added to self-report indices of conscientiousness increase the predictability of supervisor ratings. Do these results imply that the hypothetical trait of conscientiousness is strongly related to job performance? Note that all the ratings of conscientiousness in this study are based on observations of performance in a job-related context. Supervisors, co-workers, and customers all rely on their observations of a person on the job. It is not surprising that their ratings relate to supervisor ratings of performance.

Would ratings of conscientiousness based on observations of performance in non-job-related contexts also be good predictors of job-related performance? There is some reason to think that they might. We know that ratings of conscientiousness by others can be used to predict performance in school situations. Digman (1972) obtained a correlation of .70 between a composite rating of conscientiousness by elementary school teachers and high school grades. While Digman's results are longitudinal, indicating that conscientiousness in elementary school is predictive of performance in high school, the initial observation and the performance measure were both obtained in school settings. Would conscientiousness ratings made by spouses or friends who have not observed a person in situations similar to those used as measures of performance be as predictive? We suspect that they might not be as accurate. At the same time, aggregates of different kinds of measures of personality would probably be more predictive in many situations than measures based on a single source of data such as self-reports. From this perspective, the uncorrected correlation of approximately .2, which has been reported as the usual correlation between conscientiousness and job-related performance, is probably a lower-bound estimate of the true relationship between conscientiousness and job performance.

The relationship between conscientiousness and measures of job performance may also depend on the nature of the job. Barrick and Mount (1993) obtained supervisor ratings for 146 middle managers and also obtained a measure of the job autonomy of each manager. Some worked in settings that enabled them to define how their jobs should be performed; others did not. They found that the relationship between conscientiousness and ratings of job performance was influenced by job autonomy. Figure 12.4 presents a summary of these relationships. Conscientiousness is a much more critical determinant of job performance in jobs that are autonomous than in jobs that provide limited opportunity to structure how one will perform the job. Note that Figure 12.4 indicates that conscientiousness is not related to supervisor ratings at all when the job is low in autonomy.

Conscientiousness has been assumed to be the trait that is measured by **integrity tests.** These tests have been widely used to assess responsibility, long-term job commitment, consistency of performance, proneness to violence, moral reasoning, hostility, work ethics, and dependability in the workplace. Ones, Viswesvaran, and Schmidt (1993) reported the results of an extensive meta-analysis of various integrity test measures. They were able to find 222 studies of the validities of these measures, involving over 500,000 subjects. The studies reported correla-

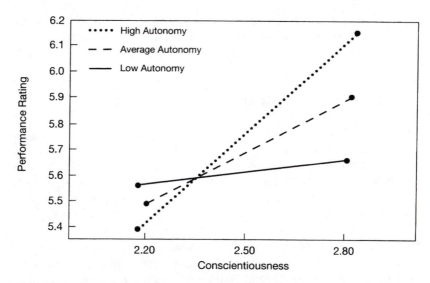

FIGURE 12.4 Performance as a function of conscientiousness in jobs differing in autonomy. (Based on Barrick and Mount, 1993)
Reproduced with permission of the American Psychological Association.

tions between scores on integrity tests and two kinds of measures of job-related performance. For measures of job performance based on ratings and indices of productivity, the average uncorrected correlation between integrity test scores and performance was .21. They estimated that the hypothetical "true" validity of these tests for job performance when the correlation was corrected for restrictions in range of talent and unreliability of measurement was .34. They also studied correlations between integrity test performance and measures of counterproductive behavior such as theft, illegal activities, absenteeism, tardiness, and violence. The mean correlation between integrity tests and unproductive behaviors was .33; the corrected correlation was .47.

Integrity tests may be used to predict the performance of employees and of applicants for jobs, both future performance and concurrent performance. Since scores on integrity tests are unrelated to scores on tests of intelligence, performance on these tests may be combined with performance on tests of general intelligence to predict the performance of potential employees. Ones et al. estimate that the combined predictive validities for various jobs when both intellectual ability and integrity tests are included would range from .47 to .71. While these correlations are based on a number of corrections that have been challenged, there does seem to be good evidence for the notion that the construct assessed by various integrity tests may be added to measures of general intelligence to predict performance in many job settings.

Why do integrity tests work as well as they do? Apparently they are measures of conscientiousness. Individuals apparently differ in their tendency to exhibit responsible or counterproductive behaviors in workplace settings, and this tendency can be assessed by self-report measures or ratings of previous workplace behavior. To the extent that these behavioral tendencies are consistent and enduring over time, they may be used to predict behavior in various jobs.

UNEMPLOYMENT AND SELF-EFFICACY

The world of work encompasses not only job performance but also the reaction to job loss. Individuals who are unemployed may suffer a loss in self-esteem and, with continued unemployment, their belief in their ability to attain a new job may decline (Eden & Aviram, 1993). Eden and Aviram attempted to change job-seeking behavior by increasing self-efficacy. They studied a group of 66 unemployed Israelis. First they obtained measures of generalized self-efficacy by asking subjects to respond to items such as "I give up easily" (those who agreed with this item were assumed to have low self-efficacy). Then they randomly assigned their subjects to a control group and to a group that attended eight workshop sessions designed to provide information about job-seeking skills and to increase self-efficacy beliefs. They found that the length of unemployment among their subjects at the start of their study was correlated $-.74$ with scores on the measure of self-efficacy. Can you explain this finding? Did self-efficacy decline as a result of unemployment? Did individuals with low self-efficacy remain unemployed? Or are both hypotheses correct?

Eden and Aviram also assessed self-efficacy two months after the beginning of training and found that it was increased by self-efficacy training. The training also increased job search activity for individuals who were initially low in self-efficacy. Figure 12.5 reports results for the amount of job seeking activity for individuals in the experimental group (those who received self-efficacy training) and for individuals in the control groups, who differed in initial levels of self-efficacy. The results indicate that those who were initially low in self-efficacy who were assigned to the experimental group exhibited a large increase in their job seeking behavior; the benefits of self-efficacy training were small, however, for individuals who had high initial self-efficacy.

PERSONALITY AND HEALTH

People have always wanted to know why they get sick. All cultures have developed explanations for illness, but it is only recently that scientifically meaningful answers have been provided. To realize how recently, consider that before the 1870s it was not known that microscopic agents can cause sickness. Despite incredible advances in the understanding of illness, we still cannot explain exactly why one person becomes ill and another doesn't. For example, not everyone who is exposed to a virus that "causes" colds actually develops a cold.

Obviously, there are biological factors that influence who gets sick. People with impaired immune systems or constitutional weaknesses in their physiological functioning are going to be at greater risk than people without such physical

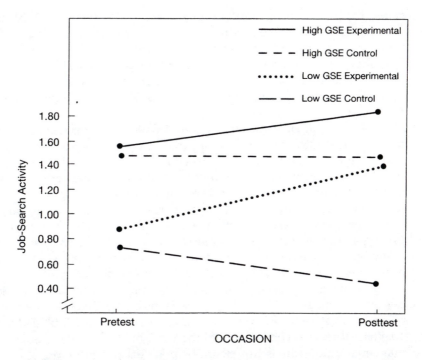

FIGURE 12.5   Change in job-search activity as a function of initial general self-efficacy (GSE) and treatment. (Based on Eden and Aviram, 1993) Reproduced with permission of the American Psychological Association.

problems. We are all familiar with such risk factors as high serum cholesterol, high blood pressure, obesity, and family history of disease. Yet despite the identification of such risk factors, the ability to predict who will get sick and who will not has been only moderately successful. For example, even combining all of the known risk factors for coronary heart disease, the ability to predict new cases is only about 50 percent (Contrada, Leventhal, & O'Leary, 1990).

STRESS AND ILLNESS

One factor of particular interest to psychologists is **stress.** When complex organisms are threatened or challenged, their bodies undergo a complex set of physiological reactions to prepare them to meet the threat or challenge. These reactions involve the autonomic nervous system, the endocrine system, and the immune system. As was discussed in chapter 6, the sympathetic adrenomedullary system responds to *acute* stressors (that is, to stressors that last for a brief duration) while the hypothalamic pituitary adrenocortical system responds to *chronic* stressors (those that endure for long periods of time). Both of these systems are known to influence immune function (Maier, Watkins, & Fleshner, 1994). Environmental stressors can promote disease when stress responses are particularly intense and/or frequent.

Stress reactions can physically damage arterial walls through blood pressure increases, can promote the production of fatty acids and the buildup of plaque on the coronary arteries, and can compromise immune system functioning (Friedman & DiMatteo, 1989). More indirectly, since stress is unpleasant, people may engage in behaviors to reduce stress that are health threatening, such as smoking, overeating, taking drugs, or engaging in various forms of risky behavior (Friedman & DiMatteo, 1989).

Is there evidence that stress promotes illness? Suppose you wanted to test this idea. What would you do? One approach might be to survey a sample of people and ask them about their recent stressful experiences and their current health status. This approach would combine a **retrospective** and **cross-sectional** research strategy. It would be retrospective because you would be asking people to report on their past life events, and it would be cross-sectional because you would be comparing people who are currently healthy with those who are currently ill. Not surprisingly, this approach for establishing cause (stress) and effect (illness) carries many problems. Even if we found that people who report worse health also report more stress, the result would be inconclusive because of many possible confounds. It is possible that not feeling well could bias memory so that less healthy people recall more unpleasant life events. Or perhaps being ill makes one more likely to experience negative life events (for example, poor health might lead to less energy to deal with threats or challenges). Or there might be a "third variable" confound such that certain individuals (for example, poor people) are more likely to experience stress *and* poor health without any causal link between them. There is also the problem of whether self-reports of health are valid (an issue we shall return to later). For these reasons, the most convincing research uses **prospective designs** and objective health outcomes such as mortality rates. In these studies, information on stressful life events is gathered from a sample of healthy people who are then followed for a number of years, during which time their health status is assessed to find out who gets sick and who stays well.

Adler and Matthews (1994) reviewed such studies and noted that they tend to support the idea that stress may play a role in cardiovascular disease and infectious disease, but not in cancer or endocrine diseases such as diabetes. Regarding cardiovascular disease, some studies show a link between stress and coronary heart disease (CHD) while others do not. Surprisingly, one of the most severe stressful life events, the loss of a loved one, does not appear to be related to subsequent CHD mortality (Adler & Matthews, 1994). One form of stress that does seem to be connected to CHD and to cardiovascular diseases (CVD) such as hypertension is **job strain.** Job strain is said to occur in occupations where there are heavy demands on the individual (such as time pressure) but where the individual has little control over his or her work, or where the job requires high effort but provides few rewards. A number of prospective studies carried out in Europe and North America have shown that workers in occupations with high job strain had higher rates of cardiac illness and mortality than those in occupations with low job strain (Schnall, Landsbergis, & Baker, 1994).

Regarding infectious disease, there is some evidence that stress can increase the chances of developing upper respiratory infections (colds or flu) upon exposure to a virus. Linville (1987) found that undergraduates' reports of stressful life events were related to increased reports of respiratory illness two weeks later. Stone, Reed, and Neale (1987) found over a three-month period that negative life events were relatively high three to four days before onset of respiratory illness symptoms. Clover et al. (1989) found that during the flu season more individuals in stressed families developed the flu than did individuals in nonstressed families.

Viral Challenge Studies

One thing you can do with respiratory infections that you cannot do with coronary disease (at least in humans) is to carry out controlled laboratory studies in which you actually try to produce the disease in healthy volunteers. These "viral challenge" studies compare individuals who get sick when given the virus to those who do not get sick when given the same virus. In this case, unlike the field studies described above, one can rule out the possibility that people experiencing greater stress may be more likely to be exposed to the virus in the first place. Stone et al. (1992) and Cohen, Tyrrell, and Smith (1993) exposed volunteers to rhinoviruses and found that subjects reporting more stressful life events were more likely to develop colds than were those reporting fewer stressful life events. These studies suggest that the effects of stress are linked to a response to the infectious agent and are consistent with evidence that stress can lower the immune response (Kiecolt-Glaser & Glaser, 1991).

Stress and Personality

Up to now we have been discussing whether stress can have an impact on health. Note that we have said nothing about personality. Where does personality fit in the stress-to-illness model? We have used the term *stressor* to mean an event that produces stress, but *stress* itself obviously is tied to an interaction between the event and the person's reaction to the event. As Lazarus (1990) stated, stress "depends on an appraisal by the person that the person-environment relationship at any given moment is one of harm, threat, or challenge" (p. 4). So stress can be thought of as having an *objective* aspect and a *subjective* aspect. Differences in the amount of stress people experience can reflect both of these aspects. Consider two individuals who have the same patterns of appraisal. Both would consider being unemployed to be threatening, hence stressful. If the first individual is unemployed while the second is employed, we can say that the individuals differ in their degree of stress for *objective* reasons. On the other hand, consider two individuals who are both unemployed. If the first individual appraises unemployment as threatening but the second individual does not, the first individual will experience more stress than the second individual for *subjective* reasons.

Personality characteristics might dispose individuals to have particularly frequent or intense threatening encounters. For example, a person who does not have the self-discipline to come to work on time is more likely to experience the stress of unemployment than one who is never late. Or certain personality characteristics might dispose individuals to appraise many situations as threatening. For example, an insecure person might believe that every time her boss barks at her she is in danger of losing her job. Thus one way that personality enters into the stress-to-illness connection is by increasing the amount of stress an individual experiences.

There can also be aspects of personality that minimize the amount of stress experienced. Some people may tend to appraise even difficult situations in ways that minimize their feelings of vulnerability. Other people, after appraising a situation as stressful, are often highly motivated to do something about it. But some ways of dealing with stress may be more effective than others. Personality may influence the **coping** strategies people use when faced with stressful situations.

Finally, people's social environments can sometimes serve as a **buffer** against the effects of stressful encounters. People who have meaningful connections to other people seem to be healthier and live longer than those who are socially isolated (House, Landis, & Umberson, 1988; Orth-Gomer, 1994). **Social support** seems to help people deal with stressful encounters. A number of studies have found that subjects exposed to a potentially stressful situation show less intense physiological stress responses if another person is present giving them encouragement and support (Gerin, Pieper, Levy, & Pickering, 1992; Kamarck, Manuck, & Jennings, 1990; Lepore, Allen, & Evans, 1993). Personality factors may play a role in whether one has a social network that can provide support in times of stress.

TYPE A, HOSTILITY, AND HEART DISEASE

Any personality trait that leads people to experience frequent or intense stress can potentially increase risk of illness. Consider these two individuals. John is laid back, takes life as it comes, knows how to relax as well as how to work hard, and prefers cooperating with people to competing with them. When John is stuck in traffic, he figures there's nothing he can do about it and listens to some music on the radio. Andrew is hard-driving, impatient, a workaholic, and acts as though life were an endless struggle to come out on top. When Andrew is stuck in traffic, he curses, blasts his horn, and feels tense and irritable.

Which of these people is more likely to get a heart attack? We have little doubt that you chose Andrew. Andrew typifies what is known as a **Type A** individual: excessively achievement oriented, competitive, never feeling that there is enough time, and easily angered. Andrew is more likely to experience frequent and/or intense stress responses than John (who would be considered a **Type B**). According to one view of Type A behavior, Andrew has a strong need to maintain control over his environment (Glass, 1977). Any situation that threatens his sense of control is appraised as threatening and calls forth a vigorous attempt to regain control. Because of his need to maintain control, Andrew also puts himself in objectively stressful circumstances (for example, by working under pressure and never taking vacations).

The Type A pattern was identified (and named) by two cardiologists who noticed that their (cardiac) patients seemed to differ from patients with other kinds of illnesses (Friedman & Rosenman, 1974). In order see if this pattern was really connected to heart disease, they developed a method for categorizing individuals as Type A or Type B and then carried out a prospective study in which 3,500 healthy men were followed for $8\frac{1}{2}$ years to see which of them developed coronary heart disease. The results of this seminal study (the Western Collaborative Group Study) indicated that Type A men were about twice as likely as Type B men to develop symptoms such as angina pectoris (chest pain) or to have myocardial infarctions (MI).

Since then many other studies have been carried out to explore the relationship between Type A and heart disease. In some of these, Type A was assessed using Friedman and Rosenman's **Structured Interview** (SI) technique. In the SI, carefully trained interviewers ask subjects a series of questions concerning competitiveness, achievement striving, time urgency, and hostility. It is not the content of subjects' answers to these questions that is of most importance. Rather, the interviewers attempt to elicit examples of Type A behavior from the subjects, by challenging their answers, deliberately speaking slowly, and using a variety of other techniques that would drive a Type A person up the wall. Under these conditions, Type A individuals interrupt interviewers before they can finish their sentences, speak with loud, "explosive" utterances, clench their fists, and express hostility directly (by making rude comments) or indirectly (by being sarcastic, condescending, or bored).

Type A has also been measured by means of a self-report questionnaire, the **Jenkins Activity Survey** (JAS; Jenkins, Zyzanski, & Rosenman, 1979). The advantage of a self-report measure is that it is relatively easy and cheap to use. However, the two measures do not correlate highly enough to consider them alternative measures of the same underlying construct. (This situation may remind you of the one regarding the measurement of need for Achievement using self-reports and the TAT, discussed in chapter 8.) Further evidence that the two methods are not equivalent is that the relationship between the JAS and CHD is much weaker than between the SI and CHD (Friedman & DiMatteo, 1989; Matthews, 1988). What may surprise you is that even when the SI is used, the evidence linking Type A to CHD is not very strong. Prospective studies that used **hard outcomes** (CHD mortality and diagnosed MI) do not show greater risk for Type A than for Type B individuals (Adler & Matthews, 1994). For **soft outcomes,** such as self-reports of chest pain, individuals classified as Type A do seem to be at greater risk than those classified as Type B.

Does this mean that the common belief that Type As are coronary prone is incorrect? Yes and no. What has become increasingly clear is that it is a mistake to think of Type A as a coherent, organized behavior pattern. Instead, each aspect or component of Type A should be thought of as a separate personality characteristic. When the various responses to the SI are examined separately, the hostility component (called **potential for hostility**) appears to play a much more important role in coronary risk than do other components (such as competitiveness, achievement striving, and time urgency) (Adler & Matthews, 1994; Dembroski et al., 1989; Rosenman, Swan, & Carmelli, 1988; Smith, 1992). As a result, there has been a great deal of recent emphasis on trying to understand the nature of hostility and how it might increase risk of coronary heart disease.

Hostility and Health

As was true for Type A itself, the study of hostility is complicated by the fact that interview and self-report measures do not correlate very highly. As was also true for Type A, the main self-report measure of hostility, the Cook-Medley Hostility Scale, tends to show weaker relationships with CHD than does the hostility score derived from the SI (Adler & Matthews, 1994; Smith, 1992). Also like Type A, hostility itself is a multifaceted concept. In some people it is primarily an internal feeling of resentment, frustration, dissatisfaction, and irritability. For these people, hostility may be part of their general tendency toward negative affectivity (the neuroticism factor of the Big Five). Other people are hostile as part a "dog-eat-dog" view of the world. They are cynical, suspicious, and expect the worst of others (Barefoot, 1992). They often express their hostility toward others overtly. This type of hostility is related to low scores on the Big Five agreeableness factor (Suarez et al., 1993).

There is some evidence that this second type of "antagonistic" hostility may be the kind that puts people at greater risk for CHD (Suarez & Williams, 1990; Suls & Wan, 1993). The constant vigilance that this attitude produces, combined with frequent anger experiences, may cause particularly strong and frequent stress responses (Williams et al., 1985). Such individuals may not be aware of their hostile attitudes. Kneip et al. (1993) found that self-reports of hostility did not predict the presence of CHD in radiological scans of the coronary arteries; however, ratings of hostile attitudes by the subjects' spouses did predict CHD. This may be part of the reason why actual behavior observed during the SI is more predictive of CHD than are self-reports.

From Hostility to Heart Disease

Is there evidence that hostile people show the kinds of stress reactions that could lead to CHD? One way to study this question is to put people into a potentially stressful situation in the lab while monitoring physiological responses such as blood pressure. A meta-analysis of such research suggested that physiological differences between people low and high on hostility may be most evident when the stressful situations involve interpersonal conflict, harassment, or provocation (Suls & Wan, 1993).

The importance of both situations and dispositions to blood pressure responses to a challenging task was demonstrated in a study by Suarez, Harlan, Peoples, and Williams (1993). Women who scored in the top or bottom quartile of the Cook-Medley Hostility Scale were instructed to solve anagrams under one of two conditions. In the high-harassment condition, the women trying to solve the puzzle were badgered by a female experimenter, who said things like "Stop mumbling, I can't understand your answer" and "You are getting paid to be in this experiment!" In the low-harassment condition, the experimenter let the subject do the task without making any comments. As Table 12.5 shows, the women who scored high on the hostility questionnaire had higher systolic blood pressure during the harassment than women who were low in hostility.

These findings and others like them illustrate the point made frequently in this book: personality dispositions do not operate in a vacuum. People high in hostility will not necessarily have larger stress responses than those low in hostility. In fact, they will do so only when the situation engages their hostile disposition. In a controlled laboratory study, the experimenter determines who gets into which situation. In real life, people often determine this themselves. Individuals with an antagonistic, hostile outlook are more likely to interpret other people's behavior as "harassment," and because of their own hostile behavior, they are more likely actually to bring forth such behavior from others.

To summarize, antagonistic hostility appears to play a more important role in the etiology of coronary heart disease than does the traditional Type A behavior pattern. The mechanism that is said to link hostility to disease has been labeled "personality-induced hyperreactivity" (Suls & Rittenhouse, 1990). In this view, hostile people appraise many situations as threatening and respond in ways that elevate health-damaging sympathetic and neuroendocrine stress reactions. Laboratory research has shown that hostile people often respond more intensely in situations of interpersonal conflict.

It is still not clear whether such reactions lead to heart disease. It is important to note that the difference between those who are high versus low in hostility in, for example, systolic blood pressure, is not very great. Some researchers have

TABLE 12.5 Cardiovascular Responses as a Function of Hostility and Harassment Condition (Based on Suarez et al., 1993)

	HIGH HOSTILITY	LOW HOSTILITY
Harassment	129.7	121.4
No harassment	119.8	118.9

Reproduced with permissioin of the American Psychological Association.

questioned whether differences of this magnitude are really enough to place highly hostile individuals at greater risk for heart disease. Laboratory studies focus on the *size* of the stress reaction because intensity is easy to measure in the typical experiment, in which subjects are studied on only one occasion. But in the real world the *frequency* of stress responses may be more important than their intensity (Contrada, Leventhal, & O'Leary, 1990; Suls & Rittenhouse, 1990). Recent advances in ambulatory monitoring, in which physiological measures are recorded as individuals go about their normal everyday activities, may help us to understand better the role of personality in heart disease (cf. Ewart & Kolodner, 1993).

The "personality-induced hyperreactivity" model is not the only one possible. Perhaps there are other ways in which hostility becomes a risk factor for heart disease. Earlier we mentioned that social support sometimes appears to help people deal with stressful situations. Hostile people appear to have lower levels of social support than nonhostile people (Smith, 1992). A recent study by Lepore (1995) also suggests that hostile, cynical people may not benefit from social support in the same way that nonhostile individuals do. Subjects were given a stressful social task (making an impromptu speech) with a supportive person present or with no support. For subjects high in cynicism, the presence or absence of social support made no difference in their blood pressure responses; for subjects low in cynicism, blood pressure was substantially lowered when a supportive person was present (see Figure 12.6).

THE BIG FIVE TRAITS AND HEALTH

The Type A construct was invented by physicians on the basis of their observations of patients' behavior. The hostility construct was derived from measures designed primarily for other purposes on the basis of empirical results linking hostility to illness. Neither of these constructs is clearly linked to existing taxonomies of personality. Recall that systems such as the Big Five are intended to provide some order to a field that has historically had a chaotically large number of constructs. The case of hostility indicates why linkage to a system like the Big Five is desirable. At least some of the conceptual confusion surrounding the hostility construct may be resolved if we can show how some aspects of hostility are linked to neuroticism and other aspects to agreeableness.

Recall that the Cook-Medley Hostility Scale is correlated with both neuroticism and agreeableness. N does not appear to be a risk factor for heart attack, but it is associated with *complaints* about chest pain (Costa & McCrae, 1987; Smith & Williams, 1992). Watson and Pennebaker (1989) found that N was related to a wide variety of health complaints, but not to objective indicators such as high blood pressure. Anxious, worried people tend to worry about all sorts of things, including their health (Stone & Costa, 1990). To the extent that any measure of hostility also measures N, that measure is unlikely to correlate with hard outcomes such as

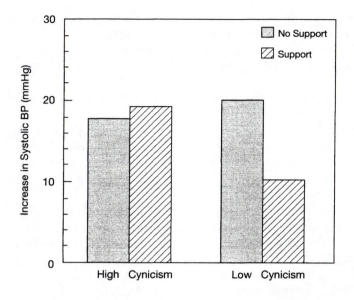

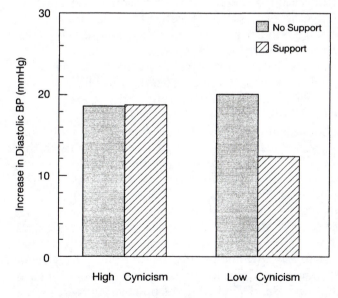

FIGURE 12.6 Interactive effects of social support and cynicism on changes in blood pressure. (Based on Lepore, 1995) Reproduced with permission of the American Psychological Association.

mortality or myocardial infarction (Smith, 1992), but it may correlate with soft outcomes such as angina pectoris (reports of chest pain). About 20 percent of individuals who complain of angina and undergo invasive procedures such as angiograms to check the state of their coronary arteries turn out *not* to have any coronary disease (Mayou, 1989). However, such patients do have high scores on measures of neuroticism (Beitman et al., 1989, cited in Smith and Williams along with others). People high in N are likely to experience more distress and to report more illness symptoms just because they *are* high on N (Depue & Monroe, 1986)! This tendency to complain about symptoms in the absence of underlying disease is one reason why self-report measures of illness can be a problem in research on stress and illness.

There are no prospective studies of health that use the Big Five. It takes many years to carry out a long-term prospective study, and measures designed to assess the Big Five have not been around for very long. As a result, we are "stuck" with measures used at the onset of such studies, measures that were not designed to measure the Big Five. Nevertheless, it is sometimes possible to use "old" personality tests, to examine their items, and to create measures that approximate more contemporary personality constructs.

This was the strategy used by Friedman, Tucker, Tomlinson-Keasey, et al. (1993) to examine whether personality measured in childhood predicted the number of years a person lived. Subjects were about 11 years of age in the 1920s when they entered the Terman Life-Cycle Study. They had been rated by parents and teachers and had filled out a variety of personality tests. Friedman et al. attempted to map the tests and ratings used in the original assessment onto the Big Five system to see if those subjects who were still alive in 1986 differed in their personalities from those who had died. They found that at least one Big Five trait was associated with longevity, and that trait was conscientiousness. In contrast, there was no association for measures linked to neuroticism, extraversion, or intelligence.

Why might conscientious people live longer then less conscientious people? In a cross-sectional study, Booth-Kewley and Vickers (1994) found that conscientiousness as measured by the NEO-PI correlated positively with "wellness behaviors" (e.g., exercising and eating healthfully) and with "accident control" (e.g., knowing first aid and fixing hazards around the home) and negatively with "traffic risk taking " (e.g., speeding, jaywalking). So one obvious possibility is that people low in conscientiousness, because they are more impulsive and less careful, are more likely to die from accidents or injury than are more conscientious people. Another is that they are less likely to take good care of themselves.

Friedman, Tucker, Schwartz, et al. (1995) checked the cause of death of deceased subjects in the Terman sample. They found no greater tendency of subjects low in conscientiousness to die as a result of accidents or injury than subjects high in conscientiousness. In fact, there was no difference in cause of death between subjects high and low in conscientiousness. Those low in conscientiousness did have worse health habits in that they drank and smoked more; however, conscientiousness was a significant predictor of longevity even when the difference in drinking and smoking was statistically controlled.

We are left with a puzzle. Conscientiousness is the strongest predictor of longevity; why this is so remains a mystery. In attempting to understand this relationship, we can focus on either the low or the high end of the conscientiousness continuum. One possibility suggested by Friedman, Tucker, Schwartz, et al. (1995) is that low conscientiousness may be associated with a generally poor social environment, such as having more problems in school. In this view, low conscientious-ness is associated with increased stress. Another possibility they suggest is that high conscientiousness may somehow protect individuals from the ravages of stress. Perhaps highly conscientious people are better able to cope with the stressors to which all people are inevitably subjected.

COPING WITH STRESS

Up to now we have focused on how personality might place people at risk for illness. There are things people think, feel, or do that increase the chances they will experience stress. Personality may be related to the probability of feeling stressed. One can also ask whether personality can protect people's health by leading to effective coping. In this view, stressful life events are considered something everyone encounters from time to time, and the question is whether there are ways of dealing with them that may have health-protecting consequences.

Coping refers to various ways that individuals deal with stressful situations. Lazarus (1990) defines coping as "constantly changing cognitive and behavioral efforts to manage specific external and/or internal demands that are appraised as taxing or exceeding the resources of the person" (p. 99). For many years, Lazarus and his colleagues have studied the ways individuals attempt to deal with stress (Lazarus, 1966; Lazarus & Folkman, 1984). On the basis of factor analyses of people's reports of how they dealt with recent stressful encounters, Lazarus and his colleagues developed the Ways of Coping Checklist (Folkman, Lazarus, Dunkel-Schetter, DeLongis & Gruen, 1986), which consists of eight scales (Table 12.6).

Emotion-Focused and Problem-Focused Coping

At a broader conceptual level, Lazarus sees two types of coping: **problem-focused coping** (dealing with the cause of the problem) or **emotion-focused coping** (dealing with the feelings about the problem). In any stressful encounter, people may try to deal with the source of the stress itself. For example, if you are unemployed,

TABLE 12.6 Scales of the Ways of Coping Checklist

1. Confrontive coping ("I stood my ground and fought for what I wanted.")
2. Distancing ("I went on as if nothing had happened.")
3. Self-control ("I tried to keep my feelings to myself.")
4. Seeking social support ("I talked to someone who could do something concrete about the problem.")
5. Accepting responsibility ("I criticized or lectured myself.")
6. Escape–avoidance ("I wished the situation would go away or somehow be over with.")
7. Planful problem solving ("I knew what had to be done, so I doubled my efforts to make things work.")
8. Positive reappraisal ("I found new faith.")

you might go to an employment agency, get additional training, or ask your Aunt Bertha for a job in her boutique. In all of these cases, you would be taking action to reduce the stress by solving the underlying problem. An alternative is to try to change how you feel. An unemployed person might get involved in a hobby, start drinking heavily, daydream about winning the lottery, or deny that the situation is really bad. Here the attempt is to reduce stress by making oneself feel better.

Most people use both problem and emotion-focused coping to some degree or another. Summarizing years of research on stress and coping, Lazarus (1990) contends that most people use all eight forms of coping in every stressful encounter. Is one form of coping better than another? Lazarus's view is that whether or not a coping strategy is effective depends on the nature of the situation and the person's resources. For example, when a situation is uncontrollable, effective emotion-focused coping may be the only way to reduce stress. In an experimental study in which subjects played the parts of hostages in an FBI training session, emotion-focused coping, particularly avoiding thinking about the situation, was most effective in minimizing stress (Strentz & Auerbach, 1988). In this situation there was little the subjects believed they could do to change the situation. In contrast, emotion-focused coping has often been found to be ineffective, and even to increase stress, in many other types of situations (Aldwin & Revenson, 1987).

Coping Strategies

Even though people typically use a variety of coping strategies, different individuals use some strategies more than others across a range of stressful situations. Emotion-focused coping has shown substantially higher cross-situational correlations than has problem-focused coping, leading Lazarus to conclude that problem-focused coping is more sensitive to contextual factors while emotion-focused coping is more influenced by personal factors (Lazarus, 1990).

The role of personality in influencing coping strategies was demonstrated in the Strentz and Auerbach (1988) hostage study. Subjects with an **external locus of control** were more likely to use emotion-focused coping than were subjects with an **internal locus of control.** Locus of control refers to a personality dimension that determines whether one believes that the important things that happen are either mostly under one's own control or mostly out of one's hands. It is not surprising that people who believe there is little they can do to influence outcomes are more likely to use emotion-focused coping.

OPTIMISM

Is there evidence that certain personality characteristics can protect people from stress? One personality dimension that has been linked to favorable psychological or health outcomes in the face of stressful situations is **optimism** (versus pessimism). Scheier and Carver (1993) describe *optimists* as people who generally have positive expectancies for their future, who believe that good things will generally occur. Because of this belief, they tend to actively engage situations that might be stressful rather than avoiding them or withdrawing from them. Pessimists believe the opposite and do the opposite in the face of stressful situations.

Optimism is measured by an eight-item test called the Life Orientation Test (LOT), which includes items such as "I always look on the bright side of things" and "I'm a believer in the idea that 'every cloud has a silver lining.'" The test–retest correlation of the LOT over three years was .69, suggesting that optimism is a fairly stable trait. Indeed, Scheier and Carver note that optimists tend to remain optimists even when unexpectedly bad things happen to them.

Optimists and pessimists differ in the types of coping strategies they say they typically use. Table 12.7 shows the five highest correlations between the LOT and scales from the COPE, a self-report measure of coping strategies developed by Carver, Scheier, and Weintraub (1989). The LOT is keyed so that high scores indicate optimism, low scores pessimism. These correlations show that optimists tend to report using active strategies, whereas pessimists tend to report withdrawal strategies.

Do these differences in coping make a difference in health outcomes? Undergraduate students filled out the LOT and a measure of physical symptoms twice during one semester. Those who scored relatively high in optimism reported fewer illness symptoms during the final exam period than those scoring low in optimism (Scheier & Carver, 1985). It is possible that this difference in self-reported symptoms is just a response bias; perhaps, like people high in neuroticism, pessimists tend to recall and report more symptoms than do optimists.

Scheier and Carver (1985) controlled for this possibility by taking into account the number of symptoms reported by the students at the time they first filled out the LOT. By statistically controlling for any differences between optimists and

TABLE 12.7   Correlations Between Optimism (vs. Pessimism) and Coping Strategies (Based on Carver et al., 1989)

Active coping   +.32
("I take additional action to try to get rid of the problem")

Planning   +.25
("I try to come up with a strategy about what to do")

Positive reinterpretation and growth   +.41
("I look for something good in what is happening")

Denial   −.27
("I refuse to believe that it has happened")

Behavioral disengagement   −.34
("I give up the attempt to get what I want")

Reproduced with permission of the American Psychological Association.

pessimists at Time 1, Scheier and Carver were able to show that the difference in symptom reporting at Time 2 (the final exam period) was not due to a response bias. Nevertheless, as we have noted before, self-reports of symptoms are not the same as verified illnesses. Unfortunately, there is little convincing data one way or another about the influence of optimism on "hard" health outcomes.

Coping with Illness

Many health psychologists take a broader view of health than just the absence of sickness. A great deal of attention has also been paid to how people cope with illness. Indeed, personality may play a more important role in how people deal with illness than in whether they get sick in the first place. Personality may influence how quickly people recover and how they live their lives in the presence of chronic illness. Two studies suggest that optimism may promote positive outcomes in such situations. Scheier et al. (1989) studied a group of middle-aged men who were recovering from coronary bypass surgery. Ratings by hospital personnel indicated that optimists tended to recover from the surgery faster than pessimists. Six weeks after the operation, optimists were more likely to say that their lives had returned to normal.

A study of women who had surgery for breast cancer showed a similar pattern (Carver et al., 1993). Self-reported emotional distress was measured before surgery, as was the LOT, and then immediately after surgery, and again at three months, six months, and twelve months after surgery. The correlation of the LOT with emotional distress prior to surgery was −.56. The correlation between the LOT and the twelve-month follow-up was almost exactly the same: −.57. When the level of distress at six months was controlled, the correlation between the LOT and distress at twelve months was −.32. This pattern of correlations indicates that self-reports of emotional distress are highly correlated with optimism–pessimism. Since emotional distress is a key aspect of neuroticism, it is fair to say that part of what the LOT measures is neuroticism. However, by statistically taking into account prior emotional distress (at six months), Carver et al. showed that optimism is related to lower distress above and beyond the influence of neuroticism.

Having shown that optimism is related to lower levels of distress in this sample, Carver et al. asked the reasonable question, Why? Recall that optimism is supposed to help people deal with stressful situations through the specific coping styles used. In order to see if that was the case, Carver et al. asked the women to indicate which coping processes they had used in the past month. They then carried out a path analysis (see chapter 2) to see whether the effects of optimism on emotional distress were due to differences in coping strategies. This analysis indicated that the correlations between the LOT and distress at the various follow-up periods were due almost entirely to the different coping strategies used by optimists and pessimists. For example, optimists used humor and acceptance more than pessimists did, and both of these were related to reduced distress at the six-month follow-up; pessimists used denial and behavioral disengagement more, and these were related to increased distress at the six-month and twelve-month follow-up, respectively.

Personality as a Buffer Against the Effects of Stress

Dispositional optimism (or pessimism) does seem to play a role in one's psychological adjustment to stress, including the stress of illness. It is less clear whether optimism actually prevents people from getting sick when they are subject to stressful situations. Another personality construct that has been assumed to protect people from the ill effects of stressful events is **hardiness.** Kobasa (1979; 1982) developed the concept of hardiness to capture the idea of a mature, growth-oriented approach to life similar to that discussed by many humanistic psychologists such as Carl Rogers. Hardiness includes three components: commitment, control, and challenge. Individuals who score high on measures of hardiness are committed to what they are doing; they feel a sense of purpose and meaning in their lives that leads them to persist even when under pressure. Individuals who score low on measures of hardiness are alienated, find little meaning in their activities, and tend to be passive in the face of adversity. People high in hardiness also believe their actions can influence the outcomes of events; that is, they have an internal locus of control. People low in hardiness, in contrast, often feel helpless and overwhelmed because of their belief that there is little they can do to influence what happens to them (external locus of control). People high in hardiness see change as challenging rather than threatening. What a person low in hardiness views as threatening, a person high in hardiness views as an opportunity for personal growth and a normal part of living. Kobasa (1979) maintained that these three "stress-resistent resources" lead hardy people to appraise situations as less stressful and to engage in coping strategies that minimize the ill effects of stressful encounters.

Is hardiness related to health? A number of studies indicate that individuals high in hardiness report fewer illness symptoms than do people low in hardiness (as reviewed by Funk, 1992). Most of these studies have been retrospective, and none has included verified hard outcomes such as mortality or diagnosed myocardial infarctions. Furthermore, it is unclear whether hardiness actually buffers the ill effects of stress or whether it directly affects illness reports regardless of the presence of stressful events. Such direct effects might reflect the presence of neuroticism in measures of hardiness. Examination of various hardiness scales indicates that the majority of items seem to ask about low rather than high hardiness. For example, the measure of "commitment" could just as well, or perhaps even more, be considered a measure of "alienation." Correlations of hardiness with neuroticism scales usually range from .4 to .5, indicating a substantial degree of overlap.

PERSONALITY AND HEALTH: SOME FINAL THOUGHTS

There are two ways of thinking about personality and health. On the one hand, personality may be a risk factor for illness, either through direct physiological effects (e.g., increased blood pressure responses) or indirect behavioral effects (e.g., smoking). There is compelling evidence that hostility may function as such a risk factor. On the other hand, personality may play a protective function in the face of stressful life events. Stress may increase the chances that a person will become ill. Personality characteristics such as optimism and hardiness are associated with coping strategies that tend to reduce stress, and consequently, ought to protect against the ill effects of stress. However, there is not yet convincing evidence that such personality characteristics play such a protective role, perhaps in part because of the lack of relevant prospective studies using hard health outcomes.

Because personality traits are treated as continua, it is often unclear whether the high scores are more related to health, whether low scores are more related to health, or whether both ends of a dimension are related to health. For example, conscientiousness seems to be an important predictor of longevity. Is this so because careful, highly conscientious people do things that prevent them from dying or because low-conscientious people do things that cause them to die? Clearly we need more information about how personality influences health and illness.

13

Conclusion: Personality in the Twenty-First Century

In this book we have reviewed research on traits, genes, affects, thoughts, and self-concepts, but we have said relatively little about the ways in which different approaches to personality may be combined. We believe that future progress in personality research depends on our ability to combine different techniques and methods in order to develop a more coherent and integrated view of personality. We cannot really anticipate future directions of personality research—we do not have a clear crystal ball—but we will sketch some directions that we think are desirable.

BIOLOGICAL INTEGRATION

Of all of the ways in which personality psychology might evolve in the twenty-first century, we think that the clearest prediction that can be made is that biological perspectives will be increasingly important. The availability of neuroimaging techniques to observe brain processes is enhancing the knowledge of the relationship of brain and behavior. These advances, combined with a better understanding of neurochemistry, are likely to contribute to the development of more sophisticated models of the biological basis of individual differences.

We are likely to witness the development of research that relates three kinds of biological approaches to personality. Research based on twins and adoption studies is now widely accepted as providing evidence for genetic influences on personality. This research will be used in attempts to discover the specific genes that are related to individual differences in personality. While most personality dimensions are likely to be tied to several different genes and their combinations, making it difficult to determine the influence of individual genes, progress in mapping the locations of genes that influence various neurotransmitters is likely to lead to the discovery of individual genes that influence personality dimensions. This research may integrate several different biological approaches to personality. Specific genes that influence individual differences will influence the structure and functioning of the brain. In order for us to begin to understand their role (and to discover their locations), it will be necessary to develop concepts that relate genes to brain functioning, and to relate brain functioning to personality characteristics. This type of research should ultimately lead to a better understanding of the biological basis of personality. It should also be clear that this research will require collaboration among scientists trained in molecular genetics, brain sciences, and personality (or individuals who are trained in several relevant scientific disciplines).

Although we believe that there will be progress in understanding genetic and biological influences on personality, we do not believe that a reductionist model in which personality is understood in biological terms is possible. While individuals may differ in their personalities for genetic and biological reasons, the influence of these characteristics can be understood only within specific social contexts. Personality characteristics are embedded in a particular social and historical context. Caspi (in press) discusses the following example: Jones (1981), in a study of men born in the 1920s, found that low ego control in adolescence predicted midlife drinking problems. Block, Block, and Keyes (1988) studied individuals born in the 1960s and found that children with low ego control at ages 3 and 4 were likely to be marijuana users at age 14. This example illustrates something that is both general and historically specific. Those with low ego control are more likely to be attracted to the use of drugs, irrespective of the historical era in which they were born, but the drug of choice is clearly determined by the availability of different drugs in different historical periods.

Historical changes may also influence phenotypes for genetically influenced traits in profound ways. We know that average levels of intelligence have increased in many different countries around the world (Flynn, 1984; 1987). We don't really understand these changes, however; they may be attributable to better educational opportunities or perhaps to changes in nutrition. Whatever their cause, it is clear that the phenotype for intelligence has increased substantially over the last 50 years.

There is also evidence that depression and a variety of other mental health problems are increasing (Achenbach & Howell, 1993; Lewinsohn, Rohde, Seeley, & Fischer, 1993). These changes cannot be understood without a considerion of changes in our culture that may increase the probability of mental illness for those who are genetically vulnerable. These changes cannot be understood in biological terms. While a genetic and biological theory of individual differences may provide us with an understanding of the characteristics that make a person vulnerable to various stresses, we shall have to understand the kinds of stresses that occur in a particular culture in order to understand how genotypes influence phenotypes.

CROSS-METHOD INTEGRATIONS

We have considered various approaches to measuring personality, such as traits, motives, and attributions. Personality psychologists use various methods to measure personality and interpret their results using various theories. At some point we shall have to find ways of integrating different research traditions. We believe this is a promising direction for personality research. We will discuss three different approaches to the integration of different research traditions.

Traits and Motives

In chapter 8 we reviewed research using the TAT to measure individual differences in motivation. How do these kinds of measures relate to traits?

John, Winter, Stewart, Klohnen, Duncan, and Peterson (1993, as reported in Winter, 1996) obtained measures of affiliation motivation and extraversion from college women. They interviewed these women twenty years later and obtained information about divorce and about difficulties in intimate relationships. They found that affiliation motivation and extraversion were not related to each other. Winter indicates that affiliation motivation may be thought of as a measure of goals or desires and that extraversion refers to behavioral style or tendencies. Individuals who are high in both affiliation motive and extraversion might both desire interpersonal relationships and have behavioral tendencies and skills that are compatible with these desires. So too, individuals who are low on both of these dimensions might find their behaviors and their goals congruent. What about individuals who are high on one of these measures and low on the other? Those high on affiliation motivation but low in extraversion might want to form close relationships with others but be hampered by a personal style and skills that are not compatible with their goals. Individuals who are high in extraversion and low on affiliation motivation might be adept at forming social relationships but this might not be a central goal for these individuals.

John and his colleagues found that introverts who were high on affiliation motivation were more likely to divorce and to report difficulties in intimate relationships than extraverts who were high in affiliation. Extraverts who were low in affiliation motivation had more difficulties in intimate relationships than introverts who were low on affiliation motivation.

The research of John and his colleagues indicates that it is possible to combine different methods to study personality. Much of the research on variables such as extraversion and affiliation motivation is embedded in a particular intellectual tradition. Rarely do psychologists attached to different methods of studying personality use methods derived from other intellectual traditions in the same investigation. Yet it is precisely this type of research that may provide us with a better understanding of the person.

The Overt and the Covert

We can ask people to respond directly to questions about their personality and we can study unconscious influences on personality. We have considered some research in chapter 9 that indicates that individuals whose self-reports are distorted may behave in ways that are different from those whose self-reports are not distorted. We know that there are both conscious and unconscious influences on human behavior. It would be interesting to study individuals whose conscious and unconscious characteristics are either congruent or incongruent.

We can get a hint of how to proceed with this type of study by considering research on covert attitudes. Fazio, Jackson, Dunton, and Williams (1995) used a priming task to measure evaluative attitudes about blacks and whites. This procedure provides a subtle and difficult-to-fake measure of how a person evaluates a particular stimulus. The evaluation is based on a priming procedure (see chapter 9) in which individuals are presented with a stimulus followed by evaluative words such as *good* or *bad*. The subject's task is to indicate as rapidly as possible whether the word he or she is viewing is either positive or negative in its meaning. Priming occurs when a stimulus that precedes the word facilitates the judgment, thereby decreasing the amount of time it takes to evaluate the word. If a first or prime stimulus elicits a positive response and is followed by a positive word, the time taken to indicate that the word has a positive meaning is decreased. The stimulus is said to prime the target word. If the prime has a negative meaning for the individual, it will increase the amount of time required to indicate that a word has a positive meaning. In this case the prime interferes with the processing of the word whose evaluative meaning is different from that of the prime.

Fazio and his colleagues presented both black and white subjects with pictures of black and white individuals as primes, followed by positive and negative words. If an individual has a negative feeling about black people, it should take longer to process positive words preceded by black faces than to process positive words preceded by white faces. Similarly, such an individual should process negative words more rapidly when they are preceded by a picture of a black face. By studying the effects of priming on the evaluative judgments of words, it is possible to obtain a measure of an individual's emotional reaction to black and white people. Fazio et al. found that this measure of covert attitudes indicated that white subjects tended, on average, to hold negative attitudes toward black individuals. Judgments of positive words were facilitated for these subjects when the words were primed by white faces, and judgments of negative words were facilitated when they were primed by black faces. The black subjects' judgments of positive words were facilitated when primed by black faces.

Bargh, Chen, and Burrows (1996) demonstrated that subliminal primes of attitudes could influence social behavior. They presented Caucasian subjects with subliminal pictures of African American or white faces. They required their subjects to perform a boring task and then informed them that the computer had lost their data and that they would have to perform the task again. When this request was made, the subjects' facial expressions were videotaped. The facial expressions were evaluated for hostility by raters who were not aware of the stimulus to which the subjects had been exposed in the first part of the experiment. They found that subjects who had seen African American faces responded in a more hostile way to the request than subjects who had been exposed to Caucasian faces. Furthermore, the influence of these subliminal exposures was not related to the subjects' overt attitudes toward African Americans. Apparently, whether subjects claim to hold favorable or unfavorable attitudes toward African Americans did not influence the way in which they responded to the presence of a subliminal prime stimulus. These results suggest that the presentation of subliminal representation of an African-American face may trigger a hostile response in some Caucasian students even though they do not profess any overtly hostile or negative attitudes toward African Americans.

We believe that the availability of indirect measures of covert attitudes provides an interesting research technique for the study of discrepancies between self-reports and behavior. This technique might be used to study individuals who say they do not feel hostile toward a partner but who nevertheless display a pattern of negative evaluation of the person in a priming task. Ultimately, techniques like this should enable us to explore the meaning of congruence and lack of congruence between overt and covert measures. Such research might contribute to a better understanding of the ways in which conscious and unconscious characteristics combine to influence behavior.

Narratives and Other Personality Indices

Personality psychologists are interested in narratives—the life stories that people tell about themselves that provide a sense of their identity. McAdams writes, "Identity is a life story—an internalized narrative integration of past, present, and anticipated future which provides lives with a sense of unity and purpose" (1990, p.161). Some psychologists are interested in the study of narrative for its own sake as a way of understanding a person in his or her own words. Narratives constitute an idiographic way of studying an individual's personal identity. They may also be related to other ways of measuring individual differences. We will discuss two examples of research relating narratives to other approaches to the study of personality.

In the first, Moffitt et al. (1994) asked college students to provide autobiographical memories for positive and negative events in their lives (see Singer &

Salovey, 1993, for a discussion of the role of narrative memories in understanding the self and personality). They used a standardized method to analyze the student's narratives. Each positive and negative narrative was scored for the presence of either single events or summaries of events. Single-event narratives are particularized; they are descriptions of unique occurrences in a person's life. Summary narratives lack connections to particular moments in time; they lack detail and imagery and are usually part of a larger generalized narrative.

Moffitt et al. related measures of narrative characteristics to scores on an index of depression based on adjectives that individuals assigned to themselves. Table 13.1 presents their results. Individuals who were high in depression tended to provide summary narratives in response to requests for positive memories. Individuals who were low in depression tended to provide single-event narratives. As Table 13.1 indicates, those who differed in depression did not differ in the kinds of narratives that they created for negative memories. These data suggest that depression is related to a tendency to remember positive things in the past in a generalized rather than specific manner.

The Moffitt et al. study is a nice example of the possibility of relating individualized narratives to traditional nomothetic measures of personality. It provides evidence that the kinds of narratives people develop about their lives are related to other indices of personality. Although we find the study exemplary in all respects, we are interested in a number of questions that are not addressed by the authors of this paper. An examination of Table 13.1 indicates that some individuals who are classified as being high in depression present narratives characteristic of individuals low in depression and vice versa. Why? What are the implications of this pattern of behavior? If you say that you are depressed but your positive memories are of single events redolent of specific imagery and tied to a particular occurrence, what does this recollection imply about you? Is it likely that you are not really depressed? Would a psychiatrist who interviews you describe you as being only mildly depressed? Would you be more likely to recover from depression than someone who says she is depressed and exhibits the kinds of narratives about positive events that are typical of depressed individuals?

TABLE 13.1   Percentages of Single-Event and Summary Memories by Memory Request and Depression Group (Based on Moffitt et al., 1994)

| | MEMORY REQUEST | | | |
| | POSITIVE | | NEGATIVE | |
Depression	Single event	Summary	Single event	Summary
Low	65	35	44	56
High	26	74	40	60

Note: $N = 45$ for each memory request.
Reproduced with permission of the American Psychological Association.

To ask these questions is to begin to inquire about a more fundamental question. What is the role of narratives in personality? Assume that our narratives are related to other ways of measuring personality. McCrae and Costa (1990) argue that the themes of narratives are related to the Big Five. Clearly narratives are subtle and nuanced descriptions of individual lives. But once they are developed, how do they change a person? Do they summarize our past and current behavior or are they guides for that behavior? Are they idle chatter in the mind or causes of an individual's behavior? What do we gain from studying narratives that we do not gain from studying other measures of personality? Surely we are provided with a rich interpretative statement by a person about himself. But we would like to know what can be predicted from an analysis of a person's narrative that cannot be predicted without knowing the narrative. It could be argued that the goal of the study of personality is not prediction but understanding. Without entering into that complex philosophical debate, we think that the question about prediction is legitimate. And we believe that it cannot be answered unless we study the relationships between narratives and other measures of personality and classify people simultaneously on more than one type of measure.

The second example of the study of narrative in personality psychology poses many of the same kinds of questions. McAdams and de St. Aubin (1992) studied narratives about *generativity*. Generativity narratives are those that contain themes about the influence of the person on those who survive her or him—about what endures after the person is gone. Generativity is a concept that is related to concern for the next generation and a need to influence it in positive ways. McAdams and de St. Aubin asked subjects to provide autobiographical narratives about five experiences in their lives, including one of commitment and one involving a goal. These narratives were coded for the presence of generativity as indicated by themes related to creating new things; maintaining products, projects, or traditions; offering of oneself or one's products to others; references to the next generation; or references to symbolic immortality. People whose narratives contained many generative themes were more likely to report that they had engaged in behaviors that were assumed to be indicative of generativity. For example, they were likely to draw upon their past experience to help a person, to teach someone a skill, and the like. A score for generativity themes in narratives correlated .45 with a score for reported frequency of generative acts. Generative narrative theme scores also correlated with a questionnaire measure of generativity that contained such items as "I try to pass along the knowledge that I have gained through my experience" and "I feel as though my contributions will exist after I die." The correlation between generativity scores based on narratives and scores on the questionnaire measure of generativity was .40.

The results of the McAdams and de St. Aubin study indicate that three methods of measuring generativity are interrelated: narratives, questionnaires, and behavioral acts that are assumed to reflect generativity are positively related to each other. This study, like the Moffitt et al. study of depression, does not provide us with much insight about the role of narratives in a person's life. While narratives may provide meaning and coherence to an understanding of one's own personal life, it is not clear whether the insights they provide about someone's personality tell us something about the person (other than the structure of his or her narratives) that cannot be learned by other methods of measuring personality. Again, the way to begin to answer this kind of question is to study people whose narratives are and are not congruent with other related indices of personality. In this way it should be possible to discover the role of narratives in personality.

CONCLUSION

Personality psychologists have many different methods available to study personality. We believe that progress in understanding personality will occur when psychologists begin to study individuals using the full range of concepts and tools available to them.

Glossary

acquiescence tendency—A tendency to agree (rather than disagree) with personality test items. Also called *yea-saying tendency*.

actual self—One's representation of the attributes that oneself or others believe one actually possesses. Sometimes called the *real self*.

adaptation—A mechanism that increased fitness in the ancestral environment by "solving a problem" relevant to survival and/or reproduction.

additive genetic influences—Genetic influences that produce variations in phenotypes proportional to their number, so that the greater the number of additive genetic influences shared by two individuals, the more similar will be their phenotypes. Thus, two individuals who share four of five target genes would be more similar than two individuals who share only one of the five.

aggregating—Combining data over multiple observations. Aggregation can be across occasions, situations, instruments, or observers.

ancestral environment—The environment experienced by the ancestors of our species. The earliest fossil of the genus *Homo* is dated to about 2.5 million years ago. The earliest fossil of the genus that preceded *Homo*, *Australopithicus*, is dated to about 4.4 million years ago. Fully modern humans (our species, *Homo sapiens*) are believed to have emerged about 100,000 years ago. Also called the *natural environment* and the *environment of evolutionary adaptedness*. It is important to note that mechanisms that have evolved were "designed" to solve recurrent problems faced by our ancestors, not necessarily those faced by us.

anxiety—An unpleasant emotional state that often occurs when people feel threatened. Anxiety can range from "low-level" general feelings of threat to acute responses to immediate danger. It differs from fear in that it tends to have a slower onset and dissipation and often an only indistinct cause.

appraisal—The meaning one gives to situations and events that one encounters.

approach tendencies—A motivational tendency to approach stimuli and situations that might provide rewards. Sometimes called *appetitive* tendencies.

archival material—Information that already exists that can be used in research. Examples include letters, diaries, speeches, home movies, statistical documents such as the census, and many others.

arousability—The degree to which stimulation produces arousal, often indicated by the magnitude of responses to stimuli.

ascending reticular activating system—A network of cells that plays a role in sleep and wakefulness and serves to alert or activate the cerebral cortex, especially in response to stimulation.

assortative mating—Nonrandom mating in which individuals preferentially mate with others who are similar to themselves in some phenotypic characteristic.

attachment—A bond that develops between an infant and its primary caretaker. The quality of the attachment may influence how secure the individual feels and how the individual relates to others over the course of development.

attenuation—Reduction in the size of a correlation because of error of measurement.

attributional style—A person's tendency to typically make certain types of attributions rather than others.

Barnum effect—Tendency of subjects to agree with results of personality tests even when those results are not based on the subjects' actual responses (McKelvie, 1990).

baseline—The measurement of a physiological response when the individual is not exposed to any particular conditions of stimulation. It is used as a point of comparison for responses to experimental conditions. In practice, psychophysiological baselines are often measured under so-called "resting" conditions, in which subjects sit or lie down and external stimulation is minimized.

basic emotions—A relatively small set of emotions that are believed by some theorists to be biologically fundamental in humans, and to be the base from which all other emotions are derived. Although the actual emotions vary from one theorist to another, they usually include at minimum fear, sadness, anger, and happiness.

behavioral activating system (BAS)—A motivational brain system that activates behavior in the presence of signals of reward.

behavioral deficits—Performance on tasks at a level substantially below that found in the general population. Studying such deficits in brain-damaged patients can provide clues to the normal functioning of the brain.

behavioral inhibiting system (BIS)—A motivational brain system that inhibits behavior in the presence of signals of punishment.

behavioral potential—The strength of the tendency to engage in a specific behavior, based on the probability of a certain outcome and the value of that outcome.

biological determinism—The complete determination of human behavior by biological factors. Few scientists believe in biological determinism, although critics of biological approaches to understanding human behavior often accuse their more biologically oriented colleagues of endorsing this view.

biologically prepared—Having an innate tendency to learn certain things more easily than other things.

blends—Variables or dimensions that load highly on more than one factor.

buffer—Anything in the environment or in the person that serves to protect an individual from the negative effects of stressful situations.

case study—Intensive study of a single individual, often using qualitative descriptive methods. Case studies often consist of clinicians' reports of patients with unusual or interesting histories.

causal modeling—A mathematical technique used to estimate the relationships among sets of variables in a way that permits inferences about cause and effect. Also known as *path analysis* and *structural equation modeling.*

certainty of paternity—A problem faced by human males because they cannot be sure whether a woman's offspring is theirs or another male's. As a result they risk devoting resources to someone else's offspring, which would reduce their fitness.

coefficient alpha—A measure of internal consistency of a set of responses such as items on a test or scale. It estimates the correlation of each item with all other items and is equivalent to all possible split-half reliabilities. Also known as *Cronbach's alpha.*

cognitive dissonance—A hypothetical psychological state of tension that occurs when people experience inconsistency between their cognitions, beliefs, or actions.

cognitive dissonance theory—A theory in social psychology of how people resolve inconsistencies among their thoughts, feelings, beliefs, and actions, often by altering their experience of one of the conflicting elements.

cognitive style—The tendency to use certain types of information-processing strategies across a wide range of tasks and situations. Cognitive styles differ from abilities in that each style may have its advantages and limitations, whereas high ability is usually considered more desirable than low ability.

collective motives—Motives that characterize a whole society.

conditions—The different experiences provided by the experimenter to different groups of participants in a research study.

confounding—The situation in research studies when a variable that is extraneous to the hypothesis could account for results. This happens when the experimenter inadvertently manipulates or selects a variable in addition to the one intended. For example, if one were intending to study gender differences but all of the women in the sample were in their twenties and all the men were in their forties, gender would be confounded with age. Such confounds are a major threat to the internal validity of studies.

congenital adrenal hyperplasia (CAH)—A condition in which the adrenal glands produce abnormally large quantities of androgens. Also known as *adrenogenital syndrome*.

construct—A concept used to make sense out of phenomena. Constructs allow us to define, think about, and interpret events.

construct validation—The process by which one empirically evaluates the validity of a construct.

content analysis—Methods for analyzing the content of (usually) written material. It usually involves a set of rules for quantifying the material with regard to particular variables or dimensions.

content validity—Complete coverage of the target domain of the measure; adequate representation of all aspects of the construct that a measure is designed to assess.

continuous—A continuous variable is one that can theoretically take any value between two end values. In contrast, a *discrete* variable is one that is divided into separate categories or classes. IQ is a continuous variable; gender is a discrete variable.

control for—Remove effects of possible sources of systematic error in a study either through the research design or test construction, or through statistical means such as analysis of covariance. For example, one could control for age in an experiment by being sure that the average age of subjects in the treatment conditions is the same, or one could use statistical techniques to remove the effects of age on the dependent variable.

convergent validity—Agreement among alternative measures of the same construct. Also called *congruent validity*.

coping—Efforts to deal with stressful situations. Although *coping,* as used in everyday speech, often implies that one has dealt successfully with a stressful situation, in the psychological literature coping can be successful or unsuccessful (Aldwin & Revenson, 1987).

core relational theme—The specific pattern of appraisals that is linked to each different emotion.

correlation—Generally, a description of the relationship between two variables, most often indicated by the *correlation coefficient*. Although most of the correlations in personality psychology involve linear relationships, correlations can also be curvilinear (e.g., quadratic). Correlations can also be used to describe relations among sets of variables (as in multiple correlation or canonical correlation). The size of a correlation is determined by a number of factors, only one of which is the actual relationship between the constructs being measured. The most important factor is that the size of the correlation is limited by the degree of unreliability of the measures. Also, the greater the variance of a particular variable, the more chance there is of finding relationships between that variable and others. One consequence is that failure to include the full range of low and high scores on a variable may produce smaller (attenuated) correlations than might be found if the full range were included (called *restriction of range*). For example, correlating years of education with income in a sample of college-educated individuals will produce a lower correlation than the same correlation using a sample that includes the full range of education in the population.

correlation coefficient—A statistic used to describe the degree of relationship between variables. There are a number of slightly different correlation coefficients that can be computed, depending upon the type of measurement involved. The most frequently used correlation coefficient is the Pearson *r*. Others include the Spearman *rho* and the Kendall *tau*.

correlational research—Research in which all of the variables are measured rather than manipulated. Such variables are most often characteristics of people or measures of their behavior. The research seeks to discover relationships among these variables.

cortical arousal—State of activation or responsivity of the cerebral cortex. It is used to refer to the magnitude of reactions to stimuli and the individual's state of alertness or "mental excitement."

criterion—A standard to which measures can be compared.

cross-sectional design—A design in which the data are collected from two or more groups of subjects at the same point in time. For example, older subjects might be compared with younger subjects as a way of evaluating whether aging has an effect on a particular behavior. One problem with such a design is that often the two groups differ on variables other than the one that is the basis of classification. For example, in comparing individuals of different ages, one is also comparing individuals who have grown up during different historical periods.

death instinct—The instinct to return to a state of inactivity; the instinct to destroy life.

defense mechanisms—Strategies and maneuvers used by the ego to prevent unacceptable thoughts and feelings from becoming conscious and thus causing extreme anxiety. People are not aware of engaging in defense mechanisms, since they derive from the portion of the ego that is unconscious. Examples of defense mechanisms are repression, displacement, projection, intellectualization, reaction formation, and sublimation.

deindividuation—The condition in which people lose a sense of themselves as individuals. This is often related to a reduced reliance on internal standards of behavior.

design—The formal characteristics of a research study, including the number and types of conditions, the type of variables used, and the order in which participants experience one or more conditions.

dimension—An attribute that can be placed on a continuous scale of measurement. In personality psychology, the term is often used loosely as a synonym for a trait continuum.

disattenuation—Increase in the size of a correlation obtained by taking into account error of measurement in the variables being correlated.

discriminant validity—Lack of correlation between measures that are intended to measure different constructs. This becomes an issue when measures that are supposed to assess different constructs actually correlate highly with each other, that is, when discriminant validity is *not* found. Also called *divergent validity*.

disposition—A tendency to exhibit certain behaviors under specified conditions. Note that the popular use of the term refers to emotional tone, which personality psychologists call *temperament*.

dissociated—Separated, especially referring to aspects of a phenomenon that ought to show a consistent pattern.

distal goal—A goal that one hopes to achieve at some time in the future that constitutes the end point for a series of actions.

distribution—The array of scores used in a given analysis. Distributions can be plotted on graphs with the score on the X axis and the number of cases having each score on the Y axis.

dominance—In genetics, a form of nonadditive influence in which one of a pair of genes at a given location (the dominant gene) influences the phenotype while the other (the recessive gene) has less influence on it.

double blind—A design frequently used in medical research in which neither the patient nor the physician knows whether the patient is receiving the experimental treatment or a placebo.

EEG alpha asymmetry—The relative amount of alpha wave activity from the left and right sides of the brain as measured by the electroencephalograph. It is assumed that the more alpha wave activity that is present from a brain region, the lower is the activation level of that region. Thus, a pattern in which there is more alpha wave activity over the right than over the left hemisphere would indicate that the left hemisphere is more activated than the right hemisphere. This pattern would be labeled "relative left-hemisphere activation."

effect size—A way of expressing the magnitude of a difference in standard deviation units. An effect size of 1.00 corresponds to a difference equal to one standard deviation.

ego—The part of the mind that deals with the demands of reality as well as those of the id. Also used as a synonym for the self.

electrodermal activity—Changes in the conductivity of the skin due to changes in arousal. The changes are detected by electrodes attached (usually) to the fingers or palms. Also called *galvanic skin response* and *skin conductance*.

Embedded Figures Test—A test in which subjects try to find a simple geometrical figure that is hidden within a complex pattern.

emotion-focused coping—Coping that attempts to change how one feels about a stressful situation.

endogenous events—Events that individuals encounter as a result of their own actions or characteristics.

environmental influences—In behavior genetics, any influence on a phenotype that is not genetic. These can include both prenatal and postnatal events and can range from biological influences such as nutrition to social influences such as culture.

epiphenomenal—Referring to an event that accompanies another event but has no causal relationship to it.

epistasis—A form of nonadditive genetic influence in which genes at different locations interact in their influence on the phenotype.

equal-environments assumption—The assumption that the environments experienced by pairs of MZ twins are no more similar (or different) than the environments experienced by DZ twins. This assumption permits the inference that greater similarities among MZ twins than DZ twins reflect the greater genetic similarity of MZ twins.

error of measurement—The degree to which a measurement differs from the "true" value of the underlying variable. The only way *not* to have some error of measurement is to have perfectly reliable and valid measuring instruments. Measurement of almost anything involves some amount of error; measurement of personality variables always involves fairly large amounts of error.

exogenous events—Events that individuals encounter that have nothing to do with their own actions or characteristics.

expectancy-value theory—A general approach to understanding the role of motives and beliefs in determining action. *Expectancies* are beliefs about the likely outcome of a particular action under a particular set of circumstances. *Value* indicates the importance or significance of that outcome to the individual. Values can be positive (desired) or negative (undesired). For any particular action, there may be more than one possible outcome, each with its own value. The product of each expectancy-value pair represents the behavior potential for that action. The action with the highest positive behavior potential is the one that will be engaged in. The "computation" of behavior potentials usually occurs automatically rather than deliberately.

experience-sampling method—A method of obtaining information about subjects' experiences as they happen. In one version, subjects wear a beeper that randomly goes off one or more times a day. They then record whatever is happening at that moment.

explicit memory—Memory that can be intentionally recalled.

external locus of control—The tendency to believe that the important outcomes of life are due to forces beyond the individual's control (such as fate, luck, powerful others, institutions, etc.).

extremity tendency—A tendency to use the endpoints of scales rather than the intermediate points (for example, using only 1 and 7 on a 7-point scale).

extrinsic motivation—The notion that the motivation to perform an act derives not from the performing of the act itself but from an external reward.

face validity—Judgment of validity based on inspection of the test content.

factor analysis—A set of mathematical techniques used to reveal the underlying structure of a group of variables by examining how they cluster together. The aim is to see if a large number of variables or dimensions can be reduced to a smaller set of dimensions. The factors are hypothetical dimensions that are estimated on the basis of observed patterns of correlations among the variables.

fertility—Capacity for bearing children.

field dependence-independence—An individual-difference dimension related to characteristic ways of dealing with information. More field-dependent people tend to rely on information "as given" and to be strongly influenced by the most prominent aspect of a situation they encounter. More field-independent people tend to "restructure" information and to be less influenced by prominent aspects of situations. This dimension is measured by cognitive performance tasks such as the Rod and Frame Test and the Embedded Figures Test. The dimension is sometimes referred to simply as *field dependence.*

fitness—In evolutionary biology, a technical term that refers to the degree to which an individual's genes are transmitted to future generations. More fit individuals transmit more copies of their genes than do less fit individuals.

free association—Verbalizing anything that comes into one's mind, especially under conditions that minimize a sense of threat.

g, **general intelligence**—The common element in all possible measures of intelligence; whatever it is that causes such tasks to be intercorrelated and form a positive manifold.

genotype—In genetics, refers to the total genetic makeup of the individual.

gravitation hypothesis—The idea that over time people tend to end up in job situations that are commensurate with their characteristics.

habituation—A decrease in response to a stimulus when it is repeated many times. The faster the habituation, the fewer repetitions are needed before the individual ceases to respond to it.

hard outcomes—In research on illness, outcomes with high reliability and validity, such as a diagnosed heart attack or death.

hardiness—A dimension of personality derived from existential personality theory. It is comprised of three components: commitment, control, and challenge. Hardy people are said to deal with life in an engaged, energetic manner, an attitude toward life hypothesized to help protect hardy individuals from the negative effects of stressful situations.

heritability—The proportion of variance in an observed characteristic (phenotype) that can be attributed to differences among individuals in their genetic makeup (genotype). The heritability statistic (h^2) is influenced by the variability of the trait in the population under study, the variability of the genotypes in that population, and the variability of the relevant environmental factors experienced by that population. Since it is a proportion, heritability can range from 0 to 1.00.

heritable—Transmitted through the genes. In behavior genetics the term has a specific technical meaning (see *heritability*).

heterotypic continuity—The idea that underlying characteristics may take different behavioral forms at different developmental periods. Therefore, even if specific behaviors change, the underlying characteristic may show consistency over the life span.

heuristic—As a noun, a rule of thumb that enables people to make relatively rapid judgments. Use of heuristics can sometimes lead to erroneous or illogical conclusions.

human nature—The totality of psychological and behavioral mechanisms assumed to exist in all human beings as a result of our species' evolutionary history.

humors—Bodily fluids that were believed in ancient times to determine certain biological characteristics of individuals, including health and temperament.

hypothesis—A statement of the presumed consequences of certain things being true. *Theories* are ideas about what might be true. Thus theories are the "if" and hypotheses are the "then" in an "if–then" statement: if theory A is correct, then one consequence is that we ought to observe B. Theories are stated at a more abstract level than hypotheses, and any one theory can generate a large number of hypotheses. In order to be testable, a hypothesis must involve a consequence that is observable. If research supports a hypothesis, then the theory from which the hypothesis was generated *might* be true; however, since any specific hypothesis can usually be generated by more than one theory, and since any theory can generate more than one hypothesis, psychologists are careful not to assume that support for a specific hypothesis provides strong support for a specific theory. This caution is one reason why many studies must be done before there is consensus about the truth value of any theory.

id—That part of the mind that is closely connected to bodily functions and is the underlying source of motivation. The id seeks immediate gratification of impulses toward pleasure. It is an evolutionarily primitive motivational system, hence "animalistic" and "nonrational."

ideal self—One's representation of the attributes oneself or others would like one ideally to possess, which would lead to the fulfilling of desired goals or wishes. These attributes may or may not also be part of the actual self.

idiographic—An approach to research, advocated by Gordon Allport, that focuses on the unique individual. The underlying assumption of this approach is that the terms that describe a given individual do not necessarily describe all people. Generalizations that are derived from studying groups of people are inadequate to capture the organized personality of the individual.

implicit memory—Memory that influences behavior but cannot be intentionally recalled by the subject.

incentive—A condition or outcome that serves to satisfy a motive.

inclusive fitness—An extension of the concept of fitness to include the transmission of genes shared by an individual with others. For example, individuals who help others who share their genes could help send copies of those genes to future generations through the reproductive success of those being helped.

independent variable—In an experiment, the variable that is manipulated or controlled by the experimenter in order to evaluate the effect of that variable on behavior. In personality research, characteristics of people are sometimes loosely considered as independent variables. For example, if one wanted to study whether extraverts differ from introverts in their preferences for types of music, scores on a measure of extraversion/introversion might be thought of as the independent variable. Strictly speaking, however, such a study would really be an example of *correlational research* rather than a true experiment, first because there is no random assignment and second because neither variable was manipulated or controlled by the experimenter.

individual response specificity—A tendency of different individuals to display a characteristic pattern of idiosyncratic psychophysiological responses across a range of situations.

inhibited—Characteristically fearful, shy, and reticent, especially in the presence of novel stimuli or unfamiliar people.

inspection time—The shortest time an individual needs to inspect two stimuli in order to discriminate reliably between them.

integrity tests—Tests designed to identify employees who are likely to present problems at work.

inter-rater reliability—The degree to which two or more observers of a response agree on the score that should be assigned to it. Depending on the type of ratings, it can be expressed as a correlation or as a proportion of scores on which there is agreement. Also known as *inter-judge reliability.*

internal locus of control—The tendency to believe, in general, that the important outcomes in life are due to one's own actions.

internal consistency—The degree to which items within a test or scale are related to each other.

internal validity—The ability to conclude correctly from the results of a study that the target behavior was influenced by the different treatment conditions. True (randomized) experiments are meant to maximize internal validity.

intervention—A field study in which an attempt is made to change an outcome in a specific set of circumstances.

intrinsic motivation—The notion that motivation for an act derives from the behavior itself.

ipsative—Measurement in which scores on tests for a single individual are compared with each other. For example, in ipsative measurement "high" means "higher than other scores of the same individual."

isomorphism—With respect to brain–behavior relationships, refers to the concept that there is a direct correspondence between specific types of behavior and specific neural systems.

Jenkins Activity Survey—A self-report measure designed to assess Type A personality.

job strain—A form of stress that occurs when there is a mismatch between the requirements of a job and the opportunities to meet those requirements, or between the requirements and the rewards the job provides.

lexical decision task—A task in which the subject makes a rapid judgment as to whether or not a set of letters is a legitimate word in the subject's language.

lexical hypothesis—The idea that the words in a language—the lexicon—accurately represents the structure of personality. The assumption is that language develops to encode important aspects of people's social reality, and personality is such an important aspect.

libido—The basic driving force of motivation; the energy of the id. Also used just to refer to the life instinct or sexual drive.

life instinct—The instinct to produce and sustain life.

life tasks—Problems people believe they are working on that are related to particular life transitions.

limbic system—A group of brain structures believed to be related to emotions, including the hippocampus, amygdala, septum, prefrontal cortex, and other structures.

loading—The correlation between a variable (or dimension) and a factor. One interprets the meaning of a factor by examining the variables that load highest on it. Conventionally, loadings below .3 or .4 are often ignored in interpreting the meaning of a factor.

main effect—A result in which an experimental situation has a uniform impact on people regardless of any other variables measured or manipulated in the study.

manipulate—A term used to describe the process of producing different experiences for participants in an experiment.

marker—An observable characteristic that reflects an underlying genetic or biological factor. Markers are often used to trace genetic similarities in populations.

marker variables—Variables (or dimensions) that load very high on one factor and very low on all other factors.

mating strategies—Adaptive mechanisms designed to solve problems related to mating (such as selecting mates, attracting mates, and keeping mates).

mean—The arithmetic average of scores. A measure of the central tendency of a set of scores.

measurement—In personality psychology, the process of assigning numerical values to characteristics of individuals or their behavior.

metatrait—The trait of having a trait, as indicated by consistency of responses to elements that comprise the trait (usually items on questionnaires). In questionnaires that use rating scales, two individuals could obtain the same score yet be very different in the consistency of their responses. The consistent person would be described as "traited" while the inconsistent person would be described as "untraited."

minimal investment—The least amount of resources an individual must expend in order to produce offspring.

moderator variable—A variable that alters the relationship between two other variables.

mood congruence—The biasing of attention, perception, memory, or judgment in a direction similar to one's ongoing mood state.

mood incongruence—The biasing of attention, perception, memory, or judgment in a direction opposite to one's mood state. This can happen when people attempt to shift their mood from bad to good.

motive dispositions—Motivational tendencies that persist over time in a traitlike way.

multiple determination—The idea that any specific behavior can have more than one cause. In personality psychology this also refers to the possibility that the same behavior in different people is caused by different factors.

multivariate—Analysis of more than two variables at one time. Examples include multiple regression analysis, factor analysis, and structural equation modeling.

natural selection—The fundamental principle of evolution discovered by Darwin and Wallace in the nineteenth century. Individuals who are more successful in their survival and mating are more likely to send their genes to future generations than are individuals who are less successful. Therefore, any genetically influenced characteristic that increases the individual's success in survival and reproduction will itself be passed to future generations in greater numbers than characteristics that do not increase this success. Over generations, the "successful" genes will tend to replace the "unsuccessful" genes, thus altering the genetic makeup of the species and eventually producing new species. Those characteristics that make the most difference for survival and reproduction (that are most subject to "selection pressure") will become "species typical" relatively quickly.

necessary and sufficient—A condition is considered a "necessary" cause when an effect cannot occur in its absence (e.g., clouds are necessary for rain to occur); a condition is considered a "sufficient" cause when the presence of the condition is all that is required for the effect to occur (e.g., "if you prick us, do we not bleed?"). A cause can be necessary but not sufficient, or sufficient but not necessary, or it can be necessary and sufficient—in which case the condition will invariably be present when the effect occurs.

nomothetic—An approach to research that seeks to discover generalizations that can be applied to all people or subsets of people. The term was introduced by Gordon Allport.

nonadditive genetic influences—Genetic influences that reduce the similarity of individuals who do not share a particular set of genes. Thus two individuals may share four out of five target genes and be no more similar in their phenotypes than two who share only one of the five genes.

nonshared environmental influences—Environmental factors that are not shared by members of the same family or household and that serve to make the phenotypes of family members different from one another.

nonspecific—Systems or processes that have general effects on behavior rather than effects limited to particular functions.

normative—Measurement in which scores on tests are compared with other people's scores on the same tests. For example, in normative measurement "high" means "higher than other people's scores on a given test."

norms—Information about tests based on responses of large numbers of people from the same population as the subjects.

objective threshold—The level of presentation of a stimulus at which subjects have no knowledge or information about any aspect of the stimulus.

observational learning—Learning based on observing the behavior of other individuals.

optimal arousal level—The level of arousal or stimulation at which an individual feels most comfortable or functions most effectively.

optimism—A dimension of personality that affects beliefs about what is likely to happen to oneself in the future. Optimists believe that the things that happen to them will be generally positive; pessimists do not share this belief as strongly and may even believe that the things that happen will be generally negative.

ought self—One's representation of the attributes that oneself or others believe one should or ought to possess, and that reflect a sense of one's duty, obligations, or responsibilities. Failure to have these characteristics is felt to lead to disapproval and punishment. These characteristics may or may not be part of the actual self.

outcome expectancy—Belief about the likely consequences of a particular behavior.

parental investment—The amount of resources a parent devotes to a particular offspring relative to resources available for other potential or existing offspring.

path analysis—See *causal modeling.*

pattern mask—A visual stimulus (often random letters or lines) presented immediately after a target stimulus which prevents further visual processing of the target stimulus. It is used to prevent the target stimulus from entering conscious awareness.

percent of variance—"Accounting for variance" refers to how much we reduce error of prediction of one score when we have knowledge of another score. The greater the percent of variance accounted for, the greater the reduction in error of prediction. The percent of variance accounted for by a correlation of $r = .40$ is 16% $(r^2 \times 100)$.

percentiles—Scores that divide a distribution into hundredths. A percentile score of 30 indicates that 30% of the scores fall below that score; a percentile score of 83 indicates that 83% of the scores fall below that score.

perceptual defense—Selectively failing to perceive or misperceiving stimuli that could cause anxiety if perceived accurately. In studies of subliminal presentation, perceptual defense is given as the explanation for the higher threshold (longer exposure time) required to perceive threatening words.

person-centered—Research that focuses on the individual case without comparing one person with another. The emphasis is often on the organization of characteristics within the individual or on the individual's unique biography.

person–situation interaction—A pattern of results in which an experimental situation has different effects on the behavior of individuals with different characteristics.

personal strivings—The things individuals believe they are typically trying to accomplish in their lives.

personology—The study of the total personality of individuals.

phenotype—In genetics, refers to any observed or measured characteristic of an individual.

placebo control—Providing a placebo to a group of subjects as a way of controlling for possible placebo effects in the experimental treatment. The measure of efficacy of the experimental treatment is any change beyond that seen in the placebo control group.

placebo effect—A change in a person's health or psychological status as a result of exposure to a treatment when the components that are assumed to cause change are omitted (e.g., in the case of medicine, no active ingredient is present).

pleasure principle—The motivational principle that governs the id—the blind seeking of pleasure and avoidance of pain. See *psychological hedonism.*

positive affectivity—The tendency to experience states of positive affect frequently. See *positive emotionality.*

positive emotionality—The tendency to experience positive emotions, especially energetic enthusiasm. Also called *positive affectivity.*

positive manifold—A pattern of correlations in which all variables are positively correlated with all other variables.

postnatal—Occurring after birth.

potential for hostility—A score derived from the Structured Interview that involves behaviors coded as evidence of overt and covert hostility and antagonism.

power motive—The desire to have impact on other people's behaviors, thoughts, or feelings. This was not in Murray's list of motives but resembles his "need for dominance."

press—Stimuli or events that are important to individuals because of relevance to their needs. Plural of *press* is *press.*

primary appraisal—One's understanding of the significance of a situation or event as regards its potential benefits or harms.

priming—Using one stimulus to alter the response to a subsequent stimulus.

principle of indifference of the indicator—The idea that the particular set of tests or items that is used to measure intelligence is irrelevant. As long as one samples widely from items or tests that form a positive manifold, the aggregate scores tend to be similar.

private self-consciousness—A dimension of individual differences relating to the tendency to be aware often of one's inner thoughts, feelings, and attitudes.

problem-focused coping—Coping that attempts to change the stressful situation by dealing with its causes or how it is understood.

projective technique—A psychological measure in which individuals produce written or spoken material in response to an ambiguous stimulus. The material is then analyzed for clues to underlying motives, concerns, or conflicts of which the individual may be unaware. Examples include the TAT, Rorschach, and sentence-completion tests.

prospective design—Design in which the outcomes of interest (dependent variables) have not yet occurred at the time that other data (independent variables) are obtained.

protective inhibition—A process that serves to reduce cortical arousal under conditions of intense stimulation, presumably to protect neural tissue from overactivation. Also called *transmarginal inhibition*.

prototypic emotion script—A description of the situations that elicit an emotion, the characteristic responses to that emotion, and the methods used to control the emotion.

proximal goal—A goal that can be achieved close in time to one's actions but that is typically not the desired end point of the actions. Proximal goals can be thought of as "way stations" toward distal goals.

psychological hedonism—The doctrine that all action is motivated by the desire to maximize pleasure and minimize pain.

psychological mechanisms—As used in evolutionary psychology, complex information-processing and decision rule systems designed by the processes of evolution to solve problems of survival and reproduction faced by members of a species.

psychometric—Referring to the study of psychological measurement.

psychophysiology—The study of brain–behavior relations using measures of physiological activity.

random assignment—The placing of a research participant in a treatment condition on a purely random basis (such as flipping a coin or using a random numbers generator). This is done to minimize the chances that the individuals in the different conditions could differ in some systematic way that could influence the behavior under investigation.

readiness potential—A change in electrical activity, recorded in the EEG, from scalp locations above motor areas of the cortex that occurs prior to the onset of a motor response.

reality principle—The motivational principle that drives the ego to attempt to take into account the demands of the physical and social environment while attempting to gratify the demands of the id.

regression toward the mean—A statistical phenomenon that occurs as a result of error of measurement. When individuals are measured twice, those who obtain scores at the extremes of the distribution on one measurement occasion will tend to obtain less extreme scores on the other occasion, for purely statistical reasons; as a result, the average score of those individuals is likely to be closer to the mean of the distribution of the other measurement occasion. Regression toward the mean can be a serious threat to the internal validity of studies in which subjects are not randomly assigned to different treatment conditions.

reliability—The degree to which a given measurement can be reproduced. A reliable measuring instrument is one that always gives the same results under the same conditions—that is, is free of random error. Reliability also refers to generalizability over time, items, and judges.

representative sample—A sample that preserves the frequencies of characteristics found in the general population. The only way to ensure a completely representative sample is randomly to sample individuals from the target population.

repress—Actively keep material (thoughts and feelings) out of conscious awareness.

reproductive value—The number of offspring an individual is likely to have over his or her lifetime. Reproductive value is related to variables such as age and health.

resources—Time, effort, energy, food, shelter, protection, and anything else that helps an organism survive and reproduce.

response tendency—A tendency to respond systematically to test items in a way not related to the construct the test is designed to measure. Also called *response styles* and *response sets*. Response tendencies are a source of systematic, as opposed to random, error of measurement.

restriction in range of talent—A sample that does not include the full range of scores on a measure of ability (or any other variable of interest) that occurs in the population to which one wishes to generalize. Restriction in range reduces the magnitude of obtained correlations below what would be found if the full range were sampled.

retrospective design—A design in which the data refer to events or experiences that have already occurred at the time the data are gathered.

Rod and Frame Test—A test used to measure field dependence-independence in which subjects are asked to set a rod to the true vertical position when it is presented within a tilted square frame.

sample—The subjects in a study who come from a larger population to which one wishes to generalize the results. The fact that many samples in personality research are "samples of convenience"—undergraduate volunteers, individuals who respond to ads, etc.—may limit the ability to generalize to other populations. In order to generalize to the general population, it is necessary to use *probability sampling* or representative sampling. These methods are often used in survey research.

scale—Sometimes used to refer to a personality test.

secondary appraisal—Beliefs about one's capability of dealing with situations one encounters, especially situations that are appraised as potentially harmful.

selective breeding—Purposeful breeding for desired characteristics through selection of individuals for breeding who manifest those characteristics.

self-attributed needs—Needs or motives that people believe they possess. Self-attributed motives are part of the self-concept and are measured by self-report questionnaires. Also called *explicit* or *respondent* motives. They are contrasted with *implicit* or *operant* motives, which are measured through thought-sampling (projective) techniques.

self-efficacy—A belief that one is capable of performing an action.

self-esteem—One's evaluation of oneself.

self-regulation—Processes and strategies individuals use to control their own behavior or internal states.

self-report—People's responses to questions about themselves. On questionnaires, this often takes the form of "agree/disagree" or ratings of the degree to which an item accurately describes the person.

sexual selection—Evolution of characteristics that occurs because of direct effects on reproduction rather than survival, usually through increasing opportunities for mating. It includes characteristics that help the individual compete for mates (as in male elephant seals fighting over access to females) or that are preferred by individuals of the opposite sex (as in peahens' preference for peacocks with large tails).

sexually dimorphic—Referring to physical and behavioral characteristics that have different forms in females and males. In some species, there appear to be few sexually dimorphic physical characteristics other than reproductive organs. In others, the entire physical appearance of females and males differs. Similarly, species differ in the degree to which behavior is sexually dimorphic.

shared environmental influences—Environmental factors that are shared by people living in the same family or household that cause them to be more similar to each other than to individuals living in different families or households. See *shared family environment*.

shared family environment—Environmental factors that are experienced by members of the same family or household that cause them to be more similar to each other than they are to non-family members.

skin conductance response—Increases in skin conductance occurring either in response to a stimulus or spontaneously.

social desirability tendency—A tendency to respond to test items in a way that promotes a favorable social image. Items differ in their probability of eliciting this tendency. For some items, it is obvious that certain responses promote a more favorable social image than others (for example, answering "false" to the items "I often feel I am not as good as others" and "I usually cheat on tests"). Such items call forth a social desirability tendency in some subjects.

social motives—Motives that are related to actions involving other people or one's status in the social environment.

social support—The help or opportunity for social interaction for individuals facing stressful situations. It can take the form of direct helping (such as providing financial resources), providing information, giving comfort and sympathy, or just being available for social interactions.

soft outcomes—In research on illness, outcome measures that have questionable validity as indicators of illness. Self-reports of symptoms are usually considered soft outcomes.

specialized—"Hemispheric specialization" refers to the idea that the two sides of the brain differ in the functions for which they are primarily responsible (for example, the left hemisphere is specialized for language functions—it plays a larger role in language than does the right hemisphere).

split-half reliability—The correlation of scores based on one half of the items on a test or scale with scores based on the other half of the test or scale.

stability—The consistency of scores over time. Over short time periods, stability is used to estimate reliability. Over longer time periods, stability refers to the degree to which people's scores on the underlying variable change or remain the same.

standard deviation—A measure of variability computed as the square root of the variance of a set of scores. In a normal distribution a fixed proportion of the scores will fall 1, 2, and 3 standard deviations from the mean.

state—Condition of a person at a given time. In personality psychology the term usually refers to relatively short time frames (minutes, hours, and days rather than months and years).

stimulus response specificity—The elicitation of different and specific patterns of psychophysiological activity by different stimulus conditions.

stress—A psychological and physical condition in which the individual is subjected to some form of threat or challenge. The term is also used by some to refer to the environmental conditions that produce stress; others use the term *stressor* to refer to any condition that produces stress.

Structured Interview—A procedure for assessing Type A behavior pattern. The behaviors of individuals in the interview are coded for various manifestations of Type A behavior, resulting in a Type A score. Also called the *Type A Interview*.

subception—Showing differential responses to stimuli that subjects claim they cannot perceive. These responses can take the form of a psychophysiological response such as skin conductance or of changes in response parameters such as increased or decreased reaction times.

subjective threshold—The level of presentation of a stimulus at which subjects believe they have no information about the stimulus even though they are able to emit responses that indicate that some information has been obtained.

subliminal perception—The obtaining of information about a stimulus when it is presented below the threshold for conscious awareness.

superego—The part of the mind that represents the strictures of society, especially as communicated by the parents. It includes the rules that prohibit unacceptable behavior as well as images of socially desirable behavior. Often used as a synonym for "conscience."

surgency—An alternate label for the extraversion factor of the Big Five, characterized by talkativeness, assertiveness, and high energy.

sympathetic nervous system—The division of the autonomic nervous system that prepares the individual for high-intensity, emergency reactions (sometimes called "fight–flight" reactions).

taboo—Socially unacceptable.

temperament—An individual's characteristic emotional tone, usually assumed to be biologically based.

test–retest reliability coefficient—The correlation of scores on tests taken at two different points in time. Usually the time difference is days, weeks, or months. As the time difference gets larger (say, a year or more) the emphasis shifts from reliability of measurement to the stability of the underlying characteristics being measured.

threats to validity—Anything that undermines the validity of measurements.

trait—A characteristic of an individual. For some personality psychologists, traits are simply observed consistencies in behavior; for others, they are underlying dispositions to behave in characteristic ways under certain conditions. Traits often are assumed to be *continuous,* as opposed to *types,* which are defined as discrete categories into which people can be classified.

true experiment—A study in which subjects are randomly assigned to different treatment conditions. The consequences of the different treatments on some target behavior is then assessed.

Type A—A pattern of behavior characterized by impatience, competitiveness, and hostility.

Type B—A pattern of behavior that is opposite to that of Type A.

uncertainty orientation—A dimension of individual differences in the motivation to acquire new knowledge about oneself and one's environment. Uncertainty-oriented people accept that their views may be incomplete or wrong and are open to seeking new information to adjust their views, including new information about themselves. More certainty-oriented people are made uncomfortable by the idea that their views may not be correct and avoid situations that might lead them to have to rethink their views, including those about themselves.

uninhibited—Characteristically open to and interested in novel situations and new people. Generally fearless and outgoing.

valence—The positivity or negativity of an outcome.

validity—The degree to which a given measurement accurately reflects the underlying variable it is designed to measure.

variable—Anything that can be assigned or take on more than one value. In personality research, differences among individuals on measurable characteristics often constitute the variables of interest.

variable-centered—Research that focuses on one or more specific variables by comparing people who differ on those variables. The emphasis is often on relationships among variables.

variance—A statistic that describes the amount of variability in a set of scores, that is, the degree to which the scores differ from each other. The variance is computed as the average squared difference between each score and the mean.

veridical—Accurately reflecting the true state of things.

wait-list control—A control group consisting of individuals who have sought therapy but who are told that no therapists are currently available. The object of this control group is to ensure that those receiving therapy do not differ from the control group in their intention to receive therapy.

withdrawal/avoidance tendencies—Motivational tendencies to maintain distance from possibly threatening stimuli or situations.

References

ACHENBACH, T. M., & HOWELL, C. T. (1993). Are American children's problems getting worse? A 13-year comparison. *Journal of the American Academy of Child and Adolescent Psychiatry, 32,* 1145–1154.

ADLER, N., & MATTHEWS, K. (1994). Health psychology: Why do some people get sick and some stay well? *Annual Review of Psychology, 45,* 229–259.

AGGLETON, J. P., & MISHKIN, M. (1986). The amygdala: Sensory gateway to the emotions. In R. E. Plutchik & H. Kellerman (Eds.), *Emotion: Theory, research, and experience: Vol. 3. Biological foundations of emotion* (pp. 281–299). San Diego: Academic Press.

AHERN, F. M., JOHNSON, R. C., WILSON, J. R., McCLEARN, G. E., & VANDENBERG, S. G. (1982). Family resemblances in personality. *Behavior Genetics, 18,* 261–280.

AINSWORTH, M. D. S., BLEHAR, M. C., WATERS, E., & WALL, S. (1978). *Patterns of attachment: A psychological study of the strange situation.* Hillsdale, NJ: Erlbaum.

AJZEN, I., & FISHBEIN, M. (1977). Attitude-behavior relations: A theoretical analysis and review of empirical research. *Psychological Bulletin, 84,* 888–918.

ALDWIN, C. M., LEVENSON, M. R., SPIRO, A., & BOSSE, R. (1989). Does emotionality predict stress? Findings from the normative aging study. *Journal of Personality and Social Psychology, 56,* 618–614.

ALDWIN, C. M., REVENSON, T. A. (1987). Does coping help? A reexamination of the relation between coping and mental health. *Journal of Personality and Social Psychology, 53,* 337–348.

ALLEN, L. S., & GORSKI, R. A. (1992). Sexual orientation and the size of the anterior commissure in the human brain. *Proceedings of the National Academy of Sciences, USA, 89,* 7199–7202.

ALLPORT, G. W. (1937). *Personality: A psychological interpretation.* New York: Holt, Rinehart & Winston.

ALLPORT, G. W. (1961). *Pattern and growth in personality.* New York: Holt, Rinehart & Winston.

ALLPORT, G. W. (1965). *Letters from Jenny.* New York: Harcourt, Brace, & World.

ALLPORT, G. W., & ODBERT, H. S. (1936). *Trait names: A psycholexical study.* Albany: Psychological Review Company.

ALMAGOR, M., TELLEGEN, A., & WALLER, N. G. (1995). The big seven model: A cross-cultural replication and further exploration of the basic dimensions of natural language trait descriptors. *Journal of Personality and Social Psychology, 69,* 300–307.

AMABILE, T. M. (1982). Children's artistic creativity: Detrimental effects on competition in a field setting. *Personality and Social Psychology Bulletin, 8,* 573–578.

AMABILE, T. M. (1985). Motivation and creativity: Effects of motivational orientation on creative writers. *Journal of Personality and Social Psychology, 48,* 393–399.

AMBADY, N., & ROSENTHAL, R. (1993). Half a minute: Predicting teacher evaluations from thin slices of non-verbal behavior and physical attractiveness. *Journal of Personality and Social Psychology, 64,* 631–641.

AMELANG, M., & BORKENAU, P. (1984). Versuche einer Differenzierung des Eigenschafts-konzepts: Apekte intraindividueller Veriabilitat and differentieller Vorkersagbarkeit. [Efforts to differentiate the trait construct: Aspects of intra-individual variability and differential predictability.] In M. Amelang & H. J. Ahrens (Eds.), *Brennpunkte der persona lichkeitsforshung.* Gottingen: Hogrefe.

ANGELINI, A. L. (1959). Studies in projective measurement of achievement motivation in Brazilian students. *Acta Psychologica, 15,* 359–360.

ANGLEITNER, A. (1995). *Bielefeld twin study.* Unpublished manuscript, Department of Psychology, University of Bielefeld.

ASCH, S. E., & WITKIN, H. A. (1948). Studies in space orientation. II. Perception of the upright with displaced visual fields and with body tilted. *Journal of Experimental Psychology, 38,* 455–477.

ASENDORPF, J. B., & SCHERER, K. R. (1983). The discrepant repressor: Differentiation between low anxiety, high anxiety, and repression of anxiety by autonomic-facial-verbal patterns of behavior. *Journal of Personality and Social Psychology, 45,* 1334–1346.

ASHMORE, R. D. (1990). Sex, gender, and the individual. In L. A. Pervin (Ed.), *Handbook of personality* (pp. 486–526). New York: Guilford.

ATKINSON, J. W. (1964). *An introduction to motivation.* New York: Van Nostrand.

ATKINSON, J. W. (1982). Motivational determinants of thematic apperception. In A. Stewart (Ed.), *Motivation and society* (pp. 3–40). San Francisco: Jossey-Bass.

ATKINSON, J. W., & LITWIN, G. H. (1960). Achievement motive and test anxiety conceived of as motive to approach success and motive to avoid failure. *Journal of Abnormal and Social Psychology, 60,* 52–63.

ATKINSON, J. W., & McCLELLAND, D. C. (1948). The projective expression of needs. II. The effect of different intensities of hunger drive on thematic apperception. *Journal of Experimental Psychology, 38,* 643–658.

BACHMAN, J. G. (1970). *Youth in transition: Vol. 2. The impact of family background and intelligence on tenth-grade boys.* Ann Arbor: Survey Research Center, Institute for Social Research, University of Michigan.

BAILEY, J. M., & PILLARD, R. C. (1991). A genetic study of male sexual orientation. *Archives of General Psychiatry, 48,* 1089–1096.

BAKER, L. A., & DANIELS, D. (1990). Nonshared environmental influences and personality differences in adult twins. *Journal of Personality and Social Psychology, 58,* 103–110.

BANDURA, A. (1977). Self-efficacy: Toward a unifying theory of behavioral change. *Psychological Review, 84,* 191–215.

BANDURA, A. (1989). Self-regulation of motivation and action through internal standards and goal systems. In L. A. Pervin (Ed.), *Goal concepts in personality and social psychology* (pp. 19–85). Hillsdale, NJ: Erlbaum.

BANDURA, A., ADAMS, N. E., & BEYER, J. (1977). Cognitive processes mediating behavioral change. *Journal of Personality and Social Psychology, 35,* 125–139.

BANDURA, A., & SCHUNK, D. H. (1981). Cultivating competence, self-efficacy, and intrinsic interest through proximal self-motivation. *Journal of Personality and Social Psychology, 41,* 586–598.

BANKS, W. C. (1976). White preference in Blacks: A paradigm in search of a phenomenon. *Psychological Bulletin, 83,* 1179–1186.

BARASH, D. P. (1982). *Sociobiology and behavior.* New York: Elsevier.

BAREFOOT, J. (1992). Developments in the measurement of hostility. In H. S. Friedman (Ed.), *Hostility, coping, and health* (pp. 13–31). Washington, DC: American Psychological Association.

BARGH, J. A., BOND, R. N., LOMBARDI, W. J., & TOTA, M. E. (1986). The additive nature of chronic and temporary sources of construct accessibility. *Journal of Personality and Social Psychology, 50,* 869–878.

BARGH, J. A., CHEN, M., & BURROWS, L. (1996). Automaticity of social behavior: Direct effects of trait construct and stereotype activation on action. *Journal of Personality and Social Psychology, 71,* 230–244.

BARRICK, M. R., & MOUNT, M. K. (1991). The big five personality dimensions and job performance: A meta-analysis. *Personnel Psychology, 44,* 1–26.

BARRICK, M. R., & MOUNT, M. K. (1993). Autonomy as a moderator of the relationships between the big five personality dimensions and job performance. *Journal of Applied Psychology, 78,* 111–118.

BATES, J. E. (1989). Concepts and measures of temperament. In G. A. Kohnstamm, J. E. Bates, & M. K. Rothbart (Eds.), *Temperament in childhood* (pp. 3–26). New York: Wiley.

BAUMEISTER, R. F., HEATHERTON, T. F., & TICE, D. M. (1993) When ego threats lead to self-regulation failure. Negative consequences of high self-esteem. *Journal of Personality and Social Psychology, 64,* 141–156.

BAUMEISTER, R. F., & TICE, D. M. (1988). Metatraits. *Journal of Personality, 56,* 571–598.

BEITMAN, B. D., MUKERJI, V., LAMBERTI, J. W., SCHMID, L., DEROSEAR, L., KUSHNER, M., FLAKER, G., & BASHA, I. (1989). Panic disorders in patients with chest pain and angiographically normal coronary arteries. *American Journal of Cardiology, 63,* 1399–1403.

BELSKY, J., STEINBERG, L., & DRAPER, P. (1991). Childhood experience, interpersonal development, and reproductive strategy: An evolutionary theory of socialization. *Child Development, 62,* 647–670.

BEM, D. J., & ALLEN, A. (1974). On predicting some of the people some of the time: The search for cross-situational consistencies in behavior. *Psychological Review, 81,* 506–520.

BEM, S. L. (1974). The measurement of psychological androgyny. *Journal of Consulting and Clinical Psychology, 42,* 165–172.

BEN-PORATH, Y. S., & TELLEGEN, A. (1990). A place for traits in stress research. *Psychological Inquiry, 1,* 14–17.

BENEDICT, R. (1934). *Patterns of culture.* New York: Houghton Mifflin.

BENSON, V. E. (1942). The intelligence and later success of sixth grade pupils. *School and Society, 55,* 163–167.

BERENBAUM, S. A., & HINES, M. (1992). Early androgens are related to childhood sex-typed toy preferences. *Psychological Science, 3,* 203–206.

BERMAN, J. S., & NORTON, N. C. (1985). Does professional training make a therapist more effective? *Psychological Bulletin, 98,* 401–406.

BERNARD, L. L. (1924). *Instinct: A study in social psychology.* New York: Holt, Rinehart & Winston.

BETZIG, L. (1986). *Despotism and differential reproduction: A Darwinian view of history.* Hawthorne, NY: Aldine de Gruyter.

BIRAN, M., & WILSON, G. T. (1981). Treatment of phobic disorders using cognitive and exposure methods: A self-efficacy analysis. *Journal of Counseling and Clinical Psychology, 49,* 886–899.

BLACKWELL, H. R. (1952). Studies of psychophysical methods for measuring visual thresholds. *Journal of the Optical Society of America, 42,* 606–616.

BLANEY, P. H. (1986). Affect and memory: A review. *Psychological Bulletin, 99,* 229–246.

BLOCK, J. (1961). *The Q-sort method in personality assessment and psychiatric research.* Springfield, IL: Thomas.

BLOCK, J., BLOCK, J. H., & KEYES, S. (1988). Longitudinally foretelling drug usage in adolescence: Early childhood personality and environmental precursors. *Child Development, 59,* 336–355.

BLOCK, J., & ROBINS, R. W. (1993). A longitudinal study of consistency and change in self-esteem from early adolescence to early adulthood. *Child Development, 64,* 909–923.

BOOTH-KEWLEY, S., & VICKERS, R. R. (1994). Associations between major domains of personality and health behavior. *Journal of Personality, 62,* 281–298.

BORKENAU, P., & LIEBLER, A. (1993). Convergence of stranger ratings of personality and intelligence with self-ratings, partner-ratings, and measured intelligence. *Journal of Personality and Social Psychology, 65,* 546–553.

BOTWIN, M. D., & BUSS, D. M. (1989). Structure of act-report data: Is the five-factor model of personality recaptured. *Journal of Personality and Social Psychology, 56,* 988–1001.

BOUCHARD, T. J., JR., & McGUE, M. (1981). Familial studies of intelligence: A review. *Science, 212,* 1055–1058

BOWER, G. H. (1981). Mood and memory. *American Psychologist, 36,* 129–148.

BOWER, G. H. (1991). Mood congruity in social judgments. In J. P. Forgas (Ed.), *Emotion and social judgments* (pp. 31–53). Elmsford, NY: Pergamon Press.

BOWLBY, J. (1969). *Attachment and loss: Vol. 1. Attachment.* New York: Basic Books.

BOWLBY, J. (1973). *Attachment and loss: Vol. 2. Separation.* New York: Basic Books.

BRAND, C. R. (1987). The importance of general intelligence. In S. Modgil and C. Modgil (Eds.), *Arthur Jensen: Consensus and controversy.* New York: Falmer.

BRAZELTON, T. B. (1983). *Infants and mothers: Differences in development.* New York: Delta/Seymour Lawrence.

BREEDLOVE, S. M. (1994). Sexual differentiation of the human nervous system. *Annual Review of Psychology, 45,* 389–418.

BRETHERTON, I. (1985). Attachment theory: Retrospect and prospect. *Monographs of the Society for Research in Child Development, 50,* 3–35.

BRITT, T. W. (1993). Metatraits: Evidence relevant to the validity of the construct and its implications. *Journal of Personality and Social Psychology, 65,* 554–562.

BRODY, N. (1988). *Personality: In search of individuality.* New York: Harcourt Brace Jovanovich.

BRODY, N. (1992). *Intelligence.* San Diego: Academic Press.

BRODY, N., GOODMAN, S. E., Halm, E., Krinzman, S., & Sebrechts, M. (1987). Lateralized affective priming of lateralized affectively valued target words. *Neuropsychologia, 25,* 935–946.

BROWN, D. E. (1991). *Human universals.* Philadelphia: Temple University Press.

BROWN, J. D., & MANKOWSKI, T. A. (1993). Self-esteem, mood, and self-evaluation: Changes in mood and the way you see you. *Journal of Personality and Social Psychology, 64,* 421–430.

BROWN, L. L., TOMARKEN, A. J., ORTH, D. N., LOOSEN, P. T., KALIN, N. H., & DAVIDSON, R. J. (1996). Individual differences in repressive-defensiveness predict basal salivary cortisol levels. *Journal of Personality and Social Psychology, 70,* 362–371.

BURLEY, N., & SYMANSKI, R. (1981). Women without: An evolutionary and cross-cultural perspective on prostitution. In R. Symanski (Ed.), *The immoral landscape: Female prostitution in Western societies* (pp. 239–274). Toronto: Butterworths.

BURNSTEIN, E., CRANDALL, C., & KITAYAMA, S. (1994). Some neo-Darwinian decisions rules for altruism: Weighing cues for inclusive fitness as a function of the biological importance of the decision. *Journal of Personality and Social Psychology, 67,* 773-789.

BUSS, A., & PLOMIN, R. (1984). *Temperament: Early developing personality traits.* Hillsdale, NJ: Erlbaum.

BUSS, D. M. (1989). Sex differences in human mate preferences: Evolutionary hypotheses tested in 37 cultures. *Behavioral and Brain Sciences, 12,* 1–49.

BUSS, D. M. (1991). Evolutionary personality psychology. *Annual Review of Psychology, 42,* 459–491.

BUSS, D. M. (1994). *The evolution of desire: Strategies of human mating.* New York: Basic Books.

BUSS, D. M. (1995). Evolutionary psychology: A paradigm for psychological science. *Psychological Inquiry, 6,* 1–30.

BUSS, D. M., ABBOTT, M., ANGLEITNER, A., ASHERIAN, A., ET AL. (1990). International preferences in selecting mates: A study of 37 cultures. *Journal of Cross Cultural Psychology, 21,* 5–47.

BUSS, D. M., LARSEN, R. J., WESTEN, D., & SEMMELROTH, J. (1992). Sex differences in jealousy: Evolution, physiology, and psychology. *Psychological Science, 3,* 251–255.

BUSS, D. M., & SCHMITT, D. P. (1993). Sexual strategies theory: A contextual evolutionary analysis of human mating. *Psychological Review, 100,* 204–232.

CACIOPPO, J. T., KLEIN, D. J., BERNSTON, G. G., & HATFIELD, E. (1993). The psychophysiology of emotion. In M. Lewis & J. Haviland (Eds.), *Handbook of emotions* (pp. 119–142). New York: Guilford.

CAIRNS, R. B. (1986). An evolutionary and developmental perspective on aggressive patterns. In C. Zahn-Wexler, E. M. Cummings, & R. Ionnotti (Eds.), *Altruism and aggression.* New York: Cambridge University Press.

CALDERA, Y. M., HUSTON, A. C., & O'BRIEN, M. (1989). Social interactions and play patterns of parents and toddlers with feminine, masculine, and neutral toys. *Child Development, 60,* 70–76.

CALDWELL, B. M., & BRADLEY, R. H. (1978). *Home observation for measurement of the environment.* Little Rock: University of Arkansas Press.

CAMPBELL, J. B., & HAWLEY, C. W. (1982). Study habits and Eysenck's theory of extraversion-introversion. *Journal of Research in Personality, 16,* 139–146.

CAMPOS, J. J., BARRETT, K., LAMB, M. E., GOLDSMITH, H. H., & STENBERG, C. (1983). Socioemotional development. In P. H. Mussen (Ed.), *Handbook of child psychology: Vol. 2. Infancy and developmental psychobiology* (pp. 783–915). New York: Wiley.

CANDIOTTE, M. M., & LICHTENSTEIN, E. (1981). Self-efficacy and relapse in smoking cessation programs. *Journal of Counseling and Clinical Psychology, 49,* 648–658.

CANTOR, N. (1990). From thought to behavior: "Having" and "doing" in the study of personality and cognition. *American Psychologist, 45,* 735–750.

CANTOR, N. (1994). Life task problem solving: Situational affordances and personal needs. *Personality and Social Psychology Bulletin, 20,* 235–243.

CANTOR, N., ACKER, M., & COOK-FLANNAGAN, C. (1992). Conflict and preoccupation in the intimacy life task. *Journal of Personality and Social Psychology, 63,* 644–655.

CANTOR, N., & LANGSTON, C. A. (1989). Ups and downs of life tasks in a life transition. In L. A. Pervin (Ed.), *Goal concepts in personality and social psychology* (pp. 127–167). Hillsdale, NJ: Erlbaum.

CANTOR, N., & ZIRKEL, S. (1990). Personality, cognition, and purposive behavior. In L. Pervin (Ed.), *Handbook of personality: Theory and research* (pp. 135–164). New York: Guilford.

CAPRON, C., & DUYME, M. (1989). Assessment of effects of socio-economic status on IQ in a full cross-fostering study. *Nature, 340,* 552–554.

CARLSON, R. (1971). Where is the person in personality research? *Psychological Bulletin, 75,* 203–219.

CARROLL, JOHN. (1993). *Human cognitive abilities: A survey of factor-analytic studies.* New York: Cambridge University Press.

CARVER, C. S., POZO, C., HARRIS, S. D., NORIEGA, V., SCHEIER, M. F., ROBINSON, D. S., KETCHAM, A. S., MOFFAT, F. L., & CLARK, K. C. (1993). How coping mediates the effects of optimism on distress: A study of women with early stage breast cancer. *Journal of Personality and Social Psychology, 65,* 375–390.

CARVER, C. S., & SCHEIER, M. F. (1981). *Attention and self-regulation: A control approach to human behavior.* New York: Springer-Verlag.

CARVER, C. S., SCHEIER, M. F., & WEINTRAUB, J. K. (1989). Assessing coping strategies: A theoretically based approach. *Journal of Personality and Social Psychology, 56,* 267–283.

CASPI, A. (in press). *Personality development across the life course.* Department of Psychology, University of Wisconsin.

CASPI, A., & BEM, D. J. (1990). Personality continuity and change across the life course. In L. Pervin (Ed.), *Handbook of personality: Theory and research* (pp. 549–608). New York: Guilford.

CASPI, A., ELDER, G. H., & BEM, D. J. (1987). Moving against the world: Life-course patterns of explosive children. *Developmental Psychology, 23,* 308–313.

CASPI, A., ELDER, G. H., & BEM, D. J. (1988). Moving away from the world: Life course patterns of shy children. *Developmental Psychology, 24,* 824–831.

CASPI, A., & HERBENER, E. S. (1990). Continuity and change: Assortative marriage and the consistency of personality in adulthood. *Journal of Personality and Social Psychology, 58,* 250–258.

CASPI, A., & MOFFITT, T. E. (1991). Individual differences are accentuated during periods of social change: The sample case of girls at puberty. *Journal of Personality and Social Psychology, 61,* 157–168.

CASPI, A., & SILVA, P. A. (1995). Personality traits in young adulthood: Longitudinal evidence from a birth cohort. *Child Development, 66,* 486–498.

CATTELL, R. B. (1965). *The scientific study of personality.* Baltimore: Penguin.

CHAPIN, W. F., & GOLDBERG, L. R. (1985). A failure to replicate the Bem and Allen study of individual differences in cross-situational consistency. *Journal of Personality and Social Psychology, 47,* 1074–1090.

CHAPLIN, J. P. (1968). *Dictionary of psychology.* New York: Dell.

CHEEK, J. (1982). Aggregation, moderator variables, and the validity of personality tests. A peer-rating study. *Journal of Personality and Social Psychology, 43,* 1254–1269.

CHESS, S., & THOMAS, A. (1989). Issues in the clinical application of temperament. In G. A. Kohnstamm, J. E. Bates, & M. K. Rothbart (Eds.), *Temperament in childhood* (pp. 377–386). Chichester, UK: Wiley.

CHRISTENSEN, A., & JACOBSON, N. S. (1994). Who (or what) can do psychotherapy: The status and challenge of nonprofessional therapies. *Psychological Science, 5,* 8–14.

CLARK, K. B. (1955). *Prejudice and your child.* Boston: Beacon Press.

CLARK, K. B., & CLARK, M. P. (1939a). The development of consciousness of self and the emergence of racial identification in Negro pre-school children. *Journal of Social Psychology, 10,* 591–599.

CLARK, K. B., & CLARK, M. P. (1939b). Segregation as a factor in the racial identification of Negro pre-school children: A preliminary report. *Journal of Experimental Education, 8,* 161–163.

CLARK, K. B., & CLARK, M. P. (1947). Racial identification and preference in Negro children. In T. M. Newcomb and E. L. Hartley (Eds.), *Readings in social psychology* (pp. 169–178). New York: Holt.

CLARK, K. B., & CLARK, M. P. (1950). Emotional factors in racial identification and preference in Negro children. *Journal of Negro Education, 19,* 341–350.

CLARK, R. D., & HATFIELD, E. (1989). Gender differences in receptivity to sexual offers. *Journal of Psychology and Human Sexuality, 2,* 39–55.

CLONINGER, C. R. (1986). A unified biosocial theory of personality and its role in development of anxiety states. *Psychiatric Developments, 3,* 167–226.

CLOVER, R. D., ABELL, T., BECKER, L. A., CRAWFORD, S., & RAMSEY, J. C. N. (1989). Family functioning and stress as predictors of influenza B infection. *Journal of Family Practice, 28,* 535–539.

COHEN, S., TYRRELL, D. A. J., & SMITH, A. P. (1993). Negative life events, perceived stress, negative affect, and susceptibility to the common cold. *Journal of Personality and Social Psychology, 64,* 131–140.

COLLAER, M. L., & HINES, M. (1995). Human behavioral sex differences: A role for gonadal hormones during early development? *Psychological Bulletin, 118,* 55–107.

COLOMBO, J. (1993). *Infant cognition: Predicting later intellectual functioning.* Newbury Park, CA: Sage Publications.

CONTRADA, R. J., LEVENTHAL, H., & O'LEARY, A. (1990). Personality and health. In L. Pervin (Ed.), *Handbook of personality: Theory and research* (pp. 638–669). New York: Guilford.

COREN, S., & HALPERN, D. F. (1991). Left-handedness: A marker for decreased survival fitness. *Psychological Bulletin, 109,* 90–106.

COSMIDES, L., TOOBY, J., & BARKOW, J. H. (1992). Introduction: Evolutionary psychology and conceptual integration. In J. H. Barkow, L. Cosmides, & J. Tooby (Eds.), *The adapted mind* (pp. 5–15). New York: Oxford University Press.

COSTA, P. T., & McCRAE, R. R. (1988). From catalogue to classification: Murray's needs and the five factor model. *Journal of Personality and Social Psychology, 55,* 258–265.

COSTA, P. T., & McCRAE, R. R. (1987). Neuroticism, somatic complaints, and disease: Is the bark worse than the bite? *Journal of Personality, 55,* 299–316.

COZZARELLI, C. (1993). Personality and self-efficacy as predictors of coping with abortion. *Journal of Personality and Social Psychology, 65,* 1224–1236.

CRANK, J. N., & BULGREN, J. (1993). Visual depictions as information organizers for enhancing achievement of students with learning disabilities. *Learning Disabilities Research & Practice, 8,* 140–147.

CRONBACH, L. J., & SNOW, R. E. (1977). *Aptitudes and instructional methods.* New York: Irvington.

CROSS, W. E. JR. (1991). *Shades of black: Diversity in African-American identity.* Philadelphia: Temple University Press.

CSIKSZENTMIHALYI, M. (1975). *Beyond boredom and anxiety.* San Francisco: Jossey-Bass.

CUNNINGHAM, M. R. (1979). Weather, mood, and helping behavior: Quasi experiments with the sunshine samaritan. *Journal of Personality and Social Psychology, 37,* 1947–1956.

CUNNINGHAM, M. R., ROBERTS, A. R., BARBEE, A. P., DRUEN, P. B, & WU, C. (1995). "Their ideas of beauty are, on the whole, the same as ours": Consistency and variability in the cross-cultural perception of female physical attractiveness. *Journal of Personality and Social Psychology, 68,* 261–279.

DAGENBACH, D., & CARR, T. H. (1985). Awareness, attention, and automaticity in perpetual encoding: Conscious influences on unconscious perception. Unpublished manuscript, Michigan State University, East Lansing.

DALY, M., & WILSON, M. (1983). *Sex, evolution, and behavior* (2nd ed.). Belmont, CA: Wadsworth.

DALY, M., & WILSON, M. (1988). *Homicide.* New York: Aldine de Gruyter.

DARWIN, C. (1872). *The expression of the emotions in man and animals.* New York: Philosophical Library.

DAVIDSON, K. W. (1993). Suppression and repression in discrepant self-other ratings: Relations with thought control and cardiovascular reactivity. *Journal of Personality, 61,* 669–691.

DAVIDSON, R. J. (1992). Emotion and affective style: Hemispheric substrates. *Psychological Science, 3,* 39–43.

DAVIDSON, R. J., & FOX, N. A. (1989). Frontal brain asymmetry predicts infants' response to maternal separation. *Journal of Abnormal Psychology, 98,* 127–131.

DAVIDSON, R. J., & TOMARKEN, A. J. (1989). Laterality and emotion: An electrophysiological approach. In F. Boller & J. Grafman (Eds.), *Handbook of neuropsychology* (Vol. 3, pp. 419–441). Amsterdam: Elsevier.

DAVIS, M. (1992). The role of the amygdala in fear and anxiety. *Annual Review of Neuroscience, 15,* 353–403.

DAVIS, M., HITCHCOCK, J. M., & ROSEN, J. B. (1987). Anxiety and the amygdala: Pharmacological and anatomical analysis of the fear-potentiated startle paradigm. *The psychology of learning and motivation, 21,* 263–305. New York: Academic Press.

DECI, E. L. (1975). *Intrinsic motivation.* New York: Plenum.

DECI, E. L. (1992). On the nature and functions of motivation theories. *Psychological Science, 3,* 167–171.

DECI, E. L., CONNELL, J. P., & RYAN, R. M. (1989). Self-determination in a work organization. *Applied Psychology, 74,* 580–590.

DECI, E. L., & RYAN, R. (1985). *Intrinsic motivation and self-determination in human behavior.* New York: Plenum Press.

DECI, E. L., & RYAN, R. (1992). The initiation and regulation of intrinsically motivated learning and achievement. In A. K. Boggiano & T. S. Pittman (Eds.), *Achievement and motivation: A social-developmental perspective* (pp. 9–36). New York: Cambridge University Press.

DEMBROSKI, T. M., MacDOUGALL, J. M., COSTA, P. T., & GRANDITS, G. A. (1989). Components of hostility as predictors of sudden death and myocardial infarction in the Multiple Risk Factor Intervention Trial. *Psychosomatic Medicine, 51,* 514–522.

DEPUE, R. A., LUCIANA, M., ARBISI, P., COLLINS, P., & LEON, A. (1994). Dopamine and the structure of personality: Relation to agonist-induced dopamine activity to positive emotionality. *Journal of Personality and Social Psychology, 67,* 485–498.

DEPUE, R. A., & MONROE, S. M. (1986). Conceptualization and measurement of human disorder in life stress research: The problem of chronic disturbance. *Psychological Bulletin, 99,* 36–51.

DIENER, C. I., & DWECK, C. S. (1978). An analysis of learned helplessness: Continuous changes in performance, strategy, and achievement cognitions following failure. *Journal of Personality and Social Psychology, 36,* 451–462.

DIENER, C. I., & DWECK, C. S. (1980). An analysis of learned helplessness: II. The processing of success. *Journal of Personality and Social Psychology, 39,* 940–952.

DIENER, E., & LARSEN, R. A. (1993). The experience of emotional well-being. In M. Lewis & J. M. Haviland (Eds.), *Handbook of emotions* (pp. 405–415). New York: Guilford.

DIGMAN, J. M. (1972). High school academic achievement as seen in the context of a longitudinal study of personality. *Proceedings of the Annual Convention of the American Psychological Association 1972, 7,* 19–20.

DRAPER, P., & BELSKY, J. (1990). Personality development in evolutionary perspective. *Journal of Personality, 58,* 141–162.

DuBOIS, W. E. B. (1903). *The souls of black folks.* Chicago: McClurg.

DUNCAN, O. D., FEATHERMAN, D. L., & DUNCAN, B. (1972). *Socioeconomic background and achievement.* New York: Seminar Press.

DUNN, J., & PLOMIN, R. (1990). *Separate lives: Why siblings are so different.* New York: Basic Books.

DURLAK, J. A. (1979). Comparative effectiveness of paraprofessional and professional helpers. *Psychological Bulletin, 86,* 80–92.

DWECK, C. S., & LEGGETT, E. L. (1988). A social-cognitive approach to motivation and personality. *Psychological Review, 95,* 256–273.

EAGLY, A. H. (1987). Reporting sex differences. *American Psychologist, 42,* 756–757.

EAGLY, A. H. (1987). *Sex differences in social behavior: A social-role interpretation.* Hillsdale, NJ: Erlbaum.

EAGLY, A. H. (1995). The science and politics of comparing women and men. *American Psychologist, 50,* 145–158.

EAGLY, A., H., & STEFFEN, V. J. (1986). Gender and aggressive behavior: A meta-analytic review of the social psychological literature. *Psychological Bulletin, 100,* 309–330.

EATON, W. O. (1994). Methodological implications of the impending engagement of temperament and biology. In J. E. Bates & T. D. Wachs (Eds.), *Temperament: Individual differences at the interface of biology and behavior* (pp. 259–274). Washington, DC: American Psychological Association.

EAVES, L. J., EYSENCK, H. J., & MARTIN, N. G. (1989). *Genes, culture and personality: An empirical approach.* San Diego: Academic Press.

EBSTEIN, R. P., NOVICCK, O., UMANSKY, R., PRIEL, B., OSHER, Y., BLAINE, D., BENNETT, E. R., NEMANOV, L., KATZ, M. S., & BELMAKER, R. H. (1996). Dopamine D4 receptor (D4DR) exon III polymorphism associated with the human trait of Novelty Seeking. *Nature Genetics, 12,* 78–80.

EDEN, D., & AVIRAM, A. (1993). Self-efficacy training to speed reemployment: Helping people to help themselves. *Journal of Applied Psychology, 78,* 352–360.

EHRHARDT, A. A., EPSTEIN, R., & MONEY, J. (1968). Fetal androgens and female gender identity in the early-treated adrenogenital syndrome. *Johns Hopkins Medical Journal, 122,* 160–167.

EHRLICHMAN, H., & EICHENSTEIN, R. (1992). Private wishes: Gender similarities and differences. *Sex Roles, 26,* 399–422.

EHRLICHMAN, H., & HALPERN, J. N. (1988). Affect and memory: Effects of pleasant and unpleasant odors on retrieval of happy and unhappy memories. *Journal of Personality and Social Psychology, 55,* 769–779.

EHRLICHMAN, H., & WIENER, M. S. (1980). EEG asymmetry during covert mental activity. *Psychophysiology, 17,* 228–235.

EKMAN, P. (1992). Are there basic emotions? *Psychological Review, 99,* 550–553.

EKMAN, P. (1994). Strong evidence for universals in facial expressions: A reply to Russell's mistaken critique. *Psychological Bulletin, 115,* 268–287.

EKMAN, P., & FRIESEN, W. V. (1978). *The Facial Action Coding System: A technique for the measurement of facial movement.* Palo Alto, CA: Consulting Psychologists Press.

ELDER, G. H., & MacINNIS, D. J. (1983). Achievement imagery in women's lives from adolescence to adulthood. *Journal of Personality and Social Psychology, 45,* 394–404.

ELKIN, I., SHEA, T., WATKINS, J. T., IMBER, S. D., SOTSKY, S. M., COLLINS, J. F., GLASS, D. R., PILKONIS, P. A., LEBER, W. R., DOCHERTY, J. P., FIESTER, S. J., & PERLOFF, M. (1989). National Institutes of Mental Health treatment of depression collaborative research program: General effectiveness of treatments. *Archives of General Psychiatry, 46,* 971–982.

ELLENBERGER, H. F. (1970). *The discovery of the unconscious: The history and evolution of dynamic psychiatry.* New York: Basic Books.

ELLIOT, A. J., & DEVINE, P. G. (1994). On the motivational nature of cognitive dissonance: Dissonance as psychological discomfort. *Journal of Personality and Social Psychology, 67,* 383–294.

ELLIS, B. J., & SYMONS, D. (1990). Sex differences in sexual fantasy: An evolutionary psychological approach. *Journal of Sex Research, 27,* 527–556.

EMMONS, R. A. (1986). Personal strivings: An approach to personality and subjective well-being. *Journal of Personality and Social Psychology, 51,* 1058–1068.

EMMONS, R. A. (1989). The personal striving approach to personality. In L. A. Pervin (Ed.), *Goal concepts in personality and social psychology* (pp. 87–126). Hillsdale, NJ: Erlbaum.

EMMONS, R. A., & DIENER, E. (1986). Influence of impulsivity and sociability on subjective well-being. *Journal of Personality and Social Psychology, 50,* 1211–1215.

EMMONS, R. A., & KING, L. A. (1988). Conflict among personal strivings: Immediate and long-term implications for psychological and physical well-being. *Journal of Personality and Social Psychology, 54,* 1040–1048.

EMMONS, R. A., & KING, L. A. (1989). Personal striving differentiation and affective reactivity. *Journal of Personality and Social Psychology, 56,* 478–484.

EMMONS, R. A., & MCADAMS, D. P. (1991). Personal strivings and motive dispositions: Exploring the links. *Personality and Social Psychology Bulletin, 17,* 648–654.

EPSTEIN, S. (1979). The stability of behavior: I. On predicting most of the people much of the time. *Journal of Personality and Social Psychology, 37,* 1097–1126.

EPSTEIN, S. (1983). The stability of confusion: A reply to Mischel and Peake. *Psychological Review, 90,* 179–194.

ERDELYI, M. H. (1992). Psychodynamics and the unconscious. *American Psychologist, 47,* 784–787.

EWART, C. K., & KOLODNER, K. B. (1993). Predicting ambulatory blood pressure during school: Effectiveness of social and nonsocial reactivity tasks in black and white adolescents. *Psychophysiology, 30,* 30–38.

EYSENCK, H. J. (1952). *The scientific study of personality.* New York: Praeger.

EYSENCK, H. J. (1967). *The biological basis of personality.* Springfield, IL: Charles C. Thomas.

EYSENCK, H. J. (1990a). Biological dimensions of personality. In L. Pervin (Ed.), *Handbook of personality: Theory and research* (pp. 244–276). New York: Guilford.

EYSENCK, H. J. (1990b). Genetic and environmental contributions to individual differences: The three major dimensions of personality. Special Issue: Biological foundations of personality: Evolution, behavioral genetics, and psychophysiology. *Journal of Personality, 58,* 245–261.

EYSENCK, H. J. (1991). Dimensions of personality: 16, 5, or 3? Criteria for a taxonomic paradigm. *Personality and Individual Differences, 12,* 773–790.

EYSENCK, H. J., & EYSENCK, S. B. (1968). A factorial study of psychoticism as a dimension of personality. *Multivariate Behavior Research, Special Issue,* 15–31.

FAHRENBERG, J. (1992). Psychophysiology of neuroticism and anxiety. In A. Gale & M. W. Eysenck (Eds.), *Handbook of individual differences: Biological perspectives* (pp. 179–226). London: Wiley.

FAZIO, R. H., JACKSON, J. R., DUNTON, B. C., & WILLIAMS, C. J. (1995). Variability in automatic activation as an unobtrusive measure of racial attitudes: A bona fide pipeline? *Journal of Personality and Social Psychology, 69,* 1013–1027.

FEINGOLD, A. (1992). Gender differences in mate selection preferences: A test of the parental investment model. *Psychological Bulletin, 112,* 125–139.

FENIGSTEIN, A., SCHEIER, M. F., & BUSS, A. H. (1975). Public and private self-consciousness assessment and theory. *Journal of Consulting and Clinical Psychology, 43,* 522–527.

FESHBACH, S., ADELMAN, H., & FULLER, W. (1977). Prediction of reading and related academic problems. *Journal of Educational Psychology, 69,* 299–308.

FINCHAM, F. D., & BRADBURY, T. N. (1993). Marital satisfaction, depression, and attributions: A longitudinal analysis. *Journal of Personality and Social Psychology, 64,* 442–452.

FLYNN, J. D. (1984). The mean IQ of Americans: Massive gains 1932–78. *Psychological Bulletin, 95,* 29–51.

FLYNN, J. D. (1987). Massive IQ gains in 14 nations: What IQ tests really measure. *Psychological Bulletin, 101,* 171–191.

FOLKMAN, S., LAZARUS, R. S., DUNKEL-SCHETTER, C., DELONGIS, A., & GRUEN, R. (1986). Dynamics of a stressful encounter: Cognitive appraisal, coping, and encounter outcomes. *Journal of Personality and Social Psychology, 50,* 992–1003.

FORGAS, J. P. (1994). Sad and guilty? Affective influences on the explanation of conflict in close relationships. *Journal of Personality and Social Psychology, 66,* 56–68.

FORGAS, J. P. (1995). Mood and judgment: The affect infusion model. *Psychological Bulletin, 117,* 39–66.

FORGAS, J. P., & BOWER, G. H. (1987). Mood effects on person perception judgments. *Journal of Personality and Social Psychology, 53,* 53–60.

FOWLES, D. C. (1987). Application of a behavioral theory of motivation to the concepts of anxiety and impulsivity. *Journal of Research in Personality, 21,* 417–435.

FRENCH, E. G. (1955). Some characteristics of achievement motivation. *Journal of Experimental Psychology, 50,* 232–236.

FREUD, S. (1904/1948). *The psychopathology of everyday life.* London: Ernest Benn.

FREUD, S. (1930/1961). *Civilization and its discontents.* New York: W. W. Norton.

FREUD, S. (1940/1949). *An outline of psychoanalysis.* New York: W. W. Norton.

FRIEDMAN, H. S., DIMATTEO, M. R. (1989). *Health Psychology.* Englewood Cliffs, NJ: Prentice Hall.

FRIEDMAN, H. S., TUCKER, J. S., SCHWARTZ, J. E., MARTIN, L. R., TOMLINSON-KEASEY, C., WINGARD, D. L., & CRIQUI, M. H. (1995). Childhood conscientiousness and longevity: Health behaviors and cause of death. *Journal of Personality and Social Psychology, 68,* 696–703.

FRIEDMAN, H. S., TUCKER, J. S., TOMLINSON-KEASEY, C., SCHWARTZ, J. E., WINGARD, D. L., & CRIQUI, M. H. (1993). Does childhood personality predict longevity? *Journal of Personality and Social Psychology, 65,* 176–185.

FRIEDMAN, M., & ROSENMAN, R. H. (1974). *Type A behavior and your heart.* New York: Knopf.

FRIJDA, N. H. (1986). *The emotions.* New York: Cambridge University Press.

FRIJDA, N. H. (1987). Emotion, cognitive structure, and action tendency. *Cognition and Emotion, 1,* 115–143.

FRIJDA, N. H. (1988). The laws of emotion. *American Psychologist, 43,* 326–358.

FRIJDA, N. H. (1993). Moods, emotions episodes, and emotions. In M. Lewis & J. M. Haviland (Eds.); *Handbook of emotions* (pp. 381–403). New York: Guilford.

FUNDER, D. C. (1991). Global traits: A neo-Allportian approach to personality. *Psychological Science, 2,* 31–39.

FUNDER, D. C., & SNEED, C. D. (1993). Behavioral manifestations of personality: An ecological approach to judgmental accuracy. *Journal of Personality and Social Psychology, 64,* 479–490.

FUNK, S. C. (1992). Hardiness: A review of theory and research. *Health Psychology, 11,* 335–345.

GALE, A. (1983). Electroencephalographic studies of extraversion-introversion: A case study in the psychophysiology of individual differences. *Personality and Individual Differences, 4,* 371–380.

GANGESTAD, S. W., & SIMPSON, J. A. (1990). Toward an evolutionary history of female sociosexual variation. *Journal of Personality, 58,* 69–96.

GARDNER, H. (1983). *Frames of mind: The theory of multiple intelligences.* New York: Basic Books.

GEEN, R. G. (1984). Preferred stimulation levels in introverts and extroverts: Effects on arousal and performance. *Journal of Personality and Social Psychology, 46,* 1303–1312.

GERIN, W., PIEPER, C., LEVY, R., & PICKERING, T. G. (1992). Social support in social interaction: A moderator of cardiovascular reactivity. *Psychosomatic Medicine, 54,* 324–336.

GESCHWIND, N., & BEHAN, P. (1984). Laterality, hormones, and immunity. In N. Geschwind & A. M. Galaburda (Eds.), *Cerebral dominance: The biological foundations* (pp. 211–224). Cambridge, MA: Harvard University Press.

GLADUE, B. A. (1994). The biopsychology of sexual orientation. *Current Directions in Psychological Science, 3,* 150–154.

GLASS, D. C. (1977). *Behavior patterns, stress, and coronary disease.* Hillsdale, NJ: Erlbaum.

GOLDBERG, L. R. (1990). An alternative "description of personality": The big-five factor structure. *Journal of Personality and Social Psychology, 59,* 1216–1229.

GOLDSTEIN, (1994). Sex differences in toy play and use of video games. In J. H. Goldstein (Ed.), *Toys, play, and child development* (pp. 110–129). New York: Cambridge University Press.

GOLEMAN, D. (1995). *Emotional intelligence.* New York: Bantam Books.

GOODENOUGH, D. R. (1978). Field dependence. In H. London & J. E. Exner (Eds.), *Dimensions of personality* (pp. 165–216). New York: Wiley.

GOTTFRIED, A. W. (1984). Home environment and early cognitive development: Integration, meta-analysis, and conclusions. In A. W. Gottfried (Ed.), *Home environment and early cognitive development: Longitudinal research.* Orlando: Academic Press.

GOVE, P. B. (1993). *Webster's third new international dictionary of the English language unabridged.* Springfield, MA: Merriam-Webster.

GOY, R. W., BERCOVITCH, F. B., & MCBRAIR, M. C. (1988). Behavioral masculinization is independent of genital masculinization in prenatally androgenized rhesus macaques. *Hormones and Behavior, 22,* 552–571.

GRAF, P., MANDLER, G., & HAYDEN, P. (1982). Simulating amnesic symptoms in normal subjects. *Science, 218,* 1243–1244.

GRAF, P., & SCHACTER, D. L. (1985). Implicit and explicit memory for new associations in normal and amnesic subjects. *Journal of Experimental Psychology, 84,* 392–298.

GRAY, J. A. (1982). *The neuropsychology of anxiety.* London: Oxford University Press.

GRAY, J. A. (1987). Perspectives on anxiety and impulsivity: A commentary. *Journal of Research in Personality, 21,* 493–509.

GREENWALD, A. G. (1992). New look 3: Unconscious cognition reclaimed. *American Psychologist, 47,* 766–779.

GROEGER, J. A. (1988). Qualitatively different effects of undetected and unidentified auditory primes. *Quarterly Journal of Experimental Psychology, 40A,* 323–329.

GROLNICK, W. S., & RYAN, R. M. (1989). Parent styles associated with children's self-regulation and competence: A social contextual perspective. *Journal of Educational Psychology, 81,* 143–154.

GRUNBAUM, A. (1984). *The foundations of psychoanalysis: A philosophical inquiry.* Berkeley: University of California Press.

GUILFORD, J. P. (1975). Factors and factors of personality. *Psychological Bulletin, 82,* 802–814.

GUNNAR, M., LARSON, M., HERTSGAARD, L., HARRIS, M., & BRODERSEN, L. (1992). The stressfulness of separation among 9-month-old infants: Effects of social context variables and infant temperament. *Child Development, 63,* 290–303.

HAAN, N. (1981). Common dimensions of personality development: Early adolescence to middle life. In D. H. Eichorn, J. A. Clausen, H. Han, M. P. Honzik, & P. H. Mussen (Eds.), *Present and past in middle life.* New York: Academic Press.

HALGREN, E. (1992). Emotional neurophysiology of the amygdala within the context of human cognition. In J. P. Aggleton (Ed.), *The amygdala: Neurobiological aspects of emotion, memory, and mental dysfunction* (pp. 191–228). New York: Wiley-Liss.

HALPERN, D. F. (1992). *Sex differences in cognitive abilities (2nd ed.)* Hillsdale, NJ: Erlbaum.

HALPERN, D. F., & COREN, S. (1993). Left-handedness and life span: A reply to Harris. *Psychological Bulletin, 114,* 235–241.

HARACKIEWICZ, J. M., & ELLIOT, A. J. (1993). Achievement goals and intrinsic motivation. *Journal of Personality and Social Psychology, 65,* 904–915.

HARDAWAY, R. A. (1990). Subliminally activated symbiotic fantasies: Facts and artifacts. *Psychological Bulletin, 107,* 177–175.

HARLOW, H. F. (1953). Mice, monkeys, men and motives. *Psychological Review, 60,* 23–32.

HARLOW, R., & CANTOR, N. (1994). The social pursuit of academics: Side-effects and "spillover" of strategic reassurance-seeking. *Journal of Personality and Social Psychology, 66,* 386–397.

HARRINGTON, D. M., BLOCK, J., & BLOCK, J. H. (1983). Predicting creativity in preadolescence from divergent thinking in early childhood. *Journal of Personality and Social Psychology, 45,* 609–623.

HARRIS, L. J. (1993). Do left-handers die sooner than right-handers? Commentary on Coren and Halpern's (1991) "Left-handedness: A marker for decreased survival fitness." *Psychological Bulletin, 114,* 203–234.

HATFIELD, E., & SPRECHER, S. (1986). *Mirror, mirror: The importance of looks in everyday life.* Albany, NY: SUNY Press.

HAYASHI, T., & HABU, K. (1962). Research on the achievement motive: An experimental test of the "thought sampling" method by using Japanese students. *Japanese Psychological Research, 4,* 30–42.

HEATH, A. C., NEALE, M. C., KESSLER, R. C., EAVES, L. B., & KENDLER, K. S. (1992). Evidence for genetic influences on personality from self-reports and informant ratings. *Journal of Personality and Social Psychology, 63,* 85–96.

HEATH, R. G. (1986). The neural substrate for emotion. In R. Plutchik & H. Kellerman (Eds.), *Emotion: Theory, research and experience* (pp. 3–35). New York: Academic Press.

HECKHAUSEN, H. (1967). *The anatomy of achievement motivation.* New York: Academic Press.

HEDGES, L. V., & NEWELL, A. (1995). Sex differences in mental test scores, variability, and numbers of high-scoring individuals. *Science, 269,* 41–45.

HIGGINS, E. T. (1987). Self discrepancy: A theory relating self and affect. *Psychological Review, 94,* 319–340.

HOFFMAN, C., & KAGAN, S. (1977). Field dependence and facial recognition. *Perceptual and Motor Skills, 44,* 119–124.

HOLENDER, D. (1986). Semantic activation without conscious identification in dichotic listening, parafoveal vision, and vision masking: A survey and appraisal. *Behavioral and Brain Sciences, 9,* 1–66.

HOLLAND, J. (1985). *The self-directed search professional manual.* P.A.R. Florida.

HOUGH, L. M., EATON, N. K., DUNNETTE, M. D., KAMP, J. D., ET AL. (1990). Criterion-related validities of personality constructs and the effect of response distortion on those validities. *Journal of Applied Psychology, 75,* 581–595.

HOUSE, J. S., LANDIS, K. R., & UMBERSON, D. (1988). Social relationships and health. *Science, 241,* 540–545.

HOYENGA, K. B., & HOYENGA, K. T. (1993). *Gender-related differences: Origins and outcomes.* Boston: Allyn and Bacon.

HUESMANN, L. R., ERON, L. D., LEFKOWITZ, M. M., & WALDER, L. O. (1984). Stability of aggression over time and generations. *Developmental Psychology, 20,* 1120–1134.

HUESMANN, L. R., ERON, L. D., & YARMEL, P. (1987). Intellectual functioning and aggression. *Journal of Personality and Social Psychology, 52,* 218–231.

HUMPHREYS, L. G., DAVEY, T. C., & KASHIMA, E. (1986). Experimental measures of cognitive privilege/deprivation and some of their correlates. *Intelligence, 10,* 355–376.

HUNTER, J. E., & HUNTER, R. F. (1984). Validity and performance of alternative predictors of job performance. *Psychological Bulletin, 96,* 72–98.

HYDE, J. S. (1990). Meta-analysis and the psychology of gender differences. *Signs: Journal of Women in Culture and Society, 16,* 55–73.

IZARD, C. E. (1990). Facial expressions and the regulation of emotions. *Journal of Personality and Social Psychology, 58,* 487–498.

IZARD, C. E. (1993). Four systems for emotion activation: Cognitive and noncognitive processes. *Psychological Review, 100,* 68–90.

IZARD, C. E. (1994). Innate and universal facial expressions: Evidence from developmental and cross-cultural research. *Psychological Bulletin, 115,* 288–299.

JACKSON, D. N. (1984). *Personality research form manual* (3rd ed.). Port Huron, MI: Research Psychologist Press.

JACOBY, L. L., & DALLAS, M. (1981). On the relationship between autobiographical memory and perceptual learning. *Journal of Experimental Psychology: General, 110,* 306–340.

JACOBY, L. L., & WITHERSPOON, D. (1982). Remembering without awareness. *Canadian Journal of Psychology, 36,* 300–324.

JAMES, W. (1890). *Principles of psychology.* New York: Henry Holt.

JENCKS, C. (1979). *Who gets ahead? The determinants of economic success in America.* New York: Basic Books.

JENKINS, C. D., ZYZANSKI, S. J., & ROSENMAN, R. H. (1979). *Manual for the Jenkins Activity Survey.* New York: Psychological Cooperation.

JOHN, O. P. (1990). The "big five" taxonomy: Dimensions of personality in the natural language and in questionnaires. In L. A. Pervin (Ed.), *Handbook of personality: Theory and research* (pp. 66–100). New York: Guilford.

JOHN, O. P., & ROBINS, R. W. (1993). Determinants of interjudge agreement on personality traits: The big five domains, observability, evaluativeness, and the unique perspective of the self. *Journal of Personality, 61,* 521–551.

JOHN, O. P., WINTER, D. G., STEWART, A. J., KLOHMAN, E., DUNCAN, L., & PETERSON, B. I. (1993). Motives and traits: Toward an integration of two traditions in personality research. As cited in Winter, D. G. (1996). *Personality: Analysis and Interpretation of Lives.* New York: McGraw Hill.

JOHNSON, J. A., & OSTENDORF, F. (1993). Clarification of the five-factor model with the abridged big five dimensional circumplex. *Journal of Personality and Social Psychology, 65,* 563–576.

JONES, M. C. (1981). Midlife drinking patterns: Correlates and antecedents. In D. Eichorn, J. A. Clausen, N. Haan, M. P. Honzik, & P. H. Mussen (Eds.), *Past and present in middle life* (pp. 223–242). New York: Academic Press.

JUDD, C. M., SMITH, E. R., & KIDDER, L. H. (1991). *Research methods in social relations.* Fort Worth, TX: Holt, Rinehart & Winston.

KAGAN, J. (1966). Reflection-impulsivity: The generality and dynamics of conceptual tempo. *Journal of Abnormal Psychology, 71,* 12–27.

KAGAN, J., (1989). Tempermental contributions to social behavior. *American Psychologist, 44,* 668–674.

KAGAN, J., & MOSS, H. A. (1962). *Birth to maturity.* New York: Wiley.

KAGAN, J., REZNICK, J. S., & SNIDMAN, N. (1988). Biological bases of childhood shyness. *Science, 240,* 167–171.

KAGAN, J., & SNIDMAN, N. (1991). Infant predictors of inhibited and uninhibited profiles. *Psychological Science, 2,* 40–44.

KAGAN, J., SNIDMAN, N., & ARCUS, D. M. (1992). Initial reactions to unfamiliarity. *Current Directions in Psychological Science, 1,* 171–173.

KAMARCK, T. W., MANUCK, S. B., & JENNINGS, J. R. (1990). Social support reduces cardiovascular reactivity to psychological challenge: A laboratory model. *Psychosomatic Medicine, 52,* 42–58.

KARABENICK, S. A., & YOUSSEFF, Z. I. (1968). Performance as a function of achievement levels and perceived difficulty. *Journal of Personality and Social Psychology, 10,* 414–419.

KELLY, E. L., & CONLEY, J. J. (1987). Personality and compatibility: A prospective analysis of marital stability and marital satisfaction. *Journal of Personality and Social Psychology, 52,* 27–40.

KENDLER, K. S., NEALE, M. C., KESSLER, R. C., HEATH, A. C., & EAVES, L. J. (1993). A longitudinal twin study of 1-year prevalence of major depression in women. *Archives of General Psychiatry, 50,* 843–852.

KENRICK, D. T. (1994). Evolutionary social psychology: From sexual selection to social cognition. *Advances in Experimental Social Psychology, 26,* 75–121.

KENRICK, D. T., & KEEFE, R. C. (1992). Age preferences in mates reflect sex differences in reproductive strategies. *Behavioral and Brain Sciences, 15,* 75–133.

KENRICK, D. T., NEUBERG, S. L., ZIERK, K. L., & KRONES, J. M. (1994). Evolution and social cognition: Contrast effects as a function of sex, dominance, and physical attractiveness. *Personality and Social Psychology Bulletin, 20,* 210–217.

KENRICK, D. T., SADALLA, E. K., GROTH, G., & TROST, M. R. (1990). Evolution, traits, and the stages of human courtship: Qualifying the parental involvement model. *Journal of Personality, 58,* 97–117.

KENRICK, D. T., & STRINGFIELD, D. O. (1980). Personality traits and the eye of the beholder: Crossing some traditional philosophical boundaries in the search for consistency in all of the people. *Psychological Review, 87,* 88–104.

KERR, M., LAMBERT, W. W., STATTIN, H., & KLACKENBERG-LARSSON, I. (1994). Stability of inhibition in a Swedish longitudinal sample. *Child Development, 65,* 138–146.

KIECOLT-GLASER, J. K., & GLASER, R. (1992). Psychoneuroimmunology: Can psychological intervention modulate immunity? Special Issue: Behavioral Medicine: An update for the 90s. *Journal of Consulting and Clinical Psychology, 60,* 569–575.

KIHLSTROM, J. F., BARNARDT, T. M., TATARYN, D J. (1992). The psychological unconscious: Found, lost, and regained. *American Psychologist, 47,* 788–791.

KITCHER, P. (1985). *Vaulting ambition: Sociobiology and the quest for human nature.* Cambridge, MA: MIT Press.

KNEIP, R. C., DELAMATER, A. M., ISMOND, T., MILFORD, C., SALVIA, L., & SCHWARTZ, D. (1993). Self- and spouse rating of anger and hostility as predictors of coronary heart disease. *Health Psychology, 12,* 301–307.

KOBASA, S. C. (1979). Stressful life events, personality, and health: An inquiry into hardiness. *Journal of Personality and Social Psychology, 37,* 1–11.

KOBASA, S. C. (1982). The hardy personality: Toward a social psychology of stress and health. In G. S. Sanders & J. Suls (Eds.), *Social psychology of health and illness* (pp. 3–32). Hillsdale, NJ: Erlbaum.

KOELGA, H. S. (1992). Extraversion and vigilance: 30 years of inconsistencies. *Psychological Bulletin, 112,* 239–258.

KOESTNER, R., & McCLELLAND, D. C. (1990). Perspectives on competence motivation. In L. A. Pervin (Ed.), *Goal concepts in personality and social psychology* (pp. 527–548). Hillsdale, NJ: Erlbaum.

KOGAN, N., & BLOCK, J. (1991). Field dependence-independence from early childhood through adolescence: Personality and socialization aspects. In S. Wapner & J. Demick (Eds.), *Field dependence-independence: Cognitive style across the life span* (pp. 177–208). Hillsdale, NJ: Erlbaum.

KRANZLER, J. H., & JENSEN, A. R. (1989). Inspection time and intelligence: A meta-analysis. *Intelligence, 13,* 329–347.

KUNST-WILSON, W. R., & ZAJONC, R. (1980). Affective discrimination of stimuli that cannot be recognized. *Science, 207,* 557–558.

LAMIELL, J. T. (1981). Toward an idiothetic psychology of personality. *American Psychologist, 36,* 276–289.

LAMIELL, J. T. (1982). "An ideothetic difficulty?": A reply to Wittig. *American Psychologist, 37,* 1059.

LANG, P. J., BRADLEY, M. M., & CUTHBERT, B. N. (1992). A motivational analysis of emotion: Reflex-cortex connections. *Psychological Science, 3,* 44–49.

LARSEN, R. J., & KETELAAR, T. (1991). Personality and susceptibility to positive and negative emotional states. *Journal of Personality and Social Psychology, 61,* 132–140.

LAVIN, D. E. (1965). *The prediction of academic performance: A theoretical analysis and review of research.* New York: Russell Sage Foundation.

LAZARUS, R. S. (1966). *Psychological stress and the coping process.* New York: McGraw-Hill.

LAZARUS, R. S. (1990). Theory-based stress measurement. *Psychological Inquiry, 1,* 3–13.

LAZARUS, R. S. (1991a). *Emotion and adaptation.* New York: Oxford University Press.

LAZARUS, R. S. (1991b). Cognition and motivation in emotion. *American Psychologist, 46,* 352–367.

LAZARUS, R. S. (1991c). Progress on a cognitive-motivational-relational theory of emotion. *American Psychologist, 46,* 819–834.

LAZARUS, R. S. (1993). Coping theory and research: Past, present, and future. *Psychosomatic Medicine, 55,* 234–247.

LAZARUS, R. S., & FOLKMAN, S. (1984). *Stress, appraisal, and coping.* New York: Springer.

LAZARUS, R. S., & McCLEARY, R. A. (1951). Autonomic discrimination without awareness: A study of subception. *Psychological Review, 58,* 113–122.

LeDOUX, J. E. (1993). Emotional networks in the brain. In M. Lewis & J. M. Haviland (Eds.), *Handbook of emotions.* New York: Guilford Press.

LEPORE, S. J. (1995). Cynicism, social support, and cardiovascular reactivity. *Health Psychology, 14,* 210–216.

LEPORE, S. J., ALLEN, K. A. M., & EVANS, G. W. (1993). Social support lowers cardiovascular reactivity to an acute stressor. *Psychosomatic Medicine, 55,* 518–524.

LEPPER, M., & GREENE, D. (1978). *The hidden cost of reward.* Hillsdale, NJ: Erlbaum.

LEVENSON, M. R., ALDWIN, C. M., BOSSE, R., & SPIRO, A., et al. (1988). Emotionality and mental health: Longitudinal findings from the normative aging study. *Journal of Abnormal Psychology, 97,* 94–96.

LEVENSON, R. W., EKMAN, P., & FRIESEN, W. V. (1990). Voluntary facial action generates emotion-specific autonomic nervous system activity. *Psychophysiology, 27,* 363–384.

LEVINSON, D. J., DARROW, C. N., KLEIN, E. B., LEVINSON, M. L., & McKEE, B. (1978). *The seasons of a man's life.* New York: Knopf.

LEVY, L. H. (1970). *Conceptions of personality: Theories and research.* New York: Random House.

LEWICKI, P. (1986). *Nonconscious social information processing.* New York: Academic Press.

LEWINSOHN, P. M., ROHDE, P., SEELEY, J. R., & FISCHER, S. A. (1993). Age-cohort changes in the lifetime occurrence of depression and other mental disorders. *Journal of Abnormal Psychology, 102,* 110–120.

LEWINSOHN, P. M., ZEISS, A. M., & DUNCAN, E. M. (1989). Probability of relapse after recovery from an episode of depression. *Journal of Abnormal Psychology, 98,* 107–116.

LEWIS, M. (1989). Culture and biology: The role of temperament. In P. R. Zelazo & R. G. Barr (Eds.), *Challenges to developmental paradigms: Implications for theory, assessment and treatment* (pp. 203–223). Hillsdale, NJ: Erlbaum.

LEWIS, M. L., RAMSAY, D. S., & KAWAKAMI, K. (1993). Differences between Japanese infants and Caucasian infants in behavioral and cortisol response to innoculation. *Child Development, 64,* 1722–1731.

LIBET, B. (1985). Unconscious cerebral initiative and the role of conscious will in voluntary action. *Behavioral and Brain Sciences, 8,* 529–566.

LINN, M. C., & PETERSON, A. C. (1986). A meta-analysis of gender differences in spatial ability: Implications for mathematics and science achievement. In J. S. Hyde & M. C. Linn (Eds.), *The psychology of gender: Advances through meta-analysis.* Baltimore: Johns Hopkins University Press.

LINVILLE, P. W. (1987). Self-complexity as a cognitive buffer against stress-related illness and depression. *Journal of Personality and Social Psychology, 52,* 663–676.

LIPPA, R. (1995). Gender-related individual differences and psychological adjustment in terms of the big five and circumplex models. *Journal of Personality and Social Psychology, 69,* 1184–1202.

LITTLE, B. (1989). Personal projects analysis: Trivial pursuits, magnificent obsessions, and the search for coherence. In D. M. Buss & N. Cantor (Eds.), *Personality psychology: Recent trends and emerging directions* (pp. 15–31). New York: Springer-Verlag.

LITTLE, B. R., LECCI, L., & WATKINSON, B. (1992). Personality and personal projects: Linking big five and PAC units of analysis. *Journal of Personality, 60,* 501–525.

LOCKE, E. A., & LATHAM, G. P. (1990). *A theory of goal setting and task performance.* Englewood Cliffs, NJ: Prentice-Hall.

LOEHLIN, J. C. (1989). Partitioning environmental and genetic contributions to behavioral development. *American Psychologist, 44,* 1285–1292.

LOEHLIN, J. C. (1992). *Genes and environment in personality development.* Newbury Park, CA: Sage Publications.

LOEHLIN, J. C., HORN, J. M., & WILLERMAN, L. (1981). Personality resemblances in adoptive families. *Behavioral Genetics, 11,* 309–330.

LOEHLIN, J. C., HORN, J. M., & WILLERMAN, L. (1989). Modeling IQ changes: Evidence from the Texas adoption project. *Child Development, 60,* 993–1004.

LOEHLIN, J. C., WILLERMAN, L., & HORN, J. M. (1982). Personality resemblances between unwed mothers and their adopted-away offspring. *Journal of Personality and Social Psychology, 42,* 1089–1099.

LUBINSKI, D., BENBOW, C. P., & RYAN, J. (1995). Stability of vocational interests among the intellectually gifted from adolescence to adulthood: A 15-year longitudinal study. *Journal of Applied Psychology, 80,* 196–200.

LUBINSKI, D., TELLEGEN, A., & BUTCHER, J. N. (1981). The relationship between androgyny and subjective indicators of emotional well-being. *Journal of Personality and Social Psychology, 40,* 722–730.

LUBINSKI, D., TELLEGEN, A., & BUTCHER, J. N. (1983). Masculinity, femininity, and androgyny viewed and assessed as distinct concepts. *Journal of Personality and Social Psychology, 44,* 428–439.

LYKKEN, D. T. (1982). Research with twins: The concept of emergenesis. *Psychophysiology, 19,* 361–373.

LYKKEN, D. T. (1995). *The antisocial personalities.* Hillsdale, NJ: Erlbaum.

LYKKEN, D. T., BOUCHARD, T. J., McGUE, M., & TELLEGEN, A. (1993). Heritability of interests: A twin study. *Journal of Applied Psychology, 78,* 649–661.

LYNN, R. (1990). The role of nutrition in secular increases in intelligence. *Personality and Individual Differences, 11,* 273–285.

MACCOBY, E. E., & JACKLIN, C. N. (1974). *The psychology of sex differences.* Stanford, CA: Stanford University Press.

MACDONALD, K. (1995). Evolution, the five-factor model, and levels of personality. *Journal of Personality, 63,* 523–567.

MACKAY, N. (1989). *Motivation and explanation: An essay on Freud's philosophy of science.* Madison, CT: International Universities Press.

McADAMS, D. P. (1980). A thematic coding system for the intimacy motive. *Journal of Research in Personality, 14,* 413–432.

McADAMS, D. P. (1988). *Intimacy: The need to be close.* New York: Doubleday.

McADAMS, D. P. (1990). Unity and purpose in human lives: The emergence of identity as a life story. In A. I. Rabin, R. A. Zucker, R. A. Emmons, & S. Frank (Eds.), *Studying persons and lives* (pp. 148–200). New York: Springer.

McADAMS, D. P. (1992a). The five-factor model in personality: A critical appraisal. *Journal of Personality, 60,* 329–361.

McADAMS, D. P. (1992b). The intimacy motive scoring system. In C. P. Smith (Ed.), *Motivation and personality: Handbook of thematic content analysis* (pp. 229–253). New York: Cambridge University Press.

McADAMS, D. P. (1992c). The intimacy motive. In C. P. Smith (Ed.), *Motivation and personality: Handbook of thematic content analysis* (pp. 224–228). Cambridge, UK: Cambridge University Press.

McADAMS, D. P., & CONSTANTIAN, C. A. (1983). Intimacy and affiliation motives in daily living: An experience sampling analysis. *Journal of Personality and Social Psychology, 45,* 851–861.

McADAMS, D. P., & DE ST. AUBIN, E. (1992). A theory of generativity and its assessment through self-report, behavioral acts, and narrative themes in autobiography. *Journal of Personality and Social Psychology, 62,* 1003–1015.

McADAMS, D. P., JACKSON, R. J., & KIRSHNIT, C. (1984). Looking, laughing, and smiling in dyads as a function of intimacy motivation and reciprocity. *Journal of Personality, 52,* 261–273.

McCARTNEY, K., HARRIS, M. J., & BERNIERI, F. (1990). Growing up and growing apart: A developmental meta-analysis of twin studies. *Psychological Bulletin, 107,* 226–237.

McClelland, D. C. (1961). *The achieving society.* Princeton, NJ: Princeton University Press.

McClelland, D. C. (1975). *Power: The inner experience.* New York: Irvington.

McClelland, D. C. (1985). *Human motivation.* Glenview, IL: Scott, Foresman.

McClelland, D. C., Atkinson, J. W., Clark, R. A., & Lowell, E. L. (1953). *The achievement motive.* New York: Appleton-Century-Crofts.

McClelland, D. C., Atkinson, J. W., Clark, R. A., & Lowell, E. L. (1953/1992). A scoring manual for the achievement motive. In C. P. Smith (Ed.), *Motivation and personality: Handbook of thematic content analysis* (pp. 153–178). New York: Cambridge University Press.

McClelland, D. C., & Boyatzis, R. E. (1982). The leadership motive pattern and long-term success in management. *Journal of Applied Psychology, 67,* 737–743.

McClelland, D. C., Koestner, R., & Weinberger, J. (1989). How do self-attributed and implicit motives differ? *Psychological Review, 96,* 690–702.

McClelland, D. C., & Pilon, D. (1983). Sources of adult motives in patterns of parent behavior in early childhood. *Journal of Personality and Social Psychology, 44,* 564–574.

McCrae, R. R. (1987). Creativity, divergent thinking, and openness to experience. *Journal of Personality and Social Psychology, 52,* 1258–1265.

McCrae, R. R. (1994). New goals for trait psychology. *Psychological Inquiry, 5,* 148–153.

McCrae, R. R., & Costa, P. T. (1990). *Personality in adulthood.* New York: Guilford.

McCrae, R. R., & Costa, P. T. (1991). Adding Liebe und Arbeit: The full five-factor model and well-being. *Personality and Social Psychology Bulletin, 17,* 227–232.

McGarvey, B., Gabrielli, W. F., Jr., Bentler, P. M., & Mednick, S. A. (1981). Rearing social class, education, and criminality: A multiple indicator model. *Journal of Abnormal Psychology, 90,* 354–364.

McGinnies, E. (1949). Emotionality and perceptual defense. *Psychological Review, 56,* 244–251.

McGue, M., Bouchard, T. J., Jr., Iacono, W. G., & Lykken, D. (1993). Behavioral genetics of cognitive ability: A life-span perspective. In R. Plomin & G. E. McClearn (Eds.), *Nature, nurture, and psychology* (pp. 59–76). Washington, DC: American Psychological Association.

McGue, M., & Lykken, D. T. (1992). Genetic influences on risk of divorce. *Psychological Science, 3,* 368–373.

McKeachie, W. J. (1961). Motivation, teaching methods, and college learning. In M. R. Jones (Ed.), *Nebraska Symposium on Motivation* (Vol. 9, pp. 111–142). Lincoln: University of Nebraska Press.

McKelvie, S. J. (1990). Student acceptance of a generalized personality description: Forer's graphologist revisited. *Journal of Social Behavior and Personality, 5,* 91–95.

McKenna, F. (1984). Measures of field dependence: Cognitive style or cognitive ability? *Journal of Personality and Social Psychology, 47,* 593–603.

McNally, R. J. (1987). Preparedness and phobias: A review. *Psychological Bulletin, 101,* 283–303.

Maddi, S. R. (1980). *Personality theories: A comparative analysis.* Homewood, IL: Dorsey Press.

Maddux, J. E. (1991). Personal efficacy. In V. J. Derlega, B. A. Winstead, & Jones, W. H., *Personality: Contemporary theory and research.* Chicago: Nelson Hall.

Mahone, C. H. (1960). Fear of failure and unrealistic vocational aspirations. *Journal of Abnormal and Social Psychology, 60,* 253–261.

MAIER, S. F., WATKINS, L. R., & FLESHNER, M. (1994). Psychoneuroimmunology: The interface between behavior, brain, and immunity. *American Psychologist, 49,* 1004–1017.

MAIN, M., KAPLAN, K., & CASSIDY, J. (1985). Security in infancy, childhood, and adulthood: A move to the level of representation. In I. Bretherton & E. Waters (Eds.), Growing points of attachment theory and research. *Monographs of the Society for Research in Child Development, 50,* 66–104.

MANNUZZA, S., KLEIN, R. G., BONAGURA, N., MALLOY, P., GIAMPINO, T. L., & ADDALLI, K. A. (1991). Hyperactive boys almost grown up. *Archives of General Psychiatry, 48,* 77–83.

MARCEL, A. J. (1983a). Conscious and unconscious perception: Experiments on visual masking and word recognition. *Cognitive Psychology, 15,* 197–237.

MARCEL, A. J. (1983b). Conscious and unconscious perception: An approach to the relations between phenomenal experience and perceptual processes. *Cognitive Psychology, 15,* 238–300.

MARKUS, H. R., & KITAYAMA, S. (1991). Culture and the self: Implications for cognition, emotion, and motivation. *Psychological Review, 98,* 224–253.

MARSH, H. W. (1993). Relations between global and specific domains of self: The importance of individual importance, certainty, and ideals. *Journal of Personality and Social Psychology, 65,* 975–992.

MARSHALL, G. N., WORTMAN, C. B., KUSULAS, J. W., HERVIG, L. K., & VICKERS, R. R. (1992). Distinguishing optimism from pessimism: Relations to fundamental dimensions of mood and personality. *Journal of Personality and Social Psychology, 62,* 1067–1074.

MARTIN, N., & JARDINE, R. (1986). Eysenck's contributions to behavior genetics. In S. Modgil & C. Modgil (Eds.), *Hans Eysenck: Consensus and Controversy.* Philadelphia: Falmer.

MASLOW, A. H. (1943). A theory of human motivation. *Psychological Review, 50,* 370–396.

MASON, A., & BLANKENSHIP, V. (1987). Power and affiliation motivation, stress, and abuse in intimate relationships. *Journal of Personality and Social Psychology, 52,* 203–210.

MATHENY, A. P. (1989). Children's behavioral inhibition over age and across situations: Genetic similarity for a trait during change. *Journal of Personality, 57,* 215–235.

MATSUMOTO, D. (1987). The role of facial response in the experience of emotion: More methodological problems and a meta-analysis. *Journal of Personality and Social Psychology, 52,* 769–774.

MATTHEWS, K. A. (1988). CHD and Type A behavior: Update on and alternative to the Booth-Kewley and Friedman quantitative reviews. *Psychological Bulletin, 104,* 373–380.

MAUSNER, B., & GRAHAM, J. (1970). Field dependence and prior reinforcement as determinants of social interaction in judgment. *Journal of Personality and Social Psychology, 16,* 486–493.

MAYOU, R. (1989). Atypical chest pain. *Journal of Psychosomatic Research, 33,* 393–406.

MEAD, M. (1928). *Coming of age in Samoa: A psychological study of primitive youth for western civilization.* New York: William Morrow.

MESSICK, S. (1980). *The effectiveness of coaching for the SAT: Review and reanalysis of research from the fifties to FTC.* Princeton, NJ: Educational Testing Service.

MEYER, D. E., & SCHVÄNEVELDT, R. W. (1971). Facilitation in recognizing parts of words: Evidence of a dependence between retrieval operations. *Journal of Experimental Psychology, 90,* 227–234.

MILGRAM, S. (1974). *Obedience to authority.* New York: Harper & Row.

MINEKA, S., & SUTTON, S. K. (1992). Cognitive biases and the emotional disorders. *Psychological Science, 3,* 65–69.

MISCHEL, W. (1968). *Personality and assessment.* New York: Wiley.

MISCHEL, W. (1979). On the interface of cognition and personality: Beyond the person-situation debate. *American Psychologist, 34,* 740–754.

MISCHEL, W. (1990). Personality dispositions revisited and revised: A view after three decades. In L. A. Pervin (Ed.), *Handbook of personality: Theory and research* (pp. 111–134). New York: Guilford.

MISCHEL, W., & PEAKE, P. K. (1982). Beyond deja vu in the search for cross-situational consistency. *Psychological Review, 89,* 730–755.

MISCHEL, W., & PEAKE, P. K. (1983). Some facets of consistency: Replies to Epstein, Funder, and Bem. *Psychological Review, 90,* 394–402.

MISCHEL, W., & SHODA, Y. (1994). Personality psychology has two goals: Must it be two fields? *Psychological Inquiry, 5,* 156–158.

MOFFITT, K. H., & SINGER, J. A. (1994). Continuity in the life story: Self-defining memories, affect, and approach/avoidance personal strivings. *Journal of Personality, 62,* 21–43.

MOFFITT, K. H., SINGER, J. A., MELLIGAN, D. W., CARLSON, M. A., & VYSE, S. A. (1994). Depression and memory narrative type. *Journal of Abnormal Psychology, 103,* 581–583.

MORAWSKI, J. G. (1985). The measurement of masculinity and femininity: Engendering categorical realities. *Journal of Personality, 53,* 196–223.

MOSKOWITZ, D. S. (1982). Coherence and cross-situational generality in personality: A new analysis of old problems. *Journal of Personality and Social Psychology, 47,* 754–768.

MOSKOWITZ, D. S., & SCHWARZ, J. D. (1982). Validity comparison of behavior counts and ratings by knowledgeable informants. *Journal of Personality and Social Psychology, 42,* 518–528.

MOUNT, M. K., BARRICK, M. R., & STRAUSS, J. P. (1994). Validity of observer ratings of the big five personality factors. *Journal of Applied Psychology, 79,* 272–280.

MURRAY, H. (1938). *Explorations in personality.* New York: Science Editions.

NADLER, A., GOLDBERG, M., & JAFFE, Y. (1982). Effect of self-differentiation and anonymity in group on deindividuation. *Journal of Personality and Social Psychology, 42,* 1127–1136.

NELSON, C. A. (1994). Neural bases of infant temperament. In G. A. Kohnstamm, J. E. Bates, & M. K. Rothbart (Eds.), *Temperament in childhood* (pp. 47–82). New York: Wiley.

NEWTON, T. L. & CONTRADA, R. J. (1992). Repressive coping and verbal-autonomic response dissociation: The influence of social context. *Journal of Personality and Social Psychology, 62,* 159–167.

NIEDENTHAL, P. M., CANTOR, N., & KIHLSTROM, J. F. (1985). Prototype matching: A strategy for social decision making. *Journal of Personality and Social Psychology, 48,* 575–584.

NISBETT, R. E., & WILSON, T. D. (1977). Telling more than we can know: Verbal reports on mental processes. *Psychological Review, 84,* 231–259.

NOLEN-HOEKSEMA, S. (1987). Sex differences in unipolar depression: Evidence and theory. *Psychological Bulletin, 101,* 259–282.

NORMAN, W. T. (1967). *Personality trait descriptors: Normative operating characteristics for a university population.* Ann Arbor: University of Michigan, Department of Psychology.

OLEA, M. M., & REE, M. J. (1994). Predicting pilot and navigator criteria: Not much more than *g*. *Journal of Applied Psychology, 79,* 845–851.

OLIVER, M. B., & HYDE, J. S. (1993). Gender differences in sexuality: A meta-analysis. *Psychological Bulletin, 114,* 29–51.

OLIVIER, L. (1982). *Confessions of an actor: An autobiography.* New York: Simon and Schuster.

OLTMAN, P. K., GOODENOUGH, D. R., WITKIN, H. A., FREEDMAN, N., & FRIEDMAN, F. (1975). Psychological differentiation as a factor in conflict resolution. *Journal of Personality and Social Psychology, 32,* 730–736.

ONES, D. S., VISWESVARAN, C., & SCHMIDT, F. L. (1993). Comprehensive meta-analysis of integrity test validities: Findings and implications for personnel selection and theories of job performance. *Journal of Applied Psychology, 78,* 679–703.

ORMEL, J., & WOHLFARTH, T. (1991). How neuroticism, long-term difficulties, and life situation change influence psychological distress: A longitudinal model. *Journal of Personality and Social Psychology, 60,* 744–755.

ORTH-GOMER, K. (1994). International epidemiological evidence for a relationship between social support and cardiovascular disease. In S. A. Shumaker & S. M. Czajkowski (Eds.), *Social support and cardiovascular disease* (pp. 97–118). New York: Plenum Press.

ORTONY, A., CLORE, G. L., & COLLINS, A. (1988). *The cognitive structure of emotions.* New York: Cambridge University Press.

PANKSEPP, J. (1982). Toward a general psychobiological theory of emotions. *Behavioral and Brain Sciences, 5,* 407–422.

PANSKEPP, J. (1992). A critical role for "affective neuroscience" in resolving what is basic about basic emotions. *Psychological Review, 99,* 554–560.

PARKER, K. A. (1982). Effects of subliminal symbiotic stimulation on academic performance: Further evidence of the adaptation enhancing effects of oneness fantasies. *Journal of Counseling Psychology, 29,* 19–28.

PARROTT, W. G., & SABINI, J. (1990). Mood and memory under natural conditions: Evidence for mood incongruent recall. *Journal of Personality and Social Psychology, 59,* 321–336.

PAUL, G. L. (1966). *Insight vs. desensitization in psychotherapy: An experiment in anxiety reduction.* Stanford, CA: Stanford University Press.

PAUL, G. L. (1967). Two-year follow-up of systematic desensitization in therapy groups. *Journal of Consulting Psychology, 31,* 333–348.

PAULHUS, D. L. (1984). Two-component models of socially desirable responding. *Journal of Personality and Social Psychology, 46,* 598–609.

PAUNONEN, S. V. (1988). Trait relevance and the differential predictability of behavior. *Journal of Personality, 56,* 599–619.

PEDLOW, R., SANSON, A., PRIOR, M., & OBERKLAID, F. (1993). Stability of maternally reported temperament from infancy to 8 years. *Developmental Psychology, 29,* 998–1007.

PENNEBAKER, J. W. (1985). Traumatic experience and psychosomatic disease: Exploring the role of behavioral inhibition, obsession, and confiding. *Canadian Psychology, 26,* 82–95.

PERVIN, L. A. (1990). A brief history of modern personality theory. In L. A. Pervin (Ed.), *Handbook of personality: Theory and research* (pp. 3–20). New York: Guilford.

PERVIN, L. A. (1994). A critical analysis of current trait theory. *Psychological Inquiry, 5,* 103–113.

PETERSON, C., & BARRETT, L. C. (1987). Explanatory style and academic performance among university freshmen. *Journal of Personality and Social Psychology, 53,* 603–607.

PETERSON, C., MAIER, S. F., & SELIGMAN, M. E. P. (1993). *Learned helplessness: A theory for the age of personal control.* New York: Oxford University Press.

PETERSON, C., SELIGMAN, M. E. P., & VAILLANT, G. E. (1988). Pessimistic explanatory style as a risk factor for physical illness: A thirty-five-year longitudinal study. *Journal of Personality and Social Psychology, 55,* 23–27.

PHINNEY, J. S. (1990). Ethnic identity in adolescents and adults: Review of research. *Psychological Bulletin, 108,* 499–514.

PLOMIN, R., CORLEY, R., DEFRIES, J. C., & FULKER, D. W. (1990). Individual differences in television viewing in early childhood: Nature as well as nurture. *Psychological Science, 1,* 371–377.

PLOMIN, R., DEFRIES, J. C., & MCCLEARN, G. E. (1990). *Behavioral genetics: A primer* (2nd ed.). New York: W. H. Freeman.

PLUTCHIK, R. (1980). *Emotion: A psychoevolutionary synthesis.* New York: Harper & Row.

PORTER, J. D. R., & WASHINGTON, R. E. (1979). Black identity and self-esteem: A review of studies of Black self-concept, 1968–1978. *Annual Review of Sociology, 5,* 53–74.

QUATTRONE, G. E. (1985). On the congruity between internal states and action. *Psychological Bulletin, 98,* 3–40.

RAZ, N., WILLERMAN, L., & YAMA, M. (1987). On sense and senses: Intelligence and auditory information processing. *Personality and Individual Differences, 8,* 201–210.

RAZ, S., & RAZ, N. (1990). Structural brain abnormalities in the major psychoses: A quantitative review of the evidence from computerized imaging. *Psychological Bulletin, 108,* 93–108.

READ, S. J., & MILLER, L. C. (1989). Inter-personalism: Toward a goal-based theory of persons in relationships. In L. A. Pervin (Ed.), *Goal concepts in personality and social psychology* (pp. 413–472). Hillsdale, NJ: Erlbaum.

REHBERG, R. A., & ROSENTHAL, E. R. (1978). *Class and merit in the American high school: An assessment of the revisionist and meritocratic arguments.* New York: Longman.

RESTAK, R. M. (1994). *The modular brain: How new discoveries in neuroscience are answering age-old questions about memory, free will, consciousness, and personal identity.* New York: Scribner's.

RISKIND, J. H. (1984). They stoop to conquer: Guiding and self-regulatory functions of physical posture after success and failure. *Journal of Personality and Social Psychology, 47,* 479–493.

RISKIND, J. H., & GOTAY, C. C. (1982). Physical posture: Could it have regulatory or feedback effects on motivation and emotion? *Motivation and Emotion, 6,* 273–298.

ROBINSON, R. G., KUBOS, K. L., STARR, L B., RAO, K., & PRICE, T. R. (1984). Mood disorders in stroke patients: Importance of location of lesion. *Brain, 107,* 81–93.

ROGERS, C. R. (1961). *On becoming a person: A therapist's view of psychotherapy.* Boston. Houghton Mifflin.

ROGERS, C. R. (1963). Actualizing tendency in relation to "motives" and to consciousness. In M. R. Jones (Ed.), *Nebraska Symposium on Motivation* (Vol. 11, pp. 1–23). Lincoln: University of Nebraska Press.

Rokeach, M. (1960). *The open and closed mind.* New York: Basic Books.

Rorer, L. G. (1965). The great response style myth. *Psychological Bulletin, 63,* 129–156.

Rose, S., & Feldman, J. (1995). The prediction of IQ and specific cognitive abilities at 11 years from infancy measures. *Developmental Psychology, 31,* 685–696.

Roseman, I. J., Spindel, M. S., & Jose, P. E. (1990). Appraisals of emotion-eliciting events: Testing a theory of discrete emotions. *Journal of Personality and Social Psychology, 59,* 899–915.

Rosenberg, M., & Simmons, R. G. (1971). *Black and White self-esteem: The urban school child.* Arnold and Caroline Rose Monograph Series. Washington, DC: American Sociological Association.

Rosenman, R. H., Swan, G. E., & Carmelli, D. (1988). Some recent findings relative to the relationship of Type A behavior to coronary heart disease. In S. Maes, C. D. Spielberger, P. B. Defares, & I. G. Sarason (Eds.), *Topics in health psychology* (pp. 21–29). New York: Wiley.

Ross, L. D., & Nisbett, R. E. (1991). *The person and the situation: Perspectives of social psychology.* New York: McGraw-Hill.

Rothbart, M. K. (1989). Temperament and development. In G. A. Kohnstamm, J. E. Bates, & M. K. Rothbart (Eds.), *Temperament in childhood* (pp. 187–247). New York: Wiley.

Rothbart, M. K., & Ahadi, S. A. (1994). Temperament and the development of personality. *Journal of Abnormal Psychology, 103,* 55–66.

Rothbart, M. K., Derryberry, D., & Posner, M. I. (1994). A psychobiological approach to the development of temperament. In J. E. Bates & T. D. Wachs (Eds.), *Temperament: Individual differences at the interface of biology and behavior* (pp. 83–116). Washington, DC: American Psychological Association.

Runyan, W. M. (1983). Idiographic goals and methods in the study of lives. *Journal of Personality, 51,* 413–437.

Runyan, W. M. (1990). Individual lives and the structure of personality psychology. In A. I. Rabin, R. A. Zukor, R. A. Emmons, & S. Frank (Eds.), *Studying persons and lives* (pp. 10–40). New York: Springer.

Russell, J. A. (1994). Is there universal recognition of emotion from facial expression? A review of cross-cultural studies. *Psychological Bulletin, 115,* 102–141.

Ryan, R. M., Connell, J. P., & Grolnick, W. S. (1992). When achievement is not intrinsically motivated: A theory of internalization and self-regulation. In A. K. Boggiano & T. S. Pittman (Eds.), *Achievement and motivation: A social-developmental perspective* (pp. 167–188). New York: Cambridge University Press.

Sabatelli, R. M., Dreyer, A. S., & Buck, R. (1979). Cognitive style and sending and receiving of facial cues. *Perceptual and Motor Skills, 49,* 203–212.

Sackeim, H. A., Greenberg, M. S., Weiman, A. L., Gur, R. C., Hungerbuhler, J. P., & Geschwind, M. (1982). Hemispheric asymmetry in the expression of positive and negative emotions: Neurologic evidence. *Archives of Neurology, 39,* 210–218.

Sacks, O. W. (1987). *The man who mistook his wife for a hat and other clinical tales.* New York: Perennial Library.

Sadalla, E. K., Kenrick, D. T., & Vershure, B. (1987). Dominance and heterosexual attraction. *Journal of Personality and Social Psychology, 52,* 730–738.

SALOVEY, P., & BIRNBAUM, D. (1989). Influence of mood on health-related cognitions. *Journal of Personality and Social Psychology, 57,* 539–551.

SCARR, S., & McCARTNEY, K. (1983). How people make their own environments: A theory of genotype environment effects. *Child Development, 54,* 424–435.

SCHACTER, D. (1987). Implicit memory: History and current status. *Journal of Experimental Psychology: Learning, Memory, and Cognition, 13,* 501–518.

SCHEIER, M. F. (1976). Self-awareness, self-consciousness, and angry aggression. *Journal of Personality, 44,* 627–644.

SCHEIER, M. F., & CARVER, C. S. (1976). Self-awareness, self-consciousness, and angry aggression. *Journal of Personality, 44,* 627–644.

SCHEIER, M. F., & CARVER, C. S. (1977). Self-focused attention and the experience of emotion: Attraction, repulsion, elation, and depression. *Journal of Personality and Social Psychology, 35,* 625–636.

SCHEIER, M. F., & CARVER, C. S. (1985). Optimism, coping, and health: Assessment and implications of generalized outcome expectancies. *Health Psychology, 4,* 219–247.

SCHEIER, M. F., & CARVER, C. S. (1993). On the power of positive thinking: The benefits of being optimistic. *Current Directions in Psychological Science, 2,* 26–30.

SCHEIER, M. F., MATTHEWS, K. A., OWENS, J. F., MAGOVERN, G. J., LEFEBVRE, R. C., ABBOTT, R. A., & CARVER, C. S. (1989). Dispositional optimism and recovery from coronary artery bypass surgery: The beneficial effects on physical and psychological well-being. *Journal of Personality and Social Psychology, 57,* 1024–1040.

SCHNALL, P. L., LANDSBERGIS, P. A., & BAKER, D. (1994). Job strain and cardiovascular disease. *Annual Review of Public Health, 15,* 381–411.

SCHWARZ, N., & CLORE, G. L. (1983). Mood, misattribution, and judgments of well-being: Informative and directive functions of affective states. *Journal of Personality and Social Psychology, 45,* 513–523.

SEAMON, J., BRODY, N. & KAUFF D. (1983). Affective discrimination of stimuli that are not recognized: II. Effect of delay between study and test. *Bulletin of the Psychonomic Society, 21,* 187–189.

SEAMON, J., MARSH, R. L., & BRODY, N. (1984). Critical importance of exposure duration for affective discrimination of stimuli that are not recognized. *Journal of Experimental Psychology: Learning, Memory, and Cognition, 10,* 465–469.

SELIGMAN, M. E. P. (1994). *What you can change and what you can't: The complete guide to successful self-improvement.* New York: Knopf.

SELIGMAN, M. E. P. (1995). The effectiveness of psychotherapy: The *Consumer Reports* study. *American Psychologist, 50,* 965-974.

SHANKS, D. R., & ST. JOHN, M. F. (1994). Characteristics of dissociable learning systems. *Behavior and Brain Sciences, 17,* 367–447.

SHAVER, P., SCHWARTZ, J., KIRSON, D., & O'CONNER, C. (1987). Emotion knowledge: Further exploration of a prototype approach. *Journal of Personality and Social Psychology, 52,* 1061–1086.

SHEA, M. T. (1994). "Placebo as a treatment for depression": Comment. *Neuropsychopharmacology, 10,* 285–286.

SHEDLER, J., MAYMAN, M., & MANIS, M. (1993). The illusion of mental health. *American Psychologist, 48,* 1117–1131.

SHIPLEY, T. E., & VEROFF, J. A. (1952). A projective measure of need for affiliation. *Journal of Experimental Psychology, 43,* 349–356.

SHODA, Y., MISCHEL, W., & WRIGHT, J. C. (1994). Intraindividual stability in the organization and patterning of behavior: Incorporating psychological situations into the idiographic analysis of personality. *Journal of Personality and Social Psychology, 67,* 674–687.

SHWEDER, R. A., & BOURNE, E. J. (1984). Does the concept of the person vary cross-culturally? In R. A. Shweder & R. A. LeVine (Eds.), *Culture theory: Essays on mind, self, and emotion* (pp. 158–199). New York: Cambridge University Press.

SIGMAN, M. D., COHEN, S. E., BECKWITH, L., & PARMALEE, A. H. (1986). Infant attention and receiving of facial cues. *Perceptual and Motor Skills, 49,* 203–212.

SIGMAN, M. D., COHEN, S. E., BECKWITH, L., & PARMALEE, A. H. (1986). Infant attention in relation to intellectual abilities in childhood. *Developmental Psychology, 22,* 788–792.

SILVERMAN, L. H. (1976). Psychoanalytic theory. The reports of my death are greatly exaggerated. *American Psychologist, 31,* 621–637.

SILVERMAN, L. H. (1983). *The search for oneness.* New York: International Universities Press.

SILVERMAN, L. H., BRONSTEIN, A., & MENDELSOHN, E. (1976). The further use for psychoanalytic activation method for the clinical theory of psychoanalysis. *Psychotherapy: Theory, Research, and Practice, 13,* 2–16.

SILVERMAN, L. H., MARTIN, A., UNGARO, R., & MENDELSOHN, N. E. (1978). Effect of subliminal stimulation of symbiotic fantasies on behavior modification treatment of obesity. *Journal of Consulting and Clinical Psychology, 46,* 432–441.

SILVERMAN, L. H., & WEINBERGER, J. (1985). Mommy and I are one. Implications for psychotherapy. *American Psychologist, 40,* 1296–1308.

SINGER, J. A., & SALOVEY, P. (1993). *The remembered self: Emotion and memory in personality.* New York: Free Press.

SMALL, S. A., ZELDIN, S., & SAVIN-WILLIAMS, R. L. (1983). In search of personality traits: A multimethod analysis of naturally occurring prosocial and dominance behavior. *Journal of Personality and Social Psychology, 51,* 1–16.

SMITH, B. D. (1983). Extraversion and electrodermal activity: Arousability and the inverted-U. *Personality and Individual Differences, 4,* 411–420.

SMITH, C. A., & ELLSWORTH, P. C. (1987). Patterns of appraisal and emotion related to taking an exam. *Journal of Personality and Social Psychology, 52,* 475–488.

SMITH, C. A., & LAZARUS, R. S. (1990). Emotion and adaptation. In L. A. Pervin (Ed.), *Handbook of personality: Theory and research* (pp. 609–637). New York: Guilford.

SMITH, C. P. (1992). Introduction: Inferences from verbal material. In C. P. Smith (Ed.), *Motivation and personality: Handbook of thematic content analysis* (pp. 1–20). New York: Cambridge University Press.

SMITH, M. L., GLASS, G. V., & MILLER, T. I. (1980). *The benefits of psychotherapy.* Baltimore: Johns Hopkins University Press.

SMITH, S. M., & PETTY, R. E. (1995). Personality moderators of mood congruency effects on cognition: The role of self-esteem and negative mood regulation. *Journal of Personality and Social Psychology, 68,* 1092–1107.

SMITH, T. W., & WILLIAMS, P. G. (1992). Personality and health: Advantages and limitations of the five-factor model. *Journal of Personality, 60,* 395–423.

SNYDER, M. (1993). Basic research and practical problems: The promise of a "functional" personality and social psychology. *Personality and Social Psychology Bulletin, 19,* 251–264.

SNYDER, M., & OMOTO, A. M. (1992). Volunteerism and society's response to the HIV epidemic. *Current Directions in Psychological Science, 1,* 113–116.

SORRENTINO, R. M., HEWITT, E. C., & RASKO-KNOTT, P. A. (1992). Risk-taking in games of chance and skill: Informational and affective influences on choice behavior. *Journal of Personality and Social Psychology, 46,* 189–206.

SORRENTINO, R. M., & SHORT, J. C. (1986). Uncertainty, motivation, and cognition. In R. M. Sorrentino & E. T. Higgins (Eds.), *The handbook of motivation and cognition: Foundations of social behavior* (Vol. 1, pp. 379–403). New York: Guilford.

SPANGLER, W. D. (1992). Validity of questionnaire and TAT measures of need for achievement: Two meta-analyses. *Psychological Bulletin, 112,* 140–154.

SPEARMAN, C. (1904). "General intelligence" objectively determined and measured. *American Journal of Psychology, 15,* 201–293.

SPENCE, J. T. (1983). Comment on Lubinski, Tellegan, and Butcher's "Masculinity, femininity, and adrogyny viewed and assessed as distinct concepts." *Journal of Personality and Social Psychology, 44,* 440–446.

SPENCE, J. T., & HELMREICH, R. L. (1978). *Masculinity and femininity: Their psychological dimensions, correlates, and antecedents.* Austin: University of Texas Press.

SPENCE, J. T., HELMREICH, R. L., & STRAPP, J. (1974). The personal attributes questionnaire: A measure of sex roles stereotypes and masculinity-femininity. *JSAS: Catalog of Selected Documents in Psychology, 4,* 43. (Ms. No. 617)

SPIVEY, C. B. & PRENTICE-DUNN, S. (1990). *Basic and applied social psychology, 11,* 387–403.

SQUIRE, L. R. (1992). Memory and the hippocampus: A synthesis from the findings with rats, monkeys, and humans. *Psychological Review, 99,* 195–231.

STELMACK, R. M. (1990). Biological bases of extraversion: Psychophysiological evidence. *Journal of Personality, 58,* 293–312.

STELMACK, R. M., & GEEN, R. G. (1992). The psychophysiology of extraversion. In A. Gale & M. W. Eysenck (Eds.), *Handbook of individual differences: Biological perspectives* (pp. 227–254). New York: Wiley.

STEPPER, S., & STRACK, F. (1993). Proprioceptive determinants of emotional and nonemotional feelings. *Journal of Personality and Social Psychology, 64,* 211–220.

STERN, R. M., & SISON, C. E. (1990). Response patterning. In J. T. Cacioppo & L. G. Tassinary (Eds.), *Principles of psychophysiology: Physical, social, and inferential elements* (pp. 193–215). New York: Cambridge University Press.

STERNBERG, R. J. (1994). Thinking styles: Theory and assessment at the interface between intelligence and personality. In R. J. Sternberg & P. Ruzgis (Eds.), *Personality and intelligence* (pp. 169–187). New York: Cambridge University Press.

STERNBERG, R. J., & POWELL, J. S. (1983). Comprehending verbal comprehension. *American Psychologist, 38,* 878–893.

STEVENSON, H. W. (1991). Japanese elementary school education. *Journal of Elementary Education, 92,* 109–120.

STEWART, A. J., & CHESTER, N. L. (1982). Sex differences in human social motives: Achievement, affiliation and power. In A. J. Stewart (Ed.), *Motivation and society* (pp. 172–218). San Francisco: Jossey-Bass.

STEWART, A. J., & WINTER, D. G. (1976). Arousal of the power motive in women. *Journal of Consulting and Clinical Psychology, 44,* 495–496.

STONE, A. A., BOVBJERG, D. H., NEALE, J. M., NAPOLI, A., VALDIMARSDOTTIR, H., ET AL. (1992). Development of the common cold symptoms following experimental rhinovirus infection is related to prior stressful life events. *Behavioral Medicine, 18,* 115–120.

STONE, A. A., REED, B. R., & NEALE, J. M. (1987). Changes in daily event frequency precede episodes of physical symptoms. *Journal of Human Stress, 13,* 70–74.

STONE, S. V., & COSTA, P. T. (1990). Disease-prone personality or distress-prone personality? The role of neuroticism in coronary heart disease. In R. Friedman (Ed.), *Personality and illness* (pp. 178–200). New York: Wiley.

STRAUMAN, T. J., & Higgins, E. T. (1987). Automatic activation of self-discrepancies and emotional syndromes: When cognitive structures influence affect. *Journal of Personality and Social Psychology, 53,* 1004–1014.

STRENTZ, T., & AUERBACH, S. M. (1988). Adjustment to the stress of simulated captivity: Effects of emotion-focused versus problem-focused preparation on hostages differing in locus of control. *Journal of Personality and Social Psychology, 55,* 652–660.

STRUPP, H. H., & HADLEY, S. W. (1979). Specific vs. nonspecific factors in psychotherapy: A controlled study of outcome. *Archives of General Psychiatry, 36,* 1125–1136.

SUAREZ, E. C., HARLAN, E., PEOPLES, M. C., & WILLIAMS, R. B. (1993). Cardiovascular and emotional responses in women: The role of hostility and harassment. *Health Psychology, 12,* 459–468.

SUAREZ, E. C., & WILLIAMS, R. B. (1990). The relationships between dimensions of hostility and cardiovascular reactivity as a function of task characteristics. *Psychosomatic Medicine, 52,* 558–570.

SULS, J., & RITTENHOUSE, J. D. (1990). Models of linkages between personality and disease. In H. S. Friedman (Ed.), *Personality and disease* (pp. 38–64). New York: Wiley.

SULS, J., & WAN, C. K. (1993). The relationship between trait hostility and cardiovascular reactivity: A quantitative review and analysis. *Psychophysiology, 30,* 615–626.

SWIM, J. K. (1994). Perceived versus meta-analytic effect sizes: An assessment of the accuracy of gender stereotypes. *Journal of Personality and Social Psychology, 66,* 21–36.

SYMONS, D. (1979). *The evolution of human sexuality.* New York: Oxford University Press.

SYMONS, D. (1992). On the use and misuse of Darwinism in the study of human behavior. In J. Barkow, L. Cosmides, & J. Tooby (Eds.), *The adapted mind* (pp. 137–159). New York: Oxford University Press.

TAJFEL, H. (1982). Social psychology of intergroup relations. *Annual Review of Psychology, 33,* 1–39.

TAYLOR, S. E., & BROWN, J. D. (1988). Illusion and well-being: A social psychological perspective on mental health. *Psychological Bulletin, 110,* 67–85.

TEASDALE, J. D., TAYLOR, R., & FOGARTY, S. J. (1980). Effects of induced elation-depression on the accessibility of memories of happy and unhappy experiences. *Behavior, Research and Therapy, 18,* 339–346.

TEASDALE, T. W., & OWEN, O. R. (1984). Heredity and familial environment in intelligence and educational level: A sibling study. *Nature, 309,* 620–622.

TELLEGEN, A. (1985). Structures of mood and personality and their relevance to assessing anxiety with an emphasis on self-report. In A. H. Tuma & J. D. Maser (Eds.), *Anxiety and the anxiety disorders* (pp. 681–706). Hillsdale, NJ: Erlbaum.

TERMAN, L. M., & MILES, C. C. (1936). *Sex and personality.* New York: McGraw-Hill.

THAYER, R. E. (1989). *The biopsychology of mood and arousal.* New York: Oxford University Press.

THOMAS, A., & CHESS, S. (1977). *Temperament and development.* New York: Brunner/Mazel.

THOMAS, J. R., & FRENCH, K. E. (1985). Gender differences across age in motor performance: A meta-analysis. *Psychological Bulletin, 98,* 260–282.

THORNHILL, R., & THORNHILL, H. (1992). The evolutionary psychology of men's coercive sexuality. *Behavioral and Brain Sciences, 15,* 363–421.

TOMARKEN, A. J., DAVIDSON, R. J., & HENRIQUES, J. B. (1990). Resting frontal brain asymmetry predicts affective responses to films. *Journal of Personality and Social Psychology, 59,* 791–801.

TOMARKEN, A. J., DAVIDSON, R. J., WHEELER, R. W., & DOSS, R. (1992). Individual differences in anterior brain asymmetry and fundamental dimensions of emotion. *Journal of Personality and Social Psychology, 62,* 676–687.

TOMKINS, S. S. (1962). *Affect, imagery, consciousness: Vol. 1. The positive affects.* New York: Springer.

TOMKINS, S. S. (1963). *Affect, imagery, consciousness: Vol. 2. The negative affects.* New York: Springer.

TOOBY, J., & COSMIDES, L. (1992). Psychological foundations of culture. In J. Barkow, L. Cosmides, & J. Tooby (Eds.), *The adapted mind* (pp. 19–136). New York: Oxford University Press.

TROPE, Y. (1986). Self-enhancement and self-assessment in achievement behavior. In R. M. Sorrentino & E. T. Higgins (Eds.), *The handbook of motivation and cognition: Foundations of social behavior* (Vol. 1, pp. 350–378). New York: Guilford.

TUCKER, D. M. (1993). Emotional experience and the problem of vertical integration: Discussion of the Special Section on Emotion. *Neuropsychology, 7,* 500–509.

TURKHEIMER, E. (1991). Individual and group differences in adoption studies of IQ. *Psychological Bulletin, 110,* 392–405.

VAILLANT, G. (1983). *The natural history of alcoholism.* Cambridge, MA: Harvard University Press.

VALLERAND, R. J., DECI, E. L., & RYAN, R. M. (1987). Intrinsic motivation in sport. *Exercise and Sports Sciences Reviews, 15,* 389–425.

VAN DEN BOOM, D. C. (1989). Neonatal irritability and the development of attachment. In G. A. Kohnstamm, J. E. Bates, & M. K. Rothbart (Eds.), *Temperament in infancy* (pp. 299–318). New York: Wiley.

WACHS, T. D., & KING, B. (1994). Behavioral research in the brave new world of neuroscience and temperament: A guide to the biologically perplexed. In J. E. Bates & T. D. Wachs (Eds.), *Temperament: Individual differences at the interface of biology and behavior* (pp. 307–336). Washington, DC: American Psychological Association.

WACHTEL, P. (1977). *Psychoanalysis and behavior therapy: Toward integration?* New York: Basic Books.

WALLER, N. G., KOJETIN, B. A., BOUCHARD, T. J., JR., LYKKEN, D. T., & TELLEGEN, A. (1990). *Psychological Science, 1,* 138–142.

WATSON, D. (1990). On the dispositional nature of stress measures: Stable and nonspecific influences on self-report hassles. *Psychological Inquiry, 1,* 34–37.

WATSON, D., & CLARK, L. A. (1984). Negative affectivity: The disposition to experience aversive emotional states. *Psychological Bulletin, 96,* 465–490.

WATSON, D., & PENNEBAKER, J. W. (1989). Health complaints, stress, and distress: Exploring the central role of negative affectivity. *Psychological Review, 96,* 234–254.

WEINBERGER, D. A., & DAVIDSON, M. N. (1994). Styles of inhibiting emotional expression: Distinguishing repressive coping from impression management. *Journal of Personality, 62,* 587–613.

WEINBERGER, D. A., SCHWARTZ, G. E., & DAVIDSON, R. J. (1979). Low anxious, high anxious, and repressive coping styles: Psychometric patterns and behavioral and physiological responses to stress. *Journal of Abnormal Psychology, 88,* 369–380.

WEINBERGER, J., & HARDAWAY, R. (1990). Separating science from myth in subliminal psychodynamic activation. *Clinical Psychological Review, 10,* 727–756.

WEINBERGER, J., & MCCLELLAND, D. C. (1990). Cognitive versus traditional motivational models: Irreconcilable or complementary? In E. T. Higgins & R. M. Sorrentino (Eds.), *The handbook of motivation on cognition: Foundations of social behavior* (Vol. 2, pp. 562–597). New York: Guilford.

WEINER, B. (1980). *Human motivation.* New York: Holt, Rinehart & Winston.

WEINER, B. (1992). *Human motivation: Metaphors, theories, and research.* Newbury Park, CA: Sage.

WEINSTEIN, N. D. (1980). Unrealistic optimism about future life events. *Journal of Personality and Social Psychology, 39,* 806–820.

WEISFELD, G. E., & BERESFORD, J. M. (1982). Erectness of posture as an indicator of dominance or success in humans. *Motivation and Emotion, 6,* 113–131.

WESTEN, D. (1990). Psychoanalytic approaches to personality. In L. Pervin (Ed.), *Handbook of personality: Theory and research* (pp. 21–65). New York: Guilford.

WESTEN, D. (1992). The cognitive self and the psychoanalytic self: Can we put our selves together? *Psychological Inquiry, 3,* 1–13.

WHEELER, R. W., DAVIDSON, R. J., & TOMARKEN, A. J. (1993). Frontal brain asymmetry and emotional reactivity: A biological substrate of affective style. *Psychophysiology, 30,* 82–89.

WHITE, K. R. (1982). The relation between socioeconomic status and academic achievement. *Psychological Bulletin, 81,* 461–481.

WHITE, R. W. (1959). Motivation reconsidered: The concept of competence. *Psychological Review, 66,* 297–333.

WHITLEY, B. E., JR. (1983). Sex role orientation and self-esteem: A critical meta-analytic review. *Journal of Personality and Social Psychology, 44,* 765–778.

WHITLEY, B. E., JR. (1985). Sex roles orientation and psychological well-being: Two meta-analyses. *Sex Roles, 12,* 207–225.

WHITLEY, B. E., JR. (1988). Masculinity, femininity, and self-esteem: A multitrait, multi-method analysis. *Sex Roles, 18,* 419–431.

WIEDERMAN, M. W. (1993). Evolved gender differences in mate preferences: Evidence from personal advertisements. *Ethology and Sociobiology, 14,* 331–351.

WIEDERMAN, M. W., & ALLGEIER, E. R. (1992). Gender differences in mate selection criteria: Sociobiological or socioeconomic explanation? *Ethology and Sociobiology, 13,* 115–124.

WILK, S. L., DESMARAIS, L. B., & SACKETT, P. R. (1995). Gravitation to jobs commensurate with ability: Longitudinal and cross-sectional tests. *Journal of Applied Psychology, 80,* 79–85.

WILLIAMS, R. B., BAREFOOT, J. C., & SHEKELLE, R. B. (1985). The health consequences of hostility. In M. A. Chesney & R. H. Rosenman (Eds.), *Anger and hostility in cardiovascular and behavioral disorders* (pp. 173–186). Washington, DC: Hemisphere.

WILSON, M., & DALY, M. (1985). Competitiveness, risk-taking, and violence. The young male syndrome. *Ethology and Sociobiology, 6,* 59–73.

WINTER, D. G. (1973). *The power motive.* New York: Free Press.

WINTER, D. G. (1987). Leader appeal, leader performance, and motive profiles of leaders and followers: A study of American presidents and elections. *Journal of Personality and Social Psychology, 52,* 196–202.

WINTER, D. G. (1988). The power motive in women—and men. *Journal of Personality and Social Psychology, 54,* 510–519.

WINTER, D. G. (1992). A revised scoring system for the power motive. In C. P. Smith (Ed.), *Motivation and personality: Handbook of thematic content analysis* (pp. 311–324). New York: Cambridge University Press.

WINTER, D. G. (1993). Power, affiliation, and war: Three tests of a motivational model. *Journal of Personality and Social Psychology, 65,* 532–545.

WINTER, D. G. (1996). *Personality: Analysis and interpretation of lives.* New York: McGraw Hill.

WINTER, D. G., & STEWART, A. J. (1978). *The power motive.* In H. London & J. Exner (Eds.), *Dimensions of personality* (pp. 391–447). New York: Wiley.

WINTON, W. M. (1986). The role of facial response in self-reports of emotion: A critique of Laird. *Journal of Personality and Social Psychology, 50,* 808–812.

WITELSON, S. F. (1989). Hand and sex differences in the isthmus and genu of the human corpus callosum. *Brain, 112,* 799–835.

WITKIN, H. A. (1949). Perception of body position and of the position of the visual field. *Psychological Monographs, 63 (7 Whole No. 302).*

WITKIN, H. A., DYK, R. B., FATERSON, H. F., GOODENOUGH, D. R., & KARP, S. A. (1962). *Psychological differentiation.* New York: Wiley.

WITKIN, H. A., & GOODENOUGH, D. R. (1977). Field dependence and interpersonal behavior. *Psychological Bulletin, 84,* 661–689.

WITKIN, H. A., & GOODENOUGH, D. R. (1981). *Cognitive styles: Essence and origins.* New York: International Universities Press.

WITKIN, H. A., LEWIS, H. B., HERTZMAN, M., MACHOVER, K., MEISSNER, P. B., & WAPNER, S. (1954). *Personality through perception.* New York: Harper.

WOIKE, B. A. (1995). Most-memorable experiences: Evidence for a link between implicit and explicit motives and social cognitive processes in everyday life. *Journal of Personality and Social Psychology, 68,* 1081–1091.

Wolf, N. (1991). *The beauty myth*. New York: William Morrow.

Wylie, R. (1974). *The self-concept*. Lincoln: University of Nebraska Press.

Zajonc, R. B. (1984). On the primacy of affect. *American Psychologist, 39*, 117–123.

Zajonc, R. B., Murphy, S. T., & Inglehart, M. (1989). Feeling and facial efference: Implications of the vascular theory of emotion. *Psychological Review, 96*, 395–416.

Zevon, M. A., & Tellegen, A. (1982). The structure of mood change: An ideographic/ nomothetic analysis. *Journal of Personality and Social Psychology, 43*, 111–122.

Zimbardo, P. G. (1969). *The cognitive control of motivation*. Glenville, IL: Scott, Foresman.

Zimbardo, P. G., Cohen, A., Weisenberg, M., Dworkin, L., & Firestone, I. (1969). The control of experimental pain. In P. G. Zimbardo (Ed.), *The cognitive control of motivation*. Glenville, IL: Scott, Foresman.

Zuckerman, M. (Ed.). (1983). *Biological bases of sensation-seeking, impulsivity, and anxiety*. Hillsdale, NJ: Erlbaum.

Zuckerman, M. (1991). *Psychobiology of personality*. New York: Cambridge University Press.

Zuckerman, M. (1992). What is a basic factor and which factors are basic? Turtles all the way down. *Personality and Individual Differences, 13*, 675–681.

Zuroff, D. C. (1986). Was Gordon Allport a trait theorist? *Journal of Personality and Social Psychology, 51*, 993–1000.

Author Index

Subject Index

DB&A